Richard D. Van Scotter
Social Issues Resources Series, Inc.

Richard J. Kraft
John D. Haas
University of Colorado

FOUNDATIONS OF EDUCATION

Social Perspectives

PRENTICE-HALL, INC., Englewood Cliffs, N.J. 07632

Library of Congress Cataloging in Publication Data

Van Scotter, Richard.
    Foundations of education.

    Includes bibliographies and index.
    1. Educational sociology. I. Kraft, Richard J.,
joint author. II. Haas, John D., joint author.
III. Title.
LC189.V28   370.19'3   78-31251
ISBN 0-13-329268-1

© 1979 by Prentice-Hall, Inc., Englewood Cliffs, N.J. 07632

All rights reserved. No part of this book
may be reproduced in any form or
by any means without permission in writing
from the publisher.

Printed in the United States of America

10 9 8 7 6 5 4

Editorial/Production supervision
   by Scott Amerman.
Interior design by Alison Gnerre
Cover design by Jayne Conte
Manufacturing buyer: John Hall

Prentice-Hall International, Inc., *London*
Prentice-Hall of Australia Pty. Limited, *Sydney*
Prentice-Hall of Canada, Ltd., *Toronto*
Prentice-Hall of India Private Limited, *New Delhi*
Prentice-Hall of Japan, Inc., *Tokyo*
Prentice-Hall of Southeast Asia Pte. Ltd., *Singapore*
Whitehall Books Limited, *Wellington, New Zealand*

CONTENTS

PREFACE

**PART ONE:
FOUNDATIONS OF AMERICAN EDUCATION   1**

1. The History of Education:
   Traditional and Revisionist Views   3
   Some Grandmasters Who Influenced American Education, 4.
   Education of the Young in Colonial America, 7.
   In Quest of a Nation of Literate and Educated Citizens, 10.
   Extending Universal Schooling Upward and Outward, 17.
   The Progressive Mood in Education, 20.
   The Illusion of Educational Reform, 24.
   Preparing the American Dream for the Twentieth Century, 26.
   Case Study: Compulsory Attendance, 32.
   Thought Questions, 33.
   Practical Activities, 34.   *Bibliography,* 35.

2. The Philosophy of Education:
   A Search for Meaning   37

   Realms of Philosophy, 38.
   Idealism, Realism, and Pragmatism, 40.
   Education and Idealism, Realism, and Pragmatism, 43.
   Philosophies of Education, 46.   Existentialism, 52.
   A Personal Philosophy of Education, 56.
   Case Study: Education in the Stone Age, 57.
   Thought Questions, 58.
   Practical Activities, 59.   Bibliography, 59.

3. The Politics of Education:
   Power and Control   61

   Who Runs the Schools? 61.   The System, 62.
   Educational Politics, 62.
   The Distinction Between "Education" and "Schooling", 68.
   Key Subjects of Educational Decision-making, 71.
   The Struggle for Control of Education, 74.
   Summary, 78.
   Case Study: Academic Freedom, 78.
   Thought Questions, 79.
   Practical Activities, 80.   Bibliography, 81.

4. The Economics of Schooling:
   Payoffs and Paradoxes   83

   A Brief Lesson in Capitalist Economic Theory, 85.
   The Imbalance of Private and Public Production, 88.
   The Economic System and Education in America, 89.
   The Economic Effects of Education, 96.
   The Contribution of Education to Economic Growth:
   The Payoff to Society, 99.
   Some Discrepant Findings, 100.
   Equality of Educational Opportunity: A Special Problem in
   Financing Schools, 104.
   New Directions for Financing Schools, 110.
   Case Study: Equalization of Educational Opportunity, 113.
   Thought Questions, 113.
   Practical Activities, 114.   Bibliography, 115.

5. The Sociology of Education:
   Socialization in Schools   117

   The Nature of a Society, 117.
   Relationship of Society, Education, and Schools, 118.
   Socialization, Education, and Schools, 119.
   The Social Functions of Schools, 120.
   Influences on Children and Adolescents, 126.
   Effects of Imposed Learning Objectives, 132.
   Multiple Domains of Education, 134.
   Configuration of Educative Institutions, 135.
   Conflict in American Public Education, 137.
   Implications of the Cremin Thesis, 138.
   Education and Social Change, 140.
   Case Study: Reporting Student Achievement, 141.
   Thought Questions, 141.   *Practical Activities,* 142.
   Bibliography, 143.

   PART TWO:
   EDUCATION IN A PLURALISTIC SOCIETY   145

6. Values in Education:
   Sacred and Secular   147

   Religious Values in American Education, 148.
   A Religion of Rationality, 155.
   Values Education: The School's Response, 162.
   The Search for Democratic Values in Schools, 170.
   Case Study: School Holidays, 173.
   Thought Questions, 174.
   Practical Activities, 175.   *Bibliography,* 176.

7. Racism and Ethnicity:
   The Recognition of Diversity   178

   Historical Overview, 179.   *Theoretical Overview,* 187.
   Research on Racial and Ethnic Attitudes, 193.
   Racism and the Schools, 195.
   The School and Racial or Ethnic Differences, 201.
   Conclusions, 205.
   Case Study: The Newly Integrated School System, 207.
   Thought Questions, 208.   *Practical Activities,* 209.
   Bibliography, 210.

8. Sexism:
   Sugar, Spice, and Sports   211

   Historical Background, 211. *Sexism and the Law*, 216.
   Athletics, 218. *Jobs and Employment*, 220.
   Language, 224.
   Aspirations and Fear of Success, 225.
   Sex Differences Are Not Deficiencies, 227.
   Sexism in the Nursery and Elementary Schools, 229.
   The Feminization of the School, 231.
   Sexism in the Secondary Schools, 234.
   Sexism in Higher Education, 237. *Conclusions*, 238.
   Case Study: The Sexist Curriculum, 238.
   Thought Questions, 239.
   Practical Activities, 240. *Bibliography*, 241.

**PART THREE:
THE SYSTEM AND THE TEACHER   243**

9. School Organization:
   The Structure of the System   245

   A Statistical Perspective on American Schooling, 246.
   The Federal Government and Education, 249.
   The State Governments and Education, 253.
   The Local School District, 256.
   School-Attendance Areas, 259.
   Levels of School Organization, 259.
   Early Childhood Education, 260.
   Elementary Schools, 262.
   The School In Between, 264. *High School*, 267.
   Case Study: Changing School Organization, 269.
   Thought Questions, 269.
   Practical Activities, 270. *Bibliography*, 270.

10. Curriculum:
    The Structure of the System   272

    The Content of the Curriculum, 272.
    Goals of Elementary Education, 274.
    Curriculum in the Junior High School and Middle School, 281.
    Goals for Modern Secondary Education, 282.
    Case Study: Controversial Elementary Curriculum, 293.
    Thought Questions, 294. *Practical Activities*, 294.
    Bibliography, 295.

11. The Professional Teacher:
    Roles and Responsibilities   296

    Is Teaching a Profession? 296.
    Professional Organizations for Teachers, 307.
    The Legal Rights of Teachers, 311.
    The Legal Rights of Students, 313.
    Case Study: Academic Freedom, 316.
    Thought Questions, 316.
    Practical Activities, 317.   *Bibliography,* 319.

    PART FOUR:
    ALTERNATIVE, GLOBAL, AND FUTURE PERSPECTIVES   **321**

12. Alternative Schooling   323

    The Promise of Alternative Schools, 325.
    A Perspective on the Alternative School Movement, 326.
    A New Concept of Alternative Schools Emerges, 333.
    Alternative Schooling in Perspective, 341.
    *Alternatives to Schooling: Complementary
    and Supplementary Institutions,* 344.
    Case Study: Alternative Schools, 346.
    Thought Questions, 347.
    Practical Activities, 348.   *Bibliography,* 349.

13. Global Survival:
    Educational Issues and Models   351

    Dimensions of the Problem, 351.
    Education: Problems and Solutions, 354.
    The Interdependence of Mankind, 377.
    Case Study: Education in the Third World, 378.
    Thought Questions, 378.   *Practical Activities,* 379.
    Bibliography, 380.

14. Futures:
    Societal and Educational   382

    A Framework of the Future, 383.
    Current and Emerging Values, 385.
    Current and Emerging Knowledge, 389.
    Current and Emerging Problems, Crises, and Fears, 396.
    Educational Futures, 399.
    Case Study: A Problem in Space Travel, 403.
    Thought Questions, 403.   *Practical Activities,* 405.
    Bibliography, 407.

    INDEX   409

PREFACE

Foundations of Education is intended for use with undergraduate students who are prepared for a serious examination of educational ideas, concepts, and issues, or for graduate students beginning their study in education. Aside from use in a standard cultural or social foundations of education course, this book can be used by teachers who view their course as a capstone to the social studies curriculum, (that is, economics, political science, sociology, and anthropology courses). For students whose major concentration of study is in the social sciences, *Foundations of Education* should be helpful in relating the threads of information and knowledge they have acquired in these several subjects. For the student who has little preparation in this area, the text will serve as ample introduction to the subjects. *Foundations* also is inviting to students who are not planning on a teaching career, but would like a comprehensive survey of the field of education.

END-OF-CHAPTER RESOURCES

As a foundations text, *Foundations* addresses several issues and problematic areas in contemporary education. These areas of study deserve more than classroom treatments, as thorough and stimulating as these might be. To this end, we have included at the close of each chapter several *Practical Activities* (five to eleven in number) and a *Case Study*. (Others are provided in the Instructor's Manual.) Each *End-of-Chapter* section also contains *Thought Questions* and a *Bibliography*—sections with which you are probably more familiar. The *Case Studies* and *Practical Activities* add an innovative and repertorial dimension to this book that we believe is tremendously important and helpful in the preparation of future teachers.

The use of these *Case Studies* and *Practical Activities* is an integral part of the courses the authors teach. Judging from the testimony of students, *Case Studies* and *Practical Activities* are among the most valuable parts of our courses. These *Case Studies* can be used in class either at the beginning of an area of study, at the end of the area, or with each chapter. Notwithstanding their importance to the development of a topic, the *Case Studies* also serve as a change of pace when students and professors are having a difficult time "getting up" for the next class. We recommend their use in short writing assignments, with a two-to-three-page typewritten analysis being about the best length.

Case Studies don't take students into classrooms, schools, or the community, but they do help bring the reality of important issues into the classroom. Most of the *Practical Activities*, however, are designed to engage students in the world of educational matters outside the confines of their college classroom. The need for this involvement became most evident after we had devised and used several of the activities. Students, in large part, became engaged in issues, explaining that observing public school classrooms, interviewing teachers and administrators, talking with students, teaching short lessons, polling parents, conducting community studies, and the like had been eye-opening and educational experiences. School personnel welcomed the involvement of prospective teachers, often commenting that they too learned much from the encounters. A standard response from classroom teachers to the use of *Practical Activities* has been, "I wish this had been part of my educational studies; I would have been better prepared for the real world of schools."

Although not as innovative or novel, the *Thought Questions* and *Bibliographies* can inspire sound thinking on issues and aspects of the topics developed in the chapter. In many cases, answers to *Thought Questions* will *not* be found directly in the chapter essay. Rather, teachers and students are to examine the questions with respect not only to information gained from the chapter, but from other pertinent sources, including (perhaps most importantly) their own personal experiences. The *Bibliographies* have been intentionally and carefully limited, to include those sources—books, magazines, pamphlets—we think will be most useful to students.

CHAPTER CONTENT

Foundations is divided into four sections (I—Foundations of American Education; II—Education in a Pluralistic Society; III—The System and the

Teacher; and IV—Alternative, Global, and Future Perspectives) with a distinct area of knowledge included in each section. Nevertheless there are common elements running through all of the chapters. In each we have attempted to present the fundamental ideas and understandings related to the topic. In addition, many chapters include a position on the subject or central issue. These positions represent our particular perspective on the topic, which is a generous way of saying that our points of view are evidenced throughout the text.

There also is an underlying theme or philosophic position that brings a coherence to the many ideas in these chapters. In our case, the essays clearly take a reformist or revisionist drift. As one reviewer accurately noted, "The authors of *Foundations* take a 'moderate reconstructionist' approach." You'll read more about educational philosophies in Chapter 2, but here we will comment on the "social reconstructionist" position. Social reconstructionists call for a thorough change in the bureaucratic, collectivist, manipulative nature of the major institutions or forces in our society. The social reconstructionist in education believes that schools need a fundamental reordering in order to foster more critical thinking in students and to create a more liberating, democratic society. Schools today are part of a larger web of institutions in our society that, for the most part, preserves the status quo, and protects the desires of the "haves," or those in control of institutions and organizations, at the expense of the "have nots," those who are obliged to follow the demands of the established order—be they consumers, patients, voters, workers, or students. Reconstructionists would have schools promote analytical and critical thinking to serve as a force for social change rather than have schools become a part of a large collection of institutions that inhibit genuine freedom, as subtle as this control might be. In a society that cherishes, in theory, a democratic life style, but often stifles this in practice, it is important that schools encourage the critical examination of our way of life.

As "moderate reconstructionists" we three authors are somewhat less than radical reformers. We are not about to recommend abandoning schools, deschooling society, or even diminishing significantly the role of schools. Perhaps the simplest way to describe "moderate reconstructionists" is to say we take the schools as they are—bureaucratic, traditional, rule-oriented, evaluative—and look for slippage in the system. That is, we believe there exists room in school systems and individual schools to bring about change in curriculum content, administrative organization, student rights, and teacher professionalism, among other areas.

FOUNDATIONS OF AMERICAN EDUCATION—PART I

In Part I, we lay the foundation for this book. The section examines the core sociological foundations of education with chapters on the history of education (Chapter 1), the philosophy of education (Chapter 2), the politics of education (Chapter 3), the economics of schooling (Chapter 4), and the sociology of education (Chapter 5). These chapters are oriented toward history, philosophy, and the social science disciplines. They represent a synthesis of ideas and concepts from the various disciplines with their relationship to the field of education.

EDUCATION IN A PLURALISTIC SOCIETY—PART II

Part II of *Foundations of Education* is an examination of crucial issues in American society and education. The major issues as we see them include: values in education (Chapter 6), racism and ethnicity (Chapter 7), and sexism (Chapter 8). These three chapters are problem oriented; given this, we take more deliberate stances on the issues. Perhaps our own positions are most poignant in this section.

THE SYSTEM AND THE TEACHER—PART III

In Part III we examine the structure of the U.S. educational system and the lives of teachers—personal and professional. This involves school organization (Chapter 9), the nature of teaching the curriculum (Chapter 10), as well as the teachers' roles, responsibilities, and lives in the classroom (Chapter 11). The end-of-chapter activities are most critical in this section. We believe a first-hand view of teaching is imperative to understanding what it "begins" to mean to be a teacher.

ALTERNATIVE, GLOBAL, AND FUTURE PERSPECTIVES—PART IV

We conclude *Foundations* with three chapters on alternatives in education, education in an international setting, and the future and education. Chapter 12 deals with alternatives *in* and *to* public education. Chapter 13 examines education in other countries, assessing the effects of schooling in these nations and the impact of American education on these systems. Chapter 14 looks into the future of education. In this chapter, we construct a view of what our social lives are likely to be like in the future, what form our education system and schools are likely to take, and what effect schools can have in shaping our future life styles.

PART ONE

FOUNDATIONS OF AMERICAN EDUCATION

1

THE HISTORY OF EDUCATION
Traditional and Revisionist Views

> The ideal of equal opportunity for education open to all has led to the development of a single and common public system of education, extending downward to the earliest age levels and upward to include secondary and higher education. . . . Again the common needs of good citizenship have led to compulsory attendance requirements on the grounds that the general welfare of society and of the individual himself cannot be left to the whims of the illiterate and the uneducated. Free schooling is not distinctively American, but the idea of equal opportunity from the lowest to the highest levels of education has nowhere else been so explicitly stated or so effectively achieved.[1]

The architects of American public schooling had visions of a bold new experiment in education. The public school was to be the forum by which values of a young republic would be spread; it also was the institution which would mobilize disparate social and cultural groups into a politically cohesive unity. Public education would be designed to bring about the equalitarian goals of American society in fostering equality of opportunity, social mobility, and economic justice.

The route to these aims was not always a smooth one, nor were the successive steps en route always clear. In fact, today there is some question as to how genuine these goals have been, how vigorously they were pursued, and to what extent they were achieved. The traditional view of education

---

[1] R. Freeman Butts and Lawrence A. Cremin, *The History of Education in American Culture* (New York: Henry Holt and Company, Inc., 1953), pp. 564–65.

holds that our quest for these democratic goals has been successful. The revisionist view challenges both the sincerity and the effectiveness of this quest.

An inquiry into the history of American education needs to sort through as much evidence as possible in order to help clarify the nature of this provocative institution. Public education has been and still is laden with promises, myths, and realities.

SOME GRANDMASTERS WHO INFLUENCED AMERICAN EDUCATION[2]

American educational thought has a rich history, though many guiding principles are rooted in the ideas of thinkers who predate our culture. Some of these "grandmasters" of educational thought are of more recent European vintage; others are ancient and time-tested, but few have lost their relevance.

ancient greek and roman antecedents

The culture and nature of education in ancient Greece represented widely different systems of value. The Greece of the city-state Sparta was militaristic, and its educational system was designed to augment this posture. Spartan education fostered physical strength and endurance, loyalty, sacredness and obedience at the expense of intellectual development. In contrast, the Athenians emphasized intellectual and aesthetic education, using physical culture, athletic, and sporting activities to complement the basic education of history, philosophy, drama, rhetoric, science, and music.

A new spirit appeared in Athens which was to leave a profound impression on the political, economic, literary, and educational thought of Western civilization. Until this time, individual freedom had been suppressed, and societies were largely static. In the Athenian culture, individual freedom, initiative, and opportunity were promoted. As a result the Greeks tended to be imaginative, artistic, and creative people. They also were curious, logical, skeptical, and critical, as manifested in an inquiring spirit that provided an initial impulse to science. It is little surprise, then, that the Western world's first great philosophers and educators, who often were one and the same, came from Athens.

Although Socrates (469–399 B.C.) left no written legacy, much is known about him through the writings of his students, friends, and critics. Despite being a penetrating, quarrelsome, and even inflammatory indi-

---

[2]We borrow the term "grandmasters" from the title of Adolphe E. Meyer's book *Grandmasters of Educational Thought* (New York: McGraw-Hill Book Company, 1975). pp. 51–52.

Figure 1-1 Plato and Aristotle

vidual, Socrates was a brilliant and just man. He was an occasional soldier and an athlete, as were most Athenians, but foremost he was a philosopher, critic, and teacher. In the end, he was executed for his unsettling teachings, but not before being offered exile, which he refused. Socrates valued not brilliancy of speech, the dominant teaching style of Sophist educators, but rather the power of thought and the analysis of experience. Truth, to Socrates, was that knowledge to which all thinking men could agree. The method of arriving at this truth brought not only his eventual death, but also eternal fame. This method was a combination of skepticism, questioning, deductive logic, and dialectic process, which he used with incomparable skill to burrow to the core of an idea, belief, or issue. The dialectic process has been named the Socratic Method.

Although a student, disciple, and fellow Athenian of Socrates, Plato (427–347 B.C.) in many ways was quite different from his mentor. Whereas Socrates was not known for the handsome figure he cut (in fact he was a rather homely sort), Plato was broad-shouldered, attractive, and very athletic. More importantly, Plato believed that the aim of education was to discover each individual's natural aptitudes, to develop his abilities, and to fit him harmoniously into the social class system. The social office to which each individual was best fit was determined by selecting, sifting, and testing. In the end, Plato believed that each person's abilities should be cultivated to serve society. A good education brings out the artistic and aesthetic, which link the practical with the theoretical to bring about useful, rational behavior.

Aristotle (384–322 B.C.), another fellow Athenian, believed, like Plato, that education's primary purpose was to bring out the best in humans, so that they might create the just society. In contrast to the essentially philosophical methods of Plato and Socrates, Aristotle's educational methods were objective, empirical, and inductive. He ushered in the rudiments of scientific thought and methodology.

The foremost Roman writer on educational practice was Marcus Fabius Quintilian (first century A.D.). The legacy left by Quintilian has become ingrained in the postulates of contemporary educational thought. Quintilian condemned the use of physical force and emphasized the necessity of making studies attractive. He also stressed the importance of home life in a child's early education, the necessity of understanding individual learner differences, and the value of play and joy as catalysts to learning. Finally, he recognized that education occurs in general experiences as well as from books.[3]

modern european thought

A trio of European educators, Jean Jacques Rousseau (1712–1778) in France, Johann Pestalozzi (1746–1827), a Swiss educator, and Friedrich Froebel (1782–1852) in Germany, laid the groundwork for what in more modern times has been labeled child-centered, humanistic, naturalistic, and informal education. To these three scholars and teachers, education was not a preparation for life, but was inseparable from living; learning was not synonymous with work, and play was valuable to learning.

Rousseau was a philosopher before becoming interested in the schooling of youngsters. In his famous and still-read treatise, *Emile*, he explains how education must grow out of the natural interests and curiosity of the child and involve direct experiences with the real world of things and activities. Rousseau reaffirmed the importance of physical activities stressed earlier by the Greeks, and he called for the teaching of industrial education, music, drawing, writing, and other purposeful activities later popularized by the progressives.

Pestalozzi, with the publication of his smashing novel *Leonard and Gertrude*, gave a fair indication of the liberal and romantic educational sentiments that were to follow in *How Gertrude Teaches Her Children*. In Pestalozzi's methods, love, empathy, and patience for the young learner were com-

---

[3]Ibid., pp. 51–52.

bined with the use of real objects and sensory perception. Froebel, though known for his contribution to educational literature, is remembered primarily for having originated the kindergarten. His major aim for education was the social and individual development of the youngster through directed self-activity that emphasized cooperation, spontaneity, creativity, and joy.

There were other European scholars who significantly influenced the nature of the educational world that new Americans inherited in some fashion; Johann Friedrich Herbart (1776–1841) stands out among these. Unlike the other three educators, Herbart could not be accused of being a naive romantic, for he took the world of the learner as he saw it, in the most concrete form, and attempted to dissect and make sense of it. The result was the first systematic organization of learning psychology and, with this, a theory of instruction. Herbart's educational psychology stressed learning by association, designated "apperception." As developed by his successors, it set forth the following sequential structure to teaching: (1) preparation—putting the student in a receptive mood, (2) presentation—unveiling the new material or ideas, (3) association—relating the new material to the old, (4) generalization—developing or synthesizing new understandings in the form of general ideas, rules, or principles, and (5) application—putting the new ideas into practice, or testing them.

EDUCATION OF THE YOUNG IN COLONIAL AMERICA

Had ideas of Rousseau, Pestalozzi, and Froebel existed, colonial educators probably would not have been responsive. The religious and social beliefs that permeated life in the colonies were more compatible with harshness and intolerance than with patience and understanding. Even after the ideas of the European humanist trio were well publicized, they were not rapidly received into American pedagogy.
they were not rapidly received into American pedagogy.

Discipline was harsh in the colonial schools, and physical punishment was quite common. At least in the beginning of this period children, and people generally, were viewed as sinful sorts who needed to be ruled dictatorially and punitively. A typical passage from the *New England Primer* reads, "Foolishness is bound up in the heart of the child; but the rod of correction shall drive it from him." The *Primer* was the most distinctive of the colonial schoolbooks, whose ostensible purpose was to teach the children to read, but which in fact served much wider functions, particularly religious indoctrination. The *Primer* was the only textbook many students knew. Teaching methods also were hardly imaginative, memorization and drill being the dominant techniques of the colonial classroom. As Lawrence Cremin and Merle Borrowman relate, pupils as a rule were taught

8 FOUNDATIONS OF AMERICAN EDUCATION

one by one. If the student did well there were words of praise and a new assignment; if the performance was poor, reprimand (sometimes physical) and ridicule followed.[4] Today's dominant learning theory, based on reward or the lack of it, with punishment frowned on, would have been thought quite silly then.

It may have been fortunate that so few youngsters had the dubious advantage of attending the early schools; their number was probably no more than 10 percent of the school-age population. Even though some influential colonists viewed the school as potentially performing very important functions for the society, most children received only a limited amount of education in school. Many never saw the interior of a schoolhouse, and few if any received all of their education in school. Most often, the distinction between those attending and not attending school was along class lines. Children of the poor and lower-class families had no formal schooling and learned trades early in life. Children of the upper class received as much education as was available, in many cases through college. In addition, colonial schools were quite small, normally one-room structures, and in session for much shorter periods of the year than they are now. Schooling, by necessity, played a limited and minor role in colonial life, but this ought not to be construed as a disadvantage to the education of colonial children and adults.

The family and the community, including the shops, workplaces, social gatherings, news media, and, particularly, the churches were major educative institutions. When one of these agencies weakened in effectiveness it was fortified with new laws, such as those requiring master craftsmen to provide apprenticeship training; or alternative mechanisms were developed, such as training schools or private academies. Cremin, in his *American Education: The Colonial Experience*, finds that the colonial family was the most flexible and instrumental educating agency in transmitting new functional and practical ideas for managing and establishing change. In Cremin's assessment, not only the number of deliberate educative institutions, but the diversity of education is impressive, and is a distinct strength of this period.[5] This is a strength that was neglected and permitted to vanish as educational policy unfolded over the next two centuries.

Signs of change were evident as early as 1642, when the colonial legislature of Massachusetts passed a general education law requiring all parents to see that their children were taught to read, to understand the major laws of the colony, to know the catechism, and to learn a trade. Five years later, in 1647, the Massachusetts legislature mandated a second educational

---

[4]Lawrence A. Cremin and Merle L. Borrowman, *Public Schools in Our Democracy* (New York: The Macmillan Company, 1956), p. 64.
[5]Lawrence A. Cremin, *American Education: The Colonial Experience* (New York: Harper & Row, Publishers, 1970), pp. 123–37, 243–48.

law requiring all towns of at least fifty families to appoint an elementary teacher, for the express purpose of teaching reading and writing, who would be paid from municipal taxes. This law also required any town of a hundred or more families to appoint a teacher of Latin grammar, or in modern terms, a secondary teacher. The wealthy families' exclusive access to formal education was beginning to erode.

Elementary schools rapidly increased in the Massachusetts Bay Colony, and with them the sale of *New England Primers*. This trend gradually extended to the other colonies along the East Coast, but with less government persuasion the impact was not as great. Latin grammar schools, not much different in structure and kind from the elementary schools, also began to flourish. Latin, not surprisingly, was the heart of the curriculum; the schools' main purpose was to prepare young men for entrance into college. Harvard was the first college to be established (1636). It was a full sixty-five years before the next college, Yale, was started (1701).

The *New England Primer*, as suggested, was more than just a basic reader of the time; it also was an instrument of religious instruction. It contained pieces of Biblical information, prayers to be recited, questions and answers on religious matters (a catechism), and an alphabet complete with complementary moral lessons. The type of religion coincided with that established in the colony. In New England, this was Puritanism, or Congregational Calvinism; in the Southern colonies, the Church of England was established by law, and orthodox Anglicanism was taught in the schools. In the middle colonies there was more heterogeneity of religion, meaning that such minority groups as Quakers, Dutch Protestants, Presbyterians, Bap-

Figure 1-2 Hornbook of the Seventeenth Century

tists, Lutherans, Methodists, and Mennonites developed their distinctive schools. To observers, schools had become an institution designed to serve the larger community by assisting in the socialization of the young to the dominant cultural values. At this time, these values were almost exclusively religious.

In retrospect, education in the colonial period was not seen by most people as a means of mobilizing individual potentials or developing free people. It was believed that most people didn't need schooling, or at best only schooling for basic reading, writing, and computation. A liberal education, or schooling in secondary schools and colleges, a requisite to educational freedom, was fitting only for the few, not for the many. Yet Freeman Butts, in assessing the state of education at the end of the colonial period, thought it appropriate to conclude that education designed to enable each individual to develop himself to the utmost was emerging as a desired goal. In his words, "Building schools for a colonial society prior to the Revolutionary War was a dress rehearsal for freedom, not the main performance."[6]

IN QUEST OF A NATION
OF LITERATE AND EDUCATED CITIZENS

The founders of the new nation took very seriously the question of what type of educational institution was appropriate for a republican government. James Madison wrote, "A popular Government without popular information, or the means of acquiring it, is but a Prologue to a Farce or Tragedy, or perhaps both." The promise of establishing a republican form of government was equality, democracy, and freedom. The task of building this educational system out of the eclectic remnants left from the colonial period was going to be messy. Not only were the schools divided along different religious lines, but they were attended by "Americans" who spoke different languages and practiced a variety of ethnic customs originating in western Europe. The answer was to be a *common* school, taught in English without religious messages and attended by children from families of all backgrounds, regardless of spoken language, religious beliefs and economic status. Furthermore, schooling was "free" in the sense that it was funded by taxes collected from everyone. This was imperative to the existence of a representative government. Yet, there was a sharp limit to the amount of education that was considered necessary and tolerable. As Freeman Butts concluded, the republican ideal was to provide *some* education for all and *much* education for a few.[7]

---

[6]R. Freeman Butts, "Search for Freedom—The Story of American Education," *NEA Journal*, March, 1960, p. 37.
[7]Ibid., p. 42.

Many of the political leaders of the Revolutionary period also were educational leaders; most notable among these were Benjamin Franklin and Thomas Jefferson. Franklin's ideas on education were set forth in a pamphlet titled *Proposals Relating to the Education of Youth in Pennsylvania* (1749). In a striking break from tradition, Franklin proposed a new kind of secondary school—an academy—designed to prepare youth for the practical affairs of life, namely business, vocation, and leisure. The colonial secondary school, aptly named Latin grammar school because the primary curriculum was Latin, existed to serve only the few who would enter college and later go on to professional careers. Franklin antedated later practice in his suggesting that the emerging nation needed secondary schools that were useful and practical, and that would serve a much larger segment of the populace. English was to replace Latin and Greek, and the general curriculum was to include such heretofore pedestrian subjects as history, science, and agriculture.

Thomas Jefferson was a prolific writer on education, and if the inscription on his tombstone is accurate testimony, he wished to be remembered more for his work in this field than as the third president of the country. Jefferson's most significant ideas for education were set forth in a piece of legislation he proposed while a member of the Virginia Assembly, titled *Bill for the More General Diffusion of Knowledge* (1779). On the surface Jefferson's entrance into education did not appear successful: the bill was defeated; yet it had a significant influence on the future course of educational thought and action. His plan was no less than a blueprint for the education of all youngsters in Virginia. He proposed in this bill that all free children of the state receive three years of free elementary schooling in reading, writing, arithmetic, and history. The bill carefully spelled out the location and requirements of the elementary schools. He also proposed that grammar schools be constructed in distinct areas of the state to accommodate a select group of the best male students from the elementary schools for further studies. The brightest graduates of these secondary schools were then to be granted scholarships for university study at William and Mary College. The bill clearly was the work of a person who valued the role of education in the new society. It was awesome in its comprehensiveness, fascinating in its detail, and unique in its structure.[8]

Jefferson conceived his plan to provide a broad base of intelligent citizens who would be capable of judging important issues as well as combating tyrannical leadership, and to develop enlightened leaders predisposed to ruling in a democratic fashion. The plan, ideologically, pedagogically, and

[8]Gordon C. Lee, ed., *Crusade Against Ignorance: Thomas Jefferson on Education* (New York: Teachers College, Columbia University, 1961), pp. 83–97.

economically, was too radical for the times. Jefferson, later, saw tangible effects of his labors in education, when the University of Virginia, which he conceived, was established in 1819, after years of oral and written persuasion.

Although Jefferson had only modest success with his educational inspirations, the idea of the common school was planted, and the drive toward universal elementary schooling was underway. The establishment of public schooling took strong and dedicated leadership, and the 1800s' movement produced some capable educators: Horace Mann and James Carter in Massachusetts, Henry Barnard in Connecticut, Gideon Hawley in New York, Calvin Wiley in North Carolina, Samuel Lewis in Ohio, Caleb Mills in Indiana, Ninian Edwards in Illinois, and John Swett in California. Lecturing, writing, organizing, and at times offering their personal finances, these leaders worked unselfishly for the cause of common public schooling.

Horace Mann and the common school

Perhaps the most dedicated and zealous of this group was Horace Mann (1796–1859). Although he had much in common with Thomas Jefferson, Mann, in contrast, was an uncompromising champion of equality in education. Like Jefferson, he argued for the general diffusion of basic skills and knowledge, but he was rather unconcerned with the advanced and liberal education of an enlightened and humane leadership. In his words, "The scientific or literacy well-being of a community is to be estimated not so much by its possessing a few men of great knowledge as having many men of competent knowledge." The ideas of Horace Mann were the initial break from the republican ideal that guided the nation's schooling through the first century.

Mann sacrificed a promising law career to become the first secretary of the Massachusetts State Board of Education in 1837. His presence was felt from the start, and he traveled and labored tirelessly to promote free schooling in the state. During his twelve years as the education chief of Massachusetts, Mann produced twelve annual reports on timely aspects of education. His travails brought changes, and occasional praises, but they also resulted in failures, criticism, and even attacks. The best known of his annual reports was the seventh, which followed his travels to Europe. Mann was particularly impressed with the Prussian schools that had adopted the teaching methods of Pestalozzi. His praise for the civility and progressive techniques of their teachers aroused considerable anger and protest among educators in Boston.[9]

More important for the future role of schooling in the larger society,

---

[9]Lawrence A. Cremin, ed., *The Republic and the School: Horace Mann on the Education of Free Men* (New York: Teachers College, Columbia University, 1957), pp. 54–56.

Mann perceived the school as potentially an omnipotent and omniscient force. In his Twelfth Annual Report (1848) he made the plea to business and property owners (whose financial support was imperative) that a schooled populace was a safe and tame populace: it offered more effective protection than any police force. He also wrote that schooling was the hope of eliminating poverty and ignorance, thereby fostering equality in the state. If this seems somewhat contradictory, it is! The first plea embraces the conservative functions of education and the second statement the liberating functions. Mann, however, was a first-rate politician, having served in the Massachusetts assembly, and possessed an evangelical persuasiveness. Horace Mann also viewed the school as the instrumental source in the moral education of the young. Quoting the bible, he wrote, "Train up a child in the way he should go, and when he is old he will not depart from it."[10] The decline of established religion in nineteenth-century America and the rise of public school were not merely coincidental; the schools assumed the function of character development. With this, the door had been opened to an expanding role for public schools.

the changing school

The impetus to establish public schools was not an isolated movement particularly during the first half of the nineteenth century. William Ellery Channing referred to the 1830s as "an age of great movements." By 1830, several forces or movements had developed that significantly influenced the course of education through the rest of the century and beyond. Among these were immigration, the growth of democracy, urbanization, industrialization, and organized labor.

In 1852, just four years after Horace Mann left his state educational post, Massachusetts enacted the nation's first compulsory school attendance law. By 1890, twenty-seven states and territories had passed similar legislation, and in 1918 Mississippi became the last state to mandate compulsory schooling. Subsequently three states, including Mississippi, repealed their laws during the 1950s. Not only was the cause of free public schooling advanced by the leadership of Mann, James Carter, Henry Barnard, and other educators, but with the growth of democracy (and the concomitant decline of the Federalist party, aristocracy, and Hamiltonian politics) the common man was able to lobby for more common schools. While the common family began to see the social and economic advantages of schooling, the business and political leadership saw how schools could be a convenient and efficient means not only of educating the masses for responsible citizenship, but also of training them for industry and socializing them to the conventions of the nation's life style. Even reformists joined these forces in

[10]Ibid., p. 100.

Figure 1-3 Early Classroom Setting

supporting compulsory attendance as a way to curb abuses of child labor by the rising industrialists. This combination was a case of "strange bedfellows," perhaps, but nonetheless a potent political force.

During the second half of the nineteenth century, when schooling had become established in the nation, character development was an increasingly important function of the schools. Diane Ravitch writes, "There was no thought of moral relativism: honesty, loyalty, patriotism, industry, charity, frugality and courage were forthrightly and unselfconsciously taught as virtues of good American children."[11]

By 1850, 12 percent of the citizens were foreign born, most of these immigrants from Ireland, Germany, and Italy. Their numbers, including groups from Southern and Eastern Europe, grew precipitously for the next hundred years. In large part, the character-development thrust of the schools functioned to assimilate the immigrants into the dominant American culture. Along with learning accepted forms of behavior, children from diverse native lands were taught to speak a common language, while studying the heroics of courageous leaders, the blessings of a benevolent government, and the establishment of an extraordinary nation. In addition, these youngsters were taught accepted standards of hygiene and nutrition.

---

[11]Diane Ravitch, "The Schools are for Learning," *Journal of Current Social Events*, 13, no. 3 (Summer, 1976), p. 7.

A large number of the immigrants came to live in the burgeoning cities, hoping to find work in the industrial developments of the new nation.

Urban life, however, was disproportionately characterized by social and economic problems, and industrialization demanded both work skills and modes of behavior often quite foreign to the worker. Character-development education in the schools served as a solution to both problems in the growing nation. Education was one area in which industrial management and labor organizations could agree: both supported more and "better" schooling for the working class. Labor saw education as the primary means of increasing the economic welfare of the industrial employee. To better one's position in the system, the worker had to learn new and technological skills. Just as importantly he was obliged to develop compatible work behaviors, such as obedience, industriousness, reliability, neatness, modesty, and loyalty.

By 1900, the public schools not only were securely established, but had come to serve various economic, social, and pedagogical functions. When industry needed skilled workers, schools initiated manual training courses and vocational programs. When specific values, beliefs, and behaviors were required for a smoothly functioning society, the schools were the most accessible and effective agency to carry out such teachings. If the needs of community were in the areas of home care, health, or recreation, the schools were responsive in developing appropriate programs. Schools, in effect, became implements for economic growth, social reform, and community harmony. As expectations grew, the school took on jobs once performed by families, churches, local businesses, settlement houses, and other community agencies. This they did—in our judgment with admirable success in the short run, but with dubious consequences over the long haul.

the emerging bureaucratic structure

As the common school became more elaborate, ubiquitous, and universal, a formal organizational structure was sought. A number of revisionist historians point out that industrialization during the nineteenth century dictated the development of school organization. Among the writers is Michael Katz, who explains that the creation of organizations, in form and characteristics, assumed special importance to Americans. Organizations became a national issue because the American culture lacked established and traditional organizational forms, and because the public correctly perceived that the structure of an organization creates its purposes and effects.[12]

The kind of school organization that emerged during the nineteenth

---

[12]Michael B. Katz, *Class, Bureaucracy, and Schools: The Illusion of Educational Change in America* (New York: Praeger Publishers, Inc., 1975), pp. 4–5.

century was what Katz labels *incipient bureaucracy*. Its appeal coincided with the beginning growth of industrialization and urbanization. School bureaucracies were an answer, particularly, to the size and heterogeneity of urban schools. Katz posits that by 1880 the basic structure of American education was fixed and that it has not been altered fundamentally since. Educators during the first half of that century, however, had alternative models from which to choose, states Katz, namely: paternalistic voluntarism, democratic localism and corporate voluntarism.[13] Examples of each existed plentifully, but the bureaucratic model was clearly the choice of early reformist educators.

Reformers such as Horace Mann and Henry Barnard worked to create a rational system out of what they saw as chaos. They were dismayed, even appalled at the inadequacies of the typical public school. As David Tyack describes, the rapidly increasing number of students were attending schools in which teachers were inexperienced, untrained, and lacking any semblance of professionalism; where curricula were haphazard, and textbooks miscellaneous; where students varied widely in age and ability, attended irregularly, and behaved intractably; where school buildings were rough and messy, often serving as community centers for virtually all of the town or neighborhood's social, political, and religious activities.[14] Ironically, reform led to standardization and stereotyping, as school personnel graded classes, prescribed uniform curricula and texts, trained teachers in particular methods, and appointed proper supervising officials. Incipient bureaucracy prevailed essentially because of the functions, and the privileged people, that it served.

---

[13]In Katz's model, examples of paternalistic voluntarism were early schools administered by distinguished and capable, but largely disinterested, men who gave rudimentary training in literacy and morals to lower-class children. Voluntarism in effect was a form of *noblesse oblige*, of one class helping to civilize another. The New York Free School Society operated an extensive network of these schools for several decades in the early 1800s.

The democratic localism model consisted of neighborhood or community schools run by elected boards which valued variety, local autonomy from city supervision, and symbiotic school and community relations, while disdaining any professionalization of school teaching and administration. Democratic localists had an uphill struggle from the start, for their conception was essentially a rural viewpoint incompatible with what educators saw as the needs of urban education.

Corporate voluntarism schools were single institutions operated by self-perpetuating boards of trustees, financed through endowment and tuition. Academies and colleges for secondary and higher education were widely used examples of this model at the time. These schools in effect were extensions of private and public business organizations, with general political support from the middle class. In the late eighteenth and early nineteenth centuries, the states did offer financial assistance to these schools; extending such aid downward to elementary schools would have made it possible to operate universal, common, and free schools on the corporate model.

For a detailed analysis and comparison of these four school models, see Chapter 1 of Michael Katz's, *Class, Bureaucracy and Schools*.

[14]David Tyack, "Bureaucracy and the Common School: The Example of Portland, Oregon, 1851–1913," in *Education in American History: Readings on the Social Issues*, Michael B. Katz (New York: Praeger Publishers, Inc., 1973), p. 165.

Katz believes there is sufficient evidence indicating that the poor and the working classes, threatened by industrialization, supported democratic localism during times of technological change. The middle class, however, sought to obtain advantages for their children as technology increased the importance of formal schooling; they therefore supported an elaborate, business-oriented, graded school system. In Katz's analysis this system was *bureaucratic* in organization and *class biased* in function: two characteristics that are interrelated and mutually supportive. Modern bureaucracy is a bourgeois invention, representing a crystallization of bourgeois social attitudes.[15] The irony, Katz adds, is that school reformers thought they were promoting value-free and classless schools; the structure undermined them. The character traits promulgated in the schools represented a chauvinistic, Protestant position appropriate for proper urban living as portrayed by Victorian middle-class values. Unable to perceive the cultural bias and lack of social mobility, school reformers were persuaded that such a system fostered equality of opportunity. The results were precisely the opposite of the reformers' intent. Bureaucracy, it turns out, simply reinforced the notion that education is something that the better part of the community does to others, so that they are orderly, moral, and tractable.[16]

EXTENDING UNIVERSAL SCHOOLING UPWARD AND OUTWARD

For most of the nineteenth century, the efforts of public school advocates and educational reformers focused on the early school years, and by the late 1800s universal elementary schooling had been established. By 1900 a substantial majority of children aged six to thirteen were in elementary schools; today virtually every child is enrolled in some form of elementary school. Most attend the modern version of public-supported common school; some choose parochial or other private schools; and a few are obliged to attend special schools. In contrast, only about 10 percent of young people aged fourteen to seventeen were in school at the turn of this century. During the next fifty to sixty years there was a remarkable increase in secondary school enrollment: by 1930 more than 50 percent of this age group were in schools, and by 1960 enrollment had climbed to about 90 percent, where it appears to have stabilized, if not showing a slight tendency to decline.

Freeman Butts has described this period from roughly the 1870s to the 1970s as a century of democratic education. In the republican era (the century from the 1770s to 1870s) the ideal had been to provide *some* educa-

---

[15] Katz, *Class, Bureaucracy and Schools*, p. xxl.
[16] Ibid., pp. 32–39.

tion for all and *much* education for a few; the democratic ideal, in contrast, was to provide *as much education as possible for all*. The conventional view of educational history teaches that the underlying goal during this democratic era was *more education for more people*.[17]

What reasons account for this phenomenal growth in secondary schooling? The impetus of an ideal is not sufficient; Americans are too pragmatic to fit this interpretation neatly. Historical observers generally explain that the major force was the shift in the economic or productive base of our society. According to Butts, a republican education was sufficient for a society with a relatively small population scattered over large areas of richly endowed land with most of the workers engaged in agriculture and agriculture-related occupations. In a society that was highly industrialized, that was based on steam, electric, or nuclear power, and that relied on science and technology, the demands were quite different. Since this was a society which had the alarming potential to be controlled and managed by an elite few, more schooling, it was argued, was required to prevent autocratic use of political and economic power.[18] Yet, for a nation founded on the principle of democracy, it is peculiar that this case for a universal liberal education for all had not been made a century earlier. In retrospect, perhaps the more important reasons have been the host of corporate-industrial needs that extended public schooling has helped to satisfy. These include not only more knowledge, greater literacy, and higher quantitative skills, but also certain basic industrial skills and work habits.

the high school

The institution that became associated almost exclusively with secondary education by 1900 was the public high school. The term "high school" has a familiar ring today, but this was not so only a little more than a century ago. During that period, the Latin grammar school had become the dominant secondary institution. Its major aim was to prepare young people for further college study (tertiary or higher education). The concept of grammar school was borrowed from the Europeans, but it was challenged as the dominant secondary school by the academy, the nation's first uniquely American educational institution. The first academy, as mentioned earlier, was started by Benjamin Franklin in Philadelphia in 1751.

The high school, which was to become a distinctively American institution in ways never imagined by its early supporters, convincingly superseded both the Latin grammar school and the academy. The decisive act in this development was a series of 1870s' court decisions concerning

---
[17]Butts, "Search for Freedom," p. 42.
[18]Ibid., pp. 42–43.

the legality of publicly supported high schools. The most important was the Kalamazoo, Michigan, case in 1874, in which the courts established the principle that people of the states could start and support public high schools with tax funds. High schools, along with public elementary schools and public universities, were part of a total formal educational scheme already established in the state and the republic. Thereupon the public high school movement gained momentum.

shaping the high school

With the increasing numbers and diversity of students attending secondary school, new subjects periodically were added to the school curriculum. The result was that high schools tended to lack a uniform course of study, and colleges had different, as well as at times arbitrary entrance requirements. In 1892 the Committee of Ten on Secondary Studies of the National Education Association (NEA) was formed to standardize the high-school curriculum and to secure uniform college entrance requirements. The Committee of Ten, chaired by Charles Elliot, then president of Harvard University, also set out to "broaden the channel" from high school to college. At that time, the prevailing standard for college preparation was the Classical Course, with four years of Latin and two or three years of Greek; an English Course was accepted for terminal high-school students. President Elliot and a few other committee members sought to make the English Course acceptable for college entrance.

The result was a controversial compromise outlining four courses of study: (1) Classical (including Greek and Latin), (2) Latin-Scientific (with no Greek required), (3) Modern Language (requiring neither Latin nor Greek), and (4) English (requiring only one foreign language). More important than the details of this plan was the committee's position that secondary schools existed primarily to prepare for life, and secondarily for college. The plan also established English, one foreign language (either modern or ancient), history, mathematics, and to a lesser extent science as the core high-school curriculum. In addition, the committee recommended that high school consist of grades seven through twelve, that students should be permitted few electives, and that the Carnegie Unit (one course taken daily for one year) be established as the standard of measurement. To Elliot's delight, the Committee of Ten recommended that colleges accept students who had completed any one of the four courses. Latin and Greek were no longer the foundation for college preparation.[19]

Around the turn of the century, high-school enrollments increased substantially, and shortly there was the call to make the American high

---

[19]Edward A. Krug, *Salient Dates in American Education, 1635–1964* (New York: Harper & Row, Publishers, 1966), pp. 95–99.

school even more comprehensive. Since a majority of the students now were not continuing on to college, preparation for further schooling was becoming less and less important. The NEA responded by appointing another committee, the Commission on the Reorganization of Secondary Education. In 1918, the Commission published a drab 32-page pamphlet called the *Cardinal Principles of Secondary Education*, an unimpressive looking little publication that ironically shaped the dimensions of the discussion on secondary education for the next several decades. In recommending that all "normal boys and girls" be encouraged to attend school full-time until age seventeen or eighteen, this report offered the first call for universal secondary education. The report also called for *comprehensive* high schools that include a variety of programs. These programs were to be guided by the seven aims of education: health, command of fundamental processes, worthy home membership, vocation, citizenship, worthy use of leisure time, and ethical character. The report was received favorably, and the "Seven Cardinal Principles," as they were popularly called, inspired educators. As a result, the pattern of American education for the next fifty years or more began taking shape.[20]

THE PROGRESSIVE MOOD IN EDUCATION

The 1890s were a time of progressive reform in America, and reformist thought took a critical and indignant look at the squalor of urban slums, the harsh conditions of industrial workplaces, the corruption of local and state governments, and eventually at the dullness of public schools. This was a period when "muckrakers" such as Jacob Riis wrote about poverty in the cities, Lincoln Steffens exposed the alliance between corrupt government and corrupt business, and Ida Tarbell detailed the power-accruing practices of Standard Oil Company. Muckraker journalism reached the schools initially as a result of a series of articles during 1892 in a rather unimpressive, unobtrusive New York monthly, *The Forum*.

Joseph Rice, a young pediatrician with deep interest in the methods used in treating and teaching children, prepared a first-hand appraisal of American schools for *The Forum*. Rice visited 1,200 classrooms in 36 cities, and in a vividly documented report charged that schools and teachers "dehumanized, immobilized, and automized the children." The results of his investigations, however, were not uniformly bleak; Rice found examples of humane, resourceful, imaginative, or progressive teaching in a scattering of schools. The most noteworthy of these probably was the famous Cook County Normal School in metropolitan Chicago, run by the then-venerable educator Francis Parker. In his final article for *The Forum*, Rice called on the people of local communities to demand "progressive schools" for their

[20]Ibid., pp. 117–20.

children. He argued that the educational spirit of the country was progressive and that the stimulation and warmth of these schools were within the reach of all citizens.[21]

Cremin pointed out in *The Transformation of the School* that progressive education began as part of a broader social and political progressive reform movement. In his words, "the Progressive mind was ultimately an educator's mind, and . . . its characteristic contribution was that of a socially responsible reformist pedagogue." For all their sense of rage, Cremin pointed out that progressives were diligent, thoughtful, and patient moderates.[22] About this time the young philosopher John Dewey, an example *par excellence* of this model, began to make his incomparable mark on educational thought and American schools.

John Dewey and the liberal transformation of schools

As a village schoolteacher in his native Vermont, John Dewey saw the sterility, inactivity, and numbness of the traditional classroom. In 1894, when he arrived at the Unviersity of Chicago as head of the department of philosophy, psychology, and pedagogy, Dewey began working out new ideas for America's schools. Two years later he started the Laboratory School in order to test his ideas in practice and refine his theory on learning experiences, teaching methods, and school organization. Dewey wanted to demonstrate that individuals learned best by "doing," be it learning to walk, talk, swim, hurdle, and draw, or to solve problems and conceptualize. For the best results, he hypothesized, learning should involve using not only books, but also tools and related materials. and it should involve interaction with people as much as possible in a community, i.e., a working and social, setting. Dewey explicated this theory in *The School and Society* (1899), where he added that the occupations and associations in life that serve human social needs should be the basic context of education, and that the most reliable measure of learning is the ability of the individual to act intelligently in new social situations.

Dewey took great pain in many subsequent writings to elaborate on this theme of learning and action in real-life experiences. The teacher, he wrote, must know the individual character of the learner (implying a knowledge of the pupil's background, experiences, and abilities), understand the present moment in learning, and have a sense of what is to follow. Likewise, the teacher must have the intellectual ability to know both what information is needed in a learning situation and where to retrieve and how to organize this subject matter, so that the learner may gain new insights and knowledge as the material is presented. These two interrelated

---

[21]Cremin, *The Transformation of the School*, pp. 3–6.
[22]Ibid., pp. 88–89.

processes Dewey labeled the "continuity" and "interaction" effects, respectively.

Dewey took the relationship between the school and larger society a step further, however, with his idea of education as an "embryonic community." In practice the school would offer many new learning environments for the student, including libraries, gymnasiums, working areas, art and music rooms, science laboratories, gardens, and playgrounds. Beyond the "classroom walls," he envisioned the school as a dynamic center of the community. In addition, but no less important, the school was to be a lever for social change and reform in the immediate community and society at large. Dewey believed that experimental, investigative, and intelligent behavior is essentially progressive in that it tends to improve the conditions of life for people. In response to zealots for social reform, he cautioned that schools could not effect this reform alone, for it was only one institution among many having significant educational impact on the community.

In addition to *School and Society*, Dewey developed his educational ideas in numerous speeches, articles and other books; most influential among them were *How We Think* (1909), *Schools of Tomorrow* (1915) and *Democracy and Education* (1916). In Cremin's view, Dewey's elaboration on the distinction between education in schools and education in the community, particularly in *Democracy and Education*, is very instructive with regard to the problems of education today. Although, as Dewey pointed out, schools are only one agency among many for transmitting culture, they are the only means adults really have for systematically and deliberately educating the young. While education in its broadest sense is continuous, ubiquitous, pervasive, and powerful, there is a difference between the education one receives from actively living life and that offered in school. As Cremin states, "In the ordinary course of living, education is *incidental*; in schooling, education is *intentional*." Dewey acknowledged this distinction but summarily ignored its implications in restricting his analysis of education to the role of schooling. The paradox is that Dewey increased the scope and impact of schools while tacitly recognizing their limitations. In short, schools are simultaneously crucial but limited. This is a dualism that ironically Dewey never resolved, and a dilemma that today still underlies much educational discontent. Over time this polarity in Dewey's analysis has led to an overreliance on schooling, while creating flurries of disenchantment with the schools.[23]

the progressive education association

In 1919 the Progressive Education Association was inaugurated with the ambitious goal of reforming the entire school system of America. At the heart of its program was the fullest development of the individual youngs-

[23]Lawrence A. Cremin, *Public Education* (New York: Basic Books, Inc., Publishers, 1976), pp. 4–8.

ter using modern scientific knowledge of physical, mental, moral, and social growth, but allowing the student optimum natural expression and self-governance. Most progressive educators emphasized the child's natural goodness and stressed the importance of experience. Both the systematic organization of subject matter and a recognition of the teacher's central role were neglected. At its worst the progressive classroom has been caricatured as one in which the student asks, "Do we have to do what we want to, again?"

The aims and direction of the Progressive Education Association were a source of no small frustration to John Dewey. He refused the invitation to be its first honorary president; Charles Elliot subsequently was chosen. Dewey acquiesced after Elliot's death in 1926, though he never became active in the Association, and remained critical of its viewpoint for some years.[24] In fact, one of his last works, *Experience and Education* (1938), was a lucid, concise, and perhaps final effort to set the record straight on precisely what progressive education *is* and *isn't*. *Experience and Education* is a retrospective analysis of both traditional and progressive education: the so-called "old" and "new" education. The book's view is that as practiced in most schools, neither theory is adequate and that for the most part both are mis-educative because their proponents have neglected to carefully develop and apply a theory of experience. "Progressive education," Dewey admonishes, "knows what it is against, but not what it is for!" In response, the progressives exalt the learner's experiences, impulses, and desires at the expense of the orderly development of subject matter built on these experiences. Both interest and content are essential, but neither is a sufficient condition for *educative* experiences.[25]

the withering of the progressive education movement

Progressive education reached its peak in the late 1930s, then declined precipitously in the forties. During its surge no school in the country completely escaped its influence. Among the reasons for the collapse of this movement were the inordinate demands that progressive learning placed on the teacher. Perhaps more telling was the mood of the nation, which had shifted to an uneasy conservatism with the advent of World War II and the postwar years. The wave of literature on education and the schools announced in harsh and no uncertain terms that the schools were too soft and intellectually bankrupt.[26]

---

[24]Cremin, *The Transformation of the School*, pp. 246–50.
[25]John Dewey, *Experience and Education* (New York: Collier Books 1963), pp. 70–75.
[26]Some of this antiprogressive literature was reactionary to the point of irrationality and paranoia. Other criticism was thoughtful and responsive. The more popular works from these writings include Idding Bell's *Crisis in Education* (1949), Arthur Bestor's *Educational Wastelands* (1953), Robert Hutchins's *The Conflict in Education* (1953), Albert Lynd's *Quackery in the Public Schools* (1953), and two books by Mortimer Smith, *And Madly Teach* (1949) and *The Diminished Mind* (1953).

The nation was changing in another crucial way. The educative (and, frequently, mis-educative) role of the mass media—including radio, television, an expanded journalism, film, and eventually the recording industry—was increasing vastly. Society as a whole had always been a source of education; but with profound changes in the agencies of communication and in the shape of community life generally, non-school education had never been so pervasive, at least not since the early impact of industrialism.

THE ILLUSION OF EDUCATIONAL REFORM

The 1940s and 1950s were a period of retrenchment and return to a concentration on traditional American values and basic skills. The practices of most schools, despite some progressive infiltration, never really abandoned these perennial goals; it just appeared that way to many traditionalists. In 1957, with the launching of the Sputnik and the publicized advances in Soviet technology, science as well as education strengthened the conservatives' hand. By 1960, a general tightening of school methods and curricular programs was established. The climax was a report of a study financed by the Carnegie Corporation (through the Educational Testing Service) and conducted by James Conant, an internationally respected chemist of impeccable personal credentials, past president of Harvard University, and a former United States Ambassador to the Federal Republic of Germany. Conant reported his findings in his widely read *The American High School Today* (1959).

It should not have been surprising when Theodore Sizer, then Dean of the School of Education at Harvard, remarked that the high-school academic programs recommended by President Charles Elliot of Harvard in 1885 and James Conant, another president of Harvard in 1959 were in essence not very different. In both, the "mainline" subjects of language, mathematics, science, and social science (largely history) predominate. In addition, the two are strikingly similar in the form of instruction, the relationship between pupils and teachers, and the ways schools are run in these two separate times.[27]

reshaping the high school

Conant was not in total agreement with essentialist critics who, in contrasting American schools with their European counterparts, argue that our schools need to be geared foremostly for intellectual and academic study.

---

[27]Theodore R. Sizer, *Places for Learning, Places for Joy: Speculations on American School Reform* (Cambridge, Mass.: Harvard University Press, 1973), p. 29.

He argued that in a nation as diverse as the United States, the schools must be "comprehensive" if they are to meet the needs of all students. "Comprehensive" implies a general education for all students, a sound nonacademic elective program for those who will join the work force after graduation, and a solid academic program for those whose vocations require study in college.[28] The focus of Conant's study, then, was the "comprehensive" high school: a uniquely American phenomenon.

In this regard, Conant has been placed in the line of famous educational reformers, extending back to Jefferson through Dewey, Elliot, and Mann, who struggled for popular, universal common schooling.[29] Despite this kinship, he demonstrated a distinct concern for the studies of those whom he labeled the "academically talented" (the top 15 to 20 percent with the most promising intellectual potential). In his view, these students are not sufficiently challenged, do not work hard enough, and their programs are not of sufficient range. He was specific in documenting the shortcomings in the programs for the academically talented in the schools he investigated, and equally specific in the number of full-year courses these students should have in the academic disciplines of mathematics and science, foreign language, English, and social studies. The general educational recommendations required of all students were not so rigorous, yet the subject areas mentioned form the core of this program.[30]

A major influence of the Conant study was to reinforce the emphasis on the essential disciplines, and indirectly, on traditional subject matter and teaching methods. Furthermore, according to Conant's own overview, there were, with one exception, simply no radical alterations necessary in the basic pattern of American education. The major change he singled out was to reduce drastically the number of small high schools (those with fewer than a hundred students in the graduating class), a size which he judged utterly inadequate to offer or maintain solid academic programs.[31]

instutional rigidity

Academic conservatives have a fondness for using the progressives, particularly John Dewey, as "whipping boys" when criticizing the schools. To be sure, progressivism had its effects; but they have not been significant with respect to the essential form and substance of schooling. As Sizer

---

[28]James B. Conant, *The American High School Today* (New York: McGraw-Hill Book Company, 1959), p. 26.

[29]Merle Borrowman, "Conant, The Man," *Saturday Review* (September 21, 1963), pp 58–60.

[30]Conant, *The American High School Today*, pp. 53–56, 62–63.

[31]Ibid., pp. 44–45. Interestingly, by the late 1970s even this one major change is being questioned. A growing number of educators, observing the impersonalization and vastness of many modern high schools, argue that we should return to the decentralized school of 400-500 students.

explained, the critics' chagrin has been misplaced; it should have been directed at the traditions that the American schools institutionalized in the 1890s. According to Sizer's analysis, Americans are unfortunately caught in a *web of assumptions* about the operation and management of schools which retard imaginative steps to act upon the rising pedagogical expectations of the last hundred years. These assumptions, including those that are blatantly false, go unchallenged by all except either the cynical or the so-called utopian or visionary critics, and they constitute a set of institutional verities.[32]

The first and key "verity" assumes there is a *national consensus on the general purposes of education*; the only questions are those of execution. One does not have to sit in too many meetings of school administrators to see this pattern emerging: Few people ask what purpose is to be served, or what education is for. Education is simply what goes on in schools. Charles Silberman poignantly labeled this syndrome "mindlessness." Other verities or assumptions in this web include: the importance of *formal* education and the goodness bequeathed with degrees, diplomas, and academic symbols, in contrast to the triviality of incidental education; the necessity of *compulsory attendance* through a certain age; the central role of the public school in *nurturing the common culture*; yet, paradoxically, the wisdom of separating *school and politics*; similarly, the desirability of *teaching values*, but the horror of teaching religion; finally, the anachronistic allegiance to *local control*. The result is that school practices have changed imperceptibly little in the past century: students still are grouped by ages; children are taught in clusters of twenty to forty; schools were and are organized around an autonomous teacher responsible for a group of students; the principal assignments involve texts, tests, reading, some memorization, and workbook exercises; and the time allotment to the basic subjects—English, mathematics and others—is about the same.[33]

PREPARING THE AMERICAN DREAM FOR THE TWENTIETH CENTURY

Lawrence Cremin ends his thorough documentation of progressivism in American education, *The Transformation of the School*, with these parting words:

> And for all the talk about pedagogical breakthroughs and crash programs, the authentic progressive vision remained strangely pertinent to the problems of mid-century America. Perhaps it only awaited the reformulation and resuscitation that would ultimately derive from a larger resurgence of reform in American life and thought.[34]

[32]Sizer, *Places for Learning*, pp. 17, 30.
[33]Ibid., pp. 17–24.
[34]Cremin, *The Transformation of the School*, p. 353.

While our analysis is much the same as Cremin's, it's not so clear that the majority of the educational community shares in this perspective. The general mood, as we trace it over the past twenty to twenty-five years, is to place much stock in breakthroughs, crash programs, expansions in the role of schools, and innovations, while neglecting the pertinence of authentic progressive thought. This is so mainly because progressive educational thought has been poorly understood—for more like seventy-five than twenty-five years!

For all the criticism given our schools, the truth, when we permit ourselves to realize it, is that our schools and educators have done an amazingly good job in providing what the public demands. And we have demanded a great deal, perhaps more than has been educationally prudent. Nevertheless, schools as described have taught democracy, capitalism, and patriotism, the virtues of hard work, obedience, cleanliness, and competitive sport, as well as the evils of communism and daydreaming; they have acculturated the immigrant, socialized the native born, tooled up the future worker, taught boys industrial skills, girls clerical and homemaking skills, and everybody how to drive the automobile. It is virtually heresy to suggest that the schools cannot do some of these tasks as well as other agencies in the community, or that none of this is truly educational and therefore ought not to be functions of schools.

In effect, the schools serve not as a distinct social agency, but as an agent for the society. Schools have succeeded in teaching the young to adjust to the society but have not provided them with the skills, attitudes, and intellectual knowledge that would enable them to adjust the society. In part, our message is that schools cannot, and should not, do all that we expect of them. Ironically, we have John Dewey, in large part, to thank for this accumulation of events. He more than anyone else legitimized the omnipresence of the school. Dewey, however, never envisioned the school as extending so far. To his mind, the school should educate the whole child, but it would be sheer folly for it to try to provide the whole education for the child.

deschooling society

The humanistic reform writers of the 1960s focused on making the schools more decent, civil, liberating, individualized, and therefore more educative places for young people. In this respect, they were very much like Dewey and the host of earlier reformers who saw better schools as the means for achieving improvement of education. To be sure, Dewey caught glimpses of the educational potential in the rest of society, as did some of the later reformers, particularly Paul Goodman (who took incidental education very seriously) and John Holt in *Freedom and Beyond* (1960s). But in the view of another group of educators who took a hard look at our educational society in the 1970s, most of the so-called radical reformers were mere moderates.

According to Ivan Illich, Everett Reimer, and in some respects Carl Bereiter, the fatal flaw of educators, even those who take the most critical view of school operations, is that they envision only a "schooled society."

Although Ivan Illich is most popularly associated with the "deschooling" critique of education, it is inappropriate to consider his ideas apart from Everett Reimer's. In fact Reimer's work and ideas in education precede those of Illich's; the two actually met during 1956 in Puerto Rico; Reimer was doing government work on the human resources and education needs of that country, Illich (himself a priest) had come to organize a training program for New York priests whose parishes burgeoned with Puerto Rican migrants. By 1960 both had left Puerto Rico separately for other parts of Latin America. Reimer joined the Alliance for Progress and Illich left for Mexico, but they maintained close intellectual contact. They came to recognize clearly that the problems of education in these Third World nations were intertwined with the politics, economics, and social structure of the countries; such problems would not be solved simply either by making it possible for more citizens to attend school, or by developing a school system patterned on those of the United States and other industrialized nations. In 1968, Reimer and Illich began a systematic study of this dilemma and of possible solutions to it.[35]

The similarities between Reimer's *School is Dead* and Illich's *Deschooling Society*, both published in 1971, are immense. Whether in the developed or developing parts of the world, schools serve, or self-serve, several functions; some are explicitly recognized, but most prevail at the tacit level. Schools rest much of their case on the claim of teaching cognitive skills—particularly language and mathematics; this they do mostly with intermittent success, the lack of success falling largely on the poor of a nation. Cognitive teaching, however, is not the schools' most important function. Their crucial services to the larger society stem from their unrecognized functions of child care, social screening or sorting, and values-teaching or state indoctrination.[36] Reimer and Illich label this dimension of learning in schools the "hidden curriculum." The purpose of the hidden curriculum is to propogate the social myths of society, such as equality of opportunity, freedom, progress, and efficiency. Social myths are not totally deleterious in their effects, (nor necessarily untrue), for they do distinguish one society from another, and they help to build a society. The distortion and injustice occur when they serve to sustain beliefs that increasingly cease to represent the reality of a society, and when they function to segregate and favor one or more groups of people over others.[37] The effect of present schooling systems and of the "hidden curriculum" is, first, a failure to educate in a

---

[35]Everett Reimer, *School is Dead: Alternatives in Education* (New York: Doubleday & Company, Inc., 1971). pp. ix–x.
[36]Ibid., pp. 13–23.
[37]Ibid., p. 39.

basic literate sense, most of the students of the society's lower class; and second, a failure to truly educate the more privileged students: to nurture their authentic talents and their lifetime capacity and desire to learn.[38]

Schools are not the only modern institution that intentionally educates, or as Illich observes, "has as its primary purpose the shaping of man's vision of reality." There are "hidden curricula" in family life, health care, social services, the legal structure, and the media, serving essentially the same purpose as that of the school. The school, however, is the most powerful of these agents, for only it is granted the *official* sanction to shape the beliefs, attitudes, perceptions, and critical judgment of individuals, and only the school is able to do this in a way that maintains the dependency of the learner on the institution.[39]

To replace schooling, i.e., the central "manipulative" agency, Illich and Reimer would substitute "convivial" learning agencies called "learning webs": networks of people, places, and things. These networks would be designed to provide people with convenient and economical access to deliberate learning in such traditional places as libraries, laboratories, museums, theatres, hospitals, factories, farms, and shops; economical use of and instruction in such educational objects as books, records, film, tools, machines, computers, games, and natural preserves; informal and convenient means of gathering in small groups to share ideas or discuss books; and access to professionals, paraprofessionals, consultants and free-lancers prepared to teach particular skills.[40] This would be an arrangement that acknowledged both the potential educative nature of other socially pertinent institutions and the teaching dimensions inherent in all skilled work.

Carl Bereiter subscribes almost totally to the model of deliberate, ubiquitous, convivial education outlined above. He would institutionalize personal choice, reduce extensively the role of schooling in education, and render cultural resources much more accessible to the learner. Bereiter, in contrast to Illich and Reimer, delineates a specific role to the school. At present, he observes, schools serve three universal functions: child care, skill training, and education (the last meaning values-teaching, socialization, or indoctrination). The efforts toward humanistic educational reform fail because to develop a sufficient number of teachers who are masters of all three functions is an impossible task.[41] We would be wiser on practical and moral grounds (because values education rightly belongs within the

---

[38]Ibid., pp. 4–10. Reimer also draws what he calls an inescapable conclusion that no country in the world can afford the school systems they want, and only a few of the richer nations can afford accepted means of formal education at the current unit costs. We examine the reality of schooling, and the attempts of some Third and Fourth World countries to emulate the United States' education system in Chapter 13.

[39]Ivan Illich, *Deschooling Society* (New York Harper & Row, Publishers, 1971), p. 47.

[40]See Reimer, *School is Dead*, Chaps. 8 and 9, and Illich, *Deschooling Society,* Chap. 6.

[41]Carl Bereiter, *Must We Educate?* (Englewood Cliffs, N.J.: Prentice-Hall, Inc., 1973), chap. 6.

domain of the family and other institutions) to reduce the scope of schooling to child care and training. Furthermore, these two functions should be separated. One cadre of teachers would be charged with child care and another with skill training. "Good training and good child care," Bereiter explains, have almost nothing in common. Training is authoritarian by its very nature. . . . Child care on the other hand allows maximum reasonable freedom. Training has definite goals and aims to reach them; child care flows along indefinitely like life itself."[42]

Paul Goodman, in his assessment of and prescription for education, has a great deal in common with Bereiter, and in turn Illich and Reimer. Among other things, both Goodman and Bereiter place substantial emphasis on the early years of schooling (Bereiter more so than Goodman), request greater educational opportunities for adults (Goodman more so than Bereiter), and call for freeing adolescents from the chains of compulsory high school. In the final work before his death, *New Reformation: Notes of a Neolithic Conservative* (1969), Paul Goodman outlines his thoughts on reformation, which in part include making incidental education the chief means of learning and teaching; eliminating most high schools, with various youth communities assuming their social functions; having college education generally follow, rather than precede, entry into the professions; and designing elementary pedagogy in such a way as to delay socialization and to protect the child's free growth.[43]

These four radical, and in many respects anarchistic, educators are linked to John Dewey in their pursuit of a theory of education founded on quality of experiences: experiences selected to enhance the individual's present moment, to actualize the person's already existing humanity, and to offer the promise of future development. Furthermore, the dilemma inadvertently posed by Dewey several decades back assumes new importance with the rise of the deschooling ideology. If we consider the construct of Reimer and Illich alone, the predicament is not substantially relieved. While Dewey was left precariously perched on one horn of the dilemma (the potential of the school), Illich and Reimer are perched on the other horn (the potential of the community). With the problems of Goodman and Bereiter, strategies for resolving the dilemma are available.

prospects for institutionalized pluralism

The American public school system has been described as the consummate monopoly, nearly unrivaled with respect to the degree of control over its clients and constituents. Our nineteenth century forebears struggled quite openly to forge a "single-omnipotent system." The American common and

---
[42]Ibid., p. 93.
[43]Paul Goodman, *New Reformation: Notes of a Neolithic Conservative* (New York: Random House, Inc., 1969), pp. 85–86.

comprehensive school was meant to enculturate, socialize, and politicize: to effectively assimilate the disparate many.

But the nature of our political-economic society has changed fundamentally. Our lives have become channeled, calculated, and classified; we have been computerized, urbanized, and suburbanized to the point where growing numbers are rebelling at the collectivized quality of life. These people want to be recognized as self-styled individuals. Many Americans are in pursuit of a "neoethnicity," and no longer want to be assimilated—nor need to be.

Schools do have unique functions that they perform better than society's other educating institutions. As Diane Ravitch explains, "They are the most appropriate institution for teaching literacy. They are institutions where rational inquiry and critical intelligence is developed and encouraged."[44] When we cut through the clamor of the recent "back-to-basics" movement and the renewed attacks on schools, the blame again is ill-conceived and misplaced. It's true schools are doing a poor job in teaching basic skills; achievement test scores don't lie. "Basic skills" in this context refers to reading, writing, and computation. But we've been neglecting even more an equally important basic skill—reflective, critical inquiry.

Our schools have been providing precisely the "education" demanded by the larger society—vocational education, career education, sex education, drug education, economic education, drivers education, and so forth. No mistaking, these are important, important to surviving in our society. But schools are merely the most convenient, not necessarily the best, agency for providing this learning. Because this is so, the *essential* function of our schools has been diluted and its effectiveness reduced.

Illich, Reimer, Bereiter, John Holt, and particularly Paul Goodman provide a wholistic and communal vision toward an educational pluralism. They argue for revising the role of the schools and reducing their scope, and for increasing the functions of other community agencies. They call for nothing less than redefining the conventional meanings of education and schooling. The reality is that schooling and education never have been synonymous, though we've come to associate the one with the other. With their new vision and blueprints, education becomes a total community responsibility; simultaneously, the present concept of school becomes less encompassing, but more specific. There will be many "schools" (a multiplicity of institutions), where people of all ages intentionally are educated.

In his *Public Education* (1976), Lawrence Cremin speaks of an *ecology of education*, in which this "multiplicity of institutions," and, we add, individuals or professionals, affect a person's life educatively. These individuals and institutions, Cremin explains, include parents, peers, siblings, and friends, as well as families, churches, synagogues, museums, summer camps, agricultural fairs, settlement houses, factories, television networks, and the

---

[44]Ravitch, "The Schools are for Learning," p. 9

like. They also include writers, journalists, doctors, dentists, lawyers, social workers, mechanics, electronics specialists, farmers, plumbers, and many others. Together, these agencies and people interact with one another and with the larger society to form a "configuration of education."[45] In the eighteenth-century version of this configuration, these agencies interacted in an incidental, and largely educative, way. Today their effects are hardly coordinated and too often mis-educative, so as to foster helplessness, dependency, and misunderstanding in the learner (who is more commonly referred to as client, customer, patron, patient, and student). The new configurations of education would be a systematic, deliberate, community-based arrangement to bring out the potentially educative qualities of all the institutions and people who affect all learners today, young and old.

Paradoxically, we are back where we were two hundred years ago, when education was relevant, communal, and lifelong. And with this, John Dewey's school-community dilemma is resolved. The difference between then and now is that yesterday's learning was spontaneous and incidental; today's must be systematic and intentional. The intervening years of industrialization, technological development, specialization, and urbanization have turned the basic manipulative character of society upside down. Once it was the things and institutions that were manipulated by the people; in modern times it is the people that are being manipulated by things and institutions. This prescription for a new pluralism, configuration, ecology, and conviviality of education promises to change this dehumanizing arrangement. It is intentionally progressive!

CASE STUDY: Compulsory Attendance

The "League of Parents of School Students" has written a "model law" which would lower the cumpulsory attendance laws in your state from sixteen to twelve. The establishment of compulsory attendance laws is a state function, and the proposed bill which was introduced in the current session is under discussion now by the state legislature's Education Committee. The bill has attracted interest throughout the state, but the discussions have been particularly intense in your community as a result of an incident with a family who decided to educate their children without assistance from the schools.

The incident involved a local newspaper editor who had four children in the public schools, the youngest in first grade and the oldest in eleventh grade. Last year the family pulled all four children out of school and began their own education program. The children now are home in the morning completing math, spelling, literature, and history lessons under the mother's tutorage. They spend afternoons at the newspaper office reading,

[45]Cremin, *Public Education*, pp. 85–86.

writing (sometimes for the paper), and generally helping with the publication of the weekly newspaper. The father's work takes him to many businesses, shops, and farms in the area. Often the older children will remain for several afternoons at an establishment where there are skills or knowledge to be learned. Evenings are spent reading and discussing local, state, and national events (social studies). Basic course plans had been obtained through the community college, and the family was preparing to begin instruction in Spanish and the physical sciences.

The family's home- and work-study program was progressing this year, but not without considerable excitement in the community. Some people strongly supported the family, arguing that the schools were inadequately staffed and equipped. In fact, a group had been trying to convince the "League of Parents of School Students" to work for elimination, not just reduction, of compulsory school laws. Other citizens condemned the editor's family as lawbreakers and irresponsible parents.

Last month the superintendent of schools brought charges against the editor and his wife. In their hearing the parents were charged with breaking a state law and put on bail.

The family is now under legal pressure for their children to return to school. What should the family do and why? Where do you stand on the compulsory education bill in the state legislature? Should the bill be withdrawn or defeated? Should it be revised to abolish compulsory attendance?

THOUGHT QUESTIONS

1. How do you explain the harsh, dictatorial, punitive, drill-oriented character of early American schools, when there were examples of more thoughtful and humane ideas on schooling available from modern and earlier European sources?

2. What similarities and differences do you see in "modern" elementary schools and those of colonial times? In answering this, consider school architecture, the curriculum, teaching methods, teacher training, and student-teacher relations.

3. Using Michael Katz's models (see footnote 13), describe what education, and schools, would be like today if the "democratic localism," rather than the "incipient bureaucracy" form of school organization had prevailed. How might the effects of such a form differ from what Katz describes as the effects of bureaucracy.

4. Ralph Tyler, an eminent educator, identified six basic functions of public schools: individual self-realization, citizen literacy, social mobility, preparation for the world of work, wise choices of non-material services, and learning how to learn. Place these in their order of importance as you view them. Defend your first choice. Do you agree that all six should be functions of the schools? If so, which should not be, and why?

5. "What kind of education will best develop the free citizen and the free person?" According to R. Freeman Butts, this question runs through the history of American education and has been answered in different ways at different times. Briefly explain how this question was answered during the colonial, republican, and democratic phases of American education? Has a new response to this question developed in very recent years? If so, what is it?

6. Explain how the secondary schools in this century have served the goals of the "Seven Cardinal Principles" set forth in 1918. Are these goals appropriate for this last quarter of the twentieth century? If they need revising, what would you eliminate, add, or change?

7. If Dewey's theories of progressive education had been properly practiced in early decades, what would schooling have been like with respect to classroom arrangements, curriculum organization, and teaching methods? Was it reasonable to expect that schools and teachers could fully implement these progressive principles? What characteristics of society and schools made the philosophy difficult to implement? What changes in community attitudes, school organization, and teacher training would have been necessary?

8. Do you agree with George Counts that our schools should have as their central aim the reconstruction of society? Why is this necessary or unnecessary? A wise or unwise course of action? Is Counts's goal any more or less pertinent today? Explain.

9. Considering the present popularity of open-space schools, modular scheduling, inquiry methods, simulation games, student projects, and work-study programs, would you describe the basic nature of today's schooling as traditional, progressive, or something else? What do you believe Dewey's response to these innovations would have been?

10. How realistic do you think it is to expect schools to assume a reduced educational role in the future, and subsequently to expect community institutions to take a more active part in educating citizens? Do you see any indicators that this is developing? What problems might exist? How could the "back-to-basics" movement be used to support this change?

PRACTICAL ACTIVITIES

1. Do a pictorial or photographic essay showing the changes in school architecture and classroom organization over the past hundred years in your state. Comment on the relationship between these arrangements and the nature of education over time. Prepare your work for display.

2. Interview a grandparent, another older relative, or friend, and report what schooling was like in the past. Find out about the curriculum, methods, class size, school size, student's role, discipline procedures, and administrative personnel. Relate any anecdotes that would provide today's students with a picture of yesterday's schools.

3. From school records, news clippings, interviews, or any other source, write a brief history of one school. Select a school you attended, one in your

college or university community, or any public or private school that significantly interests you.

4. Interview an older public school teacher, active or retired, who taught during the 1930s or early 1940s. Inquire specifically about the effects of progressive education on the schools in those days: What changes took place? What debates went on about the nature of schooling? How did this teacher's school and colleagues respond to progressivism? Ask also about changes in the school curriculum and organization during the later 1940s and early 1950s. Write up the results, highlighting the effects of both progressive and traditional ideas about schools during this era.

5. Devise a questionnaire assessing people's reaction to a comprehensive community education program, and administer it to students, teachers, administrators, and parents. Areas to survey include shifting to community agencies curricular areas such as industrial arts, business education, and home economics; using the community to develop theatre groups, orchestra, and band, plus art, photography, film-making, and related programs; conducting all competitive athletic programs both for various age groups and with total community support; actively engaging businesses, organizations, institutions, and members of the professions in the formal educational configuration of the community. Tabulate the results and write a summary of your findings.

6. Design an "ecological system of education" for a community with which you are familiar. The schools should be only one of many learning centers. What businesses, organizations, associations, and other institutions would you include? How would these agencies operate, and what would their responsibilities be? What businessmen, entrepreneurs, artisans, and professionals would you enlist in the system, and how would they function? How would you organize and administer this system?

7. Examine the selected bibliography at the end of this chapter, and choose one book by an author who offers a particular historical interpretation of education. Write an analysis and critique or summary exploring this work's educational implications in terms of ideas and events that are significant in today's educational policy and practice.

BIBLIOGRAPHY

books

BESTOR, ARTHUR E., *Educational Wastelands: The Retreat from Learning in Our Public Schools*. Urbana, Ill.: University of Illinois Press, 1953.

BRUNER, JEROME S., *The Process of Education*. New York: Random House, Inc., 1960.

BUTTS, R. FREEMAN, AND LAWRENCE A. CREMIN. *A History of Education in American Culture*. New York: Henry Holt and Company. Inc., 1953.

CONANT, JAMES B., *The American High School Today*. New York: McGraw-Hill Book Company, 1959.

CREMIN, LAWRENCE A., *The Republic and the School: Horace Mann on the Education of*

Free Men. New York: Bureau of Publications, Teachers College, Columbia University, 1962.

———, *American Education: The Colonial Experience, 1607–1783*. New York: Harper & Row, Publishers, 1970.

———, *Public Education:* New York: Basic Books, Inc., Publishers, 1976.

DEWEY, JOHN, *Democracy and Education*. New York: The Macmillan Company, 1916.

———, *Experience and Education*. New York: The Macmillan Company, 1938.

DWORKIN, MARTIN S., *Dewey on Education*. New York: Bureau of Publications, Teachers College, Columbia University, 1959.

GOODMAN, PAUL, *Compulsory Mis-education*. New York: Random House, Inc., 1962.

HUTCHINS, ROBERT M., *The Conflict in Education*. New York: Harper & Row, Publishers, 1953.

ILLICH, IVAN, *Deschooling Society*. New York: Harper & Row, Publishers, 1971.

KATZ, MICHAEL B., *The Irony of Early School Reform*. Cambridge, Mass.: Harvard University Press, 1966.

KRUG, EDWARD A., *Salient Dates in American Education, 1635–1964*. New York: Harper & Row, Publishers, 1966.

———, *The Shaping of the American High School*. New York: Harper & Row, Publishers, 1970.

LEE, CORDON C., ed., *Crusade Against Ignorance: Thomas Jefferson on Education*. New York: Bureau of Publications, Teachers College, Columbia University, 1961.

MEYER, ADOLPHE E., *Grandmasters of Education Thought*. New York: McGraw-Hill Book Company, 1975.

PERKINSON, HENRY J., *The Imperfect Panacea: American Faith in Education, 1865–1965*. New York: Random House, Inc., 1968.

REIMER, EVERETT, *School is Dead: Alternatives in Education*. Doubleday & Company, Inc., 1971.

SILBERMAN, CHARLES E., *Crisis in the Classroom: The Remaking of American Education*. New York: Random House, Inc., 1970.

SIZER, THEODORE R., *Places for Learning, Places for Joy: Speculations on American School Reform*. Cambridge, Mass: Harvard University Press, 1973.

periodicals

BUTTS, R. FREEMAN, "Search for Freedom: The Story of American Education," *National Education Association Journal*, 49, no. 3 (March, 1960), pp. 33–48.

Harvard Educational Review, 46 no. 3 (August, 1976). A Special Issue on History and Education.

Phi Delta Kappan, 58, no. 1 (September, 1976). A Special Bicentennial Issue.

RAVITCH, DIANE, "The Schools are for Learning," *Journal of Current Social Issues*, 13, no. 3 (Summer, 1976), pp. 5–9.

2

THE PHILOSOPHY OF EDUCATION

A Search for Meaning

All of us search for meaning in our lives. In the affairs of community, nation, and world, we seek purpose and relatedness. We pursue inner harmony amid the restlessness and uncertainty created by our impersonal, industrial society. In the maelstrom of change, we secure a precarious survival.

As a species, we are organisms possessed of self-consciousness and capable of learning. Through the prolonged childhood of our species, the person learns the knowledge and skills necessary to survival. Survival in our species, however, is not merely physical, but also psychological, social, and cultural: a combination of elements which impels societies toward education.

> In the fundamental sense, education is the cultural process by which successive generations of men take their places in history.... Through education men acquire the civilization of the present, and make the civilization of the future. In short, the purpose of education is threefold: inheritance, participation, and contribution.[1]
>
> Education "serves to initiate young people into the ways of thinking and behaving characteristic of the culture into which they were born, and to promote the survival of succeeding generations."[2]

---

[1] Israel Scheffler, ed., *Philosophy and Education* (Boston: Allyn & Bacon, Inc., 1966), p. 17.

[2] Maxine Greene, *Teacher as Stranger* (Belmont, Calif.: Wadsworth Publishing Company, Inc., 1973), p. 3.

As individuals possessing self-consciousness, we are obliged to reflect on our existence, to be the philosophers of the earth. Our personal encounters with consciousness are often lonely and fearful: lonely as one ponders purpose in existence; fearful as one contemplates mortality. Philosophy has its wellsprings in those feelings of uniqueness and separateness, in the feeling of being a stranger in a strange land, in the peculiar attributes of human curiousity and wonderment. Philosophy is a primal subject!

Philosophy is a way toward and a perspective on the Real, the Beyond the Real, the Truth, the Good, and the Beautiful. Philosophy deals with the "wholes" of human experience, and the "destinies" of human enterprises. It is a mode of posing questions, the answers to which allow one to "create" meanings. "To do philosophy, then, is to become highly conscious of the phenomena and events in the world as it presents itself to consciousness."[3]

As a way and means for viewing education, philosophy allows one to pursue problems emerging from education-as-a-whole, such as dealing with educational concepts and arguments or probing the value dimensions of educational aims, goals, and objectives. Philosophy applied to education can be used to clarify the processes and products of education, as well as the individual and social dimensions of the enterprise.

Educational philosophy today is both analytical and normative. As an analytical approach, the concerns are the substantive meanings of educational concepts and terms, and the logic of educational theories and debates. As a normative approach, the concerns are the value aspects of educational goals, programs, and outcomes, as well as the religious and moral considerations implicit in educational decisions or choices.

George Kneller states the relationship of educational philosophy to philosophy in this way:

> Just as general philosophy attempts to understand reality as a whole by explaining it in the most general and systematic manner, so educational philosophy seeks to comprehend education in its entirety, interpreting it by means of general concepts that will guide the choice of educational ends and policies.[4]

REALMS OF PHILOSOPHY

Although there are many philosophical arenas, three basic realms of philosophy are *ontology*, *epistemology* and *axiology*. Two divisions of axiology are ethics and esthetics. *Logic* is a primary methodology of philosophy.

For each of the three realms of philosophy, there are several key ques-

---

[3]Ibid., p. 7.
[4]George F. Kneller, *Introduction to the Philosophy of Education* 4th ed. (New York: The Macmillan Company, 1974), p. 3.

tions or topics which guide the search for meaning in the particular realm. These questions and topics help to define the areas of concern in each realm.

Ontology is the study of the nature of reality, the search for what is real. Some philosophers extend ontological concerns to the nature of the universe, to attempts to create meaning in the cosmos, in the whole of universal being. A popular synonym for ontology is metaphysics.

Epistemology, the realm of the theory of knowledge, deals with questions about the nature and limits of human knowledge, about knowing and the known, and about what is truth and how one validates knowledge. It is also concerned with the question (partly psychological) of how we know what we know.

Axiology poses questions of value, of goodness and beauty, of valuing and valuation. It is a realm which probes the sources, the roots, of normative issues, of substantive values (e.g., human dignity) and procedural values (e.g., the preference for a particular process such as scientific method), and of standards for judgment. The two branches of axiology are ethics and esthetics. Ethics is concerned with the quality, the morality of human personal and social behavior. Ethics is the study of the good person, the good society, and the good life. Esthetics is the determination of criteria of beauty—in art, in experience, in person, in environment, in life.

Logic is the method, the process employed when one does philosophy. It defines the rules of the philosophical enterprise, the rules of inference. The two forms of logic are formal or deductive and scientific or inductive.

In many respects, philosophy has lost or abandoned its lofty mission of defining and guiding all the disciplines of knowledge. It has become preoccupied with its methodology. Such methods or approaches as *logical positivism*, *linguistic analysis*, and *mathematical logic* have captured the interests of philosophers.

Logical positivism is not a system of philosophy, but an approach to philosophical problems. August Comte was one of its most forceful advocates during the nineteenth century, when it was becoming clear that new disciplines of knowledge and new formulations in the older disciplines were obviating the need for much of what had previously been the provinces of philosophy. In response to this seemingly diminished role for philosophy, Comte and others claimed that philosophy, in this new world of science, was only useful in *clarifying* the theories and concepts of science. Philosophy also must abandon, said Comte, the subjective realm of metaphysics, where problems and questions do not permit experimental, scientific analysis and verification.

In the twentieth century, logical positivism is generally termed *analytic philosophy*, and is concerned with precision and verifiability. Analytic philosophers seek more precise language or symbol systems, and insist that statements, claims, and hypotheses be formulated in ways that allow for scientific verifiability. In a sense, this school of thought has applied science-as-method to traditional philosophical problems, and mathematics-as-language to traditional logical constructs. The analysis of propositions, by use of linguistic analysis has become the exclusive focus for analytic philosophers. (Linguistic analysis is focused on clarifying propositions which are stated in the language of normal discourse.) Other analytic philosophers are concerned with developing new languages, chiefly relying on mathematics as the exemplar of a precise language.

In educational philosophy, the impact of analytic philosophy has been through the use of linguistic analysis applied to those concepts used in education, such as teaching, curriculum, motivation, needs, or equality of educational opportunity. Smith and Ennis claim the following benefits from applying analytic philosophy to education:

1. To discover the neglected meanings which particular educational terms and expressions are given through the ways they are used in different contexts.
2. To uncover conceptual blunders and to lay bare erroneous lines of reasoning which result from failure to understand how language is being used in a given situation.
3. To clear away pseudo-problems and pseudo-questions that exist only as a result of confused and unclear conceptions and the vague, ambiguous use of language.
4. To explore the dimensions of educational terminology and to gain a clearer understanding of the relationships between thought, language, and reality, and thus to broaden the basis upon which we ground our beliefs about reality and our convictions of value.
5. To lay bare unrecognized logical inconsistencies which result from the uncritical use of language.[5]

Newsome put the matter more concisely, by concluding that "by and through philosophical analysis (logical and linguistic) what men say (statements, sentences, or propositions) can be clarified and made meaningful or exposed as nonsense."[6] This is also the claim for analytic philosophy applied to education.

IDEALISM, REALISM, AND PRAGMATISM

In the Western philosophical tradition, two positions have historically vied for predominance: *idealism* and *realism*. A third, younger tradition, and a distinct minority position, is *pragmatism*. Each of these three philosophies

---

[5]B. O. Smith and Robert H. Ennis, *Language and Concepts in Education* (Chicago: Rand McNally & Co., 1961), pp. iv, v.

[6]George L. Newsome, Jr., "Analytic Philosophy and Theory of Education," in *Selected Readings in the Philosophy of Education*, 4th ed., ed. Joe Park (New York: The Macmillan Company, 1974), p. 13.

is a relatively complete system; that is, each makes claims within the realms of ontology, epistemology, and axiology.

Among the three traditional philosophical positions, idealism traces its heritage from Plato and the theologies of Judeo-Christian religions; realism from Aristotle, Thomas Aquinas, and various forms of naturalism; and pragmatism from Charles S. Peirce, William James, John Dewey, and the emergence of modern science.

idealism

Advocates of idealism postulate a world of mind and ideas, of microcosm *and* macrocosm (e.g., minds of men *and* Mind of God), of forms and shadows of forms. To the idealist, the human mind creates what it knows, and those creations are ideas. Only ideas enter consciousness; only mind is capable of creativity, cognition, and volition. Only humans (or gods) create ideal ideas of truth, goodness, and beauty.

In the tradition of idealism, an Absolute Mind (or God or pantheon of gods or revealed idea) created reality, knows all, continues to create, and regulates the world. The truth of an idea can be determined by the degree to which it corresponds to or is in coherence with a body of knowledge already in existence—revealed literature, "great" books, wisdom of the past, the process of formal deductive logic. Values are manifest in concrete forms and discrete behaviors; value is "merely" human, never adequate and always imperfect; justice is temporal. On the other hand, Values, Value and Justice (ideal types, underlying forms) are infinite and eternal conceptions, never totally understood or achieved by humankind. Yet, human behavior is purposive (volitional); it does not merely react to stimuli. Free will exists, though motivation for its exercise is internal, emanating from the individual's quest for value.

realism

The proponents of realism postulate a world of things, of material existence, of "real" concrete objects, of "commonsense" reality. The realist "sees" an external world (including himself or herself) which exists independent of mind. This external world is created and determined by matter (what exists) and process (evolution). To the realist, humankind *can* know the real nature of this world independent of a priori conceptions of Mind. Both human mind and external object exist separately though at times in interaction (e.g., person-to-person interaction).

A proposition can be said to be true if it is agreed that it corresponds to scientifically validated knowledge, which is to say it is observable and its *qualities* are independently (of the observer) verifiable. Anything that exists possesses quantity and quality. Idea (perception and conception) and reality are the same, thus everything is knowable. Nature possesses discoverable plan, order, structure, and law. The world, the natural order is permanent, though evolving, and can be predicted and controlled. Value inheres in the laws of nature; beauty inheres in the elegance of nature and its laws; goodness is harmony with natural law. Realism is dependent on the ways of both formal/deductive and scientific/inductive logic.

Realism is an umbrella term, under which are clustered several separate schools of thought. For example, although all realists assert belief in the reality of matter, of the physical material world, they disagree as to the origin of this world which exists separate from and independent of the observer. For the religious realist, both matter and spirit are created by God, and spirit is the more significant mode of being or existing. The classical realist, on the other hand, sees no need for divine intervention as an explanation for the origin of the universe, and extols the rational mind over material existence. Both of these schools of thought harbor several variants. A type of religious realism, for example, is scholasticism or Thomism (after Thomas Aquinas), which is one of the philosophies of the Roman Catholic Church. An example of a type of classical realism is natural or scientific realism, which grew out of the early scientific movement, specifically the work of Francis Bacon.

Today, two prominent realist schools of thought are neorealism and neo-Thomism. Neorealism is the attempt to apply the rigor and methodologies of modern science and mathematics to philosophical problems, as in the writings of Bertrand Russell and Alfred North Whitehead. The neo-Thomists accept the duality of matter and spirit as articulated by Aquinas, but add a second duality of faith and reason (and, for some, intuition and revelation are added to faith and reason) as sources of knowledge, operating in harmony.

pragmatism

Pragmatism had its birth in the American nation—in the mid-nineteenth century with Peirce and in the late nineteenth and early twentieth centuries with James and Dewey. It grew out of the emergence of science and the scientific method, but especially out of the works of Charles Darwin. Later, in the twentieth century, the work of Albert Einstein provided additional ammunition for pragmatists. Thus, from scientific method, Darwinian evolution, and Einstein's theories of general and specific relativity came pragmatism's emphasis on process and relativism.

To the pragmatist, ideas have consequences; the meaning of a proposition is in its consequences. If an idea were acted upon, the consequences of that action define (attribute meaning to) the idea. Thus, a "meaningful"

Table 2-1 Synopsis of Idealism, Realism, and Pragmatism

	Ontology	Epistemology	Axiology	Logic
Idealism	Reality is Mind and Form.	Knowledge is the idea, vis á vis the Idea.	Value is the reflection of and imitation of the Ideal Mind and Idea.	Formal/ Deductive
Realism	Reality is things, objects, matter.	Knowledge is the correspondence of ideas to observable facts.	Value is the emulation of Nature and Natural Law.	Formal/ Deductive and Scientific/ Inductive
Pragmatism	Reality is human experience.	Knowledge is the consequences of an idea which can be acted on.	Value is derived from experience. Valuing yields criteria which can be used to evaluate experience.	Scientific/ Inductive and Formal/ Deductive

idea is one which can be tested, can be acted on, can be tried out in practice. To Peirce, consequences are amenable to experimental verification, which is to say they are grounded in human experience. To the extent one cannot experience God or love, these "ideas" have no consequences, are untestable, and lack meaning. To the extent Mind (or mind) has no location or physiology (structure or function), it does not exist; on the other hand, brain and cognitive and affective processes do exist. In the axiological realm, pragmatists allow the existence of ethical and esthetic ideas to the extent that such ideas affect human behavior. Here such concepts as cultural relativism, ethical relativism, and artistic relativism have meaning for pragmatists.

Pragmatism is a philosophy of action—of actors who act on the world. Its focus is the realm of epistemology, with some axiological claims, and little concern for ontology. It is the process of humankind's interactions and the propositions derived from these interactions which are at the heart of pragmatism.

EDUCATION AND IDEALISM, REALISM, AND PRAGMATISM

Few of the advocates of idealism, realism, or pragmatism have considered education as a key topic or a cluster of problems within their own particular philosophical positions. There are, however, many implications for education which can be drawn from each of these three philosophical schools. Often, the educational implications of a particular philosophical position are more evident in the theory of knowledge (epistemology), for example, than in the realms of ontology or axiology; for other schools of thought, the implications might be more obvious in the values domain (axiology). Thus, for relating the educational implications of a philosophical school, the realms of ontology, epistemology, and axiology will not be used as organizers; rather, the particular school of thought will be examined as a whole for its implications for education.

idealism and education

Since the idealist believes in the primacy of mind and ideas, the clear implication for education is to emphasize training the mind, cultivating the soul, and mastering ideas. A human being is considered either dichotomous: body and mind; or trichotomous: body, mind, and spirit. In the first case, mind is supreme, but in the second, spirit is foremost. In the former, education should be focused on the mind; in the latter, education should emphasize the spirit.

Freedom and rationality are two important and related concepts to idealists. By freedom is meant the exercise of free will in personal decisions, accompanied by responsibility for the consequences of personal actions. By rationality is meant the processes of discovering and evolving ideas. These two concepts imply that teaching is Socratic in nature, that the curriculum's content is the subjects, ideas, and rational thinking processes which have withstood the tests of time and which are the foundations of Western civilization, and that the student is an emerging soul, spirit, mind, possessing the capability of becoming a rational thinker and a purposive, free being. Sensory learning must always be subservient to learning based on reason.

Because, for idealists, ultimate values are enduring and transcendent, school policies and procedures should reflect and accentuate those traditional values which "great" persons and "great" societies have considered precious.

realism and education

For realists, the physical, material universe exists, independent of mind. Matter is real and not illusion. Thomists and neo-Thomists, however, go a step further than the other Realists in asserting that matter and mind are creations of a God who consistently acts in an orderly and rational manner.

Education, for most realists, should emphasize both the natural laws which control all matter, including the human organism, and the world of the mind, which discovers order and harmony in all aspects of existence.

For religious realists, of course, both matter and mind are viewed as divine creations. The curriculum implied by realism comprises an essential core of humanistic and scientific subjects (harmonized by religious beliefs for the Thomists) that are considered necessary in preparing students not only to adapt to physical and cultural reality, but also to surmount this reality through personal creativity and spirituality.

Realists don't demean ideas, but do demand that ideas be verified by sensory experience; that is, an idea or theory must correspond to concrete, physical existence. Thus, students should learn scientific and experimental methods, as well as processes of rationality.

Since realists assert the existence of a universal moral law, values are fixed and available to human beings through reason (combined with faith for Thomists). If values are timeless, the teacher has an obligation to inculcate established moral principles in all students. For Thomists, the fixed values are those revealed in the Bible and those proclaimed by the Church.

pragmatism and education

The pragmatist views the universe as matter in motion; change is continual and pervasive. Not only is reality changing, but values are also relative to time, place, and circumstances.

Since little endures or is permanent, pragmatism implies that the curriculum should emphasize processes, such as learning how to learn and science-as-method. Further, teaching and learning should be active and interactive enterprises; the ends and means of education should be reciprocal and mutually reinforcing.

For pragmatists, human beings create their world by a continuous reconstruction of experiences, by social and biological interactions with their environment. In order to encourage increased and more complex reconstructions, teachers should extend and build upon students' experiences. The learning environment should be evocative of multiple varied student responses and interactions. In addition, since learning is interactive, it includes interactions with others; it is social. Thus, the educational transactions are student-environment, student-teacher, and student-student.

Pragmatists emphasize processes, especially those of intelligence or rationality, the methods of science, and problem solving. But none of these processes is to be learned as *merely* academic ritual or formula. The individual motivations to engage in the processes grow out of intellect or of felt perplexities, and the culminations of processes are conclusions, new constructions, and some form of action. The subjects in the curriculum should be viewed as spurs to interest and as sources for problems and student projects, rather than as fixed products or collections of facts.

For the student, the development of values occurs in the same ways as the creation of knowledge—by the reconstruction of experience. This yields a kind of situation-specific ethics, where personal and social (i.e., collective) values interact to suggest the appropriate ethical response for the individual.

John Dewey, a prominent advocate of pragmatism, saw living as an interactive process of learning; education as a process to encourage and enhance learning; and democracy as the mode for a learning society.

PHILOSOPHIES OF EDUCATION

Although *aspects* of educational philosophy can be derived from each of the traditions of idealism, realism, and pragmatism, another approach provides a more coherent pattern of educational philosophies. Four discrete philosophies of education have emerged in Western societies. These are: perennialism, essentialism, progressivism, and reconstructionism.

Each of these four philosophies of education has roots in one or more of the three philosophical traditions of idealism, realism, and pragmatism. For example, pragmatism spawned both progressivism and reconstructionism; aspects of both idealism and realism can be found in essentialism; and perennialism evolved primarily out of idealism.

The choice of developing the educational philosophies of perennialism, essentialism, progressivism, and reconstructionism is made partly because these four positions derive from questions of *both* an educational *and* philosophical nature rather than from primarily philosophical interests, and partly because of the relationships of these philosophies of education to American educational history.

In American education, the dominant philosophy of education has been essentialism. One protest to essentialism has been perennialism, though much of colonial American education tended to be perennialist. Other protests have been progressivism and reconstructionism, though these two philosophies are essentially twentieth-century phenomena. Essentialism, however, is basically a conservative position. This is understandable, for a society expects its educational institutions to *reflect* the traditions and the status quo (even though it may be changing) of the society. Cultural lag in educational institutions is not merely the result of encrusted bureaucracy or unwillingness to change on the part of educational personnel; it is an intended result of the conserving function assigned to schools by a society. To induce rapid change in education, it seems, requires *first* a society which has undergone rapid change in its cultural, political, and economic institutions. Revolution, such as in modern Cuba and China, brings drastic and profound change to education.

A philosophy of education, in addition to asking basic ontological, epistemological, and axiological questions, probes topics peculiar to education. Not only are claims concerning the nature of knowledge necessary, but also judgments and justifications for what knowledge is of most worth. Further, educational philosophy seeks meanings for those global concepts which define the educational process: education, learning, teaching, curriculum, and others. Since the process of education occurs in particular social contexts, educational philosophy also overlaps social, political, and economic philosophy. For example, John Dewey found it necessary to speculate on the relationships of school and society, of child (student) and curriculum, and of democracy and education, as well as on other relationships peculiar to education. Finally, a particularly important topic in educational philosophy has been the aims or goals of education, both in terms of individual growth or self-realization, and in terms of the relationships between educational goals and those of society.

essentialism

As the dominant educational philosophy in American education, essentialism possesses constant currency and appeal, especially for those who are the leaders in society and in education. Being a conservative position, essentialism attracts adherents who believe in conserving the best of the traditions of a particular society (e.g., United States) and civilization (e.g., Western), and in promoting intellectual growth of the individual. Essentialists agree on these *primary* purposes of education. They disagree, however, as to what, if any, *secondary* purposes should be served by education. Some argue that education should simply deal only with transmission of the cultural heritage and intellectual training. Others would affirm the priority of these two goals, but allow for such secondary goals as physical health, emotional health, vocational competency, and avocational pursuits.

To the essentialist, the core of the curriculum must be the "essentials." In the elementary school, the essentials are reading, speaking, writing, spelling, and arithmetic, and later the introduction of history, geography (and perhaps a few other social sciences, but always as separate subjects or disciplines), physical and biological science, and foreign languages (usually Latin, Greek, French, or German). Less essential are art, music, and physical education. In the secondary school, the essentials of the elementary school are made broader, more specialized, and more rigorous. For example, arithmetic becomes mathematics (algebra, geometry, trigonometry, calculus); physical science becomes physics, chemistry, and geology. Less essential are art, music, and physical education, with the addition of vocational and avocational subjects. All forms of extracurricular activities such as clubs, athletics, band, or chorus are tolerated, but of low priority.

Throughout the curriculum, essentialists demand that values be taught, and the values are to be those of a particular reference group: namely, the social and cultural values of the dominant class in the society, of the political and intellectual leaders (both dead and alive) of the nation, and of the "great" writers of Western civilization. To teach the traditions of the society one must also teach the traditional values of the society.

Essentialists regard teaching as the transmission of essential knowledge, skills, and values. The teacher is the agent of society whose primary task is to insure continuity. The teacher is also the model: of intellectual competency, of knowledgeability in the cultural heritage, and of the traditional social values. The teacher (and the school) should reflect the best of what was and is the society.

perennialism

Also in the conservative tradition, yet opposed to much of essentialism, stands perennialism. The perennialists abhor much in the modern world, such as the results of the industrial revolution, the scientific revolution, the secularization and proletariatization of values, and the technological and electronic revolutions.

As a philosophy of education, perennialism is an assertion of the primacy of the past, especially of that past represented by the "great" writers and their works. Perennialism is a plea for permanencies, for the unchanging nature of the universe, human nature, truth, knowledge, virtue and beauty. The desirable is what is perennial. As Robert Hutchins remarked,

> ... the function of man as man is the same in every age and in every society, since it results from his nature as man. The aim of the educational system is the same in every age and in every society where such a system can exist: it is to improve man as man.[7]

For perennialists, the answers to all educational questions flow from the answer to one question: What is human nature? To the perennialist, human nature is constant. Humankind's most distinctive characteristic is the ability to reason; the ideal, adult human being is perfectly rational (or at least pursues the rule of reason in all human affairs). Only the human species can comprehend the physical and spiritual constancies of existence. All humanity has the same potential to realize perfection in personal and social achievement. From this conception of human nature flows the perennialist philosophy of education.

If human nature is always and everywhere the same, education must be the same for all, always and everywhere. The goal of education is constant, absolute, and universal: to develop the rational person. This is not to say that ethical dimensions are ignored; on the contrary, rationality is a broad concept which includes the application of the process of reasoning to *all* domains of human affairs.

---

[7]Robert M. Hutchins, *The Conflict in Education: In a Democratic Society* (New York: Harper & Brothers, 1953), p. 68.

To the perennialist, teaching is an art; the art of stimulating and directing the development of the individual's inherent powers to think rationally, powers possessed by all humans. Teaching is primarily exhortation, explication, Socratic discourse, and oral exposition.

The perennialist curriculum is derived from ancient Greek and Latin conceptions of a liberal education, of the liberal arts represented in the medieval trivium and quadrivium. The trivium is composed of grammar, rhetoric, and dialectic; the quadrivium consists of arithmetic, geometry, astronomy, and music. From these seven liberal arts flow the perennialist emphasis on language and mathematics, on arts as opposed to sciences. Also, since the arts were firmly established early in the history of Western civilization, the perennialist considers them as permanent, perennially fixed. The liberal arts (i.e., literary and mathematical arts) are represented in the great books, which have become confirmed as "great" by having stood the tests of time (immortality) and significance (they are the choices of the literati and intelligentsia in successive eras); they are "contemporary" for any age. Among the "great books" are the works of Plato, Aristotle, Marcus Aurelius, St. Augustine, St. Thomas Aquinas, Copernicus, Galileo, Erasmus, Shakespeare, and so on. Obviously, if one is to read these writers in the languages in which they wrote, Latin and Greek must be studied by all students.

The classical education advocated by perennialists appeals to only a minority of American citizens, but these are frequently the intellectual leaders of the society, who are able to articulate and make visible the perennialist position. Although perennialism is a conservative philosophy of education, its chief target is the other conservative philosophy, essentialism.

progressivism

The peculiarly American philosophy of pragmatism gave birth to the two educational philosophies of progressivism and reconstructionism. The progressive philosophy of education emerged in late nineteenth century America and reached its peak of influence in the 1920s and 1930s. Reconstructionism had numerous intellectual and sociological roots, but its lineage is most readily traced to progressivism. Reconstructionists formed a faction of the progressive education movement during the 1930s.

As a protest to essentialism, progressivism is spurred by dissatisfaction: that American democracy has become perverted from its enabling ideology; that American schools have become oppressive to children and youth. Progressivism is the educational manifestation of the liberal, humanitarian reform movement sought to combat the political and economic evils of industrial society. Progressives pursued reform and change in both educational *and* social affairs.

Figure 2-1 John Dewey: Father of Progressive Education

In his most comprehensive work, *Democracy and Education*, John Dewey argued that democracy is not merely a political form, but is a total way of social living, and that the greatest strength of a democratic way of life lies in democratic education. To Dewey, democracy and education are key interactive actors: the democratic society is an educative model to its citizens; democratic education flows naturally, organically from a democratic society. Progress in a democratic society is change; in a Hegelian sense, progress is represented by new syntheses which emerge from the resolutions of conflicts between theses and antitheses. Progress for the individual is growth, becoming, maturation. At any point in time, enjoyable and effective personal or social living is at stake, is being risked in the crucible of intra- and inter-personal interaction and conflict. Democratic society and democratic education are participatory and emergent, not preparatory and absolute. Living *is* learning; education (like democracy) *is* living, *is* a way of life.

To learn is to change! Given interest, curiosity, or a disturbing situation, the human organism is impelled to action. To act is to experience and experiment, to bring intelligence to bear, to direct goal-oriented behavior, to solve problems, and to make decisions. Action leads to relief of the disturbance (or to a new motivation to act), to a reconstruction of experience, to new truths (or to new dilemmas and paradoxes), to conclusions which call forth commitments to act on the conclusions. The cycle goes on, as it were, forever.

It is the individual who learns, alone or in groups, but always in the interactive mode, in interaction with the environment, with other persons, or with oneself. One of the ways in which human evolution operates is through individual differences resulting in human variability in groups, cultures, and societies. To cultivate human variability is to value human dignity and to insure the survival of the species.

In education, in schooling, the progressive philosophy leads to education as an end in itself. Education is a way, a process to discover ends. Learning is the reconstruction of personal and social experience, and an individual's experience is the infrastructure for learning. Respect for individual differences is the starting point for planning instruction. Democratic group living is the preferred mode in classrooms and schools. The application of intelligence to problems and projects is the basis for determining the curriculum. Individual freedom, within the constraints of the democratic social contract, is a goal for all members (students, teachers, administrators, and others) of the school community.

reconstructionism

During the Great Depression of the 1930s, when the "progressive education" (progressivism) movement was at its height of popularity, many Americans, and especially a significant minority of progressive educators, became disillusioned with American society and impatient with the pace of reform in both education and society. A "radical caucus" of progressives argued that progressivism was in need of redirection: to place less emphasis on child-centered (individualistic) education and more emphasis on society-centered (social reform) education; less interest in the growth of the person and more interest in the reform of society. This splinter group of progressives became the founders and advocates of reconstructionism (also called social reconstructionism).

As a spinoff of progressivism, the reconstructionists adhered to the philosophy of pragmatism and the principles of progressivism, but extended these positions to include the explicit reform of society as a major goal of education. Reconstructionists believe that an image of the ideal society should be the basis of determining educational programs; schools should seek to educate future citizens for a society of the future, a society that is "becoming" rather than one that currently exists. This challenge was presented by George S. Counts at the 1932 national convention of the Progressive Education Association in a speech entitled "Dare the School Build a New Social Order?" Counts had the audacity to suggest that the educational institution of a society might *lead* the society in the quest to realize its values and ideals. For Counts, the schools could become the social reform institution, the change agent, of a society. In the rhetoric of a "romantic," he wrote:

The weakness of Progressive Education thus lies in the fact that it has elaborated no theory of social welfare, unless it be that of anarchy or extreme individualism.... If Progressive Education is to be genuinely progressive, it must ... face squarely and courageously every social issue, come to grips with life in all its stark reality, establish an organic relation with the community, develop a realistic and comprehensive theory of welfare, fashion a compelling and challenging vision of human destiny, and become less frightened than it is today at the bogeys of *imposition* and *indoctrination*.[8]

Another reconstructionist, Theodore Brameld, has observed that reconstructionism is a crisis philosophy, appropriate for a culture or a society in crisis, which is the essence of a democratic society. Little wonder, then, that reconstructionism has had its greatest appeal in the America of the 1930s and 1960s, the two periods in twentieth-century American history when disillusionment became the prevailing ethos.

Not only is reconstructionism an educational philosophy, it also harbors the strategies of socio-political action and the collectivization of teacher power, both as means to promote social reform. For the reconstructionist, analysis and conclusion are insufficient; they must lead to commitment and action, by both teachers and students.

In education, the reconstructionists advocate the commitment of teachers (and students) to the creation of a new, progressive, reconstructed view of society. The emerging, "becoming" society must be democratic, based on communalism rather than individualism. The school must model this new society, for it is the young who will bring the new society to fruition. Cooperative endeavors must replace individualistic and competitive striving. Group living and action will replace individualistic leadership and achievement as the motivating forces of the future.

EXISTENTIALISM

The four philosophies of education—essentialism, perennialism, progressivism, and reconstructionism—command the stage in debates on educational issues. There is, however, another philosophical position which has enjoyed some appeal in the past three decades and which has some implications for education. The philosophy of existentialism is of European origin and only became popular in the period just prior to, during, and after, World War II. It is a highly individualistic philosophy, heavily dependent on subjective factors—intuition, introspection, emotional commitment, and the feeling of aloneness. As such, its educational implications are for the teacher and student *as individuals*.

[8]George S. Counts, *Dare the School Build a New Social Order?* (New York: The John Day Company, 1932), pp. 7–8.

Table 2-2 Synopsis of Four Philosophies of Education

Essentialism	Perennialism
1. Preserving the "best" of the cultural traditions of a particular society and civilization.	1. The enhancement and promotion of the superiority of the past and the permanency of the "classics."
2. Promotion of the intellectual growth of the individual.	2. Human nature is constant, its most distinctive trait being the ability to reason.
3. Providing a curriculum composed of "essentials": subjects with intellectual substance and basic skills.	3. Promoting the development of the rational person.
4. Explicit teaching of values: those traditional values prized by the dominant class.	4. Teaching is an art which helps students to use their inherent power to think rationally, and employs exhortation, explication, Socratic discourse, and oral exposition.
5. Teaching should be the most effective and efficient transmission of "essentials."	5. The curriculum centers on the seven liberal arts and the "great books" of human history.

Progressivism	Reconstructionism
1. Education is growth and development, the continuous reconstruction of experience, a living/learning process rather than a preparation for later adult life	1. Education has the mission of leading society to realize its values via goals and programs of social betterment.
2. Democratic social living includes democratic education, being both participatory and emergent.	2. Schools should become the agents of change and social reform.
3. Learning is active and leads to change in behavior.	3. The curriculum should be based on an image of the ideal society.
4. The curriculum emerges from the needs of students and of society and involves the application of intelligence to human problems.	4. Learning is active, and leads to involvement in programs of social reform via citizen political action.
5. Teaching is the guiding of inquiry.	5. The school, the teacher, the students should model the new, more perfect, democratic society.

Perhaps the greatest appeal of existentialism is to those who see little else but meaninglessness and absurdity, cruelty, and horror in modern living; to those who feel oppressed by the institutions created by industrial, technological societies; and to those who feel anonymity and the loss of freedom.

If the dilemma of Western civilization is between analysis and commitment, between reason and passion, the existentialist asserts the primacy of commitment and passion. One's existence—the dangers, the risks, the choices—precedes one's essence—the models, theories and concepts of human nature.

The individual human being is born, enters existence, grows, becomes aware of his or her existence, his or her aloneness, his or her mortality. A person becomes what he or she decides to become; a person is free to choose his or her essence—in spite of or even in defiance of hereditary and environmental influences. One acts, asserts personhood; or one becomes *merely* the product of external forces, which amounts to the loss (or abdication) of freedom. Existentialists proclaim the individual as the exemplary philosopher, the person willing to freely choose, when all else seems to overwhelm.

Though the roots of existentialism are to be found in the nineteenth century, in the writings of Sören Kierkegaard, Friedrich Nietzsche, and Fyodor Dostoevsky, existentialism did not gain widespread appeal until World War II. Leading contemporary existentialists are Albert Camus, Jean-Paul Sartre, Martin Heideigger, and Maurice Merleau-Ponty. Because it lends itself to all forms of literary expression, existentialism seems to pervade the writings of Franz Kafka, Edward Albee, Harold Pinter, Kurt Vonnegut, Jr., Samuel Beckett, William Burroughs, John Barth, Rainer Maria Rilke, Joan Didion, Saul Bellow, and Joseph Heller. The most articulate and literate American educator to espouse existentialism is Maxine Greene.

As one might expect, the individual human experience is the primary unit of explanation for the existentialist. One *is* alone—apart from the physical universe, and, for the most part, apart from other human beings. Living is a passionate confrontation with the dangers of and threats to existence, especially freedom and death.

Reality is defined by the individual, "becoming" human being, who must contend with things and others. A human may create things and goods, but primarily a human creates himself or herself. A person is free to choose to become what he or she will. And to be free is to choose, to act, and to be responsible for one's acts. Freedom is an awesome and dreadful potential: for good or evil, to oneself or to others.

To the existentialist, what we know are the events and phenomena which are perceived in consciousness. What is perceived directly we ascribe meaning to, creating, as it were, our own separate universes—sometimes "hells," sometimes "heavens," usually both.

Clearly, it is virtually impossible to have schools or educational systems based on existentialism. What *is* possible is the individual existentialist teacher or student, a person who passionately opposes the forces which deny the individual his or her freedom. The existentialist teacher values, prizes his or her freedom, and respects the freedom of others, of students, other teachers, and administrators. Further, the existentialist teacher expects students to accept the consequences, the results, the outcomes of all his or her actions. Mutual respect for mutual growth characterizes the existential interaction. But human growth and interpersonal interaction always combine joy and tragedy, hope and despair.

The subjects of the existential curriculum are unspecified, although any subject can be, at the right moment, the tool, the vehicle to engage the individual in his or her striving to "become." The educational methods appropriate to existentialism are dialogue, reflective inquiry, and individual introspection.

It should be apparent that existentialism as a philosophy has limited application as an educational philosophy. This is only true because education as a concept has been interpreted in all Western societies as necessitating some form of schooling. Schooling involves an institutionalized socialization process which requires group instruction and bureaucratic organization. Schooling is a process which proscribes freedom and mirrors those social conditions and forces which the existentialist opposes. Yet, if the individual existentialist can exert his or her will regardless of deterministic forces, the will can survive even in the crucible of the school.

Figure 2-2 Developing a Personal Philosophy of Education

A PERSONAL PHILOSOPHY OF EDUCATION

It is doubtful if any person or teacher ever lives by or teaches by a carefully thought out, systematic philosophical position. Nevertheless, the search for meaning goes on, by each person and by each teacher.

In the pursuit of meaning by persons-as-teachers, the interaction of all facets of life is focused on the behaviors called teaching. In those arenas where teaching (and learning) as interpersonal interaction occurs, the person-as-teacher needs some moorings, some beliefs he or she can rely on, a harmony of purposes. Though these may change with experience, a set of assertions concerning education is a useful beginning.

The following schema of questions about education, a beginning in the search for meaning in educational philosophy, is designed to stimulate reflection by the person-as-teacher.

questions for a philosophy of education

I. Ontology: Questions of Reality and Humanness.
   A. What is the nature of "reality"?
      1. What is "universe"?
      2. What are the ecological relationships in physical and biological existence?
   B. What is the nature of "humanness"?
      1. What are the characteristics of the human species?
      2. What are the aspects of relatedness and aloneness of humankind?
II. Epistemology: Questions of Knowing and the Known.
   A. What is the nature of "knowledge"?
      1. What is "truth," "knowledge," "the known"?
      2. How do human beings validate (prove) knowledge?
      3. What are the sources of knowledge?
   B. What are the ways of "human knowing?"
      1. What are the cognitive processes?
      2. What are the affective processes?
   C. What knowledge is most worth knowing?
      1. Is science or humanities most worthwhile?
      2. Is self-knowledge or publicly verifiable knowledge most worthwhile?
      3. Are products or processes of knowledge most worth knowing?
   D. What are the meanings of global (abstract at high level) educational concepts such as
      1. "democracy"
      2. "freedom"
      3. "human dignity"
III. Axiology—Ethics: Questions of Value.
   A. What is the nature of "values"?
      1. Are values transient, permanent, relative, absolute?
      2. Are values solely human creations, mystical creations, inherent in the physical universe?

B. What values are manifest in the process of education?
   1. What are the values of the society in which the educational institution exists?
      —The values of the human species?
      —The values of Western civilization?
      —The values of the particular nation-state?
      — The values of the local community?
   2. What are the values underlying the goals of education?
      —The goals of education in a society?
      —The goals of education in a school district?
      —The goals of education in a school?
      —The goals of education for a person-as-teacher?
   3. What are the values underlying the selection of (and omission of) curricular content? What subjects should be included in the curriculum? What content (knowledge, skills, and attitudes) should be included in a particular course?

Clearly, a teacher needs to know far more than has been presented in this chapter in order to respond adequately, thoughtfully, and honestly to each of the questions posed in the preceding outline. Throughout a person's teaching career, however, it might be helpful periodically to ask these questions, to compare current responses to earlier responses, and to compare one's positions with those of one's colleagues. In fact, it is usually only after several years of teaching experience that teachers recognize the need for and helpfulness of educational philosophy. It is then that the complexity and profundity of the educational process becomes evident, and it is then also that justifying and conceptualizing this process becomes a helpful tool.

CASE STUDY: Education in the Stone Age[9]

A million years ago, a concerned and dedicated reformer turned his attention to the problems of survival of his tribe: How were the tribal ways of life to be passed on to the young?

Inno the Younger asked himself, "What are the skills we members of the Ugo tribe need to know in order to survive?" He reflected, analyzed, synthesized, and finally concluded there were three survival skills: (1) catching fish with bare hands in the river, (2) capturing and killing small, deerlike animals with clubs and rocks, and (3) driving away the feared sabertooth tigers with fire.

So Inno created the first curriculum, composed of three subjects. Soon all the young of the tribe (ages five through ten) were studying the

---

[9]Adapted from Harold Benjamin, *The Saber-Tooth Curriculum* (New York: McGraw-Hill Book Company, 1939).

three skills of the tribe's new "Education for Survival." Schools were set up and conducted, first by the river, in the forest, and by the campsites, and later only in a grove near the campsite. Thus, education became schooling. The curriculum was standardized, and the young were segregated from the rest of the tribe in order to receive instruction. Inno the Younger had become the first of the great educators of the Ugos, and when he died, his loincloth was hung on a tree limb in the educational grove.

As long as the conditions and ways of life of the Ugos remained unchanged, the curriculum of Inno had a direct relationship to reality and insured tribal survival. But one day, one of the Ugos surveyed the entire area for hundreds of miles around the tribe's home, and discovered, to her amazement and to the amazement of the entire tribe, that there were no more saber-tooth tigers. Either the tigers had changed habitats or had become extinct.

What educational philosophy did Inno seem to prefer? What would you expect might happen to the third subject in Inno's curriculum, "Driving away saber-tooth tigers with fire," after the disappearance of saber-tooth tigers? Today, what is a "Curriculum of Survival?"

THOUGHT QUESTIONS

1. From your own experience as a student in the American educational system, which philosophical position would you say is the most prevalent: essentialism, perennialism, progressivism, or reconstructionism? Supply as much evidence as you can muster to support your decision.

2. As a newly employed first-year teacher in a public school, which philosophical position is most appealing to you? Give your reasons for your choice of position.

3. As a teacher, you will be intervening in the lives of children and youth. As a form of self-examination, try to probe your deepest motives in order to answer for yourself: "Why do I want to teach?"

4. Teachers must devise some form of "economy of knowledge," since it is impossible to teach everything that is known. For you as a teacher in a public school, what is it that everyone needs to know? What knowledge is of most worth?

5. Probably the most radical educational position is that of reconstructionism. Why has this position seldom been a viable philosophy for public education in the United States? In what situations or historical eras would one expect reconstructionism to become popular and win adherents?

6. One form of realism is Thomism (or neo-Thomism). In what ways is this philosophy appropriate or inappropriate as a basis for public education in the United States?

PRACTICAL ACTIVITIES

1. Obtain a copy of the goals for your school or for a local school district, and discuss these goal statements in terms of one or more of the educational philosophies presented in the chapter.
2. Using the "Questions for a Philosophy of Education" as a basis, attempt to state your philosophical assertions regarding education.
3. Visit a local elementary or secondary school. Talk to an administrator and two or three teachers about the general, overall goals they have for education at the school. See if you can determine which philosophy of education seems to prevail.
4. From your knowledge of existentialism as a philosophy applied to education, describe what you imagine might be "A Day in the Life of an Existentialist Teacher."
5. Ask a practicing teacher to indicate for you how what he/she does in the classroom is related to a more general philosophy of education. Ask for three or four philosophical principles upon which this teacher bases his/her teaching.
6. Many school districts use teacher application forms that contain a page where the teacher applicant is asked to state his/her philosophy of education in about 200–400 words. As succinctly as possible, what would you write on this form?

BIBLIOGRAPHY

BRAMELD, THEODORE, *Education for the Emerging Age*, 244. New York: Harper & Row, Publishers, 1965.

BROUDY, HARRY, AND OTHERS, *Philosophy of Education*. Urbana, Ill.: University of Illinois Press, 1967.

BRUBACHER, JOHN S., *Modern Philosophies of Education* (4th ed.). New York: McGraw-Hill Book Company, 1969.

BUTLER, J. DONALD, *Idealism in Education*. New York: Harper & Row, Publishers, 1966).

COUNTS, GEORGE S., *Dare the School Build a New Social Order?* New York: The John Day Co., Inc. 1932.

DEWEY, JOHN, *Democracy and Education*. New York: The Macmillan Company, 1916.
———, *Experience and Education*. New York: The Macmillan Company, 1939.

FRANKENA, WILLIAM K., *Three Historical Philosophies of Education*. Chicago: Scott, Foresman & Company, 1965.

GREENE, MAXINE, *Teacher As Stranger*. Belmont, California: Wadsworth Publishing Company, 1973.

HORNE, HERMAN H., *Philosophy of Education*. New York: The Macmillan Company, 1927.

HUTCHINS, ROBERT MAYNARD, *The Conflict in Education*. New York: Harper & Row, Publishers, 1953.

KNELLER, GEORGE F. *Existentialism in Education*. New York: Philosophical Library, 1958.

MORRIS, VAN CLEVE, *Existentialism in Education: What it Means*, pp. xii, 163. New York: Harper & Row, Publishers, 1966.

―――――, *Modern Movements in Educational Philosophy*. Boston: Houghton Mifflin Company, 1969.

NASH, PAUL, *Authority and Freedom in Education: An Introduction to the Philosophy of Education*. New York: John Wiley & Sons, Inc., 1966.

PARK, JOE, ed., *Selected Readings in the Philosophy of Education* (4th ed.). New York: The Macmillan Company, 1974.

PETERS, RICHARD S., *Ethics and Education*. Chicago: Scott, Foresman & Company, 1967.

PHENIX, PHILLIP H., *Philosophies of Education*. New York: John Wiley & Sons, Inc., 1961.

WHITEHEAD, ALFRED N., *The Aims of Education and Other Essays*. New York: The Macmillan Company, 1929.

WINGO, MAX, *The Philosophy of American Education*. Boston: D. C. Heath & Company, 1965.

WIRSING, MARIE E., *Teaching and Philosophy: A Synthesis*. Boston: Houghton Mifflin Company, 1972.

3

THE POLITICS OF EDUCATION
Power and Control

Public education in the United States is a gigantic operation involving, in one way or another, approximately one-fifth of the nation's population. As a public service, public education is a governmental responsibility. Unlike schooling in most nations, however, public education in the United States is not primarily the responsibility of the federal or national government. Since education is not an enumerated power in the U.S. Constitution, it is assigned through the "reserve clause" in the Constitution, to the separate states or to the people. All fifty state constitutions, on the other hand, declare education to be one of the primary responsibilities of the states.

WHO RUNS THE SCHOOLS?

Educational personnel in the U.S. public school system are a curious, complex mixture of professionals and laypersons, of teachers, specialists, administrators, and support staffs. Some are elected, though most are appointed; some are credentialed, though many are not; some make policy, some administer policy, some determine procedures to implement policies, and some implement policies by teaching or cooking or driving buses or doing any one of the dozens of functions necessary to the operation of a public institution for the education of children and youth.

Those who operate public schools are joined by another group also having an interest in public education, the general citizenry: the parents of school students, and the taxpayers whose local, state, and federal taxes support the public schools. Since the United States is a republican form of democracy, all who are involved in or concerned about public education have representatives for these interests in organization lobbies and in governmental bodies. Organization lobbies are the National Association of School Boards, the National Education Association (NEA), the American Association of School Administrators, the American Federation of Teachers (AFL-CIO), state education associations (affiliated with NEA) and state federations of teachers (affiliated with AFL-CIO), local teacher associations and federations of teachers, a variety of other trade and craft unions, other professional organizations of educational personnel, and a variety of parent and taxpayer organizations.

Governmental bodies dealing with educational matters are far too numerous to list; among the most influential are local boards of education (usually composed of elected laypersons), state legislatures, state boards of education (elected or governor-appointed laypersons), the U.S. Congress, the U.S. Supreme Court, and the U.S. Office of Education. Leading officials in American education are the U.S. Commissioner of Education (who reports to the Secretary of Health, Education, and Welfare), state commissioners of education or superintendents of public instruction (who report to the governors and/or state boards of education), and local superintendents of schools (who report to the local boards of education).

THE SYSTEM

The educational system in the United States is, to put it succinctly, a complex, public, state-local-federal enterprise, with a private and parochial school alternative available at parent option. Figure 3-1 is a simplified diagram of this system, showing the lines of direct control and indirect influence for the various levels of government and for the public and private/parochial educational subsystems. Placing the state educational system in the center of the schematic diagram reflects the reality that public education in the United States is primarily a creation of each of the states, with most educational responsibilities delegated to local school boards.

EDUCATIONAL POLITICS

Curious as it may seem, given the enormous potential and actual influence of the American schooling process, there exists an ideological tenet in American society that educational affairs should be apolitical and

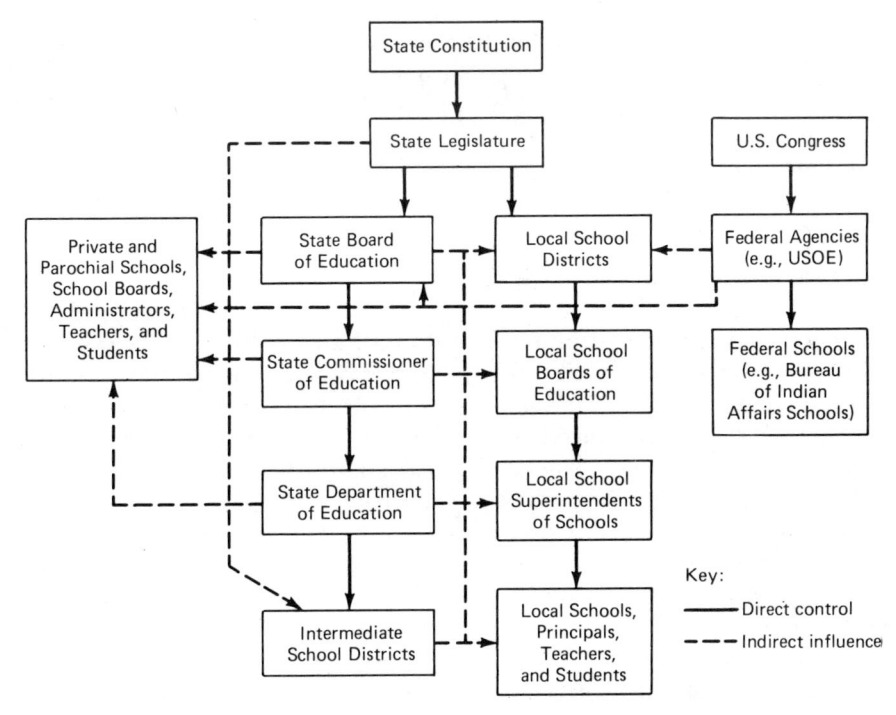

Figure 3-1 The Educational System in the United States

nonpartisan. Upon careful observation, however, such a claim soon appears a myth, perpetuated by myopia and silence. As Nicholas A. Masters argues:

> It is obvious that any social institution that performs such a significant role is not going to be allowed to roam freely within the political structure. Groups and individuals which possess the resources of power and influence exert, or will exert when they feel the occasion demands, tremendous efforts to shape and mold the system to their way of thinking and to tailor the curriculum to meet their special technological and scientific needs.[1]

It isn't only that decision-making in formulating policy is a political process. It isn't only that elections, referenda, initiatives, and appointments of leaders are all political activities present in the normal functioning of the educational system. It isn't only that dozens of organizations that are clear representatives of education interests employ paid, registered political lobbyists. It isn't only that schools as societal institutions socialize the young into the values, norms, and mores of the society, and that one form of this socialization process is political socialization (e.g., respect for the nation's

---

[1]Nicholas A. Masters, "The Politics of Public Education," in *Criticism, Conflict, and Change: Readings in American Education*, eds. Emanuel Hurwitz, Jr., and Robert Maidwent (New York: Dodd, Mead & Co., 1970), p. 175.

flag). It isn't only that, at times, the schools become the battleground for resolving highly crucial socio-political issues, such as desegregation. All these activities and many others place education as one of several significant national political arenas and as possibly the most significant state and local political arena; by no means is education an apolitical process at any government level.

a definition of politics

Focusing on the structures and functions of government tends to obscure the presence of political activities. Politics may be defined as the acquisition and effective use of power—a process involving interplay among the possessors of political resources and influence. The dynamics of the political process occur within the rules and constraints of the system, but also within those arenas where it is considered legitimate to use power to achieve goals (i.e., desired policies and programs). Applied to education, the political process displays some of the same characteristics that it does in other political arenas. Educational politics, like all forms of politics, involves the promotion of an individual's or group's interests by the use of such resources as power, money, jobs, information, status, and prestige, Control of such resources constitutes *potential* power, whereas the dispensing of the resources to achieve certain ends constitutes *actual* power.

Also, however abhorrent such practices may be, educational politics is not above corrupt, immoral, and, infrequently, illegal actions. The governor of Arkansas, for example, was taken to court and found guilty of disregarding the U.S. Supreme Court's school desegregation decision, and there can be little doubt that his actions reflected political intent. Although this example is rather atypical, there are many documented instances of the practice of favoritism in the hiring of school administrators and teachers. Though a public interest with lofty goals and with a clientele composed of the malleable and impressionable young, education, like any human social creation, is not without its share of rascals, devious opportunists, and even criminals.

a definition of educational politics

Educational politics may be defined as *that process by which educational values (or resources) are distributed (or allocated) within a society by the legitimate uses of power through governmental actions.* In this definition, "educational values" are such tangibles and intangibles as teacher and school administrator jobs; curricular content; necessary qualifications to be a student (for example, minimum age of a child, or presence or absence of a kindergarten); sources of funds to operate schools and the formulas determining which taxpayers pay what amounts to support public schools; and the many status and prestige factors which can be awarded to or withheld from students or teachers or other educational personnel (for example, letter grades for students or merit pay increases for teachers). The verb "distributed" refers to decision-making acts that determine policies, procedures, and programs for a particular school system or school district, or even for a single school or a single teacher's class. By "the legitimate uses of power" is meant the use of legal and ethical means or practices to arrive at educational decisions. Ethical practices are those consistent with the values of a democratic society, such as respect for human dignity and reliance on rational thought and rational consent. "Governmental actions" in the realm of public education are those quasi-legislative and quasi-judicial decisions made by local school boards and local school administrators (and in some cases by teachers), and those legislative, judicial, and administrative decisions relating to education, made by state and federal bodies and officials.

a case study in educational politics

Our abstract definition of educational politics can be more easily understood when related to an actual case study. The brief example to be considered is drawn from a local controversy in a small rural school district in northern New Mexico. Although it is an actual case, fictitious names for the district and for persons involved are used, and some liberties in interpretation are taken.

In August, 1976, only a few weeks prior to the scheduled opening of the school year, Cerca school district was without a school superintendent. At a school board meeting the evening of August 17, Superintendent Carl Brodbelt made a proposal to the Cerca Board of Education concerning his role in administering the schools. This led to a highly emotional shouting exchange between Brodbelt and Monica Sandoval, school board president, over differing conceptions of the responsibilities of a superintendent of schools. The ostensible issue was over Brodbelt's request to take a *paid* leave of absence to attend the University of New Mexico from September through December. For the past two years, however, there had been continual friction between Brodbelt and Sandoval, usually over such issues as the hiring of Spanish-surnamed teachers and the funding and development of bilingual-bicultural education programs.

At the August 17 board meeting, Brodbelt not only requested a four-month paid leave, but also asked the board to clarify the respective authority and powers of the board of education and the superintendent of schools. Specifically, he asked that personnel records in the school district central office be designated confidential material not subject to open perusal or discussion by school board members; that the school board desist from blocking personnel appointments on arbitrary and capricious grounds; that refusal by school administrators to carry out orders from the superintendent be considered insubordination and grounds for dismissal; and that school board members refrain from using pressure on the superintendent to obtain school jobs for friends and relatives without regard for needs, qualifications, or standard personnel procedures.

After lengthy heated exchanges involving the superintendent, board members, and members of the audience, the school board voted to recess the August 17 meeting until a week later without taking action on Brodbelt's request, and to appoint Felix Lucero, the director of instruction, as temporary superintendent during the week interim.

an analysis of the case study

It is worth repeating our definition of educational politics: *"that process by which educational values (or resources) are distributed (or allocated) within a society by the legitimate uses of power through governmental actions."* In the following analysis, this definition is related to the Cerca school district case.

In the Cerca case, the relevant social unit ("within a society") is the community served within the boundaries of the local school district. The relevant governmental body and officials ("through governmental actions") are the Cerca school board, the school board president, Ms. Sandoval, the superintendent of schools, Mr. Brodbelt, and indirectly, the director of instruction and temporary superintendent, Mr. Lucero. The school board president usually controls the agenda and pace of board meetings; the school board is the quasi-legislative representative of the State of New Mexico and determines all policies of the school district by majority votes on agenda items; the superintendent serves as the chief administrator of the school district at the pleasure of the school board, and acts by making administrative decisions; the director of instruction is hired by the school board, but is responsible to the school superintendent.

The "uses of power" in this case are the influence of the audience and, though only implicit, the influence of the Chicano (or Spanish-American or Mexican-American) community in the school district, the influences of the personalities of Ms. Sandoval and Mr. Brodbelt, the vested legal authority of the school board, the administrative discretionary power of the superintendent, and the alleged "improper," if not "illegal," use of personnel records and "favoritism" in hiring practices by the school board and its president.

What was at stake as "values" or resources in the Cerca controversy

Figure 3-2 Community Interest in the Control of Education

were the administrative job of superintendent, teaching jobs, funds for bilingual-bicultural education, the programmatic concepts or ideas and goals of bilingual-bicultural curricula, and the information contained in district personnel folders. Of these values, jobs and funds are more tangible resources than curricula and personnel information; yet all are valued, in one way or another, by the participants in the political controversy. In fact, the controversy itself hinged on how these resources were to be allocated in the school district: who was to make what decisions, who was to hold what positions, what programs were to be funded and developed, and who was to have access to what information.

How was the Cerca controversy resolved? Brodbelt was given a four-month paid *terminal* leave of absence. Lucero's appointment was changed from temporary superintendent to superintendent of schools on a one-year renewable contract. The school board reaffirmed one of its own policies that, except for the appointment of a superintendent of schools, all personnel records were to be confidential. Bilingual-bicultural education programs received school endorsement, and affirmative action hiring policies were developed and approved. Finally, the board of education, the superintendent, and all other school district administrators hammered out the meaning of the penalties for insubordination.

One key aspect of educational politics illustrated by the Cerca case is that the surface issue at stake often obscures the long-standing root issues which have divided the community and educational leaders in the past, and which constantly seethe just beneath the surface of present events.

THE DISTINCTION BETWEEN "EDUCATION" AND "SCHOOLING"

Education is an extremely broad term that includes not only the effects of successfully completing twelve, sixteen, or more years of school, but also the more pervasive collective effects of child-rearing practices, of parental life styles, of television, books, magazines, and other media, of friends, of churches, political parties, clubs, and other membership groups, and of family and personal travel, and the myriad experiences from which one learns and changes. Thus, schooling, in the formal, institutional sense, is merely *a part* of one's education.

Schooling, especially at the elementary and secondary school levels, can be considered a decentralized national industry, with identifiable economic products. As we explain in Chapter 4, Kenneth Boulding identified these products as (1) knowledge (i.e., changes in the cognitive structures of an individual), (2) skills (i.e, the possession of both the know-how and the know-what of doing something like writing a book or carving a soap sculpture), (3) custodial care (i.e., the care and feeding of children and youth during the normal working hours of their parents), (4) certification (i.e., the awarding of certificates and diplomas presumed to attest to the recipient's possession of special competencies, but usually inflated and not to be trusted exclusively as a surrogate for job-related tests or trials), and (5) community activity (i.e., those socially unifying school activities which serve as a focus for the entire community, such as athletic events, musical performances, and adult recreation and education programs).[2]

why schooling is political

As products of the schooling industry, these five economic benefits are differentially distributed among client groups (that is, students, parents, and general citizenry), and it is this unequal distribution of benefits, combined with the conflict over underlying beliefs and values, that makes schooling in the United States a political enterprise. For example, whether or not to provide free, public schooling for five year olds (i.e., to provide kindergartens) is an economic and a political question. But a tacit policy to automatically promote all elementary students, regardless of achievement records, is also an economic and political decision; so also is a policy requiring minimum mathematics and reading scores as criteria for receiving a high school diploma.

Because schooling has economic consequences which are unequally

---

[2]Kenneth Boulding, "The Schooling Industry as a Possibly Pathological Section of the American Economy," *Review of Educational Research*, 42, no. 1 (Winter, 1972), pp. 129–43.

distributed, and because certain individuals and groups desire either the status quo or change in the schooling process, educational politics operates in a changing milieu of countervailing forces, where the parties concerned are often different from issue to issue. This means that there are constant pressures in public education for stability and for change in a variety of directions, from both outside the educational establishment and from within.

political pressures on education

Those local, state and national pressure groups outside the formal, public education structure are *external forces*, while those within the structure represent *internal forces*. The National Association of Manufacturers, for example, is a national lobby and an *external force* that, on occasion, exerts influence on educational decision-makers; the National Education Association, on the other hand, is a strong, national *internal force* representing over one million American teachers.

External forces. Among the more prominent external forces that influence educational matters are:

> large corporations, such as those in the oil, transportation, synthetics, electronics, and publishing industries
>
> prestigious college and university administrators and faculty members who want the schools to emulate institutions of higher education
>
> large unions, such as the United Auto Workers and the AFL-CIO, especially in support of the activities of the American Federation of Teachers at the national, state, and local levels
>
> the press: newspaper, magazine, and television; at local and national levels
>
> Chambers of Commerce at local, state, and national levels, and similar organizations like the National Association of Manufacturers
>
> religious organizations (e.g., National Council of Churches), particularly sects (e.g., Roman Catholicism), and local churches
>
> local politicians in town, city, and county governments
>
> businesses with high local impact (such as General Electric in Schenectady, New York; International Business Machines in Poughkeepsie, New York, and San Jose, California; United States Steel in Pittsburgh, Pennsylvania) and the many nationally insignificant businesses which tend to influence all aspects of the political life of the small towns in which they are the chief economic institutions.
>
> the Republican and Democratic political parties, other parties such as the Socialist Labor Party, and unique political organizations such as the John Birch Society, the Daughters of the American Revolution, and the American Legion
>
> the thousands of local parent and taxpayer organizations, some temporary and some ongoing.

Figure 3-3   A New Force in School Politics

Internal forces. Of the many internal forces representing education's own vested interests, the more influential groups are:

- the two teachers' professional unions: the American Federation of Teachers (local, state, and national union; affiliated with the AFL-CIO) and the National Education Association (local, state, and national union)
- the National Association of School Boards (with local and state affiliates)
- the American Association of School Administrators (composed chiefly of school superintendents, their associate and assistant superintendents, and professors of educational administration; with local and state affiliates)
- the American Association of Colleges of Teacher Education (composed chiefly of administrators and faculty from the hundreds of departments, schools, and colleges of education that train and recommend for state certification educational personnel of all types)
- the many national professional education associations and fraternities and sororities, such as the Association for Supervision and Curriculum Development, the National Council of Teachers of Mathematics, the National Council for the Social Studies, Phi Delta Kappa and Kappa Delta Pi (with local and/or state affiliates and/or chapters)
- local and state boards of education
- the national Parent-Teacher Association and local and state parent-teacher

organizations, some, though not all, of which are affiliated with the national association

prestigious and highly visible educators, such as the United States Commissioner of Education, state superintendents of public instruction, a few deans of education, and some journalists and education writers.

KEY SUBJECTS OF EDUCATIONAL DECISION-MAKING

Pressures, from individuals and groups, both informal, *ad hoc* groups and formal, permanent organizations, from within and without the public education establishment, are directed toward influencing certain kinds of decisions by supportive advocacy or by forceful opposition. In public education, "the most significant subjects for decision ... concern the curriculum, the facilities, the units and organization of government, and personnel; and partly shaping them all is the omnipresent issue of finance."[3]

These "subjects for decision" manifest themselves in curious and diverse specific instances, all colored by local and state peculiarities and national concerns and trends. A few examples from each subject area will reveal the flavor of educational politics and issues.

curriculum decisions

Curriculum decisions, when they are not too controversial, are usually reserved for analysis and action by the school's or school district's professional staff: by administrators, curriculum specialists, and teachers. Except when embroiled in a community controversy over curricular emphases, inclusions, or exclusions, the school board and superintendent rarely deal with curriculum decisions. Exceptions to this rule are decisions such as high school graduation requirements and state-mandated courses in United States history and government.

Some examples of curricular decisions that have become heated political controversies involving community and school forces are:

> to include (or exclude) particular courses or units of instruction on religion or on sex, courtship, and marriage or on radicalism, civil disobedience, and social revolution or on personal philosophies and life styles or on race relations and conflict resolution or on sensitivity training, meditation techniques, and psychotherapy.
>
> to use, in courses or in school libraries, particular textbooks or trade books, especially works including various forms of profanity, or those describing any kinds of sexual acts, or those denigrating or stereotyping any race, sex, or

---

[3]Thomas H. Eliot, "Toward an Understanding of Public School Politics," in *Criticism, Conflict, and Change, . . .*, p. 165.

ethnic group; among these are *Lord of the Flies, Brave New World, Slaughterhouse Five, Little Black Sambo, The Merchant of Venice, Catch-22, Go Ask Alice, Fahrenheit 451*, the *Man* series, and *Soul on Ice.*

to allow student publications to exercise complete "freedom of the press," or to allow student organizations the right to invite any guest speakers to their meetings, or to permit principals and/or teachers and students to invite anyone of their choosing to be assembly speakers, or to allow teachers complete "academic freedom" to pursue any topics (i.e., controversial issues) in their courses, as long as they are competent to discuss the topic and the topic is relevant to the course and the issue is given a balanced treatment.

physical facilities decisions

Examples of decisions about physical facilities are:

the cost per square foot of a new school building; and whether or not to accept the lowest bid for construction

to include or exclude esthetically appealing landscaping or interior decorating (e.g., carpeting) when budgeting a new facility

to include special recreational features, such as a swimming pool, in the plans for a new junior or senior high school

to close or renovate an older school

to allow particular organizations (e.g., churches) to use public school facilities for meetings and other activities; and whether or not to charge a fee for the use of school facilities

specific regulations about the conduct of students and others in their normal use of school buildings

to plan, fund, and construct a new school or to allow various kinds of "overcrowding," such as larger student enrollments per class or separate double sessions (i.e., duplicate schedules for two separate high school student bodies in the same building)

to include food preparation, serving and eating areas in all, some, or no schools.

decisions on units and organization

Most of the decisions relating to public education's units and organization of government are made by a state government: by the legislature and the executive branch through the state board of education and the state department of education. The remaining decisions on governmental units and organization are made either by a local school district's board of education or by the electorate of a local school district. Some examples of this type of decision are:

to reorganize two or more existing school districts into a single district; or to subdivide a large urban school district either into new, smaller districts or into community-monitored subdistricts

The Politics of Education 73

to create new, multidistrict intermediate school districts or boards of cooperative educational services

to set attendance boundaries for specific elementary, middle, junior high, or senior high schools, which, in lieu of an open enrollment policy, determine which schools students in a district will attend

to elect the members of a local school district either at-large or precinct by precinct; or to elect or appoint (usually by the governor) the members of a state board of education.

personnel decisions

Decisions about personnel deal with hiring and firing administrators, coordinators, specialists, teachers, and support staffs (e.g., food service personnel); with the specific school assignments, transfers, and teaching loads of teachers; and with the conditions of employment for all educational employees. Examples of personnel decisions are:

to fire a superintendent of schools or to appoint a federal or a state commissioner of education

to hire, as teachers or administrators, persons who are avowed or acknowledged homosexuals, lesbians, communists, fascists, or racists, or persons with "unusual" appearances such as long hair and beards or "peculiar" clothes, or physically handicapped persons such as those who are blind or deaf

to determine fair and legitimate procedures and criteria for dismissing educational personnel

to determine an operational and official definition of tenure, and the criteria and procedures for awarding or denying tenure

to determine regulations for the certification of teachers, administrators, counselors, and other educational specialists

to establish and administer a state retirement plan for all public education personnel

to reach a contractual agreement between a local school board and a local teacher's union through the process of collective negotiations.

financial decisions

Few educational decisions lack fiscal implications. Among the more significant economic decisions in public education are:

to determine the budget and the necessary tax base to operate educational programs in a local school district

to determine the allocation of state general funds to each school district in a state, and to equalize this state support according to the comparative effort (level of taxation) and available tax base (assessed valuation of property) of each district in the state

to obligate the taxpayers in a school district to the bonded indebtedness (including accrued interest) necessary to pay for construction of a new school to determine the salary schedule or the salaries for teachers and school administrators

to allocate funds for new, special educational programs, such as career education, special education, and bilingual-bicultural education

to purchase equipment, supplies, textbooks, library books, buses, food, and all other materials necessary to operate the schools.

THE STRUGGLE FOR CONTROL OF EDUCATION

The extent to which schooling is valued in a society determines, in part, the amount of energy and effort devoted to controlling this institution. If those in power see the system of schooling as a means of enhancing and achieving the objectives they espouse, they will insure that this social institution fosters their goals and prospers as a "public corporation." Conversely, to the extent that those in a society who are relatively powerless see schooling as denying them and their children the attainment of desired economic, political, and social goals, these individuals and groups will either withhold support of the schools or will attempt to obtain and use power to change the ways schools operate.

In the United States, the tensions between entrenched power groups and minority racial and ethnic groups are present in every arena where significant social issues are contested, and one of these arenas is public education. "Schools are important political instruments ... that play a vital function in social mobility, political socialization, and preservation of the political system."[4] Thus, regardless of the nature of the society or the type of political ideology and system it adopts, any attempt to control the institution of schooling in that society is always worth the effort. This generalization is not ignored in the United States by those possessing relatively great power, nor by those with relatively little power.

five battlegrounds in educational politics

Although the tensions among individuals and groups seeking to control the schools in American society are present to a greater or lesser degree in all education decisions, recently five battlegrounds in the contest for control of the schools have received more attention than the others. These are: (1) local school board elections, especially in large and medium-sized cities, (2) court decisions, especially from federal courts and the Supreme Court, (3) votes on legislative bills, especially in Congress and in state legislatures, (4) collective bargaining sessions between teachers' unions and local school boards, and (5) local referenda, especially those required by law to

[4]Masters, "Politics," p. 177.

approve bond issues and increases in school taxes. Currently, these are the forums from which decisions emanate on the most highly contested issues in American public education.

fifteen political issues in education

What are those crucial, contemporary, political issues around which educational debate is centered and political power is brought to bear? Needless to say, even when limited to public education at the elementary and secondary levels, there are today dozens, perhaps even hundreds, of important political issues facing educational decision makers. The decisions taken on these issues will affect the present generation of children and youth, as well as one or more future generations. Among these many issues, the following list is representative rather than comprehensive:

1. Due to federal civil rights laws, all public institutions which receive *any* federal funds must institute and implement affirmative action employment policies. The issue is how to achieve racial, ethnic, and sex representativeness among school administrator and teacher groups without violating any applicant's or employee's civil rights, especially the Constitutional guarantees of "due process" and "equal protection of the law."

2. Parents, businesspersons, and others have become concerned in the past few years that high school graduates lack competency in basic skills, especially those of computing, reading, writing, and speaking. This has resulted in clarion appeals for "back to the basics." The issue is one of priorities among educational goals: If skills are to receive renewed emphasis, what is to be de-emphasized?

3. By the 1954 *Brown* v. *The Board of Education* decision of the Supreme Court and by subsequent decisions of that court and other federal courts, it has been established that "separate but equal" (by religion, race, sex, or ethnicity) has no place in public education; that is, official, *de jure* segregation in facilities or programs by reason of religion, race, sex, or ethnicity is illegal in public schools. The issue is how to achieve desegregated schools to the mutual satisfaction of all involved groups, especially through avoiding "excessive" busing, loss of "white" student populations in the nation's largest cities, and violence.

4. All citizens are lamenting the increased bureaucracy and unresponsiveness of bureaucrats in every governmental unit. Of all levels of government, citizens complain, those closest to them should be the most responsive to their wishes. Local electorates are now demanding that elected school boards and professionals in the local school bureaucracies be held accountable to the citizenry for what students learn or fail to learn in the schools. The issue in the cry for accountability is how to determine what learning outcomes are priorities for the community, both at large and for each interest group, and then to decide precisely to what extent, considering all the out-of-school influences on students, the public school educators can be legitimately held accountable for which specific learning outcomes.

5. Although it is questionable whether the public schools are a powerful enough institution to effect such changes, more and more since the 1960s the nation's leaders, legislators, and general public have placed the burdens of social reform on public education. The schools have been mandated to eliminate such deep-rooted societal problems as racism, sexism, cultural deprivation, and poverty, and other

impediments to social and economic equality. Since the public schools are ill-equipped and unprepared to address such monumental tasks, the issue is not only how to approach such problems and what programs offer the most promise, but also whether or not the schools are the best agency to attack the problems.

6. As the teacher shortage in the United States disappears and a condition of over-supply emerges, and as teacher turnover in school districts slows to a trickle, two particular questions become crucial personnel matters: how to rid the schools of incompetent and insensitive teachers, and how to screen new applicants so as to insure hiring and retention of outstanding teachers. The practice of tenure is related to both of these questions, in that it is difficult to dismiss tenured teachers and it is becoming more difficult and taking longer to attain tenure. The issue is whether or not states should abolish tenure for public school teachers, or failing this, what changes should be made in the criteria for awarding tenure.

7. In recent years, many administrative decisions made by school administrators or school boards are being challenged in the judicial appeal channels by the parties affected—parents, students, and teachers. In many of these cases, the bases of appeal are claims that either "due process" or "equal protection of the law" has been denied the plaintiffs. The issue is what administrative review procedures are necessary to satisfy constitutional provisions in situations involving alleged violations of policies or rules by students or teachers. Stated differently, the issue is what legitimate rights do students and teachers have as clients and employees of public schools.

8. In 1975, Public Law 94-142 was passed by Congress, providing a "bill of rights" and program development funds for the education of the nation's almost eight million handicapped children and adolescents. By 1980, over three billion dollars in federal funds each year will be channeled to state and local education agencies to help support education for the handicapped. The issue is a complex one, including problems in defining the many categories of handicaps, in determining for handicapped students how much instruction should occur in regular classrooms and how much in special classrooms, in preparing and certifying both regular and special teachers who will be expected to teach the handicapped, and in the civil rights of handicapped students.

9. After more than two decades marked by vigorous merging of contiguous school districts into single, larger districts, thus justifying expanded curricula, especially in junior and senior high schools, the trend is now in the opposite direction, especially in large and medium-sized cities. Bigness in education, as in other institutions, has led to cumbersome, impersonal bureaucracies. Secondary schools with 750–1,000 students can offer a full range of general and vocational programs; yet large junior and senior high schools (1,500–3,000 students) often become factory-like, tend to "process" students (and sometimes teachers also), and may ignore the desires of students, parents, urban subcommunities, and racial and ethnic enclaves. Generally, however, the larger the school district, primarily in urban areas, the greater the taxable wealth available for the support of schools. The issue, then, is how to achieve smaller, more responsive units (school districts, subdistricts, schools), while maintaining tax bases sufficient to support diverse, comprehensive curricula.

10. Almost all states in the nation, either in their constitutions or their statutes, mandate that a *free* public school education must be made available to all residents. But the operational and legal meaning of "free" is often an issue. What materials and services must public schools provide without charge to students: textbooks? uniforms, soap, and towels for physical education classes? band uniforms and instruments? outfits for vocal music groups? costumes for plays and musicals? breakfasts, snacks, lunches? uniforms and equipment for athletic teams? uniforms for cheerleaders? notebooks, paper, pencils?

11. Most teachers are represented in salary and benefits matters by a collective bargaining agent, usually an affiliate of the NEA or AFT, which enters into collective negotiations with the school board (and superintendent) or its paid, professional negotiator. Out of the negotiating sessions comes a contractual agreement signed by both parties. This employee-employer negotiating process involves several issues: Who represents taxpayer, parent, and student interests? Should public school teachers have the right to strike? Besides salaries and fringe benefits, what other conditions of employment should be negotiated: number of students per class or per day? number of paid professional leave days per year? amount of pay for participation in any "after hours" extracurricular activities? financial support for professional travel? paid sabbatical leaves? special toilet facilities, lounges, and mini-cafeterias? acceptable forms of disciplining students? grievance procedures? provision of a desk and coat closet for each teacher? number of paraprofessional teacher aides per teacher?

12. Because the myth of the melting pot has "died," and the concept of cultural pluralism is now valued, the public schools, just since the late 1960s, have been expected to develop new multiethnic and multicultural curricula, particularly, but not exclusively, for the historically oppressed and neglected racial and ethnic minorities in the nation. Ethnic studies programs which have received the most attention and funds are black or Afro-American studies; American Indian or Native American studies; Mexican-American, Spanish-American, or Chicano studies; and Oriental-American (Japanese, Chinese, Vietnamese, Korean) studies. When a student's language is not English, bilingual education added to ethnic education, although some educators and political leaders would claim that multiethnic, multicultural, bi- or multilingual education is essential for *all* Americans. The issue here is where to place emphases from region to region, state to state, and community to community; for which groups of students are programs intended; who is to administer and teach these programs; and who pays.

13. It has been argued that equality of educational opportunity is above all else a function of equality of financial support, as measured by average per pupil expenditures for *all* schools in a school district or for *all* school districts in a state. A few even argue equality among *all* states in the nation. The issue is how to operationally define "equality of educational opportunity" and how to equalize all the factors included in the definition. Also involved is who—federal government, state government, local school district—is to pay what share of any financial equalization formula.

14. A key political issue, regardless of the kind of election held, is voter qualifications. In educational politics, the question of who is eligible to vote relates primarily to three types of local school elections: elections of school board members; elections to approve selling bonds to raise funds for new facilities; and elections to approve increases in regular school taxes to support operating expenses (mainly salaries of teachers and administrators). The debate is usually focused on the lower voting-age limit; on who, for *school district* elections (as distinguished from local, state, and federal government elections), is a registered voter; and on whether to allow only property owners or both property owners and renters to vote.

15. Today, all states have compulsory school-attendance laws, with age ranges from five or six to fourteen or sixteen. Some now argue that it is no longer necessary to require schooling beyond age eleven or twelve, whereas others argue for increasing the required age to eighteen or until a student graduates from high school. The issue appears to hinge on how much coercive power and influence a state should have over its young citizens; on how old one must be to make decisions about one's own welfare; and on how valuable a given number of years of formal schooling is held to be.

The above fifteen political issues by no means exhaust the current array of contested educational decisions, and in fact they include almost none of those decisions made primarily within individual schools by administrators, groups of teachers, and individual teachers. Furthermore, other observers of the educational landscape might produce different and longer lists, though we are confident most of our issues would be on almost all lists.

SUMMARY

Far from being apolitical or even nonpartisan, public education in the United States is engulfed by politics. Hundreds of political decisions, some contested and some tacitly accepted, some routine and some momentous, are made each day in the schools, in school board meetings, in state capitals, in the courts, and in Washington, D.C. With its complex and multidimensional structure, it is difficult to establish the loci of power in the U.S. public education system; clearly, however, the state legislatures and local boards of education wield the greater share of the power.

Educational politics is affected by numerous pressures or forces, some external to the education establishment and some internal, and all interacting in the many decision-making forums. Since the benefits of public education are unevenly distributed among citizens, it is a political enterprise rife with issues, major and minor, calling for attention and resolution. In many respects, the way these educational issues are resolved will partly determine the nature of American society in the next decades.

CASE STUDY: Academic Freedom

As an experienced junior high school English teacher, you prefer to select your own works of literature for class study rather than relying on a published anthology. One of the books you are using this year is a good, well-known piece of writing by an American winner of the Nobel Prize. The book, however, does contain some profanity, a few explicit sexual scenes, and some references which might be offensive to people of conservative or right-wing politics.

A few parents of students in your class have called you and your principal requesting that this book, which you are having all students read, be eliminated from any and all English courses in your school. After reading the book your principal asks you to withdraw it from required reading in all your classes.

What will you do? When a teacher's values and professional judgment conflict with the norms of some parents or other community members, who should prevail? In the case described, should it matter if the parents who are making the demands represent a majority of all parents of school students? Should community members have *any* say in curricular matters?

THOUGHT QUESTIONS

1. Why are there so many local public school districts in the United States?

2. Using the definition of "educational politics" given in this chapter, analyze the following local educational situation in terms of the implied political controversy:

> EDUCATOR EXPLAINS "ACCOUNTABILITY"
>
> According to the state legislature, educational accountability is a program "designed to measure objectively the adequacy and efficiency of the educational programs offered by the public schools."
>
> To Jim Armitage, assistant superintendent of the Boulder Valley Public Schools, it is "meeting the needs of the students and showing evidence as to how goals and objectives have been met."
>
> He comments, "Teachers should not just do what they feel like doing (in the classroom) but what the parents and community want. But they should do it in the way they want."
>
> Since the Educational Accountability Act of 1971 was adopted for the state legislature many of the 181 school districts in the state have struggled to identify just what their programs are and how much they cost. From that they have to determine whether or not they are getting their money's worth.
>
> The local accountability committee recently reported to the school board four recommendations for the coming school year:
>
> —That the board develop by 1978 a budgeting and accounting process that will identify programs and their costs and that the board consider allocating in the 1977 budget necessary funds to accomplish this. The committee recommends this process begin with the 1977 budget planning.
>
> —That the board direct the administrators to prepare an alternative proposal for graduation requirements, based on competency, before any new policy for graduation requirements is adopted.
>
> —That the committee be a steering advisory committee on accreditation by contract.
>
> —That a work session with the board and committee be scheduled early in the year to improve communications.
>
> *Daily Camera*, Aug. 10, 1976, Boulder, Colorado

3. What *external* and *internal* forces would you expect to exert pressure on a state department of education mandate to revise the criteria for awarding teaching certificates?

4. Of the fifteen political issues in education described in this chapter, which three seem to have the highest visibility in your state or region? Explain why you suspect these three issues have become important.

80 FOUNDATIONS OF AMERICAN EDUCATION

5. Which level of educational governance might have primary responsibility for each of the following decisions? Use "L" for local school district, "S" for state department of education *or* state legislature, and "F" for any kind of federal involvement.

_____ awards high school diplomas
_____ purchases classroom textbooks
_____ requires all schools to offer a state history course
_____ establishes equalization formulas
_____ determines minimum number of days of attendance for students
_____ certifies school administrators
_____ operates overseas schools for dependents of military personnel
_____ hires a superintendent
_____ funds Head Start programs
_____ establishes compulsory attendance laws

6. If a foreign visitor asked you, "Who runs the schools in the United States?" how would you respond?

PRACTICAL ACTIVITIES

1. If a nearby school or district is out on strike, visit the picket line and talk with the teachers about the issues involved. If possible, obtain materials on the school board's, parents', or students' reactions to the strike. Also, obtain any literature on the teachers' position. Give your own reaction and evaluation of the situation.
2. Attend a meeting of a local or state teachers organization (State Federation of Teachers *or* State Education Association). Report on topics discussed and your reactions to the meeting.
3. Attend a local school board meeting. Report on what issues were discussed, who raised them, and the board's vote on the issues. Where did the power appear to reside: with the school board, teachers, administrators, the parents, or some other group?
4. Attend a teachers' meeting in a local school. (First obtain permission to attend.) What issues were discussed? Who presided at the meeting? How did teachers and administrators participate? Which person or group appeared to have the greatest influence on the decisions? Give your general reaction to the meeting.
5. Attend a "Parent-Teacher Organization" meeting. Who ran it? What issues were discussed? Did the parents seem to have any power in significant educational matters? What was the apparent relationship between the parents and teachers? What was your general reaction?
6. It is usual for Head Start programs (for preschoolers from impoverished families) to be run by not-for-profit organizations outside the

public school system. Each separate local Head Start program is governed by an elected governing board. Attend a monthly meeting of a Head Start governing board and report on the educational/political issues raised and discussed.

7. For several months, read your town or city's daily newspaper and clip out all the news articles, editorials, and letters to the editors that touch on matters of educational politics. Next, set up categories into which your clippings can be placed. Then, create a scrapbook of these issues in educational politics. See if you can find items at all political levels: local, state, and national.

BIBLIOGRAPHY

ASSOCIATION FOR SUPERVISION AND CURRICULUM DEVELOPMENT, *Freedom, Bureaucracy, and Schooling*. Washington, D.C.: ASCD, 1971.

BENDINER, ROBERT, *The Politics of Schools*. New York: Harper & Row, Publishers, 1969.

BERKE, JOEL S., AND MICHAEL W. KIRST, *Federal Aid to Education: Who Benefits? Who Governs?* Lexington, Mass.: D. C. Heath, 1972.

CAHILL, ROBERT S., *The Politics of Education in the Local Community*. Danville, Ill.: Interstate Printers and Publishers, 1964.

CAMPBELL, ROALD, AND OTHERS, *The Organization and Control of American Schools*. Columbus, Ohio: Charles E. Merrill Publishing Co., 1970.

GAUERKE, WARREN, *School Law*. New York: Center for Applied Research in Education, 1965.

GITTELL, MARILYN, *Participants and Participation*. New York: Center for Urban Education, 1967.

GROSS, NEAL, *Who Runs Our Schools?* New York: John Wiley & Sons, Inc., 1958.

HOUSE, ERNEST R., *The Politics of Educational Innovation*. Berkeley, Calif.: McCutchan Publishing Corporation, 1974.

IANNACCONE, LAURENCE, AND FRANK W. LUTZ, *Politics, Power and Policy: The Governing of Local School Districts*. Columbus, Ohio: Charles E. Merrill Publishing Co., 1970.

KIMBROUGH, RALPH B., *Political Power and Educational Decision Making*. Chicago: Rand McNally & Company, 1964.

KIRST, MICHAEL W., ed. *The Politics of Education at the Local, State, and Federal Levels*. Berkeley, Calif.: McCutchan Publishing Corporation, 1970.

KOERNER, JAMES, *Who Controls American Education?* Boston: Beacon Press, 1968.

MASOTTI, LOUIS H., *Education and Politics in Suburbia*. Cleveland: Western Reserve University, 1967.

MASSIALAS, BYRON, *Education and the Political System*. Reading, Mass.: Addison-Wesley Publishing Company, Inc., 1969.

MASTERS, NICHOLAS, ET AL., *State Politics and the Public Schools*. New York: Alfred A. Knopf, Inc., 1964.

MERANTO, PHILIP, *The Politics of Federal Aid to Education in 1965*. Syracuse, New York: Syracuse University Press, 1967.

WYNNE, EDWARD, *The Politics of School Accountability*. Berkeley, Calif.: McCutchan Publishing Corporation, 1972.

ZEIGLER, HARMON, *The Political Life of American Teachers*. Englewood Cliffs, N.J.: Prentice-Hall, Inc., 1967.

THE ECONOMICS OF SCHOOLING
Payoffs and Paradoxes

American schools are in an economic turmoil today. School bond issues fail at an alarming rate; there is an oversupply of teachers; many teachers who do have jobs are faced with diminishing real incomes because of the strong bite of inflation; overcrowded classrooms are the rule rather than the exception; schoolhouses, and not just inner-city schools, are becoming more shabby in appearance. Indeed, we can identify exceptions to this trend. There are districts where enrollments are growing, school construction has not let up, new buildings are or will be in use, attractive family incomes are solid and secure, unemployment is virtually nonexistent, and the industrial tax base is strong. This generous support of schools, however, is the exception.

The economic peril of public schools is not a recent phenomenon. Construction of schools in the past several decades has been one step behind the influx of students and the need for more classrooms. Inside the schoolhouse, classrooms, lunch rooms and faculty lounges appear austere in contrast to the bright, carpeted, attractive surroundings of most private businesses. The incomes of schools' professional staffs are pale by comparison with incomes of professionals in private business and industries. It is no secret that teachers, even those with doctorate degrees, command considerably lower salaries than physicians, dentists, lawyers, engineers, and architects. The average annual salary of a public school teacher in 1975 was $11,513.[1] This figure was slightly higher for secondary teachers, and

---

[1] *Annual Estimates of School Statistics* (Washington, D.C.: National Education Association, 1975).

slightly lower for elementary teachers. By any comparison, the school teacher today generally earns less than corporate managerial, sales, and accounting personnel who generally have less formal education than the classroom teacher.

On the other hand, total expenditures for what Kenneth Boulding calls the "schooling industry" amounted to a whopping $120 billion in 1976.[2] The schooling industry by this accounting includes the formal institutes of public education: kindergartens, schools, colleges, and vocational-technical centers. This figure today is approximately 8 percent of the gross national product (GNP), the federal government's most inclusive measure of the nation's productivity during a year.[3] This represents a gain of over 4 percent since 1950. On this basis, it appears that the public schools, or the schooling industry, are receiving more than their share of the economic pie. This discrepant information is accounted for simply by the even more impressive jumps in the number of students attending colleges and junior colleges, and to a lesser extent, a rise in the number completing high school. It does not follow that schools, colleges and universities have an abundance of operating funds.

The foregoing is not meant to suggest that we don't spend enough money on formal schooling.[4] We are also not implying that what funds are allocated for public schools could not be spent more wisely or efficiently; that waste and excesses don't exist; that perhaps even American youngsters wouldn't be better off with less formal education. What is interesting, sometimes puzzling, but hardly amusing is the paradoxical state of the importance of education in America, and its subsequent financing. Our society places great stock in formal education; education has been called our new state religion in the twentieth century, and the school, according to Ivan Illich, has become the New Church.[5] The paradox is that while education or formal schooling is virtually worshipped, we don't support it financially in a generous fashion. Schools in this deprivation are in the same predicament as numerous other social or public institutions, including sanitation services, street and highway maintenance, medical assistance, police protection, and social services. John Kenneth Galbraith, the prolific institutionalist economist, has labeled this situation one of "private opulence and public squalor."[6]

[2]*Digest of Educational Statistics*, 1975 (Washington, D.C.: National Center for Educational Statistics, U.S. Department of Health, Education and Welfare, Education Division), Table 22, p. 26.
[3]Ibid., Table 24, p. 27.
[4]We use the term schooling (rather than education) deliberately. Schooling is what is done in schools and other places of formal instruction; education is a much larger process that occurs in many other institutions more often incidentally than deliberately, and that occurs outside institutional arrangements.
[5]Ivan Illich, *Deschooling Society* (New York: Harper & Row, Publishers, 1971).
[6]John Kenneth Galbraith, *The Affluent Society* (Boston: Houghton Mifflin Company, 1958), p. 257.

A BRIEF LESSON IN CAPITALIST ECONOMIC THEORY

Many economic beliefs in our culture even today are rooted in classical capitalist theory, or the doctrine of laissez-faire capitalism. One of the earliest, and perhaps still the most eloquent and thorough, treatments of laissez-faire theory was the Scottish philosopher Adam Smith's *The Wealth of Nations*, written in the timely year of 1776. Classical economists for more than the next century were to further develop the theory, revising it with the changing social environment. As a form of economic decision-making, laissez-faire capitalism never really existed in its pure, theoretical version; nevertheless, the basic tenets have had profound effects on the thought patterns of American people.

There is an inviting simplicity, neatness, and efficiency to the theory of laissez-faire capitalism. The American economist Robert Heilbroner, though far from a laissez-faireist, captured the essence of this appeal in his book *The Making of Economic Society*. Heilbroner first explains how *traditional* and *command* economies solve the basic economic problem of scarcity—scarce goods and services—and with it the question of how to produce and distribute these scarce goods. He then turns to the *market* organization of society, the guiding principle of laissez-faire capitalism, as a solution to the economic problem. He asks readers to assume they are economic advisors for a developing nation. As he describes,

> We could imagine the leaders of such a nation saying, "We have always experienced a highly tradition-bound way of life. Our men hunt and cultivate the fields and perform their tasks as they are brought up to do by the force of example and the instruction of their elders. We know, too, something of what can be done by economic command. We are prepared, if necessary, to sign an edict making it compulsory for many of our men to work on community projects for our national development. Tell us, is there any other way we can organize our society so that it will function successfully—or better yet, more successfully?"
>
> Suppose we answered, "Yes, there is another way. Organize your society along the lines of a market economy."
>
> "Very well," say the leaders. "What do we then tell people to do? How do we assign them to their various tasks?"
>
> "That's the very point," we would answer. "In a market economy, no one is assigned to any task. In fact, the main idea of a market society is that each person is allowed to decide for himself what to do."
>
> There is consternation among the leaders. "You mean there is no assignment of some men to mining and others to cattle raising? No manner of designating some for transportation and others for weaving? You leave this to people to decide for themselves?
>
> But what happens if they do not decide correctly? What happens if no one volunteers to go into the mines, or if no one offers himself as a railway engineer?"

"You may rest assured," we tell the leaders, "none of that will happen. In a market society, all the jobs will be filled because it will be to people's advantage to fill them."

Our respondents accept this with uncertain expressions. "Now look," one of them finally says, "let us suppose that we take your advice and allow our people to do as they please. Let's talk about something specific, like cloth production. Just how do we fix the right level of cloth output in this 'market society' of yours?"

"But you don't," we reply.

"We don't! Then how do we know there will be enough cloth produced?"

"There will be," we tell him. "The market will see to that."

"Then how do we know there won't be too much cloth produced?" he asks triumphantly.

"Ah, but the market will see to that too!"

"But what is this market that will do all these wonderful things? Who runs it?"

"Oh, nobody runs the market," we answer. "It runs itself. In fact there really isn't any such thing as 'the market.' It is just a word we use to describe the way people behave."

"I am afraid," says the chief of the delegation, "that we are wasting our time. We thought you had in mind a serious proposal. What you suggest is inconceivable. Good day, sir."[7]

Despite the skepticism of these leaders entrusted with monumental economic decisions and having no prior conception of the market solution, this simple, but sophisticated economic mechanism does arouse a wonderment in observers. As Adam Smith remarked, the market is guided only by an "invisible hand." This efficient, parsimonious mechanism which makes but a minimum appeal to government intervention, has had a captivating effect on the American public and business community. Nevertheless, the changing nature of our nation's industrial state, and the almost catastrophic economic slumps and inflations resulting from the lack of any external and deliberate controls during the past two centuries, have resulted in very significant changes in the prevailing nature of the market system and capitalism. A small but articulate group of classical conservatives (most notable among them, journalist William Buckley and economist Milton Friedman) serve as modern spokespeople for the enduring principles underlying this laissez-faire economic system.

A crucial force supporting capitalist theory is that human beings naturally will search for economic gain: the highest wages, greatest profits, and optimum prices (whether one is a consumer or producer) obtainable

---

[7] Robert Heilbroner, *The Making of Economic Society*, 2nd ed. (Englewood Cliffs, N.J.: Prentice-Hall, Inc., 1968), pp. 14–15.

on the market. People, it is believed, also will naturally compete in order to maximize their gains. It makes no difference whether one is selling a produced good or personal skills; free, unfettered competition is central to the smooth, efficient, productive operation of this system. Any government intervention as a rule represents an unnecessary intrusion that seriously risks production inefficiencies and personal injustices. Given this logic, it follows that the role of government should be minimal: it should be limited to providing a medium of exchange (money) for economic transactions; providing for the national security, i.e., military protection; preventing the rise of artificial monopolies; and helping to support very basic educational needs.

The reality of our economic life is that such a world never existed, even in smaller, nonindustrialized, shopkeeper and agrarian societies. In the scientific-industrial corporate complex that dominates our society in this later part of the twentieth century, government, particularly the federal government, plays a strategic role. To enumerate, for the better part of this century:

> The federal government has not permitted bankruptcy for certain businesses which cannot make a profit.
>
> The number of business firms has decreased, small farms and businesses being consumed or eliminated by larger corporations.
>
> Despite antitrust laws, corporations have gained monopolistic power in the market place.
>
> Price competition has not been totally free: tacit establishing of price levels (price fixing) has been common practice.
>
> Particularly in recent decades, price inflation has resulted more from price setting, i.e., corporate establishment of prices (often spurred by labor demands), than from the natural stimulus of consumer and investment demand.
>
> Labor organizations have grown, and have affected production, market prices, and control over job entrance.
>
> The federal government has discriminately subsidized selected businesses and industries.
>
> Since the Great Depression (even earlier in a few states) governments have drafted major legislation to minimize unemployment, reduce poverty, and increase the living standards of many citizens.
>
> Fiscal and monetary controls have been implemented to eliminate or reduce cyclical fluctuations and to induce growth in the economy.

The list could go on!

The result in America is a mixed economic system: a system that bears but remote similarity to the pure capitalist model. The system now is a complex mixture of capitalist and socialist programs, prompting the new label of "welfare capitalism." The related economic beliefs (or myths) of most people are compatible with capitalist theory, but the realities of our economic society confuse matters. As a result of huge doses of government production, regulation, and welfare (the latter extended to both rich and poor, business, industry, and families) and because of the existence of corporate market control, the lay person tends to hold many inaccurate and contradictory beliefs about our economic system. Most telling for the public schools is the myth that when private enterprises spend money it is their own money and generally for productive purposes; when the government or public enterprises spend money, it is a drain on the taxpayer.

THE IMBALANCE OF PRIVATE AND PUBLIC PRODUCTION

One striking consequence of the persuasive power of capitalistic beliefs is the public's bias towards private production and expenditures. The most conspicuous bellwether, or gadfly of this phenomenon, depending on where one's sympathy lies, has been Professor Galbraith. In 1958 Galbraith wrote in *The Affluent Society* how the disparity or social imbalance between private and public production is manifested. According to his analysis, our concern for production of goods is traditional and at times irrational. Privately produced goods and services are considered an addition to the nation's wealth, even when the product is clearly frivolous. Public services, by comparison, are sterile of productive potential, thus a burden on the economy, even when they serve the most important ends. As he comments, "At best public services are a necessary evil; at worst they are a malign tendency against which an alert community must exercise eternal vigilance."[8]

This attitude has led to some unfortunate contradictions. The expansion of telephone services is welcomed as an improvement of the general welfare, but the reduction of postal service is viewed as a necessary economy. The proliferation of goods elaborately packaged, easily disposed of, and prematurely obsolescent is a consumer convenience, but garbage collection is allotted low priority. As automobiles became larger, and more numerous, city parking facilities became comparatively scarce and the local roads relatively narrow. In general, we take great satisfaction with increases to our personal wealth, but complain about the added cost of police protection to guard it. Finally, while we persuade young people to stay in school longer, and make it most difficult for them to secure decent employment if they reject this advice, local bond issues for public school construction regularly fail and state allocations for colleges lag behind costs.

Espousal of traditional beliefs in the market mechanism is one explanation for the different views of the private and public sectors in our

---

[8]Galbraith, *The Affluent Society*, p. 133.

economy; another reason is the nature of the product or services provided. Public production with few exceptions is collectively consumed. That is, when society provides highways, street lights, police and fire protection, a standing army, and scientific research, they must be available to everyone if they are available to anyone. Still another reason is the division between profitable and unprofitable enterprises. When a good or service can be provided at a profit to others, it will be undertaken by private productive means, regardless of whether the good is important or urgent. When profits are not readily forthcoming, as in the case of disease control, reduction of poverty, recreation, sanitation services, and mail delivery, government action will be obliged to fill the vacuum.

Galbraith warned there would be a serious price eventually to pay if this disparate provision of private and public outlays were not brought into balance. The quality of life, he argued, would diminish to intolerable levels from such a single-minded concentration on the production of salable goods. Congestion, pollution, and deterioration of inner cities would be a major result; in fact, the environment in general would be a casualty. Indeed, the private economy itself would suffer from the lack of strategic support services by public agencies and facilities. It is imperative, he stressed, that we forge appropriate public policy to expediently realign this misallocation. The initial reaction to this thesis was skepticism and rejection. The Galbraithian argument was considered a misrepresentation of our economic situation, supported by those with a socialistic perspective. Today, needless to say, the general public has come to see the wisdom of this once unconventional view.

THE ECONOMIC SYSTEM AND EDUCATION IN AMERICA

Intellectual, cultural, and economic historians of education agree there is causal relationship between the functioning of our economic society and the goals of our society in general. However, various spokespersons disagree as to the effect of this relationship on students and the general public.

the conventional wisdom

In the traditional interpretations of educational history, the expansion of schooling over time is viewed as an increasing benefit to a wider range of young people. As schooling became accessible to more people, and as the schools expanded or diversified the curriculum, economic opportunities accrued to the learner.

Schooling expanded substantially once the quest for the common school became a reality. As educational historian R. Freeman Butts pointed out, by 1870 elementary schooling was beginning to be established; by 1900 the majority of elementary age children were in school; and by 1960 universal elementary schooling had been won.[9] More remarkable, however, was the march of secondary schools. In 1890 fewer than 7 percent of high-school-age people were enrolled in school, but this was to change in geometric leaps. Within ten years, the enrollment had nearly doubled, and by 1920 the figure had more than quadrupled. By 1930 more than 50 percent of the fourteen- to seventeen-year-old population were in school, and by the early 1960s the total had passed 90 percent.

In the mid-twentieth century, college education also expanded rapidly. By 1950 about 30 percent of high school graduates were attending college; by 1970 this figure was over 50 percent. This growth prompted Butts to write that it might not be long until we are back where we were in 1900, with 75 percent of high school graduates bound for college; but in 1900 only 10 percent of the youth were in high school; today 90 percent are there.[10] College enrollments have leveled in the past few years, but even if this trend should prevail, higher education will have witnessed a tremendous expansion.

Evidence supporting the notion that economic benefits followed the growth of schooling is less vivid, but still widely acclaimed. More schooling, it is argued, leads to a wider range of job opportunities, resulting in better jobs which bring higher pay, which in turn creates higher standards of living and general social mobility. Though educators would agree that schools serve some people faster and more effectively than others, most would maintain that schools have advanced the education and economic well-being of all clients. If industry and other businesses also benefited, this was only a natural spill-off of the system, not the primary driving force behind school goals and operation.

Economic development and the growth of schooling have been closely interrelated, in fact mutually supportive. In the conventional wisdom, the rewards of more and better educational facilities to business are obvious: trained and educated individuals are more valuable employees. In turn, industrial development requires more sophisticated education and training.

With the expansion of industrialization and decline of agriculture, young people were less able to find work in family farming or local shops

---

[9]R. Freeman Butts, "Search for Freedom—The Story of American Education," *NEA Journal*, 49, 3 (March 1960), p. 42.

[10]Ibid, p. 46.

and crafts. Advances in science and technology created especially tight employment conditions in the agrarian community, where gains in technology were most pronounced. The percentage of workers employed in agriculture declined precipitously with twentieth-century gains in productivity. Industrialization, it was argued, called for better-trained and better-educated people to carry out the tasks required by increasingly sophisticated technology and management. Manufacturers and managers not surprisingly took interest in the school's curricula. Organizations such as the National Association of Manufacturers, the American Federation of Labor and the Grange actively supported the addition of vocational-technical programs. But "the bread is buttered on both sides"; having access to more schooling, young people found that opportunities for economic advancement in corporate enterprises multiplied. Industry held out the promise of higher pay, shorter work days, in some cases better working conditions, and financial security.

The argument for more schooling, as normally is the case, included the requirements of a democratic society. As Butts concluded,

> A society based on steam power, electric power, or nuclear power can be managed and controlled by relatively few people. Technical power leads to political power. To prevent autocratic dictatorial use of political and economic power by a few, everyone must have an education devoted to freedom. There is no other satisfactory way to limit political or economic power.
> So it became increasingly clear that the opportunity to acquire an expanded and extended education must be made available to all . . . . Equality of opportunity stood alongside freedom as the prime goals of education.[11]

With industrialization came the rise of big labor, first with the American Federation of Labor (AFL) in the late 1900s, and later with the Congress of Industrial Organization (CIO) in the 1930s. Labor organizations have been consistent supporters of increased resources for education. When schools were attended by a small minority of youngsters, the pupils came almost exclusively from the business and propertied class. The curriculum of the schools was college preparatory, or elitist. It served primarily those families whose children were destined for life in politics, professions, and the arts. The common-school movement had as its raison d'etre the accommodation of children from all socio-economic backgrounds. In turn, labor recognized the public school as a partner in advancing the academic skills and economic opportunities of working class families. While perhaps not as instrumental as other forces, the growth of organized labor benefited the cause of public schooling.

[11] Ibid., p. 42

the counter-viewpoint

The unconventional interpretation of the relationship between the individual and our economic society distinctly contrasts with the image portrayed in the traditional interpretation. This unconventional, revisionist, or radical critique, as it is variously called, pictures the corporate society and schools on a self-serving venture. The goal is to shape the young learner to accept the values compatible with the business ethic, to learn skills useful to economic operations, and to acquire knowledge that is not disruptive to the functioning of the political and economic establishment. In effect schools function as an intermediary, augmenting and perpetuating the dominant social institutions, particularly the modern corporation.

One current spokesperson for the counter-viewpoint, Clarence Karier, commented that the history of American education demonstrates that changes in the means of production result in significant changes in social institutions and life styles.[12] The growth of large urban centers in the last quarter of the nineteenth century, and the subsequent development of the American high school (an urban school), the decline of the academy (appropriate for a rural setting), the development of industrial education, manual training, and vocational guidance, as well as the enactment of child labor and compulsory education laws—all are historical developments, directly or indirectly related to education, and traceable to new forms of production. The creation of our mass education system, Karier adds, followed the shift from handicraft to mass-production enterprises and the adoption of production-line techniques. In turn, the American system of mass education has performed three salient and overlapping functions: training, testing and sorting, and holding.[13]

The overriding function of *training* has been to assist youth in meeting occupational requirements for an increasingly complex system. Trade classes, woodworking, mechanics, cooking, home economics, typing, clerical skills, and agricultural instruction have been a substantial part of the comprehensive school. There was a time during the early part of this century when many corporations operated their own trade classes, physical education programs, literary activities, foreign language training, and even kindergartens. It was important to corporations that these functions exist; not surprisingly, corporations also saw the economic advantage in having the schools assume this instruction. The National Association of Manufacturers at the turn of the century passed a resolution calling for high schools to teach commercial courses and modern languages. Languages were advantageous for employees who would work in the companies' growing

---

[12]Clarence J. Karier, "Business Values and the Educational State," in *Roots of Crisis: American Education in the Twentieth Century*, ed. Clarence J. Karier, Paul Vilas, and Joel Spring (Chicago: Rand McNally & Company, 1973), pp. 6–8.
[13]Ibid., p. 16.

foreign markets, particularly, at this time, in South America. Organized business continued up to the present to call for the expansion of work- and life-related courses.

Vocational programs received a noteworthy boost from the Conant Report, *The American High School*, published in 1959. From his observations, James Conant spoke highly of the vocational-technical curriculum of high schools, and encouraged their continued support as an important function in preparing many youth for life after high school.[14]

Conant also observed that few of the "academically talented" students were carrying adequate course loads in science, mathematics, and a foreign language, and were not sufficiently challenged in their academic program. Given the rapid advances that were being made in science, along with the expanding use of more sophisticated technology in industry, the schools were not maintaining the quality of education which would assure a talented and trained work force.[15] His recommendations for considerably stronger academic loads in these subject areas were based squarely on the manpower needs of industry and the military might of the nation.

The Conant Report also recommended that the high school diploma, a fundamentally ornamental document, be supplemented with a durable record of courses a student had completed with the grade received. This record, Conant stated, could be in the form of a card, carried in a wallet. Such a card would prove expedient to future employers when considering an applicant for employment.[16] As educational historian Joel Spring remarked, "Conant wanted all Americans to be card-carrying graduates of the high school.[17]

In his book *Education and the Rise of the Corporate State*, Spring writes that the purpose of corporate programs for employees is to foster the kind of worker who later would be called an organization person. He states, "A socialized and cooperative individual was the type needed both on the assembly line and in the management team . . ."[18] Since many programs extended corporate control over the social life of the worker, they could be used to increase his efficiency. Later business extended its support to public schooling as a more effective way of achieving the same ends.

Even today, the analogy between school, classroom, and the factory is frequently drawn. Such commonplace characteristics as drab interior settings, bells signifying when to start and stop work, assigned work places (desks), rules specifying that students should be in a classroom or study

---

[14] James B. Conant, *The American High School Today* (New York: McGraw-Hill Book Company, Inc., 1959), pp. 30–32.
[15] Ibid, pp. 33–36.
[16] Ibid., p. 50.
[17] Joel Spring, *The Sorting Machine: National Policy Since 1945* (New York: David McKay Company, Inc., 1976), p. 48.
[18] Joel H. Spring, *Education and the Rise of the Corporate State* (Boston: Beacon Press, 1972), p. 32.

place at all times, the assumption that if they are in the halls or lunch room they are wasting time, hall permission slips, assembly-like lunch rooms, teacher-chosen subjects, teacher-established classroom rules, teacher-directed lessons, and so on, are conducive to the production of obedient, "good" workers.

Another major function of schools in our economic society, according to the counter-viewpoint, is that of *testing* and *sorting* students. Test instruments became popular during World War I as a method of classifying military personnel. After the war, educational researchers and psychologists applied what had been learned to the expanding school system. With more and more children coming to school from various socio-economic backgrounds, and with wider variance in intellectual ability, tests were used ostensibly to measure what children knew, what and how fast they could be expected to learn, and even how they might learn best. The essential aim of more sophisticated testing devices was to increase the response of schools to the individual student—to individualize learning.

Aside from this, it turned out that most intelligence tests during the last half-century or more reflect the values of middle-class, Protestant, industrial America. For example, in response to the question, "What is the difference between work and play?" the Stanford-Binet IQ test tallies as "plus" answers:

> You work to earn money and you play for fun. One is for amusement and the other for a living. Play is a pleasure and work is something you should do, your duty. Work is energy used for doing something useful and play is wasting energy. One's recreation, and one's labor. Play is an enjoyment and work is something you have to do. One is something that most people like to do; the other is a duty. When you're working, you're generally doing what has to be done—when you're playing you're just doing what you feel like. Work you take seriously and play you don't.[19]

At the secondary level, aptitude, achievement, and intelligence tests were used widely to determine what courses students should take and in what track they should be fitted. Conant in *The American High School Today* strongly recommended that students be grouped according to ability in nearly all academic subjects, throughout the high-school years. The lone exception to this was the senior-year social studies course, which, he argued, should be designed to bring together students from disparate backgrounds to help build a democratic community. Tests would be an important device to sort students.[20]

Another major recommendation of the Conant Report, central to the testing and sorting function of schools, was a guidance program. Conant

---

[19]Lewis M. Terman and Maud A. Merrill, *Stanford-Binet Intelligence Scale* (Boston: Houghton Mifflin Company, 1960), p. 213.
[20]Conant, *The American High School Today*, pp. 49–50.

believed there should be one full-time counselor for every 250 to 300 students, a vast increase over what had existed. The major task of the counselor was to see to it that students were fitted for appropriate academic and vocational offerings.[21]

Upon graduation, all students were to carry Conant's record card. This was particularly important for those concentrating in vocational studies. This device could be readily used to match high school graduates with the needs of the labor. In fact, Conant suggested that if it were discovered that a particular trade was saturated in a specific geographic area, the schools should cease operating that program.[22]

Vocational programs are important to the success of another school function, *holding* young people out of the job market temporarily. Colleges perform this function for those who are destined to fill white-collar, managerial positions. In most trades (and even professions), youngsters could be more efficiently trained as apprentices on the job; but this would shift a burden back on the business community and disturb the existing employment arrangements. What schools lack in providing effective training of future workers for industry, they make up by regulating the supply of young workers who otherwise would flood the job market.

A major device that the schools and businesses use to maintain this hold on the individual, argue the revisionist critics, is the credentialing or certifying process. Before a person can gain entrance to a particular job, he or she must have earned a high school diploma, a bachelor's degree, or whatever the required credential is. In many cases, studies completed in order to earn the credential have little relation to job experiences that follow. While this process may serve well to regulate the supply of workers, it tends to produce disenchantment and waning interest in jobs.

In the judgment of revisionist educators, the school has consistently been an instrument of social, political, and economic control. Those in control have been businessmen, professionals, school administrators, public instruction bureaucrats and political leaders, as the composition of school boards and other power groups indicates. The most important feature of the school in the twentieth century, Joel Spring argues, is its role as the major institution for socialization. Schooling prepares for the acceptance of control by dominant institutions and elites, and tends to create dependence on professional and institutional expertise. As he concludes,

> Dependence upon institutions and expertise represents a form of alienation which goes far beyond anything suggested by Karl Marx in the nineteenth century. . . . The triumph of the school in the twentieth century has resulted in the expansion of this concept of alienation. Technology and state capitalism still make work meaningless to the individual and create a condition of aliena-

[21]Ibid., pp. 44–46.
[22]Ibid., pp. 51–52.

tion from the product of labor. The school increases this alienation by making alien the very ability of the individual to act or create. In school the ability to act is no longer an individual matter but is turned over to experts who grade, rank, and prescribe. Activity, itself, no longer belongs to the individual but to the institution and its experts. In the nineteenth century man lost the product of his labor; in the twentieth century man lost his will.[23]

THE ECONOMIC EFFECTS OF EDUCATION

Economists find it useful to distinguish between education as an *investment* and education as a form of *consumption*. (They mean schooling and not education as we have defined the terms.) Schooling is an investment if at some future time it affects the performance of the economy. The training of skilled specialists is an investment in that it contributes to the economic growth, assuming learners use the acquired skills. Education for leisure, or education that involves literature, the arts, and music, is also an investment in that it affects the demand for performing arts and literary works. To the extent the student uses this education as a teacher or artist, it is all the more an investment. Schooling taken merely for the present satisfaction and enjoyment, or to meet certain requirements (which may not be so enjoyable) is a consumption good. Education as consumption may include courses in history, mathematics, poetry, physical education, even economics, plus a host of extracurricular activities and sports. As you may be thinking, deciding when schooling is an investment or consumption involves "splitting hairs."

Economists, at least those few concerned with the economics of schooling, prefer to observe the tangible aspects of schooling, namely incomes earned and growth in the economy, that appear related to schooling. To some economists, and a lot more of the general public, the thought of investments in human beings, or the concept of "human capital," is offensive. Some of the criticism, namely that benefits of education resulting in human growth and social change are not amenable to quantitative techniques, is reasonable. Nevertheless, even the most devout humanists in turn must admit that schooling costs money and is undertaken by many people in order to earn more money. Therefore, it is subject to the scrutiny of those concerned with the allocation of scarce resources in the economy.

education and earnings: the payoff to individuals

While there are immediate satisfactions of education or schooling, economists argue that more importantly the benefits accrue over a long period of time, and for all purposes can be ignored as a consumption item.

[23]Spring, *Education*, pp. 154–55.

Table 4-1 Annual Income of Men by Age and by Years of School Completed: United States, Selected Years, 1956–1972

Years of Schooling Completed (age 25 and over)	1956	1960	1964	1968	1972
Elementary					
Less than 8 years	$2,574	$2,988	$3,298	$3,981	$5,235
8 years	3,631	4,206	4,520	5,467	6,756
High School					
1 to 3 years	4,367	5,161	5,653	6,769	8,449
4 years	5,183	5,946	6,738	8,148	10.433
College					
1 to 3 years	5,997	7,348	7,907	9,397	11,867
4 years or more	7,877	9,817	10,284	12,938	16,201

Source: *Digest of Educational Statistics, 1975*, National Center for Educational Statistics, U.S. Department of Health, Education and Welfare, Education Division, Washington, D.C.

Table 4-1, showing the annual incomes earned with various years of schooling, is one method of assessing the investment value of schooling.[24]

Comparing the earnings streams of individuals does assume that earnings are an accurate reflection of productivity, a big assumption. As we shall discuss, earnings are even an inaccurate measure of monetary benefits from schooling.

The data in Table 4-1 show that additional schooling is associated with higher average incomes for males. For example, in 1972 the average annual income of those over twenty-five years old was $6,756 for elementary school graduates, $10,433 for high school graduates, and $16,201 for college graduates. This relationship between income and years of schooling has persisted through the years, even though the amount of schooling attained by the population has increased. In fact, the income differentials for various schooling levels have either been maintained or increased over time. In 1956, the average high school graduate had an income 43 percent greater than the elementary school graduate; the figure in 1972 was 55 percent. In turn, the average college graduate had an income 52 percent greater than the high school graduate in 1956, and 55 percent greater by 1972. The information in Table 4-1 is not sufficiently elaborate to illustrate, but individuals with the most education benefit progressively more from the number of years on the job. That is, the income differentials, for the same amount of schooling, become wider as the age of the worker increases.

Earnings from schooling also can be measured in terms of lifetime in-

---

[24] Although the rationale for this may change in the near future, the earnings data in this table includes only men. Women are excluded because the relationship between their income and education may be distorted. A large proportion of the female population in the past either have not entered the labor force or were employed only on a part-time basis.

Table 4-2   Lifetime Income of Men, by Years of School Completed: United States, Selected Years, 1956 to 1972

Years of School Completed	1956	1961	1964	1968	1972
	\multicolumn{5}{c}{*Income from Age 18 to Death*}				
Elementary					
Less than 8 years	$131,432	$151,881	$170,145	$213,505	$279,997
8 years	178,749	205,237	223,946	276,755	343,730
High School					
1 to 3 years	201,825	235,865	255,701	308,305	389,208
4 years	244,158	273,614	311,462	371,094	478,873
College					
1 to 3 years	278,227	335,100	355,249	424,280	543,435
4 years or more	372,644	454,732	478,696	607,921	757,923
5 years or more	*	475,116	500,641	636,119	823,759

*Data not available. Source: *Digest of Educational Statistics, 1975*, National Center for Educational Statistics, U.S. Department of Health, Education and Welfare, Education Division, Washington, D.C.

come. As Table 4-2 indicates, in 1972 the lifetime earnings of a college graduate were nearly $300,000 greater than a high school graduate's earnings. This represents approximately a doubling of both groups' expected career earnings over 1956 figures. It doesn't take a mathematic wizard to figure that this difference means the spread between the total earnings of high school and college graduates has been widening over time. The same relation holds between elementary school and high school graduates.

    Economists attempt to account for the fact that extended years of schooling delay the individual's income-earning years. Said another way, income earned in the near future is more valuable than that earned in the distant future, inasmuch as cash in hand may be put to money-making purposes, i.e., invested. Even using generous discounting procedures, a device to reduce future income to its current equivalent, the contribution of additional schooling to earnings is positive and significant.

    It comes as no surprise to college students that schooling costs money. So far we have considered only the monetary returns to schooling without any mention of costs. Another measure of the value of schooling is what economists call the "rate of return on investment in education"; the costs of schooling are needed to arrive at this figure. "Private costs" include (1) tuition and fees paid by individuals, (2) opportunity costs incurred by individual (namely, income foregone while in school), and (3) incidental school-related costs, e.g., books, supplies, travel. (Purchases of term papers and examination answers occur in the black market and aren't included in this accounting.) One group of economists computed the rate of return on the individual's investment in education by comparing the costs of additional years of schooling with the income earned from that schooling. Their findings are a bit dated now, but nonetheless impressive. For example, a first-grade boy in 1949 could expect a 25.6 percent return on the private money needed to complete high school, and a return of 18.2 percent from his investment in schooling through college.[25] These are handsome returns. If it seems strange that the return from schooling through college is less than through high school, remember that despite the much higher incomes earned by college graduates, the private costs in all three expenditure categories are substantially greater during the college years.

Ultimately, the financial gains to an individual, from a macroeconomic perspective, are of value to the whole society. That is, incomes earned are returned to the economy through personal consumption expenditures, personal savings invested in capital consumption, and personal taxes that end up as public expenditures. The size of the nation's gross national product and income is dependent on these factors. For the society's investment in schooling, the rate of return is computed in the same manner as for individuals, except that school costs (i.e., teachers' salaries, supplies, building maintenance, interest, depreciation on capital) are substituted for individual tuition and fees. As one should expect, the return to society is less than that to the individual; by last count, which again was based on figures of three decades ago, this return was 13.6 percent on schooling from first grade through high school, and 12.1 percent through college.[26] All in all, this is still a sound economic investment. We've been considering the payoff of schooling to individuals, but this last measure, investment in schooling, brings up the value of schooling to society.

THE CONTRIBUTION OF EDUCATION TO ECONOMIC GROWTH: THE PAYOFF TO SOCIETY

Still another method of determining the economic value of an investment in schooling, and another way of measuring schooling's social benefit, is to compute the growth in our economy that might be attributed to schooling. The most significant and recent work in this area was accomplished in the early 1960s by economists Theodore Schultz and Edward Dennison. (The economics of education has not exactly been a thriving field.) Schultz and Dennison, using different techniques, came up with similar findings. In brief, Schultz calculated the increase in workers' real income in 1957 over 1929, computed the increase in capital investment for education (i.e., the social costs of schooling), and used various rates of return on the investment in education. From these figures he found what percentage of the increase in earnings per worker could be attributed to schooling; applying

---

[25] Jon T. Innes, Paul B. Jacobson, and Roland J. Pellegrin, *The Economic Returns to Education: A Survey of the Findings* (Eugene, Ore.: Publication of the Center for the Advanced Study of Educational Administration, University of Oregon, 1965), p. 28, Table 16.
[26] Ibid., p. 27, Table 15.

the figures (36–70 percent) to the growth of national income, he concluded that "education" accounted for *between 16.6 and 32.2 percent* of this growth in national income (economic growth) from 1929 to 1957.[27]

Dennison chose to compare figures he calculated on the output per laborer due to education with increases in the national income. Adjusting for what he estimated were increases in labor's output (or earnings) arising from factors other than schooling, he found that *23.5 percent* of the growth in the economy from 1930 to 1960 resulted from increased "education" of the labor force.[28]

Maybe you've felt uneasy with the analysis on the economic returns to education. It may seem cut and dried, calculating and materialistic; somehow the benefits of education aren't so simple, and this analysis feels inadequate, perhaps for puzzling reasons. One major problem we find with the economic approach is that it is based on group, (i.e., total-population) norms and characteristics. Missing are important factors unique to individual situations in life. It is clear that college graduates earn more than high school graduates; but what would these same college graduates have earned had they only completed high school? It is not likely to be the same as the average high school graduate (or the same as a random individual selected from the population of high school graduates). Individuals who go on to further years of schooling tend to have a variety of personal attributes working in their favor, factors such as intellectual ability, motivation, ambition, imagination, family position in society, and access to economic and educational opportunities. (To his credit, Dennison attempted to account for these "noneducational" factors in his assessment of education and economic growth.) Educators also point out that in spite of the increasing number of people now pursuing higher education, differentials have persisted among individuals' incomes within any given educational level. Schooling, they note, may not be the only factor in determining future economic returns, though surely it is an important one.

SOME DISCREPANT FINDINGS

Kenneth Boulding, economist and internationally recognized scholar, has pointed out that the essential elements of productivity in our schooling system have not increased a great deal over the past fifty years. The real products of schooling, according to Boulding, are knowledge, skills, custo-

---

[27] Theodore W. Schultz, "Capital Formation by Education," *Journal of Political Economy*, 68, 12 (Dec. 1960), pp. 571–83.
[28] Edward F. Dennison, *The Sources of Economic Growth in the United States and the Alternatives Before us* (New York: Committee for Economic Development, 1962). For a concise summary of both Dennison and Theodore Schultz's findings, see Innes and others, *Economic Returns*, pp. 33–38.

Table 4-3   A Comparison in the Growth of the Schooling with the Increase of Its Physical Product

Year	Total School Expenditure as Percentage of Gross Capacity Product	Percent of "Children" (Age 5–18) in School
1930	3.3	80
1940	2.7	85
1950	2.9	91
1960	4.7	90
1969	6.0	93

dial care, certification, and community activity. Measures of these products are very hard to come by, and those that exist are at best indirect. One rough method Boulding offers for assessing productivity is to compare two ratios: the current dollar cost of the schooling industry as a proportion of the total economy ("total product"); and the number of school years as a proportion of the school-age population. It can be seen from Table 4-3 that the schooling industry as a proportion of the total economy has risen much faster than its physical product, indicating a substantial increase in the "real price" of education.[29]

Professor Boulding doesn't hold much hope for new ways to increase the productivity of knowledge and skills that are being tried in the schools, e.g., performance contracting, accountability, programmed instruction. So little is known about the nature of learning that increasing these products is difficult. The other three, custodial care, certification, and community activity, though secondary products, are equally elusive of gains in productivity. The most expedient, but probably unacceptable, means of increasing the productivity, according to Boulding, is to decrease schooling costs.[30]

The liberal orthodoxy in the United States concerning economic development and education has been that generous expenditures on schooling are central to productivity increases. Society and the individual alike are the beneficiaries of more abundant educational opportunities. The pervasive slogan throughout the land is "Education pays; stay in school." As we've seen, a few economists have carefully calculated the precise extent to which schooling pays. Ivar Berg, a sociologist and a manpower expert at Columbia University, in his research booklet under the suggestive title *Education and Jobs: The Great Training Robbery*, takes a skeptical view of this human capital paradigm. Berg does not question either the methodology or the calculations of economists Schultz, Dennison, and others; rather, he makes a simple point that these economists have jumped over the actual variables of productivity and concentrated on incomes earned, a spurious correlate.

[29]Kenneth E. Boulding, "The Schooling Industry as a Possibly Pathological Section of the American Economy," *Review of Educational Research*, 42, no. 1 (Winter, 1972), pp. 129–36.
[30]Ibid., pp. 137–38.

As another manpower expert, Eli Ginzberg, summarizes in the foreward to Berg's book,

> The critical point is not whether men and women who complete high school or college are able subsequently to earn more than those who don't, but whether their higher earnings are a reflection of better performance as a result of more education or training or of factors other than the diplomas and degrees they have acquired.[31]

This is a point mentioned at the end of the last section, but one worthy of emphasis.

Berg's study of the relationship between schooling and employment revealed some telling and discrepant findings. To start, he found that additional academic credentials help the worker to obtain better-paying jobs; far less clear is how much schooling actually contributes to productivity. He also found that with the passage of time there has been a tendency for more and more people to be in jobs that utilize less education than they have acquired.[32] While the data are a little general, it does suggest caution in pursuing "Back to School Drives." The most direct effect of more schooling is likely to be an increase in job dissatisfaction.

In questioning employers, Berg discovered that they continuously raised educational requirements for employment because they believed this would lead to a more ambitious, disciplined, thus productive, work force.[33] Many employers, however, were unaware of the extent to which they had workers with wide differences in education in the same job categories. Employers tend to assume erroneously that employees in the high-paying job areas are the more educated. In some areas, such as selling insurance or real estate, workers with less education but more experience perform better and earn more. Indeed, the frequency of job turnover is positively related to schooling level.[34] Employers also tend to justify higher schooling demands as a hedge on the future, when workers will be promoted into higher ranks where the education is needed. Ironically, Berg found that only a small percentage are promoted substantially over time, and that the more highly qualified are likely to have departed out of dissatisfaction in search of better jobs.[35]

According to Berg there is little evidence to support the belief that workers with educational credentials are more productive. This, combined with the findings that many workers are underemployed (i.e., in jobs requiring less education and skills than they possess) and that there is a lack

---

[31] Ivar Berg, *Education and Jobs: The Great Training Robbery* (New York: Praeger Publishers, Inc., 1970), p. xii.
[32] Ibid., pp. 51–60.
[33] Ibid., pp. 70–75.
[34] Ibid., pp. 87–101.
[35] Ibid., pp. 76–80, 89–90.

Figure 4-1 Inequality of Opportunity

of demand for workers in many lower job categories, leads to an interesting though perhaps unsettling policy. The solution to unemployment and productivity with certain groups is not sending the dropout back to school, or assuring that women are educated to their full potential, or extending vocational training, but rather upgrading those underemployed now, filling the open ranks with those suitably qualified, and generally matching much more accurately job requirements and worker competencies.

Christopher Jencks added another twist to the economics of education controversy in his study of economic inequality and equal educational opportunity. Jencks and his colleagues at Harvard's Center for Educational Policy Research reassessed much of the data surrounding the interrelation of family background, schooling, and earnings and came up with convention-shattering findings. There is little evidence, they found, that school reform can substantially reduce the extent of cognitive inequality, as measured by tests of verbal fluency, reading comprehension, or mathematical skill.[36] Inadequate basic cognitive skills, Jencks argued, is the key reason given by reformers to explain why poor children cannot escape poverty. It is believed that without these skills they are unable to obtain well-paying jobs. In turn, educational reform is claimed to be the best mechanism for undermining this plight of the poor, an assumption Jencks concluded was unfounded. Even if it were true that schools could substantially affect cognitive skills, it is not true, adds Jencks, that the economic status of many people would be affected. The reason some people end up richer than

---

[36]Christopher Jencks and others, *Inequality: A Reassessment of the Effect of Family and Schooling in America* (New York: Basic Books, Inc., Publishers, 1972), pp. 86–102.

others depends on things other than cognitive skills, or schooling, and family background.[37] What these things are is not clear, but Professor Jencks and his co-researchers offer some suggestions that by now sound familiar: specialized competencies (unrelated to intellectual abilities), personality, job market conditions, weather, availability of natural resources, and luck, for a start.[38]

If the ultimate aim of social policy makers is to eliminate poverty and generally distribute incomes more equally in our economy, then Jencks has some suggestions: constrain employers to reduce wage disparities among their workers; make taxes more progressive; provide income supplements to the needy; provide free public services for those who cannot afford adequate services in the private sector. Unless we are willing to invoke such direct socialistic measures, poverty and inequality will remain in our nation.

EQUALITY OF EDUCATIONAL OPPORTUNITY: A SPECIAL PROBLEM IN FINANCING SCHOOLS

A major dimension of the rationale for support of public schooling has been to promote social and economic equality in the United States. The quest for fairness, justice, and equality has been an elusive pursuit of Americans, but one solidly ingrained in the ethic of our culture. The public school, needless to say, has been the primary instrument in this search. "Equality of educational opportunity" has been its rallying principle.

In the United States, educational opportunity has taken on a special importance as the handmaiden to economic opportunity; it has become a major pillar on which the nation's appeal rests. Equality has been an inseparable ingredient of educational opportunity. The meaning of equal educational opportunity as historically applied included several elements:

1. Providing a *free* education through a given grade level, which constituted the principal entry point to the labor force.
2. Providing a *common curriculum* for all children, regardless of background.
3. Providing that children from diverse backgrounds attend the *same school*.
4. Providing equality within a given *locality*, since local districts defined the area of tax support and attendance.[39]

Historically there have been persistent flaws preventing the fulfillment of each of these criteria. The first two criteria in large part have been attained. Criteria three and four, however, have been stormy issues in recent years; the last is of special importance for school finance.

---

[37] Ibid., *Inequality*, pp. 221–25.
[38] Ibid., *Inequality*, pp. 226–32.
[39] James Coleman, "The Concept of Equality of Educational Opportunity," *Harvard Educational Review*, 38, no. 1 (Winter, 1968), p. 11.

case in point

Several court cases since 1970 illustrate the challenge and debate over local school funding and the pursuit of educational equality. *Serrano* v. *Priest* (1971), tried in the California Supreme Court, is the landmark case. This suit and others involving school finance are anchored in the "equal protection" clause of the Fourteenth Amendment to the U.S. Constitution, which prohibits federal and state governments from discriminating unfairly between classes of people. This clause requires all people to be treated by law in the same manner, unless a case can be made for differential treatment in the best interest of society.

The plaintiffs in *Serrano* alleged that as a result of the public school financing plan in California they are required to pay a higher local property tax rate than residents of other districts in the state to obtain the same or lesser educational opportunities. In examining the state public school financing plans, the court found that over 90 percent of public-school funds came from (1) local real property taxes and (2) the state school fund. Of these two, the local property tax is the primary source. This tax, they added, is based mainly on the value of private property within a school district; this is a value per pupil that varies widely throughout the state. They also found that the various methods for allocating state school funds to local districts do not offset the disparities created by local financing, and in part widen the gap between the rich and poor districts.

On the evidence, the court argued that allotting more educational dollars to one district than another, on the basis of local family, commercial and industrial wealth, is relying on irrelevant and arbitrary factors. The court ruled that the level of spending on children's education must not be a function of wealth, other than that of the state itself.[40] This was a decision that would shake the financial foundations of American public-schooling finance. Its reverberations immediately were felt with other similar legal interpretations in Minnesota, Texas, and New Jersey.

the financial picture

The United States Constitution makes no mention of federal responsibilities for the education of citizens. This function is delegated to the states, and every state constitution provides for the establishment of a system of public schools. Legislatures in all states have the responsibility to provide financing for public education from resources available in the state. By and large, the primary revenue base has been the local school district, with state funds providing a substantial addition. In recent years, as a

---

[40]Thomas A. Shannon, "Has the Fourteenth Done It Again?" *Phi Delta Kappan*, 53, no. 8 (April, 1972), pp. 466–71.

Table 4-4 Estimated Expenditures for Public Elementary and Secondary Schools per Pupil in Average Daily Attendance 1974–75 in Selected States

New York	$2,005
Alaska	1,624
Nebraska	1,211
Missouri	1,078
Michigan	1,547
Minnesota	1,423
Tennessee	903
Alabama	871
Mississippi	834
National Average	$1,207

Source: *Financing the Public Schools: A Search for Equality* (Bloomington, Ind.: Phi Delta Kappa, 1975).

result of the perceived national need for particular programs (e.g., federal lunch program and compensatory programs for low income communities), federal government contributions have augmented local school resources.

The percentage distribution of revenue, for all states, from local, state, and federal sources currently stands at 50.1 percent, 41.4 percent, and 8.5 percent, respectively.[41] Local support has reached as high as 66.5 percent (Nebraska) and as low as 22.9 percent (Alabama). State support, in turn, spreads from 63.1 percent (Alabama) to only 22.9 percent (Nebraska). Federal funds to public schools in 1975 ranged from 3.8 percent (Michigan) to 17.4 percent (Louisiana).[42]

More important for the issue of equality in education are the resources available and actual expenditures among the states and within each state. In 1973–74, approximately 58.2 billion dollars were expended for operation of the nation's elementary and secondary schools. As illustrated in Table 4-4, the level of support ranged from $2,005 per pupil in New York to $834 per pupil in Mississippi. The national average was $1,207 per pupil.[43]

The differences between New York and other northeastern and northern states) and most southern states is significant. Much of this difference is explained by the available wealth in the states. For example, in 1972 the per capita personal income in New York was $5,242; in Alabama it was $3,420. Granted, personal income is not the source of school revenue, but it is a reasonable, if not precise, indicator of private property value. The unequal wealth of states does not account for the total difference in school

[41]*Digest of Educational Statistics*, 1975, Table 65, p. 65.
[42]*Financing the Public Schools: A Search for Equality* (Bloomington, Ind.: Phi Delta Kappa, 1975), p. 17.
[43]While the level of support figures for the states are based on 1974–75 data, the national average is based on 1973–74 data.

Figure 4-2 New York

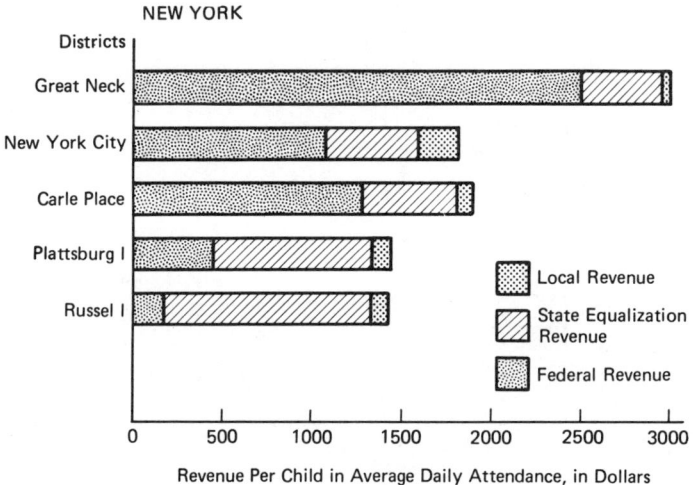

revenue; unfortunately, many of the poorer states "make less of an effort." That is, they levy lower tax rates on private property to support schools than do wealthy or moderately wealthy states such as New York, Minnesota, and Wisconsin. Federal support to states, which is less than 10 percent of total school revenue, would not offset this difference even if more federal grants were based on need. Short of a fundamental change in financial structure of American schooling, which may take a constitutional amendment, the differential in revenue among the states is not likely to be closed significantly.

As great as the financial difference is among states, it is even greater among school districts within most states. In California, for example, the wealthiest district had fifty times as much local wealth per pupil as the poorest, and about triple the total revenue per child (after state and federal grants). In New York the richest district in per pupil wealth had approximately fourteen times as much local wealth as the poorest, while the revenue disparity was approximately two to one. In Texas the richest district is 1,000 times richer than the poorest; the difference in local revenue is over twice as much.[44] Figures 4-2, 4-3 and 4-4 depict the school revenues in these states.

The revenue gap among districts has been reduced by both federal and state funds, but mostly state. The basic method of providing state revenue has been the *foundation system* of shared financing. In principle this system has the potential to equalize school revenues within a state; in practice it has not been applied vigorously. As it is applied, a state establishes a

[44]*Financing the Public Schools*, pp. 18–21.

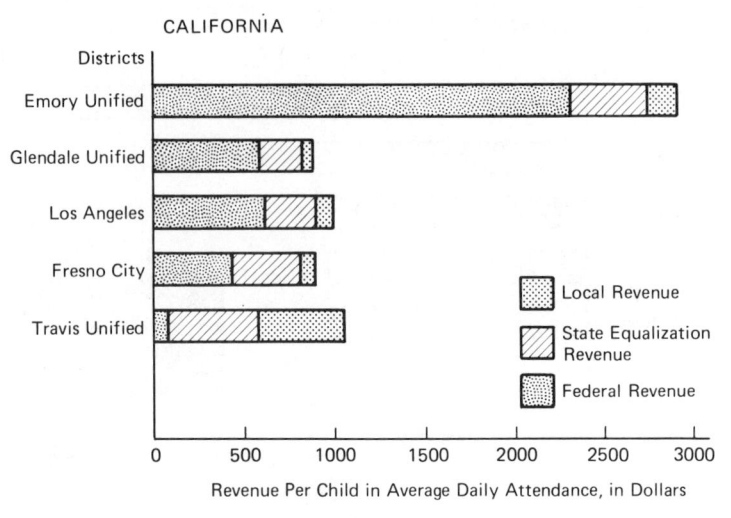

Figure 4-3 California

minimum dollar level (floor or foundation) of spending per pupil, which it guarantees to every district. To qualify for the guarantee, a district must meet a minimum property-tax rate. For example in Minnesota (in 1976) a district must vote a tax rate of at least $29 for each $1,000 of assessed value. At that level the state guarantees at least $900 to educate each pupil annually.

This minimum foundation rate is chosen in reference to some district in the state, so that this rate will yield enough local money (in the referent district) to meet the foundation level of revenue. In theory, the district and rate chosen are the richest district and a minimum rate low enough for the poorest district to afford, yet high enough to discourage raising extra funds in wealthier districts. In practice, the "key" district selected as the foundation standard tends to be average in wealth; thus state funds close the gap only somewhat. Critics of the basic foundation system are numerous; the most stinging criticism comes from those who claim it serves the rich. With the "key" district modestly chosen, the foundation tax rate generally needs to be set higher to insure a reasonable foundation level of revenue. The result is that poorer districts raise more money locally and are thus given less state money than otherwise. Ironically, a formula that gives some state aid to richer-than-average districts is more equalizing, because the poorer districts can tax at a lower rate, thus receiving substantially more state aid. The foundation system has not proved to be the best of all worlds.[45]

[45]John E. Coons, William H. Clune, and Stephen Sugarman, "School Financing: Its Uses as an Apparatus of Privilege," in *Foundations of Education: Dissenting Views*, ed. James J. Shields, Jr., and Colin Greer (New York: John Wiley & Sons, Inc., 1974), p. 80.

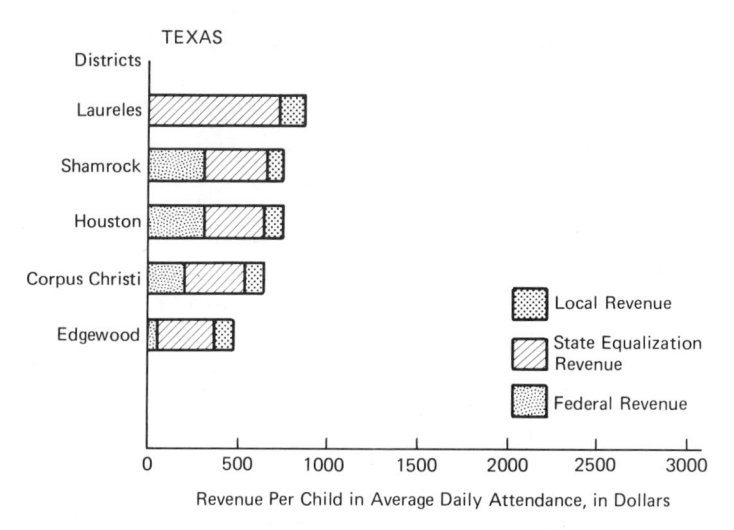

Figure 4-4 Texas

the impact of school resources

So far, this discussion of the equality of educational opportunity has focused on the resources (or inputs) for schooling. But in order for this approach to be valid and useful, the money provided for school buildings, teacher salaries, books, programs, and the rest must have positive effects on the learning of youngsters. The concept of equality in education, treated as equality in inputs, is based on the assumption that such inputs lead to substantial outputs, i.e., affect the child's education.

James Coleman, who headed a major study survey of equal educational opportunity in the mid-sixties, was the first to empirically detect this gap between input and output. Coleman's group carried out their study under a mandate in the Civil Rights Act of 1964. It pointed out the meaning of "equal educational opportunity" had undergone modification as a result of the historic *Brown* v. *The Board of Education* Supreme Court decision in 1954. Here the court ruled that separate-but-equal school facilities were not enough. Implicit in this argument, Coleman pointed out, was the position that we need to assess the effects of schooling on the student. That is, equal school resources were no guarantee of equal school effectiveness. Unfortunately, this notion was largely overshadowed by the emphasis on racial aspects of the decision. In Coleman's subsequent review of existing studies and new data, his group came up with interesting, though disturbing findings.[46]

The Coleman group examined the relation of school inputs to their

[46]Coleman, *Concept of Equality*, p. 15.

effects on the academic achievement of black and white students. The order of importance in inputs, both in schools attended by black children and those attended by white children, were: facilities and curriculum materials least important; teacher quality next; and educational backgrounds of fellow students the most important. The difference in the availability of these same inputs in those schools was precisely the same: facilities, and curriculum materials were the least variant between schools; teacher quality the next; and student backgrounds the most variant. Said differently, those resources over which the school has the most control are the least important, and vice-versa.[47] This is not to say that educational resources have no effect, or even very little effect, on learning, but rather that the effect is remarkably the same for everyone.

In large part, the controversy over equality in education still continues to focus on such indirect, and perhaps invalid, elements as the amount of expenditures and quality of inputs. We can make sure that schools have equal library, classroom, and playground resources, but this does not mean that the quality of schooling is equal. The situation, however, is not irreversibly dismal. Educational researcher Herbert Walberg found ample evidence, in contrast with Coleman and Jencks, to show that the amount of schooling, the opportunity to learn, and the quality of schools do enhance learning.[48]

Even if the inputs to learning are minor, or overshadowed by family and neighborhood factors, this is not justification for maintaining a system of unequal resources. Every school child has a right to an equal share of the state's resources.

NEW DIRECTIONS FOR FINANCING SCHOOLS

The institution of education is enshrined in the hearts and minds of Americans, yet financial support has not been particularly generous, especially considering the economic resources we are willing to devote to private production. The economic benefits of schooling—both to the individual and society—are widely acclaimed. Though schooling tends to raise levels of economic achievement, it far from guarantees this, and in many instances creates greater disparities. The state has the obligation to provide each person with the opportunity to develop his or her economic potential, but presently it falls considerably short of this goal.

[47]James S. Coleman and others, *Equality of Educational Opportunity* (Washington: U.S. Department of Health, Education and Welfare, Office of Education, 1966), pp. 20–22.
[48]Herbert J. Walberg and Sue Pinsur Rasher, "The Ways Schooling Makes A Difference," *Phi Delta Kappan*, 58, 9 (May 1977), pp. 703–7.

In light of the latest decisions related to *Serrano* v. *Priest* in California, it's very likely that states will be adopting new school financing systems. The Supreme Court of California has said that the state will have to find an equitable plan. However, we can't stress too much that equalizing expenditures does not mean equalizing the quality of education.

school finance reform

One possible solution is for *states* to assume *full funding* of public schools. All revenues for schooling would be collected by the state and distributed to school districts on an equal per-pupil basis. This is a simple, precise way of eliminating the wide differences in money that now exist among schools. It would also cut school finance ties from the regressive and sluggish property tax.

Hawaii is the only state with a state-wide school system and the only state maintaining this funding plan. Opponents of full state funding muster several objections to the alternative, including the arguments that it would burden current state tax revenue sources and create even larger state educational bureaucracies.

A second solution is to *equalize local initiative* in financing schools. With this proposal, the amount of school money for a district would depend on the local tax effort (i.e., the tax rate local citizens are willing to levy) rather than the wealth of a community. More accurately, the relation to wealth would be substantially reduced. Theoretically, richer districts feel the burden of higher tax rates less than poorer districts; nevertheless, poorer districts often tax themselves as high as or higher than wealthier districts but are unrewarded for the sacrifice. A local-initiative system increases the state aid to districts in proportion to the local units' success in raising local tax revenues. Those districts with a low tax base would receive a larger share of state funds, assuming they make a modicum of tax effort.[49]

Though equalizing local initiative substantially reduces the revenue disparity among districts, this approach does not necessarily eliminate such disparity. A radical variation on this solution, *district power equalizing*, is designed to accomplish this goal. In practice, with a district-power-equalizing plan, the state would establish a given amount of revenue to be guaranteed to local districts for each level of tax effort. If a local tax levy raises less than the guaranteed amount for that level of taxation, the state makes up the difference from a fund generated by general taxes. If the local tax pro-

---

[49]*Financing the Public Schools: A Search for Equality* (Bloomington, Ind.: Phi Delta Kappa, 1975), p. 17.

duces an excess (this is the controversial part), that excess goes into the general fund to be redistributed to poorer districts.[50] In effect the state places a lid on the amount rich districts may spend. In states where limits have been placed on spending, the wealthy districts, such as New Trier in Illinois, have strongly complained that its high-quality program is in jeopardy.

The preceding proposals totally ignore school revenue differences among states. Short of massive federal infusions or full federal funding, a significant inequality will remain. Neither of these federal plans is likely to be implemented. Education, as we pointed out, is a state function; barring a constitutional amendment, it doesn't appear that any federal schemes to substantially reduce inequities would be held constitutional.

reducing the burden on schools

Despite one of the underlying themes in this chapter—that our public schools are relatively underfinanced—the ultimate solution to school financial woes no doubt is, as Kenneth Boulding implies, to reduce costs—through a reduction in programs and services. Taxpayers are most reluctant to continue to assess themselves higher taxes to support education or any other local and state needs. This cutback (in programs and services) will not necessarily diminish the quality of schooling, and may enhance it. Don't say we didn't warn you that the economics of education is paradoxical.

Many responsibilities related to the "general education" of young people have been heaped on the schools. In addition to teaching basic verbal, writing, mathematical, and critical-thinking skills (the last is largely neglected by "back-to-basic" advocates, though it is the most neglected basic), schools are asked to teach cooking, sewing, auto mechanics, woodworking, mechanics, typing, bookkeeping, driving, trumpet playing, and the forward pass, as well as about drugs, alcohol, money, and sex. There is no question these are important skills and knowledge for survival in our society. In fact, those in the latter group (i.e. drug group, et. al.) rightfully belong in the school curriculum, as long as they are an integral part of basic literacy and thinking. Teaching them in the schools for purposes other than this demands large expenditures of resources and time, as well as considerably more staff. All this costs the schools millions of dollars annually and detracts from the basic learning that is the primary task of schools. This, as we've argued in other chapters, is what schools do best, and what they justly can be held accountable for. The other general-survival competencies are more efficiently taught in the larger community—in homes,

[50]While the level of support figures for the states are based on 1974–75 data, the national average is based on 1973–74 data.

churches, community organizations, vocational-technical centers, and even businesses.

CASE STUDY: Equalization of Educational Opportunity

Your state always has taken pride in its educational systems, but the property tax base varies considerably from one school district to another. Some districts have large manufacturing firms, some are havens for wealthy people who have built expensive homes, and a few are fortunate enough to have oil wells. These districts can raise considerably more money than the majority of districts in small cities with modest tax bases, or poor rural areas, or financially pressed urban centers.

Place yourself in the role of a state legislator dealing with the question of equality of educational opportunity. Debate a state school-tax plan that would distribute revenue from the wealthy districts to aid poor districts. Also consider whether or not you should limit the amount of money that rich districts can spend per pupil, how much poor districts should be forced to raise before they are given aid, and the minimum (and maximum) levels of money per pupil a district should have to support its schools.

THOUGHT QUESTIONS

1. Define the term "free enterprise system." Does it adequately describe our economic system? How does the meaning of free enterprise differ from profit system, capitalism, democracy? Does the term have a clear meaning for you? What is the best term to describe our economic system, if free enterprise isn't the best?

2. Are public schools and other public buildings more austere and generally less attractive than private corporate buildings? What evidence from your observations illustrates this? How do you explain your observations?

3. The cost of schooling in America is now over $100 billion a year, and rising. Do you think it is justified that we spend this much on schooling? Is the money we spend on schooling in America wisely spent? What can be done to reduce these high costs?

4. Why are many people refusing to pay any more taxes for schools?

5. How much money should a teacher make at the start of his or her career? After twenty years? Should teachers receive salary increases for acquiring more college credits or advanced degrees? Why is or isn't this system rational? What would be a better system?

6. Why do teachers earn modest incomes when compared with other professionals of equal or less formal schooling? Is this justified? Are economic earnings really an important issue in considering the satisfactions of professional careers?

7. Has education in America provided the individual with otherwise unattainable economic opportunities that enhance one's freedom, or has the individual been accommodated to the needs of big business? What arguments presented in the text are the most convincing? How do these meet with your personal observations?

8. What are you worth in "human capital" terms—in a dollar figure? Is it possible to say with any accuracy? Some people say a price cannot be put on a human life. What do you believe? Do you believe in capitalist theory? Capitalism holds that everything is a commodity with a monetary value. Are there any contradictions in your beliefs?

9. Robert Hutchins remarked that there has been a nasty rumor spreading for several decades to the effect that an individual could become rich by going to college. Not only is this not true, Hutchins believed, but also vocational, technical, professional studies—and economically beneficial training in general—should have no part in education. How would you support Hutchins' statement? Disclaim it? What do you believe in terms of this issue?

10. If James Coleman, Christopher Jencks, and others are correct in their analysis that effects of schooling on cognitive abilities and economic earnings are negligible, how do you explain the large individual and social expenditures on schooling? Is it more reasonable to challenge the Coleman-Jencks theses? What difference does it make, then, if there is an unequal distribution of resources among school districts in the nation?

PRACTICAL ACTIVITIES

1. Attend a school board meeting or public hearing on the school budget for the coming year. Briefly describe the major budget items, the discussion or presentation of the budget, and your reactions.

2. Obtain a map of school districts in your state, and list each district's per-pupil expenditure. Color-code your map to illustrate the variations in per-pupil expenditure. If possible, locate and include other related data, such as medium family income in each district and tax effort (tax revenue raised for public schools as a percent of personal income in the district). Indicate your data source and discuss your results.

3. Obtain a copy of the current salary schedule for some school district. If possible, select the district where you plan to teach, or an area where you would like to teach. Using information about the cost of living, prepare a budget for a family of four and see if you can live within the starting salary.

4. Devise a short questionnaire concerning citizen reasons for support of public schools. Areas to survey include major purposes of schools in a community; the benefits of public education to society; most and least important areas of the school curriculum; most important areas of a high school economics course (e.g., economic theory, consumer economics, business organizations); reasons for students to get a college education; the benefits of college to the individual, to the nation. (If you can obtain a large

enough sample, separate the responses from high school students and adults.) Tabulate the results and write a summary of your findings.

5. Design a semester course in economics for either a high school or a junior high school curriculum. Include in your design the units to be covered, major ideas or topics in each unit, and at least one general objective for each unit.

5a. If you are preparing to be a history, geography, or government teacher, design a major unit on economics as it relates to your subject area. Include general objectives, an outline, and potential learning activities to employ.

5b. If you are preparing to be an elementary school teacher, design a plan for including economics in your social studies curriculum. Either select a grade level and develop a detailed plan, or present a general scheme for including economics in the K–6 curriculum.

BIBLIOGRAPHY

books

BENSON, CHARLES S., *The Economics of Public Education* (2nd ed.). Boston: Houghton Mifflin Company, 1968.

BERG, IVAR, *Education and Jobs: The Great Training Robbery*. New York: Praeger Publishers, Inc., 1970.

BERKE, JOEL S., ALAN K. CAMPBELL, AND ROBERT J. GOETTEL, *Financing Equal Educational Opportunity, Alternatives for State Finance*. Berkeley, Calif.: McCutchan Publishing Corporation, 1972.

BOWLES, SAMUEL, AND HERBERT GINTIS, *Schooling in Capitalist America, Educational Reform and the Contradiction of Economic Life*. New York: Basic Books, Inc., Publishers, 1976.

COLEMAN, JAMES S., AND OTHERS, *Equality of Educational Opportunity*. Washington: U.S. Department of Health, Education and Welfare, Office of Education, 1966.

COONS, JOHN, WILLIAM H. CUNE, AND STEPHEN D. SUGARMAN, *Private Wealth and Public Education*. Cambridge, Mass.: The Belknap Press of Harvard University Press, 1970.

GALBRAITH, JOHN KENNETH, *The Affluent Society* (2nd ed.). Boston: Houghton Mifflin Company, 1969.

———, *Economics and the Public Purpose*. Boston: Houghton Mifflin Company, 1973.

GREER, COLIN, *The Great School Legend, a Revisionist Interpretation of American Public Education*. New York: The Viking Press, 1972.

HEILBRONER, ROBERT L., *The Making of Economic Society* (5th ed). Englewood Cliffs, N.J.: Prentice-Hall, Inc., 1975.

JENCKS, CHRISTOPHER, AND OTHERS, *Inequality: A Reassessment of the Effect of Family and Schooling in America*. New York: Basic Books, Inc., Publishers, 1972.

KNELLER, GEORGE F., *Education and Economic Thought*. New York: John Wiley & Sons, Inc., 1968.

SPRING, JOEL H., *Education and the Rise of the Corporate State*. Boston: Beacon Press, 1972.

———, *The Sorting Machine, National Educational Policy Since 1945*. New York: David McKay Company, Inc., 1976.

periodicals and pamphlets

BANE, MARY JO, AND CHRISTOPHER JENCKS, "The Schools and Equal Opportunity," *Saturday Review—Education*, 55, no. 38 (October 1972).

BENSON, CHARLES A., AND THOMAS A. SHANNON, *Schools Without Property Taxes: Hope or Illusion?* A Phi Delta Kappa Fastback, no. 1. Bloomington, Ind.: The Phi Delta Kappa Educational Foundation, 1972.

———, *Equity in School Financing: Full State Funding*. A Phi Delta Kappa Fastback, number 56. Bloomington, Ind.: The Phi Delta Kappa Educational Foundation, 1975.

Financing the Schools: A Search for Equality (2nd ed.). Bloomington, Ind.: Phi Delta Kappa, 1975.

GUTHRIE, JAMES, *Equity in School Financing: District Power Equalizing*. A Phi Delta Kappa Fastback, Number 57. Bloomington, Ind.: The Phi Delta Kappa Educational Foundation, 1975.

INNES, JON T., PAUL B. JACOBSON, AND ROLAND J. PELLEGRIN, *The Economic Returns to Education: A Survey of the Findings*. Eugene, Ore.: The Center for the Advanced Study of Educational Administration, University of Oregon, 1965.

Phi Delta Kappan, Vol. 55, no. 3 (November 1969). A special issue in school finance.

THE SOCIOLOGY OF EDUCATION
Socialization in Schools

We have come to know that every individual lives, from one generation to the next, in some society; that he lives out a biography, and that he lives it out within some historical sequence. By the fact of his living he contributes, however minutely, to the shaping of this society and to the course of its history, even as he is made by society and by its historical push and shove.[1]

Society can survive only if there exists among its members a sufficient degree of homogeneity; education perpetuates and reinforces this homogeneity by fixing in the child, from the beginning, the essential similarities that collective life demands.[2]

People are schooled to accept a society. They are educated to create or recreate one.[3]

THE NATURE OF A SOCIETY

A relatively large, cohesive group of people possessing a common culture is termed a society. By this definition, every nation is a society, but also every tribe and ethnic or racial group within a nation (or sometimes within

---

[1]C. Wright Mills, *The Sociological Imagination* (New York: Oxford University Press, 1959), p. 6.
[2]Emile Durkheim, *Education and Sociology* (New York: The Free Press, 1956), p. 70.
[3]Everett Reimer, *School Is Dead* (Garden City, N.Y.: Doubleday & Company, Inc., 1972), p. 121.

two or more nations, such as the Basques in Spain and France) is a society. As a matter of logical convenience, however, such groups in the United States today as blacks, Mexican-Americans, and native American Indian tribes are classified as subsocieties or subcultures.

The primary goal of every society, and to a greater or lesser extent of each subculture within a society, is to survive. Secondary goals concern the quality of life, the degree of health, stability and change, and justice desired by the collectivity. In order to continue to exist, a society must meet at least these six survival requirements:[4]

1. The population has to be reproduced, or the group will die out.
2. The population also has to be reproduced culturally and socially; its children must be educated and trained in the values and skills needed to function as adequate adults.
3. Goods and services have to be produced and distributed.
4. Order must be maintained both internally and externally.
5. The population must be maintained at a reasonable level of physical and mental health.
6. The society's members must see enough meaning and purpose in life to be motivated to perform their various tasks.

These survival tasks are carried out by social institutions: "the family, the educational system, the economy, the polity, the health and welfare system, and the religious or moral system." Each of these social institutions "is a major area of organized social activity required for social continuity."[5]

RELATIONSHIP OF SOCIETY, EDUCATION, AND SCHOOLS

Clearly, then, education is a social institution charged with cultural and social reproduction, that is, with the education of children and youth for individual and social survival. To state that education is a social institution, however, is not to equate education with schools and schooling. During the Golden Age in ancient Greece, Pericles asserted that Athens served as an education to the world, that the entire way of life in Athenian society was a model educational environment to its citizens, as well as to outside observers and visitors to the city-state.

The culture of Athens was educative, but Athens also had schools such as Plato's academy. The point here is that the education of a person is only partly the result of schooling, and mainly the result of other educative

---

[4]Melvin M. Tumin, *Patterns of Society: Identities, Roles, Resources* (Boston: Little, Brown & Co., 1973), p. 272.
[5]Ibid., p. 171.

agencies (and individuals) such as the family, the community, and the communications media. School or schooling is but one influence, one "teacher" among several which form the social institution of education.

Each of the six social institutions—family, education, polity, economy, health/welfare system, and religious/moral system—is to some extent an educative agent. Although each of these institutions influences the cognitive and affective "maps" of all members of a society, their greatest impact is on the society's younger members—children and youth. Sociologists refer to this pervasive process of initiation and conditioning as socialization.

SOCIALIZATION, EDUCATION, AND SCHOOLS

Socialization is a process of "teaching" and "learning," where the culture, the society, the community, and the other social institutions combine to be the "teacher," and where all members of the society are the "learners." In this context, each individual societal member is both a "teacher" and a learner": a "teacher" when in the role of group member, and a "learner" when, as an individual, others influence one's behaviors. A person, then, is both a part of the "We" and a separate, unique "I." Schwartz describes socialization this way:

> Socialization ... produces social patterns in that it provides both a body of expectations and ways to meet them that are more or less shared by other members of a social group. . . . From the point of view of individuals, socialization helps them to cope with the demands of their social groups by giving them the capacity to meet these demands. From the point of view of a group, socialization contributes to its stability and continued existence by transmitting established behavior and value patterns to its members.[6]

If each of the six social institutions plays a part in the socialization process, then one can refer to the subprocesses as political socialization or economical socialization—or education-as-socialization. Education, however, is more than merely external impositions, implicit or explicit, of a social institution on the individual members of a society. It is also the process of self-development initiated by the individual. Education involves both the demands of socialization, of societal membership, of community, *and* the drives for individuality, for personal growth, for self-actualization, and self-realization. In addition, education is both process and product. It is societal and individual efforts as well as the outcomes of those efforts. Cremin's definition of education successfully combines these four elements of social control, individual self-development, process, and product:

---

[6]Audrey James Schwartz, *The Schools and Socialization* (New York: Harper & Row, Publishers, 1975), p. 2.

I have found it fruitful to define education as the deliberate, systematic, and sustained effort to transmit, evoke, or acquire knowledge, attitudes, values, skills, or sensibilities, as well as any outcomes of that effort.[7]

One social agency created to enhance the processes of socialization *and* education is the school. In one form or another, schools exist in almost every society on earth. In some societies, the school is only a secondary agent of socialization, with the family, religion, and the community as the primary socializing agencies. In other societies, especially those of Western Europe, Japan, and North America, the school has become the primary agency of socialization. In the United States, the school emerged as the primary educative agency only during the past two centuries. Before the nineteenth century, American society relied more heavily on the family and the church as primary educative agencies.[8]

As agents of society, schools perform a number of socialization functions, the kinds being dependent on the nature of the society. For today's schools in almost all nations, Reimer identifies four social functions they all perform. These are: (1) custodial care, (2) social-role selection, (3) indoctrination, and (4) education.[9] From a different vantage point, Boulding, an economist, describes five outcomes or products of the schooling industry: (1) knowledge, (2) skills, (3) custodial care, (4) certification, and (5) community activity.[10] Of Reimer's four functions and Boulding's five outcomes, three from these two lists concern what is commonly regarded as *education*. Reimer uses the term, "education," while Boulding employs the two words, "knowledge" and "skills." Both writers include "custodial care" as a function/product of schooling. It appears as though Boulding's term "certification" would be subsumed as a part of Reimer's broader concept "social-role selection." Reimer's term "indoctrination" and Boulding's use of "community activity" seem to be distinct and mutually exclusive concepts.

THE SOCIAL FUNCTIONS OF SCHOOLS

Those socialization functions performed by schools include at least the five alluded to above: (1) education (including not only knowledge and skills, but also attitudes, values, and sensibilities), (2) social-role selection (including not only the highly visible act of certification but also the more subtle forms of sorting and selecting), (3) indoctrination, (4) custodial care, and (5) community activity.

[7]Lawrence A. Cremin, *Public Education* (New York: Basic Books, Inc., Publishers, 1976), p. 27.
[8]Ibid., p. 37.
[9]Reimer, *School Is Dead*, p. 13.
[10]Kenneth Boulding, "The Schooling Industry as a Possibly Pathological Section of the American Economy," *Review of Educational Research*, 42, 1 (Winter, 1972), pp. 129-43.

Although education is a form of socialization which today is performed primarily by schools, education is also a function of other agencies affecting children and youth, *and* of the individual's own actions directed toward self-development. Such groups as family, peer groups, church, mass media, and youth-serving organizations all play roles in the education of the young. In or out of schools, the individual child or adolescent is an agent in his or her own education.

the function of education

As a social function of schools, education comprises knowledge, skills, attitudes, values, and sensibilities. Most of these types of learning are in the category of what is termed "general education," as distinguished from "specialized education." In this context, "general education" refers to learning needed to function effectively as a citizen and member of a particular society, which in the United States includes several modes of communication (reading, writing, speaking, computing, etc.), several modes of thinking (problem-solving, scientific method, etc.), the values of human dignity and the rational consent of the governed, coupled with materialism and capitalist economics, the attitudes of racism, sexism, competitiveness, individualism, and elitism, coupled with egalitarianism, communalism, and cooperativeness, and the many other cognitive and affective attributes needed for membership in contemporary U.S. society.

By "specialized education" is meant here the variety of optional "elective" activities which schools provide to cater to individuals' interests, leisure choices, occupational tendencies, and desires for higher, continuing education. Thus, social studies is a subject in the domain of general education, although for some students it is also a subject of individual interest (for purposes of leisure, occupation, or college admission) and therefore falls into the domain of specialized education. Although home economics and industrial arts generally are considered general education, for some students these areas are specialized education, usually for occupational preference purposes.

All school subject areas can be both general and specialized education, though it is common for some subjects to be thought of as primarily general education (e.g., English or mathematics) and other subjects as primarily specialized education (e.g., building-construction trades, cosmetology, physics, or advanced placement courses). At the elementary school level, almost all education is general education, while there are increasing specialized education options as students enter middle schools, junior high schools, high schools, and colleges. Virtually all graduate school education is specialized education.

It should be obvious that, as a social function of schools, education (both general and specialized) is what most persons would consider the major reason for the existence of schools in the United States. It will become increasingly clear, however, that other social functions of schools interfere with the school's function of education, especially that aspect of education referred to as individual self-development or self-realization.

the function of social-role selection

The schools in the United States engage in numerous activities which are carried on ostensibly to complement the educational function, but which, in effect, perform a different socialization function—that of social-role selection. Sociologists use the concepts of *role* and *status* to describe the social positions held by the individual members of a social group.

> While closely related, the terms *status* and *role* have somewhat different meanings: status properly signifies a social position without reference to the behavior it entails; role, on the other hand, refers to the dynamic aspects of status, to the behavioral expectations that all persons who hold similar social positions are expected to meet. . . . A role, then, is a collection of *prescribed*, *proscribed*, and *permitted* behaviors associated with a social position or status.[11]

While the term *student* refers to a status, the expected behaviors of someone holding the status of *student* comprise the role of a student. Thus, *student* is a term that denotes both a status and a role.

Each of us holds, simultaneously, many social statuses and roles. Over time we drop certain age-specific statuses and roles and acquire other new ones. Also over time we desire, pursue, and sometimes achieve new, valued, and rewarding statuses and roles, usually in the realm of occupations. Unfortunately, or fortunately depending on one's sense of justice and preference for a particular social ideology, every society possesses a differential reward system with respect to occupational statuses. As Goslin observes: "Although the number and variety of positions to be filled varies from society to society, it has thus far been true in every society that the available positions have carried with them unequal responsibilities for and demands upon their occupants."[12] Even more important, "the world has not yet seen a society in which the occupants of all positions were accorded equal rewards or status. As a result there is competition among the members of the society . . . for those positions receiving the greatest rewards and carrying with them the greatest responsibility and prestige."[13]

Groupings of statuses can be identified within any society by clustering those statuses which possess relatively similar (1) qualifications for membership, (2) level of responsibility, (3) supply and demand ratio, (4) degree of prestige, (5) types and levels of rewards, (6) level of difficulty or

---

[11]Schwartz, *The Schools*, pp. 9–10.
[12]David A. Goslin, *The School in Contemporary Society* (Glenview, Ill.: Scott, Foresman & Co., 1965), p. 8.
[13]Ibid.

risk, and (7) degree of desirability. Such status or social-role groupings are usually termed *social classes*, and these are invariably weighted, scaled, and stratified in a hierarchical pattern. Havighurst and Neugarten describe the nature of social class stratification this way: "All human societies that we know about exhibit social inequality: that is, inequality in power, prestige, and material goods." Then, quoting David Riesman: "Everywhere and in every epoch there has existed some form of stratification with those at the top holding more privilege, power, and enjoying greater rewards than those at the bottom."[14]

As a basis for describing the characteristics of each social class and for ranking social classes, Kahl used the following seven dimensions:[15]

1. prestige
2. occupation
3. possessions, or wealth, or income
4. social interaction (i.e., patterns of differential social contacts; people stick with their own kind)
5. class consciousness (i.e., awareness of belonging to a class, such as "working class" or "middle class")
6. value orientations
7. power, or control

For some persons, and especially for children and youth, their positions on the continuum of each of these dimensions are mainly the result of ascribed or inherited characteristics, that is, of having been born into families which are in particular social classes. For other persons, and especially for those in complex, industrialized, and technologically "advanced" societies, their positions are more the result of acquired characteristics, of ability and achievement, than of ascribed characteristics.

There are a number of ways to stratify social classes. For our general needs, we will use the five-level category system Kahl favors for describing cities in the United States. The five classes are upper, upper-middle, lower middle, working, and lower. An average American city would have a distribution of its population by these five classes that approximates the following:[16]

Upper Class	1%
Upper-Middle Class	9
Lower-Middle Class	40
Working Class	40
Lower Class	10
Total	100%

[14]Robert J. Havighurst and Bernice L. Neugarten, *Society and Education*, 4th ed. (Boston: Allyn & Bacon Inc., 1975), p. 7.
[15]Ibid., p. 20.
[16]Joseph A. Kahl, *The American Class Structure* (New York: Holt, Rinehart and Winston, Inc., 1959), pp. 184–220.

A person's social position and social class membership are determined by both ascribed (i.e., inherited) and acquired (i.e., achieved) statuses or characteristics. For example, a person who is black and female, who is a first-born child in a family of four children, whose family belongs to a Methodist church, and is classified as lower-middle class possesses these statuses and social class position as a result of ascribed or inherited characteristics. If this woman, during her adult life, becomes wife and mother, completes a Ph.D. in economics, works her way to president of a large banking institution, and, together with her husband, achieves upward social mobility into the upper class, these new statuses and social class would be results of acquired or achieved characteristics.

In U.S. society, ascribed and acquired statuses combine to determine social position and class. Although American values stress acquired characteristics as preferred criteria for determining social position and class, ascribed statuses still weigh heavily in the allocation of social positions. The schools of America play a part in this determination of social position. It is the school in modern, complex, industrial, technological societies which, on the one hand, reinforces the individual's ascribed statuses and, on the other hand, provides arenas and activities for the individual to perform and achieve acquired characteristics. Teachers and other school personnel subtly reward student behaviors which they consider acceptable and desirable according to the standards of their social position and class. The school tests and certifies (by diplomas, degrees, and transcripts of letter grades); the school promotes and graduates; it rewards and punishes; and the school sorts students along continua or in either-or categories for its many curricular and extra-curricular activities. Goslin describes the part the school plays in social status selection this way:

> With the rise of mass education the school functions as an integral part of the process of status allocation in four ways: (1) by providing a context in which the individual can demonstrate his abilities, (2) by channeling individuals into paths that lead in the direction of different occupations or classes of occupations, (3) by providing the particular skills needed to fulfill the requirements of various positions, and finally (4) by transferring to the individual the differential prestige of the school itself.[17]

Also describing the school's role in status allocation, Reimer is more critical of this function than most other observers, chiefly because he views it as seriously undermining the more important function of schools—education. He calls this status-allocation function "the sorting of the young into the social slots they will occupy in adult life," and for Reimer the "aspect of job selection in school is wasteful and often personally disastrous. . . . The major part of job selection is not a matter of personal choice at all, but a matter of survival in the school system. . . . Age at dropout determines whether boys and girls will be paid for their bodies, hands, or brains, and

[17]Goslin, *The School*, p. 9.

the function of community activity

The fifth and final function that we have identified is that of community activity, by which we mean those activities initiated by the school which serve as a focus for the entire community and therefore serve as vehicles for the enhancement of social cohesiveness. This function includes such highly visible activities as athletic contests (mainly football and basketball), drama performances, musical events, and special ceremonies such as commencements and pageants, and such less visible activities as recreation clubs and leagues (e.g., chess, skiing, basketball, softball) and various self-improvement, vocational, or avocational adult education courses (e.g., painting, Volkswagen repair, macrame, "Great Books," mysticism and the occult, photography). The point here is that schools are often community-oriented and thus become community centers that foster identification with a community. The school's community activities serve to coalesce those who participate to a sense of community.

INFLUENCES ON CHILDREN AND ADOLESCENTS

There are many influences on the lives of children and youth, among which three of the most important and potent are the family, the peer group, and the school, with the media, and especially television and the recording industry, vying with the other three to mold the young. Since children and youth also hold the status and role of student, these same influences have an impact on students' performance and behavior in school. Thus, a duality of influence exists, where family, peer group, school, and media (and others such as churches) all affect children and youth *both* as individuals and as students. It is the latter impact which is of greater concern to us in education, although the impact of schooling on the lives of individuals *after leaving school* is also of interest.

the influence of family

From birth onward, the baby and then the child become progressively more and more humanized, primarily as a result of social interaction and social learning. "The family, as the major socializing agency in the society, acts to teach the child the culture and subculture."[22] As the family socializes and humanizes the child for participation in the arenas and activities of socio-cultural life, one of the institutions for which the child is prepared is the school.

In preparing the child to participate in school life, there is too much

[22] Havighurst and Neugarten, *Society*, p. 134.

diversity among families in the United States to identify one pattern of preparation. One factor which accounts for differences in family attitudes toward schooling is that of social class. This is to say that the family not only "educates" the child to the values, norms, and mores of the social class to which the family belongs; it also "educates" the youngster to the entire social structure, which includes all social classes, and also to the possibilities and ways of social class mobility, both upward and downward. Although there may be upward and downward social mobility of many individuals from each of the social classes, nearly all families support, and "educate" their children to support, the nature of the total social class structure of the society. When the children of all social classes enter the public schools, it is then that the differences of family social class backgrounds come into sharp contrast.

Because schools have come to play an ever-increasing role in the lives of all children and youth, often to the age of twenty-five, families of all social classes prepare their children, in different ways to be sure, to cope with twelve or more years of school attendance. As Havighurst and Neugarten have observed, "different families create environments that influence children's intellectual growth and educational motivation in different ways."[23] Some of the factors which vary from one family environment to another, and which appear to affect children's educational progress are: (1) language spoken in the home, (2) educational reading materials present in the home, (3) quality and amount of family talk, (4) methods and consistency in disciplining younger family members, (5) quality and amount of family engagement with community activities, family visits to local attractions, and extended family travel, and (6) parents' attitudes toward learning and schooling. As might be expected, many of these factors also correlate significantly with the social class status of the family, and often also with the racial and ethnic background of the family.

the influence of peer groups

Besides belonging to families, children and adolescents also belong to peer groups, to age-similar and status/role-similar groups. These groups are many and varied, but one child or youth will be a member of only a few groups at a time. Some of the kinds of peer groups to which children may belong are neighborhood play groups, friendship groups and cliques in school, clubs, street gangs, Scouts, athletic teams, student governments, student newspapers and yearbooks, cheerleaders, religious classes and clubs, dating groups, and the many group tags students use to refer to other students such as "jocks," "heads," "freaks," and "cowboys."

Like families, peer groups exert influence on individual members, and many peer group influences affect the school performance of members

[23]Ibid., p. 145.

as students. This is especially true for adolescents in middle, junior high, and senior high schools, but it is also true to a lesser degree for children in elementary schools. As the influence of family wanes and becomes less monopolistic over time, the influence of peer groups increases as individuals move from childhood to adolescence to adulthood. From mid- to late-teens, peer group influence is most pervasive.

As one agency of socialization, the peer group "teaches" children and youth many coping skills, especially those which may or may not be helpful in the social settings of schools. "The peer group teaches children their sex roles, building upon, but changing and elaborating the earlier teaching of the family."[24] Other functions of peer groups are to suggest aspects and modes of social mobility, to provide models of new social roles, and to assist in the process of becoming independent from adults.[25] "Further, peer groups provide a social arena away from adults where members can work out new social identities."[26]

Parents and teachers are well aware of the impact peer groups have on children and youth as students in the schools. "Pupils, more than other people in the school, experience conflict between formal school expectations and the informal expectations of their peers."[27] Peer groups that are the outcasts at school tend to drop out of school at the earliest possibility and to influence new members to do the same. On the other hand, a peer group in which planning to attend college is a norm tends to attract and reinforce members who are "college material." "More commonly, though, the child's peer culture tends to be oriented away from the educational process in the direction of leisure time activities, recreation, and fun."[28] Although peer groups can and do function to enhance academic achievement and positive attitudes toward school, they more commonly promote non- and even anti-educational goals and attitudes.

the influence of school

Not only do the family and peer group influence students as individuals, the climate, structure and organization of the school and classroom affect student attitudes and behaviors. This type of influence is mainly implicit in the ways schools and classrooms are organized and conducted; it is thus often referred to as "the hidden curriculum," in order to distinguish this form of "teaching" from the more generally recognized curriculum of teaching the subjects (e.g., science, mathematics, and social studies) in the curriculum. Dreeben contends "that what children learn derives as much

[24]Ibid., p. 163.
[25]Ibid., p. 164.
[26]Schwartz, *The Schools* p. 151.
[27]Ibid., p. 153.
[28]Goslin, *The School*, p. 33.

from the nature of their experiences in the school setting as from what they are taught."[29]

What students experience in schools, separate from the explicit, educational, curricular experiences, are (1) a social-class bias reflected by the values and norms schools promote, (2) a bureaucratized institution, and (3) a set of imposed goals designed to change students' behaviors. Although there are other components of the schools' hidden curriculum, these three appear to have the greatest impact on students as individuals.

The social class bias in schools and school districts is that of the middle class. With some exceptions, elected school board members tend to come from the upper class (very few), the upper-middle class (most), and the lower-middle class (perhaps 20 to 40 percent). For school administrators (i.e., superintendents and principals), a preponderance is from the upper-middle and lower-middle classes, while teachers mainly come from the upper-middle, lower-middle, and working classes. This distribution of those in control of schools and classrooms leads to the conclusion that "the orientation of the American school is predominantly that of the middle class," which in turn means that school personnel will tend to place "strong emphasis upon the character traits of punctuality, honesty, and responsibility. Respect for property is stressed. There is a premium upon sexual modesty and decorum. While both competitiveness and cooperation are valued to varying degrees, there is always stress upon mastery and achievement."[30]

In a broader view, Dreeben claims that in schools in the United States, students learn, among other things, four crucial social norms, which upon closer inspection are also middle-class values. These norms-values are: (1) independence, (2) achievement, (3) universalism, and (4) specificity.[31]

By "independence" Dreeben means "that individuals accept the obligations . . . to act by themselves (unless collaborative effort is called for) and accept personal responsibility and accountability for their conduct and its consequences." By "achievement" he means that students are obliged "to perform tasks actively and master the environment according to standards of excellence." Finally, by "universalism" and "specificity" Dreeben means that "students must acknowledge the right of others to treat them [i.e., students] as members of categories often based on a few discrete characteristics rather than on the full constellation of [characteristics] representing the whole person."[32]

These definitions of independence, achievement, universalism, and specificity take on fuller meanings in the contexts of specific school and classroom activities. For example, students learn the norm-value of inde-

---
[29]Robert Dreeben, "The Contribution of Schooling to the Learning of Norms," *Harvard Educational Review*, 37, no. 2 (Spring, 1967), 211.
[30]Havighurst and Neugarten, *Society*, p. 139.
[31]Dreeben, "The Contribution," p. 215.
[32]Ibid., p. 216.

pendence as they are required by teachers and other school personnel to do their homework assignments on their own, to take both teacher-made and standardized achievement tests as individuals, to avoid, in most cases, cooperative tasks with other students, to avoid cheating, to be graded (i.e., letter grades such as A, B, C, D, and F) as individuals, to be individually responsible for personal possessions such as notebooks, writing paper, pencils, and articles of clothing, and to be responsible for school property such as textbooks, desks, library books, and lockers. Even though teachers and principals mouth the goals of cooperation and working with others, "judging the product according to collective standards, however, is another question. . . . In the last analysis it is the individual assessment that counts."[33]

Schools "teach" achievement by encouraging, and even commanding, students to succeed in doing school tasks, to always do their best, to master certain skills, to compete with other students, to take all tests and assignments very seriously, and in general to accept and strive to excel on the many external standards set up by schools. Achievement standards are evident in every activity which teachers evaluate: homework assignments, quizzes, tests, number of absences, times tardy, physical prowess (i.e., number of push-ups or number of baskets made), and extent of oral participation in discussions. For each task, a student receives a symbolic reward or punishment, an "A" or an "F," a "plus" or a "minus"—some type of indicator of success or failure. These indicators in the aggregate determine whether a student has earned promotion to the next grade level or graduation from a middle, junior high or senior high school. To learn achievement is to learn to cope with success and failure as perceived and determined by others.

Through the contrasting norms/values of universalism and specificity, students learn to accept the school's practices of categorization. In school, a student's complex individuality is mostly denied as a result of treating individuals as members of categories, but categorization has its positive aspects "especially when contrasted to nepotism, favoritism, and arbitrariness." The distinction between universalism and specificity hinges on "whether individuals are treated as members of categories [universalism] or as special cases [specificity]."[34] As a member of a family, a child is usually treated with specificity, whereas in school the treatment he or she receives is most frequently based on universalism. For example, a child in a family may be fed at a time (later or earlier) and in a location (perhaps other than the kitchen or dining room) that are different from other family members, but in school this child may be required to get in line to be served at a time and place that is the same for all students in a particular classroom, or for a particular grade level, or in a particular school.

Universalism is fostered in schools by such procedures and activities

[33]Ibid., pp. 224–25.
[34]Ibid., p. 228.

as group instruction (30:1 pupil-teacher ratios), grouping of students by grade levels which approximates like-age grouping, annual (and automatic in elementary schools) promotions, sex-segregated lavatories and locker rooms, tracking (often based on career interest and academic ability) in secondary schools, getting in line ("no cutting-in") for a variety of activities like lunch and assemblies, and raising of hands and remaining in seats in individual classrooms.

The norm-value of specificity is promoted in schools by special-case treatments of students, such as when an individual is singled out for a special honor or approbation due to an outstanding performance in one or more curricular or extra-curricular areas. Such commendations may take the form of a varsity letter or a certificate or honor or merely a verbal compliment. Although favoritism by teachers for certain students is frowned upon ("teacher's pet"), teachers do single out students for compliments or reprimands based on classroom behaviors. Specificity is also learned from the friendships that develop in classes, corridors and lunchrooms, on teams, in clubs, bands and orchestras, among cheerleaders, and between student and student, student and teacher, and student and coach, director, or sponsor. In these instances, students are treated not as merely representative of all students, but as special students possessing special, individual characteristics.

Figure 5-1 The Mass Media: An Influence and Distraction

EFFECTS OF IMPOSED LEARNING OBJECTIVES

Perhaps the most subtle and significant impact that schools have on students is the intentional imposition of adult and professional educator goals and objectives *on* the scope and sequence of students' learning. The school's curriculum is chiefly the result of the past and present collective, considered judgments of community leaders and professional educators, and often represents a series of historical compromises between groups competing for control of the curriculum. The point here is that adults, living and deceased, have made and continue to make curricular decisions *for* children and adolescents. In support of this decision-making process adults invoke a number of arguments. One is the "common sense" approach, which assumes that only adults know what is best for the young and for the continued existence of the society. Another is the "appeal to tradition," which points to the history of most societies where the elders have always prescribed and proscribed a "curriculum" for the young. A third argument draws attention to the "physical and psychological risks and dangers" inherent in any educational scheme that would allow children and adolescents to decide crucial educational issues for themselves. A final argument, perhaps for many the most persuasive, appeals to the logic of the production and system models. The production model takes as a starting point a precise blueprint, with specifications, of the desired final product; while the system model assumes that among the inputs in a guided or goal-directed or cybernetic ("steered") system are a number of specific aims or objectives. Both models were devised to achieve efficiency, precision, and predictability. Both have enjoyed successful applications in a variety of enterprises in industrial-technological societies. Applied to education, however, these models treat students as products or outputs, delegating to adults the role of architect, designer, or planner.

Each of the four arguments for adult imposition of learning objectives on students has some merit, but they all omit or ignore several pertinent matters having to do with the nature of U.S. society and the nature of learning. As Margaret Mead has pointed out, there are other alternatives to exclusive reliance on just one age-dependent learning in which the young learn from the old. Other potential interactions are prefigurative learning (the old learn from the young), cofigurative learning (members of an age-group learn from each other), and self-guided learning, where an individual is, so to speak, "self-educated."[35]

Another often ignored consideration relates to the value base of U.S. society, which includes the valuing of democracy, freedom, and equality. If the younger members of the society are to cherish these values, then

---

[35]Margaret Mead, *Culture and Commitment* (Garden City, NY: Doubleday & Company, Inc. 1970).

families and schools, as well as other social institutions, need (to some degree in their organizational structures and decision-making processes) to model these values and to provide experiences in which students feel that these values apply to their lives and are not mere platitudes. To these ends, it seems inappropriate for schools to specify precisely all the goals and objectives for student learning.

In living and learning, two facilitating and enhancing conditions are spontaneity and enthusiasm, both of which appear to occur when situations possess elements of risk (*some* danger), indeterminacy, and ambiguity. In such situations, the goals of individuals as well as of the group are emergent rather than prior stipulations. The directions of learning tend to emerge somewhat haphazardly and with the aid of considerable serendipity. The desirability of having *some* school learning occur under such conditions and in such situations mitigates the need for precise and ubiquitous educational objectives.

In a society characterized to some extent as pluralistic, it seems contradictory, if not impossible of attainment, to attempt to formulate a consensus set of clear, behaviorally stated, fixed, unambiguous educational goals and objectives for *all* the children and youth in a community, a state, or the nation. This is not to deny the need for some "general education" or "common learnings." It does, however, suggest that the level of specificity of educational objectives should reflect the plurality of perceptions of and meanings attached to statements of objectives; and that the number of common objectives for all students should be considerably limited.

Finally, there seems to be a relationship between personal alienation in Western societies and the techniques, procedures, and processes most generally relied upon by social institutions in these societies. In many respects, these techniques (e.g., systems analysis and scientific methods) dictate which problems are solvable and which ends are attainable, with the result that ends are subordinated to means, person to process, and human to machine. In the context of discussing the "Search for an Image" of the future, the French critic of technological society, Jacques Ellul, states his case against the predetermination of precise goals:

> That toward which we move cannot be a mountain placed before us nor a heavenly Jerusalem all decked out to delight us. That toward which we move must come into existence as we live and advance toward it. This is why the young try to experience what adults often reproach them about: a revolt that does not appear to have any goal and is without any kind of program. What matters is to live and not to attain an objective; the objective creates itself through lived experience. This in turn implies the complete subordination of all organizational means to our project.[36]

---

[36] Jacques Ellul, "Search for an Image," in *Images of the Future*, ed. Robert Bundy (Buffalo, N.Y.: Prometheus Books, 1976), p. 33.

MULTIPLE DOMAINS OF EDUCATION

Because of the societal values of freedom, equality, human dignity, and rational consent of the governed, because of the pervasive preference for a democratic way of life, and finally, because education is at once a public and a private concern, a society-wide and a local community interest, there exist in American society perpetual disagreements and conflicts over the goals and methods, the ends and means of public education. Even this state of affairs itself is cause for dispute, since some people consider perpetual conflict as dysfunctional, while others regard it as desirable, a sign of health in a democratic society. Regardless, what is clear is that there is an intimate relationship between a society pursuing democracy and the process of education in that society.

Not only is there conflict over ends and means within the public school domain of public education, often there is conflict within and between other public education domains: the family, religious institutions, the workplace and marketplace, libraries, radio, television, museums, daycare centers, Scout troops, and so on.[37] It may seem peculiar to refer to domains of public education *other than* public schools, because public schooling has become so ubiquitous and monopolistic in Western nations. But there are several crucial distinctions upon which this concept of "multiple domains in public education" depends. First, as was discussed earlier, schooling and education are not the same or coterminous. Cremin has noted that Dewey and other progressive reformers tended "to focus so exclusively on the potentialities of the school as a level of social improvement and reform as to ignore the possibilities *of other educative institutions* [emphasis added]."[38] This overemphasis on schooling tends to obscure the educational agendas and significance of other societal agencies.

Second, Cremin observes that although Dewey viewed education as a broad, pervasive concept, he split it into *intentional* and *incidental* types. In this duality, education in schools is considered *intentional*, whereas education elsewhere—in the family or neighborhood or marketplace—is categorized as *incidental*. This bifurcation tends both to obscure the educational role played by educative agents such as the family and the media, and to relegate the educational influences of nonschool agencies to a category of unplanned, haphazard, capricious, and unintentional. It is misleading in contemporary American society to consider powerful social influences like families and media either as having only *incidental* effects on the learning of children and adolescents, or as having no explicit educational goals for the sons/daughters or listeners/viewers whom they influence. In support of his contention that schools are only one of many intentionally educative agencies in society, Cremin quotes Charles Silberman, who argued that

---

[37]The analysis drawn here and throughout the remainder of this section draws heavily on Cremin, *Public Education*.
[38]Cremin, *Public Education*, p. 3.

If our concern is with *education*, . . . we cannot restrict our attention to schools, for education is not synonymous with schooling. Children—and adults—learn outside school as well as—perhaps more than—in school. To say this is not to denigrate the importance of schools; it is to give proper weight to all the other educating forces in American society: the family and the community; the armed forces; corporate training programs; libraries, museums, churches, Boy Scout troops, 4-H clubs . . . .[39]

Further, Silberman expanded the concept of "teacher" or "educator" to include not only school, college, and university instructors, but also parents, community leaders, media directors and journalists, sponsors and leaders of community organizations (e.g., Boy and Girl Scouts), religious educators (e.g., pastors, priests, rabbis, and church school teachers), lawyers, doctors and dentists, business and corporate executives and trainers, textbook writers and publishers, military leaders and instructors, and others who *intentionally* and as part of their roles or occupations teach others.[40]

One crucial point in Cremin's analysis, then, is that U.S. society contains numerous educative agencies and educators, all of which have curricula that have been as intentionally planned and developed as those of the public schools. Public education, conceived broadly as the education of the American public, includes many educative agencies, only one of which is the public school system. Pursuing this point, Cremin suggests

> . . . a theory of education whereby each of the major educative agencies performs a mediative role with respect to the others and with respect to society at large. The family mediates the culture, and it also mediates the ways in which religious organizations, television broadcasters, schools, and employers mediate the culture. Families not only teach in their own right, they also screen and interpret the teaching of churches, synagogues, television broadcasters, schools, and employers. One could go on and work out all the permutations and combinations. What is more, these various institutions mediate the culture in a variety of pedagogical modes and through a range of technologies for the recording, sharing, and distributing of symbols. In effect, they define the terms of effective participation and growth in the society. . . . The theory of education is the theory of the relation of various educative interactions and institutions to one another, and to the society at large.[41]

CONFIGURATION OF EDUCATIVE INSTITUTIONS

As "the multiplicity of institutions that educate" interact with one another at a particular time and place, Cremin calls this cluster of interacting educative agencies a "configuration of education." For example, a student in a particular U.S. community, in a particular grade-level class, of a particular elementary school, from a particular family which holds mem-

[39]Ibid., pp. 11–12.
[40]Ibid., pp. 11–14.
[41]Ibid., pp. 23–24.

bership in a particular church, with a particular set of radio listening and television viewing habits, will be influenced, that is, *educated*, at that age and in that locale by a configuration of educative agencies. He or she will be educated by family, by local community, by school, by peers, by religion, and by media, all within the milieu and ethos of the larger national culture and society, which itself forms a part of the interdependent, global network of cultures and societies.[42]

In the world, in a society, in a community, and even in a family, seldom if ever are all parties or all educative agencies in harmony concerning either the goals of public education or the education of a single citizen. Cremin theorizes that the interacting institutions in a configuration of education may have "complementary or contradictory, consonant or dissonant" relationships. For example, the parents of a high school student may desire that their son or daughter be accounted for and supervised every moment from the time the youth leaves home for school until he or she returns home. The school's administrators, teachers, and most other parents, however, favor the concept of the "open campus" high school, where students are only required to be at and in school when they have scheduled classes. In this situation, the educative agencies of the school and *most* families are *complementary* and *consonant* in their relations concerning the "open campus" concept and the value of allowing adolescents some freedom in the use of their time; whereas for the school and one set of parents the relationship concerning the "open campus" and freedom for youth is *contradictory* and *dissonant*.

> Or, to take another example, family and school may share a mutual concern for the child's intellectual development [a complementary and consonant relationship], but the teacher may be more demanding at the same time as the parent is more sustaining [a contradictory and dissonant relationship, but perhaps a healthy tension].[43]

An obvious illustration of contradictory and dissonant relations among educative agencies in a configuration of education is the differing emphases on particular modes of communication by the television medium (visual and oral), the family (oral), and the school (written and oral). Note, however, that all three agencies, to some degree, employ oral communication, which makes their relationship also somewhat complementary and consonant. The ideal for totally complementary and consonant configurations of education is to be found in the literature of utopias. In this regard, Cremin quotes an aphorism of John Dewey's: "The most utopian thing about utopia is that there are no schools at all."[44] Presumably, in utopia all

[42] Ibid., pp. 30–31.
[43] Ibid., pp. 31–32.
[44] Ibid., p. 7.

educative agencies, all configurations of education, all social institutions, the total environment, would be perfectly complementary and consonant, obviating the need for any specialized agency like a school.

CONFLICT IN AMERICAN PUBLIC EDUCATION

In the U.S. educational system, however, conflict among educative institutions and configurations of education is the rule rather than the exception. This is due to at least two crucial factors: the pluralist nature of American society and the decentralized, parent-option nature of the American school system. As a nation composed of many native American Indian societies and many immigrant groups from other national societies in Africa, Asia, Europe, Latin America, Canada, and Mexico, the United States is a conglomerate of diverse racial, ethnic, and religious subcultures tenuously held together by a national language, territorial sovereignty, an economic system combining capitalism and welfare state, a political system based on constitutional and representative democracy, and a collection of borrowed social values which form a hierarchical value structure, but *without* a single, pinnacle value to which all others are subordinate. For such a society, conflict is indigenous to its way of life.

The educational system in the United States also induces conflict among educative agencies. Since education is not one of the enumerated functions of the national or federal government (i.e., education is not specifically mentioned in the U.S. Constitution), it is a power reserved to the states or to the people. This means that each of the fifty states could have preempted the field of education, by state constitution or statute, and could have required all children and youth between specified ages, say five and sixteen, to attend only state-operated public schools. Historically, no state did totally monopolize public education to the extent of prohibiting all private and parochial schools. Although one state, Hawaii, created a unitary system without any local school boards or school districts (i.e., there is but one school district—the entire state), even in this atypical case parents have the options, at their expense and without public tax monies, of enrolling their children in private or parochial schools. In all states except Hawaii, the state government has delegated most of its public education powers to voters in local school districts created by state statutes and to local school boards. Thus, conflict is virtually certain to occur both among local, community educative institutions and between community educative agencies and those at the state, regional, and national levels. For example, in a community with public, private, and parochial schools, potential conflict exists in the competition for the educational dollar, in the different philosophies and goals of education, and in the differential attitudes toward each of the three kinds of schools by community leaders and organizations. Also, there is potential conflict among the community's many educative agencies (including all three kinds of schools) and educative agencies at other levels, such as the state government, major state-wide media (newspapers, radio, television stations), national, society-at-large communications media (especially network radio and television), the federal government, and nationwide professional associations and lobbyist groups.

IMPLICATIONS OF THE CREMIN THESIS

From the foregoing discussion of Cremin's concepts of "multiple educative institutions" and "configurations of education," several implications for public education, or the education of the public, can be drawn. Cremin states: "When seeking the sources of social stability and change (and especially of social reform and resistance to reform), one must consider the possible contributions of all the institutions that educate, bearing in mind that the decisive elements may still lie elsewhere."[45] At another place he states:

> In its most general sense, the process of education is on the one hand a series of transactions between an individual with a particular temperament and life history and one or more institutions of education that tend to relate to one another in configurations, and on the other hand a series of deliberate efforts toward self-development. It is a complex process, fraught with irony and contradiction. The teacher and the taught often differ in educational aim and outlook, as do both in many instances from the sponsor. What is taught is not always what is desired, and vice versa. What is taught is not always what is learned, and vice versa. And when what is taught is actually learned, it is frequently learned over lengthy periods of time and at the once, twice and thrice removed, so that the intended and the incidental end up merging in such a way as to become virtually indistinguishable."[46]

Cremin considers his conception of education, of multiple educative institutions, and of configurations of education, to be an "ecological approach" which embodies three ways of thinking about education: "thinking *comprehensively*, thinking *relationally*, and thinking *publicly*." By thinking *comprehensively* is meant taking into consideration all the many educative influences on a student beside the obvious ones of school and teacher. It means recognizing that the successes and failures attributed to schools result from complementary or contradictory educational configurations in

[45] Ibid., p. 37.
[46] Ibid., pp. 43–44.

which the school is but one educative institution among many. "And the moral is simple: the public school ought never to take the entire credit for the educational accomplishments of the public, and it ought never to be assigned the entire blame."[47]

By thinking *relationally* is meant "to be aware of the problem of allocation of financial and human resources and of resultant educational outcomes."[48] The point here is that decision-makers, either inside or outside the school system, need to make educational policy decisions in relation to all the educative institutions in the society. Seen relationally, the school always operates as a part of an interactive system composed of such other parts as the family, the community, and the communications media.

By thinking *publicly* is meant "that public thinking about education and public policy making for education go on at a variety of levels and in a variety of places."[49] Decisions are made by parents, teachers, principals, school district central office personnel, school superintendents, local boards of education, directors of Boards of Cooperative Educational Services, state departments of education, state commissioners of education, state boards of education, a variety of regional consortia, local and state radio and television stations, the U.S. Office of Education and other federal agencies, local, state, and national professional associations, state and federal courts, local, state, and federal councils and legislatures, mayors, governors, and the President and his cabinet, and hundreds of others holding positions which influence the education of the American public. Further, rationales for each and every educational decision should arise out of public dialogue and debate, should involve a maximum of citizen input, and should lead to public decisions which are a matter of public record. Cremin justifies such a process by appeal to Dewey's conception of democracy:

> A democracy is more than a form of government; it is primarily a mode of associated living, of conjoint communicated experience. The extension in space of the number of individuals who participate in an interest so that each has to refer his action to that of others, and to consider the action of others to give point and direction to his own, is equivalent to the breaking down of those barriers of class, race, and national territory which kept men from perceiving the full import of their activity.[50]

Then, in Cremin's own words: "In the last analysis, the fundamental mode of politics in a democratic society is education, and it is in *that* way over all others that the educator is ultimately projected into politics."[51]

[47]Ibid., p. 58.
[48]Ibid., p. 61.
[49]Ibid., p. 69.
[50]John Dewey, *Democracy and Education* (New York: The Macmillan Company, 1916), p. 101, quoted in Cremin, *Public Education*, pp. 72–73.
[51]Cremin, *Public Education*, p. 76.

EDUCATION AND SOCIAL CHANGE

At the height of the Great Depression in 1932, George S. Counts asked the conventioneers attending the annual convention of the Progressive Education Association: "Dare the schools build a new social order?" At that time, most institutions in the United States were under siege and were considered incapable of countering the human devastation wrought by economic collapse. Curious, that at this moment an American educational leader should call for the schools to lead the way toward social reform, toward the reconstruction of society. It is indeed curious because, as a social institution, the schools in all modern, industrial, technological societies typically play a conserving, conservative, perpetuation-of-the-status-quo role. How realistic was Counts or anyone else who looks to the schools as a vehicle for social change?

Some educational historians and most educational polemicists assert that American schools have changed or can change the social order, but such claims do not square with the facts. Perhaps the soundest argument that the schools can bring about social change has to do with the Americanization of European and Asian immigrant groups. It is argued that the schools were primarily responsible for acculturating these racial and/or ethnic groups to the language and ways of their newly adopted country. This may have been the case with some earlier waves of immigration during the nineteenth and early twentieth centuries, but not for the later immigrant groups such as the Puerto Ricans, and not for the "original" natives of North America, and not for very early settlers like the Mexican-Americans, and certainly not for black Americans. In short, the American school system never created a melting pot and never achieved *E Pluribus Unum*.

If crises are the times when social change can be most readily accomplished, such moments in the history of the United States do not reveal the schools or educators in the vanguard of reform movements—not in 1776 to 1789, or in 1861 to 1865, or in 1914 to 1918, or in 1928 to 1939, or in 1940 to 1945. A possible exception to this generalization is the role of teachers and students in high schools, colleges, and universities during the Vietnam era (c. 1966 to 1972). Although the social changes during these years may have begun a cultural revolution yet to be documented, the school provided only the forum for the actors: The explicit curricula of these educational institutions rarely if ever included societal reform as a goal, either of instructors or governing bodies.

Since about 1960, public policies and funds have been focused on the schools as agencies for the conduct of "wars" on racism (and racial isolation), poverty, cultural "deprivation," environmental degradation, sexism, and depletion of natural resources, among others. Unfortunately, and probably inevitably, such pervasive ills of a society cannot be cured by a single institution, let alone one of society's weakest institutions, its public school system. It might even be considered deception and deviousness on the part of the leaders of a society to expect the public schools alone to undertake basic social reforms.

If a society includes many educative institutions, its public schools being only one of them, and if these multiple agencies form various clusters or configurations of education whose interaction may be complementary and consonant or contradictory and dissonant, then social change can be best expedited when the educative institutions and configurations act and interact in near-harmony of purpose. To rely exclusively on any one of them for social reform is to deny or ignore the complex, interactive, multifaceted nature of social change.

CASE STUDY: Reporting Student Achievement

You are a sixth-grade teacher of English in a middle school (grades 6, 7 and 8) where there are two ways of reporting pupil progress to parents: (1) a report card containing letter grades for each subject, and (2) a narrative description of a student's strengths and weaknesses. Both reports also serve as the basis for parent conferences with parents willing to schedule conferences and to come to the school.

There are 150 students in your five sections or classes of English. For the first quarter (nine weeks), your report card letter grades are distributed as follows:

A = 10
B = 20
C = 30
D = 70
F = 20

Justify this distribution, *not* in terms of individual achievement, but rather in terms of the *social function* of schools. Also, justify to a parent the awarding of a "D" to his or her daughter. For both justifications, you will need to assume many specifics of classroom behavior and performance.

THOUGHT QUESTIONS

1. What are some desirable goals in the two domains of *general education* and *specialized education*?
2. Explain the quotation "People are schooled to accept a society. They are educated to create or re-create one."

also how much they will be paid. This in turn will largely determine where they can live, with whom they can associate, and the rest of their style of life."[18]

the function of transmission of social values

Closely related to the school's function of status and class selection is the socialization function of indoctrination, as Reimer calls it, or the transmission of social values. Of course, here as with other socialization functions, the school is not the only social institution charged with the transmission of cultural and social values. In fact, all social institutions transmit these values in the normal course of their activities. The schools transmit and reinforce social values, both overtly and explicitly as well as covertly and implicitly. For example, through simulated economic activities, such as "playing store" in the primary grades, schools teach the value of free enterprise capitalism. This is overt and explicit socialization to a particular societal value. But schools also transmit values in less obvious, implicit ways, such as through the organizational structure of a school itself, which is hierarchical in nature, mirroring the hierarchical structure of virtually all organizations in contemporary, industrial societies. These are examples of the inculcation or indoctrination of socio-cultural values.

the function of custodial care

Our fourth function of schools is also one that interferes with and diverts attention from the function of education. This is the child-care or custodial care function, sometimes referred to pejoratively as baby-sitting or keeping the kids off the streets. Goslin calls this "the role of the school in providing mothers with relief from the task of taking care of their children during a significant part of the day, which in turn makes possible the addition of large numbers of married women to the labor force."[19] Schools in the United States today, at all levels from pre-kindergarten through the college years, provide extensive and progressively more expensive custodial care. Reimer and others have pointed out that "packaging custody" has the consequence of extending "childhood from age twelve to twenty-five...."[20] Reimer claims that "child care is the most tangible service schools provide, and since parents are naturally concerned about the quality of such care, this function has a priority claim on school resources. Other functions must compete for what is left after prevailing local standards of safety, comfort, and convenience have been met."[21]

[18]Reimer, *School Is Dead*, p. 17.
[19]Goslin, *The School*, p. 11.
[20]Reimer, *School Is Dead*, p. 15.
[21]Ibid., p. 14.

3. How do the school's social functions of social-role selection, indoctrination, custodial care, and community activity interfere with, and often preclude, the school's function of education?

4. Explain the statement "Every social institution is to some extent an educative agency."

5. List several ways in which the schools teach each of the following values– norms:

—independence
—achievement
—universalism
—specificity

6. How can educators resolve the I/We dilemmas? How can teachers balance personal and social learning objectives for students?

7. What are some arguments for and against "adult imposition of learning objectives on students"?

8. List some of the "educators" in American society other than schools. What is the "content" or "curriculum" of each educative agency on your list?

9. Describe a "configuration of education" which impinged on you during a particular stage in your development.

10. To what extent to you think schools can bring about social change in a society?

PRACTICAL ACTIVITIES

1. Devise a questionnaire that assesses community satisfaction or dissatisfaction with the schools.

2. Attend a school board meeting and do an informal survey of who is in attendance and who is on the board of education. Deal with factors such as age, sex, race, apparent social class, apparent educational level, etc. Describe any school-community issues which were discussed.

3. Get or make your own map of a school district, then color-code the ethnic, religious, and socio-economic group boundaries. Indicate the data source for your map-making (school records, census data, etc.). Make sure your finished product is a *map*, not a sketchy diagram.

4. Visit an elementary or secondary school classroom, and observe and record examples of the "teaching" (usually implicit rather than explicit) of

—independence
—achievement
—universalism
—specificity

5. Interview a number of local "educators" other than those connected with schools, and try to determine what they "teach" children and adolescents. The following is a suggested list:

—local government officials
—newspaper journalists and editors
—radio announcers or program directors
—scout troop leaders
—4-H Club leaders
—church officials and teachers
—business and corporation leaders
—several parents
—public librarians
—museum curators
—television journalists and program directors
—community recreation officials

6. Interview school personnel who are responsible for extracurricular activities, and try to ascertain what educational goals are achieved in their extracurricular areas. Also, try to determine to what extent such activities contribute to the function of "community" activity.

7. Try to document a local example of a case in which a "configuration of educative agencies" have contradictory, dissonant relationships. You may wish to select a single student, and chart the effects of family, local television, and so forth.

8. Draw a geometric model that shows the many interactions of societal institutions with the schools. Then explain the interactions you have diagrammed.

BIBLIOGRAPHY

BANKS, OLIVE. *The Sociology of Education*. New York: Schocken Books, 1968.

BROOKOVER, WILBUR, AND EDSEL ERICKSON, *Society, Schools, and Learning*. Boston: Allyn & Bacon, Inc., 1969.

CALLAHAN, RAYMOND C., *Education and the Cult of Efficiency*. Chicago: University of Chicago Press, 1962

COLEMAN, JAMES S., *The Adolescent Society: The Social Life of the Teenager and Its Impact on Education*. New York: The Free Press, 1961.

CORWIN, RONALD G., *A Sociology of Education*. New York: Appleton-Century-Crofts, 1965.

CREMIN, LAWRENCE A., *Public Education*. New York: Basic Books, Inc., Publishers, 1976.

DEWEY, JOHN, *The Child and the Curriculum/The School and Society*. Chicago: University of Chicago Press, 1902.

DEWEY, JOHN, *Democracy and Education.* New York: The Macmillan Company, 1960.
DREEBEN, ROBERT, *On What Is Learned in School.* Reading, Mass.: Addison-Wesley Publishing Company, Inc., 1968.
DURKHEIM, EMILE, *Education and Sociology.* New York: The Free Press, 1956.
ERIKSON, ERIK H., *Identity: Youth and Crisis.* New York: W. W. Norton & Company, Inc., 1968.
FLACKS, RICHARD, *Youth and Social Change.* Chicago: Markham, 1971.
FRIEDENBERG, EDGAR Z., *Coming of Age in America.* New York: Vintage-Random House, Inc., 1970.
GOSLIN, DAVID, *The School in Contemporary Society.* Chicago: Scott, Foresman & Company, 1965.
HAVIGHURST, ROBERT, AND BERNICE NEUGARTEN, *Society and Education* (4th ed.). Boston: Allyn & Bacon, Inc., 1971.
HIEMSTRA, ROGER, *The Educative Community.* Lincoln, Neb.: Professional Educators Publications, 1972.
HUMMEL, RAYMOND C., AND JOHN M. NAGLE, *Urban Education in America: Problems and Prospects.* New York: Oxford University Press, 1973.
HUNT, MAURICE, *Foundations of Education.* New York: Holt, Rinehart, & Winston, 1975.
PRICHARD, KEITH W., AND THOMAS H. BUXTON, *Concepts and Theories in Sociology of Education.* Lincoln, Neb.: Professional Educators Publications, 1973.
SARASON, SEYMOUR B., *The Culture of the School and the Problem of Change.* Boston: Allyn & Bacon, Inc., 1971.
SCHWARTZ, AUDREY JAMES, *The Schools and Socialization.* New York: Harper & Row, Publishers, 1975.
SILBERMAN, CHARLES E., *Crisis in the Classroom.* New York: Random House, Inc., 1970.
WALLER, WILLARD, *The Sociology of Teaching.* New York: John Wiley & Sons, Inc., 1932.

PART TWO

EDUCATION IN A PLURALISTIC SOCIETY

6

VALUES IN EDUCATION
Sacred and Secular

A *value* is an enduring belief that a specific mode of conduct or end-state of existence is personally or socially preferable to an opposite or converse mode of conduct or end-state of existence. A value system is an enduring organization of beliefs concerning preferable modes of conduct or end-states of existence along a continuum of relative importance.[1]

Milton Rokeach

Values are beliefs, attitudes or feelings that an individual is proud of, is willing to publicly affirm, has been chosen thoughtfully from alternatives without persuasion, and is acted on repeatedly.[2]

Louis Raths

Values are our standards and principles for judging worth. They are the criteria by which we judge "things" (people, objects, ideas, actions, and situations) to be good, worthwhile, desirable; or, on the other hand, bad, worthless, despicable; or, of course, somewhere in between these extremes, we may apply our values consciously. Or they may function unconsciously, as part of the influence of our frame of reference, without our being aware of the standards implied by our decisions.[3]

James Shaver

[1]Milton Rokeach, *The Nature of Human Values* (New York: The Free Press, 1973), p. 5.
[2]Louis E. Raths, Merrill Harmin, and Sidney B. Simon, *Values and Teaching* (Columbus, Ohio: Charles E. Merrill Publishing Co., 1966), pp. 28–30.
[3]James P. Shaver and William Strong, *Facing Value Decisions: Rationale-building for Teachers* (Belmont, Calif.: Wadsworth Publishing Company, Inc., 1976), p. 15.

147

Values pervade our schools. Shaver and his coauthors distinguish three types of values: *esthetic*, or standards by which we judge beauty—in art, music, nature, personal appearance, dress, classroom displays; *instrumental*, or methods we judge most effective for achieving some end—recitation, dialogue, lecture, competition, grouping; and *moral*, or principles by which we judge whether aims or actions are proper.[4] Moral values include personal or situational preferences (e.g. solitude, participation, loyalty, cooperation, religiosity, even honesty) and those basic to a society (e.g., sanctity of human life, due process, equal protection under the laws, freedom of speech). Private values become public when a person's behavior invades the basic rights of another. What style of clothing a person wears, how one seeks spiritual guidance, or what music someone plays is private. But if an individual chooses to wear no clothing, or preach at unwilling listeners, or play a stereo at 100 decibels, this becomes a moral consideration.

This chapter is about moral—and religious—values in schools. Moral and religious values have been entwined because religious authority for centuries was an omnipotent ethical force in Western culture. Religious values assumed a basic moral character. But the function of religion needs to be distinguished from moral authority.

Religious values or beliefs serve to guide people in coping with the unknown and mysterious. A religious experience, R. Bruce Raup explained, occurs when we sense our human inability to understand and to control; when, faced with the unpredictable and the precarious, we feel perpetual unreadiness for what is to come; when we move, hardly knowing why, from doubt and despair to faith and courage during moments of great personal crisis or triumph which are indelibly part of us thereafter. These experiences prompt an individual to elicit the intuitive and imaginative from within, and to shape metaphysical beliefs. Religions may sanction a particular moral value but they do not have license to dictate that a specific value is its own authority.[5] When religious and moral values coincide, the ethical fiber of a community or society is reinforced.

RELIGIOUS VALUES IN AMERICAN EDUCATION

Congress shall make no law respecting *an establishment of religion, or prohibiting the free exercise thereof*; or abridging the freedom of speech, or of the press; or the right of the people peaceably to assemble, and to petition the government for a redress of grievances.
                First Amendment to the United States Constitution

[4]Ibid., pp. 19–22.
[5]R. Bruce Raup, "Moral Authority and Religious Sanction," in *Intellectual Foundations of American Education, Readings & Commentary*, ed. Harold J. Carter (New York: Pitman Publishing Corporation, 1965), p. 99–102.

colonial schools

A practice known as the "establishment of religion" was common throughout Europe in the 1600s. As R. Freeman Butts relates,

> the laws of the state required all people to accept the doctrines of the established church, and taxes were levied to support the empowered religion. The new American colonies followed this European tradition, and the town (or "public") schools taught the doctrines of the dominant religion. In most northern colonies, Congregational Calvinism was the church established by colonial legislatures; in southern colonies orthodox Anglicanism, beliefs of the Church of England, were taught in the schools.[6]

As we described in Chapter 1, the content of the basic primers employed to teach reading and writing was essentially religious, and the church catechism was an integral part of the schoolchild's elementary education.

During the 1700s minority religious groups such as Presbyterians, Baptists, Lutherans, Methodists, Quakers, Dutch Reformed, who had increased in number, objected to the dominant religious beliefs taught in the colonial schools. The solution at this time was to permit these minority religious groups to conduct their own schools alongside the established "public" school. Despite some attempts to develop secular colleges, most institutions of higher learning also assumed a distinctively religious perspective. Harvard (1636), Yale (1701), and Dartmouth (1769) were founded by Congregationalists; William and Mary (1693) and Columbia (1754) by Anglicans; Princeton (1946) by Presbyterians; Brown (1964), Baptist, and Rutgers (1746) by Dutch Reformed.

As separate religious schools proliferated, some educational reformers expressed concern on at least two fronts. First, there was a question of true freedom of access to education when all schools had a religious base. Only secular schools, these reformers argued, could be genuinely open to all families and have the potential to be nondoctrinaire. Second, there was the concern that so many separate schools would be a divisive element in a new society with the basic goal of national unity.

building a wall of separation

Against this background, the First Amendment to the Constitution was written. The governments of the several colonies were giving not only legal and moral, but also financial support to the established Church. Butts argues that when James Madison and others took a leading part in framing

---

[6]R. Freeman Butts, "Search for Freedom—The Story of American education," *NEA Journal*, 49, 3 (March, 1960), 35.

the first clause of the First Amendment (prohibiting Congress from making any "law respecting an establishment of religion") they had in mind strict separation between the state and all religions.[7] Thomas Jefferson, general watchdog of religious indoctrination and critic of religious teachings in the schools, was perhaps the leading spokesman for strict separation.

In 1779, Jefferson introduced into the Virginia Assembly a Bill For Religious Freedom; with minor revisions, the bill eventually was passed in 1786. Jefferson wrote extensively in pursuit of religious freedom, expressing the belief that religion is a matter which lies solely between man and God. Religion as a matter of conscience, belief, and faith is a natural right of the individual, and therefore is not a *legitimate* power of others or government. Religious belief is a natural right (or matter of conscience) precisely because "man" is an intelligent, reasoning being. Jefferson wrote, "that Almighty God hath created the mind free, and manifested his supreme will that free it shall remain by making it altogether insusceptible of restraint."[8] By the same logic, he explained, religious beliefs should be subjected to reason and free inquiry—the only effective agents against error. "It is error alone," he wrote, "which needs the support of government."[9]

Schools, many early democratic statesmen argued, must be free from the persuasion of religious teachings. In Jefferson's words, it was necessary to build a "wall of separation between Church and State." Until approximately 1930, the court's interpretation of the Establishment Clause of the First Amendment was to build that wall higher and more solid—after which notable exceptions were made.

interpreting the relationship between church and state

Religious schools still exist today, but with only the most cautious support of the state. A 1925 U.S. Supreme Court decision in Oregon (*Pierce* v. *Society of Sisters*) permitted children to attend approved nonpublic schools in order to meet state attendance laws. However, approximately 90 percent of all school-age children today attend public, secular schools. Of those who select private or religious schools, most attend Catholic institutions.

In the application of the "separation" principle to education over the years, two basic issues emerged: (1) the use of public funds to help support religious schools, and (2) religious instruction in the public schools. Generally, public funds have not been provided to religious schools, and religious

---

[7]R. Freeman Butts, "Church and State in American Education," in *Intellectual Foundations of American Education, Readings & Commentary*, ed. Harold J. Carter (New York: Pitman Publishing Corporation, 1965), p. 115.

[8]The 1779 version of Jefferson's Bill for Religious Freedom is contained in Gordon C. Lee, ed., *Crusade Against Ignorance—Thomas Jefferson on Education* (New York: Bureau of Publications, Teachers College, Columbia University, 1961), pp. 66–68.

[9]Taken from Jefferson's Notes on the State of Virginia, also reproduced in Gordon C. Lee's *Crusade Against Ignorance*, pp. 60–66.

instruction not permitted in the public schools—but, as we suggested, these are not "watertight" maxims today.

The courts have been reasonably clear and steadfast with respect to prohibiting religious instruction in the public schools. The U.S. Supreme Court first ruled in *McCollum v. Board of Education* (1948) that released time for religious instruction could not be given inside the public school, even if students who did not wish to participate were permitted to pursue secular studies. In this case, classes were taught separately by Protestant and Catholic teachers. The Court ruled that such instruction clearly violated the First and Fourteenth Amendments (the latter making the Establishment Clause of the former applicable to the states). In 1952 (*Zorach v. Clausen*) the Court declared that a released-time program in New York City involved neither religious instruction in public school classrooms nor expenditures of public funds. In this case, unlike *McCollum*, the Court explained that students left the public school premise for religious instruction, and all costs were assumed by the religious organization. Whatever the merits of this argument, released time for teaching religion is permissible if it is conducted outside the public school and without any expense to the taxpayer.[10]

In the 1960s, prayer and Bible reading in the public schools came under fire. Heretofore, prayer and Bible-reading exercises were a common practice in school, and considered little more than a mild and reasonable means of fostering character and moral development. An official prayer composed by the New York State Board of Regents, and made mandatory at the start of each school day, was declared unconstitutional. In this case, *Engel v. Vitale* (1962), the majority opinion argued that the prayer violated both the Establishment and Free Exercise Clauses of the First Amendment. A year later in *Abington v. Schempp* (1963), the Court ruled unconstitutional a Pennsylvania statute that ten verses from the Bible be read without comment each day in the public schools, with the provision that participation be voluntary. This statute, they stated, abridged the Establishment Clause, but not the Free Exercise Clause, since no coercion existed. The State, the judges emphasized, must be steadfastly neutral in all matters of faith, neither favoring nor inhibiting religion.[11]

---

[10]Lawrence Byrnes, *Religion and Public Education* (New York: Harper & Row, Publishers, Inc., 1975), pp. 59–60. The dissenting judges in *Zorach v. Clausen*, however, raised the subtle point that the state nevertheless is aiding religion by using a portion of the school day for religious purposes, and is tacitly persuading students to attend this instruction.

[11]*School District of Abington Township v. Schempp* (1963) in E. Edmund Reutter, Jr., and Robert R. Hamilton, *The Law of Public Education*, 2nd ed. (Mineola, N.Y.: The Foundation Press, Inc., 1976), pp. 44–48.

It is of interest to note in the *Abington* case that the Court elaborated on the neutrality question in pointing out the justification for chaplains in military and state penal institutions. This may seem an establishment of religion, but in such instances, providing religious services, instruction, and resources is necessary to insure religious liberty as guaranteed by the Free Exercise Clause. While the state cannot aid religion, neither can it display hostility toward religion.

With respect to the first issue—use of public funds to support religious schools—the courts have been less clear. We mentioned that the turning point in constructing a skyscraper with the "wall of separation" was 1930. That year in *Cochrane* v. *State of Louisiana* the Supreme Court permitted Louisiana to spend tax funds for free textbooks to children in private schools. Seventeen years later in *Everson* v. *Board of Education* (1947), the Court declared that it is constitutional to reimburse parents for money spent for public bus transportation of their children to public and parochial schools. In doing so the Court made a point that this aid was given not to the schools, but to the families. This they deemed was taxation in the interest of public welfare rather than direct support of religion. Furthermore, it is significant in the *Everson* case that Justice Hugo Black stated in effect that while the New Jersey statute in question extended public welfare benefits to all citizens (and therefore is not a constitutional violation), the "wall of separation" erected by the First Amendment must be kept high and impregnable, without the slightest breach.[12]

In 1968 (*Board of Education* v. *Allen*) the Court held that a State of New York law requiring local public school authorities to lend textbooks free of charge to all students in grades seven through twelve, private schools included, did not violate the Constitution. The Court reasoned that inasmuch as parochial schools serve a secular educational function and the textual material itself is secular, no religious cause is promoted.[13] First in the *Everson* case and then in *Allen*, the Supreme Court made it clear that providing transportation and textbooks per se is not prohibited by the First Amendment.

Shortly thereafter in two cases, *Lemon* v. *Kurtzman* (1971) and *DiCenso* v. *Robinson* (1971), concerning Pennsylvania and Rhode Island statutes, respectively, the Court ruled that each violated the Establishment Clause. In both cases, financial aid was available for secular services, teachers' salaries, textbooks, and other instructional materials. The hooker in both statutes was the provision for teachers' salaries. In delivering the majority opinion, Chief Justice Burger remarked, "Unlike a book, a teacher cannot be inspected once so as to determine the extent and intent of his or her personal beliefs and subjective acceptance of the limitations imposed by the First Amendment." To provide aid for teachers' services is to invite "excessive and enduring entanglement." The Pennsylvania statute (*Lemon* case) had an additional defect in providing aid directly to the church-related schools, rather than to parents and children.[14]

Most recently in *Wolman* v. *Walter* (1977), a majority opinion of the Supreme Court stated that the State of Ohio could appropriate $88 million to the state's 720 nonpublic schools (96 percent of which were sectarian) for

---

[12]*Everson* v. *Board of Education of Ewing Township* (1947) in Reutter, *The Law*, pp. 36–37.
[13]*Board of Education of Central School District No. 1* v. *Allen* (1968) in Reutter, *The Law*, pp. 49–51.
[14]*Lemon* v. *Kurtzman* (1971), in Reutter, *The Law*, p. 58.

textbooks to be lent to students or their parents. The Court also approved the use of state funds for educational testing and diagnostic services and therapeutic health services, as well as for guidance, counseling, and remedial help for disturbed and handicapped children. They rejected provisions, however, for aid for field trips and instructional materials (e.g., projectors, tape recorders, and maps) retained by schools. In effect, the majority opinion drew the line upholding aid that helped students directly, but struck down expenditures directly supporting the schools. Any law, the Court reaffirmed, must not advance (or prohibit) religion and must avoid excessive entanglement with religion.

As we warned, the picture of public aid to parochial schools (parochiaid, as it's called) is somewhat ambiguous. Although we believe that a legitimate distinction exists between particular categories of assistance—teachers vis-à-vis textbooks or transportation; aid directly to schools vis-à-vis aid to students or parents—it is not clear that the second categories in these two pair do not at least indirectly promote religious schooling. Any attempts to neatly distinguish between sacred and secular aspects of a total curriculum also seem simplistic and spurious. This concern doesn't mean we are convinced that the State should remain "steadfastly neutral" with respect to advancing religious schools.

Opponents of the "strict constructionist" position taken by courts over the years argue that there are abundant contradictions in the courts' handling of the impervious "wall of separation" in the Establishment Clause. These critics offer several examples of deliberate church and state collaboration, including postal privileges for religious organizations, tax exemptions for churches, GI loans to students attending religiously controlled colleges, chaplains in Congress, religious services in federal hospitals and prisons, and the distribution of food to sectarian schools under the National School Lunch Act.[15]

Supporters of more generous parochiaid emphasize that any theory of the Establishment Clause ought to include an intimate connection with the Free Exercise Clause. In that public schools have a virtual monopoly over schooling in our educational system, a sensitive reading of these two clauses in juxtaposition would not favor absolute neutrality by the state. In some situations, it is either imperative or proper, we think, for the government to assist parochial schools in the furtherance of religious freedom.

prayers, promises and paradoxes

What is the present status of religion in the public schools? Prayers, Bible readings, and compensation for teachers' salaries are clearly out. Permitted are funds for student transportation to parochial schools (via public trans-

[15] Byrnes, *Religion and Public Education*, pp. 17–18.

portation and presumably school buses) and for textbooks or other curricular materials (assuming they are secular in nature), providing this aid is given directly to parents and students, or "comprehensive measures of surveillance and control" accompany the grants. (The surveillance and bureaucratic ramifications of such control could be awesome!) Finally, students may be released during school time to receive religious instruction, even though this occurs during normal school hours and possibly entails a subtle coercion.

Some religious education is permissible—not teaching religion, but teaching about religion—in public schools. It is legal to teach virtually anything about religion so long as it is nonsectarian and nonproseletyzing. Courses or topics on comparative religion, the history, sociology, and psychology of religion, the Bible as literature, and other religious studies can be taught. In *Abington* v. *Schempp* (the aforementioned Bible-reading case) Justice Clark wrote:

> It is insisted that unless these religious exercises are permitted a "religion of secularism" in the sense of affirmatively opposing or showing hostility to religion, thus "preferring those who believe in no religion over those who do believe." . . . We do not agree, however, that this decision in any sense has that effect. In addition, it might well be said that one's education is not complete without a study of comparative religion or the history of religion and its relationship to the advancement of civilization. It certainly may be said that the Bible is worthy of study for its literary and historic qualities. Nothing we have said here indicates that such study of the Bible or of religion, when presented objectively as part of a secular program of education, may not be effected consistent with the First Amentment.[16]

Yet unresolved in any legal constitutional sense is the celebration of religious holidays (e.g., Christmas, Chanukah, and Easter) in the public school classroom. Most schools handle the issue by accommodating the dominant religious values of the community with mildly celebrative gestures of observance and support. Even this, however, it appears would be declared unconstitutional (if ever challenged) on possibly two counts. First, celebration in schools is in effect the support of one or more religious beliefs; second, celebration involves a subtle coercion of student beliefs toward particular religions (usually to the exclusion of minority or non-Western religions) and religion generally (as opposed to nonbelieving).

School officials could assume a strict-constructionist stance and prohibit all religion in the schools, but there is some question whether this is necessary and in fact might represent hostility to or obstruction of religion. Given Justice Clark's opinion in *Abington* that the secular or objective study of religions in a comparative, historical, or other academic context is not only permissible but encouraged, would it be permissible to augment the

[16]Reutter, *The Law*, p. 47.

secular study with celebrations for instructional purposes? If celebration is appropriate, does the Free Exercise Clause call for some celebration of all possible religions, or only those represented in the local community? What sort of religious celebration, if any, is constitutionally permissible remains yet unresolved.

A RELIGION OF RATIONALITY

There is considerable danger that we have established a "religion of secularism" in our schools and society, not through any particular hostility toward religion, as Justice Clark warned, but in our neglect of it. In our culture, religion generally is viewed as an impediment to "progress." Science, rationality, and intellect are understood to be responsible for progress, while the religious experience is something to be graciously tolerated like an aged family member.

The "cries" by part of our population in recent years for religious, metaphysical, and mystical expression testify to the century-long scientific bias in our cultural perspectives. Since Thomas Jefferson's empirically based approach to religion and curricular modernization, up to the present emphasis in education theory, schools and colleges have become a citadel of science and rationality. We have fully developed in our society (as well as other Western societies) what Theodore Roszak calls the Scientization of Culture.

scientization of culture

The mindscape of our culture that has been forged and shaped over the past three centuries, with ever more urgency since the advent of industrialization, Roszak explains, is the creation of modern science.[17] For more than a century after our nation was founded, science, the psychology of science, and the scientific perspective on reality gradually crept into our life style, our ways of thinking and perceiving. During the present century, science, technology, and their derivatives—quantification, computerization, automation, impersonalization, expertise, complexity and remote control—have virtually exploded on the American (and Western) culture.

From one vantage point—the popular view—we have never been more affluent, surrounded as we are by modern conveniences. An elaborate web of technological amenities, including radio, television, telephone, washer and dryer, refrigerator, air conditioner, automobile, credit money,

---

[17]Theodore Roszak, *Where the Wasteland Ends* (Garden City, N.Y.: Doubleday & Company, Inc.,1972), p. xxiv.

and automated banking, are accessible to the average American family. Such conveniences, according to the conventional wisdom, signify progress and victory for both science and our economic system. The problem is that the popular view, as is usually the case, misses the deeper meaning of this scientific-technological development. That we have more does not mean that we *are* more. Even when it is not conspicuous, many people recognize that advancement in one area of our life is accompanied by deterioration elsewhere. It's as if things get worse as they get better!

The problem facing humans in this modern context appears to have at least two disturbing dimensions.

1. The web of technological amenities that is supposed to bring us to "leisure world" is in reality like a long string of decorative lights: when one light is missing and the link is broken, the entire system malfunctions. As Roszak explains, each element (appliance or convenience) "is wedded to the total pattern of existence; remove any one and chaos seems to impend. As a society we are addicted to the increase of environmental artificiality; the agonies of even partial withdrawal are more than most of us dare contemplate."[18] The addiction we develop for this elaborated technology is abetted by techniques of persuasion (advertising and media imagery) that are imbedded in the style of our economic system. John Kenneth Galbraith, in *The New Industrial State*, described this pattern as the Revised Sequence: the situation in which the corporate business firm (scientific-industrial complex) arranges consumer behavior to satisfy its productive needs, rather than the consumers exercising their sovereignty by guiding production decisions in the marketplace.[19]

2. This web of technological amenities also is viewed by the individual as a complex, mysterious electronic labyrinth, understandable to only the technical expert. In Galbraith's analysis, the technostructure (technicians, specialists, and technocracy) of national and supernational corporations that creates and designs the new public and household technology ultimately exercises the decisive power in our political-economic culture. The consumer, citizen or individual, in the face of this mounting technological complexity, has become confused, has lost control of the immediate environment, and even has drifted into a state of culture anomie. As Roszak explains in quoting Kenneth Boulding, "We live in the age of 'superculture'—the culture of airports, throughways, skyscrapers, hybrid corn and artificial fertilizers, birth control and universities. It is worldwide in its scope.... It even has a world language, technical English, and a common ideology, science." Roszak adds,

[18]Ibid., p. 32.
[19]John Kenneth Galbraith, *The New Industrial State* (Boston: Houghton Mifflin Company, 1967), Chap. 19. Galbraith's concept of the techno-structure, commented on in the following paragraph, is examined in Chapter 6 of this book.

An age, in short, built hopelessly beyond the scale of the ordinary citizen. For most of us that language and that ideology are what the Latin of the mass was to the medieval peasantry: the hocus-pocus of social domination. If, then, the experts tell us that the ship of state must be steered along a certain course, at a certain speed, that it must go here and cannot go there . . . who are we to say them nay?[20]

True, the implements of daily living have become excessively complex, and we must rely on experts for daily survival; but the problem is deeper than this. In our culture the primary business of educational systems is to train experts (i.e., specialists, technicians, and "tinkerers,") who not only see merely part of the picture, but who see it in a very peculiar way—the scientific view. Still, the problem extends further: in our culture, schools and other major institutions, have endorsed unqualifyingly this scientific positivist view. Roszak, alluding to the poet William Blake, called this the "single vision": the orthodox consciousness of urban-industrial society. This is a consciousness that philosophically and psychologically legitimizes a particular world-view, by subliminally screening, filtering, censoring, and generally shaping our powers of perception and cognition.[21] It is the deification of rationality! Left submerged in the wake of this psychology of science and culture of industrialization are our unconscious potentials of the imaginary and visionary—potentialities that are summarily discouraged, debased, and ridiculed in conventional culture. While the scientific mindset is esteemed, art and religion are trivialized.

expanding the vision

At the turn of this century, William James wrote:

> Our normal waking consciousness, rational consciousness . . . is but one special type of consciousness, whilst all about it, parted from it by the flimsiest of screens, there lie potential forms of consciousness entirely different. We may go through life without suspecting their existence; but apply the requisite stimulus, and at a touch they are there in all their completeness. . . . No account of the universe in its totality can be final which leaves these other forms of consciousness quite disregarded.

In the past few pages we have referred liberally to Theodore Roszak's work *Where the Wasteland Ends*. This book is about the religious dimension of our political existence, and how our religious sensibilities have been repressed or "exiled from our culture." The religion Roszak unravels is not

---

[20]Roszak, *Wasteland Ends*, p. 53.
[21]Ibid., pp. 75–78.
[22]William James, *The Varieties of Religious Experience—A Study in Human Nature* (London: Longmans, Green and Co., 1902), p. 388.

that of the churches and doctrine, but religion in what he calls its perennial sense—vision, transcendent knowledge, or mysticism. His purpose also is to offer insight as to how this religious impulse can be, and in nascent respects is being, revived.

Today in America there thrives a renewal of religious spirit expressed by the plethora of religious, consciousness-raising, and human potential cults. This recent consciousness revolution, as it is called, combines aspects of modern Western psychotherapy and ancient Eastern religious experiences. Humanistic psychology, also known as Third Force psychology to distinguish it from psychoanalysis and behaviorism (the first two forces), is one ingredient of the new awakening. Carl Rogers began promoting "personal growth" encounters as early as the 1940s; later his ideas were related to the behaviors and methods of classroom teachers. By the 1950s, the Gestalt therapy techniques of Fritz Perls and others were used to help people gain contact with their inner selves, and Abraham Maslow described the path to "peak experiences," which in effect are ultimate, mystical contacts of individual with self. It is not surprising that the abundance of theorizing and experimentation in the 1960s and 1970s has inspired a Fourth Force, namely Transpersonal Psychology, in which individual (sub)consciousness expands into mystical union with the totality of humanity or "cosmic consciousness."

The architects and practitioners of the new human potential groups have borrowed eclectically from Zen Buddhist, Tibetan Buddhist, Hindu, Yogic, and Taoist sources in forging this amorphous trans-cultural movement. The result has been a proliferation of human potential religious and quasi-religious cults. The individual, in search for avenues of sensitivity, spontaneity, introspection, and relatedness, has various options; these include Transcendental Meditation, Transactional Analysis, Gestalt Therapy, Yoga, biofeedback, guided fantasy, and even nude marathons. A person also can obtain physical and emotional relief through any one of several processes that have been developed and marketed: Rolfing (or structional integration, created by Ida Rolf), EST (Erhard Seminars Training, named after the inventor Werner Erhard), Silva Mind Control (developed by José Silva), Arica, bioenergetics, and psychosynthesis. With this range of assumptions, interests, and inputs, it is little wonder there is no common framework and spirit to the movement—still there appears to be within these cults the potential for significant reformation of our cultural vision.

The religious revival today also includes the more traditional back-to-Christ groups. The total resurgence of religious expression—counterculture and conventional—defies a simple explanation. We believe religion serves at least two separate, personal needs in contemporary society: (1) religion is a way of coping with the complex and uncontrollable, and (2) it is a means of gaining touch with intuitive thought and inner feelings.

It is no coincidence that the upswing in consciousness-raising and religiosity has increased sharply during the past ten years, as life in our society has become increasingly complex. The seventies were destined to be the threshold of this development. The twenties were too early for the scientific-technological impact; the Great Depression in the thirties slowed its development and implementation; the war years of the forties diverted productive facilities to military goods, while the economically sluggish and socially frivolous fifties prevented its realization. Science and technology swept through the sixties with fervor, but a high interest in social reform and skepticism toward materialist values also characterized the decade. When the unfulfilled social hope of the 1960s diminished in the early seventies, we (as a nation) had to face reality. The new religious movement has its share of critics who argue that it uncourageously avoids reality by indulging in narcissistic awareness flings that divert serious social efforts. Certainly, there is the risk of escape into the simplistic and trivial that many (individuals and groups) have followed in attempting to cope with the overwhelming complexity of their cybernetic environment.

This new religious spirit also has the potential to revive an intuitive style and viewpoint: a complementary vision that summons feelings, fantasy, imagination, and creativity. This vision doesn't replace the classical and intellectual, but supplements it with analogic and metaphoric ways of the mind that help render our environment both understandable and hospitable. This is what Richard Jones, for example, had in mind when he showed how feelings, emotions, and fantasies can be infused in a curriculum with the intellectual and cognitive. Both dimensions are integral to the human condition.[23]

The secularization of our culture has inexorably unfolded over the past few centuries, and with this our religious sensibilities have been repressed. Somewhere, all but those people authentically on the "cutting edge" of scientific knowledge have acquired a very simplistic concept of science. There is abundant evidence from those on the frontiers of scientific development that research (in the laboratory and study) is not conducted in a strictly objective, methodological, and "antiseptic" fashion. That is, there exists a clear personal or intuitive dimension to the scientific process, laced with inspiration, hunches, interests, and biases, as testified to in the writings of Michael Polanyi, Thomas Kuhn, James Conant, Jonas Salk, David Hawkins and others.[24]

[23]Richard Jones, *Fantasy and Feeling in Education* (New York: New York University Press, 1968).

[24]We recommend to the reader Michael Polanyi's *Personal Knowledge* (University of Chicago Press, 1959) and *The Tacit Dimension* (Doubleday & Company, Inc., 1966), Thomas S. Kuhn's *The Structure of Scientific Revolution* (University of Chicago Press, 1970), James Conant's *Two Modes of Thought* (Trident Press, 1964), Jonas Salk's *The Survival of the Wisest* (Harper & Row, Publishers, 1973), and David Hawkins's *The Language of Nature*, an essay in the philosophy of science (W. H. Freeman Company, 1964).

The trouble, Roszak points out, is that "science presents itself professionally and publicly as that discipline in which taste, inspiration, and intuition do not prove anything and are, in themselves, insufficient to constitute knowledge." The product of scientific thought, he adds, has been purged of its personal characteristics," with the result that scientific knowledge and its technology are peculiarly amenable to standardization and proliferation.[25] Scholars such as Jerome Bruner and Robert Ornstein (psychology), Jacob Bronowski (physics and biology), and Alexander Marshack (anthropology), John Kenneth Galbraith and Kenneth Boulding (economics), Freeman Dyson and Victory Weisskopf (physics), Loren Eisley (biology), James Conant (chemistry), and Carl Sagan (astronomy) have acknowledged the personal dimension of "Research," and legitimized its development.[26] In response to a statement attributed to Isaac Newton that "the purpose of the scientist is to sail the oceans of the unknown and discover the islands of truth," Jerome Bruner retorted, "The purpose of the scientist is to sail the oceans of the unknown and INVENT the truth."[27]

Science-based industrialism, Roszak believes, must be disciplined, scaled down, decentralized, accessible, and manipulatable if it is to be spiritually and physically livable. Science and religion, or the intellectual and metaphoric, can and must coexist.

the metaphoric mind

The metaphoric mind, Bob Samples explains, is the mirror image of the rational mind. In effect, we have two minds! All this talk about the intuitive and creative potential within us may not be obscure and mysterious. The belief that some people are inclined towards the sciences and others toward the arts (the former tending to be conventional, conforming, and intellectual and the latter inventive, introspective, and metaphoric) is oversimplified and not totally accurate. Researchers, notably Robert Ornstein, posit the theory that there is a neurophysiological basis for the existence of two minds, actually located in different areas of the brain. As Samples reports, our brain is divided into two cerebral hemispheres separated by a thick bundle of nerve fibers called the corpus callosum that serves as a communication conduit between the hemispheres. In the left cerebral hemisphere lies the rational-linear mind that requires structure and order, and lends us logical, organizing, analyzing, and reasoning capabilities. (This is the de-

---

[25]Roszak, *Wasteland Ends*, p. 154.
[26]Also relevant in this context are Marshack's *The Roots of Civilization* (McGraw-Hill Book Company, Inc., 1972), Jerome Bruner's *On Knowing: Essays for the Left Hand* (Harvard University Press, 1962), Loren Eisley's *The Immense Journey* (Random House, Inc., 1957), and Kenneth Boulding's *The Image; Knowledge in Life and Society* (University of Michigan Press, 1956).
[27]This incident is related by Bob Samples in his book *The Metaphoric Mind—A Celebration of Creative Consciousness* (Menlo Park, Calif.: Addison-Wesley Publishing Company, 1977), p. 97.

pository of reading, writing, and arithmetic.) Across the corpus callosum in the right cerebral hemisphere lies the metaphoric mind, carrying our capability to invent, create, dream, fantasize, and challenge conformity.[28]

The nervous system of the human being as it branches out from its core terminal, the brain, is reversed so that sensations on the right side of the body are connected to the left half of the cerebrum, and those on the left side are connected to the right side of the cerebrum. Jerome Bruner, alluding to this, refers to subjective knowing and creative attributes as left-handed knowledge. Left-handed knowing is the metaphoric way.

The metaphoric mind is a maverick, Samples exclaims.

"It follows us doggedly and plagues us with its presence as we wander the contrived corridors of rationality. It is the metaphoric link with the unknown called religion that causes us to build cathedrals—and the very cathedrals are built with rational, logical plans. . . . Albert Einstein called the intuitive or metaphoric mind a sacred gift . . . the rational mind was a faithful servant."[29]

But the intuitive or artistic within us must coexist with the rational or artistic. As Jonas Salk in *The Survival of the Wisest* points out,

The artist draws largely upon that part of the mind that functions beneath consciousness, even in sleep, while the scientist by and large . . . uses that part of the mind that functions in consciousness. The part of the mind that functions beneath the consciousness also operates during consciousness; but it is necessary to learn how to . . . employ it for solving the problems of life, survival, and of evolution. Wisdom arises from both parts of the mind.[30]

Perhaps this balance once existed; more likely the human species has evolved through periods where one aspect of the mind—intellectual or metaphoric—dominated. In modern times the rational, logical-linear thinking has dominated the intuitive-analogic functioning. The time for a balanced equilibrium is long overdue. In addition to the religious expression we considered in the last section, other indicators of natural mystical expression prevail. The surging athleticism of jogging and running, dance and movement, as well as forms of the martial arts such as aikeido are more than avenues to physical fitness. To those who participate seriously, they are nothing short of artistic, spiritual, and psychological releases. Running, for example, to the disciple becomes a mentally, physically, and psychically energizing form of "healthy" addiction.[31]

[28]Bob Samples, "Mind Cycles and Learning," *Phi Delta Kappan*, 58, no. 9 (May, 1977), 688.

[29]Samples, *The Metaphoric Mind*, pp. 26, 62.

[30]Jonas Salk, *The Survival of the Wisest* (New York: Harper & Row, Publishers, 1973), p. 83.

[31]George Leonard in his book *The Ultimate Athlete* (New York: The Viking Press, Inc., 1975) offers a fascinating account of how movement, exercise, and physical fitness unite and transform physical and psychic being.

Figure 6-1. Developing Values at an Early Age

VALUES EDUCATION: THE SCHOOL'S RESPONSE

Values education is one of the popular items in pedagogical circles these days. If it isn't already, it is about to become one of the ingrained areas of the school curriculum. Textbooks, curricular materials, teacher workshops, and professional journals all can be found sporting titles associated with values education, and offering various paths to valuing in the classroom. Take your pick—values education comes in assorted packages: values awareness, values clarification, values analysis, moral reasoning, values action, and more.

For years values either were ignored (though to be sure they indirectly permeated the school curriculum) or rejected as being too controversial and not properly academic. Values education has arrived, but, not surprisingly, in faddish style. The need to study values has been overdue, and in the 1970s educators began responding to this need. There are several *competing* approaches, but as yet the topic seriously lacks any core purpose and organizing framework.

values clarification

Values clarification was the first approach proposed by educators in response to the neglect (and implicit indoctrination) of values in schools. Originally constructed and explicated by Louis Raths, Merrill Harmin, and Sidney Simon, the clarification approach is designed to help students (and others) rationally examine personal behavior patterns and more clearly realize values. There is a high affective content to this approach; values, according to the authors, are illusive, personal, and relative. Their professed interest is not what people believe or in teaching people what to believe, but rather in the process of valuing. The development of values, they add, is a personal and life-long pursuit.[32]

In their original work, Raths and his coauthors promulgated (what now has become widely known) seven criteria for legitimate valuing. Values, they submit, must be chosen (1) freely, (2) from alternatives, (3) after thoughtful consideration of the consequences, and an individual must (4) cherish, (5) be willing to publicly affirm, (6) act on the value, and (7) do so repeatedly. In a more recent statement on the clarification process, Raths takes considerable care in stressing that valuing is a thoughtful, reflective, highly intelligent act that in the final analysis must be freely expressed.[33]

A substantial number of values-education materials on the market reflect the clarification approach. Those specifically designed by Raths, Simon, and their colleagues are intended to develop valuing abilities related to one or more of the above seven criteria. A few are included here to illustrate the approach. Some of the clarification strategies are quite brief and can be used for periods as short as ten minutes. An example is the *Values Voting* strategy, in which the teacher asks the class a series of questions prefaced by: "How many of you . . ." e.g., dream about being famous? . . . feel religion is an important part of your life? . . . think familiarity breeds contempt? and so on. A popular strategy is the *Values Continuum*, in which students identify their individual positions along a continuum on a particular issue such as:

How much do you talk to other people?

Tight-lipped   Blabber-mouth
    Timmy : : : : : :Bertha

How would you raise your child?

Super-permissive   Super-strict
    Polly : : : : : :Sally

---

[32]Louis E. Raths, Merrill Harmin, and Sidney B. Simon, *Values and Teaching: Working Values in the Classroom* (Columbus, Ohio: Charles E. Merrill Publishing Co., 1966), pp. 36–37.
[33]Louis E. Raths, "Freedom, Intelligence and Valuing," in *Values, Concepts and Techniques* (Washington, D.C.: National Education Association, 1976), pp. 12, 16.

How do you feel about premarital sex?

Virginal Virginia	Mattress Millie
Wears White	Wears a Mattress
Gloves on	Strapped to Her
Every date : : : : : :	:Back[34]

The Values Clarification Approach has come in for harsh criticism in recent years. James Shaver, writing as then-president of the National Council for the Social Studies, remarked that this approach is anti-intellectual, has the potential to promote relativism, and pays little attention to whether certain principles (values) might not have special validity, particularly in a democratic society. The VC approach totally ignores any decision-making processes.[35] Perhaps the most telling testimony comes from classroom teachers who relate that while clarification exercises generate much initial interest and enthusiasm, they "don't seem to lead anywhere", that is, to further thinking and valuing.

Several of the clarification exercises provided by the VC authors are insensitive to the feelings of young people and foster a reliance on peer pressure. The values continuum exercises above illustrate this point: many students are unlikely to want to be associated with a "blabber-mouth," "super-permissive," and "mattress Millie" identity. Demeaning and pejorative options such as these encourage students to select a middle or mean position to protect their dignity. Shaver also is critical of the emphasis given public confirmation of values in the clarification approach. A person may genuinely hold a value even though he has not publicly affirmed it. There may not have been the opportunity for such action, the action may have involved an unreasonable risk, or the value in question conflicted with another more pressing one at the time.[36] Forcing someone, particularly a young person, to publicly affirm a position runs the risk of a rigid stance with respect to future decisions or pronouncements by the individual.

John Stewart provides what we consider a very comprehensive and thoughtful critique of values clarification, particularly the Raths, Simon, and Harmin approach. Stewart takes special note of their ambiguous relativism, which he labels "absolute relativism." While the VC authors purport to believe that values are personal, situational, individually derived, and relative, they make some very inconsistent exceptions. According to the values clarification premise, remarks Stewart, "*All* values statements are

---

[34]Sidney B. Simon, Leland W. Howe, and Howard Kirschenbaum, *Values Clarification: A Handbook of Practical Strategies for Teachers and Students* (New York: Hart Publishing Company, Inc., 1972). Value Voting is included as Strategy Number 3 in this work, pp. 38–57, and Values Continuum is Strategy Number 8, pp. 116–26. In total, 79 value clarification strategies are included.

[35]James P. Shaver, "A Critical View of the Social Studies Profession," *Social Education*, 41 no. 4 (April, 1977), pp. 305–6.

[36]James P. Shaver and William Strong, *Facing Value Decisions: Rationale Building for Teachers* (Belmont, Calif.: Wadsworth Publishing Company, Inc., 1976), pp. 120–21.

relative—*except* (1) this one, (2) those that are essential for the Values Clarification theory and methodology, and (3) those deemed absolute by groups or organizations who want to use Values Clarification but keep their own value systems intact, e.g., parochial schools.[37]

The point is not that values clarification activities should be disregarded by teachers. Rather, the movement is rooted in a spurious philosophy of relativism and needs to develop a more cohesive conceptual framework. Another part of this framework could be the moral reasoning approach.

moral reasoning

If you had entered the field of education several years ago, you would have been bombarded with materials related to values clarification. Today the deluge of articles, books, and teaching materials is about moral reasoning or development. The popular approach to teaching moral reasoning in the classroom is based on the theory and research of Harvard psychologist Lawrence Kohlberg.

Kohlberg has postulated three levels of moral development, the preconventional, conventional, and postconventional, each level containing two distinct stages. Kohlberg's conceptual schema is derived both from John Dewey's original theoretical postulates of moral development and Jean Piaget's later empirical studies on the moral reasoning of children as they cognitively mature. The levels they defined were: (1) premoral, (2) conventional (Dewey) or heteronomous (Piaget) and (3) autonomous.[38]

A description of Kohlberg's six stages is presented, in abbreviated form, in Table 6-1. At the preconventional level, the individual responds to cultural rules of good and bad, right or wrong in terms of the physical consequences from those who enunciate the rules. At the conventional level, he or she conforms to the personal expectations of significant others while maintaining, supporting, and justifying the ruling social order. At the postconventional level, there is a clear effort to define valid moral values and principles apart from the authority of the groups or individuals holding them.

Kohlberg's moral stages were refined and validated through several multi-year cross-cultural studies, including a twenty-year study of fifty Chicago-area boys, middle and working class; a small, six-year longitudinal study of Turkish village and city boys; and a variety of other cross-sectional studies in Canada, Britain, Israel, Taiwan, Yucatan, Honduras, and India.

[37]John S. Stewart, "Clarifying Values Clarification: A Critique," *Phi Delta Kappan*, 56, no. 10 (June, 1975),.p. 68.
[38]Lawrence Kohlberg, "The Cognitive-Developmental Approach to Moral Education," in *Moral Education . . . It Comes With the Territory*, eds. David Purpel and Kevin Ryan (Berkeley, Calif.: McCutchan Publishing Corporation, 1976), pp. 176–77.

Table 6-1   Stages of Moral Development[39]

I. Preconventional Level
   Stage 1: *Punishment and obedience orientation*—where physical consequences determine what is good and bad, and avoidance of punishment is valued irrespective of underlying moral order.
   Stage 2: *Instrumental-relativist orientation*—where right action is what satisfies one's own needs, and human relations are viewed in terms of reciprocity and equal sharing; in effect the marketplace disposition.
II. Conventional Level
   Stage 3: *Interpersonal concordance or "good boy–nice girl" orientation*—where there is much conformity to stereotypic images of norm behavior, and good is defined in terms of what pleases or helps others.
   Stage 4: *"Law and Order" orientation*—where maintaining the social order, doing one's duty, and showing respect for authority are valued for their own sake.
III. Postconventional Level
   Stage 5: *Social contract–legalistic orientation*—where values agreed upon by the whole society, including individual rights and rules for consensus, determine what is right, and honor is given to emphasis on the legal viewpoint with the possibility of changing the law in terms of national considerations.
   Stage 6: *Universal ethical–principle orientation*—where right is a matter of conscience in accord with self-chosen and consistent ethical principles appealing to logical comprehensiveness and universality.

The stages, by his account, form an *invariant sequence* where individuals always move forward, except under conditions of extreme trauma, and never skip stages. The stages are also *hierarchical integrations*, where a higher stage includes or comprehends lower-stage thinking and is preferred to those below it.[40]

Moral reasoning approaches to values education are designed to aid students in advancing to higher stages of development. The technique employed in the Kohlberg framework is to present a hypothetical or factual value-dilemma story which students discuss, then take a position regarding the dilemma, giving their supporting reasons. The following is a description of an activity:

> The students read an actual story about a "Mercy Death"; a man is charged with the mercy killing of his wife, who has been ill and despondent for some time. The class is to decide whether Mr. Waters, the husband and defendant, should be set free or not, and why. Students break into small groups to discuss their reasoning. The teacher may propose an alternative dilemma if the class strongly favors one of the choices, e.g., what if the prosecutor established that Mr. and Mrs. Waters had been having marital problems the past few years, as

---

[39]Lawrence Kohlberg, "The Cognitive- Developmental Approach to Moral Education," in *Values, Concepts and Techniques* (Washington, D.C.: National Education Association, 1976), p. 20.

[40]Kohlberg, "The Cognitive-Development Approach," in *Moral Education*, p. 178.

a result mainly of her depression, or what if Waters' attorney could establish that Mrs. Waters had been suffering from a rare, painful and incurable disease? The teacher also is instructed to ask probing questions, such as: "Does a person have the right to decide when he will die, or should a person suffering from a terminal and painful illness be allowed to end his life?" Through the discussion, each student is encouraged to reflect on the various positions, and come to his or her own answer.[41]

Kohlberg makes clear that in contrast to the relativist position of values clarification, the moral development approach has the definite aim of stimulating movement to higher stages of moral reasoning. This approach, however, restricts values education to Kohlberg's concept of what is moral, namely to the concept of *justice*. In Kohlberg's words,

> Value education in the public schools should be restricted to that which the school has the right and mandate to develop: an awareness of justice, or of the rights of others in our Constitutional system. While the Bill of Rights prohibits the teaching of religious beliefs, or of specific value systems, it does not prohibit the teaching of the awareness of rights and principles of justice fundamental to the Constitution itself.[42]

Moral education, when centered in justice, Kohlberg explains, is something different than value or affective education, and essentially the same as civic education.

Various criticisms or reservations have been directed at the Kohlberg-based moral reasoning approach, the most common being its claim of universality. Jack Fraenkel argues that although Kohlberg has identified his six stages in nine separate cultures, this is too small a sample from which to draw such a sweeping generalization. There are cultures with substantially different patterns of life and value systems—enough so as to question any universal application. Be that as it may, Kohlberg and others probably have no intent of applying the framework to all corners of the earth.[43] A related and more serious skepticism is provided by those who question his reliance on a Western, Kantian framework of morality. Justice is only one of several alternative bases for what is moral: there are conceptions of morality based on, to name a few, utilitarianism, courage, and romanticism.[44] Then there is the difficulty of providing enough adequately qualified teachers to skillfully conduct moral-dilemma discussions. A basic requirement, it seems, is postconventional functioning (at least on the Stage

---

[41]Ronald E. Galbraith and Thomas M. Jones, *Moral Reasoning—A Teaching Handbook for Adapting Kohlberg to the Classroom* (Minneapolis: Greenhaven Press, Inc., 1966), pp. 137–40.
[42]Kohlberg, "The Cognitive-Development Approach," in *Moral Education*, pp. 185–87.
[43]Jack R. Fraenkel, "The Kohlberg Bandwagon: Some Reservations," *Social Education*, 40, no. 4 (April, 1976), p. 217. This also is in David Purpel and Kevin Ryan, eds., *Moral Education*, pp. 294–95.
[44]Richard S. Peters, "A Reply to Kohlberg," *Phi Delta Kappan*, 56, no. 10 (June, 1975), p. 678. This also is in David Purpel and Kevin Ryan, eds., *Moral Education*, with the title "Why Doesn't Lawrence Kohlberg Do His Homework?" pp. 288–90.

5 level) by the classroom teacher. If no more than 10 percent of the adult population reaches postconventional operations, and there is little reason to suspect that the teacher population is significantly (to say nothing of miraculously) different, the number of potentially qualified teachers appears to be insufficient.

values analysis

The analysis approaches are similar to moral reasoning in that they are essentially cognitive, emphasize rationality, and are judged by most of their architects to be the basis of civic education. The roots of values analysis are deeply embedded in American educational thought by now, dating at least to the prolific writing of John Dewey. Of more recent vintage, the ideas of Maurice Hunt, Lawrence Metcalf, James Shaver, Donald Oliver, Jack Fraenkel, and Michael Scriven stand out. Hunt and Metcalf were the first to develop a teaching model for values analysis: a model that recognizes that value conflict is inevitable, that policy-making in our socio-political environment involves value judgment, and that the consequences of value decisions merit serious consideration.[45]

Influenced by Gunnar Myrdal's monumental examination of America's racial problem, *An American Dilemma* (1944), Oliver and Shaver constructed an analysis approach designed to teach students to examine value conflicts embedded in public issues. Value conflict, the authors pointed out, can be either interpersonal or intrapersonal, and can involve issues central to the political philosophy of our nation. A popular example of interpersonal conflict from their work involves the case of a soapbox speaker who has aroused the gathering crowd to a potentially riotous state. At issue are two conflicting positive values: freedom of speech and public security. Oliver and Shaver would have the class investigate the facts surrounding the incident, analyze the evidence supporting both value positions, and after considering the consequences of alternative actions, reach a *qualified* decision (i.e., one that recognizes subsequent evidence may call for a different decision). Central to their theory are the understandings that value conflict is inevitable and certainly not undesirable, that critical and rational thinking are vital to our society, and that certain principles or values have special validity in our democratic order. These certain values are namely, the principles established in the Constitution, the use of rational thinking, and ultimately the appeal of human dignity.[46]

Interpersonal and intrapersonal values conflict cuts across virtually

---

[45]Maurice P. Hunt and Lawrence E. Metcalf, *Teaching High School Social Studies: Problems in Reflective Thinking and in Social Understanding*, 2nd ed. (New York: Harper & Row, Publishers, 1968), pp. 133–39.
[46]Donald W. Oliver and James P. Shaver, *Teaching Public Issues in the High School* (Boston: Houghton Mifflin Company, 1966), chap. 6 and 7.

Alternatives	Consequences		Desirability from Various Points of View						
	Short-range	Long-range	Moral	Legal	Aesthetic	Ecological	Economic	Health and Safety	Ranking

Figure 6-2 Values-Analysis Chart

every area of the school curriculum. In addition to the freedom-of-speech example above, interpersonal conflict involves other "basic" issues (values) concerning equality of opportunity, majority rule, and public welfare. Interpersonal conflict also is derived from "specific" issues such as conservation and economic growth, artificial foods and public health, as well as abortion, euthanasia, student rights, space exploration and many more. Intrapersonal conflict may involve these same issues and others, including questions of honesty, cooperation, competition, cleanliness, and the like. Too often the individual escapes from internal inconsistencies by compartmentalizing conflicting values, or by rationalizing. According to the value analysis school of thought, the forthright and thoughtful examination of social-ethical issues, inter- and intrapersonal, is central to responsible citizenship education.

Jack Fraenkel has developed a values analysis model similar to that of Oliver and Shaver, with value conflict the focus. Fraenkel uses what he calls a value dilemma as a springboard to critical analysis. After clarifying the nature of the conflict, students are asked to: (1) examine the *facts* in the dilemma; (2) suggest reasonable alternative courses of action; (3) consider possible short- and long-range consequences of the alternative policies. Eventually students will be obliged to judge which alternative is best, but before doing so they are encouraged to evaluate their policy with respect to a variety of criteria: moral (how would the lives and dignity of humans be affected?), legal (would any laws be broken?), esthetic, ecological, economic, health, and safety. Figure 6-2 illustrates a chart that can be used to organize the Fraenkel analysis.[47]

---

[47]Jack R. Fraenkel, "Analyzing Values Conflict," in *Values, Concepts and Techniques* (Washington, D.C.: National Education Association, 1976), pp. 77–86.

Among these approaches to values-moral-civic education, we are partial to values analysis, mainly because of its potential to effectively prepare young people for critical, intelligent decision-making in our increasingly complex and manipulative society. We certainly do not suggest scuttling values clarification and moral reasoning approaches; if due consideration is given the reservations discussed, these approaches can fruitfully augment the values curriculum.

THE SEARCH FOR DEMOCRATIC VALUES IN SCHOOLS

Ultimately the examination of values in school and society comes back to the quest to promote a democratic environment. Concerning the relationship between religion and public education, the centuries-long debate over separation of Church and State has been argued in the interest of individual freedom—the basic democratic value. Values clarification and analysis approaches, as well as moral reasoning, are developed essentially to combat prejudice, closedness, conformity, absolutism and authoritarianism, or to promote personal freedom. Despite the underlying democratic ideals of our society, we are not in practice skilled in critical thinking or tolerant of divergent and dissenting viewpoints. We struggle to provide a semblance of our democratic ideal, and do a lot of compartmentalizing and rationalizing to live with any inadequacies.

perceptions and socio-political behavior

How democratic values develop in our schools will be determined to a significant degree by the extent of democratic-promoting and authoritarian-promoting perceptual systems of our teachers and administrations, and of the general populace. The work of social psychologist O. J. Harvey on perceptual belief systems is particularly germane to this question.

A belief system, as Harvey describes it, is a kind of psychological filter which renders the individual selective in making discriminations as to what is attended to, admitted into and kept out of one's system. It represents a set of predispositions to perceive, feel toward, and respond to ego-involving stimuli and events in a consistent way. Especially pertinent to schooling is the fact that a person's belief system influences the kind of cues on which a person relies and utilizes in decision-making. Whereas one person, namely Harvey's *System 1*, will be disposed to rely on cues implying status and authority, another, *System 4*, will be inclined to use a variety of information carefully assessed for reliability.

Harvey and his research associates designed a conceptual framework to represent the varying degrees of differentiation and integration that in-

```
Concreteness                                    Abstractness
|------▲---------▲----------▲----------▲------|
       |         |          |          |
   System 1  System 2   System 3   System 4
```

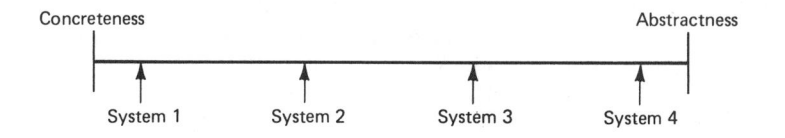

Figure 6-3 Belief Systems Continuum

dividuals display in their ways of thinking. They conceived a continuum which accounted for the extent of concreteness and abstractness in thinking. The concrete end of this continuum, Harvey explains, "represents the state of minimal differentiation within the concepts and little or no integration among them. The more abstract end of the continuum is represented by high differentiation and integration across a wide range of domains."[48] An infinite number of points, representing different individual perceptual and conceptual preferences, can be identified along the continuum. Harvey found the most workable classification, however, involved four basic systems of concreteness-abstractness, though there exist mixtures of the four (see Figure 6-3).

These levels or systems also were found by Harvey to have developed out of the background and environment of the individual. The systems, extending from the concrete to the abstract, can be characterized as follows:

System 1 functioning has evolved from a training history in which the individuals were restricted in the exploration of their environment, especially that portion concerned with values and power relationships, while rewards and punishments were contingent upon conformity and non-conformity to traditionally accepted standards. Consequently representatives of this system manifest such characteristics as high absolutism and closedness of beliefs, high conventionality, high dependence on institutional authority, high evaluativeness and strong beliefs that American values should be instituted as a world model.

The *System 2* representative comes from a background of capricious and arbitrary childrearing practices which offer unstructuredness and diversity in excess of the optimal. This results in feelings of uncertainty, distrust of authority, and rejection of socially approved guidelines. While struggling for autonomy, this person expresses rebellion against such objects as God, national unity, police, perhaps teachers and other traditional referents that serve as positive guides for the System 1 representative.

System 3 functioning, next to the highest level in abstractness, tends to emerge out of a childhood of over-protection and over-indulgence, buffering persons from an exploration of their physical environment and restricting the exploration of the social world to the manipulation of and dependency upon

---

[48]O. J. Harvey, "Belief Systems and Education: Some Implications for Changes," in *The Affective Domain*, ed. Jack Crawford (Washington, D.C.: Communications Service Corporation, 1970), pp. 68–71.

people. As a result, this individual develops skill in effecting desired outcomes by having others do it; the ability to achieve goals by the manipulation of others. Likewise, System 3 persons are concerned with the attitudes of peers, social acceptance, and standards of behavior prescribed by particular referent groups. Although they tend to find security through identification with a group, they nonetheless develop more autonomous internal standards than the previous two systems.

The *System 4* individual is a consequence of childhood freedom to explore the physical and social world deriving values from one's own experience and thought. More than others, this person has a set of internal standards more independent of external criteria, sometimes coinciding with social norms, sometimes not, but always displaying flexibility, creativity and relativism in thought and action. There is little concern with social position. System 4s are not given to moralizing about others, but do have a clearly defined moral code applicable universally.[49]

proportions of system types in schools and society

Harvey's postulate on the number of system types among us reinforces the position that there prevails an underlying authoritarianism, closedness, and rule-orientation in our society. He reports that in the general adult population approximately 50 percent are System 1 representatives, and only *five percent* System 4, while 20–25 percent are System 3s and about 10 percent System 2s; the remainder are admixtures, mostly System 1–3 combinations and to a lesser extent System 3–4 combinations. More importantly with respect to public schools, Harvey's studies indicated that teachers were distributed as follows:

System 1—50–55 percent
System 2—less than 1 percent
System 3—20–25 percent, including 3–4 combinations
System 4—at most 5 percent

The distribution of abstract functioning among new teachers is higher than among their established colleagues; the degree of abstractness decreases with experience, due both to the higher attrition of System 4 teachers and the gradual accommodation to institutional norms. The amount of concrete functioning among principals and superintendents is even greater; the percentage of System 1s among this group is as high as 90 percent. Among his study of several thousand college students in the liberal arts, Harvey found a lower percentage of System 1 individuals (35–40 per-

---

[49]O. J. Harvey, "Beliefs and Behavior: Some Implications for Education," *The Science Teacher*, 37, no. 9 (December 1970), pp. 11–13.

cent), a significantly higher proportion of System 4s (7–8 percent); System 3s remained about the same (20%). Among those undergraduates preparing to be teachers, the concreteness process begins to take effect during the junior and senior years of college; approximately 45 percent are System 1, 5 percent System 2, 25 percent System 3, and 5 percent System 4. For liberal arts majors who will go on to professional or graduate school or into the business world, this concretization process is delayed until that entry.[50]

Given Harvey's statistics, it is not surprising that the state of values in education—secular and sacred—is so inadequate. If openness, reflective thought, creativity, and democratic-oriented values in general are to flourish, our schools must foster more abstract thinking, and our society must be less hostile to such behavior. There is much to do in education in order to prepare young people to deal insightfully and effectively with the crushing tide of scientific and institutional control. Given the pace of modern events, the task of creating a genuinely democratic existence is nothing less than urgent.

CASE STUDY: School Holidays

It was to be a quiet and short school board meeting, so the superintendent thought, in which the only major item was the approval of next year's school calendar. The discussion had just begun when the parent moved that Yom Kippur and Rosh Hashannah, two major Jewish holidays, be included as open dates. They were to be observed on September 20 and September 29, both regularly scheduled school days. There was considerable support for the motion among a vocal group of parents.

As the discussion continued, several complaints surfaced about school practices with respect to minority religious holidays. One person mentioned that exams regularly were scheduled without regard for non-Christian religious groups. Nearly 10 percent of the student body was Jewish, and a significant number of other students were members of the Seventh Day Adventists, Black Muslims, and Latter Day Saints. One basketball player this past season lost his starting position on the varsity team for missing practice on a religious holiday. Most coaches also have expressed discontent and even anger with players whose religious observances have conflicted with practices and contests.

Do you believe religious holidays for various sects should be added to the school calendar? Which ones? What should the school policy be with respect to religious holidays? with respect to the religious freedom rights of students and teachers?

[50]Ibid., pp. 13–14.

THOUGHT QUESTIONS

1. From your contact with schools, list examples of esthetic, instrumental and moral values you find. Do you believe that schools have a legitimate concern with the moral values of students? If so, what sort of moral values would you exclude? If you have had experiences with both public and parochial schools, are there any significant differences in the esthetic, instrumental, and moral values they attend to? Explain.

2. What are examples of moral values (or authority) that you believe are basic to the American culture? Are all of your moral values consistent with this guideline? If not, which ones are not? How do you explain the discrepancy?

3. Thomas Jefferson's call for building a "wall of separation" between Church and State has been interpreted in various ways. How literally or metaphorically should this statement be taken? Explain what this statement or metaphor means to you with respect to the place of religion in public schools today.

4. Based on your own (public) schooling, what moral values did your teachers attempt to convey to students? What, if any, values in your school were clearly religious values?

5. From your reading of what and how much parochiaid is legally permitted, do you believe the Courts should take a more conservative or liberal position towards parochiaid? What is your reasoning?

6. How valid do you believe the authors' point to be, when they say that as we acquire more technological amenities, we become more dependent upon them, less able to understand and repair them, and therefore less well off? What so-called technological amenities, e.g., automobile, television, telephone, hair dryer, are an important part of your life? What would life be like without any one of them? Which could you get along without if for some reason they became in short supply? Which of these can you diagnose normal mechanical problems for and repair?

7. How does Theodore Roszak's idea of the "scientization of culture" apply to the subject area in which you will be or are teaching? Does it seem to make any difference what one's subject is, i.e., is this concept more pertinent to the physical sciences, than to, say, English, history, social studies, home economics, or vocational technology? Discuss some ways (activities or exercises) that can be used to teach this concept in your class—secondary or elementary level.

8. Which part of your mind—the rational or metaphorical—do you regard as the dominant? Are you content with the degree of balance or imbalance between the two domains? Explain!

9. Discuss Carl Bereiter's argument that schools ought not become involved with "education," i.e., values; rather this should be left to the family and to the groups, churches, or clubs with whom families choose to affiliate. (You may want to review Chapter 1 for this question.) Given Bereiter's position, do you believe he would make an exception for values clarification

exercises? How about moral reasoning dilemmas? Values analysis approaches?

10. Considering the subject that you will be teaching, in what ways could you integrate values clarification exercises into the curriculum? (After thinking up your own ideas, check out Merrill Harmin, Howard Kirschenbaum, and Sidney Simon's *Clarifying Values Through Subject Matter* (Minneapolis: Winston Press, Inc., 1973). Think up a moral reasoning dilemma or two that is appropriate to your curriculum.

11. Where do you place yourself on Harvey's concrete-abstract continuum? Are there areas in your life or issues on which you might shift to another region of the continuum? What in the operations or nature of schools do you think causes teachers to shift over time to more concrete levels, i.e., System 1 functioning?

PRACTICAL ACTIVITIES

1. Attend a school board meeting. Do an informal survey of who is on the Board of Education. Note such factors as age, sex, race, apparent social class, and educational level. What values and belief positions did they appear to hold? Explain. Observe the people attending the meeting. To what extent did they participate? What interests or interest groups did they appear to represent? What values or beliefs did they assume?

2. Study the values education curriculum of a local school, or the school you teach in, and list the courses, grade levels, and materials used. Observe a few class sessions, describe how values were being taught, and note your reactions to this.

3. Take part in one of the new consciousness-raising groups, e.g., Transcendental Meditation, Transactional Analysis, Yoga, biofeedback. What effects does it appear to have on you? On others who participated? Describe the religious-spiritual implications of this experience for you. Explain what practical benefits there are, or applications to your future professional aspirations.

4. Using some of the exercises from the book *Values Clarification* (Sidney Simon and others) in conjunction with a local public school teacher, conduct a values inquiry session. Report on how you selected the activity, what grade level it was used for, and what success or failure you feel you achieved with the exercise. Discuss how you would organize VC exercises in your own future classroom.

5. Using a moral dilemma developed by Lawrence Kohlberg and his colleagues, conduct a moral reasoning session in a local elementary, junior high or senior high classroom. Report on the class and grade level, how the students dealt with the issue, the moral reasoning they displayed, and the results of your discussion.

6. From a discussion with teachers or administrators, relate one or more recent incidents concerning the place of religion in the schools. What was

the incident? How was it handled? Should it have been dealt with differently? Analyze it from your perspective.

7. From your observation of several classrooms in a local elementary or secondary school, what appear to be the dominant values of the children or young people? From where do they seem to be getting most of their values? Are they different from yours? Do you see much change since you were their age?

BIBLIOGRAPHY

books

BRUNER, JEROME S., *On Knowing: Essays for the Left Hand.* Cambridge, Mass.: Harvard University Press, 1962.

BYRNES, LAWRENCE, *Religion and Public Education.* New York: Harper & Row, Publishers, 1975.

EISLEY, LOREN, *The Immense Journey.* New York: Random House, Inc., 1957.

GALBRAITH, RONALD E., AND THOMAS M. JONES, *Moral Reasoning—A Teaching Handbook for Adapting Kohlberg to the Classroom* (Minneapolis: Greenhaven Press, Inc., 1976).

GORDON, W. J. J., AND T. POZE, *The Metaphorical Way of Learning & Knowing.* Cambridge, Mass.: Porpoise Books, 1973.

JONES, RICHARD M., *Fantasy and Feeling in Education.* New York: Harper & Row Publishers, 1968.

LEONARD, GEORGE, *The Transformation.* New York: Delacorte Press, 1972.

———, *The Ultimate Athlete.* New York: The Viking Press, 1975.

MARSHACK, ALEXANDER, *The Roots of Civilization.* New York: McGraw-Hill Book Company, 1972.

MASLOW, ABRAHAM H., *The Farther Reaches of Human Nature.* New York: The Viking Press, 1971.

OLIVER, DONALD W., AND JAMES P. SHAVER, *Teaching Public Issues in the High School.* Boston: Houghton Mifflin Company, 1966.

ORNSTEIN, ROBERT E., *The Nature of Human Consciousness.* San Francisco: W. H. Freeman Company, 1973.

PURPEL, DAVID, AND KEVIN RYAN, eds., *Moral Education . . . It Comes with the Territory.* Berkeley, Calif.: McCutchan Publishing Corporation, 1976.

RATHS, LOUIS E., MERRILL HARMIN, AND SIDNEY B. SIMON, *Values and Teaching: Working with Values in the Classroom.* Columbus, Ohio: Charles E. Merrill Publishing Co., 1966.

ROKEACH, MILTON, *The Nature of Human Values.* New York: The Free Press, 1973.

ROSZAK, THEODORE, *Where the Wasteland Ends.* Garden City, N.Y.: Doubleday & Company, Inc., 1972.

SALK, JONAS, *The Survival of the Wisest.* New York: Harper & Row, Publishers, 1973.

SAMPLES, BOB, *The Metaphoric Mind—A Celebration of Creative Consciousness.* Menlo Park, Calif.: Addison-Wesley Publishing Company, 1976.

SAMPLES, BOB, AND BOB WOHLFORD, *Opening—A Primer for Self-Actualization*. Menlo Park, Calif.: Addison-Wesley Publishing Company, 1975.

SHAVER, JAMES P., AND WILLIAM STRONG, *Facing Value Decisions: Rationale-Building for Teachers*. Belmont, Calif.: Wadsworth Publishing Company, Inc., 1976.

SIMON, SIDNEY B., LELAND W. HOWE, AND HOWARD KIRSCHENBAUM, *Values Clarification—A Handbook of Practical Strategies for Teachers and Students*. New York: Hart Publishing Company, Inc., 1972.

Values, Concepts and Techniques. Washington, D.C.: National Education Association, 1976.

periodicals and booklets

Phi Delta Kappan. A Special Issue on Moral Education, 56, no. 10 (June 1975).

Social Education. "Moral Education: Learning to Weigh Human Values," 39, no. 1 (January 1975).

Social Education. Edwin Fenton, guest editor. "Cognitive-Developmental Approach to Moral Education," 40, no. 4.

GORDON, W. J. J., *Strange & Familiar*. Cambridge, Mass.: Porpoise Books, 1972.

GORDON, W. J. J., AND TONY POZE, *Activities in Metaphor*. Cambridge, Mass.: Porpoise Books, 1973.

7
RACISM AND ETHNICITY
The Recognition of Diversity

Among the most cherished parts of the American creed are these words from the Declaration of Independence.

> We hold these truths to be self-evident, that all men are created equal, that they are endowed by their Creator with certain unalienable Rights, that among these are Life, Liberty and the pursuit of Happiness.

The statement of such ideals, particularly in 1776, can be looked upon with a great deal of pride by the American people. The actual practice of them, however, leaves much to be desired. Ours is a history in which all too many minorities have been deprived of life, liberty, and happiness, and not all people have been looked upon as brothers or equals. This is not to say that the United States is unique in its prejudices. Most nations of the world contain as much or more discrimination based on race or ethnicity, but this fact does not excuse us from dealing with it in our society and in our time. This chapter will present an historical account of minority groups within the American society, in addition to dealing with the role of the school in perpetuating and alleviating inequalities.

Although in one sense, all Americans are members of some type of racial, religious or ethnic minority, this chapter will concentrate on four major groups who are set apart by their physical differences, and who thus have suffered greater degrees of discrimination than have the immigrants and their descendants from Great Britain and Europe. These four groups meet the criteria of a minority laid down by anthropologists working with the data from a UNESCO study on world minorities.

> (1) Minorities are subordinate segments of complex state societies; (2) minorities have special physical or cultural traits which are held in low esteem by the dominant segments of the society; (3) minorities are self-conscious units bound together by the special traits which their members share and by the special disabilities which these bring; (4) membership in a minority is transmitted by a rule of descent which is capable of affiliating succeeding generations even in the absence of readily apparent physical or cultural traits.[1]

The four major minority groupings in the American society which meet the above definitions are the Spanish-surnamed, consisting of Americans of Mexican, Puerto Rican, Cuban, or other Latin American descent; blacks; Orientals, primarily of Chinese, Japanese, and Filipino ancestry, but more recently including Vietnamese and Laotians; and finally, Native Americans. Although one can make a strong case for racism and prejudice against the Jews, Irish, Catholics, Polish, and other groups, the discrimination against the four "minorities" listed above has been more pervasive and long-lasting. The four groups also lend themselves well to analysis, as they were brought into the American society by four different means. The Mexicans found themselves a colonized people when their territory was annexed by the United States. The Orientals immigrated to this country, though not always of their own free will, while the blacks were brought here in slavery. The Native American populations were conquered peoples, and have recently spent much time in the courts attempting to regain that which was lost on the battlefield or in broken treaties.

HISTORICAL OVERVIEW

blacks

Blacks were first brought to this country in 1619, with a similar status to other indentured servants. Later in the seventeenth century, however, their status declined as the large plantations needed greater amounts of human labor. By the middle of the eighteenth century, slavery had been legalized in every colony, and tens of thousands of slaves were brought in from West Africa. By 1776, there were over a half million Negroes in slavery or indentured servitude in this country, one sixth of the total population. In 1783, Massachusetts abolished slavery, and other northern states

---

[1]Charles F. Marden and Gladys Meyer, *Minorities in American Society*, 3rd ed. (New York: American Book, 1968), p. 23.

soon followed suit. The South, however, was too dependent upon slavery, and although it was banned from the Northwest Territory, Congress was prohibited from restricting the slave trade until 1808. Blacks served in the Revolutionary Army, as they have in every war since that time, but their use has consistently been more out of a desperate need for manpower than out of any sense of equality. An early indication of the black's status in American society was their being counted as only three-fifths of a person in determining the number of representatives of a state to Congress.

Slaves could own no property, could enter into no contract, not even a contract of marriage, and had no right to assemble in public unless a white person was present. They had no standing in courts. Without legal means of defense, slaves were susceptible to the premise that any white person could threaten their lives or take them with impunity.[2]

Free blacks fared little better, suffering from a great deal of prejudice and discrimination. By 1860, four million blacks were enslaved, and although an abolitionist movement had gained strength, not all its supporters were sincere in their efforts. The Dred Scott decision in 1857 confirmed that blacks were not citizens and thus not protected by the Constitution. Blacks were initially rejected for service in the military during the Civil War, but when a shortage of men developed, they were quickly admitted. With the Union victory, Negroes were given their freedom, but not equality or freedom from aggression. Lynchings and other forms of violence were perpetrated on the black population until well into the twentieth century and, many would argue, up to the present day. The Thirteenth, Fourteenth and Fifteenth Amendments gave blacks the right to vote and the promise of equality, and the Civil Rights Act of 1875 gave them the right to equal accommodations but the Act contained no effective enforcement. During the Reconstruction period, blacks served in every Southern legislature and in the House and Senate. Through the pressures of the Ku Klux Klan and a barrage of laws that followed the 1883 ruling that the Civil Rights Act of 1875 was unconstitutional, blacks were effectively eliminated from participation in the political process and from equality of treatment or opportunity. This culminated in the important Supreme Court case, *Plessy* v. *Ferguson*, which established that "separate but equal" facilities were permissible by law.

At the beginning of the twentieth century, the black was politically disenfranchised, economically kept at the bottom of the ladder, and subject to every form of legal and illegal discrimination.

In the early twentieth century, Booker T. Washington exemplified the position of accommodation, conciliation, and gradualism in contact between the races, while men such as W. E. B. Du Bois in the Niagara Movement sought equality through agitation and protest. The National Associa-

---

[2]National Advisory Commission on Civil Disorders, *Report* (New York: Bantam Books, 1968), p. 209.

tion for the Advancement of Colored People (NAACP) took many forms of legal action and carried on a nationwide propaganda effort to fight prejudice and discriminatory statutes. Marcus Garvey led a movement "back to Africa," where he hoped to liberate both African and American blacks from their oppressors. Numerous riots by whites against blacks occurred before and after World War I, a war from which Negroes were also excluded until their manpower once again became necessary. The Ku Klux Klan gained a great deal of power and influence between the wars, and during the Depression blacks suffered more severely than whites, due to many forms of discrimination in aid and work opportunities. With the New Deal and the CIO's policy of nondiscrimination, the plight of American blacks slowly began to improve.

During World War II, blacks again were initially prevented from fighting but later were accepted in separate, mostly noncombat units. It was not until 1949 that the Armed Forces outlawed segregation. During the Depression, war, and early postwar period, the legal pressures began to build, leading in 1954 to the crucial court decision *Brown* v. *Board of Education*, in which the court reversed its "separate but equal" doctrine of 1896 and declared that segregated schools give black children

> ... a feeling of inferiority as to their status in the community that may affect their hearts and minds in a way unlikely ever to be undone.... We conclude that in the field of public education the doctrine of separate but equal has no place.

With the major 1954 decision, the dam broke and a series of court decisions and Civil Rights Acts outlawed all forms of discrimination on the basis of race or ethnicity. Without the moral leadership of Dr. Martin Luther King and the political action of such groups as the NAACP, the Southern Christian Leadership Conference, the Student Non-Violent Coordinating Committee, the Black Muslims, and a variety of black power advocates, it is unlikely that many of the laws would have been passed, much less enforced. A great deal of legal progress has been made by black America in the past thirty years, but prejudice still exists. The role of the school in alleviating and perpetuating that prejudice will be dealt with later in the chapter.

Spanish-Americans

The second largest "minority" in the United States is the 9 million persons of Spanish descent, with two-thirds being of Mexican origin. This total compares with over 22 million blacks. Although there are large numbers of Puerto Ricans, Cubans, and other Latin Americans in the United States, it is the history of the Mexican-Americans which will be dealt with here. Unlike the blacks, Mexican-Americans became citizens by conquest and annexation. Concentrated in the southwestern part of the United States, many Mexican-Americans can trace their ancestry in the area of 150 or more years prior to the annexation of New Mexico in 1848, after the war with Mexico. Anglo-Americans are but the most recent of a line of conquerors, from Spain, to France, to Mexico, none of whom took much interest in what now comprises the states of California, Arizona, New Mexico, Texas, and Colorado.

Trade routes, set up in the 1840s, were replaced by the railroads later in the century as the Anglo-Americans set up forts and trading posts. Cattlemen moved in and claimed vast amounts of land for themselves, as did the mining and forestry interests. Indian and Hispanic systems of land ownership were invalidated and replaced by Anglo deeds and titles. By 1892, the land grab was complete, with the opening of grazing privileges to people other than the Hispanos from whom they had been taken. The traditional ties to the land were effectively broken, and the "original" citizens of the Southwest soon were forced into the mines and lumber camps, and into the bottom layer of the economy of the Southwest. Where once citizens of Mexican origin could be found in all levels of society, by the end of the nineteenth century, most had been forced from their lands to become part of the lower, working class. Millions of acres of common or group-owned land were declared to be government land and sold to Anglos throughout the last half of the nineteenth century.

The label "Spanish-American" came into social usage after the exodus from Mexico following the Revolution in 1909. Hispanos of many generations' residence, not wishing to identify with the impoverished Mexican immigrants, took on the name Spanish-Americans, while labeling the others as Mexicans or Mexican-Americans. Of more recent origin is the word Chicano, which has rapidly replaced the other names as that preferred by the more militant groups.

Article IX of the Treaty of Guadalupe Hidalgo, bringing the Southwest in to the United States, guarantees that the people in the territories annexed would have "all the rights of citizens of the United States." Most historians agree that the treaty has been more breached than honored and that the Anglo-American power structure, through land grabs, economic exploitation of migrant labor and *braceros,* numerous discriminatory laws, and outright violence, has kept the Chicano in economic and political powerlessness for the past century and a quarter.

Housing discrimination against the Mexican-American was practiced throughout the Southwest, and segregated schools could be found until the Supreme Court declared them unconstitutional in a series of cases from 1948 until the famous *Brown* decision of 1954. Amazingly, however, a circuit court in Houston in *Ross* v. *Eckels* declared Mexican-Americans were part of "the larger American majority" and paired them with black schools, leaving the dominant Anglo schools segregated. Numerous other forms of

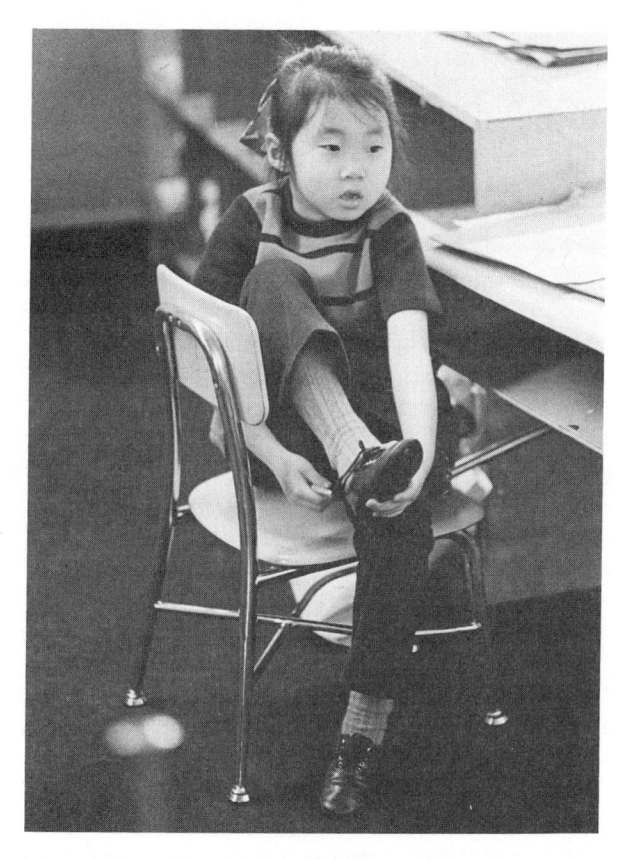

Figure 7-1 Ethnic Diversity Characterizes American Schools

school discrimination can be found in textbooks, IQ tests, tracking, language, and cultural training, all of which will be dealt with in greater detail later. Like other racial and ethnic minorities, the Mexican-American population has been the subject of ethnic jokes and racial slurs, with many of the forms of discrimination practiced in the South against blacks being practiced against Chicanos in the Southwest.

Elwyn Stoddard lists five recognizable periods in the struggle for equal rights. The first was the 450-year period from the Spanish Conquest until the Mexican Revolution in 1910, during which the people were kept in a subordinate position. From 1910 until World War II, Mexican-Americans, like other hyphenated Americans, attempted to assimilate totally into the "melting pot." Separatism followed the war, when veterans discovered that they were still not accepted into the dominant society. During the larger civil rights movement, Chicano activists came to the forefront to pressure the society for greater justice and the abolishment of discrimination. Men such as Cesar Chavez and Rudolfo "Corky" Gonzalez came to the forefront of the movement, which included boycotts and a variety of public confrontations. Stoddard concludes that the movement is now entering its fifth stage, in which overt actions are declining in favor of penetrating professional, political, and economic organizations at all levels.[3]

Oriental-Americans

The Chinese- and Japanese-Americans are the largest sectors of the growing Oriental-American minority in the United States. These two groups, in particular, are held up as examples of the economic, political, academic, and social success available to minorities in this country. Their "success," however, has been limited by a long history of maltreatment, racism, and prejudice, beginning with the arrival of the Chinese workers for the railroad in 1850 and in the mining camps of the nineteenth century. Japanese immigrants to the plantations on Hawaii provided cheap labor, but when they came to San Francisco in the late nineteenth century, American laborers felt threatened, and cries of the "yellow peril" were heard. This led in 1907 to an informal agreement between the United States and Japan to ban further immigration. The Japanese tended to settle in rural areas rather than urban "Chinatowns." With Japanese success in small farming, the American farmers soon felt threatened and succeeded in getting the Alien Land Law passed in 1913, prohibiting "foreign" ownership of land. When that failed, they got a prohibition on the leasing of land passed in 1920, and with its failure, the Alien Exclusion Act of 1924 prevented further immigration to the United States by Japanese.

Many of the same forms of discrimination practiced against blacks in the South and Mexican-Americans in the Southwest could be found in areas of urban and rural California where many Oriental-Americans settled. In addition, the stereotype of the "slant-eyed, treacherous, and subversive Oriental" pervaded the newspapers and popular thinking for the first half of the twentieth century. This led to perhaps the greatest violation of constitutional and civil rights in American history, with the internment of tens of thousands of Americans of Japanese descent, including many American citizens, due to the fear of the "yellow peril" that was so prevalent during World War II. The decision involved such liberal leaders as President Roosevelt and Earl Warren, who later became Chief Justice of the Supreme Court. The Japanese and Japanese-Americans were deprived of property, freedom of movement, and numerous other civil rights, a further evidence of the racism so prevalent in American society.

Chinese were crowded into Chinatowns, and the chances of their moving outside its confines or even working in other locations were ex-

---

[3]Elwyn R. Stoddard, *Mexican-Americans* (New York: Random House, Inc., 1973), pp. 242–43.

tremely limited. The Chinese immigrants and their descendants were cut off from the dominant American society, and although there has been an awakening among Chinese youth, the Chinese-Americans have not been accepted nor have they attempted to enter the dominant culture in large numbers.

Of more recent origin are the Filipinos, Koreans, and Polynesians; and since the end of the Indochinese war, large numbers of Vietnamese and Laotians have entered the Oriental-American community. It is too early to state with any assurance what the treatment of these newer groups will be, but one can conclude that it will probably not differ too greatly from the overt racism of the past or the not-so-subtle racism presently experienced by Chinese- and Japanese-Americans. Skin colors and features still play a role in American society.

Native Americans

The fourth and final minority to which we shall turn our attention is the *Native American* or *American Indian*. Through four centuries of conquest, cultural extermination, genocide, and coercive assimilation, the Native American has borne the brunt of the most pervasive physical, economic, political, and cultural discrimination in this country's history. That over 300 tribes have survived is remarkable indeed.

The European explorers and the settlers who followed saw the Indians as savages in need of conversion to Christianity. Almost all saw them as inferiors whose lands could be taken and rights as human beings violated. Alvin M. Josephy in his *The Indian Heritage of America* puts the destruction of Indian peoples in its starkest reality:

> The European conquest of the Americas had been termed one of the darkest chapters of human history, for the conquerors demanded and won authority over the lives, territories, religious beliefs, ways of life, and means of existence of every native group with which they came in contact. No one will ever know how many Indians or how many tribes were enslaved, tortured, debauched and killed.... The stain is made all the darker by the realization that the conflict was forced upon those who suffered; the aggressors were the whites, the scenes of tragedy the very homelands of the victims.[4]

Throughout the colonial period and through the nineteenth century, involving both warfare and treaties, the Indians were forced to abandon their tribal lands in exchange for money, "guarantees" on other lands, hunting and fishing rights, educational programs, and a variety of other promises, all too often broken as the pressures of new settlers were brought to bear. The treaties raised questions concerning the legal status of the In-

[4]Alvin M. Josephy, Jr., *The Indian Heritage of America* (New York: Bantam Books, 1969), p. 277.

dians, with the Supreme Court ruling that they had some of the attributes of sovereignty, although not to the same extent as foreign nations. This led to the federal government's role as "guardian" and regulator of the Indians, primarily through the Bureau of Indian Affairs (BIA). This status of limited sovereignty has led in recent days to the courts' upholding the rights of Indian tribes in various parts of the country to retake lands, be paid for lands taken illegally, and to regain traditional hunting and fishing privileges. These cases have been one factor in the continued animosity and prejudice of the dominant society towards the Native American population.

If blacks, Mexican-Americans, and Oriental-Americans were segregated in their ghettoes or barrios, the Native Americans were treated even worse. Indians were placed on reservations throughout the nineteenth century in the American equivalent of South African apartheid. They were often made to move hundreds of miles from their homelands, placed in inhospitable environments, prevented from practicing their traditional religion, forced to adopt private land ownership patterns, and perhaps as an ultimate indignity, had their children taken away from them and placed in white-run boarding schools. Indian political leadership was replaced by BIA bureaucrats, and Indians were forced into a near total dependency relationship with the dominant power structure of the society.

The Indian Reorganization Act of 1934 attempted to remedy some of the worst conditions by encouraging tribal self-government and the retention of traditional cultures, in addition to placing all tribal lands in trust, to prevent their being taken over by non-Indians. Tribal religions and customs were permitted again, and medical and educational facilities were upgraded. The paternalism of the BIA continues to the present, however. A policy of "termination" of the reservation system throughout the fifties and sixties has placed additional hardships on the Indian peoples and forced many of them into urban centers. The Civil Rights Bill of 1968 included an Indian Rights Section, extending civil rights protections to Indians, subject to tribal courts, and prevented the further erosion of Indian jurisdiction on the reservations.

Equal rights for Indians are a product of legislation of the past ten years. Into the 1970s there were school districts which prohibited Spanish-speaking children from using their native language. Fifteen years ago, black activists were boycotting buses for the right to sit wherever they pleased, and only thirty-five years ago, Japanese-Americans were deprived of their civil rights and placed in detention camps. American racism has run the gamut from prejudicial beliefs and behavior to segregating peoples on the basis of race. Concentration camps and apartheid policy have been part of our history, as has extermination through lynchings and Indian massacres. It is not a pretty history, and to say that other nations are filled with racism and prejudice is no excuse. Progress has been made through the courts and in the mass media, economic opportunities, and rising political involvement, but prejudice still exists, and it is to where it comes from and why it still exists that we now turn our attention.

THEORETICAL OVERVIEW

the melting pot and cultural pluralism

Throughout much of American history, the concept of the "melting pot" was a dominant theme. The phrase did not come into popular usage until Israel Zangwill's play of the same name in 1909; nevertheless, the basic idea prevailed that the immigrants of the eighteenth, nineteenth and early twentieth centuries were somehow supposed to melt into the dominant American culture. Although the Scandinavians of the upper midwest, the Germans in Missouri and Wisconsin, and the Irish of Boston maintained many aspects of their own identity, there was a significant amount of "melting" into the dominant culture which did occur. Minorities which could be identified by racial characteristics, however, did not melt. Jews and Eastern Europeans maintained much of their own identity, as did many groups from southern Europe, not to mention those from the Middle East and Asia. It can be said that the melting pot worked for those whose cultures, race, religion, and other characteristics were similar to the dominant Anglo-American society, but that it wasn't too successful with blacks, Mexican-Americans, Native Americans and Oriental-Americans. Zangwill's optimism knew no bounds.

> There she lies, the great Melting pot—listen! Can't you hear the roaring and the bubbling? There gapes her mouth—the harbour where a thousand mammoth feeders come from the ends of the world to pour in their human freight. Ah, what a stirring and a seething! Celt and Latin, Slav and Teuton, Greek and Syrian—black and yellow— . . . East and West, and North and South . . . the crescent and the cross—how the great Alchemist melts and fuses them . . . what is the glory of Rome and Jerusalem where all nations and races come to worship and look back, compared with the glory of America, where all races and nations come to labour and look forward?[5]

A related concept to that of the melting pot is assimilation. Assimilation implies a dominant and a submissive group, in which a "conquered" culture becomes a version of the dominant culture. It generally contains elements of force, in that the dominant culture demands certain behavioral patterns and adjustment to its way of doing things. The Northern European groups generally went through a fairly complete process of assimila-

---

[5]Israel Zangwill, *The Melting Pot* (New York: The Jewish Publication Society of America, 1909), pp. 198–99.

tion into the dominant American culture, whereas the other minority groups went through assimilationist phases, and outward conformity, but were never truly assimilated. The third- and fourth-generation Japanese-Americans are perhaps as fully assimilated as any of the groups dealt with earlier in this chapter, but even with them, racial prejudice has prevented complete and total acceptance into dominant American society.

Another concept related to the melting pot is that of acculturation or amalgamation. This concept is perhaps closer to what Zangwill was referring in his play, a blend of the best from all the different cultures in a give-and-take between equals. There was opposition to this among many Americans who saw little to be learned from the vast number of impoverished, illiterate European immigrants, much less the former black slaves, Chinese railroad workers, Japanese farmers, Mexican migrants, or "savage" Indians. Although large numbers of individuals within each group sought assimilation or amalgamation with the dominant culture, many more refused to mix or blend. This led to a gradual acceptance of the third pattern of interaction, namely, cultural pluralism.

Cultural pluralism was a fact of American society long before sociologists defined it in the early twentieth century. Diversity had come to be seen as a strength of American society, and as something to be preserved. Horace Kallen called American culture an "orchestra," with every type of instrument having its own timbre and tone.[6] Others have likened it to a tossed salad or stew, rather than a melting pot. Cultural pluralism denotes an acceptance of minority groups as distinct and separate elements in the nation, with public policy geared at retaining the distinctives within each culture, rather than suppressing, eliminating, or amalgamating them.

Louis Wirth has set up a typology in which minorities can be categorized as pluralistic, assimilationist, secessionist, or militant.[7] It appears difficult to categorize the minority groups from either their own perspective or from that of the dominant American culture. At one point or another, individuals and groups within the minorities have held all four perspectives, and the dominant American creed has shifted in its attitudes towards and respect for the various minority cultures. A great deal of evidence can be brought to bear, however, that the dominant trend in American society has been towards an acceptance of cultural pluralism on the part of minorities and the majority alike.

what is prejudice?

People in all societies tend to view others from their own ethnocentric frame of reference. This is as true of the United States as it is for other countries. Due to the multiplicity of subcultures and social groups in this

[6] Horace M. Kallen, "Democracy versus the Melting-Pot," *The Nation*, 100, no. 2591 (February 25, 1915), 220.
[7] Louis Wirth, *On Cities and Social Life* (Chicago: University of Chicago Press, 1964).

country, Americans have in-groups and out-groups, with judgment being passed on how closely others conform to "Our" standards. Ranking and generalizing are two characteristics of ethnocentric thinking, and the greater the differences, the more likely are gross overgeneralizations to occur. Examples of this type of generalization are the "lazy, shiftless Negroes," "hot and passionate Latins," or the "penny-pinching Scotsman." Ethnocentrism lays the groundwork for prejudice. With a lack of strong feelings about one's own group, it is difficult for prejudicial feelings to arise toward other groups. Gordon Allport defines ethnic prejudice as "an antipathy based upon a faulty and inflexible generalization. It may be felt or expressed. It may be directed toward a group as a whole, or toward an individual because he is a member of that group."[8] Prejudices may be positive or negative, but owing to the consequences of negative prejudice, most research deals only with this aspect. Prejudice contains not only intellectual and affective components, but also a predisposition to act in a certain manner, and it is when prejudice enters the realm of behavior that the courts step in. Peter I. Rose defines four basic kinds of people: (1) the unprejudiced nondiscriminator, who stands strongly for the American creed of equality, but whose effectiveness as a change agent may be limited by speaking only with people who believe as he does, i.e., the prototypical American liberal; (2) the unprejudiced discriminator, who has no basic antipathy toward any group, but will discriminate when it is in his own best interests to do so, i.e., the fair-weather liberal; (3) the prejudiced nondiscriminator, who dislikes a group but treats them as the law demands, i.e., the fair-weather illiberal; (4) the prejudiced discriminator, who actively discriminates against one or more groups and who might be called the "active bigot."[9]

By the age of four, most children have developed "distinct in-group/out-group orientations (incipient race attitudes)."[10] All studies indicate that awareness of the physical characteristics of race comes at a very early age, and although studies vary on the percentages of young children who are "clearly prejudiced," there is a great deal of evidence that by the age of seven, children have formed a variety of concepts and feelings about race, and much of it is negatively prejudicial in nature.

From what does racial prejudice spring? During much of man's history, and even up to the present day in many parts of the world, the answer has been that there are innate differences as a result of the evolutionary process, which have made the white race the leaders and the "colored" races the followers or servants. This served the racist colonialists well in Asia, Africa, and Latin America, and justified the actions of the white-Anglo power

---

[8]Gordon W. Allport, *The Nature of Prejudice* (Garden City, N.Y.: Addison-Wesley Publishing Company, Inc., 1954), p. 10.

[9]Peter I. Rose, *They and We: Racial and Ethnic Relations in the United States* (New York: Random House, Inc., 1968), pp. 80–83.

[10]Mary Ellen Goodman, *Race Awareness in Young Children* (London: Collier-Macmillan, Ltd., 1964), p. 253.

structure in the United States in its treatment of Native Americans, blacks, Mexicans, and Orientals. Strength, leadership, intelligence, and any other trait are to be found in all races, and social scientists have spent the past 200 years emphasizing a variety of social and psychological theories to explain differences. Prejudice may spring from a fear of the unfamiliar or unknown, but when "adult" data is brought to the process, it should disappear. That it doesn't disappear in the face of evidence has led researchers to look further for its cause.

Most social scientists reject prejudice as strictly a psychological deviation, as it is too widespread, and only the most narrow-minded see it as an inborn tendency. This leaves us with the conclusion that it must be a learned social behavior and attitude. Through the socialization process, prejudices are internalized, as children learn the group attitudes from their peers, family and others in their in-group. This is particularly true of individuals and groups that seek to maintain or improve their prestige by dissassociating themselves from those of lower status. Numerous studies have indicated that racial prejudice is more extreme among those whose economic and social position is under greater or more direct threat, i.e., working class white Americans. John Dollard and Clyde Kluckhohn, among others, developed a thesis dealing with the psychological advantages of prejudice.

> One goes through life seeking gratification for felt needs, and, while many such needs have their origin in the organic structure of the individual, there are others which are culturally determined. These are learned early in life and are canalized and directed toward certain goals. When goal-directed behavior is blocked, hostile impulses are frequently created in the individual, who, unable to determine the real source of his frustration and in an attempt to overcome it, manifests "free-floating aggression."[11]

Scapegoating is the mechanism used to deal with this "free-floating" aggression, with perhaps the treatment of the Jews throughout history, and particularly in Nazi Germany, as the prime example of the mechanism at work.

Another theory on the nature of prejudice comes from the psychologists who see it as a function of the authoritarian personality. A wide variety of studies have been done to describe the authoritarian personality, and perhaps the most fruitful has been the research of O. J. Harvey and his colleagues whose ideas were discussed in Chapter 6.

T. W. Adorno's classic work, *The Authoritarian Personality*, indicates that authoritarian people tend towards social discrimination, viewing

---

[11]Rose, *They and We*, p. 88.

[12]O. J. Harvey, ed., *Experience, Structure and Adaptability* (New York: Springer Publishing Co., Inc., 1960), pp. 44ff.

people as good or bad and issues as black or white, blaming others, and exhibiting out-group hostility.[13] Both Adorno's characterizations of the authoritarian personality and Harvey's studies with teachers and other school personnel would appear to lend a great deal of credence to critics who state that the public schools and their personnel are all too often perpetuators of prejudice, stereotypes, and discrimination, rather than alleviators of the problem.

the practice of discrimination

We move now from a discussion of the nature of prejudice to the practice of discrimination. Prejudice itself often has an action-effect of avoidance, and the pattern of stereotyping leads the prejudiced individual to a set of informally patterned roles which govern his behavior towards the "inferior" group or individual. At this first level, prejudice may evidence itself in derogatory words or ethnic jokes. American humor and the English language are replete with stereotypical words and phrases, many of them used by the groups who are the butt of the joke. All too often, however, throughout the history of mankind, these stereotypes have been utilized by demagogues to inflame hatred, with Hitler being only the most blatant example of the harm that can be done.

Beyond mere avoidance of people towards whom we are prejudiced, comes another level, that of deprivation or denial. Not only does the individual seek to avoid, he actively seeks to deny another individual or group some right. One doesn't need to go to Nazi Germany for examples of denial. The first section of this chapter gave numerous examples in U.S. history where Orientals were denied their right to come to this country, blacks were denied the right to vote or sit wherever they pleased on buses, and Native Americans and Mexican-Americans were deprived of their land. Not until the 1960s, with that decade's series of civil rights laws and civil liberties court cases, did most of the legal basis for denial and deprivation disappear from this country. Segregation is the institutionalized form of discrimination and restricts contact of groups or individuals. Throughout most of our history, various forms of *de jure* (legal) discrimination have been practiced in housing, hospitals, schools, and churches, to name just a few of the institutions affected. To be sure, there have been and are forms of *de facto* segregation which are completely voluntary in nature, but given the complexity of our society and economy, there have been all too many examples of *de facto* segregation which could be shown to have racial or

---

[13]T. W. Adorno, *The Authoritarian Personality* (New York: Harper & Row, Publishers, 1950).

ethnic discriminatory overtones, and this has led to many of the northern school desegregation court orders on busing.

Most segregation laws in this country have led to limiting contact in certain situations, but still permitting it in others. For example, blacks in the South, while not permitted to sit next to whites, could work in their homes or fields and shop in their stores. A more extreme form of segregation has come to be known as apartheid, or concentration camps, practiced to a certain degree in South Africa today, and used during World War II with Americans of Japanese descent. Expulsion, exile, or total removal from the society is an even more extreme form of segregation. Its practice has been somewhat limited in U.S. history, although a few "undesirables" have been so treated, and one can still hear people say, "Why don't we send them back to where they came from?" when speaking of blacks or Mexican-Americans; the speakers are rarely cognizant of the absurdity of the statement, as only the Native Americans and some Mexican-Americans have any "right to be here" under such a position.

Discrimination ultimately can become violent and in its ultimate form can lead to extermination or genocide. Violence may not be as "American as Apple Pie," but there is no denying its role in our history. The massacres of the American Indians can only be called genocide, and the hundreds of lynchings of blacks in the late nineteenth and early twentieth century are examples of extermination being practiced in a society which guarantees the "right to life." Although some militants would point to Attica and Kent State as evidence that extermination of those who differ from the societal norms is still practiced, "ultimate solutions" are no longer condoned by the power structure or society in general.

reactions to discrimination

Minority groups have reacted to their status in a variety of ways. The psychiatrist Robert Coles, in his study of black and white children in the South during the 1960s, has demonstrated the effects of discrimination on the black children and how it led to self-hatred. Numerous schools have been founded in the black community to counteract this self-hatred and to instill a pride in race. The outward evidences of this can be seen in the slogans "Black is Beautiful" and "Black Power." This move on the part of blacks has been followed by other groups and their slogans can be read in "Brown Power," "La Raza Unida," "Yellow Power," and "Gray Panthers," in addition to such historically related themes as "Custer Died for your Sins."

If the 1960s and 1970s saw an upsurge in self- and group pride, these were not the traditional reactions to discrimination. Perhaps the dominant reaction has been one of submission; it didn't take a black slave long to know who had the power, nor for the Japanese-Americans to see the hopelessness of fighting the whole U.S. government, which was caught up in a xenophobic hatred of the "Japs." Within every minority can be found those who attempt to withdraw from their group and assimilate into the dominant society. Success in this venture often depends on how closely the individual resembles the majority in racial, social-class, or other characteristics. Examples of this type of withdrawal are the straightening of the hair by blacks or the taking of new names by Jews and Mexican-Americans.

The various "power" movements and pride in race and ethnic heritage in recent American history have led to a rise in the avoidance mechanism as a reaction to discrimination or minority status. With their new-found pride, many individuals within the minority communities, and some large groups such as the Black Muslims, have rejected the inferior image of themselves and have segregated themselves from the society at large. Voluntary separation from the society at large is a difficult position to maintain, and the pressure to "give" California to the blacks or New Mexico and Arizona to the Mexican-Americans is called for only by a small percentage of those minority communities. The new militancy among Native Americans, however, has led to greater autonomy on the reservations and attempts to preserve their cultural heritage in a segregated setting. The dominant trend in American society, however, is integration, one very important aspect of which is school integration, which has become the focus of many of the legal battles in recent years.

True integration presupposes the inherent equality of opportunity for all groups, and for this reason, it would appear to be some time in the future before minority citizens will participate fully in all aspects of American culture and society.

RESEARCH ON RACIAL AND ETHNIC ATTITUDES

The classic work dealing with racial and ethnic attitudes is Gunnar Myrdal's *An American Dilemma*, published in 1944. Myrdal used a variety of techniques, including statistics from other studies and many in-depth interviews, to reach his major conclusion: namely that the "Negro problem" at its heart was not a black problem but rather the "white man's attitude toward the Negro."[14] Myrdal outlined his view of the inner-personal struggle within the soul of white America between the American creed of egalitarian ethics and the beliefs about the inherent inferiority of the black race. He also documented at length the discrimination faced by blacks in almost all

[14]Gunnar Myrdal and others, *An American Dilemma: The Negro Problem and Modern Democracy*, 2nd edition (New York: Harper & Row, Publishers, 1962), p. 43.

areas of their lives in this country: economically, politically, educationally, and healthwise. Needless to say, Myrdal's conclusion that the black problem was not due to genetic inferiority, or laziness, did not set too well with the dominant white community. It did, however, have a profound impact on post-World War II legislation and court cases, and began the process of overturning laws not in keeping with the "American Creed," and of changing white attitudes towards the blacks and other minority groups. Standard operating procedures and beliefs were being challenged by a scholar of impeccable credentials, and Americans could no longer turn their backs on the inconsistencies and contradictions in their own belief systems.

Although a great deal of evidence can be brought to bear that Americans are not free of racial prejudice, research studies since 1944 indicate a progressive liberalization in the attitudes of white Americans towards blacks. The Detroit Area Study in 1958 found 54 percent of the white community would be disturbed or unhappy if a black with the same income and education moved into the block. By 1971 this percentage had dropped to 28 percent. On the issue of segregated schools, the percentage in favor dropped from 33 percent to 17 percent in the same period. On intermarriage, which Myrdal and others have found to be the most emotion-laden interracial issue, the researchers documented a drop in opposition from 68 percent in 1969 to 51 percent only two years later in 1971. On children of different races playing together, the percentages rose from 40 percent in favor in 1956 to 79 percent in 1971. The authors of the report indicate that this liberalization of attitudes can be found among all age, educational, and income groups in the society, although not necessarily to the same extent. In the time between two studies done in 1968 and 1971, an interesting shift occurred in the black community. Fewer blacks, 28 percent in 1971 as compared to 42 percent in 1968, believed that whites were really interested in seeing blacks get a better break.[15]

Although white attitudes appear to have liberalized rather dramatically since Myrdal's study, it is obvious that the black community still feels the brunt of discrimination and sees the racist structure of American society as the major obstacle to their success. Racism runs very deep, and blacks in this society believe, probably correctly, that verbalized assent to aspects of the American creed concerning equality of all mankind, is not the same as equal treatment in the marketplace, schools and housing. The busing riots of the middle 70s, most of them racially motivated, are a living proof to blacks that much of the "liberalization" of attitudes in the white community is only skin-deep, and that the division of American society into separate and unequal groups of which Myrdal spoke in the 1940s, the Supreme Court in the fifties and the Douglas Commission in the sixties, is still a continuing reality.

[15]Howard Schuman, "Are Whites Really More Liberal: Blacks Aren't Impressed," *Psychology Today* 8, no. 4 (September, 1974), pp. 82–84.

Figure 7-2   Children Often Bear the Brunt of Ethnic and Racial Discrimination

RACISM AND THE SCHOOLS

Since 1954 and *Brown v. Board of Education*, the schools have become the major battleground in the struggle against racism and for equality of opportunity in American society. That a large percentage of both white and minority children still attend essentially segregated schools twenty-five years after the case is an indication of not only racial attitudes, but the separate and unequal nature of American society. Without a doubt, the largest and most influential study on equality of educational opportunity was conducted by James S. Coleman for the U.S. Office of Education, under mandate from the 1964 Civil Rights Act. It involved over 900,000 children of all races and from all parts of the country in a study of various aspects of the school environment, pupil achievement, and teachers.

The study found in the mid-sixties, a decade after the courts had ruled segregated schools as unconstitutional, that almost 80 percent of the white pupils in first and twelfth grades attended schools that were from 90 to 100 percent white, while 65 percent of the black pupils in first grade attended schools that were between 90 to 100 percent black, with 66 percent at grade twelve in black secondary schools. It also found that in the South most students attended schools that were 100 percent black or white.

Much progress has been made in the decade since the Coleman report was issued, particularly in the South, but the vast majority of whites still attend schools with children who are predominantly of their own race. Integration has been primarily limited to the South and large urban areas of the Northeast, Midwest, and West. In most cases, the integration has been anything but voluntary or peaceful, with the bus bombings in Pontiac, Michigan, and riots in Boston and Louisville being but the most visible evidence of public hostility to court-ordered busing programs. Not all the opposition to busing has been motivated by racism, but there can be little doubt that a significant portion of it stems from the fear which many whites still have of blacks and other minority peoples.[16]

Some of the other data that the Coleman study came up with were that black pupils attend classes that were larger than those attended by white pupils; there were 26 black students per teacher as opposed to 22 for whites; and that blacks had less access to facilities related to academic achievement, such as laboratories, books in the library, and textbooks. They also had less access to curricular and extracurricular programs related to academic achievement. As measured by types of colleges attended, years of experience, educational level of mother, and a score on a thirty-word vocabulary test, black pupils attended schools where teachers appeared to be "somewhat less able." Student body characteristics also differ between the predominantly white and black schools, with blacks attending schools where children come from larger families, whose mothers have less education, and where fewer students are enrolled in college preparatory curricula.[17]

On the tests of achievement, the Coleman study found that with the exception of Oriental-Americans, the average minority student scored distinctly lower than did white pupils, and that the differences increased as the student moved through the grades.[18] Table 7-1 indicates some of the differences found in the testing. As Coleman and his colleagues made clear in the study, the results on Table 7-1 are median scores and should not obscure the fact that large numbers of minority children perform at levels higher than many white children. The study comes to this dismal conclusion:

> Whatever may be the combination of nonschool factors—poverty, community attitudes, low educational level of parents—which put minority children at a disadvantage in verbal and nonverbal skills when they enter first grade, the fact is the schools have not overcome it.[19]

Perhaps the most important conclusion reached in the Coleman study

---

[16]James S. Coleman and others, *Equality of Educational Opportunity* (Washington, D.C.: U.S. Government Printing Office, 1966), p. 3.
[17]Ibid., pp. 9–12.
[18]Ibid., p. 20.
[19]Ibid., p. 21.

Table 7-1 Nationwide median test scores for first- and twelfth-grade pupils, fall 1965

	Racial or ethnic group					
Test	Puerto Ricans	Indian-Americans	Mexican-Americans	Oriental-Americans	Negro	Majority
1st grade:						
Nonverbal	45.8	53.0	50.1	56.6	43.4	54.1
Verbal	44.9	47.8	46.5	51.6	45.4	53.2
12th grade:						
Nonverbal	43.3	47.1	45.0	51.6	40.9	52.0
Verbal	43.1	43.7	43.8	49.6	40.9	52.1
Reading	42.6	44.3	44.2	48.8	42.2	51.9
Mathematics	43.7	45.9	45.5	51.3	41.8	51.8
General information	41.7	44.7	43.3	49.0	40.6	52.2
Average of the 5 tests	43.1	45.1	44.4	50.1	41.1	52.0

was that the differences in facilities, curriculum, or even teachers were not the crucial factors when it came to levels of achievement in school. The most important factor turned out to be the "educational backgrounds and aspirations of the other students in the school."[20] That one innocuous-sounding phrase has proved to have more policy implications for the schools than perhaps any other single statement in our education history. The racial, ethnic, and social-class makeup of each school became the criteria upon which court decision after court decision has been decided in the past decade.

Busing of students has been part of the schooling process for over half a century, with millions of children riding the buses each day in rural and urban areas alike. Black and white children have been bused away from the nearest or neighborhood school to attend segregated institutions, but for the first time the courts mandated that not only should black children be bused to achieve racial balance, but so also should white students. The court orders have encountered opposition and even the violence referred to earlier in this chapter, as parents demanded the right to send their children to the neighborhood school. For the most part, the integration orders have involved the South and the large northern urban areas to which blacks and other minorities have emigrated since World War II. The federal court order in Michigan to integrate Detroit and its suburbs was struck down by the Supreme Court, so that it appears, at least for the time being, that the urban areas—increasingly minority in population—will be integrated, while the suburban areas remain as white, Anglo, middle-class bastions.

The implications of the white flight to the suburbs have been the

[20]Ibid., p. 22.

center of a recent dispute in which Coleman stated his belief, based on studies in the 1970s, that busing had contributed to the white flight and thus has "backfired" in bringing about more segregation.[21] Under attack from a variety of critics who were unable to replicate his findings, Coleman retracted some of his positions. The man whose original research had formed the basis for much of the court-ordered busing in this country found himself invited to speak to antibusing rallies.

The studies on the effects of busing on the achievement levels of minority children are mixed, with some showing significant gains, and others indicating no gains or even slight declines. Almost all studies indicate that busing has no significant effect on the achievement levels of white, Anglo children. It may take many more years for all the effects of integrated education to be known, as they certainly go far beyond academic achievement and into intergroup attitudes, interracial lifestyles, social mobility and a host of related areas. Most studies agree that when the integration process is properly planned for and carried out in a supportive environment, numerous nonacademic benefits can result.

Not all Americans have limited the list of reasons to those given in the Coleman report for the lower achievement on the part of minority children and young people, limited as it was to environmental factors. Arthur Jensen has become a major controversial figure in the field of education by stating that the genetic differences in the races is the crucial factor. The age-old environment-*versus*-heredity battle has thus been joined once again.

The turmoil over nature *versus* nurture or heredity *versus* environment has been going on for centuries, with the emphasis shifting back and forth. In the eighteenth century, with the French and American revolutionary talk of equality, the balance tended to be in favor of the environmental causes for differences; in the nineteenth century, Charles Darwin's evolutionary concepts and the Social Darwinism of Herbert Spencer shifted the thinking towards a genetic basis. The twentieth century saw the rise of IQ testing and attempts to discover the quality of neurological structures. Differences were found within and between groups, with environmental explanations generally being accepted, until Arthur Jensen, an educational psychologist at the University of California at Berkeley, published his article, "How Much Can We Boost IQ and Scholastic Achievement?" in the *Harvard Educational Review* in the spring of 1969.

Jensen rejected the environmental explanations of difference as inadequate and unproven, and presented his evidence that 80 percent of what is measured by IQ tests is the result of genetic endowment and only 20 percent the result of environmental factors. Jensen holds that blacks in the United States score on the average about one standard deviation below

[21]James S. Coleman, "Racial Segregation in the Schools: New Research with New Policy Implications," *Phi Delta Kappan* 57, no. 2 (October, 1975), pp. 75–78.

whites on most tests of intelligence, or the equivalent of about fifteen points, and that this difference has primarily a genetic cause. The mass media soon picked up on Jensen's research, and he became the storm center of controversy throughout the early part of the 1970s, with the debates continuing to the present day. Misinterpretations of Jensen's data were common, threats on his life were made, his classes were disrupted, and professional associations, such as the Society for the Psychological Study of Social Issues (SPSSI) of the American Psychological Association (APA) and the American Anthropological Association (AAA) issued statements and resolutions "condemning" the dangers and unscientific conclusions of Jensen, as well as others, such as Richard Herrnstein and William Shockley, who had written and spoken in defense of Jensen's positions.

Jensen states that success in life is due to many factors besides IQ, and that IQ tests are an imperfect index, but that in spite of its weaknesses, the IQ test is a valid predictor of scholastic performance and occupational attainment for both blacks and whites. He also presents evidence to show that both blacks and whites achieve scores from the top to the bottom, but that "potentially talented" people are seven times more likely to appear in the white group and "mentally retarded" are seven times more likely to appear in the black group. His major genetic argument states that we already know about a vast number of genetically conditioned characteristics which differ between the races, i.e., body characteristics, hair form and pigmentation, bone density, chronic diseases and basic-metabolic rate, to name just a few. He concludes, "wouldn't it be surprising if genetically conditioned mental traits were a major exception?"[22]

Jensen also argues that since there is evidence of substantial heritability of IQ within the white community, it is likely that such also exists among blacks, and that the lower IQ is partially caused by genetic differences. He rejects the common argument that the culture-loading or bias of IQ tests accounts for differences in the white and black population. While admitting that IQ tests are not perfect, he presents a case that blacks tend to do relatively better on culture-loaded or verbal tests than on the culture-fair ones, and that such other minorities as Mexican-, Oriental-, Native, and Puerto Rican-Americans all perform at or above white levels on culturally loaded tests which were standardized with white populations. IQ tests are "colorblind" in their ability to predict performance, he claims, and an internal analysis of items indicates that although sex differences could be found on certain items, no significant racial differences were present. Jensen also rejects the argument that the tester has an effect on the scores received, indicating that in his research, tests administered by black examiners using black dialect had an effect of less than one point on the scores of the black children.

[22] Arthur Jensen, "The Differences are Real," *Psychology Today*, 7, no. 7 (December, 1973), p. 81.

He goes on to reject most of the common environmental explanations for racial IQ differences, such as socio-economic status, education, and nutritional and other health factors, stating that American Indians and Mexican-Americans rank lower on most of these scales than the black population, and yet have higher average scores on most tests at most grade levels than does the black population. Jensen concludes that his work does not "prove" a genetic cause of racial differences, but that he has shown the environmentalist theory to be scientifically unsound.[23]

Jensen rejects the charge that he is a "racist" and states that in no way does he advocate denying equality of opportunity on the basis of race or national origin. His critics, however, state that racists have taken his data and used it in a variety of ways to "prevent true equality of opportunity" from occurring. William Shockley, Nobel laureate for his work with transistors, is one person who jumped on the Jensen bandwagon, and with no training in genetics or testing, he has spent much of the past decade warning America of "dysgenics" and advocating sterilization of low-IQ people. Since such a plan would hit the black community harder than the white, it is understandable that Shockley has been the target of a great deal of hostility.

Richard Herrnstein, in the September, 1971, *The Atlantic Monthly*, accepted Jensen's basic hypothesis about racial differences and took it into the sociological realm, stating that in an open-class system such as ours, the equalization of educational opportunity would lead to a meritocracy in which those with high IQ's would pass on their abilities to their offspring, thus creating a self-perpetuating elite. Hereditary differences increase as we decrease environmental differences. Herrnstein's thesis was not well accepted in the black community either, as it was seen as a justification for not changing the poverty environment in which many blacks find themselves.

A vast amount of polemical literature has been written about the "racism" of Jensen and Herrnstein, men whom we will separate from Shockley and others who have neither their training nor scholarship in the field. Perhaps the most scholarly critic of Jensen is Theodosius Dobzhansky, a world-renowned geneticist, whose article in *Psychology Today* in December, 1973, summarizes the opposing positions without the political rhetoric of many of Jensen's cirtics or the racist rhetoric of many of his defenders.

His first major point is that human equality or inequality are "sociological designs, not biological phenomena,"[24] and that people are not born unequal, but that all people are born different from all others. Dobzhansky rejects the blank slate theory of the extreme environmentalists along with the strict hereditarians who believe that our parental genes control our des-

[23] Ibid., p. 86.
[24] Theodosius Dobzhansky, "Differences are not Deficits," *Psychology Today*, 7, no. 7 (December, 1973), p. 97.

tinies. The only real question is: how much does the environment and how much does our heredity affect our lives? He questions the 80 percent heredity-control figure of Jensen, pointing out that the degree of heritability in other organisms is considerably less. He also points out that "genes determine the intelligence (or stature or weight) of a person only in his particular environment,"[25] and that the interplay of the environment and heredity is the crucial factor. The studies on the rearing of identical twins in the same or separate environments, with greater IQ differences among those raised separately, is compelling evidence of the importance of the environment. He also points out the problems of generalizing from data collected predominantly in the white middle class to other racial and social-class groupings. In rejecting Shockley's views on dysgenics, and Herrnstein's fears of a meritocracy, Dobzhansky points out the well-known phenomenon of the regression towards the mean in which the children of parents with high IQ's will tend to have lower IQ's, with the opposite being true of low-IQ parents, whose children will tend to have higher scores.

The centuries-long racism in American society makes attempts such as Jensen's to correlate or control for social class and other environmental factors unconvincing, according to Dobzhansky. He uses the research of Scarr-Salapatek to lend support to the position that genetic variability is more important in advantaged groups than among the disadvantaged, and since a greater proportion of blacks are among the disadvantaged, at least part of the differences in IQ can be attributed to environmental causes. True to the scientific spirit, Dobzhansky concludes that there is still insufficient information with which to make definitive judgments about the percentage of difference between the races to be accounted for by either environment or heredity.[26]

THE SCHOOL AND RACIAL OR ETHNIC DIFFERENCES

Dobzhansky and other geneticists point out that no matter how strong the genetic conditioning on any particular trait, improvement of the environment can bring about positive change. The important question for the schools of America to face is not what percentage of the IQ differences between the races is environmental or hereditary, but rather how to take each child where he or she is and to maximize that potential. With bills to abolish IQ testing coming up before state legislators in the mid 1970s, it appears that a political decision might put an end to some of the discussion about the possible differences of the races, although scientists will continue to research the issue. IQ tests only measure what the test designer defines

[25]Ibid., p. 98.
[26]Ibid., p. 101.

as intelligence, ignoring a host of other characteristics which might properly be included. Anthropologists, basing their opinions on research among hundreds of groups of every racial and ethnic background, for the most part reject the simplistic notions of American and British testers. Perhaps it is inevitable that a political decision end the debate, as it has been a political decision which led to the use of IQ scores and a host of other mechanisms to institutionalize the racism in American society.

The misuse of IQ tests has not been the only form of institutional racism of which the schools might be accused. Segregated and inferior schooling of the poor and minorities has been the rule not the exception. Only with the pressures of federal courts and federal monies have the schools upgraded education in the inner cities and poor rural areas, and even today, with greater equalization of expenditures, few citizens or educators find the educational systems of our large cities to be as good as those of the suburbs. Until pressures were brought to bear on publishers, textbooks reflected the white, male, Anglo, middle-class perception of reality. Initial attempts to make materials relevant to minorities were ludicrous, with white faces being painted black, and life in the suburbs going on as usual for Dick and Jane. After ten years of pressure, books are finally available which reflect the realities of life for children in most racial and ethnic groups, using a variety of settings from the rural South, the Indian reservation, and the urban barrio.

Textbooks can be replaced, but a tenured, mostly white teaching staff is more difficult to deal with. If racism has been found in textbooks and expenditures, it can, regrettably, also be found among teachers. Teachers come from and reflect the dominant culture in American society, so it is not surprising that a certain percentage would reflect the negative racial attitudes of the society at large. Particularly with the pressures of the women's movement in recent years, affirmative-action hiring programs for women and minorities have started to make headway in bringing more minority members into teaching and administrative positions in our schools. Few systems, however, have anywhere near the same percentage of minority teachers as they have minority children.

One of the problems has been the ineffectiveness of teacher-education institutions in producing minority teachers. The hurdles have been numerous. A poor elementary and/or secondary education has not given minority young people good preparation for colleges and universities. A poor public school education has made it difficult for many minorities to do well on the SAT or other admission tests, thus preventing admission to the colleges. The shock of attending a nearly all-white university, often located in a white suburb, has caused many failures and dropouts, while those who do graduate from college are offered more money by private industry and governmental agencies, all of whom have to fill affirmative-action quotas. Teacher-education programs have not been at the forefront in the fight against racism, so that those minority members who do decide on a teaching career often do not feel at home with a curriculum which prepares them to teach in white, Anglo America. Finally, even though a great deal of progress has been made in preparing minority candidates in recent years, the tremendous drop in the number of available teaching positions has made it difficult for the best-qualified teacher candidates to get jobs. With shrinking tax bases and rising costs, city schools, which might be expected to hire the most minority candidates, are not only not hiring new teachers, but they are in many instances laying off those that are already on their staffs.

Recent state and U.S. Supreme Court decisions indicate that although strides have been made to equalize expenditures, tremendous disparities still exist. All too often, the poorest districts have been rural, Mexican-American barrios in the Southwest, Native American schools in many parts of the country, or black, inner-city ghettoes. State equalization formulas have provided extra money to many districts throughout the country, but with the dependence upon a property tax base for financing the schools, it is unlikely that districts made up of predominantly poor minorities will ever be able to provide a truly "equal" education to that of the rich suburbs. The state courts have, since 1970, begun the process of equalization, although the Federal Supreme Court in overturning *Rodriguez v. San Antonio Independent School District*, stated that equal expenditures for schools was something for the states to decide individually, and that it would not mandate it from the Federal level. A December, 1976, decision by the California Supreme Court may finally settle the question, as it declared the property tax to be inadequate as a method for funding education and for providing equality of educational opportunity. If the case stands up in the U.S. Supreme Court, the system of school finance in almost every state will have to go through a dramatic revision, with profound implications for poorer districts.

In addition to the discriminiation against minorities in textbooks, either through omission or through stereotypes, minorities have been left out of the curriculum in almost all subject areas. The history of blacks, Orientals, Native Americans, and Mexican-Americans has been ignored or distorted in most of our social science textbooks. Heroes of minority groups have too often been left out or portrayed in a less than dignified manner. Cultural contributions in music, art, and literature (oral and written) have seldom made it into anthologies, and for too long black athletes have been exploited, forced into playing only certain positions on athletic teams, and almost never given coaching responsibilities. Too often, "minority studies" programs have been set up to relieve the pressures from minority groups, but all too often the overall curriculum of the school has remained "lily white." True multicultural education is to be found in all too few schools. Racist materials are still used in all too many schools, and another generation is being brought up on many of the same old stereotypes and myths.

Until well into the 1970s, children speaking languages other than English on the school grounds could be punished and even expelled from many of our educational institutions. For most of our history, the schools were a major instrument for wiping out the linguistic heritage which immigrants brought to this country, and which our Native American and Mexican-American population had maintained long after being conquered. The absurdity of wiping out the linguistic competencies of millions of Americans, while spending millions of dollars to teach others those same languages, did not dawn on the society at large until recently. A growing acceptance of cultural pluralism in the past ten years finally led to federal and state bilingual-bicultural programs to teach children in the early grades in their native language (Spanish, French, Chinese, and Vietnamese being among the largest current programs), while at the same time building up a linguistic competency in English.

The history of the treatment of minorities in the schools of America has not been a pretty one. Recent studies by educational historians such as Colin Greer[27] have shown that much of the social mobility that was generally attributed to the schooling process was a myth, and that too often the schools best served the upper class by providing trained manpower, socializing the immigrants into certain acceptable patterns of thought, keeping people out of the job market for extended periods of time, and setting educational standards which assured the preservation of their elite status. Whether one accepts the views of the revisionist historians or not, there can be no denying that although large numbers of minority members did climb the social and economic ladder through the school system, the vast majority were pushed out or dropped out long before the schools could do them much good. Christopher Jencks's reevaluation of the Coleman Report and other research led him to the conclusion that differences in income were not attributable to one's education or cognitive skills.[28] If historically the schools have not served the minorities, and if they are not the crucial factor today in economic success, a question might legitimately be raised about the efficacy of vast expenditures on the educational system. With the failure of so many attempts at improving the education received by our poor and minorities, there appears to be a growing consensus that we have been expecting too much from our schools. To ask school-age children to bear the brunt of integration, while housing and jobs remain segregated, is only a short-term solution, although long-term attitudinal benefits will hopefully result. That social and economic equality will result in a

---

[27]Colin Greer, *The Great School Legend: A Revisionist Interpretation of American Public Education* (New York: The Viking Press, 1972).

[28]Christopher Jencks and others, *Inequality: A Reassessment of the Family and Schooling in America* (New York: Basic Books, Inc., Publishers, 1972), p. 226.

country with a 200-year history of racism is too much to hope for from token busing programs or even an equalization of school expenditures. There are things, however, which the school can do to bring the American dream of equality a little closer to reality.

CONCLUSIONS

As Myrdal astutely pointed out almost forty years ago, racism is basically a white problem, and must be dealt with by the white population. This means ridding ourselves and our institutions of all forms of racism and discrimination. The 1960s taught us that referring to minorities as "culturally deprived" or "culturally disadvantaged" was but another evidence of American racism, and that we must come to an acceptance of cultural difference, not as something inferior, but rather as something to be looked upon as a strength of American society.

Teachers and administrators have been shown to be the key factors in the successful integration of schools. Much of the violence and fear which have plagued the integration effort, particularly in the large northern cities, could have been avoided had educators and school boards been better prepared to work with minority young people and had they accepted their role in striving for an equal society, rather than "fighting against" it in the courts or through open hostility. Human behavior and attitudes change slowly, but if no change is possible, then the educational enterprise is a waste of time and money. Much more must be done in the ways of human-relations training for educators, both at the pre- and in-service levels. The education of teachers must become much more multicultural in nature and include understandings of the history and culture of minority groups.

Recent court cases on the financing of schools offer hope that the poor and minorities will have equal amounts of money spent on their education; but true equality of opportunity would dictate that more money be spent on those from poverty backgrounds to compensate for the economic deprivation experienced at home. Related to the issue of school finance has been that of the control of education. As small school districts were consolidated into larger ones during the 1940s and 1950s, control shifted to ever larger bodies, so that today some school districts consist of hundreds of thousands of children, tens of thousands of teachers, and budgets in the hundreds of millions of dollars. Minority groups have felt particularly oppressed in the large, bureaucratized white-run school systems. This has led to a wide variety of decentralization efforts, beginning in New York and spreading to many other cities throughout the country. Although there is only limited evidence available on the success or failure of decentralization efforts, it appears that a crucial component to any successful educational experience is the active involvement of parents and the community in the schools. Too many of the decentralization experiments have been paper reforms, giving little real power to the minority parents or community. It is our opinion that the dominant white power structure has failed miserably in its attempts to educate the minority children of this country, and that it is now time to turn over much of that effort to the minority community. One mechanism for returning power to the people has been the controversial voucher plan, in which parents are given a voucher for the education of their children, which can be "spent" at any school, public or private, as long as that school meets minimum standards and does not violate state or federal laws. The voucher plan appears to have died after a few brief experiments, due to tremendous opposition from the educational community who perceived in it a real threat to their power.[29]

Teachers' groups, school boards, and administrators must begin to take much stronger positions on affirmative action. All too often the educators have backed such programs only under court order. If white and minority young people are to have role models from the whole range of citizens who make up this society, the schools must be leaders in providing administrators, teachers, janitors, and other school personnel of all races and ethnic groups. Too often IQ and achievement tests have been used to discriminate against minority children, tracking them into low-achieving groups or segregating them within integrated schools. Teachers' expectations of minority young people have been shown to be a crucial factor in their success in school, and although Rosenthal and Jacobson's book *Pygmalion in the Classroom* has been roundly criticized, other research indicates the importance of a teacher's attitude towards children in its effect on their achievement.[30]

Recently developed bilingual-bicultural programs have shown success in teaching basic skills in children's first language while building up their competence in English. Such programs, when only for minority children, are extremely vulnerable from a political standpoint. Only as multilingual-multicultural education becomes something which the majority of American citizens covet for their own children will the real benefits of cultural pluralism be realized in our society. Programs such as Head Start and Follow Through have survived for a decade, and although critics claim their long-term academic effects are minimal, they have provided tens of thousands of preschool and primary grade children with a culturally sensitive, positive learning environment. Studies of self-concept have come in for a lot of criticism in recent years, but the preponderance of evidence indicates that minority children have made great strides in the area of self-

---

[29]Christopher Jencks, "Educational Vouchers: Giving Parents Money to Pay for Schooling," *The New Republic* 163, no. 1 (July 4, 1970), pp. 19–21.

[30]Jere E. Brophy and Thomas L. Good, "Teacher Expectations: Beyond the Pygmalion Controversy," *Phi Delta Kappan* LIV, no. 4 (December, 1972), pp. 276–77.

esteem, no doubt due in part to the "black is beautiful" movement and similar attitudes in society at large and the increasing recognition of minority contributions in the school and society.[31]

That schools can and do make a difference in our society is something upon which critics and defenders alike can agree. Disagreement comes over what mechanisms are most appropriate in our drive to achieve "equality of opportunity." The schools have traditionally followed dominant American values, attitudes, and behavior, and to ask them to take the leadership in changing American society in something so fundamental as race relations may be asking too much. Unless and until the society at large makes a firmer commitment to true equality and equal treatment of all minority groups, attempts at integrating schools are bound to run into hosility. This in no way excuses the schools from promoting a concept of cultural pluralism, but it is a recognition of the fact that we can no longer afford the hypocrisy of asking the schools to bear the brunt of the integration effort, while the worlds of work, housing, and church remain essentially segregated. Much progress has been made. Attitudes are changing, equal financing is slowly becoming a reality, curricula and textbooks reflect the multiethnic nature of American society, and children of different races, ethnic groups and social classes are interacting in our schools. This bodes well for the future of American society; but Myrdal's warning still rings in our ears that the problem of racism is a "white problem," and one fears that many too many Americans are unwilling to face up to that fact.

CASE STUDY: The Newly Integrated School System

Just prior to the beginning of the fall term, the Federal District Court mandated that the school system in which you teach must integrate its schools. In addition to the general mandate, the court is requiring a massive busing program to bring about racial balance in all the elementary and secondary schools in the district. The School Board has been fighting the issue in the courts for many years to prevent integration, and the climate in the community is tense. The night of the ruling fifty buses were blown up by opponents of the decision. Parents have begun to put their homes up for sale, and teachers in some of the formerly all-white schools are seeking to move to the suburbs.

The previously all-white school in which you teach will soon be made up of 50 percent minority children from black and Mexican-American homes. From remarks in the teacher's lounge in past years, you know that many of your colleagues are prejudiced against minority children and gen-

---

[31]Norma Trowbridge, "Self Concept and Socio-economic Status in Elementary School Children," *American Educational Research Journal*, 9, no. 4 (Fall, 1972), pp. 525–37.

erally believe them to be incapable of high-quality academic work. Your principal has been opposed to integration in the past, but with the court order is now desperately trying to prepare the school, the teachers, parents and children in the community for the changes, which are now about to take place.

What feeling do you have about teaching in an integrated setting for the first time? What actions can you take in conjunction with parents, the principal, and fellow teachers, to facilitate a smooth transition to a new type of school? What can you do to make the "new" children feel welcome in your school, and to prevent resentment among the other children, many of whose friends are now being bused elsewhere? What curricular and extracurricular changes do you think might be necessary, given the new makeup of your student body?

THOUGHT QUESTIONS

1. What evidence can you cite that racism and prejudice are not strictly a thing of the historical past, but are still to be found in the United States today?

2. Has any group to which you belong ever suffered discrimination in this country or abroad?

3. For what historical and other reasons have blacks, Mexican-Americans, Native Americans, and Oriental-Americans suffered comparatively greater degrees of discrimination than other ethnic groups in American society?

4. Differentiate between the concepts of cultural pluralism and the melting pot. Bring evidence to bear on which seems to be the dominant theme in American culture today?

5. In *Brown* v. *The Board of Education* (1954), the Supreme Court stated that "separate but equal" schools were inherently unequal. What impact has that court case, and subsequent ones based on it, had on American society since 1954?

6. In the debate over genetic differences of the races, scientists, educators, politicians, and others have lined up on one side or the other. What position do you hold to and what are its implications for education?

7. What mechanisms can be used to provide a truly multicultural education for children in the overwhelmingly white-Anglo suburbs?

8. Why do you agree or disagree with Myrdal's thesis that the racial dilemma facing this country is basically a "white problem?"

9. Martin Luther King and other civil rights advocates have demonstrated the effectiveness of "civil disobedience" in bringing about social and legal

change. Do you agree or disagree with utilizing it, and why? Is violence ever justified to bring about change?

10. Many minority groups in recent years have advocated separatism rather than integration. For what reasons do you back "separate development" or an integrated society?

PRACTICAL ACTIVITIES

1. Visit a bilingual program in a nearby school district and compare the activities, textbooks, teaching materials, and overall program with regular classroom situations.

2. Analyze the textbooks being used in your school for evidence of racial bias. Look for the omission of certain events and individuals, in addition to bias in statements, interpretations, pictures, and illustrations.

3. Visit a school in your district which has a significant number of children or young people of minority descent. What do you observe about the treatment of children of various racial groups? How much segregation and integration do you observe in the classrooms, lunchrooms, and on the playground?

4. Draw a map of a city with which you are familiar. In the map, include general boundary lines between racial or ethnic groups in addition to the general socio-economic class makeup of each area. Estimate the age of the homes and schools in the various parts of the city, and finally, make some generalizations, based on the information included on the map.

5. Survey the course listings of a school district, and list all the courses offered from kindergarten through twelfth grade which deal either directly or indirectly with minority groups in the United States.

6. Obtain copies of standard IQ and Achievement Tests and analyze them for items which evidence cultural or social-class bias.

7. From your own past, detail examples of bias or prejudice which you have experienced or observed, and tell how you felt in the situation.

8. Design a lesson plan, appropriate for the grade level you hope to teach, which deals with personal and societal prejudice.

9. Obtain a copy of a simulation game which deals with prejudice, i.e., Star Power, Hang-Up, or Ghetto. Play the game with a group of friends or with a class of students. Briefly describe what occurred in the game and give your analysis of what can be learned from such simulations.

10. Obtain a copy of a case in which the courts mandated some form of racial integration of schools. List the major reasons the court gave for its decision, and then using newspapers or magazines, document what happened in the community following the court-ordered integration.

BIBLIOGRAPHY

ALLPORT, GORDON W., *The Nature of Prejudice*. Garden City, N.Y.: Addison-Wesley Publishing Company, Inc., 1954.

BROWN, DEE, *Bury My Heart at Wounded Knee*. New York: Bantam Books, 1971.

DELORIA, VINE, *Custer Died for Your Sins* (New York: Macmillan Publishing Co., Inc.).

GRAMBS, JEAN DRESDEN, *Intergroup Education: Methods and Materials*. Englewood Cliffs, N.J.: Prentice-Hall, Inc., 1968.

GRIER, WILLIAM H., AND PRICE M. COBBS, *Black Rage*. New York: Basic Books, Inc., Publishers, 1968.

ITZKOFF, SEYMOUR, *Cultural Pluralism and American Education*. Scranton, Pa.: International Textbook Company, 1969.

MALCOLM X., *The Autobiography of Malcolm X*. New York: Grove Press, Inc., 1966.

MONTAGU, ASHLEY, *Man's Most Dangerous Myth: The Fallacy of Race* (5th ed.). New York: Oxford University Press, 1974.

MYRDAL, GUNNAR, AND OTHERS, *An American Dilemma: The Negro Problem and Modern Democracy* (2nd ed.). New York: Harper & Row, Publishers, 1962.

Psychology Today, 7, no. 7 (December, 1973).

ROSE, PETER I., *They and We: Racial and Ethnic Relations in the United States*. New York: Random House, Inc., 1968.

STEINER, STAN, *The Mexican Americans*. New York: Colophon Books, Harper & Row, Publishers, 1970.

―――, *The New Indians*. New York: Harper & Row, Publishers, 1968.

8

SEXISM
Sugar, Spice, and Sports

With the publication of Betty Friedan's *The Feminine Mystique* in 1963, the women's movement, although centuries old, received a new impetus. Sexism, the prescribing and limiting of roles for either sex, has been part of American society since its founding, and also goes back into the earliest history of almost every tribe and nation. Ms. Friedan touched a responsive chord for millions of Americans with her ability to express the alienation and discrimination felt by overworked housewives, underpaid women in dead-end jobs, welfare mothers, professional women who had been discriminated against, and men who saw the limitations of their own chauvinist behavior.

HISTORICAL BACKGROUND

Sexism did not spring up in the 1960s, nor did efforts to alleviate it begin at that time. Patriarchal systems go back at least as far as Old Testament times, with the Genesis account of creation stating:

> And the rib; which the Lord God had taken from man; made he a woman and brought her unto the man. . . . Unto the woman God said; I will greatly multiply thy sorrow and thy conceptions; in sorrow thou shalt bring forth children: and thy desire shall be to thy husband; and he shall rule over thee.

The apostle Paul updated the sexism and helped to institutionalize it into the Christian church. In I Corinthians 11, he states:

> The head of the woman is the man . . . the woman is the glory of man . . . for neither was the man created for the woman, but the woman for the man.

and again in I Timothy 2:

> Let a woman learn in quietness with all subjection. But I permit not a woman to teach, nor to have dominion over a man, but to be in quietness.

The Orthodox Jewish prayer which states "Blessed art Thou, oh Lord our God, King of the Universe, that I was not born a woman," and the Koranic text which states that "Men are superior to women on account of the qualities in which God has given them preeminence," show that not only Christianity, but others of the world's leading religions have promoted sexist ideology for centuries.

Although Plato in his *Republic* apppears to advocate equality of the sexes, Aristotle placed women in an inferior role in his *Politics* and other writings, and with the use of Aristotle's writing as a basis for much of his own work, St. Thomas Aquinas, the Roman Catholic theologian of the middle ages, set the basis for centuries of discrimination against women in the church and society at large. The Reformation did little to help matters, as the Protestant churches and new nation states did not emancipate women. This was as true in Puritan New England as it was in Great Britain, France, and Russia.

Patriarchies, systems built around the supremacy of the male head of the household and the inferior status of women, are not unique to religions but can be found in social, political, and economic systems throughout our collective history. Property, titles, kingships, and a host of others privileges were passed on through the male line, and women were barred from owning property or participating in any meaningful way in the political life of the community. Not until the 1920s were women given the right to vote in the United States, long after former male slaves had been given the franchise.

The litany of sexism in our history and that of almost every country of the world would take volumes to fill. Suffice it to say that although many of the outward forms of discrimination have been struck down by the courts in this country, overt sexism still reigns supreme throughout most of the world, and the centuries and millenia of sexual discrimination, even in the more progressive societies, make it a problem whose complete solution will no doubt take generations to achieve. Child-rearing practices, language usage, educational influences of our schools and mass media, stereotyping in the world of work, and a wide variety of other cultural cues make the purging of sexism in our society a long-term task.

Nature versus Liberation

The battle lines have been drawn in the United States between the feminists on one side and an assorted group of opponents on the other. Benjamin Barber suggests that it is not a war between men and women, but rather "a war between nature and liberation, between biology and self-determination, invented to reconcile men to women's aspirations—or to contain women within men's realities."[1] On the one side have been such diverse organizations as the National Organization of Women (NOW), women's political caucuses, and radical Lesbians, while in opposition one can find groups such as Fascinating Womanhood and some religious organizations, along with men such as Stephen Goldberg, proclaiming *The Inevitability of Patriarchy*,[2] and using a variety of anthropological or religious arguments. Barber deals in detail with the arguments on both sides of the issue, and concludes that the war is unnecessary, contrived, and unreasonable, but that the escalating rhetoric has clouded the real issues, and made rational debate and resolution nearly impossible.

Although agreement among all feminists on each issue is impossible to achieve, five basic premises do appear in much of the literature of the war on nature:

> Women are oppressed, both by nature and by the appeal to nature.
> Men and marriage are natural obstacles to women's human fulfillment as persons.
> Monogamous marriage and the nuclear family are crucial instruments in capitalism's system of nature exploitation.
> Romantic love is the ideology of naturalist sexism.
> Femininity and natural sexual differentiation are inimical to and ultimately incompatible with human equality and liberated personhood.[3]

It is obvious to even the most casual reader, that these positions are the extremes, and that few individuals or feminist groups would subscribe wholeheartedly to all of them, but they do form the core of the argument "against nature," and thus must be dealt with.

The argument that women are oppressed has been advanced by hundreds of writers, going back long before the Women's Movement of the 1960s and 1970s. The argument is epitomized by the expression "Woman as Nigger," used by Naomi Weinstein in her October, 1969, article in *Psychology Today*.[4] That women have been discriminated against, put down,

---

[1]Benjamin Barber, *Liberating Feminism* (New York: Dell Publishing Co., 1975), p. 1.
[2]Stephen Goldberg, *The Inevitability of Patriarchy* (New York: William Morrow and Company, Inc. 1973).
[3]Barber, *Liberating Feminism*, p. 26.
[4]Naomi Weinstein, "Woman as Nigger," *Psychology Today* 3, no. 20 (October, 1969), pp. 20, 22, 58.

and abused, there can be no disagreement; but Barber and others take exception to the use of the word "oppression," stating that to compare the injustices suffered by discontented middle-class, white, American housewives with the suffering of the starving, disease-riddled masses of the Third World or even the black citizens of our own society, is to debase the argument.

In recent years, the rhetoric against marriage appears to have lessened with the recognition that marriage, homemaking, child-rearing and other "domestic" activities are no more boring, possessive, or inimical to growth than most other institutional and personal relationships in the society. This did not prevent many people from being hurt in the process of discovering that being released from the pressures of a stifling marriage did not automatically turn one into a creative artist, an unselfish sharing human being, or whatever other goals the freedom-seeking individual might have had in mind. There can be no question but that marriage and child-rearing are difficult tasks, but to deny the evolutionary history of people and advocate their abolishment, as have some radical feminists, can only lead one to conclude that in such a narcissistic Brave New World, children might be left to raise themselves or die, and that ultimately the species would pass from the earth.

In response to the argument that the nuclear family is but a part of the oppressive capitalist system, it might be argued that rather than being part of the exploitation, it is one of the last aspects of social relations that has not been brought totally under the legal, contractual system, and that it is one of the few aspects of modern life in which trust and affection take precedence over law.

Critics of the liberationists state that androgynous personhood is not the only solution to the inequality faced by women today; that just as blacks came to prize their blackness, women must come to prize their womanhood; and that differentiation of the sexes need not imply lesser capacity on the part of one sex or the other. From a political perspective, equality of treatment and opportunity must be guaranteed, but in order to achieve such equality, there is no need to wipe out all natural differences.

The antiliberationists are a mixed group, as stated earlier, varying from the conservative religious perspectives of Helen B. Andelin and her *Fascinating Womanhood* and the pop psychology of Maribell Morgan to the critiques of Norman Mailer, Midge Decter, and Esther Vilar. Perhaps the most clearly stated of the naturalist positions is that of Stephen Goldberg in his *The Inevitability of Patriarchy*.

Given the logical inconsistency, scientific absurdity, and moral insensitivity of the arguments of Andelin and Morgan, one is tempted to dismiss their arguments out of hand, but because of the massive sales of their books, the growth of their "women's" groups, and the general popularity of their positions in the mass media and among large numbers of women and men, one must give at least some cursory attention to their positions. Their basic premise is that nature and God have placed women in a subordinate position and that it is their duty to remain happy, dependent, and feminine in that inferior position. Success by wives in careers outside the home is generally seen as a threat to the fragile male ego and a breaking of "God's Law" that woman's place is in the home. The man is the head of the household, and it is his role to serve as patriarch, priest, and provider, and the woman must do everything in her power to help him succeed. Numerous "rules" are given the housewife to follow to help her become the "Domestic Goddess." Place your faith in your man. Do not excel him in any "masculine" area. "Revere your husband and honor his right to rule you and his children."[5]

A little more difficult to deal with than Andelin and Morgan, if only because of the quality of their writing, are such "naturalists" as Goldberg and Mailer, whose basic position differs little from their less intellectual allies. Goldberg states it as:

> The three institutions of patriarchy, male dominance, and male attainment of high-status suprafamilial roles and positions are universal, possibly manifestations of biological sexual differentiation.[6]

Some naturalists, among them Montagu and Vilar, hold that women are naturally superior, but most appear to hold to their positions strictly to justify the status quo power positions of men, and attempt to ignore or gloss over the gross injustices faced by women throughout all of history. Goldberg and others hold that the male hormone, testosterone, leads to greater aggressiveness on the part of the male of the species and that male leadership and authority are thus a "natural" condition.[7] While liberationists argue that the socialization process is in need of change, in order to help females escape their second-class citizenship, Goldberg argues that the biological realities make it imperative that females continue to be socialized, so that they do not need to compete in areas in which they cannot possibly succeed. Traditional "female" emotions of love, tenderness, and kindness are things to be promoted, not the aggressiveness and power needs of the male, they claim, and if through changes in the socialization process we deny these basic realities, women are bound to lose.

The naturalist arguments can be attacked on several grounds. The first is their lack of a sense of history. People are not only shaped by their nature, but in turn help to shape and redefine it. Naturalists with their dependence upon ethology, the study of our species' nature, ignore not only history, but sociology, ethics, and political theory, all of which have a great

[5] Helen B. Andelin, *Fascinating Womanhood*, 16th printing (Santa Barbara, Calif.: Pacific Press, 1970), p. 148.
[6] Goldberg, *The Inevitability*, p. 73.
[7] Ibid., p. 47.

deal to say about the dilemmas of modern women. The bondage of nature that forced people to work sixteen-hour days to eke out an existence has been broken, as has the dehumanization of women who had to give birth to ten children in order for two or three to live. The only question remaining is not what is natural to being human, but rather what politics and values do we choose to live by. In this we are no longer slaves to "nature," and the naturalist arguments crumble. Just because we observe aggressiveness, murder, rape, and disease in the "natural" world is no reason for such to become or continue to be the norm in the world of human beings.

Barber concludes his discussion of the war between nature and liberation with the following profound statement:

> And so the warriors leave the rest of us with a terrible choice, an impossible choice: natural slavery or liberated androgyny, a natural, apolitical, inequitable heterosexuality that buys species survival with permanent injustice, or an unnatural, apolitical, equitable unisexuality that purchases personhood at the price of sexuality.[8]

Only as we discover and create the mechanisms for providing equality and justice, while continuing to permit sexual differentiation to exist, will the species continue to be propagated and nourished and neither sex be asked to be less than fully human persons.

Many issues concerning sexism in American society are being decided in the courts and it is to the legal questions and cases that we now turn our attention.

SEXISM AND THE LAW

The proposed Equal Rights Amendment (ERA) states, "Equality of rights under the law shall not be abridged by the United States or by any state on account of sex." With its passage to the Constitution by Congress in 1972, there was a great deal of hope that the long struggle for equality might finally be over, and those hopes were further strengthened by the fact that by the end of 1973, thirty of the necessary thirty-eight states had ratified the amendment. Hopes were soon dashed, however, as the opposition began to defeat the Amendment in the other twenty states, and even began the (possibly unconstitutional) process of withdrawing ratification in some of those states where it had been passed. Strong support for the amendment by both Presidents Ford and Carter, along with the active campaigning by both Mrs. Ford and Mrs. Carter, have not been sufficient cause to persuade state legislators to back the amendment, so that as of this writing, the amendment still has not been passed.

For over fifty years, feminists have attempted to get an equal rights

---

[8]Barber, *Liberating Feminism*, p. 109.

amendment to the Constitution only to find it bottled up in Congress. From 1950 to 1970, Representative Emanuel Celler (Dem.-N.Y.) kept it in his Judiciary Committee until Representative Martha Griffiths pried it loose. Legal discrimination against women goes back into British common laws and practices, and the subsequent adoption of many of the same laws and practices in the United States was based on the old common-law fiction that the husband and wife are one and that the one is the husband. fiction that the husband and wife are one and that the one is the husband. Many aspects of the modern American marriage ceremony indicate the subordinate position of the woman in the relationship, not just the promise to "love, honor, and obey," the husband. The traditions go back into Biblical passages and religious traditions of the early church, which later came to be written into law. This has come all the way down to the present day in the United States where it is estimated there are still hundreds of state laws which discriminate against a married woman's right to obtain loans in her own name, buy property, inherit or control the family's wealth. Slowly these laws are being struck down by the courts, primarily in response to the Civil Rights Act of 1964, which prohibits discrimination based on "race, color, religion, national origin, or sex." Behavior and attitudes seldom change as rapidly as the law, however; and so, married women, although they have greater legal and economic protection today than at any point in our history, generally give up their maiden name to "take on their husband's identity," wear white wedding dresses to signify their purity while the double standard permits promiscuity in the groom, generally must claim their husband's domicile as their own, and are subject to a variety of other legal and traditional constraints that make them into second-class citizens.

    Until Title VII of the Civil Rights Act of 1964 was extended in March, 1972, to cover state and local government employers, most cases involving public employees were brought under the equal protection clause of the Fourteenth Amendment. Title VII of the Civil Rights Act specifies the areas in which sexual or other discrimination is prohibited: retirement and insurance programs, promotions, sick leaves and vacations, employment advertising, recruitment, wages, conditions of employment, hiring, firing, layoff, recall, and assignment. Alleged violations of Title VII can be brought before the Equal Employment Opportunities Commission (EEOC), which investigates the complaint and seeks voluntary compliance by the employer. The commission attempts conciliation and may press for compensation if discrimination is found. If voluntary compliance fails, the EEOC may bring suit against a private employer, employment agency, or labor union; cases involving state and local government are referred to the U.S. attorney general.[9] Additional legal recourse is provided by Executive Orders 11246, 11375, and Revised Order No. 4.

[9]Charlotte B. Hallam, "Legal Tools to Fight Discrimination," *Phi Delta Kappan*, LY, no. 2 (October, 1973), p. 130.

Title IX of the Education Amendments of 1972 is without question the most powerful tool to prevent discrimination based on sex in educational establishments of this country. It states:

> No person in the United States shall, on the basis of sex, be excluded from participation in, be denied the benefits of, or be subjected to discrimination under any education program receiving federal financial assistance.

Almost all public school systems and institutions of higher education receive some form of federal assistance, and thus come under the jurisdiction of Title IX. The Revised Title IX Amendments were not submitted to Congress until June, 1975, and immediately created a whirlwind of excitement and opposition. In the years since their promulgation, however, most educational institutions have learned to live with them, and have found that many "traditional" ways of dealing with males and females in the schools could be eliminated with little or no problem.

In the area of admissions, schools may not discriminate, except in the case of all-male or -female institutions and those church-related colleges where beliefs prohibit participation of both sexes in certain activities. All students must be permitted to take any course in the curriculum, and home economics courses or shop courses may not be required unless they are required of both sexes. Guidance testing and other mechanisms used to track males or females into certain programs or occupations are prohibited, as are job employment opportunities which differentiate between boys and girls. Without a doubt, the most controversial aspect of the regulations deals with athletics and physical education, and, as might have been expected, the issue has still not been settled years after the regulation was first promulgated. Because of the nature and depth of the discussion and arguments, the effects of Title IX on athletics are dealt with in a special section.

ATHLETICS

Few things are as close to the American people as athletics, and in few other aspects of our culture are the American people as chauvinist in their attitudes as they are in sports. This chauvinism has been seen on the national scale in the Olympics in our desperate need to "beat the Russians, East Germans, Cubans," or whoever else is perceived as challenging our supremacy, but it is also seen in the sexual realm, where any suggestion that women's sports should be given equal treatment and funding leads to an outcry that athletics are doomed, the male ego will be destroyed, women can't compete, and a host of other sexist statements.

The public schools and colleges have made some progress in recent years to equalize opportunity for girls and women in intramural and interscholastic athletics, but the thornier issues of equal expenditures and facilities are a long way from being resolved. Progress has generally been made under pressure from the courts, who have ordered the integration of noncontact sports in the schools and Little League baseball, when teams for girls were not provided. Studies indicate, however, that very few school districts provide an equal number of sports for girls and boys, with the ratio still being 2 to 1 in favor of the boys in most school districts. Expenditures are even more lopsided, where ratios of 5 and 9 to 1 are not uncommon, in favor of the boys. The discrimination takes many forms other than equality of access and expenditure.

Sex-role stereotyping of the sports themselves often occurs, with girls being encouraged to go into gymnastics, figure skating, or swimming, in addition to such "noncontact sports" as golf and tennis, while the team sports such as baseball, football, soccer, and basketball are left to the boys. Even when girls are permitted into the team sports, they find them to be gender separated, so that only in a few rare instances are girls permitted to compete on the same team with boys.

Separation of the sexes in athletics is justified by coaches, administrators, and others on a variety of grounds. Females are portrayed as the "weaker" sex, even though there is a growing body of evidence that from the standpoint of resistance to disease and other medical phenomena, women are the "stronger" of the sexes. There is also evidence that variations of strength within one sex are greater than the differences between the sexes, and although males may on the average be stronger than females, this is no reason to prevent women and girls from competing with men or against each other in any sport. For centuries, women have been doing manual labor involving massive amounts of energy, so to declare the present generation of females physiologically incompetent of participation in rigorous physical activity is to ignore our whole history.

It becomes obvious that most of the arguments about female participation in athletics have to do with sex-role stereotyping, where males are seen as aggressive, competitive and strong, and the females are viewed as nonaggressive and fragile. Girls are not rewarded for strength and endurance, while boys are discriminated against if they show such signs of "weakness" as crying or supportive behavior. Other arguments state that the female is incapable of participating in the active sports due to her greater propensity for injury, but once again the evidence does not bear this out, and in the most sensitive part of the anatomy, the reproductive system, a strong case can be made that the female is more "protected" from injury than the male.

Although Title IX has begun the process of reversing discrimination against women in athletics and physical education, the discrimination has been so prevalent and long-standing that equal treatment may be several more years in the making. Girls' gymnasiums have traditionally been smaller and more poorly equipped, with inadequate locker rooms and other facilities. Until recently, one was hard put to find women coaches being paid for their extra coaching duties, although it has been traditional to pay men for the same services. Men have been thought to be capable of coaching women's sports, but even today, very few women can be found coaching male or even coeducational teams. Refereeing is a male bastion, even in interscholastic female sports, while the few female officials are generally paid on a lower scale than their male counterparts.

With the possible exception of the Iowa Girls Basketball Association, female sports have traditionally taken second place to the male sports at both the secondary and university levels. A limited number of scholarships for female athletes have now become available, some travel money is now set aside for girls' teams, girls' uniforms are finally being bought by the schools, and girls' games are no longer only played as an adjunct to the "real" contest, the boys' games. Changes have begun, but in most cases it has taken a state or federal court suit to bring about equal treatment.

The society at large is slowly beginning to accept changes in the stereotypes of appropriate behavior for each of the sexes, resulting in a rise in female teams in most sports, and even coeducational teams in such sports as soccer. Males are learning to dance, figure skate, jump rope, and express emotions other than the aggressiveness and competitiveness which the old "macho" images forced upon them, while females now have more of the necessary permissions to express aggressiveness and to escape their programmed passivity. As girls have been able to express their athletic ability, the male ego has not suffered the predicted shattering, nor has the quality of male sports declined.

Sexist behavior has been and is being changed by court order, political pressure by groups such as NOW, and laws and regulations such as those in Title IX. The battle for equal opportunity for both sexes in athletics and physical education is a long way from over, for the attitudes of far too many coaches, administrators, and parents have not been sufficiently changed; but evidence from the civil rights movement and a host of other societal changes, indicate that behavioral change can and must be legislated first, and only then will attitudes begin to catch up with the new realities.

JOBS AND EMPLOYMENT

With all the publicity surrounding affirmative action programs in various sectors of the labor market, one might expect that the place of the American woman in the marketplace had improved greatly in recent years. Advertisements proclaim that "we've come a long way baby," but the objective evidence does not substantiate this claim. Although women constitute 51 percent of the population, their low share in almost every other statistical category is grossly disproportionate.

Table 8-1 Comparison of Median Earnings of Year-Round Full-Time Workers, by Sex, 1955—1974 (Persons 14 years of age and over)

Year	Median earnings Women (1)	Median earnings Men (2)	Earnings gap in dollars (3)	Women's earnings as a percent of men's (4)	Percent men's earnings exceeded women's (5)	Earnings gap in constant 1967 dollars (6)
1974	$6,772	$11,835	$5,063	57.2	74.8	$3,433
1970	5,323	8,966	3,643	59.4	68.4	3,133
1965	3,823	6,375	2,552	60.0	66.8	2,700
1960	3,293	5,417	2,124	60.8	64.5	2,394
1955	2,719	4,252	1,533	63.9	56.4	1,911

Notes: For 1970 and 1974, data include wage and salary income and earnings from self-employment; for 1965 and before, data include wage and salary income only.

Column 3 = column 2 minus column 1.
Column 4 = column 1 divided by column 2.
Column 5 = column 3 divided by column 1.
Column 6 = column 3 times the purchasing power of the consumer dollar (1967 = $1.00).

Source: U. S. Department of Commerce, Bureau of the Census: "Money Income of Families and Persons in the United States," Current Population Reports, 1957 to 1975. U.S. Department of Labor, Bureau of Labor Statistics: *Handbook of Labor Statistics*, 1975.

Women's salaries have risen with men's over the past twenty years, but the Labor Department Statistics for 1955–1974 indicate that the gap between the two has actually widened, and that women in 1974 were only earning 57.2 percent as much as men. Recent cases before the EEOC have brought about some equalization of salaries between the sexes within certain occupational groups, but the vast majority of working women find themselves concentrated in low-paying, dead-end occupations, making up over 70 percent of all clerical workers, 90 percent or more of all household workers, and over 50 percent in service occupations. These statistics do not even include the millions of American women who are denied social security or other governmental benefits such as a minimum wage because they work in their own homes. When the salaries of people in the same general occupational categories are compared, the inequities become even more obvious.

Other interesting statistics for 1974 reveal further aspects of female deprivation in employment. Among women, 8.4 percent of those working full time earn less than $3,000 per year, and only 3.5 percent make over $15,000, while the respective figures for males are 4.6 percent under $3,000 and 28.9 percent over $15,000.[10] When educational levels are controlled for, women suffer discrimination, regardless of educational level.

[10] U.S. Department of Labor Employment Standards Administration, Women's Bureau, *The Earnings GAP Between Women and Men* (Washington, D.C., Department of Labor, 1976), p. 6.

Table 8-2 Total Money Earnings of Civilian Year-Round Full-Time Workers, by Occupation Group and Sex, 1974(Persons 14 years of age and over)

Occupation group	Women	Men	Dollar gap	Women's earnings as a percent of men's	Percent men's earnings exceeded women's
Total	$6,772	$11,835	$5,063	57.2	74.8
Professional, technical, and kindred workers	9,570	14,873	5,303	64.3	55.4
Managers and administrators	8,603	15,425	6,822	55.8	79.3
Sales workers, total	5,168	12,523	7,355	41.3	142.3
Retail trade	4,734	9,125	4,391	51.9	92.8
Other sales workers	8,452	13,983	5,531	60.4	65.4
Clerical workers	6,827	11,514	4,687	59.3	68.7
Craft and kindred workers	6,492	12,028	5,586	54.0	85.3
Operatives (including transport)	5,766	10,176	4,410	56.7	76.5
Service workers (except private household)	5,046	8,638	3,592	58.4	71.2
Farmers and farm managers	*	5,459	—	—	—
Farm laborers and supervisors	*	5,097	—	—	—
Nonfarm laborers	5,891	8,145	2,254	72.3	38.3
Private household workers	2,676	*	—	—	—

*Base fewer than 75,000.
Source: U.S. Department of Labor, Bureau of Labor Statistics: Current Population Reports, P-60, No. 101.

Salaries of women with less than an eighth grade education are 63.5 percent of comparably educated males' salaries, while women with five or more years of college make 64.7 percent of the males' salaries at the same educational level.[11]

In most broad job categories, such as education, women are concentrated in the lower-paid teaching positions, while males hold over 80 percent of higher-paid administrative posts. This is true in almost every line of work, but even when women and men are found in identical professional positions, women's salaries have been found to be on the average only 76.3 percent that of men's salaries, with a low of 67.3 percent among chemists and a high of 86.9 percent among linguists.[12] Federal pressure for affirmative action in the early 1970s helped to equalize salaries in many large universities and in corporations doing business with the federal government, and pressures to hire women in administrative and managerial positions

[11] Ibid., p. 10.
[12] National Science Foundation: "National Register of Scientific and Technical Personnel," 1970.

have brought about some equalization; but for women who work in low-paying jobs, such as waitresses, or as homemakers, little has changed.

Discrimination can also be seen in a variety of other statistics, and in the attitudes women must face in the job market. The unemployment rate for women is higher than for men, and the figures do not include the large numbers of women who have given up looking for a job simply because nothing was available. The lowest salaries and highest unemployment rates tend to be among black women, who suffer from the double discrimination of both race and sex.

Lower pay for women is often justified by the statement that their salaries are strictly "luxury," and that they can live off their husbands' income and really do not need to work. This ignores a basic reality of American life in the final quarter of the twentieth century: namely, that over 40 percent of the working women in this country need to work in order to support their families because of death or disablement of a spouse or divorce. Some statistics indicate that over two-thirds of all the adult poor in this country today are women, and also that many women work because their husbands' salaries are too inadequate to support the family even at a basic poverty level.

Women of child-bearing age have been denied jobs because they might get pregnant, and until recently, pregnant women were dismissed or forced to take leaves of absence, even when their health or that of the fetus were in no way influenced by the work involved. Absenteeism among women is lower than for men in almost all age groups, and significantly more so among older people. Even though women hold a disproportionate number of dead-end jobs, their turnover rates are no higher than for men. With automation, few jobs today require strength, yet there still can be found obsolete job descriptions listing weight and height limits. For centuries women have labored in the fields, mines, and factories; yet today find themselves kept out of many jobs which their female ancestors competently filled.

An overt example of discrimination in employment has been sexually segregated want-ads. It was not until 1968 that the EEOC found that Male/Female want ads, like ones that listed white and black, were a violation of the civil rights of the individual job seekers. Segregated want-ads were generally justified on the basis that there are fundamental differences between the sexes which manifest themselves in job preferences. A study by Bem and Bem at Carnegie-Mellon University indicates that sex-segregated want-ads discouraged women from applying for jobs under the male-interest category, even when they were trained for the position. Women preferred jobs listed under the "female-interest" category, when the ads were sex-segregated. When the jobs were listed alphabetically and "male" and "female" advertisements were integrated, women's true preferences came out, with 81 percent preferring jobs previously listed under the "male interest" category.[13]

Mothers who work must all too often be prepared to take not only a full-time job outside the home, but continue to carry the load of housework and child care, unless the husband shifts his own priorities to pick up a greater share of the homemaking responsibilities. There is still a great deal of latent prejudice against the idea of working mothers, particularly those with pre-school-age children. The wife of one of the authors was told to "choose between her career as a nurse and her family." Many women are caught between their own needs for job fulfillment and the pressures of their husbands "to keep the house and cook the meals as you did before you went back to work." Unless the husband's position permits him the flexibility to care for the children, unless there are adequate, affordable day-care facilities, children are often left to their own devices, bringing about one of the important societal questions being asked in the late seventies, "Who is raising the kids?" All too often, no one is, and it is the working mother who takes an unfair share of the blame in modern society.

The effects of "maternal deprivation" on very young children have not been clearly established. Most of the studies have used children who had been in institutionalized settings, twenty-four hours a day, and in these studies, detrimental effects, including retardation, appear to occur with greater than normal regularity. Children separated from their parents during working hours and in stable care situations appear to suffer few, if any, ill effects, and some research would indicate that such children exhibit greater independence, possibly because of their ability to interact with several adults. Studies done in other countries, such as the Soviet Union and in Israel on the kibbutz, do not indicate any harmful effects of communal childbearing patterns, but one cannot extrapolate from these communal child-rearing settings to the highly individualistic family settings found in the United States.

LANGUAGE

The campaign to do away with sexist aspects of English language usage by the United States has provoked a considerable backlash, not only by male chauvinists, but also by linguists and others who see it as an attack at one of the foundations of our society. Burr, Dunn, and Farquhar in their article in *Social Education* set the stage for the battle by stating:

> A language is not merely a means of communication, it is also an expression of shared assumptions. Language thus transmits implicit values and be-

---

[13]Sandra L. Bem and Daryl J. Bem, "Sex-Segregated Want Ads: Do They Discourage Female Job Applicants?" (Pittsburgh, Pa.: Know, Inc.).

havioral models to all those people who use it. When basic assumptions change, the idioms which express them become obsolete.[14]

The authors go on to make a strong case that our language usage has operated to exclude females, by the use of the words "men" or "man" as generic terms, the use of "he" when both he and she are meant, and through the naming of such anthropological discoveries as the Java Man, when it is obvious that the race must have included females. They argue that ambiguity alone would be enough reason to replace sexist words with more all-inclusive or neutral terms, for example, "people" or "citizens" for "men" or "mankind," or the use of "ancestors" for "forefathers." Under present usage, women are not permitted to represent people, while men are.

The linguistic backlash has often taken a more chauvinist than scholarly turn, with such absurdities being raised as changing the names of literary masterpieces to *A Person for All Seasons*, or *Death of a Sales-Person*, or the names of capitals to Amperson, Jordan, or Personila, Philippines. Such put-downs do little but show the insensitivity of many persons to the psychological implications of a sexist language, and are but a further indication of the kind of language which is used to keep women in their place. Real strides have been made in dealing with sexist pictures and materials in textbooks, but the depth to which male terminology dominates the language of the mass media and popular usage indicates a long battle.

ASPIRATIONS AND FEAR OF SUCCESS

In 1968, Matina Horner completed her research dealing with why women fear success, and her results were published in a variety of scholarly and popular journals and newspapers. She had obviously touched a responsive chord, and was dealing with a problem first pointed up some years before by David McClelland, John Atkinson, and others in their work on "achievement motivation," using the Thematic Apperception Test (TAT). Women were generally excluded from most of the early research on achievement motivation, so Horner and a growing number of psychologists since that time have attempted to deal with the issue.

Horner hypothesized that fear of success (FOS) would be far more prevalent among women than among men, that FOS would be more characteristic of women capable of success than of the population at large, and that for such women anxiety would be greater in competitive situations than in noncompetitive situations. She used the standard Thematic Apperception Test and also asked the 178 students in the sample to tell a story based on the following clue: "After first-term finals, John (Anne) finds him-

[14]Elizabeth Burr, Susan Dunn, and Norman Farquhar, "Women and the Language of Inequality," *Social Education* 36, no. 8 (December, 1972), p. 841.

self (herself) at the top of his (her) medical-school class." Sixty-five percent of the girls wrote stories which evidenced anxiety about the girl (Anne) becoming unpopular, unmarriageable, lonely, and unfeminine, or denying that any women could be so successful. Only 10 percent of the boys showed the same FOS. In a related study, she found that when placed in a competitive situation, girls who evidenced fear of success did more poorly, while a much larger percentage of boys thrived on the competitive situation.[15] Horner concludes:

> In recent years many legal and educational barriers to female achievement have been removed; but it is clear that a psychological barrier remains. The motive to avoid success has an all-too-important influence on the intellectual and professional lives of women in our society.[16]

Others have picked up on the same theme and have suggested that the basic problem is one of aspiration, not ability, as there is abundant evidence that girls graduating from high school and going on to college do so with higher achievement records than boys.

David Tresemer, in *Psychology Today* in 1974, reported on his research, which calls into question many of the basic assumptions and findings of Horner's work. He reviewed sixty-one studies done following Horner's pioneering work and found that "fear of success" themes varied among the women from 11 percent to 88 percent with a median of 47 percent, while among the thirty-six studies that included men, the FOS themes ranged from 14 to 86 percent, with a median of 43 percent. In addition, he found that in no less than seventeen of the studies, men exhibited higher levels of FOS than did the women. Tresemer suggests that the inability of many of the follow-up studies to replicate Horner's findings is due to several factors: problems in scoring the stories, the muddled meaning of "success," and the fact that Horner did not validate the motive by comparing the story themes of aroused and nonaroused groups. As a result, the FOS may have been the cause, or the cause may have been some other undisclosed anxiety. Tresemer concludes that the research does not really bear up under scrutiny, and that fear of success is only one of many reason why people, men and women, fail to reach their full potential.[17]

Part of the discrepancy in the findings of Horner in the sixties and those of the studies reviewed by Tresemer in the seventies might also be a result of the changing environment and opportunities for women. Discrimination has been outlawed in employment, textbooks have been changed to portray women in a variety of roles, affirmative action programs have helped to place women in many positions from which they had

---

[15]Matina Horner, "A Bright Woman is Caught in a Double Bind, In Achievement Oriented Situations She Worries Not Only About Failure But Also About Success," *Psychology Today* 3, No. 6 (November, 1969), pp. 36–38.
[16]Ibid., p. 62.
[17]David Tresemer, "Fear of Success: Popular, but Unproven," *Psychology Today* 7, No. 10 (March, 1974), pp. 82–85.

previously been excluded, and women are entering the job market at all levels. With a growing number of successful role models, one can speculate that "fear of success," while still present and perhaps more dominant among females, is on the wane.

SEX DIFFERENCES ARE NOT DEFICIENCIES

That there are physical differences between the sexes is both obvious and universal; but which aspects of psychological difference are culturally induced and which are "innate" is an argument that is a long way from being settled. Some extremists in the liberation movement seek to overcome any and all biological differences and attempt to show that one's sex is of no consequence beyond that of child-bearing, while a few radical feminists would even go so far as to do away with even that female function. A far larger group would suggest that differences are not deficiencies, and whether the differences are biological in nature or culturally induced, many of them play a positive social role. This group holds that stating that we are not the "same" in no way implies that we are not "equal."

Rather than resurrecting all the arguments on "nature *versus* nurture," the following section will deal with the differences that have been found in a variety of research studies, and leave with the reader the arguments as to how those differences came about. In one of the largest studies ever conducted, the National Assessment of Educational Progress (NAEP) tested approximately 26,000 individuals each year between 1969 and 1973, in eight different subject areas. The samples were drawn from nine, thirteen, and seventeen year olds and young adults between twenty-five and thirty-six years of age. The results of the assessment are shown in Table 8-3.

Table 8-3 Percentage of correct answers, by age and sex, on achievement tests administered by the National Assessment of Educational Progress.

	At Age 9		At Age 17		Young Adults (25–36)	
	Females	*Males*	*Females*	*Males*	*Females*	*Males*
Writing	29.0	27.6	64.2	60.8	60.2	56.6
Music	54.1	53.5	50.0	48.3	42.4	40.6
Reading Competence	72.7	68.1	79.5	75.5	83.3	83.8
Literature	44.5	43.2	62.3	60.2	63.9	64.0
Mathematics	36.0	37.4	54.9	59.4	54.3	64.7
Science	62.2	64.0	37.3	42.3	43.3	52.6
Social Studies	71.8	72.6	73.2	74.4	70.2	74.7
Citizenship	64.0	64.2	61.3	62.3	58.8	62.0

Source: National Assessment of Educational Progress, "Males Dominate in Educational Success," *Spotlight* (October, 1975), pp. 1–2.

Among its findings, NAEP found that males generally do better than females in four major subjects: mathematics, science, social studies, and citizenship, while females outperform males to a significant degree only in writing, have a slight advantage in music, and while surpassing the males in reading and literature at the younger ages, they are surpassed in adulthood in both. At age nine, in the male-dominated subjects, the girls are at about the same level as the boys, but they fall behind at age thirteen and continue the decline on into adulthood.

National Assessment does not have the answers as to why the disparity exists, but the director, Roy H. Forbes, suggests that the answers may lie in the "different and systematic cultural reinforcements that are tied to old stereotypes of male-female behavior, interests, and abilities."[18]

Michael Lewis suggests that sex-role stereotyping begins even before birth, as parents start to discuss their preference for the sex of the child, and that mothers respond in sex-appropriate fashion to an active kicking and moving child, seeing it as more likely to be a male than a female. An inordinate amount of attention is paid to the sex of a child in our society, rather than to the health, activity level, or aspects of the child's behavior. Lewis and his colleagues have discovered that mothers exhibit more proximal behavior towards boys in the first six months, that is, more touching, hugging, and kissing. They hypothesize that this has several possible causes:

1. boys are more valuable to the mother than girls;
2. boys are more fretful and upset at birth than girls;
3. boys quiet more to physical stimulation than do girls, while girls quiet more to verbal stimulation than do boys.[19]

From the current research they state that it is impossible to say what is the major explanation, but the evidence shows that boys cry more as infants and more often experience traumatic births than do girls. Interestingly, by six months the pattern changes so that girls receive more proximal behaviors, which might be a function of the value placed on male autonomy and independence in our society.

Maccoby and Jacklin summarize the research on "What We Know and Don't Know about Sex Differences." They suggest that none of the following myths are borne out by the research data currently available to us.

Myth One: Girls are more "social" than boys.
Myth Two: Girls are more suggestible than boys.
Myth Three: Girls have lower self-esteem than boys.
Myth Four: Girls lack motivation to achieve.

[18]National Assessment of Educational Progress, "Males Dominate in Educational Success," *Spotlight* VIII, no. 5 (October, 1975), p. 1.
[19]Michael Lewis, "Parents and Children: Sex Role Development," *School Review* 80, no. 2 (February, 1972), p. 236.

Myth Five:	Girls are better at role learning and simple repetitive tasks. Boys are better at high-level tasks that require them to inhibit previously learned responses.
Myth Six:	Boys are more "analytic" than girls.
Myth Seven:	Girls are more affected by heredity, boys by environment.
Myth Eight:	Girls are "auditory," boys "visual."[20]

Differences which can be found on most of the above dimensions are differences in kind rather than in degree. For example, boys are more likely to move in a larger peer group, whereas girls associate in pairs or small groups; but no greater or lesser degree of sociability can be imputed from these results. On aspects of self-esteem, girls rate themselves higher on social competence, boys on strength and power.

In reviewing the literature, Maccoby and Jacklin found some sex differences that had been fairly well established. Aggression on the part of the male has been observed in most cultures and at most age levels, whereas girls, who mature more rapidly, have greater verbal abilities. Boys have been observed to excel in visual-spatial and mathematical abilities, particularly during adolescence. The researchers found ambiguous results or too little evidence in such areas as differences in tactile sensitivity, fear, anxiety, activity, passivity, competitiveness, dominance, compliance, and nurturance.[21]

The percentage of the differences caused by hormonal or other physical factors is hard to sort out, and one is forced to take the position of most anthropologists in their discussion of differences, namely, that heredity and environment are so fundamentally interrelated that to attempt to separate out the different elements is probably futile. Without question, numerous cultural and educational factors have negatively influenced both males and females in their success in certain ways and it is appropriate to examine the role of the school.

SEXISM IN THE NURSERY AND ELEMENTARY SCHOOLS

Sex-role stereotyping begins at or even before birth and is deeply embedded in the treatment of children by their parents. Institutionalized stereotyping is carried on in the preschools and elementary schools of this country in a wide variety of ways. One of the most obvious forms of sexism in the lower grades is the sex of the individuals making up teaching and administrative groups. Preschools are almost exclusively female in both their teaching and administration, while in the elementary grades women

[20] Eleanor Emmons Maccoby and Carol Nagy Jacklin, "What We Know and Don't Know about Sex Differences," *Psychology Today* 8, no. 7 (December, 1974), pp. 109–10.
[21] Ibid., pp. 110–12.

make up well over 80 percent of the teaching force, but less than 20 percent of the administrators. Critics have decried the feminization of such schooling and the negative effects on the boys who make up half the school population; equally devastating is the not-so-subtle message given to the children, that men are to be found in positions of power and responsibility, and that boys can aspire to such positions, while girls must look forward to positions of secondary influence and control. The few males who do find themselves in preschools or the early grades are often seen as "potential administrators," who are only serving a limited time in their current positions. Those males who do elect to remain in the classroom do so often at expense to their own egos, owing to the lack of status attributed to their positions by the society at large. In addition, the male early-grade teacher often is placed in difficult positions by his fellow teachers, who expect him to play the role of the disciplinarian.

Another area in which sex-stereotyping is prevalent is in the textbooks and other teaching materials used in the nursery, primary, and intermediate classrooms. Countless studies have been conducted throughout the country in recent years, and all of them show the overwhelming bias in elementary readers and other books. A study of readers and story books in use in Boulder, Colorado, from 1972 to 1974 is representative of findings of studies throughout the country. Of the main characters in 163 stories in first through sixth-grade readers, 32 percent were boys, 23 percent adult males, 16 percent animals, 9 percent boy and girl, 8 percent girl, 6 percent adult females, 4 percent adult man and adult woman, and 1 percent object or place. Not only were the stories overwhelmingly male in their characters, but the roles played by the characters were also revealing. Adult males were found in eighty-seven different roles, from astronaut and animal trainer to woodsman, while women could only be found in seventeen roles, mostly in traditional female positions such as teaching or housekeeper.[22] For the most part, women are portrayed as eccentric, dependent, or just downright stupid, with the need to be rescued by a smart boy or man. Males are the protagonists in stories characterized by "typical" male traits, i.e., aggressiveness, cleverness, rational-scientific-problem-solving behavior, and bravery.

Sexism is not only found in the language arts readers, but even in materials in mathematics, where girls are "unable to measure, figure out, or do other things involving mathematical skills," because "it is well known that girls are no good at math." Science is also often portrayed in a sexist manner, with boys actively involved in experimentation, while the passive girls are "wowed" by their prowess. Although millions of American mothers of school-age children work outside the home, all too often the portrayal of the American woman in elementary social studies textbooks is that of the

[22]Education Task Force: Boulder Chapter, National Organization of Women, "Sex Role Stereotyping in the Boulder Schools System," 1974 (Mimeographed).

housewife with iron in hand or bending over a sinkful of dirty dishes. With only a small minority of all American families consisting of the "typical" father, mother, boy, girl, and dog living in the suburbs, social studies texts in the early grades still continue to emphasize this family configuration, generally ignoring the millions of single-parent homes and single-child or childless homes, much less communal or other styles of family arrangement.

Sexism in the nonformal aspects of the elementary school has been as pervasive as that in the curriculum itself. Children receive very strong messages from their peers and their teachers about the sex-appropriateness of various activities, and only as a concerted effort is made to help change these perceptions, can sexist attitudes be changed. Such things as always having the boys carry the projector or serve as crossing guards while girls water the plants, or boys playing "male" brass instruments while girls play the strings and woodwinds, indicate the depth of sexist attitudes. Having children line up by sex can only encourage children to make unnecessary distinctions between the sexes.

THE FEMINIZATION OF THE SCHOOL

Differential grading procedures and differing treatment by sex in discipline are two other areas numerous critics have pointed to as examples of sexism in the elementary school. This is also true at the secondary level, where passivity and obedience are often rewarded in grading students and where the severity of punishment differs by sex. One of the authors recognized sexism in his own teaching at the junior high school level, when in the first semester, the girls received 80 percent of the A's in a social studies course. Upon some introspection it was discovered that the learning style required of the students was generally that of passive learning and memorization of facts, things which the girls had been socialized into doing to a much greater extent than the boys. An additional insight gained from the experience was that 80 percent of the students disciplined during that initial year were boys, who tended to act out their aggression in highly distractive ways, while the girls tended to "get away with" behavior such as note passing and whispering, which might be characterized as equally disruptive, but which by the standards of the school and society were not nearly as worthy of punishment.

Boys receive a mixed message in that they are "programmed" at home and by much of their environment to be aggressive and independent, but in the school these traits are often downplayed or can even lead to punishment. The statistics on the effects of this conflict are devastating. Nearly two-thirds of all grade-repeaters are boys; classes for underachievers and poor readers are predominantly made up of boys; and boys tend to make up a large majority of the population among stutterers, schizophrenics, and groups of almost every conceivable pathologic condition. Boys who can live with the mixed messages from home, society, and school can become high achievers, while those who cannot deal with them become the failures and dropouts. One would be hard put to state that all aspects of the school environment are more detrimental to boys than girls; there can be little argument, however, that traditionally the schools have treated the sexes differently, and that this has been a contributing factor to the success and failure of young people, not only in the school setting, but also in later life. An apocryphal story indicates the degree to which many boys find schooling difficult to put up with. A new kindergartner was sent out to the school garden to get a plant for use in a class project. He later recounted the experience to his parents, stating that he was outside "all alone. I could have escaped."

In order to deal with the "feminization" of the elementary schools, some schools have begun sex-segregated classes in which large-muscle activities, vocational skills, and "boys'" subjects are emphasized. Although there appears to be some benefit to be derived from such a curricular organization of the classroom, feminists have rightly pointed out that girls can and do benefit just as much from such an approach as the boys, and that segregation of the sexes ignores the broader societal questions in its attempts to deal with the symptoms. Too often sex-segregated classrooms have perpetuated the rigid role definitions which they are attempting to get away from. There appears to be some disagreement among the experts on the effects of a predominately female teaching force on the "feminization" of the elementary schools. Brophy and Good conclude that the sex of the teacher is not the major factor in determining the success of boys and girls in the school setting, but that the societally determined sex roles for girls mesh more closely with that of the student role than it does for boys, thus leading to typically reported sex differences in student behavior, attitudes, and achievement. They conclude that adding more males to the teaching profession will not change the basic teacher-student roles and will thus have a minimal effect on the "success" of boys in schools. Only changes in definition of the "student role" and the societally determined sex roles for boys and girls will bring about improvements in school achievement.[23] Smith disagrees with this conclusion and cites research that indicates the following:

1. Boys appear to receive more disapproval and blame from their female teachers than do girls.
2. Female teachers are more likely to use a harsh tone when criticizing boys and a normal tone with girls.
3. Girls are more likely to receive higher grades for equivalent work.

[23]Jere E. Brophy and Thomas L. Good, "Feminization of Elementary Schools," *Phi Delta Kappan* LIV, No. 8 (April, 1963), pp. 569–66.

4. Female teachers structure the classroom environment in such a manner as to alienate boys.[24]

Smith concludes that to change curriculum and environment of the school is not enough, and that more males are needed in the early grades to serve as role models and meet the needs unique to boys.[25]

There can be little doubt in the late 1970s that boys and girls differ in their success rates in school and that many factors contribute to this differential. The masculinization of the elementary school, either in curriculum or teaching role, is not the answer; but surely the schools must provide positive male and female role models for all boys and girls, while treating them as unique individuals capable of a complete range of passive and aggressive behavior, conformity and creativity, and all the other characteristics that have traditionally limited both males and females in our society. Pessimism is perhaps the order of the day, however, given the na-

Figure 8-1 Changing Sex Roles

[24]Dan F. Smith, "Yes, American Schools Are Feminized," *Phi Delta Kappan* LIV, no. 10 (June, 1973), p. 703.
[25]Ibid., p. 704.

ture of sexism in the society at large, as it relates to children. Books on child-rearing still tend to reinforce sex-stereotyped roles; toy manufacturers continue to encourage boys to be active and girls passive, and through their advertising suggest that girls aspire to be mothers, nurses, and teachers, while boys can become almost anything they can imagine. Television and other mass media do their part to reinforce traditional sex roles, with even such a progressive educational program as Sesame Street being greatly criticized for its lack of nontraditional female roles.

SEXISM IN THE SECONDARY SCHOOLS

Perhaps the most obvious and blatant example of sex discrimination in secondary schools has been in physical education and interscholastic athletics. The vast differential between the funding for girls' and boys' sports has been brought to the attention of many school districts, and the courts are now mandating more nearly equal expenditures and opportunities for girls in our secondary schools. Sex-segregated gym classes, except in the contact sports, have been eliminated in many school districts, and women's coaches are now receiving pay equal to the men in many districts. With the nationwide educational budgetary crises, the reallocation of funds and the offering of opportunities for girls have had an effect on boys' athletics, often bringing out the most blatant chauvinism among coaches and parents of boys, who fail to see the need for equity between the sexes. No longer can girls be given the "old" gymnasium and locker room. No longer can girls be made to buy their own uniforms, pay their own travel costs to games, and buy their own meals on athletic trips, while the boys go free. These changes are long overdue, and one can only hope that the girls' sports programs do not follow the same pattern of overemphasis on interscholastic sports as boys' sports have done, at the expense of physical fitness and intramural sports for all young people.

A second important area in which there has been blatant discrimination in the secondary schools is that of vocational study. Until very recently, many districts had sex-segregated home economics and technical courses. Even when these have been integrated voluntarily or under court order, the prevailing sexism of the school and society prevents truly equal access to the courses. Boys are still hesitant to enroll in home economics and cosmetology courses, while certain vocational courses are not too popular with the girls (although status reasons have caused girls generally to be more likely to enroll in formerly "all-boy" courses). Subtler forms of discrimination still occur in many settings, however, as girls are "programmed" into typing and shorthand courses leading to generally lower-paying business jobs, while boys are pushed into business-management preparatory programs. Work-study programs have traditionally placed girls in lower-paying positions or in what might be considered "dead-end" occupations.

Family living and child-rearing courses have been offered to girls for many years, ignoring the obvious fact that males live in family situations and are becoming more actively involved in child-rearing. Within courses, activities are often scheduled to appeal to one sex more than the other, as in sewing when only women's clothing is made, or in cooking classes which emphasize chef training.

Vocational and regular guidance programs at the secondary level have also been fraught with sexism. In the past, young people were encouraged to prepare for "realistic" occupations, in keeping with traditional sex roles, so that girls became nurses and teachers and boys were channeled into courses which would better prepare them for pre-medical and pre-law work in the colleges. Sex-biased vocational interest and preference tests have been administered to generations of American young people, and boys and girls have been channeled on the basis of their scores. Only very recently have newer instruments been developed to get around this blatant form of sexism. Although discrimination in counseling has been significantly lessened in recent years, covert and subtle disapproval of courses and jobs is more difficult to eliminate, to say nothing of the discrimination which young people face when attending sexist institutions of higher education or choosing to enter nontraditional jobs. Appropriate role models are hard to find, particularly for girls entering certain traditionally male-dominated professions. Thus an extra effort is needed by counselors to ensure that secondary-age girls do not close any doors just because of past discrimination. In addition to actively encouraging young people to enter nontraditional training programs and jobs, counselors have the responsibility to train students in their legal rights, including how to file a complaint when they have been discriminated against on the basis of their sex. In other words, passive change on the part of counselors is not enough to overcome decades or centuries of discrimination. Only an activist counseling profession can help to turn the tide.

Anthologies used in secondary school level literature classes have proven to be almost as sexist as the elementary school readers. A much smaller number of the main characters of stories tend to be females than males, and the large majority of stories are written by male authors. Females derive their status from the males in the stories and are all too often stereotyped into traditional roles. Illustrations are overwhelmingly male, perhaps because of the "exciting" roles in which authors place male characters. With the exception of a few well-known women in American or world history, libraries are almost devoid of biographies of women, whereas biographies of males in school libraries often number in the hundreds, with versions at all reading levels. As was pointed out in another section of this chapter, the sexist aspects of language pervade the linguistic patterns of teachers and not just the general public; and few textbook companies have made any concerted effort to use sex-neutral wording where it is appropriate.

History, as it is taught in most secondary schools, is exactly that: "his" story. Many texts do not even list women in their index of topics, and most include no more than a page or two on women's contributions to the history of the United States or to that of other countries. This is partially because of the military, heroic, political perspective that so often pervades the textbooks and the classroom, and since these have been traditional male preserves, it is no wonder that women have been slighted. Even where women have made national and international contributions to our society and other societies, they have been slighted by the writers of history textbooks. One can only hope that as history writers move more into the social and cultural aspects of our nation, the crucial role of women will receive its proper place. Sexism too often pervades the discussion of current events or contemporary history, and only as teachers, male and female, become aware of the role of American women in history and in the present can the problem be solved.

The legal status of women throughout our history and in the states today is seldom dealt with adequately in social studies courses, while the economics of discrimination against women—those who elect to remain in the home as well as those who hold paying jobs—has only recently been added to the curriculum in secondary schools and colleges. Study of the social conditioning for traditional sex roles has just entered the sociological curriculum, while psychology courses have all but ignored the research on the similarities and differences of men and women. In family and sex education classes, the changing roles of men and women in the family structure and the possibilities for new structures need to be raised, while dealing honestly with double-standard moralizing and the Freudian bias in assumptions about female sexuality.

Math and science suffer from the same forms of sexism at the secondary level as they do at the elementary, namely, in the kinds of problems and illustrations used, and in the society-wide bias, also to be found among educators, that girls are somehow incapable of success in these disciplines. Conscious efforts must counteract the societal bias against women in these courses, for it is the advanced mathematics and science courses which are so necessary to get into engineering schools, pre-medical programs, and a wide variety of other higher-paying occupations that have traditionally been male dominated.

The extracurricular activities in the typical junior or senior high school are another place to be scrutinized for evidence of sexism. It is still all too true that the girls cheerlead while the boys are cheered, and that all too many clubs are dominated by one sex or another. Seldom are the sponsors of clubs, usually women faculty, paid for their services, whereas males who coach receive additional salary. Students with academic and disciplinary problems at the secondary level tend to be overwhelmingly male, and the schools must make a concerted effort to analyze what aspects of the formal curriculum, in addition to the extracurricular and "hidden" curriculum of the school, are perhaps a cause for such difficulties.

If role models for boys in the elementary school are a problem, the same can be said for girls at the secondary level. Although women make up close to half of the teaching force in the junior and senior high schools of this country, they made up less than 1 percent of the superintendents and only 3 percent of the secondary principals in 1972–73.[26] All these percentages are down from the period before and shortly after World War II, when many more women could be found in positions of responsibility. Women can be found in curriculum directorships, counseling, and consultantships, but positions of real power are still reserved for the men. Listing the qualities necessary for a successful high school administrator, Louise Bach has stated that he or she must:

1) be adept at helping young people control themselves and even more adept at controlling him/herself;
2) be attuned to the needs of others;
3) be as good at listening as at talking;
4) be good at counseling;
5) know when to be firm and when to bend;
6) know how to give another person room to go around rather than over him/her;
7) lead without appearing to dominate; and
8) be able to share the process of planning and direction with others.[27]

Ms. Bach then concludes with the comment, "The ideal principal must now cultivate all the virtues that have always been expected of the ideal woman. Women have finally lucked out by having several thousand years to train for jobs where muscles are out and persuasion is in."[28] One can only hope that as the courts, women's groups, and others pressure to bring women into positions of power that the men, who will continue to dominate administrative positions for some time to come, will evidence these same traits and that they will replace the "macho" style so prevalent in the administrative profession.

SEXISM IN HIGHER EDUCATION

If higher education can be considered the capstone of the American educational system, there is much evidence that it might also be considered the most sexist part of that system. Since the focus of this book is the

---

[26]Suzanne S. Taylor, "Educational Leadership: A Male Domain?" *Phi Delta Kappan* LV, no. 2 (October, 1973), p. 124.
[27]Louise Bach, "Of Women, School Administration, and Discipline," *Phi Delta Kappan* 57, no. 7 (March, 1976), p. 465.
[28]Bach, p. 465.

elementary and secondary schools, space does not permit any real analysis of the problem of sexism in higher education. Suffice it to say that the "old-boy" network has kept higher education in both teaching and administration as an almost total male preserve, and that despite token efforts at women's studies programs, curricular changes to deal with sexism have been minimal.

CONCLUSIONS

As with other reform movements in our history, it is perhaps too much to ask of the school that it lead the way and reform or reconstruct the society's attitudes towards and treatment of women. Schools have traditionally been conservative in nature and tend to reflect or mirror whatever is true of society at large. This does not, however, excuse the educational system from cleaning up its own house, and thus contributing to the greater societal change, particularly as far as the next generation is concerned. That educators have all too often only changed under court order does not speak well for the profession. That sexism dominates our society and schools has been only too clearly portrayed in countless books and articles over the past decade. That some progress has been made to bring about greater justice and equality is also true, if not quite so self-evident. The challenge laid down to the schools and those of us who teach in them is to deal with the sexism within ourselves and our institutions, and thus make a contribution to the broader task of eliminating it in families, business, industries, religious institutions, and other parts of American society.

The more overt aspects of sexism, such as discriminatory policies in admissions, promotions and tenure, use of sexist language, omission of facts and illustrations about women, and the like, can be more easily dealt with, through legal means if necessary. The patterns which come down to us through centuries of patriarchal thinking and behavior are more difficult to get at, but it is education which is best equipped to deal with them. If those whose consciousness has been raised cannot or will not change, there is little hope for the rest of the society.

CASE STUDY: The Sexist Curriculum

After you are assigned to your first teaching position, it becomes obvious to you that the curriculum, in general, has a strong sexist bias in what it does and does not cover throughout the thirteen years the children attend the public schools in your district. In addition, the materials the school district has selected for use at your grade level are fraught with sexism. The illustrations are overwhelmingly male, showing boys and men in a wide variety of exciting roles, while those portraying girls or women show them exclusively in traditional roles, and often "helping" men. The books are, for the most part, written by males and about males, with girls being portrayed as flighty, unintelligent, and generally not every exciting.

Women are pretty much ignored in the history books, with a few of the usual exceptions. Questions at the end of chapters connote many forms of sexism. Teachers in your school tend to discipline boys more harshly, and the grading system appears to discriminate against the boys. In certain classes, girls are dominant, partly because of sex biases in the society at large, but partly also because of the counseling they receive; other classes are mostly boys. In athletics, the girls are limited to two sports, whereas the boys can participate on nine different school-sponsored athletic teams.

As a new teacher who is well aware of the sexism in the schools and society, you feel an obligation to change not only your own classroom and your own teaching, but to work on the rest of the school and system as well. What steps would you take to deal with sexist aspects of the curriculum and materials within your own classroom? How would you then begin to deal with the problem on a school- and system-wide basis?

THOUGHT QUESTIONS

1. What physiological differences are there between males and females and what effects, if any, should or do these differences have in the emotional and psychological makeup of people, and in the roles they play in society?

2. What differences are there in the educational achievement of the sexes? What are some possible explanations for these differences?

3. Few, if any, schools have gone to completely equal funding for girls' athletics, although some strides have been made in that direction. What effects would such a policy have on secondary and higher educational institutions?

4. Throughout the chapter numerous examples of sexism were shown in the schools of this country. Take one level—nursery, elementary, secondary, or higher education—and document the major forms of sexism at play at that level.

5. In what ways are racism and sexism similar or different? How might each be defined?

6. What are the basic presuppositions of traditional groups such as Fascinating Womanhood and The Total Woman? about women's role and place in the home and in society? What are the presuppositions of radical feminists?

7. What are the societal reasons for discrimination against women in the economy?

8. How have the roles of men and women changed since your grandparents' time? Deal with such things as child-rearing, jobs, relationships with spouses and others of the same or opposite sex, and any other differences. In what ways have things remained the same?

9. List, from memory, women who have made a major contribution to our history. Why have women been so ignored by historians?

10. What characteristics and behaviors are male and which are female as defined by today's standards? What effects on society would there be if they were reversed?

PRACTICAL ACTIVITIES

1. Do a thorough evaluation of a textbook currently in use in an elementary or secondary school. Look for examples of sexism in the illustrations, use of language, end-of-chapter questions, sex of the authors, sex of main characters (if it is a reading or literature book), sexism through omission, roles of men and women, and anything else you can find.

2. Conduct a study of the curricular offerings in a school district. Look for places where the role of women might properly be included in the curriculum. Document places where the school district has attempted or is attempting to change, along with places where women, and their role in American society, are being ignored.

3. Attend a meeting of NOW, Fascinating Womanhood, Total Woman, a Women's Political Caucus, League of Women Voters, Church Women's Group, or any other organization made up predominantly of women. Deal with the issues discussed at the meeting and your reaction to the issues and the participants.

4. Write a nonsexist short story. After writing the story, list the conscious attempts you made to make it a nonsexist story.

5. Do a study of the number of male and female teachers and administrators at each level of schooling in a school district. Calculate the percentages of male to female in each type of position, i.e., teacher, principal, assistant principal, coordinators, central administrators, etc. Do the percentages indicate any sexism at work in the school district?

6. Spend an afternoon or an evening watching television, both the advertisements and the regular programming. What roles do you see portrayed by men and by women? What overt and covert forms of sexism are evident? How closely does what is portrayed on TV parallel society in general?

7. List the words you use or hear regularly which are gender-related, e.g., mankind, he (when referring to both male and female), etc. What words could be substituted for them? Which of them do you feel are nonsexist and should be left alone?

8. Spend some time in the school library. Count the number of biographies and autobiographies of women and estimate the number about

men. Why the big difference? Compare the sex of the authors of the biographies.

9. Ask several children, boys and girls, what they would like to be when they grow up. Ask them if they would still want to be in that type of job if they were a member of the opposite sex. Did you find any examples of sex-role stereotyping among the children? If so, where do they get the messages from?

10. Make a collage or draw a picture of the "ideal man" and the "ideal woman," then explain that ideal, including descriptions of the physical, emotional, and psychological aspects which make such a person your ideal. With the exception of obvious physiological differences, how do your ideal male and female differ from each other?

11. List all the ways that you have benefited from or have been negatively affected by the fact that you are male or female.

BIBLIOGRAPHY

ANDELIN, HELEN B., *Fascinating Womanhood*. Santa Barbara, Calif.: Pacific Press, 1970.

BARBER, BENJAMIN, *Liberating Feminism*. New York: Dell Publishing Company, 1975.

FIRESTONE, SHULAMITH, *The Dialectic of Sex: The Case for Feminist Revolution*. New York: William Morrow and Company, Inc., 1970.

FRAZIER, NANCY, AND MYRA SADKER, *Sexism in School and Society*. New York: Harper & Row, Publishers, 1973.

FRIEDAN, BETTY, *The Feminine Mystique*. New York: W. W. Norton & Company, Inc., 1963.

GOLDBERG, STEPHEN, *The Inevitability of Patriarchy*. New York: William Morrow and Company, Inc., 1973.

GOUGH, PAULINE, *Sexism: New Issue in American Education*. Bloomington, Indiana: The Phi Delta Kappa Educational Foundation, 1976.

GREER, GERMAINE, *The Female Eunuch*. New York: McGraw-Hill Book Company, 1971.

HEILBRUN, CAROLYN G., *Towards a Recognition of Androgyny*. New York: Alfred A. Knopf, Inc., 1973.

MILLETT, KATE, *Sexual Politics*. Garden City, N.Y.: Doubleday & Company, Inc., 1970.

MORGAN, ROBIN, ed., *Sisterhood Is Powerful, An Anthology of Writings from the Women's Liberation Movement*. New York: Vintage, Random House, Inc., 1970.

National Education Association, *Sex Role Stereotyping in the Schools*. Washington, D.C.: NEA, 1973.

STACEY, JUDITH, SUSAN BEREAUD, AND JOAN DANIELS, eds. *And Jill Came Tumbling After: Sexism in American Education*. New York: Dell Publishing Company, 1974.

PART THREE

THE SYSTEM AND THE TEACHER

9

SCHOOL ORGANIZATION
The Structure of the System

Unlike school systems in many other countries, public education in the United States is a function of more than one level of government. Constitutionally, education was left to the states, who in turn delegated authority to local districts. The federal government has become increasingly involved in financing educational programs in a multiplicity of areas, and the constitutional and political debates over federal aid to education continue to the present day. Not only is education a function of at least three levels of government, it is also influenced by the executive, legislative, and judicial branches. Wide differences can be found in the way the various states and local school districts implement educational prescriptions, but in spite of such diversity, trends can be perceived, and as a result of professional, social, economic, political, and judicial pressures, the American educational system is homogeneous to a large extent. Before detailing formal organization, a statistical overview of public and private education in the United States will be given. Although statistics soon become obsolete, they can be used to perceive definite trends and to make projections. Almost one in every three Americans is involved either as a student or in some other capacity in the public or private educational institutions of the United States.

A STATISTICAL PERSPECTIVE ON AMERICAN SCHOOLING

The fifty state school systems contained 16,561 local school districts in 1974.[1] The trend towards the consolidation of school districts becomes evident when one compares the total of 127,531 local districts in 1931–32 with the 1974 total.[2] Most of the consolidation occurred during the 1950s and 1960s, for a variety of political, educational and economic reasons that will be dealt with later in this chapter. The number of school districts in the states varies from a high of 1,238 in Nebraska to one statewide district in Hawaii.[3]

Enrollments for the fall of 1975, from kindergarten through higher education, were 58,940,000, down slightly from 1974.[4] A further decline is projected by the U.S. Office of Education to around 54,000,000 by 1983.[5] Fluctuations in birthrates, societal expectations, and the state of the economy have upset numerous demographic predictions in the past, so projections are at best tentative; but it does appear that the peak enrollments have been reached. Table 9-1 gives some indication of the rapidity and extent of growth, particularly at the secondary and higher education levels.[6]

Perhaps more revealing than the gross numbers of enrollees at each level is the percentage of attendance throughout our educational history. In 1889, only 6.7 percent of fourteen to seventeen year olds were enrolled in gades nine through twelve. By 1929–30, this had risen to 51.4 percent, with a high of 93.5 percent in 1971, and a slight decrease since that time. This statistic indicates the recent nature of mass secondary education in the United States.[7] The changing nature of attendance at American educa-

Table 9-1 Enrollment in Educational Institutions, 1899–1973

	1899–1900	1929–30	1959–60	Fall, 1973
All levels	17,961,841	29,652,377	45,227,620	59,080,117
K–8th grade	16,261,846	23,739,840	32,412,266	35,135,441
Grades 9–12	699,403	4,811,800	9,599,810	15,426,526
Higher Education	237,592	1,100,737	3,215,544	8,518,150

[1] W. Vance Grant and C. George Lind, *Digest of Educational Statistics, 1975* (Washington, D.C.: U. S. Government Printing Office, 1976), p. 56.
[2] Ibid., p. 57.
[3] Ibid., p. 56.
[4] Ibid., p. 6.
[5] Kenneth A. Simon and Martin Frankel, *Projections of Educational Statistics to 1983–84* (Washington, D.C.: U. S. Government Printing Office, 1975), pp. 21, 23.
[6] Grant and Lind, *Digest*, p. 7.
[7] Ibid., p. 37.

Table 9-2 Estimated Retention Rates, 5th Grade through College Entrance 1924–32 to 1966–74*

School Year Pupils Entered 5th Grade	5th Grade	6th Grade	9th Grade	High School Graduate	First-Time College Student
1924–55	1000	911	612	302	118
1934–55	1000	953	803	467	129
1944–55	1000	952	848	522	234
1954–55	1000	980	915	642	343
Fall, 1964	1000	988	975	748	433
Fall, 1966	1000	989	985	744	449

*Number of students per 1000 completing fifth grade who also complete sixth, ninth, and twelfth grades and enter college with their respective classes.

tional institutions can also be seen in Table 9-2, which shows retention rates.[8] In the early part of the twentieth century, growth was most rapid in secondary education, whereas higher education has been the major center of educational growth since World War II. With declining birth rates and changing job and familial patterns as two of the causes, it is quite likely that preschool education and child-care programs will be the growth area in the last quarter of the century. By 1974, the percentage of three year olds enrolled in nursery schools had risen to 19.9 percent with 37.6 percent of the four year olds and 78.6 percent of the five year olds.[9]

During the rapid growth years of the 1950s and early 1960s there was a great need for teachers, so that in most fields the teacher candidate had a choice of location and job almost anywhere in the country. Colleges and universities geared up to produce teachers in what was thought to be an ever-increasing demand field. With the stabilization of birth rates and enrollments, and actual declines in many states and cities, the bottom dropped out of the teacher market, so that by the early 1970s, there was an excess of teachers on the job market.

Teachers salaries rose considerably between 1929–30 and 1974–75, the average annual earnings increasing from $1,420 to $12,070. When adjusted for inflation, however, and placed in 1974–75 dollars, the rise is considerably less, from $4,297 to $12,070.[10] Gross numbers, however, can be somewhat misleading, for there are considerable differences between states and between individual districts within any given state. For 1969–70, the range was from a low state average of $8,235 in Mississippi to $13,988 in New York and $15,076 in Alaska.[11] The high point in 1974–75 dollars was

[8]Ibid., p. 14.
[9]Ibid., p. 47.
[10]Ibid., p. 55.
[11]Ibid., p. 54.

Table 9-3 Percentage of Revenue Receipts for Public Elementary and Secondary Schools from Federal, State and Local Sources, 1919-20 to 1973-74

School Year	Federal	State	Local (Including Intermediate)
1919-20	0.3	16.5	83.2
1929-30	0.4	16.9	92.7
1939-40	1.8	30.3	68.0
1949-50	2.9	39.8	57.3
1959-60	4.4	39.1	56.5
1969-70	8.0	39.9	52.1
1973-74	8.5	41.4	50.1

reached in the 1971-72 school year, when the nationwide average salary was $12,713, with the decrease to $12,070 in 1974-75. With the exception of the Depression years, this is the first time in the past fifty years that teachers have suffered a decrease in purchasing power.[12]

The size of the American educational establishment becomes even clearer when the expenditures on all levels of education are detailed. In the forty-five years from 1929 to 1974, the gross national product rose from 10.1 billion to 1.4 trillion, while the expenditures on education at all levels rose from slightly over 3million dollars to over 108 billion dollars annually. As a percentage of the gross national product, educational expenditures went from 3.1 percent to 7.8 percent in the same period.[13] Educational institutions take the largest percentage of state and local funds, some 38.3 percent in 1971-72. The growing trend toward state and federal financing of schools can be clearly seen in Table 9-3.[14] In 1974-75, the percentage of support from the federal government varied from a low of 2.8 percent in New Hampshire to a high of 23.0 percent in Mississippi. State funding of schools also varied greatly, with a low of 7.2 percent in New Hampshire to a high of 88.7 percent in Hawaii, with its one statewide school district.[15]

Educational expenditures are projected to reach a total of 172.8 billion dollars annually by the 1983-84 school year, with 127.1 billion dollars for the elementary and secondary schools, and 45.7 billion dollars for institutions of higher education.[16]

The number of students in private educational institutions rose from approximately 1,500,000 in 1899-90 to a high of over 7 million in 1959-60. Even with a growth of over 64 percent between 1959-60 and the fall of 1973, in private higher education the total number of students enrolled in private schools of all kinds and levels fell to less than 7 million by 1973.[17]

[12]Ibid., p. 55.
[13]Ibid., p. 27.
[14]Ibid., p. 65.
[15]Ibid., p. 63.
[16]Simon and Frankel, *Projections*, p. 88.
[17]Grant and Lind, *Digest*, p. 7.

Much of the drop occurred in the Catholic parochial schools, whose enrollment rose from 1.9 million students in 1919–20 to 4.6 million in 1964, only to be confronted with a large number of school closings and a drop of enrollment to 3.5 million in 1974–75.[18]

Although the disparities still exist between the white and nonwhite populations in the United States, dramatic gains have been made by the nonwhite population, to the extent that if only the 25-to-29-year-old age group is dealt with, the median amount of schooling in 1975 was 12.8 years for whites compared to 12.6 years for nonwhites.[19]

THE FEDERAL GOVERNMENT AND EDUCATION

The federal role in education is a concern that has troubled the American people since the adoption of the Constitution in 1789. The schools have been the battleground for testing many of the principles of federalism in other areas, such as freedom of speech and press, powers of Congress, and issues concerning states' rights. Precedents formed in the field of education have led to changes in the respective roles of the federal and state governments.

federalism and constitutional authority

The concept of federalism, with its division of authority between the national and state governments, was laid down by the U.S. Constitution. The relationships between the two levels of government are taken from Articles I, IV, and VI and the Tenth Amendment. The Tenth Amendment provides: "The powers not delegated to the United States by the Constitution, nor prohibited by it to the States, are reserved to the States respectively, or to the people." Since the Constitution makes no reference to education, the States have been given the basic responsibility for public education. The constitutional provisions are subject to constant interpretation and reinterpretation. Strict constructionists have held and continue to hold that powers not expressly provided to the federal government are reserved for the states, and that the increasing encroachment on the part of the federal government into the field of education is a violation of the Constitution.

The most frequently used argument by those in favor of federal involvement in the educational process, is the phrase in the Preamble to the Constitution, which states that the government of the United States was formed to "promote the General Welfare." Further justification for federal involvement is found in the "elastic" clause of Article I, Section Eight, which

[18]Ibid., p. 44.
[19]Ibid., p. 14.

states that Congress shall have the power "To make all Laws which shall be necessary and proper for carrying into Execution the foregoing Powers, and all other powers vested by this Constitution in the Government of the United States. . . ." Proponents of federal aid to education see in this clause the constitutional authority for the federal government to act in accordance with its stated power over taxation, commerce, and other powers provided for in the Constitution.

The failure to mention education in the Constitution has been the source of much debate among educational historians. It appears that a major reason for the omission was that education in the eighteenth century was primarily private and limited to those who could afford it. An additional reason was that with the many other critical problems facing the new nation, education was not seen as a high national priority. This is not to say that the founding fathers were not concerned with educational matters; Jefferson was actively involved in the founding of the University of Virginia and wrote extensively on education, while Washington and Madison, among others, expressed interest in establishing a National University and raised no Constitutional arguments against such a "federal" institution.

While there is general agreement that the states have the primary jurisdiction over educational matters, the federal government has certain educational functions about which there is little disagreement. Among these are the education of residents of special federal areas, Native Americans on the reservations, and peoples of the territories; the training of people to serve the national government, cooperative educational programs with other countries, scientific research, and the collection and diffusion of information about education. Even before the Constitution was adopted in 1789, the national government found itself involved in educational activities beyond these roles.

history of federal programs

Historians trace federal involvement in education to the Northwest Ordinance of 1787, the third article of which stated that "religion, morality, and knowledge being necessary to good government and the happiness of mankind, schools and the means of education shall be forever encouraged." Taking its cue from the Land Ordinance of 1785, the Northwest Ordinance set aside every sixteenth section for the support of education. In addition to the funds raised from the sale of this property, the Congress established a policy providing that 5 percent of the proceeds from the sale of federal public lands within the various states would revert to the states, provided the states agreed not to tax federal property. Many states used the proceeds from these sales to establish common school funds in the 1830s.

Following the Civil War, rudimentary education was provided for the newly freed slaves by the Bureau of Refugees and the Freedman's Bureau.

Public land grants were made available in 1862 through the Morrill Act to establish and maintain agricultural and mechanical colleges. In 1867, Congress passed the Department of Education Act, for

> ... the purposes of collecting such statistics and facts as shall show the condition and progress of education in the several States and Territories and of diffusing such information respecting the organization and management of schools and school systems, and methods of teaching as shall aid the people of the United States in the establishment and maintenance of efficient school systems, and otherwise promote the cause of education throughout the country.

Recent activities by the National Institute of Education and the National Assessment Project trace their justification back to the creation of the Department of Education, which has since become the U.S. Office of Education, still under a Commissioner, as specified in 1867.

Beginning with the Smith-Lever Act of 1914, which provided programs of agricultural extension, and the Smith-Hughes Act of 1917, supporting vocational education, Congress passed a series of educational acts geared at helping the states improve their vocational and agricultural training programs. The relief measures of the Great Depression had a profound effect on schooling, beginning with the Civil and Public Works administrations, which constructed, altered, and repaired school buildings. The Civilian Conservation Corps (CCC) and National Youth Administration (NYA) provided employment, housing, food, and medical care for hundreds of thousands of young people.

By 1950, federal involvement in education totalled close to three hundred separate activities, located in nine different departments and 27 independent Federal agencies.[20] Although, as has been noted, federal involvement in education predates the Constitution itself, the major growth has occurred since World War II. Since that time, millions of veterans have used the various "GI bills" to obtain college education or vocational training, and the expenditures of federal funds in these programs total in the billions of dollars. With the National Science Foundation in 1950 and the Cooperative Research Program of 1954, the federal government found itself deeply involved in promoting basic research. The National Defense Education Act (NDEA) was passed in 1958 to counter Sputnik and the advances of the Soviet Union in the production of engineers and scientists. During the next decade, NDEA appropriations totaled close to $4 billion. The Vocational Educational Act of 1963 added greatly to federal support n the area, so that by 1967 appropriations were over the $225 million mark.

The most extensive federal involvement in education came with the Elementary and Secondary Education Act of 1965 (ESEA), an act President

---

[20]Edgar L. Morphet, Roe L. Johns, and Theodore L. Reller, *Educational Administration: Concepts, Practices and Issues* (Englewood Cliffs, N.J.: Prentice-Hall, Inc., 1959), p. 183.

Johnson pointed to as one of his greatest accomplishments. Initially passed for the period 1965–68, it has continued in existence to the present day and is the major reason for the rise in federal grants to elementary and secondary schools from $666 million in 1964 to almost $5 billion in 1975. Through its various titles, ESEA deals with (1) education of children from low-income families, (2) improvement of school-library resources, (3) the establishment of regional centers to provide services to districts unable to receive them in other ways, (4) research and training in education, and (5) the improvement and strengthening of State Departments of Education.

Congress has passed numerous other programs since ESEA in 1965, covering such areas as the health professions, higher education grants, the National Foundation on the Arts and Humanities, student loan programs, the International Education Act, the Education Professional Development Act, environmental education, drug-abuse activities, manpower development, and juvenile delinquency programs. With the passage of ESEA in 1965, the federal share of costs at the elementary and secondary level rose from 4.4 percent to 7.9 percent; with the additional moneys provided by ESEA amendments and subsequent federal programs, that percentage rose to a high of 8.9 percent in 1971–72.

federal involvement in education: a position

The debate over federal aid to education has lessened in recent years, but the cry of states' rights can still be heard from many political platforms. The size and depth of involvement by the federal government in education at all levels makes it unlikely that its presence will disappear. Federal aid is a fact of our times and has a long and generally honorable history in the United States. The issue then becomes one of, first, the amount of control the federal government exercises when it distributes funds to the states and, second, the expansion of national power at the expense of the states and local governments. Critics on the right state that any expansion of national power is destructive of individual rights and that we must place a high value on individualism and laissez-faire government. These critics believe the state and local governments to be closer to the people and more responsive to their constituents. On the other hand, critics on the left are often those who favor a strengthening of national government in order to provide an adequate education for all children, regardless of race, sex, national origin, state, or region in which they might have been born. These persons argue that an increase in federal power does not necessarily lead to any decrease in the rights of the individual.

There is little disagreement that the young people of the United States should be educated at public expense. Where the money should come from and who should control the educational systems are questions that will continue to occupy Americans for decades to come. Issues with national import, such as education of the poor, no doubt have lent themselves to national solutions and probably will continue to do so. School system administrators are hard put to turn down money from the federal government in times of budget crises and bond issue rejections. Numerous citizens are asking a major political question of the 1970s, however, as to whether federal control and bureaucracy are necessary adjuncts to federal aid.

The Congress through its appropriation of funds, the executive branch through its bureaucratic controls and research, and the federal judiciary through its rulings on race, religion, and school finance will all continue to influence the American educational system. The lack of empirical results on the reform and upgrading of education through the massive federal programs of the 1960s has led to a more cautious mood in the 1970s and a slowing in the pace of federal financing, control, and administration of American schools. The major trend in recent years has been the shift in financing and control from the local to the state level.

THE STATE GOVERNMENTS AND EDUCATION

The state is the level of government charged with the responsibility for education, and most states' constitutions contain provisions giving them the authority to govern schools. Most states have chosen to delegate much of the constitutional authority to local districts. The operational powers for education come not only from the state constitutions, but also from the legislatures and the courts.

state organization

All the laws, rules, regulations, and judicial opinions affecting education are published in state school codes, documents which have become sizable, owing to the growing complexity of the educational enterprise. State codes deal with the whole range of activities in which schools engage: financial responsibility, accountability laws, certification of teachers, buildings, organization and administration, elections, special programs, school taxes, tenure, and literally hundreds of other laws and judicial opinions affecting the everyday operation of schools throughout the state. At one time, most districts consisted of any area which could support a one-room school, but with the consolidation laws of the 1950s, the number of districts was cut from 127,000 to fewer than 17,000 today, with over 40 percent of the current total being found in only six states.

In forty-eight of the fifty states, State Boards of Education have been given the responsibility of supervising the elementary and secondary school districts. State Boards vary in size from three to twenty-one members and attain office either through election in partisan or nonpartisan elections or by appointment by the governor. Their functions vary, but generally consist of appointing a State Superintendent of Public Instruction or supervising his election, and passing rules and regulations concerning certification, state aid, special programs for the handicapped, vocational education, and the distribution of federal funds.

The chief state school officers or superintendents of public instruction trace their history back to Gideon Hawley, appointed to that post in New York in 1812. Since that time, some of the most important names in American educational history have been state superintendents—Horace Mann in Massachusetts and Henry Barnard in Connecticut, to name just two. The superintendent in each state supervises the work of the State Department of Education, made up of educators whose job it is to administer the policies set by the state boards, the legislature, and the courts. State Departments enforce the laws, rules, and regulations governing education in the state, distribute the funds allocated by the board, state legislature, and federal government, certify who may teach and administer schools in the state, enforce building, curricular, and other codes, and provide leadership and services to local districts.

the growing state role

Numerous questions in the area of education now face the states. Is local control an anachronism in the last quarter of the twentieth century? How can the state provide the majority of funds for schools while still maintaining some semblance of local control? Can statewide minimum standards be set without destroying the creative and dynamic in the schools? What are the minimum funding levels necessary to maintain a high-quality educational program?

At the heart of the shift to educational power and decision-making is the financial crunch facing the schools. With schooling costs rising at double the rate of the gross national product, dramatic variations in different school districts' ability to raise taxes, the public's disenchantment as expressed in the failure of bond issue elections, and the overloading of the property tax as the basis for school finance, the states have been forced to take an ever greater role. In 1976 the states provided 43.6 percent of the funds for schools (nationwide), only slightly less than the 48.6 percent from local sources;[21] if present trends continue, state sources of financing will make up considerably more than half of the school revenues by 1980.

[21]Grant and Lind, *Digest*, p. 63.

Court challenges to the inequities in local financing, such as *Serrano* in California, *Rodriguez* in Texas, and *Cahill* in New Jersey, have forced many state legislatures to rewrite their school foundation acts to provide more equitable statewide levels of funding, regardless of the ability of the local district to raise funds. States have also been forced to move away from the local property tax as the only or major source of school funding and to shift to sales or income taxes to support the schools.

Reorganization of the schools into larger, consolidated school districts was not generally popular with many local school districts, who found themselves legislated out of existence by state law. This action further strengthened the movement towards the centralization of power at the state level. States have the responsibility for making many programmatic decisions in addition to the organizational and financial ones. All states have compulsory attendance education laws, but the inclusion of kindergartens and junior colleges in the local school districts varies from state to state. Preschool education, other than kindergarten, is a growing state and federal concern, as are programs for the handicapped and various kinds of adult and vocational education.

Accountability laws have been passed in recent years to aid in providing better equality of education. The public is pressuring the schools to define more clearly what they are doing and how well they are succeeding at achieving their objectives. Minimum standards in such areas as the curricular offerings, promotion of students, instructional materials, and more recently, graduation requirements stated in achievement rather than credit terms, are other mechanisms whereby the states have exercised their growing power. Textbook selections are sometimes mandated, either in the form of statewide adoptions of one set of texts or in approved listings from which local districts may choose. In recent years, textbooks and nationally developed curricular materials have provided local and state battlegrounds in such subjects as religion, values, and evolution. Statewide courses of study can also be found. Program decisions have traditionally been made more at the local rather than the state level; with the increase in state funding, however, it is likely that these prerogatives will shift more to the state boards of education and become more embroiled in the legislative and political arenas.

The certification of teachers is a function of the state, having shifted from the local level in the past half century. Most states currently approve teacher training programs at institutions of higher education and then automatically certify their graduates. Minimum standards on such things as course work and student teaching, however, are generally laid down by law, so that great variation does not exist between programs. Accrediting organizations, such as the National Council for the Accreditation of Teacher Education (NCATE), have also had an impact on the quality of certification programs and have helped to facilitate reciprocal certification agreements between states. Teachers' groups such as the National Education Association (NEA) and the American Federation of Teachers (AFT) have begun to exercise an increasingly greater influence over teacher preservice and inservice programs; but the legal control still rests firmly with the states.

Schools' physical facilities are generally built with local funds, through the passage of bond issues, although some states have created special programs to help needy districts. The quality of school buildings is controlled by state rules and regulations, both in the initial planning and building, and also in the standards for maintenance and safety.

The right for private and parochial schools to exist was guaranteed in 1925 in the Oregon case, *Pierce* v. *Society of the Sisters of the Holy Names of Jesus and Mary*. The control of the various states over private schools varies greatly, all the way from those which do not even keep records as to what schools exist, to others which require private schools to conform to all statutes applying to the public schools.

THE LOCAL SCHOOL DISTRICT

The decentralized nature of the administration of American schooling is one of its most distinctive features. Although education is a growing federal concern and the legal responsibility of the state, it is at the local level that much of the decision-making power still rests.

historical background

Educational historians trace the beginnings of local control of education to the Massachusetts Bay Colony, which in 1647 decentralized education down to the level of the town or township and mandated that local officials provide for the education of the young. Despite the inability of towns to serve the rural areas very satisfactorily and the lack of resources in many of the smaller districts, the Massachusetts model of small local districts was adopted throughout many parts of the United States. In the Midwest, Far West, and Northwest large numbers of rural school districts were formed, and only in recent years has consolidation led to larger, more economically viable districts in these parts of the country. In the South, during Colonial days, much of the education was a function of the Church of England, which was organized on a parish or county basis. With the adoption of the Constitution and the separation of church and state, the county unit of schooling was maintained and has since been adopted outside the South by Utah and Nevada.

the nature of local districts

Through legislative action or constitutional mandate, the states create local governments. These governmental units—cities, counties, water districts, or school districts—are created to serve a particular function or set of functions and are delegated the authority to achieve their purposes. Historically, the schools were founded by local communities, and thus there is a long tradition of having the most power at the local level. Receiving their delegated authority from the states, rather than from municipal or county governments, they often function autonomously from other local governmental bodies. The local school district possesses quasi-corporate powers, but the legislature has the power to create, destroy, or reorganize school districts as it sees fit. This legislative supremacy has been well established in the courts, but politicians are wary when it comes to changing what have been traditional prerogatives at the local level. Whereas the local school district often encompassed only a one-room school, today "local" districts may enroll hundreds of thousands of students, employ tens of thousands of teachers, and have a budget in excess of one-half billion dollars. With these changes have come recent pressures to decentralize the large, impersonal, urban school systems.

organization of local districts

Groups of lay citizens, known as the board of education, school board, school trustees, or some similar name, are elected by the public, and given legal authority by the legislature to carry out an educational program at the local level. Board members are appointed by the mayor in a few large-city school districts, but most are elected in nonpartisan elections. Terms of office are generally from three to five years, and the size of boards varies from three to as many as fifteen, with seven considered the ideal number by many experts. Most board members serve without pay, although a few cities pay expenses. Traditionally, boards of education have been dominated by businessmen and professionals, with a large underrepresentation of the poor, minorities, and women. In recent years, gains have been made by these previously underrepresented groups.

Certain functions performed by the local board of education are mandated by state law. The state school code must be adhered to in such matters as curriculum, finance, building codes, certification, and attendance, but if the board wishes to go beyond the minimums stated in the laws, they enter the discretionary part of their work. With demands by the public for accountability in the schools, and the increasing pressure by many community groups for inclusion in the decision-making process, the role of the school boards has changed. Without question, one of the most important functions performed by the school board is the selection of a superintendent and the approval of the staff of administrators and teachers.

It is the superintendent of schools who is delegated the responsibility for efficient management of local education. The superintendent and his staff are charged with carrying out the instructional program, making personnel decisions, and administering the business end of the schooling process. With increasing pressures from teachers' organizations and community groups, and the budget crises facing many districts today, the superintendency of schools is one of the most difficult positions in society. School boards have often been proving grounds for politicians wishing to make a name for themselves, with the resultant use of the schools and the superintendents as pawns in political game-playing.

the local district: a position

Local control of education has a long and honorable history in American history. Self-government, dispersion of power, and freedom of choice are phrases which are used often in local school elections. With the exception of California, Illinois, Nebraska, and Texas, most states have already gone through the traumatic reorganization of small, inefficient rural school districts. Many still remain, but most districts in the country today are viable from the standpoints of both student population and economics. The challenges to local school district organization in the last quarter of the twentieth century, are the maintenance of positive educational traditions in the declining rural population, and the reorganization of the urban, metropolitan areas. Residents of our large cities, often minority groups, are demanding a greater participation in their schools, with decentralization and citizen participation becoming increasingly more important political themes. The shrinking tax bases in the large cities and the migration of the upwardly mobile middle class to the suburbs have left the city schools without enough funds to carry out their educational programs. Metropolitan-wide districts that include the "wealthy" suburbs may be necessary in the not-too-distant future. But with this trend towards financial centralization must also come the decentralization of much of the decision-making, or the alienation felt by many parents, teachers, and students will only continue to rise. The challenge, then, is, how can school organization move towards ever-increasing centralization of finances and other services at the metropolitan, state, or federal levels, while still retaining some semblance of local control and initiative. In an era of financial crisis, the schools must also take a hard look at their traditional autonomy from other governmental entities and decide how they can best cooperate with cities, counties, and states to prevent the overlap of buildings and services.

SCHOOL-ATTENDANCE AREAS

The final level of school organization and administration we shall deal with is the school-attendance area, or district. Attendance areas are designated by the school board and administration, and all children within a given area must attend the "local" school. The lines between attendance areas and busing between attendance areas are the cause of many disputes and even violence, as has been evidenced in the battles over court-ordered busing for racial reasons. Attendance areas vary in size, with several elementary schools within one junior high school area, two or more junior high schools within a high school area, and several high schools in a junior college attendance area.

School boards have the legal right to assign students to any school within the district, provided the distance is not too far, the safety of the children is not endangered, or that it is not done on the basis of race to maintain segregation. Many schools have adopted some form of limited open enrollment, in which students can attend a school other than that to which they have been assigned, provided there is space available in the new location. Voluntary enrollment programs have become popular during the time of "forced" busing, and where the courts permit it.

School attendance areas are set up for a variety of geographical, administrative, or socio-political reasons. The size of an area to be served provides some limitation, as do such natural barriers as mountains or rivers and man-made barriers such as superhighways. The socio-political reasons for attendance areas have generally been struck down by the courts but even though racial segregation, de facto or de jure, has been denied the schools, the integration of social classes is nevertheless a long way off. This is particularly true in the large metropolitan areas, where the poor and minorities are often integrated in the inner city, while the more affluent white-Anglo population remains segregated in the suburbs. The courts have attempted to deal with this problem by cross-district busing programs as mandated by the lower court decision in Detroit, but a five to four Supreme Court reversal in 1974 prevented the regionalization of the desegregation effort.

LEVELS OF SCHOOL ORGANIZATION

The pattern of school organization varies throughout the United States. Theoretically, the organization of schools should be determined by the purposes and needs of the children being served, but as with many other aspects of education, historical precedent has often proven to be more persuasive than logic. Size and location of buildings or financial considerations have led to numerous school-district grade patterns. All too often, an old high school is turned into a junior high school, or when student enrollment demands some pattern other than a traditional 6-3-3 or 6-2-4 plan, a middle school is created.

Until 1910, the 8-4 plan, with an 11-year variant, 7-4, was dominant throughout the United States. This slowly gave way, except in rural areas, to some plan involving a 2- or 3-year junior high school. The 6-3-3 has become the most popular form, although defenders of the 6-2-4 system hold that it is superior, especially in certain areas of the Midwest where there are both elementary school districts covering grades K-8 and separate secondary districts covering 9-12. Other reasons for clinging to the two-year junior high school are the perception that a four-year high school is a better college preparatory institution, a two-year junior high school is more economical, as it doesn't need all the facilities of the three-year institution, and the age range in a three-year junior high school is too broad.

Another trend in school organization has been the addition of the junior college to the top end of the scale. At one time there were quite a number of four-year junior colleges (11-14), particularly in California, but these have disappeared, and the grades 13 and 14 are almost universal today. At the lower end of the school district organization, nursery schools have been added. The biggest impetus to the inclusion of preschool education in the public sector has come through the Head Start program begun in the 1960s. Numerous bills are pending in Congress to provide publicly financed day-care and nursery school programs for working parents, and the battle has begun as to whether these programs should form part of the public school system, be run by private individuals or corporations, or be some mixture of the two. The stakes are tremendous, with billions of dollars involved and hundreds of thousands of jobs.

EARLY CHILDHOOD EDUCATION

The most extensive part of early childhood education is the kindergarten. The extent of growth in the kindergarten movement can be seen in its enrollment figures: 225,394 in 1899-1900, compared with 2,838,190 in fall, 1973.[22] The kindergarten movement traces its history back to Friedrich Froebel, who founded the first kindergarten (literally, "garden for children") in Blankenburg, Germany in 1837. It had a sound theoretical base and was an idea whose time had come. The first public American kindergarten was founded in St. Louis in 1873, and by the

[22] Ibid., p. 7.

early 1880s they could be found in almost every major city in the United States. The first private kindergarten was opened by Mrs. Carl Schurz in 1855, in Watertown, Wisconsin. Although kindergarten is not mandatory throughout the United States, by October, 1974, over 100 years after the start of the movement in this country, 78.6 percent of all five year olds were enrolled in some form of preprimary education.[23]

Early childhood education for three and four year olds is an even newer phenomenon than the kindergarten. In 1920 there were only three recognized nursery schools in the United States. By 1974, 19.9 percent of three year olds and 37.6 percent of four year olds were enrolled in public or nonpublic nursery school programs. In that year, 685,000 three year olds and 1,322,000 four year olds were attending some kind of early childhood education program.[24]

Although early childhood education is an accepted part of the American educational scene, it is still not a formal part of most school systems. At the three- and four-year-old stage, most schooling is conducted by private nursery schools. In the 1972 and 1976 political campaigns, public provision of early childhood education became an important issue of debate, and Congress and many state legislatures continue to debate day-care and early childhood education programs, financed by state and federal funds. The precedent for public involvement can be found in the Head Start program, begun in the 1960s as part of the federal poverty program. Research on the effects of Head Start finds important short-term gains when children enter the regular school, but the long-term benefits appear to be lacking. The program has become popular among the poor, developed a strong political base, and withstood many efforts to kill it. It has filled an important need in the lives of children and families with its individualized, child-oriented, educational environment.

The pioneering developmental psychology studies of Jean Piaget and the writings of Maria Montessori have given early childhood education a solid theoretical base upon which to build. Early childhood education is concerned with the physical, emotional, and social growth of children, and in providing places which can prepare the child for the shift from home to school. Formal, pressured, competitive learning situations are frowned upon in most preschools, but much in the way of readiness activities is made available to the children to prepare them for the primary grades.

Critics of early childhood education blame it for the break-up of the home and the taking away of further responsibility from parents; but as long as there are working parents, poverty for many children, and the need to help children make the adjustment from home to school, it is likely that such schooling will continue to be the growth edge in school enrollment.

[23] Ibid., p. 47.
[24] Ibid., p. 47.

ELEMENTARY SCHOOLS

If the social and emotional development of the child takes precedence during preschool education, the intellectual development is the major function of the elementary school. This is not to say that socialization or the development of self-awareness, -understanding, and -realization are left out of schooling, but rather that American elementary education has academic achievement as its basic goal.

organization

Elementary education, as has been indicated earlier, generally consists of six years of schooling, preceded by kindergarten. New organizational plans, however, have limited elementary education to four or five years followed by middle schools; others have created two nearly separate institutions—primary education consisting of grades 1–3 and intermediate, grades 4–6. Even more revolutionary in its attempt to get away from the traditional K– vertical organization is the multigrading system, in which a given class contains pupils from more than one grade, and pupils progress at their own pace in each subject area. For example, a student might be at a sixth-grade level in science, fourth grade in reading, and fifth grade in mathematics. Nongraded schools have also made their appearance, generally being divided into a nongraded primary unit and a nongraded intermediate unit. Individual progress is the key to the reclassification of students, not their age. The purpose of doing away with grade labels is to make it easier for each individual child to learn.

Except for institutions modeled on the British Infant School, most elementary schools in the United States assemble children into class-sized learning groups based on some criterion. Age is the most often used, but groups can also be formed based on intelligence test scores, achievement in subject matter areas, emotional, physical, or social maturity, or other factors. Research does not bear out the value of homogeneous grouping when based on intelligence or achievement, even though a large percentage of teachers claim better results when children are homogeneously grouped. Flexible grouping, in which pupils are grouped in a number of different ways throughout the school day, appears to be the dominant form in use today in American elementary schools.

Taking their lead from the British Infant School movement and such programs as Follow Through (the elementary continuation of Head Start), many schools in Vermont and North Dakota, as well as hundreds of individual schools throughout the United States, have rejected traditional grading and grouping practices. In their place have been substituted activity-centered, child-centered informal teaching and learning situations. Rigid timetables have been abandoned, but unlike the progressive schools of the 1920s and 1930s, these schools recognize the central role played by the teacher. Teachers do not deliver lectures to young children, but are actively involved in creating the learning environment and in helping the children to achieve.

Another aspect of organization in the elementary school is whether the classroom should be self-contained or departmentalized. In the self-contained classroom, the teacher is responsible for all aspects of the curriculum. A partially self-contained classroom, perhaps the dominant mode today, has the teacher involved in all the "basic" subjects, with specialists handling art, music, and physical education. At the intermediate level, the trend appears to be in the direction of departmentalization, with each teacher being responsible for only one or two subjects, similar to that found at the junior and senior high school level. Self-contained classrooms are generally defended on the grounds that children feel more secure relating to one teacher and that curriculum integration is more likely than under a departmentalized scheme. The reality of teacher preparation and interest dictates against any one teacher being a master of all aspects of the curriculum, and critics maintain that certain areas, often science and mathematics, suffer as a result. The dual progress plan of organization attempts to combine the best aspects of both the self-contained and departmentalized forms of organization. Under this plan, students receive their language arts and social studies in the morning with one teacher, and then rotate in the afternoon with specialists in science, mathematics, art, and music.

Team teaching is another innovation, in which two or more teachers, working together, are given the responsibility for the instruction of the same group of students. The teachers share the responsibility for planning, teaching, and evaluating. A team of three teachers would be assigned seventy-five to one hundred pupils. Unless the teams are carefully selected, with compatibility of personality and competencies, they can often lead to turn-teaching, or to negative learning environments created by hostility among members of the team. In addition to personal attributes, appropriate schedules and space are needed for successful team teaching. Team teaching has never fulfilled the high expectations of its proponents. Tradition, the design of school buildings, constant evaluation by peers, and lack of effective team leaders are some of the probable causes for its lack of widespread acceptance.

The relatively new deployment of teachers and staff is known as differentiated staffing. Under this organization, the staff of a school are broken down into new categories, with a highly trained master teacher serving as leader of a team made up of senior teachers having master's degrees, staff teachers with bachelor's degrees, associate teachers, teacher assistants, educational technicians, and clerks. Proponents of differentiated staffing claim that it takes greater advantage of the differing abilities and interests of teachers, in addition to allowing the real professional to remain in the classroom, rather than go into administration for higher salary or prestige. Teachers' associations have generally been skeptical, seeing it as a mechanism for rewarding the few teachers at the top, while keeping salaries and prestige for the vast majority at relatively low levels. As a means for introducing paraprofessionals (often minorities who have not gone through teacher preparation programs) into the classroom, this staffing pattern has something to offer. The time for widespread deployment of differentiated staffing has not arrived, and until further experimentation and research establish its effectiveness, it remains one of those organizational innovations that may improve the quality of education; but given the lack of success with most other "reforms," dramatic change is unlikely.

THE SCHOOL IN BETWEEN

Until the early twentieth century, education in the United States was organized on a 6–6 or 8–4 system. In rural areas and some big cities, this type of school organization can still be found, but the dominant pattern has changed to a 6–3–3 system. Although Richmond, Indiana, set up the first two-year junior high school in a separate building in 1896, two educational systems more nationally known for their schools, Columbus, Ohio, and Berkeley, California, are credited with beginning the junior high school movement in 1909. It was a movement whose time had come, and must go down in history as one of the more rapidly adopted educational innovations. By 1917, there were 217 junior high schools, and by 1960, over 80 percent of the appropriate age group were enrolled in junior high schools.[25]

Even as it achieved its near total dominance, the junior high school began to come in for criticism from psychologists and educators who believed that the "ideal" school organization was not the 6–3–3 system, but rather a 5–3–4 or a 4–4–4, the school in between being called a "middle-school," rather than a junior high school. The trend since 1960 has been away from the junior high school towards the middle school, to the extent that in 1965 Paul Woodring stated that "it now appears that the 6–3–3 plan, with its junior high school, is on the way out."[26]

The news of their death, however, failed to reach most of the junior high schools, for they appear to be alive, if not well, in the middle of the

[25]William M. Alexander and others, *The Emergent Middle School* (New York: Holt, Rinehart and Winston, Inc., 1968), p. 46.
[26]Paul Woodring, "The New Intermediate School," *Saturday Review*, 48, no. 42 (October 16, 1965), p. 77.

1970s. A strong case can be made for the middle school from a variety of pedagogical, psychological, and developmental perspectives, and it appears that the slowness with which the idea has caught on results from economic and not educational reasons. The massive building boom has slowed in much of the country, an effect of the leveling-off of enrollments and the public's failure to pass bond issues. Without new school buildings to move into, many aspects of the middle school movement lost their momentum. The innovative period of the 1960s peaked, and the pendulum appears to have swung back towards a return to the basics, so that parents and school boards have not looked so kindly on massive reorganization of the schools. These and other reasons have slowed, but not stopped, the movement away from the junior high school.

purposes of the junior high school

The junior high school began as the mechanism for providing students with a secondary education at an earlier age. It has kept this basic goal throughout its history, and it is precisely this purpose that most advocates of the middle school point to as a basic reason for abolishing it. The junior high school has developed into a mini-high school, with interscholastic athletics competition, bands and orchestras, and a curriculum that mirrors that of the high school. Teaching methods tend to be those of the high school and college, with little to appeal to the "in-between-ager," as the child from eleven to fourteen has been called by some observers. Other traditional purposes of the junior high school have been to serve as a place in which children can explore a variety of subjects before they "specialize" in high school and college; to serve as a transition from the self-contained classroom at the elementary level to the departmentalization of the high schools; to serve as a weaning area in which children are given greater independence; to provide greater depth in the subject matter than is found in the elementary school; and to provide academic and vocational guidance.

the middle school and its purposes

Advocates of the middle school give the junior high school failing marks in its attempt to fulfill most of its basic purposes. Middle school proponents give numerous justifications for its existence, among them: to provide a program meeting the wide range of individual differences and needs; to provide specialization in subjects that most upper elementary teachers are not prepared to teach; to start pupils earlier in certain subjects such as foreign languages; to prevent the academic, social, and athletic patterns of the high school from becoming the dominant pattern for the eleven to fourteen year olds; and to these are added, interestingly enough, most of the same purposes given at the founding of the junior high school early in the twentieth century. It is our opinion that the middle school advocates make a strong case for the new organizational structure, particularly when they use the arguments of developmental and child psychology.

children, in-between-agers, and adolescents

Since its founding in 1909, the rationale for some kind of junior high school or in-between school has found a solid base in the research done on human growth and development. This same research has also led many educators to advocate that the in-between institution begin at age ten or eleven instead of waiting until children reach twelve or thirteen, the traditional age to enter junior high school. As every parent can attest, dramatic physiological, emotional, and intellectual changes occur during this three- to five-year period in the life of every young person. It is also true that these changes can occur any time during a several year span. Fifth- and sixth-grade boys may be as immature, physiologically, as seven or eight year olds, whereas girls in the same class may be as mature as fifteen year olds;

Figure 9-1   Instruction Must Be Geared to the Needs of the Age Group

and the range in the eighth grade may be from ten to seventeen for the boys or girls. This dramatic range of differences makes it necessary that the middle school offer a program geared to the needs of each individual child, not to some mythical norm. Dramatic changes in metabolic rate have been found for children in this age group, causing rapid changes in behavior, and Piaget has pointed up the differences between children who are still in the concrete stage of their development and those in the formal-operations stage.

Although they are often ignored in the traditional junior high school, the personality changes occurring in children as they progress into adolescence is perhaps the most important part of the process which the school must take into account. The concept of self, one's sex role, the identification with one's peers are all going through often painful and wrenching changes. Relationships with parents and all authority figures go through a redefinition, moral values come up for examination, and abstract thinking becomes a part of the intellectual arsenal of the new adolescent.

the middle school: a position

As the reader has no doubt discerned, we believe the junior high school is an obsolete institution, in desperate need of replacement by something more geared to the needs, interests, aspirations of this age group. The middle school seems to have developed a solid research base and rationale for its existence, and would appear to be a good alternative. Given the emotional, physiological, and intellectual changes which children begin to experience as early as fifth grade, it is imperative to create some type of institution specifically geared to meeting their individual needs. We fear, however, that the middle school will cause the schools to become departmentalized down to the fifth grade, and that instead of a new, more humane institution, we will have the high school and university brought down to the elementary school child. Unless teachers are specifically trained for the middle school, special materials and teaching methods are developed, and the community accepts the rationale and program of the middle school, we believe the risks of failure may outweigh the benefits gained from the organizational change.

HIGH SCHOOL

It is little known to the general public that the comprehensive secondary school, enrolling most of the fourteen to seventeen year olds in the community, is a comparatively recent invention. In the year 1889–90, only 6.7 percent of this age group was enrolled, and in 1909–10, only 15.4 percent; by 1929–30, over 50 percent of the age group were in attendance. Since 1960, the enrollment has remained around the 90 percent mark, with slight fluctuations up and down.[27]

historical background

The modern comprehensive high school didn't suddenly spring into existence in the early part of this century. Its roots can be traced back to the Latin grammar schools of the Middle Ages throughout Europe and particularly those of England. The early Latin grammar schools in America were institutions geared at producing ministers for the Puritan churches of New England, and thus took on a more religious flavor than the "humanistic" institutions of Europe. The Latin grammar school with its academic and religious emphasis never really caught on in the New World, though some of the early institutions have survived to the present day. Private-venture academies, such as that envisioned by Benjamin Franklin, soon replaced the Latin grammar school as the dominant secondary institution in the Colonies. The academies offered a more practical and scientific curriculum, with such subjects as drawing, accounting, astronomy, mechanics, and commerce, in addition to the more traditional humanities. Academies often turned themselves into college preparatory schools, and the demand built up again for a new kind of institution. The first "high school" was founded in Boston and was named the Boston English Classical High School. High schools soon spread throughout the frontier, and were generally day schools, operated by a school board, with little or no fees. The academies that continued to exist alongside the new institution were generally fee-charging boarding schools operated by private organizations. An important court case in 1874 in Michigan recognized the "common-school" nature of the high school and held that it was permissible for tax funds to be used to support the public high school, not just the elementary common school.

The battle over the nature of the high school began back in colonial times and has not ended even today. Some saw the secondary school as an elitist, academic, college preparatory institution, while others found in it the possibilities of a democratic institution, preparing students not only for college, but, should they not care to go on for more schooling, one giving them the necessary vocational training. Numerous commissions were appointed to deal with the structure of secondary education, and as a result of the 1918 Commission on the Reorganization of Secondary Education, many current practices were begun. The concept of fifteen or sixteen units of work in six basic disciplines was instituted, and is still alive and functioning in most institutions. The four- or six-year nature of secondary educa-

[27]Grant and Lind, *Digest*, p. 37.

tion was recognized, and graduation from secondary school replaced examinations as the dominant requirement for entrance to the universities. The same Commission enunciated for the first time the Seven Cardinal Principles. The seven principles helped to shift the focus away from the strictly academic nature of secondary education up until that time, and placed some other priorities on the schools. Since 1918, numerous other commissions have listed appropriate goals for secondary education, many of them stated in much more sophisticated, behavioral terms, but almost all of them include in one form or another the Seven Cardinal Principles.

(These principals as well as descriptions of elementary and secondary school curricula are found in Chapter 10.)

CASE STUDY: Changing School Organization

Place yourself in the position of an intermediate or junior high school teacher who has been asked to help organize the new middle school, recently voted in by the Board of Education. The system will be moving from the current 6–3–3 system of organization to 4–4–4, with a four-year middle school. You have been asked to serve on a committee made up of administrators, teachers, parents, and students.

You have already taught for several years at your current school, and a major shift in organization will no doubt entail many changes in the curriculum, teaching methods, and textbooks. The parents in the community fear that the change will have a negative effect on their boys' athletic opportunities, and that the move is really only another of those "radical" ideas by the new superintendent.

What concerns do you feel the teachers have when moving over to the new system? How are you going to facilitate the adjustment of teachers and students to the new school? What can be done about the parents who have decided to actively oppose the move? Deal with changes that will need to occur in curriculum, teaching methods, athletics, guidance programs, extra-curricular activities, facilities, and any other changes you think need to be considered.

THOUGHT QUESTIONS

1. What advantages and disadvantages can you see to having three levels of government, federal, state, and local, involved in financing and administration of the schools?

2. What is meant by equalizing educational opportunity within a state? What should a state do to guarantee or not guarantee it?

3. What strengths and weaknesses can you see in a system such as ours, which places much of the power to control education at the local level?

4. The schools and other local and state governmental agencies duplicate many facilities and programs. Given the financial crises facing most governmental agencies, what can be done to save money and prevent duplication?

5. What are some of the causes of the increase in secondary education since 1890, when only 6.7 percent of fourteen to seventeen year olds were enrolled, to the more than 90 percent enrollment today? What are the positive and negative effects of the increase in enrollment?

6. Schools today in the United States are organized by age-level in a variety of ways: 6-3-3, 6-2-4, 4-4-4, to name only a few. Taking into consideration physiological, emotional, intellectual, and other factors, which do you believe is the most appropriate organizational scheme?

7. It is often said that the group or individual that pays the bills "calls the tune." Can you see any way for local control of schools to be retained in the face of ever greater state and federal centralization of financing?

PRACTICAL ACTIVITIES

1. Visit a local school district's administrative offices to obtain a copy of the organizational chart and administrative hierarchy. In addition, obtain a copy of the goals and purposes of the district. How compatible are the goals and purposes with the organizational and administrative structure of the district?

2. Attend a state or local school board meeting and note the ethnic, sexual, and socio-economic makeup of the board and the audience. What can you tell about the superintendent's relationship with the board?

3. Obtain a copy of a local school district budget. Note the sources and percentages of funds from various sources, and how these funds are expended.

4. From local school district sources, find out what federal educational programs are in operation in the district, and what control the federal government exercises over those programs.

5. Find out what early childhood programs operate in your school district and whether they are in publicly or privately run institutions.

6. Discuss the educational philosophy of his or her institution with a middle school or junior high school teacher or administrator.

BIBLIOGRAPHY

ALEXANDER, WILLIAM M. AND OTHERS, *The Emergent Middle School*. New York: Holt, Rinehart & Winston, Inc., 1968.

ANDERSON, LESTER W., AND LAURA A. VAN DYKE, *Secondary School Administration* (2nd Edition) Boston: Houghton Mifflin Company, 1972.

BRUBAKER, DALE L., AND ROLAND H. NELSON, *Creative Survival in Educational Bureaucracies*. Berkeley, California: McCutchan Publishing Corporation, 1974.
CAMPBELL, ROALD F. AND OTHERS, *The Organization and Control of American Schools* (3rd Edition.). Columbus, Ohio: Charles E. Merrill Publishing Co., 1975.
CORWIN, RONALD G., *Militant Professionalism: A Study of Organizational Conflict in High Schools*. New York: Appleton-Century-Crofts, 1970.
FRANKLIN, MARIAN POPE, *School Organization, Theory and Practice*. Chicago: Rand McNally & Company, 1967.
HAUBRICH, VERNON F., *Freedom, Bureaucracy and Schooling*. Washington, D.C.: Association for Supervision and Curriculum Development, 1971.
MILSTEIN, MIKE M., AND JAMES A. BELASCO, eds. *Educational Administration and the Behavioral Sciences: A Systems Perspective*. Boston: Allyn & Bacon, Inc., 1973.
NOAR, GERTRUDE, *The Junior High School, Today and Tomorrow*. Englewood Cliffs, N.J.: Prentice-Hall, 1961.
POPPER, SAMUEL H., *The American Middle School: An Organizational Analysis*. Waltham, Mass.: Blaisdell Publishing Company, 1967.
SMITH, LOUIS M., AND PAT M. KEITH, *Anatomy of Educational Innovation: An Organizational Analysis of an Elementary School*. New York: John Wiley & Sons, Inc., 1971.

CURRICULUM
The Structure of the System

Curriculum is one of the most commonly used words of educational jargon and one of the most poorly defined. It is given a most restricted definition by some, while others see it as all the educational experiences of a learner in the school environment, or as "something that happens to learners." Rather than waste time in a futile debate of the concept and definition, this chapter will deal with some of the societal and other sources of what occurs in schools, and then detail what it is that happens within the boxes which we label as subject areas.

THE CONTENT OF THE CURRICULUM

Inlow suggests that there are three basic sources from which we draw the substance of what goes on in our schools: (1) the age-old disciplines, (2) the emerging disciplines, and (3) the contemporary world.[1] Goodlad gives the three sources as societal pressure, the learner, and the organized subject matter itself.[2]

---

[1] Gail M. Inlow, *The Emergent in Curriculum* (New York: John Wiley & Sons, Inc., 1966), p. 13.
[2] John I. Goodlad, *School, Curriculum and the Individual* (Waltham, Mass.: Blaisdell Publishing Company, 1966), pp. 148–162.

One of the most important sources of curriculum and curricular change has been the knowledge explosion. Since it is manifestly impossible to teach everything there is to know, educators must select from among a growing number of options that which is most appropriate and important for a child to know. With the expansion of knowledge, the ability of students to think for themselves and act like scientists became important curricular objectives, in addition to the traditional mastery of information. Modern technology in the form of computers, machinery of all types, and the mass media have also had profound curricular implications, not only from the standpoint of the kinds of jobs for which the schools must prepare their students, but also in the way in which technology can be put to instructional use. Numerous other societal influences, such as the environmental crises, issues of war and peace, life expectancy and other demographic factors, and economic factors of wealth and poverty, affect what happens to the child in the school setting.

Equally significant for curricular change and reform have been understandings about how and when children learn, ideas gleaned from developmental and educational psychologists. In such areas as physical, emotional, and social maturation and their effects on learning, much research has gone into the concept of pupil readiness. The research of Piaget has been most important in helping to develop appropriate materials for children in school, while the concepts of Maria Montessori have given additional impetus to the movement to provide students with tasks appropriate to their stage of development. Moving children from the specific and the concrete to the general and more abstract is another curricular principle taken from research on children's styles of learning.

Jerome Bruner in his book *The Process of Education*[3] set forth most clearly the third major source of curricular decisions, namely the academic disciplines themselves. Numerous school subjects went through a dramatic reform in the early 1960s as a result of Bruner and his colleagues' emphasis upon the disciplines. Inlow lists the basic points made by the disciplinary theorists as follows:

1. Each discipline has its own unique structure.
2. Structure within each discipline consists of the fundamentals (and/or concepts, and/or powerful ideas) that are sequential and related.
3. Because mastery of copious detail is impossible and undesirable, details should be grouped into a structured pattern of concepts, formulas and theory from which nonspecific as well as specific transfer may be made.
4. Each discipline has its own methods and tools of discovery—sometimes discrete, sometimes shared with other disciplines.
5. Teaching and learning should follow the methods that brought the discipline into being in the first place, and act, on a continuing basis, to refine its conceptualizations.

[3]Jerome S. Bruner, *The Process of Education* (Cambridge, Mass.: Harvard University Press, 1960).

6. A discipline is never to be converted into a teaching arrangement; it is the teaching arrangement. It is to be learned as the scholars learned it and developed it.
7. A study of, and in, the disciplines should constitute educational effort from the earliest elementary grades until general education terminates, and study at all levels should be organized around the central themes of each discipline.[4]

Bruner and his colleagues felt that American schools had paid too much attention to the learner and his environment in previous decades, and sought to redress the imbalance. If the 1960s was the decade of the disciplines, the pendulum kept in motion, and many educators by the late 1960s and early 1970s were calling for a more humane schooling and a new emphasis upon the emotional side of the learner. In the mid 1970s the call had gone up for a return to the basics. Whether the curriculum is caught on a pendulum or goes through some type of cyclical reform movement is difficult to say, but in the area of what should be taught and the methods for teaching it, there is a constant call for change and reform.

Many observers of curriculum at all levels have placed it on a continuum from subject-centered on the one extreme to learner-centered on the other extreme, with the one emphasizing content and the other process. Table 10–1 compares the extremes of the two curricular positions.

Few schools fit into one extreme or the other completely. Individual classrooms that vary from the dominant mode can be found within most schools. With all the publicity attending the progressive-school movement of the 1920s and 1930s, many felt that the student-centered curriculum had come to be the dominant mode. Critics of the schools, however, point out that even at its height, progressive education was dominant in only a small percentage of American elementary or secondary schools. In spite of changes in the schools during the 1960s, making them more humane and student-oriented, only a small percentage of schools changed towards the more open, free environments envisioned by advocates of alternative education. All of this is to say that the elementary and secondary curricula in the 1970s are still basically subject- and content-oriented as opposed to student- and process-oriented.

GOALS OF ELEMENTARY EDUCATION

objectives

Education at the elementary level in colonial times was usually a function of the church and had as its basic purpose the salvation of the child from sin. With the development of mass education in the nineteenth century, social and economic objectives took primacy. The immigrants flooding American

[4]Inlow, *The Emergent in Curriculum*, p. 15.

Table 10-1

Traditional, Subject-Centered Schools	Contemporary, Student-Centered, Humanistic Schools
1. Teacher controls all aspects of learning.	1. Learning enviroment is cooperatively developed by parents, students, and teacher.
2. Facts dominate the curriculum.	2. Discovery, inquiry, and meaning are more important than discrete facts.
3. Rigidity	3. Flexibility
4. All students do the same thing at the same time.	4. Individualized education and varying the program to meet the needs of each child.
5. Isolation from society	5. Integration with the society
6. Sterile environment	6. Creative environment
7. Emphasis on permanence and tradition	7. Emphasis upon change and the future.
8. Product	8. Process
9. Control and constraint	9. Freedom
10. External discipline	10. Internal discipline
11. Authority	11. Self-actualization
12. Subject-centered	12. Person-centered
13. Emphasis on teaching	13. Emphasis on learning
14. Competition	14. Cooperation
15. Only the best succeed	15. Everyone succeeds
16. Group works at same rate	16. Individualized rates
17. Learn only from teacher	17. Learn from fellow students
18. All education in the school	18. Education in many environments
19. Adults are responsible	19. Children are responsible
20. Children perceived as untrustworthy	20. Children perceived as trustworthy
21. Intolerance of ambiguity	21. Tolerance of ambiguity
22. Controlling	22. Freeing

shores were seen as a threat to the status quo, Christian values, and the white, Anglo-Saxon, Protestant ethic. The elementary schools, both private and later public, were seen as the mechanism to insure that the great "unwashed" mass of immigrants became good Americans and productive citizens on the farms and in the factories of the United States.

With the expansion of secondary education in the twentieth century and the impact of such men as Edward L. Thorndike and John Dewey, elementary education began to change. It was no longer terminal for all students, and began to be looked upon as a preparatory institution for the high school. Thorndike took many of the ideas of psychology and applied them to the school situation, emphasizing such concepts as the importance of readiness in the child's ability to learn, and the transferability of learned material and behaviors from one situation to another. His stimulus-response theories led to greater emphasis upon drill. John Dewey, without doubt the greatest educator America has ever produced, had a profound impact on elementary education. Basing his educational theory on pragmatic philosophy and his study of psychology, Dewey emphasized the importance of the school as a socializing agent. Education should not be preparation for life, but a slice of life itself. Schools were to become more humane and child-centered, with subject matter being a means to the end of helping each child reach his fullest potential. The social and emotional parts of the child received new emphasis, to the extent that in some of the progressive schools, critics felt that almost all cognitive goals had been abandoned. Dewey is often blamed for the decline in basic skills and the excesses within the progressive movement, but a careful reading of his work indicates his lifelong commitment to cognitive skills and the scientific method, in addition to humanizing the school environment.

The Commission on Reorganization of Secondary Education produced what became known as the Seven Cardinal Principles. These principles, although formally designed for the newly emerging secondary schools in 1918, were also applicable to and affected the elementary schools. With the possible exception of vocational training, the other six goals influenced curricular development at the elementary level. They were: health, citizenship, worthy use of leisure time, command of the fundamental processes, worthy home membership, and ethical character.[5] These goals can now be found in one form or another in the stated objectives of almost every school district in the United States and in numerous other countries. In recent years, with the growth of career education, even the vocational goals can be found at the elementary level. The National Education Association has also been active in defining objectives for the elementary schools. Its Educational Policies Commission, in its influential report in 1938, grouped forty-three objectives into four main headings: self-realization, human relationships, economic efficiency, and responsibility.[6]

The Russell Sage Foundation report in 1953, by Nolan Kearney, submitted an extensive list of objectives in nine basic categories adding to previous lists such things as physical and esthetic development.[7] In 1956, The Yale-Fairfield study of Elementary Teaching repeated the same objectives with slightly different wording.[8]

The constant restating of what appear to be obvious objectives of elementary education is of questionable value. How dominant these objectives are when compared to the reality of schooling in this country is an important area of study and concern. Charles Silberman in his important

[5] Commission on Reorganization of Secondary Education, *Cardinal Principles of Education*, U.S. Office of Education Bulletin No. 35, 1918 (Washington, D.C.: U. S. Government Printing Office, 1918), pp. 10–11.

[6] Educational Policies Commission, *The Purposes of Education in American Democracy* (Washington, D.C.: National Education Association, 1938), pp. 50–108.

[7] Nolan C. Kearney, *Elementary School Objectives* (New York: Russell Sage Foundation, 1953), pp. 52–113.

[8] C. M. Hill and others, *Yale Fairfield Study of Elementary Teaching* (New Haven, Conn.: Yale University Press, 1956).

Figure 10-1 Elementary Instruction Takes Many Forms

work, *Crisis in the Classroom*, lists four characteristics which all schools share in common: (1) Attendance is compulsory, and children must attend school whether they want to or not; (2) the length of schooling is extensive—five or more hours each day, 180–190 days a year, for twelve or more years; (3) the economics of scale demand that schooling be a collective experience; (4) schooling is an evaluative experience, and children are constantly evaluated by the power figure, the teacher. With these four characteristics as the basis, Silberman concludes that the basic purpose of American schools is "education for docility."[9]

The hidden curriculum—the unstated, but powerful lessons which children and young people learn in our schools—has been an area of great concern to educational critics for the last decade. The schools do teach basic skills and socialize in positive ways, but there can be no denying that the goals of personalizing a child's education, taking individual children where they are at and helping them reach their fullest potential, and many other beautifully stated purposes of elementary education in the United States are a long way from attainment. With the pressures for a "return to the basics" "keeping up with the Russians," and other sloganeering, it is unlikely that the humane vision of John Dewey will ever be reached in the majority of American schools.

[9]Charles E. Silberman, *Crisis in the Classroom* (New York: Random House, Inc., 1970), pp. 121–122.

elementary school subject areas

Language Arts. Without question, the dominant part of the curriculum in the primary years is the area of language arts. With impetus both from federal programs such as "Right to Read" and from the dissatisfaction of numerous parents, reading skills have taken on a new urgency in the U.S. elementary schools. The "return to the basics" movement and the establishment of numerous "fundamental" schools highlight the importance that parents and educators alike are placing on the basic language skills. Listening, writing, speaking, and spelling form other parts of the language arts curriculum.

Much of the controversy in the language arts program centers around the phonics/word-recognition battle. During the first quarter of this century, phonic approaches to learning to read dominated the schools. Under this approach, children learned to sound out words. Since the 1930s, most schools have used the word-recognition approach, involving the use of basal readers and a combination of sight and sound methods. With the increasing public recognition that many secondary school students are only able to read at a third- or fourth-grade level, many critics have called for a return to the phonics system. They believe that such a return will solve the educational problems of America today. Reading experts are moving towards a position that children learn to read in a variety of ways, and that the teacher must become more of a diagnostician to be able to prescribe the most appropriate methods for each child. Simplistic solutions and slogans will not solve the problem of the illiterate young person and adult in American society, but neither will attempts by educators to place all the blame on the family or the environment.

The "New English," with its base in linguistics, the scientific study of language, has had a growing impact on the elementary school language arts curriculum. Transformational and descriptive grammar have replaced the more traditional forms, while creative writing, and a greater emphasis upon oral language, speaking, and listening, are among the trends found in the "New English." The teaching of English as a second or foreign language to children from homes which use substandard English dialects is another aspect of the language arts program in the elementary schools. For children who speak a black dialect at home, this has involved learning to not look down on their own "language," but to also master standard English as a tool to succeeding in the mainstream of society. For children from predominantly Spanish-, Chinese-, or Vietnamese-speaking homes, as well as other linguistic groups, recent federal and state legislation have provided funds for bilingual-bicultural educational programs. In these programs, children are taught initially in their native language and then are helped to gain facility in standard English. Children come to the schools with varying amounts of English-speaking ability, and the new programs attempt to take the child where he or she is at, give them a pride and facility in their native language and culture, in addition to improving their skills in English.

Following the Russians' success with Sputnik in 1957, the National Defense Education Act provided funds for an extensive program in foreign languages for elementary schools. FLES (Foreign Language in the Elementary School) became very popular in the United States throughout the 1960s, with children taking primarily Spanish or French, but in a few cases studying Russian, Chinese, or Japanese. As with so many curricular innovations, however, once the federal money dried up, the programs began to die, so that by the mid 1970s, foreign language programs at the elementary level were primarily extracurricular, with students taking the courses paying extra for them. FLES is an interesting example cf the difficulty of something "new" cracking the traditional curriculum. Educational historians have stated that innovations take up to fifty years to enter the curriculum on a widespread basis.

Social Studies. Social studies in the elementary school developed out of the traditional disciplines of history and geography, and have expanded over the years to include parts of all the social sciences. Rather than take a disciplinary approach, the social studies have developed a pattern in which children move from an analysis of their home and school in the first grade, to the neighborhood and city in the second and third grades, on to the state and nation in the fourth and fifth grades, concluding with a study of the world in the sixth grade. Although coming in for criticism from professional historians and social scientists, the social studies program has for the most part been fairly well accepted by the public, until the past few years. During the 1960s the federal government spent money, primarily through the National Science Foundation and USOE, to develop new curricular materials in elementary social studies. As long as the social studies program remained fairly innocuous, the public said little, but some of the new programs, such as Man: a Course of Study (MACOS), dealt with more substantive questions. MACOS, with its study of taboos and values in other cultures, has stirred up a hornet's nest of protest among conservatives, who feel that it is undermining basic American and spiritual values.

The elementary social studies were not immune to the efforts of social scientists to help children think like historians or economists, and numerous curriculum materials were added to the elementary schools, bringing basic social science concepts down to the level of kindergarteners. Approaches stressing inquiry have begun to replace the more traditional memorization of facts. Topics such as values, differing economic and political systems, and questions of social justice have begun to take their place alongside the "facts" of American history. Elementary and secondary social studies programs are the focal point for much of the conservative attack on the schools today, and the cry of "back to the basics" refers not only to reading, writing, and arithmetic, but also to the traditional presentations of American history.

Mathematics. Of all of the reforms in the curriculum, perhaps the "new math" has been the most threatening to both parents and teachers. Traditional mathematics education was based upon a stimulus-response theory of learning, and consisted of memorization, drill, and repetition. This type of program gave way to a push for a rational understanding of what processes were being used in solving the problem, and finally to the "new math," which takes its lead, as did the other curricular reforms of the 1960s, from the structure of the discipline itself. Having been taught under the traditional system and having little understanding of the discipline, parents and teachers were slow in adopting the newer methods. Instead of the *What?* questions, the "new math" asks the *Why?* questions.

As with the shakedown period in any curricular reform, there were excesses during which children did not master the basic skills necessary for modern society. As a result, the "new math" came under attack, and in recent years, a new synthesis of the old and the new is developing, which will hopefully train young people in the basic computational skills of their parents' era, but also give them the basic understandings of the discipline, so necessary in our modern technological society.

Science. With the Russian space success, the United States moved into a new era in science education. The schools were looked upon as the cause for the United States' failure to beat the Russians into space, even though one educator stated that all that Sputnik proved was that "the Russians had more and better German scientists than we did." Regardless of the cause of Russia's space successes, they did have a demonstrable effect on the quality and quantity of input into elementary curriculum projects. Numerous "pure" scientists suddenly became interested in the schools, as federal funds poured into such groups as the Elementary School Science Project and many others like it.

Science teaching moved from the memorization of a few unrelated facts and the playing with animals in the classroom, to the serious business of helping children to understand the basic scientific concepts in each of the disciplines. Approaches to learning that stressed discovery replaced the more didactic classroom practices, and countless "hands-on" materials were brought into the classroom. In addition, children were taken out of the school to learn the concepts of ecology, biology, botany, astronomy, and other sciences, which can best be taught in the natural environment. Massive amounts of equipment were paid for with federal funds, and tens of thousands of teachers received training in special National Defense Education Act (NDEA) institutes. Inquiry or the scientific method forms the base of the elementary science curriculum today, but as was the case in mathematics, teachers have been slow to adopt new methods, and with the plethora of elementary science materials on the market today, it is still too early to state exactly where science in the elementary school is going.

Other curricular areas. The four areas dealt with so far form the academic core of the elementary curriculum, and because of their long history and strong public support, they will no doubt remain the core for generations to come. Physical education, art, and music are generally seen as peripheral activities in the curriculum of the elementary school. They are often taught by specialists, particularly in departmentalized intermediate programs. As a result, when the budget crisis strikes, it is these "nonessential" programs which are often the first to be cut.

Every set of goals or purposes of elementary education gives lip service to the need for the physical and aesthetic development of the child, but at its core, the school curriculum is still academic in nature. Music teachers have recently begun a radio advertising campaign, using nationally famous musicians, to "educate" the public on the importance of "music in our schools." Without doubt, the education of our young is incomplete without physical and aesthetic education. Teachers in these programs have begun to gain a "new" perspective on their role in the elementary school setting—perhaps just in time. Slowly, but surely, they have moved away from producing the star athlete or performer-musician, to a new and more relevant role of participant music and athletics for all students.

CURRICULUM IN THE JUNIOR HIGH SCHOOL AND MIDDLE SCHOOL

One of the most persuasive reasons for the replacement of the junior high school with the middle school is the traditional nature of the junior high school curriculum. If the colleges and universities of this country can be accused of dictating the curriculum for the high school, then the same charge can be leveled at the high school for the undue influence it has over the junior high school. The influence is not one of dictating entrance requirements. Rather, junior high school teachers, with few exceptions, are trained in the same manner as high school teachers, the textbooks are slightly watered-down versions of the high school texts, teaching methods are much the same, and the organization of classes tends to be similar. Even the name "junior" implies a slightly less-developed version of the high school. This is not to state that there are not some differences in the two institutions. Junior high schools are much more likely, at least at the seventh grade level, to have a block time program, in which English and social studies are combined, along with a possible science-mathematics block or some other combination of courses. This blocking of courses is defended on the grounds that the junior high school young people need more extended contact with one teacher, as was their elementary experience, and on the basis of a wide variety of justifications concerning the integration of subject matter. By ninth grade, however, block or core programs have generally disappeared, and the curriculum closely resembles that of most high schools. In fact, Carnegie units from ninth grade courses are generally counted for admission to universities, and this leads to further control of the curriculum.

The organization of the school day parallels that of most senior high schools with six or seven fifty-minute periods, although some have moved towards modular scheduling and other innovations more common at the senior high level. Required courses make up most of the curriculum for most junior high students. Despite extensive lip service to individualized education, the greatest number of students take three years of English, social studies, mathematics, and science, with a few electives in the arts, vocational training, and foreign languages. Students are grouped by ability in a majority of junior high schols; this grouping begins the tracking process, which is accentuated at the senior high level.

In services and programs provided as extracurricular activities, the junior high schools fall somewhere between the elementary schools and senior high schools. Guidance services are found in most junior high schools, with some of the guidance function being performed by a homeroom teacher. Clubs and sports, both intramural and interscholastic, are considerably more developed at the junior high school than at the elementary level. Critics see them as starting children too early in the "adult" competitive roles, social and athletic, and feel that young people in the midst of puberty don't need additional pressures placed on them by adult society.

GOALS FOR MODERN SECONDARY EDUCATION

Most of the attempts at improving on the Seven Cardinal Principles have explained in more detail what the secondary schools should do in the way of educating for citizenship, intellectual development, spiritual or ethical growth, vocational skills, and personal and interpersonal growth and skills. In the sixties and seventies, one of the people most influential in the reform of secondary education has been James S. Coleman. In a *Phi Delta Kappa* article in December, 1972, he elaborated on the skills which every young person should have before the age of eighteen. He does not claim that they are all-inclusive, but does suggest that they must be explicitly included in the educational system.

1. Intellectual skills, the kinds of things that schooling at its best teaches.
2. Skills of some occupation that may be filled by a secondary school graduate, so that every eighteen-year-old would be accredited in some occupation whether he continued in school or not.

3. Decision-making skills; i.e., those skills of making decisions in complex situations where consequences follow from the decisions.
4. General physical and mechanical skills, i.e., skills allowing the young person to deal with physical and mechanical problems he will confront outside in work, in the home, or elsewhere.
5. Bureaucratic and organizational skills; i.e., how to cope with a bureaucratic organization, as an employee, customer, or client, or as a manager or entrepreneur.
6. Skills in the care of dependent persons; i.e., skill in caring for children, old persons, and sick persons.
7. Emergency skills; i.e., how to act in an emergency or unfamiliar situation in sufficient time to deal with the emergency.
8. Verbal communication skills in argumentation and debate.[10]

Coleman's suggestions are not unique, but they do tend to strike a note of reality, in the midst of so many lists of goals and purposes which are so esoteric or abstract that the schools seldom change as the result.

The secondary school is a part of the society, and as such is often seen as part of the solution to problems confronting the society in general. Perhaps the greatest evidence of this is in the area of social class and caste, in which the schools through integration, programs for the culturally different, and busing are being asked to bear the brunt of societal and cultural change. The same is true of the changes in technology. As the economy changes rapidly, the schools are expected to keep up by introducing new courses to prepare students for a future filled with change. When a breakdown of values appears in the society, the schools are asked to teach values, and when juvenile delinquency threatens the culture, the schools are asked to deal with the problem. When young people appear to be threatening democratic values as perceived by their elders, new curricula are added in an attempt to democratize American youth. Schools traditionally reflect the society in which they find themselves. Although George Counts titled his provocative book *Dare the Schools Build a New Social Order?*, the answer through the ages has been that the schools are not equipped to change very rapidly, much less to change the whole social order. The school must continue to confront the issues of the society, or the young people will continue to see many of its activities as irrelevant; but its ability to solve the massive problems of discrimination, values changes, economic deprivation, and lack of spiritual direction is questionable.

the secondary school program

In most high schools the program is based on departmentalization, similar to that found at the university. As discussed in the previous section on the junior high school, departmentalization has come down from the university, all the way to the intermediate grades. Teachers are seen as specialists

[10]James S. Coleman, "How Do the Young Become Adults?" *Phi Delta Kappan*, LIV, no. 4. (December 1972), p. 228.

in one discipline, and knowledge tends to become compartmentalized for secondary students. Junior and senior high school young people see the world through the various disciplines, and come to expect that adults spend one hour each day "doing English," another "doing science," and on through the various subjects which are part of their schooling experience. Many experiments have been conducted on methods for breaking away from the traditional program and curriculum, but compartmentalized knowledge, offered by specialists, in fifty-minute time blocks, to thirty or forty students, for which they receive one Carnegie unit of credit towards graduation and college entrance, and for which they receive a grade, still tends to dominate the secondary schools of the United States.

The correlated curriculum, in which attempts are made to relate one course to another, is one method for breaking down the discrete nature of the secondary school curriculum. One of the more common attempts is in the areas of American history and literature, which can be easily correlated. The broad-fields approach to the curriculum combines the various social science disciplines into a social studies course, drawing concepts and approaches from each of the disciplines. The same approach can be used in a general science course or general business course. The core curriculum in its most radical form abolishes all disciplinary lines and has students working on the solutions to problems of an interdisciplinary nature. In its less radical form, it attempts to combine certain subject areas, and gives a teacher a larger block of time in which to get to know his or her students, and to stress social values, in addition to the traditional academic ones. The activity curriculum takes the students' needs and interests as its basis and structures the learning environment around them.

Another area of concern and controversy at the secondary level is the comprehensive versus the specialized high school. Comprehensive secondary schools serve the needs of a heterogeneous student population, while the specialized high schools, such as those found in the arts and sciences in New York City, and the vast number of vocational schools throughout the country, serve a more homogenous population. The comprehensive secondary school has been justified as a more democratic institution and one that prevents the slotting or tracking of students. Its critics, however, state that within most comprehensive secondary schools, students are still tracked into college preparatory and vocationally oriented programs, and that prestige and status still tend to reside in the academically oriented curricula.

Some of the innovations referred to in the section on elementary schools are also being experimented with at the secondary level. Team teaching and differentiated staffing are two concepts that have been tried in many parts of the country, but the expectations of their early advocates have never been reached. Modular and flexible scheduling are two further innovations being tentatively introduced in the secondary schools of the United States. Both concepts in scheduling are an attempt to break away from the fifty- to sixty-minute blocks, five days a week. Flexible periods of time charaterize the new approaches to scheduling, with large- and small-group instruction and time for individual study and tutoring. Some subjects are taught in larger blocks of time, while others receive shorter periods of time. On a theoretical level, it is difficult to argue with the rationale behind flexible scheduling procedures, but on a practical level numerous secondary schools have dropped it after a trial period, owing to difficulties in scheduling, a feeling that students don't know what to do with their free or independent study time, and finally the weight of tradition. In an attempt to break away from the Carnegie Units, in which a student receives one credit for a year's work in a subject, many secondary schools have recently instituted minicourses that last for four to nine weeks. Since most universities still require the student to present a certain number of units, high schools have given one-fourth, one-sixth, or one-fifth credits for the completion of each minicourse. Minicourses have helped many schools to loosen up their curriculum and have brought in many new subjects.

On an instructional level many changes have been occurring in the secondary schools. The traditional lecture-recitation method still predominates in many classrooms, but with the vast amounts of new materials available as a result of the curriculum movement of the 1960s, most classrooms today have begun to move towards inquiry and discovery approaches to learning. Technology has also had its effect on the secondary school classroom, with programmed materials now available in most subject areas, and highly sophisticated computer programs being used in science and mathematics classrooms. Individualized materials have made it possible for the teacher to give more than lip-service to the goal of individualized instruction. Simulations and gaming techniques, first used in foreign policy and military decision-making, are now available in a variety of disciplines for use at the secondary level and are providing students with greater realism when it comes to social problems, business decisions, technological change, and the environment. Television and radio are being used, though not as extensively as had been hoped in the 1950s and 1960s. Closed-circuit television can help to individualize instruction, show videotapes on demand, or perform many instructional services in the school. Television from an airplane or satellite is providing students in remote areas with many of the instructional benefits previously limited to large wealthy urban and suburban schools.

Of importance in the development of the American secondary school has been the growth of the extracurricular, co-curricular, or activities programs. For many students these programs are what keeps them in school. Special-interest clubs, student publications, dramatics, debating societies, bands, choral groups, orchestras, athletic teams, and student government activities all go into making the secondary school much more than the sum of its formal learning program. It has been suggested by some observers that the American secondary student is the busiest person in our society, "working" in the school setting for eight hours, followed by athletic programs for three or more hours, followed by several hours of homework. It is no wonder that guidance programs are needed at the secondary level to aid young people in making career choices, deal with their sex role and relationships with the opposite sex, receive academic counseling, and just cope with an incredible overload. Critics of the high schools have suggested that they are part of the cause of juvenile delinquency and teenage suicides. It is certainly true that the secondary student in most of our high schools does not lack for sensory input.

With the exception of agriculture, all subject areas in the secondary curriculum have seen an increase in their overall enrollments. English-language arts is the curricular area with the most students, 129.6 percent enrollment. Figures of over 100 indicate a pupil is enrolled in more than one course within a subject area during the school year. Other high enrollment areas are health and physical education and the social sciences. Enrollments in mathematics and the physical sciences have stabilized at about 67–71 percent of the student population, while music, art, foreign languages, business, industrial arts, and home economics enroll between 24 and 33 percent.[11] Since about 1950, there have been no dramatic enrollment shifts in the secondary curriculum, in spite of attempts after Sputnik to encourage the sciences and mathematics. The curricular changes that have come are in the form of new textbooks, teaching methods, and materials.

English-language arts

The language arts program plays a central role in the secondary school curriculum, with a majority of schools requiring students to take English courses during each of their years in the senior high school. No area of the curriculum has come in for as much criticism as the English program. Parents, college teachers, and employers all blame the schools for what they see to be vast numbers of illiterate or semiliterate young people graduating from secondary schools. Concern over the decline in college entrance scores has led many universities to institute "bonehead" English courses for some entering freshmen and has put pressure on the secondary schools to strengthen their programs. If it is true that a large percentage of graduates from our high schools are functionally illiterate, it is equally true that Eng-

---

[11] W. Vance Grant and C. George Lind, *Digest of Educational Statistics, 1975* (Washington, D.C.: U. S. Government Printing Office, 1976), p. 47.

lish teachers are not the only ones to blame. Parents, television, changing values, and a host of unknown factors must also be included in the causes.

The language arts curriculum contains not only such basic skills as reading, writing, speaking, and listening, but has come to include such things as semantics, play production, public speaking, and the use of television, to name but a few of the many topics included in a high school study guide. It is the so-called frills which critics of the secondary schools are demanding be dropped from the curriculum, but with the changing nature of modern society, it is difficult to state with any precision exactly what constitute the "basic skills" for the twenty-first century.

Attempts are being made to allocate certain skills and materials to specific grade levels, and to develop scope and sequence charts to aid teachers in dealing with the vast amounts of material without too much overlap. Reading, both remedial and developmental, is becoming an increasingly important part of the secondary school language arts program Traditional prescriptive grammar is being replaced by descriptive structural approaches, although attacks are being made on the "new English." With numerous studies showing a lack of reading on the part of the adult U.S. population, literature courses have moved away from historical and critical analysis and towards the enjoyment of the works for their own sake. As with other areas of the curriculum, the language arts have moved towards discovery and inquiry approaches to learning, and the individualization of materials. The critical use of the mass media and the importance of oral expression have become increasingly important aspects of the modern language arts curriculum at the secondary level.

social studies and history

Social studies courses are required by state law more than any other parts of the curriculum. A large majority require the study of U.S. history and the U.S. Constitution as part of the secondary school graduation requirements. History, as an area of study, has suffered to such an extent that professional historians have recently called for its "reintroduction" into the schools. With economics, psychology, geography, anthropology, and a host of contemporary problems-oriented courses all vying for a place in the curriculum, history has slowly been shunted aside.

Under the impetus of the U.S. Office of Education and the National Science Foundation, numerous new social studies curricula have been produced since the movement towards the "new social studies" began in the early 1960s. Many of the social studies projects were geared towards the teaching of subjects other than history, and this has led to its further decline in the curriculum. Inquiry approaches dominate the new curriculum materials as students are encouraged to discover information on their own, draw their own conclusions, find out their own facts, and act as professional social scientists would, given the same problem. Many of the new materials use case studies, a jurisprudential approach, and simulation games to make the material more interesting and stimulating for the student.

Traditional citizenship education and the study of history has given way to a discipline-oriented, inductive, problems-based approach to the social studies. In recent years, the social studies have begun to deal in considerably greater depth with the study of values and value-related questions. This has been both welcomed by some of the public who see the school as needing to teach values, and opposed as one more attempt at the secularization of society and the taking away of traditional responsibilities from the family. No doubt the social studies will remain embroiled in controversy as long as they continue to deal with political, social, moral, and religious questions.

science

From a cursory look at the course offerings in the sciences at the secondary level, it would appear that little has changed in the last half century. General science is still a standard at the ninth grade, followed by biology, chemistry, and physics. A great deal has happened since Sputnik, however, with vast amounts of federal and foundation money going into the preparation of new materials for the teaching of science at all levels. As with the social science curriculum reform movement, discovery and inductive approaches to the subject matter have replaced the highly didactic approaches typical of the old science classrooms. Laboratory work has become increasingly important as high school students become involved in the actual work of scientists. Students conduct their own experiments and draw their own conclusions, rather than only observe demonstrations or read about the results of prior scientific research.

In addition to the "big three" science courses—biology, chemistry, and physics—earth science courses dealing with often-ignored aspects of geology, astronomy, and particularly ecology have become increasingly popular. In addition, science courses dealing with social and moral problems, often in an integrated approach using concepts from a variety of disciplines, have been developed for high school use. Advanced placement courses for those with a scientific aptitude have been developed in many high schools along with special courses for the slow learner.

mathematics

Mathematics instruction received much of the criticism of the secondary schools in the late 1950s. Like other areas of the secondary curriculum it received large amounts of U.S. Office of Education and National Science

Foundation funding to develop new materials and approaches, and money to provide in-service training of teachers in the new mathematics. Most secondary schools still follow the traditional pattern of algebra in grade nine, plane geometry in grade ten, advanced algebra in grade eleven, followed by solid geometry and trigonometry in grade twelve. What occurs in these courses, however, changed greatly during the 1960s and 1970s, with much more emphasis upon discovery and enrichment programs, and an emphasis upon understanding, as opposed to the memorization of formulas and rules.

Many secondary schools moved beyond the traditional programs and into the study of sets, elementary analysis, properties of the number system, and the solution and graphical interpretation of algebraic inequalities. Much of the pressure has come from the changes in the elementary mathematics curriculum, where the "new math" has had a profound effect on what is taught and how it is learned. Many secondary schools set up advanced-placement mathematics courses for which advanced students can receive college credit, in addition to introducing the use of individualized, programmed material, and the computer.

foreign languages

Much has happened in the area of foreign language instruction since the days when Greek and Latin were taken by all secondary school students. In a recent year, only 124 students in the whole United States were taking Greek in the secondary schools, and by 1965, the vast majority of students were enrolled in modern foreign languages, with Spanish, French, and German heading the list. Numerous other modern languages are taught, but most are offered only when sufficient enrollment warrants it.

Methodologies of instruction have changed to emphasize speaking and understanding the language, rather than the older methods of reading and writing. Students are more often encouraged to take more than two years in a language, in order to achieve some level of mastery, rather than taking two foreign languages during junior and senior high school. Most of the curricular trends from other disciplines have also influenced instruction, i.e., team teaching, individualized instruction, inquiry approaches, and making the program interesting and relevant to the needs and interests of the young people.

fine arts

Instrumental and vocal music enrolls millions of students at the secondary level in the United States, and concerts by musical groups are attended by tens of millions of Americans. Emphasis upon performance skills is slowly giving way to the appreciation and enjoyment of music by all students, the vast majority of whom will never perform. Regrettably, many music teachers are frustrated performers, who see this as the basic goal of the music curriculum.

Art, like music, is an important part of our society, and as such, has a place in the curriculum. Along with music, however, art instruction in the past has been too often geared at producing great artists, rather than helping all people to enjoy a variety of art forms. The art curriculum today is crowded with drawing, painting, printing, sculpture, ceramics, and a host of other art forms. Children begin at the earliest ages to work in a variety of media, and with the increasing relativism concerning what constitutes "good" art, millions of Americans are learning the enjoyment of painting and pottery.

health and physical education

As with fine arts, physical educators have often seen their role as that of producing "professional" athletes, and judge the quality of their programs on interscholastic win-loss records. Gradually, pressures have built up to get rid of the sexism in sports, with girls' athletic teams competing in many sports, and girls' sports becoming as extensive as the boys' program in many secondary schools. Intramural sports programs and individual sports which can be enjoyed throughout one's life have taken on increasing importance in the physical education programs. Physical fitness, positive health habits and attitudes, and a variety of recreational skills have become basic objectives. Inordinate amounts of time and money are still being spent on boys' football and basketball teams, but times are changing, and the day of the sexist coach, bucking to become principal, may be drawing to an end.

vocational and career education

The federal government, through a fifty-year series of vocational education bills, has encouraged the development of skill-oriented programs to prepare secondary school students for the working world. Career education is a newer phenomenon, also being encouraged by the federal and many state governments, to help children in the elementary schools begin to get a feel for career opportunities, and then at the secondary level to actually experience time in a variety of occupational settings. With the increasing salaries of many of the "blue-collar" and office positions, the popularity of training programs, either within the comprehensive secondary schools or in special technical-vocational schools, has rapidly improved.

Business education has gone beyond the old typing and secretarial skills and into such things as office management, marketing, data processing, and business law. Although practical arts in the form of "shop" and

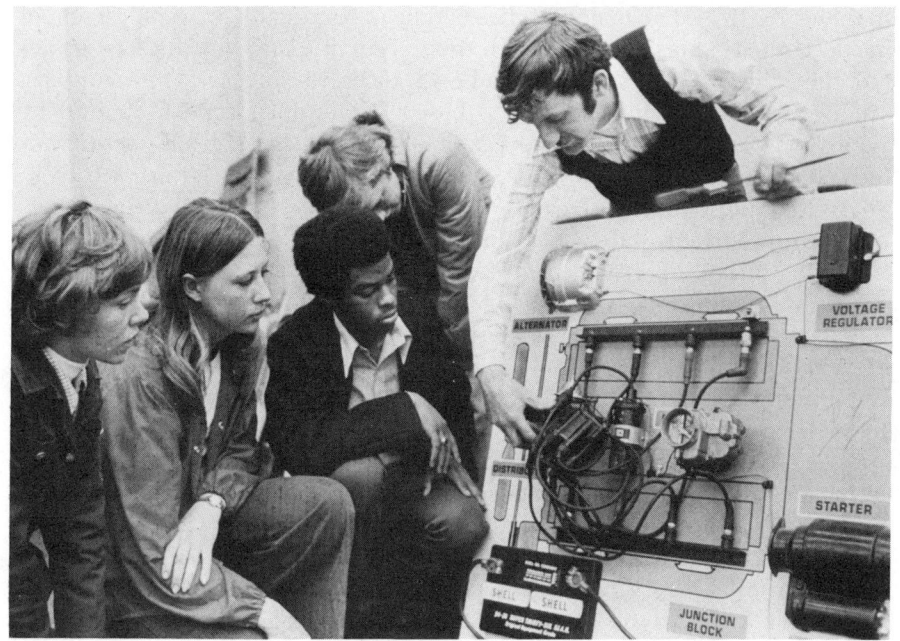

Figure 10-2 Preparing Young People for the World of Work

home economics still exist in most junior and many senior high schools, new programs geared at seriously preparing young people for the working world have been developed in countless vocational areas. Aeronautics, air conditioning, refrigeration, audiovisual techniques, commercial art, electronics, painting and paper hanging, practical nursing, vocational horticulture, and photography are just a few of the fields which have been added to the traditional carpentry, auto mechanics, and agriculture curricula.

Every recent major national commission on the reform of secondary education has advocated that *all* students graduate with some saleable skill. Those that are going on to college may not need or use it immediately, but with the hundreds of thousands of unemployed liberal arts graduates from our nation's institutions of higher education, the future of vocational and technical programs seems bright and secure.

the reform of secondary education

"Our nation's schools have turned into prisons, with guards posing as teachers, and students learning how to be docile prisoners."[12] Numerous critics of American secondary education have commented on the oppressive nature of our high schools and the irrelevance of much of what occurs

[12]Craig Haney and Philip Zimbardo, "The Blackboard Penitentiary: Its Tough to Tell a High School from a Prison," *Psychology Today*, 9, no. 1 (June, 1975), p. 26.

in them. By 1974, five major studies had been conducted on the high school in the United States, and although their recommendations differed in detail, they all called for sweeping and even radical reforms of the secondary schools. The President's Science Advisory Committee report, chaired by James S. Coleman, called for a sweeping reassessment of what goes on not only in the curriculum, but more importantly in the total transition from youth to adulthood. There can be no doubt that if the schools keep tinkering with important, but minor, adjustments in the curriculum, the major problems facing American youth will never be solved. It is helpful to remind the reader once again that secondary education for adolescents is a phenomenon of the twentieth century, and not something with hundreds of years of tradition. Although tradition already weighs heavy on them, the junior and senior high schools may be the most productive institutions to pressure for reform.

Age segregation and the isolation of youth were two problems scored in most of the reports, and all recommend some form of community participation and work experience to aid in integrating young people into the society. Varieties of nonschool settings and alternatives within the schools are important ideas. One of the most important and possibly dangerous recommendations is the lowering of school-leaving age to fourteen in order to let unmotivated young people do other things and keep them from destroying the schools. The danger results not from the obvious need for some young people to be in different settings, but from whether society will provide those settings, particularly for those from poor, inner-city homes. Secondly, the meritocracy may grow even stronger when young people from disadvantaged homes drop out, without the skills to "make it" in society.

The President's Panel on Youth suggested that educational vouchers worth the equivalent of four years of college be given to every sixteen year old, who could then use them for a wide variety of skill-training options, in addition to higher education. Action-learning in the schools should replace the passive nature of most secondary and higher education, with a variety of school and workplace options available to all students. Another set of recommendations dealt with the need to alter the time when traditional secondary education occurs, from the current fourteen-to-seventeen-year age to any time when the person wants or needs it. Schools would integrate themselves with the community, sharing art centers, guidance programs, athletic facilities, libraries, and a host of things currently duplicated by several governing agencies. Racist and sexist bias must be eliminated from all aspects of schooling, and concern with worldwide problems must replace the narrow chauvinism permeating much of what is taught in our schools today. The use of media, such as regular broadcast and cable television, must be made available for educational purposes. A major area of concern in most of the reports was in the area of student rights and obligations, and all called for the downward extension of civil rights to students, who too often have been denied them.

Whether the time is right for secondary reform remains to be seen. The growing violence, the large numbers of dropouts and push-outs in our inner-city schools, the lack of basic skill attainment, and a host of other factors would seem to indicate urgently that something must be done to prevent the collapse of much of the secondary school system. The beginnings of massive reform were evident by the late 1960s. Alternative schools of many varieties had been begun, work-study programs were underway in many schools, states began requiring minimum basic skills before receiving a high school diploma, vocational and technical schools grew in popularity, and many other aspects of the needed reform were started. The schools, like other bureaucracies, have a way of killing innovations. Only when the public demands the change and the political situation is right will true reform of the whole secondary system take place.

CASE STUDY: Controversial Elementary Curriculum

The school board in a midwestern suburban community is in the process of approving, changing, or denying approval to the new elementary school curriculum. The community is a well educated, upper-middle-class city, with only a few minorities and working-class people in the school district. The people tend to be politically, economically, and religiously conservative, and do not look upon change as a positive good.

A curriculum committee of elementary school teachers has recommended a variety of changes, including such controversial things as introducing evolution and sex education in the science curriculum in the upper grades, an emphasis upon multicultural and multinational curricula in the social sciences, a special bilingual program for the small minority for whom English is a second language, and a continuation of the successful "new math" program.

Several religious groups have come out strongly in opposition to the evolution and sex education programs, political conservatives oppose the new social studies emphases as "un-American," the white-Anglo population, in general, can see little need for a bilingual program in a time of scarce fiscal resources, and most parents and many teachers who have been frustrated by the "new math" strongly oppose its continuation.

As a school board member, how can you balance the needs of children with the rights of the community to "control" its schools? How can you maintain the tradition of academic freedom in which educators make most educational decisions without interference from "outside" groups? How can you resolve the conflicts so apparent in the proposed curriculum without alienating all concerned?

THOUGHT QUESTIONS

1. What do you consider to be the five most important educational objectives for the last quarter of the twentieth century? How would you measure their attainment?

2. The sources of the curriculum are many and varied. List in order of priority the sources which you consider to be the most important, and briefly defend your choices.

3. The curriculum has gone through some important shifts since 1900. Document the shifts and some possible causes.

4. What political, economic, or societal reasons can you give for the pendulum swing in curricular emphases since 1955?

5. From personal experience, observation, and reading, how successful do you feel the "new" English, mathematics, social studies, and science programs have been? By what criteria do you judge their success or failure?

6. In what ways should a curriculum for a junior high or middle school differ from the curriculum of an elementary or secondary school?

7. What advantages or disadvantages can you see for a correlated curriculum in the secondary schools and departmentalization in the elementary schools?

8. Why have reforms such as team teaching, flexible scheduling, differentiated staffing, to name just a few, failed to catch on in the schools of the United States?

PRACTICAL ACTIVITIES

1. Compare a curriculum guide in use in an elementary or secondary school today with the curriculum which you had when you were in that grade. How would you guess the curriculum has changed since 1650 and 1900 in this country.?

2. What evidence can you find from the textbooks and curriculum guides in use today that inquiry and discovery approaches to learning have begun to replace older methods of memorization.

3. Obtain a copy of the State School Code and list the general topics about which state laws, rules, and regulations have been passed. What anachronisms can still be found in the Code?

4. Visit an elementary and secondary school classroom and after observing subjects taught and approaches used, categorize the various aspects as being traditional, subject-centered schooling or having a student-centered, humanistic model. What is the dominant model in the classrooms you observed?

5. What curricular changes have occurred in your major subject field since about 1955? How have courses, teaching methods, texts, etc., been affected by the changes?

BIBLIOGRAPHY

BEAUCHAMP, GEORGE A., *The Curriculum of the Elementary School*. Boston: Allyn & Bacon, Inc., 1964.

BRUNER, JEROME S., *The Process of Education*. Cambridge, Massachusetts: Harvard University Press, 1960.

CLARK, LEONARD, AND OTHERS, *The American Secondary School Curriculum* (2nd Edition). New York: The Macmillan Company, 1972.

COLEMAN, JAMES S., AND OTHERS, *Youth: Transition to Adulthood*. Chicago: The University of Chicago Press, 1974.

FRYMIER, JACK R., AND HORACE C. HAWN, *Curriculum Improvement for Better Schools*. Worthington, Ohio: C. A. Jones Publishing Co., 1970.

GOODLAD, JOHN I., AND ROBERT H. ANDERSON, *The Nongraded Elementary School*. New York: Harcourt, Brace & World, Inc., 1963.

HOLTON, SAMUEL, *Understandng the American Public High School*. Boston: Allyn & Bacon, Inc., 1969.

RODGERS, FREDERICK A., *Curriculum and Instruction in the Elementary School*. New York: Macmillan Publishing Company, Inc., 1975.

SILBERMAN, CHARLES E., *Crisis in the Classroom: The Remaking of American Education*. New York: Random House, Inc., 1970.

TABA, HILDA, *Curriculum Development: Theory and Practice*. New York: Harcourt, Brace & World, 1962.

TRUMP, J. LLOYD, AND DELMAS F. MILLER, *Secondary School Curriculum Improvement*. Boston: Allyn & Bacon, Inc., 1968.

WILSON, L. CRAIG, *The Open Access Curriculum*. Boston: Allyn & Bacon, Inc., 1971.

11

THE PROFESSIONAL TEACHER
Roles and Responsibilities

The role of teacher in American culture is usually ambiguous, frequently demeaned, and generally misunderstood. Teachers earn somewhat below average salaries, for long hours of work (while continuing their own education) under conflicting and often impossible sets of expectations, in a milieu that often tends to infantilize them as well as their clients. Teachers are expected to adhere to codes, to possess impeccable credentials, and to practice to perfection the art and science of their craft.

In a nation of over 220 million people, education (teachers, students, and others) "is the primary activity of some 63.6 million Americans," of which "almost 3.2 million persons are employed as classroom teachers, and an additional 300,000 are working as superintendents, principals, supervisors, and other instructional staff members."[1]

IS TEACHING A PROFESSION?

Everyone seems to be knowledgeable concerning life in schools, what teachers do, and what teaching is. Unfortunately, teaching and the teacher have become cultural stereotypes, usually negative ones such as "classroom

---

[1]"Education in Review: 1976–75", *Innovator* (The University of Michigan School of Education), 8, no. 3 (November 25, 1976), p. 2.

cop" and "milk monitor." These pervasive caricatures are an unfortunate development because they discourage society from considering teaching and teachers as a profession, and because they tend to weaken efforts to articulate an art and science of teaching. Teaching usually is perceived as somewhere between a mere occupational group and a true profession.

> Do you remember the fine old story about two bricklayers? They were asked "What are you doing?" One replied, "I am laying bricks." The other said, "I am building a cathedral." The first man is a tradesman, the second has the soul of an artist or professional. The difference is in the meaning of the activity. It is not in how expertly or skillfully the bricklayers daub mortar onto each brick; it is not in how much information they have about the job; it is not in their loyalty to the boss; it is not in their familiarity with other constructions. It is in how they savor and feel about what they are doing, in their sensing of relationships between their work and that of others, in their appreciation of potentialities, in their sense of form, in their need for and enjoyment of significance, in their identification of self with civilized aspirations, in their whole outlook on life.[2]

In the above quotation Herbert Thelen suggests that when a group of workers consider themselves a profession, they possess a number of rather vague attitudes toward their work and toward life. A more precise definition of a profession is provided by Myron Leiberman, even though he admits there is no authoritative definition, and that his is a synthesis of characteristics derived from the analysis of several traditionally acknowledged professions. Lieberman claims that eight criteria define a kind of work and its practitioners as a profession. These are:

1. A unique, definite, and essential social service is performed by the members of the group.
2. There is an emphasis on intellectual skills in the performance of the service.
3. A long period of specialized training is required of all members.
4. The group is allowed, by the society in which it exists, a broad range of autonomy for individual members and for the total group.
5. The practitioners accept extensive responsibility for judgments and behaviors performed within the scope of their special competence.
6. There is an emphasis on the service performed (rather than the economic rewards) as the basis for organization and for judging quality *within* the group.
7. Practitioners are members of a comprehensive, self-governing, and self-regulating organization.
8. A code of ethics has been formally adopted by the organization's membership, and has been clarified, and interpreted at ambiguous points by concrete cases.[3]

We conclude, as do Lieberman and others, that the claim of teachers to professional status is at present only marginally warranted, and that this

---

[2] Herbert A. Thelen, "Professional Anyone?" in *New Perspectives on Teacher Education*, ed. Donald J. McCarthy (San Francisco: Jossey-Bass Publishers, 1973), p. 198.

[3] Myron Lieberman, *Education as a Profession* (Englewood Cliffs, N.J.: Prentice-Hall, Inc., 1956), pp. 2–6.

will probably be the case as long as we can foresee. Bureaucratization continues to force school administrators into a managerial mode and ethic, and teachers into an employee/laborer role and ethic. This then reinforces teachers' fears of being treated as mere replaceable parts in a mechanical system, and drives them to seek collective security in unions and union-like organizations. Some educators resist this tendency to equate public education with the corporation model, but the trend seems unavoidable.

the art of teaching

One who chooses the occupation *and* role of teacher, with or without credentials or portfolio, in schools and classrooms or not, appointed and paid or not, has decided to intervene with purpose in the lives of one or more human beings. These intentional acts of purposeful intervention are referred to collectively as teaching. Although a myriad of cultural, social, economic, political, psychological, organizational, historical, spatial, and environmental influences impinge pervasively on the work of teachers, we still insist that the essence of teaching is the exercise of whatever margin of freedom remains after all the external forces have exacted their toll. For us, to teach is to make decisions in an arena where the freedom to choose is severely restricted, but present in precious measure.

What it is that learners are expected to learn—the intended outcomes—are always problematical, modifiable, subject to grave risks, and constantly emerging—before, during, and after the teaching intervention—in the lives of both those who teach and those who are taught. Also, passively or actively, teacher and student are always interacting. Both are seeking satisfaction and, ideally, an even exchange of "worldly goods," both are recipients.

Finally, a teacher imposes many of his or her values on others. To try to change another person, in whatever direction, for whatever purpose, is to assume a moral obligation.

Essential to the process of teaching, then, are (1) purposeful interventions in others' lives, (2) the exercise of a modest margin of freedom, (3) decision-making in generally unpredictable contexts, (4) an interaction benefitting all participants, and (5) a moral undertaking. What, then, is required of the effective teacher? We have answered this question from our own perspective, based on many years of public school teaching and, in colleges and universities, of teaching teachers to teach.

making oneself a teacher

The person who chooses to teach undertakes a lifelong process of learning how to teach. The more one teaches and learns, the more one becomes aware of how complex relationships are between teacher and student, and between teaching and learning. The search for the most effective balance never stops.

Teaching involves the freedom to make decisions within the limits of particular situations. The effective use of this freedom depends on knowing the available options and their probable consequences, and on a willingness to risk the results of a choice.

The classroom requires that teachers possess knowledge or skill in at least eight special areas: (1) characteristics and developmental cycles of children and adolescents; (2) the ways in which people learn; (3) the structure of concepts, generalizations, modes of inquiry, and models for integrating knowledge, and also specialized knowledge in various academic disciplines; (4) methods of teaching; (5) cognitive, affective, and psychomotor learning objectives; (6) values and attitudes conducive to learning and to satisfying human relationships; (7) skills of communication, conflict management and reduction, human relations, and decision-making; and (8) skill in integrating the above seven categories with one another.

As an interpersonal art, teaching has certain analogies to the work of the surgeon, the baseball umpire, and the potter. The surgeon learns diagnosis, surgical procedures, and pre- and postoperative care, partly from reading, listening, and observing, but mainly from working with an experienced, expert surgeon and from independent and supervised practice. Excellence in a surgeon presupposes precision, neatness, simplicity, good timing, elegance in performance, *and* the success of the surgery in terms of the patient. Some judgments of excellence are made by the surgeon's peers, some by the surgeon's patients, and all by the surgeon personally.

Baseball umpires generally are former players, as children and adolescents and often as semi- or professional baseball players. The transition from player to umpire is seldom smooth and always involves "beginning over again" or "starting at the bottom." The skills of an umpire include conflict management under pressure, total recall of formal and informal rules, and most importantly, the ability to make judgments accurately, quickly, and assertively.

The potter begins by selecting the malleable clay, which is then kneaded and then pressed onto the potter's wheel, and then centered as the wheel turns. Centering is "the bringing of the clay into a spinning, unwobbling pivot, which will then be free to take innumerable shapes as potter and clay press against each other. The firm, tender, sensitive pressure which yields as much as it asserts. It is like a handclasp between two living hands, receiving the greeting at the very moment that they give it."[4] It's a mystical experience, the satisfying feeling of having found center. As the union of hands and clay mold and change each other, they both sense when harmony prevails, when both are centered.

[4]Mary Caroline Richards, *Centering* (Middletown, Conn.: Wesleyan University Press, 1964), p. 9.

A pot should this, and a pot should that—I have little patience with these prescriptions. I cannot escape paradox when I look deep into things, in the crafts as well as in poetry, in metaphysics or in physics. . . . We can't fake craft. It lies in the act. The strains we have put in the clay break open in the fire. We do not have the craft or craftsmanship, if we do not speak to the light that lives within the early materials, including men themselves.[5]

In teaching also, this is the case: when teacher and student are centered, they both will sense and feel it—a too rare rapturous experience.

behind the classroom door

The 1960s (or more precisely, 1957–1967) saw an unusually large number of administrative and curricular reforms, many were initiated with the financial support of the federal government. This period has been called the "educational decade." Some reforms were continued beyond 1967, and even a few new ones introduced, but the impact of these innovations over the next decade was not significantly different.

In the late 1960s, John Goodlad conducted a study in 150 classrooms of sixty-seven elementary schools selected from major population centers of the country. What he found in this survey of elementary schools can be generalized to secondary education as well. Goodlad and his colleagues worked from what they considered ten reasonable goals for educational change. Included in these goals were expectations that classroom practices would be guided by clear educational objectives; classroom instruction would emphasize "learning how to learn"; schools would pay attention to students' individual differences; teachers would rely on basic principles of learning and instruction and would use flexible standards of evaluation (such as observing children's actual performances, rather than comparing pupil work with grade, age, or group norms).[6]

The findings of Goodlad's search are not very heartening: on all ten counts he found little if any substantive reform. The dominant aims of most teachers still were to cover topics (selected largely from prepared courses of study and texts). Goodlad was forced to conclude that many of the changes widely recommended during the preceding fifteen years were "blunted on school and classroom door." Schools and classrooms, he observed, were characterized by a sameness regardless of location, student enrollment, and professed "typing" as provided by administrators—in spite of the talk of individualizing learning, enrichment programs, and adapting the curriculum to specific communities. In our educational system, Goodlad explains, aside from intense criticism and endless recommendations for improvement, there is not "any effective structure by means of which coun-

[5]Richards, *Centering*, pp. 11–12.
[6]John I. Goodlad, M. Francis Klein, *Behind the Classroom Door* (Worthington, Ohio: Charles A. Jones Publishing Company, 1970), pp. 12–19.

tervailing ideas and models may be pumped in and developed to the point of becoming real alternatives. . . the system is geared to self-preservation, not self-renewal."[7]

Perhaps even more disturbing, according to Goodlad's findings, was the considerable discrepancy between how innovative teachers saw themselves to be, and the actual innovation observed. Teachers sincerely thought they were individualizing instruction, encouraging inductive learning, involving children in group processes, and so on, but by any credible standard this just wasn't so. As Goodlad explains, there is no critical number of teachers, parents, and others working cooperatively on school problems; teachers are very much alone in their work. Principals remain largely in their offices, offering little pedagogical or moral support; fellow teachers stay to their respective classrooms—possibly fearing to intrude on the sanctity of the classroom. But as Goodlad concludes, it is not just the aloneness of a teacher isolated with students in a classroom cell, but also "the feeling—and in a large measure the actuality—of not being supported by someone who knows about their work, is sympathetic to it, wants to help and, indeed, does help."[8]

Goodlad also comments on the universal lack of aesthetic quality in school architecture. There are some differences among schools: "city schools were very much like their harsh surroundings; suburban schools like their softer settings." Both tended to be among the least attractive buildings in their area or neighborhood. In Goodlad's words, "these schools appeared to be artifacts of a society that didn't care."[9]

who or what is a good teacher?

Who is a good teacher? Can such be defined or described? Skepticism abounds. Grambs represents the majority viewpoint when she explains that teacher competence is whatever people think it is. A principal's perception of the good teacher is likely to be different from a parent's perception, or a student's, or even a teacher's; and one parent will differ with another just as will students or teachers. As she explains, "teachers see good teachers as those who are like themselves—whatever that may be."[10] Proponents of free schools, open schools, Montessori schools, or Basics schools may have a clearer conception than the general public of what good teaching is, but they certainly can't agree among their disparate groups.

In a 1976 Gallup Poll survey, the qualities named most often as characterizing the ideal teacher (in order) were

[7]Ibid, pp. 77–87, 97–99.
[8]Ibid, p. 94.
[9]John I. Goodlad, "The Schools vs. Education," *Saturday Review,* LII, no. 16 (April 19, 1969), pp. 60–61.
[10]Jean Dresden Grambs, *Schools, Scholars, and Society* (Englewood Cliffs, N.J.: Prentice-Hall, Inc. 1965), pp. 148–149.

the ability to communicate and understand
the ability to discipline firmly and fairly
the ability to inspire and motivate
high moral character
love and concern for children
dedication and enthusiasm for profession
friendly personality
good, clean personal appearance [11]

It seems instructive that the ability to discipline is rated ahead of the ability to inspire, and that several superficial personality factors are included in the most often mentioned list, while intellectual and critical thinking capabilities are conspicuously absent. As the writers concluded at *Phi Delta Kappan* magazine (where the survey was reported), "The ideal teacher, in effect, is one who becomes a model of behavior for the young."

Obviously, to do or be everything outlined above is a herculean task—certainly too much to ask of any one teacher. Good teachers come in an assortment of interests and talents. Some are superb speakers, others excellent discussion leaders, and others imaginative classroom organizers; from another perspective, the competent teacher may be subject-oriented, inquiry-oriented, or people-oriented.

Important as teacher personalities may be, despite a half century of research little is known for certain about what personalities are most appropriate for teaching. The study by David Ryans, however, is classic. Ryans found that effective teachers tend to be extremely generous in appraising the efforts of others, possess strong literary and artistic interests, participate in social groups, prefer nondirective classroom procedures, and employ student-centered methods. He went somewhat further in identifying three major continua of teacher behavior—democratic-autocratic, organized-disorganized, and stimulating-dull—that distinguish the effective from the ineffective teacher. As reported in Ryans's study, the behaviors associated with these three continua were

Pattern X_0—warm, understanding, friendly *versus* aloof, restricted,
Pattern Y_0—responsible, businesslike, systematic *versus* evading, unplanned, slipshod,
Pattern Z_0—stimulating, imaginative *versus* dull, routine teacher,[12]

Philip Jackson in his book *Life in Classrooms* presents new findings related to the behavior and disposition of teachers identified as outstanding

---

[11]George H. Gallup, "Eighth Annual Gallup Poll of the Public's Attitudes Toward the Public Schools," *Phi Delta Kappan*, 58, no. 2 (October, 1976), p. 195. Each year *Phi Delta Kappan* reports the findings of the Annual Gallup survey, which is informative reading for school teachers.

[12]David G. Ryans, *Characteristics of Teachers, Their Description, Comparison and Appraisal* (Washington, D.C.: American Council on Education, 1960), chap. 4.

Figure 11-1   Sensitivity to Student Needs and Interest Is Crucial

by their administrators and supervisors. Jackson's technique was to interview the named teachers. From these interviews emerged four themes that he skillfully illustrates using the teachers' own words. The first, *immediacy*, can be described as a sensitive awareness of the present situation or the "here and now." These teachers had a productive spontaneity, particularly in responding to youngsters' many-faceted needs to be understood. The second theme, *informality*, can be characterized as lack of undue routine, and an emphasis on freedom of movement and thought for students. A third theme, *autonomy*, was showed up very sharply with respect to teaching conditions, namely in a dislike both of a prescribed, inflexible curriculum and also of administration invasion of the classroom for teacher evaluation (even though these teachers presumably had the most to gain and least to lose from such evaluation). The final theme is *individuality*, as it relates to the students. Although confronted with an entire class, these teachers are keenly aware of individual student progress. These teachers' awareness of student individuality is particularly evident in their remarks about the basic satisfaction they gained from teaching.[13]

Seymour Sarason adds a comment that focuses more clearly Jackson's analysis of the good teacher. Leaving aside the unanswerable question of whether these teachers actually do all they say, Sarason states that from his experiences these kinds of teachers exist in very small numbers. But know-

[13]Jackson, *Life in Classrooms*, pp. 119–43.

ing who they are, he adds, does not answer several other important questions. How many average teachers could become significantly better with the proper training and support? Are these people a special breed, born to be top-notch teachers, or did they acquire these characteristics? Would the outstanding teacher in a suburban school also be considered so in an inner-city or rural school? (The same can be asked of good teachers in the other two settings.) Sarason emphatically comments that, based on his observations, "characteristics of individuals are always, to some extent, a reflection of the setting in which these characteristics are manifested."[14] In the right place with sufficient support, there would be many more excellent teachers.

a model of the model teacher

The good teacher can use various teaching styles and is defined differently by different people. We offer one model for identifying and developing the "desirable."

In presenting this model, we borrow selectively from psychological and clinical theories of personality and development. Psychologists have constructed and empirically tested various models of personality development. These include Carl Rogers's "Stasis Process Continuum" (explaining how healthy individuals, i.e. "fully functioning" people, have progressed from a mental state of relative rigidity to flowingness)[15] and Abraham Maslow's "self-actualization" theory (describing the healthy or self-actualizing person as one who has satisfied the basic needs for safety, belonging, love, and respect, and is free to explore his or her capacities and talents).[16] Other less popular, though hardly less rigorous theories that were useful include Jane Loevinger's "Stages of Ego Development,"[17] Philip Phenix's "Levels of Affect,"[18] Milton Rokeach's "Open and Closed Mind,"[19] Bob Burton Brown's "Experimental Mind,"[20] and the extensive writings of

---

[14]Seymour B. Sarason, *The Culture of the School and the Problem of Change* (Boston: Allyn & Bacon, Inc., 1971), pp. 170–71.

[15]Carl R. Rogers, *On Becoming a Person* (Boston: Houghton Mifflin Company, 1961). Another important source particularly applicable to the teacher is Carl R. Rogers, *Freedom to Learn* (Columbus, Ohio: Charles E. Merrill Publishing Company, 1969).

[16]Abraham H. Maslow, *Motivation and Personality*, 2nd ed. (New York: Harper & Row, Publishers, 2nd ed. 1970), and Abraham H. Maslow, *Toward a Psychology of Being*, 2nd ed. (New York: Van Nostrand Reinhold Company, 1968).

[17]Jane Loevinger, "Theories of Ego Development," in L. Berger, ed., *Clinical-Cognitive Psychology* (Englewood Cliffs, N.J.: Prentice-Hall, Inc., 1969).

[18]Phenix's theoretical position is developed in his article "Perceptions of an Ethicist About the Affective," in *Feeling, Valuing, and the Art of Growing: Insights in the Affective* (Washington, D.C.: Association for Supervision and Curriculum Development, the 1977 Yearbook), pp. 59–81.

[19]Milton Rokeach, *The Open and Closed Mind* (New York: Basic Books, Inc., Publishers, 1960).

[20]Bob Burton Brown, *The Experimental Mind in Education* (New York: Harper & Row, Publishers, 1968), chap. 3.

psychoanalyist Erich Fromm on productive and nonproductive character types.[21]

The traits outlined in the six clusters presented here represent a synthesis of the findings of these theorists and our own experiences in live classrooms. These clusters were designed to represent the personal needs, cognitive perspective, and emotional disposition that teachers bring to the classroom. Our model is hypothetical, but like the psychological theories it is a spin-off from, the construct is sequential with an inner logic, and with each successive stage building on to the preceding one. Despite the possible negative aspects of some clusters, there are positive qualities to all; each has an appropriate place in the classroom. Nevertheless, we believe that the sequence from cluster 1 to cluster 6 is hierarchical: each successive cluster is potentially more educative.

Cluster-1 representatives prefer teacher-directed learning situations, and can be described as "authority-centered." They have internalized the traditional institutional norms of the school, and are prepared to fill roles that reinforce those norms. They believe that basic skills and essential knowledge should be taught before other curriculum subjects can be considered. The classrooms of these teachers are extraordinarily disciplined environments: exactness, punctuality, orderliness and predictability are highly valued. These teachers approve of punitive measures, and use testing and grading for both evaluative and disciplinary reasons. In addition, they demand respect for and are deferential to status and authority.

Cluster-1 teachers may be remembered by their students either favorably or unfavorably. Their classroom precision, clarity, and discipline, along with their personal candor, can be impressive. Students often feel that these teachers have given them substantive and very valuable learning. Contrariwise, students may recognize an arbitrary and basic authoritarian posture, concluding that learning was greatly inhibited by the lack of spontaneity, divergence, and freedom.

Cluster-2 persons are "guardian-centered," though they often distinctly resemble the authority-centered teacher. They tend to be traditional teachers with a respect for well-behaved classes, prescribed curriculum, and the accepted norms of school and society. Likewise, they prefer teacher-directed classes, in which students assume a receptive learning role. Their curriculum is designed around basic skills and established content with little tolerance for exploratory, discovery learning, and with a low threshold for ambiguity and uncertainty.

Cluster-2 teachers, however, are mild-mannered, morally virtuous, and considerate toward students. They tend to be protective of children's welfare and to display a concern for student learning. This concern is not necessarily in response to individual student needs, but rather to the socially prescribed behavior that students ought to acquire.

[21]Erich Fromm, *Man for Himself, An Inquiry Into the Psychology of Ethics* (New York: Holt, Rinehart & Winston, 1947).

Cluster-3 character types are unique with schools and academic settings. They, too, are tradition-oritented, but in a scholarly, intellectual, and academic fashion. They are accepting of school norms, supportive of traditional curriculum and methods, and intellectually skèptical of modern or nontraditional curricula as well as many extracurricular activities. These teachers proudly fulfill the role of a dispenser of wisdom, truths, and knowledge, and are essentially content-centered.

Cluster-3 teachers prefer rational processes using reflection or empirical analysis, deduction, and induction. Noticeably absent, however, is the ability or willingness to evoke intuitive leaps, hunches or imagination, divergent thought patterns, and feelings, and to deal with student-initiated concerns. While their thinking is more differentiated and integrated than Cluster-1 and Cluster-2 representatives, they are likely to rely on traditional academic sources of authority.

Members of *Cluster-4* exhibit interest in individual student needs; still, they are best described as "self-centered." They are eager to deal with the interests of students, often creating imaginatively arranged and displayed classrooms. Like their Cluster-3 counterparts, they tend to be more abstract, less dogmatic, and less evaluative than representatives of the first two systems. Unlike Cluster-3 teachers, they practice more "progressive" teaching strategies.

Their behavior is usually empathetic and responsive, resulting from a desire for interpersonal harmony and mutual dependency. The Cluster-4 teacher is skilled at orchestrating and controlling the classroom environment by means of social engineering, but also interpersonal manipulation. Outwardly, what appears to an informal, student-centered classroom is likely to be under the subtle control of the teacher. This teacher fits very closely to the conceptual personality of Harvey's system-3 individual.[22] (See also discussion in Chapter 6.) As Harvey found, their classroom techniques often are in conflict with the exploratory, autonomous needs of students, and to their dismay, are apt to result in disharmony and rejection. Only with those students who require the same interpersonal dependency and reinforcement is a harmonious symbiosis achieved.

Cluster-5 teachers are essentially "task-centered," that is, ambitious, efficient, and productive classroom managers. Duty in this cluster is defined in terms of contractual obligations or mutually agreeable ground rules, and education is expected to be carried out in an expedient, rational way. More than representatives of the previous clusters, this person is flexible, tolerant of ambiguity, and can withstand uncertainty, largely because the process is within his or her control.

Cluster-5 teachers are the most likely to "succeed." They tend to be the most respected members of the public school faculties, though at times

---

[22]Several articles by Harvey and his associates describe his belief systems. Among these we suggest O. J. Harvey, "Belief and Behaviors: Some Implications for Education," *The Science Teacher*, 37, no. 9 (December 1970).

they are envied, despised, or both because of their ambition, productiveness, and determined leadership. They also tend to advance to more powerful positions, such as department heads, principalships, superintendencies, presidents of educational associations, leaders in teacher unions, state department of education offices, and university faculties. These teachers or educators have a deep respect for logic, empirical evidence, expertise, cooperation, and organizational planning. As character types, they are alligned closely with Kohlberg's level-5 individual.[23]

Cluster-6 representatives can be called "goal-centered" in the sense that they are motivated by ideals, conscience, and universal principles such as individual freedom, justice, and human dignity. These teachers are willing to act on such principles despite unfavorable odds and personal risk, and in other ways will pursue their goals in a persistent, open and tactful manner. Like Cluster-5 teachers, they are abstract, flexible, democratic, innovative, self-secure, and able to understand the viewpoints of others. They also are productive by almost any definition, but particularly Fromm's idea of spontaneous (in contrast to compulsive) and creative work. Unlike Cluster-5 individuals, they are more committed to personal ideals, and more clearly recognize the inseparability of emotions and intellect in learning. Cluster-6 teachers tend to use many information sources in devising their teaching approaches, though the final product is distinctly original. More than any other teachers, they have a set of internal standards independent of external criteria, sometimes coinciding with social norms and sometimes not.

The personality theories of Harvey, Kohlberg, Phenix, Fromm, Rogers, Maslow, and others are on common ground at their highest levels of functioning. This functioning is variously described as abstract and integrative (Harvey), committed to idealization (Phenix), appealing to universal principles (Kohlberg), self-actualizing (Maslow) fully functioning (Rogers), open, expressive, introspective, conscientious and so on. Cluster-6 exemplifies such an intellectually and emotionally integrated person.

The six clusters are summarized in Table 11-1 by "classroom orientation" and "personality descriptors."

PROFESSIONAL ORGANIZATIONS FOR TEACHERS

One who is a teacher is eligible to become a member of several professional organizations. An array of national, state, and local organizations compete with each other for members. Further, each of the national organizations has an affiliated state group, and some even have local affiliates.

---

[23]Likewise, the work of Kohlberg and his associates has been described in numerous educational journals. Among these articles is Lawrence Kohlberg, "The Cognitive-Developmental Approach to Moral Education," *Phi Delta Kappan*, 66, no. 10 (June, 1975), pp. 670–77.

Table 11-1　Teacher Behavior Clusters

Classroom orientation	Personality descriptors
1. Authority-centered	rule-oriented, disciplined, authoritarian, traditional, strong-willed, conforming to institutional norms.
2. Guardian-centerd	rule-oriented, mild-mannered, orderly, virtuous, low ambiguity threshold, conforming to prescribed social roles.
3. Content-centered	tradition-oriented, scholarly, academic, analytic, conforming to accepted education norms.
4. Self-centered	approval-oriented, progressive, creative, dependent, manipulative, needing strong interdependent relations.
5. Task-centered	job-oriented, analytical resourceful, achieving, pragmatic, productive, emphasizing contractual relations.
6. Goal-centered	individual-oriented, democratic, imaginative, independent, autonomous, integrative, rational, expressive, guided by internal standards.

The two most powerful teachers' professional organizations are the American Federation of Teachers (AFL/CIO) and the National Education Association. Both groups have made great strides in the past two decades in achieving economic gains for American teachers. They became effective agents in collective bargaining sessions with local school boards, and they used their political power to influence state and federal politics. But so far these organizations have been unable to do much about giving teachers control of their working conditions, or control of the curriculum, or, perhaps most significantly, control over who enters the profession, who is retained after a probationary period, and who is expelled for incompetency.

Organizations of educators appear to provide their members one or several, but seldom all, of the following benefits:

1. the political leverage of a pressure group, and sometimes of a full- or part-time lobbyist,
2. the group solidarity of a union, committed to the dual tools of collective bargaining and the threat or reality of withholding services, and employing expert contract negotiators,
3. one or more publications, such as scholarly-theoretical and/or practical-trendy yearbooks, journals, and bulletins, and newsletters,

4. the collegiality of local, state, and national conferences, workshops, and meetings,
5. preferred-buyer status for purchasing insurance, professional books, and even appliances and automobiles,
6. a reserve fund to employ legal counsel for members in cases involving academic freedom, illegal strikes, and other education-related suits, and
7. free or inexpensive professional consultation to school districts, usually from the national level to a state unit or from the state level to a local unit.

Only the American Federation of Teachers (AFT) and the National Education Association (NEA) and their respective affiliates, offer all seven benefits, in varying degrees.

the battle for control of the profession

Since about 1960 teachers' organizations have become militant, outspoken, and politically active, especially the two prominent national professional unions—the AFT and the NEA. At first the more militant but smaller group, the AFT, pushed teachers toward unionization, while the more conservative NEA deplored such an outrageous departure from the tenets of professionalism. As the AFT began to make inroads into NEA membership, however, the NEA changed its political stance and began to support collective bargaining, bargaining-agent elections in school districts, imposition of statewide or nationwide sanctions on school districts opposing or violating negotiated contracts, and even strikes (euphemistically termed withdrawal or withholding of services). Even after 1967, when the NEA accepted in principle and practice the procedures and strategies of the trade union movement, it continued to claim to be a "professional association." We consider, however, that both the NEA and the AFT are unions *and* professional organizations.

For the first time in its more than 100-year history, the NEA in 1976 endorsed a presidential candidate—Jimmy Carter. It is likely that the NEA expected from the Carter Administration and the Democratic majorities in Congress support of: (1) a new Cabinet-level executive department—a Department of Education, separate from Health and Welfare, (2) a federal law guaranteeing teachers (and probably other public employees) the rights to collective bargaining and the use of strikes, and (3) a *general* aid to public education act with appropriate funding.

The state-level education associations are probably the strongest link in the NEA's national-state-local chain. In particular as political pressure groups, the NEA's state education association affiliates have been highly successful in influencing state legislatures and state boards and departments of education. It's at this level that teachers have won significant victories and exerted crucial leverage. The victories include, among others, the passage of tenure and collective-bargaining acts; the leverage has been used to increase the public schools' appropriations and to endorse and supply campaign funds for gubernatorial and state legislature candidates.

The most heated competition between the AFT and NEA, especially in large urban and suburban school districts, occurs at the local level. What is at stake are dues-paying members and the right (determined by special elections) to become the *exclusive* bargaining agent for *all* of a district's teachers, regardless of organization membership.

The AFT is the younger and smaller of the national teachers' organizations. From its inception, the AFT at all levels has been an integral part of the American labor union movement and a member affiliate of the American Federation of Labor and Congress of Industrial Organizations (AFL/CIO).

The AFT has had its greatest successes in urban school districts and in states where organized labor in general has had its greatest impact. Although only about one-fourth the size of the NEA, the AFT membership tends to concentrate in large and moderate-sized cities, where internal unity combined with solidarity with the rest of the AFL/CIO unions have yielded pioneering gains in negotiated contracts. In addition to its organizing efforts and its fight for state and federal legislation to recognize the rights of teachers to negotiate, bargain collectively, and strike (which are now also NEA goals), the AFT seeks to strengthen state tenure laws, to eliminate classroom overcrowding by lowering pupil-teacher ratios, to eliminate excessive class interruptions, to guarantee by law free and unencumbered lunch periods for teachers, to improve teacher pensions and fringe benefits (e.g., paid hospitalization and medical insurance), and to achieve as many as possible of these improvements as parts of legislation or negotiated contracts without the use of the last resort—a strike.

During the 1960s there was furious competition between the AFT and the NEA for members and in the bargaining-agent elections. The most visible signs of this conflict were in school districts in the larger cities such as New York and Detroit. Actual teacher strikes, rather than mere threats, began to occur. By 1968, it was clear that the union movement had been successfully expanded to include America's teachers, and that the relative successes of the union strategies employed by the AFT had led to the conversion of the NEA to a union. In fact, by the early 1970s, two to four times more strikes were called by NEA affiliates than by AFT locals.

Also by 1968 it was becoming obvious that the goals, policies, and practices of the two unions were rapidly converging, and that merger in the long run was probably inevitable. Just as the paths to convergence were paved with bitterness and hostility, however, so the roads to merger thus far have been cluttered with potholes and other obstacles. Today, the NEA–AFT rivalry continues unabated, possibly awaiting a more favorable climate and more conciliatory leaders.

THE LEGAL RIGHTS OF TEACHERS

As citizens of the United States, both teachers and students have legal rights. Their rights as citizens are enumerated in the U.S. Constitution (especially in the Bill of Rights) and in the state constitutions. As citizen *and* as teacher, one has the rights and responsibilities specified in federal and state statutory law, in school district policies and regulations, and in local, state, and federal case law.

It is historically accurate that, in the same way parents emphasize their children's responsibilities rather than their rights, school boards, school administrators, parents of students, and other citizens have tended to emphasize teachers' responsibilities and to limit their rights. Ironically, teachers have tended to treat their charges similarly.

For all teachers to be able to enjoy their civil and professional rights requires that some, really only a few, test these rights in practice or in legal cases in order to establish precedents. In fact, well-publicized cases make visible to all parties some specific aspect of a teacher's rights. In a court case, both the decision itself and its "educative" value are essential to the continuous defining of teachers' rights.

A considerable body of case law relates to teachers' civil rights. These cases cover a broad range of controversy involving teachers' actions both as teachers and as citizens. Louis Fischer and David Schimmel have provided succinct set of conclusions regarding teachers' civil rights. These are presented here, under the topical headings used by these authors.[24]

freedom of expression

Twentieth-century court decisions have tended to remove restrictions on teachers' freedom to speak out on controversial issues, both in school and away from school. A distinction is still drawn, however, between in-school expression (somewhat restricted) and out-of-school expression (very few restrictions). In general, when teachers are not "at work," they enjoy the same First Amendment guarantees as any private citizen. While in school, the teacher is protected by the concept of academic freedom, *but within limits*. The limits are determined by the extent to which statements, methods or materials "can be shown [to be] irrelevant to her [or his] teaching objective, inappropriate to the age and maturity of . . . students, or disruptive of school discipline."[25]

---

[24]Louis Fischer and David Schimmel, *The Civil Rights of Teachers* (New York: Harper & Row, Publishers, 1973), pp. 146–161.
[25]Ibid., pp. 147–149.

the teacher as a person

No longer are teachers expected to "be paragons of virtue twenty-four hours a day." A teacher is autonomous in his or her values, concept of morality, leisure activities, and personal appearance. In general, "the rights of teachers to pursue a normal life consistent with others in the community receives legal protection." Here again there are exceptions, such as a teacher's immoral conduct with students or the general crime of contributing to the delinquency of a minor.[26]

loyalty and freedom

This topic deals with cases that are focused on "loyalty oaths for teachers, membership in controversial organizations, [teachers'] political activities, and membership in teacher organizations." Except for "overly broad or vague" oaths, the courts have upheld the swearing to and signing of loyalty oaths, to state and/or nation, as a condition of public school employment. Other than in the case where a teacher subscribes to the *illegal* goals of an organization, there can be no restrictions on teachers' rights to join any organization. With respect to teachers' political activities, "the judicial trend will probably reflect the recent holding that a teacher can be barred from political activity only if it materially and substantially interferes with the operation of the school." Although in some states strikes and other coercive measures may be illegal, "the right of teachers to organize and to bargain collectively is clearly established."[27]

arbitrary action, discrimination, and fair procedures

As agents of a state, school board members and administrators are delegated the power to make decisions for schools under their jurisdiction. This is discretionary power, which can be abused, and sometimes is, especially in policies and actions affecting teachers and students. If the abuse involves the "arbitrary, unreasonable, or discriminatory" use of discretionary power, the courts will find these decisions and actions to be illegal. If discrimination is involved, it is typically by race, sex, religion, or nationality.

Teachers are also protected by state tenure laws, which allow dismissal or disciplinary action only under rare circumstances, and then only when fair procedures have been scrupulously followed. The only resort for untenured, probationary teachers (usually teachers employed one, two, or three years in a given district), however, are the conditions expressly stipu-

[26]Ibid., pp. 150–151.
[27]Ibid., pp. 153–155.

lated in their one-year contracts. Their employment may be terminated at the end of any school year without notification of cause and without a hearing.[28]

The above generalizations are valid, but are not guarantees that practice in every instance will conform to them. Further, the courts, in honoring the concept of separation of powers at the state and federal levels, will refuse to hear cases involving purely educational decisions. Their rule is, "Educational matters are for educators to decide."[29]

THE LEGAL RIGHTS OF STUDENTS

Students, like teachers, historically have been exhorted ceaselessly to meet their responsibilities, but are seldom informed of their rights. This section on student rights is included in a chapter about the teacher as professional because we believe that, along with parents, teachers should be the chief advocates and defenders of children and youth, and also that schools should be places where the young do not have to pay too dearly for their mistakes. Further, a primary responsibility of teachers is the care and nurture of students.

As with teachers' rights, students' rights are most clearly defined and affirmed in case law dealing with complaints brought against teachers and school officials by students, their parents, or their legal guardians. In order to avoid the lengthy explanation of numerous precedent setting court cases, we again rely on the work of Schimmel and Fischer to summarize the relevant case law regarding students' civil rights. As before, we use their topic headings.[30]

freedom of speech

For students as for teachers, a distinction exists between freedom of expression *in* school and *away from* school. "As a general rule, students who are *away from school* have the same freedom to speak as anyone else. The *Tinker* case established that their right to speak *inside* the schools is also constitutionally protected." Only if the actual speech or symbolic statement (e.g., wearing armbands as a form of social protest) disrupts school operations, may school officials curtail students' freedom of speech *in school*.[31]

[28]Ibid., pp. 156–158.
[29]Ibid., p. 159.
[30]David Schimmel and Louis Fischer, *The Civil Rights of Students* (New York: Harper & Row, Publishers, 1975), pp. 264–84.
[31]Ibid., pp. 265–266.

freedom of the press

For this topic, again the *Tinker* case is applicable. The courts will tolerate "restrictions only to prevent substantial or material interference with school activities or the rights of others." The burden of proof for the potential disruptiveness of an article or issue of a paper is on school officials. Also, the courts have been ambivalent on the issue of "prior restraint," which is a form of press censorship prior to publication and distribution of a document. Further, student publications must refrain from the use of obscenity, especially since their readership is mainly composed of minors.[32]

freedom of association

This right has been considered by the courts as an *implied* constitutional freedom. The courts have considered it to guarantee within *reasonably* prescribed limits, public school students' rights "to organize and use school facilities, . . . [and] to protest and demonstrate." Case law, however, has upheld state statutes which prohibit minors (but not "adults") from forming or joining such organizations as fraternities, sororities, and secret clubs. The courts have held "that schools may bar all outside speakers," but that if speakers are allowed to speak in the schools of a district, school officials may not permit only those with whom they agree or are sympathetic to come in, and exclude all others.[33]

freedom of religion

The First Amendment to the Constitution prohibits the official establishment of any religion by the nation or any state. This prohibition has been interpreted by the Supreme Court to mean that a "wall of separation" must be maintained between church and state. In education, this interpretation has come to mean that religion should be kept separate from public education. The two exceptions have been to permit students "released time" to receive religious instruction and to allow teachers, usually in social studies classes, to teach *about* world religions.

The Supreme Court declared in 1962 that Bible-reading and prayers are unconstitutional in the public schools, and also made it clear that they are illegal whether required or optional. This applies only to public school classroom and schools.

A significant case involving Amish children successfully challenged one state compulsory attendance laws, but the decision emphasized the uniqueness of the Amish community and the inability to separate religious and secular aspects of the Amish way of life.[34]

[32]Ibid., pp. 266–267.
[33]Ibid., pp. 267–269.
[34]Ibid., pp. 269–271.

personal appearance

Students' personal appearance becomes a school issue particularly with respect to standards of grooming and clothing. Although most applicable court cases have held that personal grooming is a private matter, some have upheld various school rules concerning hair lengths and styles. For the issue of choice of clothing, "most courts hold there is no such constitutional right" for students. Because dress codes only apply during school hours, courts have upheld the legality of these codes when they are "reasonable and related to educational goals."[35]

racial and ethnic segregation

This crucial topic is treated in depth in Chapter 7; its economic aspects are discussed in Chapter 4.

sex discrimination

This important issue is discussed in Chapter 8.

due process

Although "today courts generally hold that students have a right to due process before serious punishment, such as expulsion or long-term suspension, can be imposed," court decisions have upheld corporal punishment *in loco parentis*.[36]

Two pieces of federal legislation in the 1970s contributed dramatically to the expansion of the civil rights of students and their families. These are: (1) The Education for All Handicapped Children Act of 1975 (Public Law 94-142), and (2) Family Educational Rights and Privacy Act of 1974, and amendments. The "Handicapped Act" has been widely hailed as the Bill of Rights for handicapped children and their parents. Its significant aspects are the concepts of "least restrictive environment" and "mainstreaming," the requirement of an "individualized Education Program" for each handicapped student (and the progressively increasing allocation of federal funds to run state and local programs). "Least restrictive environment" and "mainstreaming" are complementary concepts. Handicapped students must be individually evaluated and, depending on how severe the handicap is and how it affects learning, they must be placed in whatever school setting is least restrictive and comes closest to the climate of a "regular classroom." This will mean that many, if not most, handicapped

[35] Ibid., pp. 271–273.
[36] Ibid., pp. 276–277.

315

students will be placed in "regular classrooms" a process called "mainstreaming."

The Family Educational Rights and Privacy Act was designed to counter the abuses of unfair or exploitative uses of data collected by schools about individual students and their families. Specifically, it provides that persons who are subjects of data systems must be informed of such systems and the data on them as individuals; that they be assured the data is only used for the purposes intended when it was collected; that students or their parents or guardians be able to see the records and be able to correct them; and that they be assured that the persons responsible for data or record systems take reasonable precautions to prevent misuse of data and personal information. Another provision insures that the schools neither disclose information about their students nor permit inspection of student records without permission from the student or the student's parents or guardian.

CASE STUDY: Academic Freedom

You have assigned a book to your class to read that you realize may be controversial. You know it is regarded as a good piece of literature, fits in well with the course and age group, and is currently being used by other public schools in the country. Class discussions have been very spirited, but thoughtful and mature. The students appear to be learning more from their study of this work than they would be, in your judgment, from most other books.

As a precaution you informed your principal that you have chosen this book, gave him your reasons, and left a copy for his review. It is now a couple of weeks later and the principal asks you to withdraw the book from your reading list, explaining that he has received pressure from a group of parents. A school board member had also suggested that the principal look into the matter. A few students in your class indicated that some of the material was upsetting to them, but they were hesitant to claim that as a whole the book didn't have sound educational value.

What should you do? When a teacher's values conflict with some members of the community, whose should prevail? Should parents, students and the community have any say in curricular matters? If so, how much?

THOUGHT QUESTIONS

1. What do you consider the essential criteria for deciding whether teaching is or isn't a profession? Criticize Lieberman's eight criteria, and decide if you would include or exclude each one on your own list of criteria.

2. Evaluate as to potential usefulness for the practicing classroom teacher each of the following aspects of a teacher preparation program:

—knowledge of the characteristics of children and adolescents, and their developmental cycles
—knowledge of theories about and kinds of human learning
—knowledge of the structure of knowledge; of concepts, generalizations, and modes of inquiry; specialized knowledge in given academic disciplines
—ability to use the technical skills of teaching
—knowledge of the scope of possible educational objectives in the cognitive, affective, and psychomotor domains
—acceptance of values and attitudes that enhance learning, and lead to mutually satisfying human relationships
—mastery of the skills of communication, conflict management and reduction, human relations, and decision-making
—extensive practice in the art of effectively integrating the seven above

3. In what respects is teaching *both* an art and a science?

4. To what extent do teachers enjoy the same legal rights as all other citizens of the United States?

5. To what extent should students, as students and minors, enjoy the same legal rights as all other citizens of the United States? As a public school teacher, what rights will you accord to the students in your classes? State the rights in the form of a "Students' Bill of Rights."

6. Having considered the roles that teachers play both in school and life, what characteristics do you have that would make you particularly suited to be a teacher? What qualities in your personality might interfere with your effectiveness as a teacher? What personal needs do you have that fit in well with elementary, junior high, or senior high school teaching? Which of your needs would a teaching career tend to satisfy?

7. After reading the author's views of the "good" teacher, what words would you use to describe such a teacher? What characteristics or abilities do you ascribe to those teachers who you judged as "good"? How do these characteristics match with Ryans's X_o, Y_o, and Z_o pattern? How do they match with Jackson's themes of immediacy, informality, autonomy, and individuality? To what extent do you feel you possess the qualities that Ryans and Jackson describe?

8. Where do you fit among the six teacher clusters outlined in the chapter? Are you neatly in one cluster, or are your traits spread over several clusters? What are some characteristics of your teaching personality? Would you prefer to change any of these? If so, what characteristics would you like to have? Do most teachers fit essentially into one cluster, or are they a mixture of several?

PRACTICAL ACTIVITIES

1. Arrange to observe a teacher's classroom for several periods, preferably over a few days. Observe both teaching (e.g., large-group instruction, small-group discussion, individual work) and nonteaching functions (e.g., clerical, counseling, custodial, and policing tasks) with which the teacher is

involved. Figure out how much time is spent on "teaching" and on "nonteaching" activities. Discuss the teacher's apparent attitude towards these functions. Ask the teacher about the importance of nonteaching functions, the time spent on them, and the effect on a person's teaching. Write up the results of your findings.

2. Interview two public school teachers: one in the first, second, or third year of teaching, and one with ten or more years of experience. Plan an interview that includes asking how interesting and exciting teaching is at this point in their careers; what are the rewarding and unrewarding aspects of the work; what are the difficult and taxing aspects of teaching; how does each one's attitude toward teaching compare with what it was five or ten years ago (or what do they think it will be in five or ten years); how long they plan to stay in teaching and why? Add other pertinent questions. Interpret, compare, and contrast the two views represented.

3. Assign yourself to a group of students for a day and follow them from class to class, during study hall, recess, lunch, and the like. If necessary, explain that you are doing an informal study for a class at the college, and would like them to act as they normally do. To guide your study, develop several observation questions, including how much intellectual activity they engage in; how involved and interested or bored and inattentive are they; how do crowds, noise, delays, and intrusions appear to affect them; how much time do they spend alone or in groups, silent or talking, active or inactive, expressive or inexpressive; when do they seem the happiest and most mentally alert.

4. Attend a teachers' meeting in a local public elementary, junior high, or senior high school. What issues were discussed? What were the major concerns of the teachers? Who ran the meeting? What was the superintendent or principal's role? Describe the relationship between the principal and teachers, or among the administrators and teachers. What percentage of the teachers were present at the meeting? How many took active part in the meeting? What conclusions and generalizations can you draw?

5. Arrange to serve as a teacher's assistant for a couple of hours a day for a week. Help the teacher in any appropriate capacity, instructional, clerical, or other. In writing up your assessment of the nature of the teacher's work consider: How "professional" were the various tasks? What does the teacher need to spend more time doing, and what ought to take less time?

6. Conduct a survey of employed public school teachers to determine which of the following aspects of preservice teacher education programs they think should receive the highest priority. Have them rank items, giving a "1" to the highest ranked priority, and continuing through a "5" for the lowest priority item.

    mastery of subject matter
    competence in using a variety of teaching methods and materials
    effective use of human relations skills, including classroom management and control

understanding the nature, development, and concerns of children and adolescents

understanding the theories and principles of human learning

7. Locate a copy of a "Student Handbook" from a school in a nearby school district. Analyze it in regard to students' rights and responsibilities and write up your findings.

BIBLIOGRAPHY

BELTH, MARC, *Education as a Discipline*. Boston, Mass.: Allyn & Bacon, Inc., 1965.

BRENTON, MYRON, *What's Happened to Teacher?* New York: Coward-McCann, 1970.

CURWIN, RICHARD L., AND BARBARA SCHNEIDER FUHRMANN, *Discovering Your Teaching Self, Humanistic Approaches to Effective Teaching*. Englewood Cliffs, N.J.: Prentice-Hall, Inc., 1975.

DREEBEN, ROBERT, *The Nature of Teaching*. Glenview, Ill.: Scott, Foresman & Company, 1970.

FISCHER, LOUIS, AND DAVID SCHIMMEL, *The Civil Rights of Teachers*. New York: Harper & Row, Publishers, 1973.

FISHMAN, STERLING, ANDREAS M. KAZAMIAS, AND HERBERT M. KLIEBARD, *Teacher, Student and Society*. Boston: Little, Brown & Company, 1974.

GOOD, THOMAS L., BRUCE J. BIDDLE, AND JERE E. BROPHY, *Teachers Make A Difference*. Holt, Rinehart & Winston, 1975.

GOODLAD, JOHN I., AND M. FRANCES KLEIN, *Behind the Classroom Door*. Worthington, Ohio: Charles A. Jones Publishing Company, 1970.

GRAMBS, JEAN DRESDEN, *Schools, Scholars and Society*. Englewood Cliffs, N.J.: Prentice-Hall, Inc., 1965.

GREENBERG, HERBERT M., *Teaching With Feeling*. New York: The Macmillan Company, 1969.

HAMACHEK, DON E., ed., *The Self in Growth, Teaching and Learning*. Englewood Cliffs, N.J.: Prentice-Hall, Inc., 1971.

HARMIN, MERRILL, AND TOM GREGORY, *Teaching is* . . . . Chicago: Science Research Associates, Inc., 1974.

JACKSON, PHILIP W., *Life in Classrooms*. New York: Holt, Rinehart & Winston, 1968.

JOYCE, BRUCE, AND MARSHA WEIL, *Models of Teaching*. Englewood Cliffs, N.J.: Prentice-Hall, Inc., 1972.

LIEBERMAN, MYRON, *Education as a Profession*. Englewood Cliffs, N.J.: Prentice-Hall, Inc., 1956.

————, *The Future of Public Education*. Chicago, Ill.: The University of Chicago Press, 1960.

LYON, HAROLD C., Jr., *Learning to Feel—Feeling to Learn*. Columbus, Ohio: Charles E. Merrill Publishing Company, 1971.

MILLER, JOHN P., *Humanizing the Classroom: Models of Teaching in Affective Education*. New York: Praeger Publishers, Inc. 1976.

PROEFRIEDT, WILLIAM A., *The Teacher You Choose To Be*. New York: Holt, Rinehart & Winston, 1975.

RATHS, LOUIS E., *Teaching For Learning*. Columbus, Ohio: Charles E. Merrill Publishing Company, 1969.

RICHARDS, MARY CAROLINE, *Centering*. Middletown, Conn.: Wesleyan University Press, 1964.

RICHEY, ROBERT W., *Preparing for a Career in Education*. New York: McGraw-Hill Book Company, 1974.

ROGERS, CARL R., *On Becoming a Person*. Boston, Mass.: Houghton Mifflin Company, 1961.

SARASON, SEYMOUR B., *The Culture of the School and the Problem of Change*. Boston: Allyn & Bacon, Inc., 1971.

SCHIMMEL, DAVID AND LOUIS FISCHER, *The Civil Rights of Students*. New York: Harper & Row, Publishers, 1975.

SEABERG, DOROTHY I., *The Four Faces of Teaching*. Pacific Palisades, Calif.: Goodyear Publishing Company, 1974.

PART FOUR

ALTERNATIVE, GLOBAL, AND FUTURE PERSPECTIVES

12

ALTERNATIVE SCHOOLING

More important, we should have learned in the last decade that there is no magic in the single school system or in any set of curricular prescriptions, and that the most successful motivating device may simply be the sense that one has chosen what one wants to learn and under what conditions. In urban areas there is no reason why children in one neighborhood should be forced to attend one particular school for a specified period of time; why there should not be choice as to place, subject, style of teaching, and hours; why, for all children, French and history and algebra should have absolutely equal value; why, for some, art or dance or music should not be given more time than history; why reading a book is more of a humanistic activity than making a film or playing an instrument; why children should not be allowed to choose between permissive and highly structured situations (and many would choose the latter); why parents and children should not have the economic power to punish unsuccessful schools (by leaving them) and to reward effective ones; or why single, self-serving bureaucracies should continue to hold monopoly power in what is probably the most crucial, and certainly the most universal public enterprise in America. Wealthy children and middle-class parents have some options about schools; lower-class children have none.

Peter Schrag, *End of the Impossible Dream*[1]

The 1960s was a time of optimism. The mood of the nation was towards reform, and in education this mood was one of bold optimism. There was little question that reform could be achieved and schools im-

[1] Peter Schrag, "End of the Impossible Dream," *Saturday Review*, LIII, 38 (September 19, 1970), pp. 94–95.

plemented innumerable reform measures, including team teaching, flexible scheduling, programmed learning, multiple texts, nongraded schools, programs for the disadvantaged, computerized learning, and the "new" curricula. Educators were committed to the programs; change was just a matter of time. More dramatic, reform in education was seen as the keystone to curing many of the nation's social ailments.

The notion that reform of American public schools was necessary and imminent predates the sixties, beginning in the early fifties. First, there was the call for more intellectual rigor in the curriculum. Spokesmen such as Arthur Bestor and Hyman Rickover vigorously criticized the school system, arguing that students did not know enough history, physics and English;[2] James Conant conducted an extensive study on the curriculum of the American high school, substantiating this view;[3] Jerome Zacharias and other science educators, with the generous support of the federal government, rewrote the science curriculum. The return to "the fundamentals" and academic rigor did not subside in the 1960s, but it was flanked by another group of reformers Schrag refers to as democrats: those determined to integrate and humanize schools, while providing universal opportunity. The first group of reformers represented the aspirations of the enfranchised affluent, middle-class, who desired an Ivy League education for their kind. The second group demanded for the deprieved what they thought the privileged were getting. Now suddenly the optimism is gone. In retrospect, the sixties and seventies were decades of frustration and bafflement. The innovations, so highly regarded, did not foster basic change in our schools. Even if these reforms had lived up to expectations, people were no longer certain that the changes would have made any substantially improved economic opportunity of the disadvantaged, or the quality of life in the nation.

Meanwhile, the voices of reform shifted from those who are part of the institutionalized mainstream to those who were less sympathetic with the school system. These reformers disregarded any compensatory, innovative efforts in favor of overhauling the system; some, such as Ivan Illich, called for abandonment of the system. Nevertheless, the underlying theme of most critics—namely, greater respect for children and more diversity in approaches to learning—was hardly radical. But the words used by John Holt, James Herndon, Jonathan Kozol, Herbert Kohl, and others were imbued with outrage and indignation. Perhaps for this reason, more than any other, they failed to capture the public's support. Ironically, many of their ideas gradually become part of societal beliefs and school practices.

[2]See Arthur Bestor's *Educational Wastelands* (Champaign, Ill.: University of Illinois Press, 1953), and Hyman Rickover's *Education and Freedom* (New York: E. P. Dutton & Co., Inc., 1959).

[3]James Conant, *The American High School Today* (New York: McGraw-Hill Book Company, 1959).

If there has been a "crisis in the classroom," for the past quarter of a century, the public has not responded with any sort of alarm or mandate for reform. When widespread change is desired, it is usually to retrench, as the renewed "back-to-basics" movement indicates. People by and large are content with the schools; the schools did well by them, so they reason, and the people assume that they probably can do even better by their children. Education is a process that we all endured, that most of us have assumed was beneficial, and that few of us clearly understood. The result is that, fundamentally, our public schools have changed surprisingly little since their conception over a century ago.[4]

The most important effort at reform in the public schools in the early seventies was the "alternatives" movement. Despite good reasons for pessimism, alternatives offer some hope. Unlike nearly all the reforms of the fifties and sixties, alternative schools were offered as an option, not as a directive.

THE PROMISE OF ALTERNATIVE SCHOOLS

The alternatives movement has the potential for substantially different reform in the schools. Unlike earlier reforms, alternatives are not to be superimposed on reluctant and bewildered parents. With alternatives, the type of school a child attends is not presented as an edict but is left to the choice of parent and student. This is Schrag's message: "What I am arguing for, obviously, is a restoration of multiple options, and, as much as possible, multiple values."[5] The alternatives movement is a promising step toward educational change because it offers students, parents, and teachers a choice that takes into account a diversity of learning and reaching styles.

The meaning of "alternatives" needs to be clarified. The word "alternative" conjured various meanings to the public. The prevailing association is to the many radical schools often labeled "free" or "open." In this light, alternatives have been defined as schools or places that exist as an *alternative* to the traditional ("establishment") school. As Mario Fantini points out, when alternatives were first introduced to the mainstream, the bulk of the samples came from counterculture experiments, often in urban settings with minority children.[6] This experience accounts for the "alternative to establishment" meaning cited above; it also helps explain the white middle class's skepticism of the term "alternatives." As a result, many establishment

---

[4]Theodore Sizer in *Places for Learning, Places for Joy: Speculations on American School Reform* (Cambridge, Mass.: Harvard University Press, 1973), and Colin Greer in *The Great School Legend* (New York: The Viking Press, 1972) are two educators who reach such a conclusion after serious examination.

[5]Schrag, "End of Impossible Dream," p. 95.

[6]Mario Fantini, *Public Schools of Choice: Alternatives in Education* (New York: Simon & Schuster, Inc., 1973), p. 166.

proponents of alternatives have substituted the terms "options" or "public options in education."[7]

A more useful definition of "alternatives," in view of the direction the movement has taken in public education, is one offered by Fantini and the National Consortium on Options in Public Education. They think of alternatives as *a range of (school or classroom) options along a pedagogical contiuum.* Alternative schools that fit such a continuum can definitively be called free schools, open schools, traditional or standard schools, continuous progress or contemporary schools, and fundamental schools. There also exist less descriptive school types, such as multiculture schools, community schools, street academies, schools without walls, individualized learning schools, schools within schools, and so on. All these alternatives (options) can exist as a choice—not a fiat—for the community. Alternatives also are designed to rely on evaluative feedback from parents and students; many include parents and students in policy-making. The continuum of types of schools and the policy-making involvement of parents and students are what many advocates of alternatives consider to be the seeds for truly fundamental changes in public education. These qualities, it is argued, are the essential strength of alternatives. Vernon Smith has immodestly described the movement as "The Quiet Revolution."[8]

In this chapter, the meaning assigned to "alternatives" will be "a range of options along a pedagogical continuum." The last section in this chapter considers yet another way of looking at alternatives, as "alternative learning situations in a community that complement and supplement the schools."[9]

A PERSPECTIVE ON THE ALTERNATIVE SCHOOL MOVEMENT

Early alternatives operated within the "alternative to" framework. By and large, the first alternatives were called "free" or in some cases community schools. They were "free" in a sense that they attempted to create a free atmosphere of learning and development—the antithesis of the reality of most public schools. Typically, they were started by parents, teachers, and students, and privately financed, if only on a shoestring. Miriam Wasserman traces the contemporary roots of these schools to the freedom schools started for black youngsters in the South during the Civil Rights movement of the early sixties. The name became "free schools" when the schools were

---

[7]The national alternatives organization at Indiana University changed their name to the *National Consortium for Public Options in Education* to avoid this stigma.

[8]Vernon H. Smith, "Options in Public Education: The Quiet Revolution," *Phi Delta Kappan*, LIV, 7 (March, 1973), p. 434.

[9]This is the approach taken by Richard Saxe in his book *Opening the Schools, Alternative Ways of Learning* (Berkeley, Calif.: McCutchan Publishing Corporation, 1972).

begun by people who believed that schools should concern themselves with the individual needs of youngsters and that the children should have some freedom to choose what and how they learn.[10] Most of the schools are quite small, ranging from approximately ten to 250 students (the average size being about thirty-five). Although the schools are modestly financed, the staff-student ratio is a generous one to five. Allen Graubard, author of *Free the Children: Radical Reform and the Free School Movement,* reports that the number of free schools grew from twenty or so in 1967 to over 500 by 1972.[11] It is not clear how the movement grew or declined since then, but it is clear that a "considerable number" of free schools close after one or two or three years. It appears that the movement leveled off, perhaps even declined in the late seventies.

People in the free school movement have been strongly critical of the public schools and the larger society that the public schools serve. They see the institution of school and the society as self-serving, self-supporting and reinforcing. In response, free schools themselves often are political and one must look as closely at their politics and ideology as their pedagogy and educational philosophy. As Graubard explains, it is necessary to distinguish between the apolitical and political free schools. Within the Summerhillian tradition, there is a distinct apolitical quality and the school looks inward, sometimes consciously disengaging itself from the affairs of the larger community. (Summerhill is the famous British school started in 1921, and directed by A. S. Neill since its inception. Numerous Summerhill schools have been started on this continent by American advocates.)

In the more politically oriented middle-class free schools, (typically located in suburban or rural settings), there exist strong elements of countercultural and counterinstitutional sentiment. The constituents of these free schools believe in permissive child-rearing, and they want their schools to foster creative, spontaneous, and relatively uninhibited and unrepressed individuals. To people coming from educationally and economically "enriched" homes, skill-learning in school is less vital, and anxiety over earning a living is reduced. It is this segment of the free-school movement, and their counterparts in the public schools, that were so critical of much of American society in the 1960s.[12]

Jonathon Kozol carefully distinguishes another somewhat less political free school, this one typically found in the inner cities. In contrast to the counterculture, permissive free schools of the affluent, white middle-class, these schools are highly structured, with a premium on basic skill develop-

[10]Marian Wasserman delivered this historical sketch in a speech at the 1st International Convention for Options in Public Education, Minneapolis, October, 1973.
[11]Allan Graubard, "The Free School Movement," *Harvard Education Review* (August, 1972), pp. 364–68.
[12]Also see Allen Graubard's discussion in the April, 1973, issue of *Principal* magazine. This entire issue is devoted to the "Great Alternatives Hassle."

ment. They are only political in the sense that they want the schools to liberate their children from the racism and indoctrination and do for them what schools apparently do for the dominant white (and middle-class) people. They do not want schools that promote a free, "do your own thing" learning environment. They want schools that will provide the literacy, skill, and professional training now provided white (and middle-class) students in the public schools. Kozol makes it quite clear that he believes the inner-city community school to be the true "free school."[13]

Despite being outside the established educational system (or at best on the fringe, in the case of early street academies), and despite being relatively small (by Graubard's estimate there are about 13,000 students or less than one half of 1 percent of all school-age children), the free-school movement has helped to spark reform in the system. The alternatives movement is indebted to the writers on radical reform; and to the work of early free-school parents and teachers.

In historical perspective, free schools appear to be direct descendants of the private experimentals early in the twentieth century; examples of these early schools include Caroline Pratt's Play School, Margaret Naumberg's Children's School, Marietta Johnson's Organic School and others. Figure 12-1 is a diagrammatic view of the relationship among these and other experimental school ventures, leading to the various alternatives that began to be institutionalized by the mid 1970s.

the open classroom

Another kind of experimental school concept that was a catalyst to the alternatives movement is the open classroom, modeled on the British Infant Schools. The term "open" is misused, used inconsistently, or used synonymously with free schools and open-space schools. Both resemble the open classroom only in minor ways, and many schools called "open" ought more accurately to be called free, open-space, or individualized-learning schools. In fact, the antecedent of American open schools, the English primary schools, have a variety of labels: somewhat unsatisfactory "informal education," the "free day," the "integrated day," the "integrated curriculum," and the "open school." The term "informal education," which the English tend to favor, is the most descriptive and least confusing.[14]

Though not a majority of English primary schools, such schools do exist on wide scale in England. This approach to learning expanded rapidly after World War II. During the war, when it was necessary in Britain to

---

[13]Jonathon Kozol, *Free Schools* (Boston: Houghton Mifflin Company, 1972), pp. 7–12.
[14]There are several excellent books that describe the philosophy and practice of the English primary schools. These include John Blackie's *Inside the Primary School* (New York: Schocken Books, 1971); Mary Brown and Normal Precious, *The Integrated Day in the Primary School* (London: Wardlock Educational Publishers, 1968); and Alvin Hertzberg and Edward Stone, *Schools are for Children! an American Approach to the Open Classroom* (New York: Schocken Books, Inc., 1971).

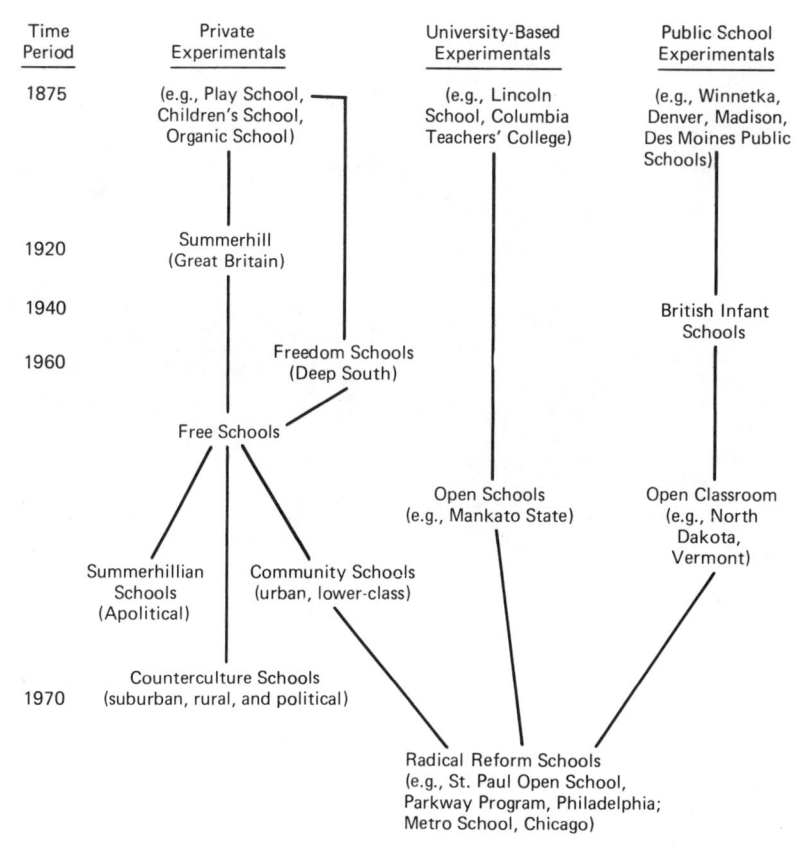

Time Period	Private Experimentals	University-Based Experimentals	Public School Experimentals
1875	(e.g., Play School, Children's School, Organic School)	(e.g., Lincoln School, Columbia Teachers' College)	(e.g., Winnetka, Denver, Madison, Des Moines Public Schools)
1920	Summerhill (Great Britain)		
1940			British Infant Schools
1960	Freedom Schools (Deep South)		
	Free Schools		
		Open Schools (e.g., Mankato State)	Open Classroom (e.g., North Dakota, Vermont)
	Summerhillian Schools (Apolitical)	Community Schools (urban, lower-class)	
1970	Counterculture Schools (suburban, rural, and political)		
		Radical Reform Schools (e.g., St. Paul Open School, Parkway Program, Philadelphia; Metro School, Chicago)	

Figure 12-1 The Development of Experimental and Alternative Schools

keep children in schools for more hours during the day and days in the week, informal teaching became not just popular but essential. In 1967 the so-called Plowden Committee called attention to this approach and urged its adoption in the primary schools.[15] As might be surmised from the labels "informal" and "open," the classroom atmosphere is casual; students are working simultaneously in small groups or individually and on different material; students are integrated across grades; and different subjects are integrated.

Charles Silberman explains that informal education is less an approach or method than a set of shared attitudes and convictions about the nature of childhood, learning, and schooling. Teachers in informal schools begin with the notion of childhood as something to be cherished and are concerned with the quality of a child's school experience in its own right, not merely as preparation for later schooling or for later life. There is, in

[15] This report was written by a Parliamentary Commission in 1967 with Lady Bridget Plowden as Chairperson.

Figure 12-2 Informal Learning Environment

addition, the conviction that learning is likely to be more effective if it grows out of what interests the learner, rather than what interests the teacher. However, Silberman hastens to add that what chiefly distinguishes the contemporary English informal schools from the American child-centered progressive schools of the 1920s and 1930s, as well as the education advocated by romantic critics like John Holt, George Dennison, and Herbert Kohl, is the clear understanding of and insistence on the teacher's central role. Teachers are more than just sympathetic, intelligent, even creative adults in the classroom who permit children to discover what they may. As Silberman puts it, they are there to teach.[16] The concept of British informal learning appears to have been introduced to Americans by Joseph Featherstone through a three-part series on the English schools in *The New Republic* in August and September, 1967. Since then Featherstone and a few other writers and educators such as David Hawkins, Vito Perrone, Roland Barth, Vincent Rogers, and Silberman have articulated the theory and practice of the informal classroom concept to Americans.

Although open or informal primary education developed in a very practical, intuitive manner in the classrooms of many teachers, the concept is supported by a substantial body of theory on the way children learn, the nature of knowledge, and the aims of education. The theoretical foundations for this concept can be found in the work of Jean J. Rousseau, Friedrich Froebel, Maria Montessori, and Susan Isaacs, but most importantly in

---

[16]Charles E. Silberman, *Crisis in the Classroom* (New York: Random House, Inc., 1970), chap. 6.

Jean Piaget's research on the mental development of children and John Dewey's philosophic treatment of instruction and learning. Both Piaget and Dewey hold that it is crucial for the child to act on his or her world. Actively manipulating, creating, and re-inventing, according to both Piaget and Dewey, are imperative to the child's understanding. It is not sufficient to tell developing children, nor even to demonstrate to them; genuine understanding occurs in the act of doing. According to Piaget, children proceed through stages of development in learning, with each stage reflecting a higher level of abstraction; but each child will develop in a particular learning area at the individual's own rate. In turn the child must work on a learning task at his or her own speed. Teachers must first decide what learning is important to the growth of a child, then arrange the classroom in such a way as to permit each child to learn at an individual's own pace and in his or her own way. Dewey's insight was that if intellectual growth is to take place, the teacher must take objects (and later ideas) from the material or external surroundings and bring them together with the experiences and interests of the child's (internal) world. Both Piaget and Dewey stressed that not only does the individual child act on material things, but each child does so with other children in a communicative or group fashion. This is important not only for social development, but also for intellectual development.[17]

Although the idea of open classroom or school has been embraced largely by people from the liberal, in some cases radical progressive, tradition in education, the concept itself is essentially pedagogical and apolitical. As described, its practice is anchored in the substructure of educational psychology and philosophy. Unlike many free schools, political and ideological matters are at most tangential. Also, in contrast to the fashionable American open-space school, architecture is irrelevant. Open, informal classrooms have been created with equal effectiveness in new structures, ancient schools, church basements, and warehouses; in classrooms, auditoriums and corridors.

Many open-school spokesmen do argue from the stance of "alternatives to," or "replacements of" the traditional school, rather than "option along a pedagogical continuum" popular in the mid 1970s. Because it is rooted in sound teaching and learning theory, they ask, "why should informal education be merely one of many options?" The theoretical and empirical evidence supporting other kinds of schools, they argue, is far less

---

[17]There are numerous publications by both Piaget and Dewey that are useful for further understanding of these ideas. We recommend to the reader Jean Piaget and Barbel Inhelder, *The Psychology of the Child* (New York: Basic Books, Inc., Publishers, 1969), as well as Frank G. Jennings, "Jean Piaget: Notes on Learning," *Saturday Review*, (May 20, 1967), and Jerome Bruner's treatment in *The Process of Education* (Cambridge, Mass.: Harvard University Press, 1961), chap. 3. As for John Dewey we suggest three of his major works: *The Child and Curriculum* (Chicago: University of Chicago Press, 1902); *Democracy and Education* (New York: The Macmillan Company, 1916); *Experience and Education* (New York: The Macmillan Company, 1938).

substantive. However, there are political obstacles to wholesale implentation of major reform ideas. Permitting public choice among competing options is more acceptable, but not necessarily more responsible.

Figure 12-1 also illustrates a historical relationship among experimental or alternative schools and open, informal schools. The informal schools in this country are descendants of early public school experimentals, many of which emerged during the progressive era, roughly extending from the 1910s to the early 1940s. Notable examples of progressive public school systems include Quincy, Massachusetts, under Francis W. Parker in the 1870s, Winnetka, Illinois, schools under Carleton Washburne in the 1920s, Bronxville, New York, under Willard Beatty, and Shaker Heights, Ohio, under Arthur K. Loomis during the 1930s.[18] A major catalyst to public school experimentals was the historic Eight-Year Study (1932–40), conducted by the Commission on the Relation of School and College of the Progressive Education Association (PEA). As a result of this experiment, progressive informal programs and classroom approaches were developed in Denver, Colorado, Madison, Wisconsin, Des Moines, Iowa, Grand Rapids, Michigan, and several other communities. With only slight differences, the aims, theory and practices of the earlier American Progressive experimentals and the informal schools in England (and America, notably in North Dakota and Vermont) are the same. The writing and work of John Dewey are the strongest links that bind the two forms. Although often misinterpreted and misconstrued, Dewey's teachings provided the basis for the early progressive schools.

After World War II, the mood of the nation was different. There was considerable disenchantment with progressive education (the PEA withered and died during the late forties), encouraged in no small part by the so-called Life Adjustment Movement, which in principal had little in common with progressivisim. The public and many educators called for a return to the basics of learning and scholarship. While the dominant mood was a concern for "essentials," the progressive ideal merely lay as if it were dormant ready to surface at the proper time.

In some respects a reformulation and resuscitation of progressivism can be detected, paradoxically, in aspects of the essentialist reforms as early as the late 1950s. As manifested in the "new math," "new physics," "new social studies," and so on, the new curriculum movement, expecially as articulated by Jerome Bruner, has been labeled (often by its critics) as neoprogressivism. As Lawrence Cremin remarked, there are "patent continuities" between Dewey's *How We Think* (1910) and Bruner's *Process of Education* (1960).[19] But there are important differences in the approach to instruction between these two groups—the early progressives and the more recent curricular reformers. One major difference stems from the false dichotomy

---

[18]Lawrence A. Cremin, *The Transformation of the School: Progressivism in American Education 1876—1957* (New York: Alfred A. Knopf, Inc., 1962), pp. 128–35, 276–77.

[19]Lawrence A. Cremin, *The Genius of American Education* (New York: Vintage Books, Random House, 1966), p. 53.

(of which Dewey warned) of assuming either a child-centered or subject-centered school. While the progressive reformers erred in the one direction, the curriculum reforms of the 1950s and 60s opted for the other, subject-centered, side of the dichotomy. Whereas the early progressives needed much more to realize the delicate balance between subject matter and the child's needs, the reformers ignored the lessons to be learned from earlier attempts at curriculum reform.

By the late 1960s, progressive education—in the form of informal, open classrooms—was reemerging. Not surprisingly, about a decade later, the pendulum had swung back to a preoccupation with the basic, essentialist curriculum. While the emphasis in education over time has shifted back and forth, the overall drift has been progressive. Even the traditional contemporary school has assumed a number of informal characteristics—small-group work, individual projects, activity periods, abundant materials, artifacts, animals, and other realia.

Today there are entire schools built on the informal concept of learning, as well as classrooms within schools. The approach has been more successful and extensive in elementary schools, but there also has been development at the secondary level. Other alternatives have sprung up, largely during the 1970s, some mainly elementary, some secondary, and a number across all grades. Alternatives such as the vocational-technical schools, are being revitalized, having existed for a better part of this century. Montessori schools, another alternative, have become increasingly popular after a long tradition of nearly a hundred years.[20]

In one respect, a couple of alternatives—private "prep" schools and parochial (mostly Catholic) schools—have always been available to some families. More recent are street academies, dropout centers, and pregnancy-maternity centers, magnet schools, learning centers and educational parks, bilingual schools, and ethnic schools, in addition to free schools, open schools, community schools, and schools for individualized learning. Together these schools form a rather unsystematic panorama of alternative offerings today.

A NEW CONCEPT OF ALTERNATIVE SCHOOLS EMERGES

Contrary to our traditional political and economic values, Americans have not been provided with diversity and choice in the selection of public schooling. In effect, the public has been offered one alternative, the standard traditional school. This school is bureaucratically organized, the

---

[20] Montessori schools are schools developed on the teachings of Maria Montessori, who wrote and taught in Italy in the early decades of the twentieth century (1870–1952). The Montessori method of teaching has become increasingly popular in the United States during recent years.

classrooms are teacher-dominated, and the curriculum emphasizes "essential" subject matter.

Several schemes for providing choice have been developed. All offer a range of alternatives with the intent of making schools more responsive and accountable to parents and students. Present channels for effecting change in public schools are very time-consuming and expensive. The political mechanism for making schools responsive operates through distant school boards and labyrinthian administrations. As such the process is cumbersome and largely ineffective. For those few people who have the time, energy, and know-how to battle organizations, some gains are made. A very few others bypass the obstacles by selecting private-school alternatives. The majority of families "pays their money and takes their chances" with the only school available. The alternative schemes are basically political, economic, and pedagogical in nature.

diversity and choice through decentralization: a political proposal

Decentralization or community control is most appropriate for urban settings, where turgid, monolithic bureaucracies operate the schools. This plan places control of neighborhood schools with the local citizens, who have the power to form their own school boards. Those neighborhood school boards in turn can effect important policies and decisions concerning school organization, staff, and curriculum. While many cities have discussed plans for decentralization and community control, New York City initiated several experimental local-control areas in 1968. The most publicized was the Ocean Hill-Brownsville community. Much controversy still surrounds the wisdom of community control within a large city, in part because of political struggles that have resulted.[21]

With regard to alternatives, decentralization is not intended to foster a range of alternative schools. Its purpose is to create a smaller, more responsive school system covering a relatively homogeneous population (for example, black, Mexican-American, Puerto Rican, lower-class white, middle-class white, or other ethnic groups) in a much larger heterogenous city or school district. As in the present traditional system, children still attend their neighborhood school. But it is reasoned that this school is the proper "choice" for a child, because the children of the community share common educational and cultural needs, and the school is operated by adults in the community who are attuned to these needs.

[21]*Challenges to Education* (New York: Dodd, Mead & Company, 1972), a book of readings edited by Emanual Hurwitz, Jr., and Charles A. Tesconi, Jr., contains several excellent articles on community control and decentralization of schools, particularly as they relate to the Ocean Hill-Brownsville experiment. See especially chapter 3.

diversity and choice through educational vouchers: an economic proposal

The idea of vouchers for schooling dates at least to the economist Adam Smith's recommendation in the eighteenth century that public monies be given to private families to pay for educational needs. Smith, laissez-faire in economic matters, is often credited as being the father of capitalism. It is no surprise, then, that like Adam Smith many contemporary classical economists, notably Milton Friedman of the University of Chicago, enthusiastically support proposals to reduce, even eliminate government control in financing education. When it comes to support for educational vouchers, conservatives are joined by many liberal educators, including Christopher Jencks, James Coleman, and Theodore Sizer. Vouchers have a wide appeal in educational circles because they afford people the purchasing power (in the case of most liberal proposals, *equal* purchasing power) to select the school, and therefore the kind of education they desire. In addition, voucher plans allow schools to free themselves from the restrictions of their traditional monopolistic position; that is, a school is able to establish goals and programs of its choosing, within the framework of basic requirements applicable to all schools.

A voucher system operates in the following way: Educational vouchers worth the average per-pupil expenditure for the district are issued to all families with school-age children. The families, upon selecting a school for each child, give the voucher to the school. Schools then exchange the vouchers for money with which to operate their programs. This exchange is carried out by a designated *Educational Vouchers Agency* (EVA), which also regulates the plan. Conservative advocates of vouchers, such as Friedman, would have the EVA's impose few if any restriction on the participating schools and parents.[22] Liberal supporters, including Jencks, carefully build in provisions to insure equality of purchasing power and to prevent discriminatory selection of students.

Several objections are raised to voucher plans. For one, opponents argue that the more affluent families would supplement the vouchers in acquiring a "better" education; on the contrary, a poor child, even with a voucher, still could not afford a suburban-type education. Second, opponents reason that ethnically, racially, religiously segregated schools would be encouraged. Third, they believed that private business persuasion and "hucksterism" would prevail, preying on parents and children who don't have an informative consumer's report on education. Finally, they argue that since vouchers are available to private schools, including those

---

[22]See Friedman's article, "Voucher Idea," in the September 23 and October 21, 1973, issues of the *New York Times Magazine*.

affiliated with churches, they would violate the First Amendment's prohibition against the "establishment of religion."

The Center for the Study of Public Policy at Harvard University, directed by Christopher Jencks, proposed an educational voucher system (for elementary education) designed to circumvent the above objections. The Center's plan calls for the establishment of an Educational Vouchers Agency (EVA) as described above. The EVA would issue vouchers to every family in a district with children of elementary school age. The vouchers issued families of "below-average" incomes would be compensatory, worth as much as twice the basic voucher. To become an "approved voucher school," a school would have to (1) accept each voucher as full payment for a child's education, charging no additional tuition, (2) accept any applicant so long as there was a vacant place, (3) in case of a surplus of applicants, fill at least half of its places randomly and the other half so as not to discriminate against minorities, (4) provide information on facilities and programs to the EVA and families, (5) maintain accounts of money received and disbursed, in a form intelligible to parents and the EVA, (6) meet existing state requirements for private schools regarding curriculum, staffing, and the like. Every spring each family would submit to the EVA the name of the school it wished to send each child to the following year. A child already enrolled in a voucher school would be guaranteed a place, as would any sibling of that student. So long as a voucher school had space, it would be required to accept any student who listed it as a first choice. Other regulations would prohibit any discrimination against racial minorities. Jencks and Judith Arien admit that the most worrisome objection to a voucher system is an EVA's willingness to vigorously regulate the marketplace so as to prevent any racial and economic discrimination. This objection, they add, is one that holds equally for any reform including the existing system.[23]

In 1972, the Office of Economic Opportunity (OEO) funded an experiment in vouchers with the Alum Rock School District in San Jose, California. The Office of Economic Opportunity wanted to study vouchers along the Jencks plan, but given its controversial elements, few schools were willing to participate. Alum Rock was the one exception, but it insisted on specific, less controversial modifications to the OEO proposal. Parents in this pilot project receive vouchers worth $680 for children in elementary school, and $970 for those in seventh and eighth grades. However, only one-third of the school district is involved, or just six schools and about 4,000 students; only public school programs participate; the Alum Rock Board of Education retains control, although it is advised by an EVA committee (composed of parents); and the plan offers a choice of programs

---

[23] Judith Areen and Christopher Jencks, "Educational Vouchers: A Proposal for Diversity and Choice," *Teachers College Record* (February, 1971), pp. 331–32.

within a school, not among competing schools. In other respects the Alum Rock program retains features of the Jencks-OEO plan. Alum Rock officials have found that close to 40 percent of the parents are selecting nontraditional programs. Note that this means that 60 percent of the students are enrolled in the familiar standard program. The Alum Rock plan is someting less than a "real" voucher plan, but the results to date have been favorable. It is possible that this "consumerism" variant of alternative schools will grow in popularity.[24]

diversity and choice through public options: a pedagogical proposal

The third mechanism for choice in education today is through "providing for choice among a range of different schools along a pedagogical continuum." These schools take into account the apparent variety of teaching and learning styles. The major spokesman for this concept, Mario Fantini, remarks that one way to consider alternatives is to place them on a continuum according to the amount of freedom or independence afforded a student.

Fantini has designed what he calls an "overlapping continuum model" (illustrated in Table 12-1). At one end the learner decides what shall be learned, with whom, when, where, and how. This *free* school alternative enables each learner to select and use his or her own resources (of which the teacher is only one), whether these are inside or outside the schoolhouse. The free school alternative is most controversial and most difficult to legitimize in the framework of public schooling, an issue discussed earlier in this chapter. At the other end of the continuum, the student has little or no choice of teacher, content, methodology, time, and place. This is the familiar traditional school, or *standard* type, in which the learner is most dependent on the procedures and requirements of the educational institution.

Between these extremes there is a range of possibilities. As Fantini describes, the learners may be free to choose certain content areas (others, such as reading, writing, arithmetic, and physical education, are required of everyone; they may have some freedom in the approach to these areas (e.g., by reading, viewing video tapes, researching, discussing, listening to lectures); they may have some freedom to choose the time and place to learn, devoting extended periods, maybe days, to one subject at a particular time; they may have access to resources in the community (including libraries, museums, artists, writers, and television and radio studios). Examples of the *open* category include open classrooms (or American versions of

[24]James Mecklenberger, "Vouchers at Alum Rock," *Phi Delta Kappan*, LII, no. 7 (March, 1972), pp. 23–25.

British infant schools), Montessori schools, and possibly "schools without walls." Open-space schools featuring ungraded continuous progress, modular scheduling, and behavior modification are typical options in the *modified* category.[25]

A number of large-city school districts have been experimenting with some form of alternatives plan at either the elementary level, secondary level, or both. Among these cities are Seattle, Washington, Quincy, Illinois, Rochester, New York, Grand Rapids, Michigan, Minneapolis, Minnesota, Berkeley, California, and Tacoma, Washington. Some were receiving support from the Office of Education while in the development stages. The Minneapolis Public Schools in 1972 initiated the Southeast Alternatives Program in the area around the University of Minnesota. Their plan uses the overlapping continuum as model. Elementary school students in the southeast area can attend any of four types of schools:

1. A *contemporary* school, Tuttle, which offers curriculum innovations but maintains a teacher-directed standard curriculum with a grade-level school organization.
2. A *continuous progress* school, Pratt, in which each child advances at an individual pace without regard to grade level, and in which instruction is given by teams and based on a deliberately sequenced curriculum in basic skills.
3. An *open* school, Marcy, which offers an informally organized curriculum with children grouped across grade levels in the style of the British infant schools. This program combines the teachers' careful organization of learning with emphasis on the children's pursuing their own interests.
4. A *free* school, Motley, which extends through the twelfth grade. Students, parents, faculty and volunteers develop courses; off-campus trips, work, and classes are an important part of the program.

A fifth school, Marshall Secondary School, completes the Southeast Alternatives plan. Marshall is a traditional school with an open school-within-a-school available to any of its students. The open program is both graded and ungraded at the junior high level, and graded only for senior high students.[26]

As a result of the Southeast Program, other alternatives have developed in Minneapolis. These, as in other cities, include fundamental schools stressing basic skills and old-fashioned discipline.

This overlapping continuum scheme seems best suited for the elementary schools. Any community with a population as small as 6,000 could offer at least three different school options, and even a community with just one elementary school could offer a variety of programs. System-

---

[25]Mario Fantini; "Alternatives Within Public Schools;" *Phi Delta Kappan*, LIV, no. 7 (March, 1973), pp. 447–48.

[26]J. K. Moss, "Alternatives: Four Schools of Choice; Minneapolis' Southeast District," *Teacher* (January, 1974).

Table 12-1 Alternatives on a freedom-to-prescription continuum

Free	Open	Modified	Standard
Learner-directed and controlled. Learner has complete freedom to orchestrate his own education. Teacher is one resource.	Learner has considerable freedom to choose from a wide range of content areas considered relevant by teacher, parent, and student. Resource centers in major skill areas made available to learner.	Prescribed content is made more flexible through individualization of instruction; school is ungraded; students learn same thing but at different rates. Using team teaching, teachers plan a differentiated approach to the same content. Teacher and programmed course of study are the major sources of student learning.	Learner adheres to institution requirements uniformly prescribed; what is to be taught – how, when, where, and with whom. Teacher is instructor-evaluator. Student passes or fails according to normative standards.
	Opening of school to the community and its resources.		
	Teacher is supportive guider.		
Noncompetitive environment.			Competitive environments.
		Teacher-student planning.	
			School is the major instructional setting.
No student failures. Curriculum is viewed as social system rather than as course of studies.			
Learner-centered.	Teacher-centered.	Subject-matter-centered.	Institution-centered.

atic development at the secondary level is less advanced but there is no reason why high schools or junior high schools in a city could not specialize in particular pedagogical positions, or why one larger high school could not offer several different learning options. School districts also may choose to develop alternatives with or without regard to grade level, such as the Berkeley plan. The Berkeley Unified School District generated some fourteen options that fall into four categories.[27]

    1. *Multiculture* schools, in which children are carefully selected on the basis of diversity of race, socio-economic status, age, and sex.

339

2. *Community* schools, in which much of the control, organization, and teaching comes from outside the school (that is, from parents and other adults with useful knowledge and teaching skills), and where a significant portion of the curriculum is conducted in the community (for example in museums, theaters, courts, offices, and local businesses).

3. *Structured skill-training* schools which are primarily in the classroom, under the guidance of a single teacher (or a team) with emphasis on learning basic skills—reading, writing, and mathematics.

4. *Schools without walls*, in which students carry out many of their studies in the resources of the city, the school being just one resource. Professionals in many skill areas are used on the job and in the schoolhouse to teach (directly and indirectly), using their know-how and experiences. A principal goal of these schools is for students to grow in self-understanding and self-esteem while developing socially and intellectually.

There are many other examples of public school alternatives, in an increasing number of communities, that take the form of either classroom alternatives, schools-within-schools, or separate alternative schools.

Mario Fantini warns that the greatest danger facing alternatives is that they will become fads like many other reform ideas. If problems are to be minimized, Fantini recommends the following ground rules: do not superimpose, rather leave as a matter of choice for all participants, teachers included; do not publicize as a replacement to the existing schools; do not practice exclusivity, racial, economic or religious; do not make exaggerated claims of accomplishments that may be deceptive in the long run; aim at a broad set of common educational objectives, spanning cognitive and affective areas, including basic skills, talent development, and self-concept development; and do not ask for more than your share of the existing school funds. Some of the developed alternatives plans have enjoyed the support of the Office of Education, such as Minneapolis Public Schools, but it can be done without extra money—though free advice from the established programs is very helpful.

In the final analysis the case for alternatives reduces to the argument that schools can increase their capacity to individualize students' programs. A student's learning style and educational needs can be matched with the methods and goals of a particular school. In the process, parents and pupils, as well as teachers, are permitted to select the learning environment that they judge best suits them. Ultimately, the privilege and also the responsibility of selection rests with the client. Although schools and their personnel are on the hot seat to meet the client's needs or "go out of business," offering alternatives reduces institutional political conflict. If constituents don't like one option they can try another; the schools collectively adapt to the learner, not the reverse.

[27] Mario D. Fantini, "The What, Why and Where of the Alternatives Movement," *The National Elementary Principal*, LII, no. 6 (April, 1973), p. 22.

ALTERNATIVE SCHOOLING IN PERSPECTIVE

assumptions and critiques

The alternative schools idea appears to be grounded in a set of assumptions. One assumption of alternative proposals is that the singular, monolithic, traditional school has not served anywhere near all of the students effectively. This assessment is observed in the deteriorating dropout rate and average daily attendance as well as the achievement scores, particularly of low-income groups.

Still, as indicated in annual Gallup surveys, upwards of 60 percent of the American public are satisfied with the existing schools. If anything, the public today wants a more structured, basic school program. According to the polls, discipline remains the number-one problem in schools, and a growing number of people want to see basic skills reemphasized. Yet Fantini argues that this support still leaves unsatisfied a critical mass of up to 40 percent who apparently want and could effectively use alternative options to the traditional school.

A second assumption underlying alternative school proposals is that choice for students and parents is desirable. This usually is argued on the ground that choice of schooling is an individual right. Harry Broudy raises a serious question about this right in regard to education. He argues education is a *public* good and not merely a *private* one. The individual student

Figure 12-3   Individualized Instruction

and family are not the only benefactors of a sound education (or the victims of an inadequate education); society has a stake in the schooling of each youngster.[28] Broudy adds that if the argument is not on the basis of individual right, then it is based on the assertion that the public good can be satisfied by whatever alternative parents choose. In other words, one form of educational experience is potentially as good as another, or that nothing we do in education makes any difference. This claim, he states, overlooks historical evidence to the contrary.[29]

A third assumption of alternatives is that they promote freedom for parents and children. Generally this freedom is in the form of freedom *from* the control of school authorities and *from* the constraints of the established school structure and curriculum. Broudy argues that some educational constraints cannot be avoided, and in fact are desirable. Contrary to the view that learning should be fun, joyous, and ecstatic, some things one must learn in school, Broudy explains, do not come naturally or easily— namely an understanding of the intellectual resources of a culture. In addition, our culture imposes certain other demands on the individual as a condition for coping with it: occupational, civic, and personal adequacy. The first is needed to earn a living, the second to plan one's role in a social order, and the third to live as a fully developed, authentic human individual. It is unrealistic and irresponsible, Broudy states, for any school to ignore these constraints.[30] To be sure, some alternative schools do. Yet many advocates of alternatives, including Fantini, insist that all alternatives schools meet a common set of educational objectives, including career development, political socialization, and talent development, as well as basic skills.

A fourth, closely related assumption is that given a choice among competing alternatives, parents and children can make intelligent selections. But intelligent choice presupposes that they can identify the best or most appropriate instruction. Because of lack of experience, the young student appeals largely to what feels right, which may be a useful guide but no guarantee of an intelligent decision. Many parents also lack the necessary knowledge, interest, and wisdom to make this choice. As a group, teachers and other educators should be more informed than parents with respect both to what is an appropriate education and to how to achieve it in the classroom. That there exist widely different viewpoints within the educational community tends to confuse the public.

When placed in the position of deciding what school to choose, parents often are at a loss and rely on the immediate and transitory interests of

---

[28]Harry S. Broudy, "Educational Alternatives, Why Not? Why Not," *Phi Delta Kappan*, LIV, no. 7 (March, 1973), p. 438.
[29]Ibid., p. 439.
[30]Again, this discussion in large part is based on Broudy's argument, pp. 439–40.

young students. Many appear to be asking for more than information about the alternatives; they want the experts to make the decisions.

Sound educative experiences, in John Dewey's terms, are not easily achieved. An educator who is a professional should be able to distinguish between "educative" and "miseducative" experiences. Interest and enjoyability are no guarantee that an experience will be educative. In assessing the potential of a learning experience, a teacher, unlike a parent, always considers (or ought to) whether or not a youngster is prepared to make the most of an experience, and where the experience is leading developmentally. The first consideration requires that educational resources be adapted to the needs and abilities of the learner; the second requires that no matter what stage of learning is involved, the teacher keep an eye on future stages as well as the present. These are simply what Dewey described as the principles of interaction and continuity.[31]

clarifying the rationale

Alternative schooling is built on two major premises. The first is that students have different dispositions toward learning and different learning styles. Therefore, they require different learning environments and teaching methods. The second is that the list of competing objectives in education is endless, and really a matter of taste; therefore, options should be available. The first premise has considerable support, but still demands the continued attention of researchers and practitioners. The second is much more suspect. Philip Jackson and others take the position that educators who operate from this belief are retreating behind the relativist, and culturally sanctioned, democratic principle. In doing so they are abdicating their responsibility as educators. Jackson argues that professional educators, teachers, and administrators must keep at the forefront of their thinking the notions that education should be a "purposeful" activity, and should entail "life-enhancing experiences." Such queries take us back to the ideas of Dewey on the nature of educative experiences. Teachers can and must plan such learning into a child's experiences.[32]

There are several central questions in considering the validity of educational alternatives:

Are all learning environments and teaching methods equally useful in providing educative experiences? In other words, if sound education in any

---

[31] John Dewey's entire book, *Experience and Education* (New York: Collier Books, 1938), originally a series of lectures, is devoted to an examination of this idea.

[32] Jackson, in "After Apple-Picking," *Harvard Educational Review*, 43, no. 1 (February, 1973), pp. 51–60, lucidly discusses this position.

school demands in some form, a command of basic reading, writing, and computing skills, as well as problem solving and inquiry skills, will any of a number of different type schools function equally well?

Are educators abandoning their responsibility in advocating alternatives?

Are parents and pupils good enough judges of the education that is best for them, or are they equally as good judges as the professionals?

Different types of alternative schools will surely have to compromise on their basic styles to accomplish these objectives. The free-school types probably will have to make special efforts toward skill-building, while the traditional and fundamental schools will have to make appropriate changes to develop problem-solving and inquiry abilities. But educators will not be irresponsible nor parents and students incapable if timely and competent guidance is provided.

ALTERNATIVES TO SCHOOLING: COMPLEMENTARY AND SUPPLEMENTARY INSTITUTIONS

Another concept of alternative education is to use the natural educative capacities of community organizations and institutions—museums, studios, parks, businesses, churches, professional and social organizations. This is the call for "configurations" or an "ecology of education" discussed in Chapters 1 and 5. There is nothing new about this idea. These agencies in the past have played an important part in "informal" education. School until the twentieth century was considered only one environment where learning took place, and a minor one for most youngsters. As the enrollment and time spent in formal education increased, learning became associated with the activities of schools. What took place informally, outside schools, was falsely considered to be quite different, namely work, play, hobbies, amusements.

During the early history of this country, informal or incidental learning was the dominant form of education. For both children and adults, the influence of the informal agencies declined as industrialization, urbanization, and automation inexorably replaced the shopkeeper, craftsman, and rural, small town way of life. With the urbanization and more recently the suburbanization of life, the natural surroundings of the young have become less utilitarian and educative. In an earlier era, adults during their daily living and working were naturally teachers; valuable learning experiences were to be found everywhere, on farms, in homes, in shops, and on the streets of every community. The call to include organizations, professionals, and other working people in the education network is recognition that these agencies potentially play a critical role in education, and that children gradually have been cut off from the natural, incidental learning of life and society around them.

Over time, schools have been asked to assume greater and greater responsibility. Schools have done this with considerable success, considering the difficulty, perhaps impossibility of the total task. Schools may be providing services and educational experiences that never existed in the past, but there exist important experiences that schools cannot provide, or only provide artificially. The schoolhouse is but one of numerous educational agencies in a community.

The new direction in the alternatives movement is a systematic attempt to return some of education to a variety of informal agents, both organizations and people. In this context, Richard Saxe defines alternatives as "planned experiences designed as activities to accomplish one or another objective of the curriculum and which do not take place within the regular classroom."[33] Investigating the functions of a local bank, writing a paper at a nearby newspaper office or publishing house, examining chemical processes at a paper mill, brewery, or other factory, surveying community problems, and studying the history of a city through the architecture of its buildings and homes are all alternatives to the routine classroom lectures, discussions, and homework. The strength of these activities is that they bring learning into a natural and perhaps more efficient setting. In effect, subject matter is related to practical affairs; that is, theory and practice are merged, and within any specific subject matter various areas of study (such as economics, politics, and architecture) are integrated. Subjects are not a secondary matter; rather, the notion is to start with reality and view it through the spectacles of disciplined study.

When possible, Saxe comments, the best agent should be employed for an educational experience. Still, according to this point of view, alternative educational agencies are a supplement and a complement to the schools, not a replacement. "Schools without walls," such as Philadelphia's Parkway Program and Chicago's Metro School, as well as many community schools, are examples of alternative schools operating in this framework. Education in the community with workers as teachers, and with organizations as schools, is a growing dimension of the alternative movement. In another sense, we need to design into our educational systems the facilities that Ivan Illich and Everett Reimer call learning net-

---

[33] Richard W. Saxe, *Opening the Schools, Alternative Ways of Learning* (Berkeley, Calif.: McCutchan Publishing Corporation, 1972).

works.[34] These are homes, meeting places, workshops, clubs, and so on, where people of all ages can systematically gather to learn how to build houses or repair automobiles or discuss literary works or make philosophic inquiries.

Alternative programs are not confined to urban areas and other communities. The wilderness programs, conducted by enterprises such as Outward Bound, are a growing complement to community alternatives. Outward Bound programs exist in many regions, some associated with public or private schools and some with independent agencies. The programs associated with school systems include summer sessions, semester seminars, minicourses, or just weekend outings. The wilderness settings in turn include mountains, rivers, lakes, woods and forest areas, and even oceans, where a variety of skills, including mountaineering, hiking, rafting, and camping are learned. Outward Bound, however, does not exist as merely a diversion from in-school activities; it has specific cognitive, affective, and psychomotor aims. For biology, botany, geology, ecology, sociology, and many other subjects, much potential academic study is available, and in an integrated, interrelated fashion. Time spent intensively living and working together provides a forum for interpersonal growth. Finally, the athletic and other physical skills of existing in a wilderness setting are legion. The threads that connect mental, emotional, and physical learning and that interrelate academic areas (seemingly disparate dimensions of life and study in a school-oriented society) are the valuable lessons to be gained from the outdoors.

CASE STUDY: Alternative Schools

The school administrators for the community in which you teach submitted a plan for the development of several alternative schools. The board of education recently approved the plan which will go into effect this coming year. The plan calls for several different elementary schools, including two traditional schools, two continuous progress schools (open space), an open school, a Montessori school, and a free school. The free school will be K–12; all others will be K–6. The school district is small enough to allow parents and students anywhere in the district to choose any one of the

[34]Ivan Illich, *Deschooling Society* (New York: Harper & Row, Publishers, 1971), and Everett Reimer, *School is Dead* (New York: Doubleday & Company, Inc., 1971). Illich and Reimer take a rather strong position against schooling of any sort, including alternative schools. They argue that schools, and the notion of schooling, are cause serious disruption in learning, thus much injustice in societies. They would have society "deschooled" in the sense that schools are the source of "legitimate" knowledge and power-conveying credentials, and in the sense that people have come to associate learning with the omnipresence and omnipotence of schools. Learning webs or networks utilizing the total physical skill and intellectual resources of a community would be the basis for education. We discussed their position more thoroughly in Chapter 1.

schools. Transportation will be provided students who live farther than one mile from the school they wish to attend.

The parents and students of the community also will be offered a choice of three junior high schools: a standard school with traditional course offerings; an open-space school based in large part on student contracts and programmed learning; an open/informal school with combined teacher-student decision-making in the curriculum. Junior high and senior high students wanting a free school environment can attend the K–12 free school in the district.

The single high school in the community has four wings, which now in effect will become four-schools-in-one-school with a different curriculum for each wing. Students may select any one of these four curricula. One wing or school will be the traditional comprehensive school emphasizing basic skills in both academic and vocational studies; a second will be traditional, but with a heavy academic or college prep orientation; a third will be largely vocational, with the minimum required general education courses and a heavy emphasis on work study courses; the last school within-the-school will be an informal program made of an array of academic courses (e.g., history, literature), special interest courses (pottery, black studies, wilderness ecology), and vocational courses (welding, typing, mechanics), in the form of either regular semester or mini-courses.

The school administration is offering the teachers of the community a choice as to which school they prefer. A major effort will be made to insure a proper mix of teacher with school; it is guaranteed that no teacher in the system will be placed in a school that is incompatible with his or her teaching philosphy and methods. Considering the school level at which you teach, elementary, junior or senior high, which would you choose? Why would this be the best setting for you? Why do you consider this school a desirable option of the district's alternative plan? What problems might occur in implementing the overall plan? How would you and other faculty members handle the problems with respect to your school?

THOUGHT QUESTIONS

1. Peter Schrag, in the opening quote of the chapter, remarks that, "Wealthy children and middle-class parents have some options about schools, but lower-class children have none." What options exist for the middle-class youngster? Should we concentrate on providing more options for lower-class students, or on developing programs for all youngsters?

2. Fantini describes four options along the freedom-to-prescription continuum. Which describes the classroom in which you are working? Which type of classroom do you hope to conduct, and why?

3. A number of advocates of the "open classroom" argue that this concept has the most solid empirical learning base, and should be the learning envi-

ronment of most, if not all, students. What support is there for this position and what objections?

4. Considering that the free school is a politically oriented, counterculture concept, does it have a legitimate position among public school options? Consider carefully arguments on all sides on this question and support a decision.

5. Assessments of the experiments on educational vouchers are just now becoming available. What does the evidence to date suggest about the success, the strengths, and the weaknesses of the idea? Should the voucher plans be modified to more closely fit the liberal proposals of Christopher Jencks and others or the conservative proposals of Milton Friedman, or should the idea be scuttled?

6. Are parents and pupils the best judges of an appropriate education? Are educators abdicating their professional responsibility if they leave the decision of what school students should attend to the family?

7. Harry Broudy questions whether or not alternatives really promote freedom for the public. What is the distinction between "freedom from" controls or constraints, and "freedom to" behave in an intelligent fashion? Of the legitimate constraints demanded as a condition of living in a society, are there any that all schools must be held accountable for? Would you add to or subtract from Broudy's list?

8. Given the increased concern for basic skills education, can this objective be achieved in all types of alternatives? Explain. Are the other educational objectives Mario Fantini outlines (career development, political socialization, talent development, and critical thinking) being met in schools today? Are they as important as basic skills?

9. Discuss the strong points of a community-based education program. Should the school remain as the primary place of learning in such a program, or should it merely be one of many relatively equal learning centers in the community?

10. How are outdoor, wilderness experiences justified as an integral part of a public education program? How can they augment the academic education of a student, the total education of a student?

PRACTICAL ACTIVITIES

1. Visit an alternative school (a free, community or open school). Write a description of the physical structure, curriculum, and administrative organization, as well as treatment of students, teacher roles, and teaching methods. Comment on how the school compares with the one you are working in, or with those with which you are familiar.

2. Visit an open-space school in your area. Discuss the physical structure, curriculum, administrative organization, treatment of students, teacher roles, and teaching methods. If possible, do so by comparing and contrasting this school with a traditional school and other alternative schools.

3. Assume you are teaching in a high school. Set up a plan for a school-within-a-school in your building. Consider the number of students and teachers, faculty teaching fields, faculty organization, courses offered, space needed, and grading system.

4. Design a comprehensive alternative schools plan for the district in which you will be teaching. Use either the elementary, middle, junior high, or senior high school level to illustrate. What types of schools would you include? Describe them briefly. How would students and teachers be selected for the different schools? Which school would you want to teach in? Why?

5. Design an educational system for your community in which the school is but one center of learning. What businesses, clubs, organizations, and public facilities could be tapped? How would these agencies fit in? What businessmen, enterpreneurs, craftsmen, and other professionals would you enlist as teachers?

6. Take the subject you will be teaching (if you are an elementary teacher, select one subject area) and outline a curriculum, learning resources, and room arrangement for "opening" or informalizing your classroom. Explain your rationale for this arrangement. (For example, how does it help students to learn and you to teach?)

7. Participate in an outdoor or wilderness program offered at your college, or in the community. Of what value was the program to you? What place should such experiences have in the public schools?

8. Design a wilderness program for your school. What would the setting for the experience be? How long would the program be and how many students would participate? Write five or six major objectives (knowledge, attitude, and skill) for the program.

BIBLIOGRAPHY

books

BARTH, ROLAND S., *Open Education and the American School.* New York: Agathon Press, 1973.

BLACKIE, JOHN, *Inside the Primary School.* New York: Schocken Books, Inc., 1971.

BREMER, JOHN, AND ANNE BREMMER, *Open Education: A Beginning.* New York: Holt, Rinehart & Winston, 1972.

BREMER, JOHN, AND MICHAEL VON MASCHZISKER, *The School Without Walls: Philadelphia's Parkway Program.* New York: Holt, Rinehart & Winston, 1971.

COX, DONALD WILLIAMS, *The City as a Schoolhouse: The Story of the Parkway Program.* Valley Forge, Pa.: Judson Press, 1972.

DENNISON, GEORGE, *The Lives of Children: The Story of the First Street School.* New York: Random House, Inc., 1969.

FANTINI, MARIO D., *Public Schools of Choice: Alternatives in Education.* New York: Simon & Schuster, Inc., 1974.

FEATHERSTONE, JOSEPH, *Schools Where Children Learn.* New York: Liveright, 1971.

GLATTHORN, ALLAN, *Alternatives in Education: Schools and Programs*. New York: Dodd, Mead & Company, 1975.
GRAUBARD, ALLEN, *Free the Children: Radical Reform and Free School Movement*. New York: Pantheon Books, 1972.
GROSS, RONALD, AND BEATRICE GROSS, eds., *Radical School Reform*. New York: Simon & Schuster, Inc., 1970.
HERNDON, JAMES, *How to Survive in Your Native Land*. New York: Simon & Schuster, Inc., 1971.
HERTZBERG, ALVIN, AND EDWARD STONE. *Schools are for Children*. New York: Schocken Books Inc., 1971.
HOLT, JOHN, *Freedom and Beyond*. New York: E. P. Dutton & Co., Inc., 1972.
KOHL, HERBERT, *The Open Classroom*. New York: Random House, Inc., 1970.
KOZOL, JONATHAN, *Free Schools*. Boston: Houghton Mifflin Company, 1972.
NEILL, A.S., *Summerhill: A Radical Approach to Child Rearing*. New York: Hart Publishing Company, 1960.
SAXE, RICHARD W., ed., *Opening the School: Alternative Ways of Learning*. Berkeley, Calif.: McCutchan Publishing Corporation, 1972.
SILBERMAN, CHARLES E., *Crisis in the Classroom: The Remaking of American Education*, Parts II and III. New York: Random House, Inc., 1970.

periodicals

AREEN, JUDITH C., "Alternative Schools: Better Guardians than Family or State," *School Review* (February, 1973).
AREEN, JUDITH, AND CHRISTOPHER JENCKS, "Educational Vouchers: A Proposal for Diversity and Choice," *Teachers College Record* (February, 1971).
Harvard Educational Review, August, 1972. A special issue on alternative schools.
MCCARTHY, ROBERT B., "Critical Factors in Alternative Education," *National Association of Secondary Principals Bulletin* (April, 1975).
National Elementary Principal (April, 1973). A special issue on alternative schools.
Phi Delta Kappan (March, 1973). A special issue on alternative schools.

13

GLOBAL SURVIVAL
Educational Issues
and Models

DIMENSIONS OF THE PROBLEM

Even a cursory review of the popular press in the last quarter of the twentieth century gives the reader some understanding of the dimensions of the problems facing mankind. Excessive population growth and the resultant malnutrition and starvation are no longer Malthusian predictions of the future, but are the reality of today. Population estimates for the year 2000 are for 7.5 billion people. Robert Heilbroner in his 1974 book *An Inquiry into the Human Prospect* predicted the possibility of 20 billion people by the year 2050. Moreover, the growth is unequally distributed, with the largest numbers of people being born into the poorer nations of the world.

Whereas some of the developed countries have reached near zero population growth, many poor nations have birth rates in excess of 3 and 4 percent per year. Further, the world's population is becoming increasingly urbanized, not just in the developed nations of the Western world, but also in the poorer nations of the southern hemisphere and Asia. Some experts have predicted that by 1990 over half of the world's people will be living in cities of 100,000 or more.

energy

Although the world has been moving towards a crisis in energy for a long time, it was not until the 1970s that the dimensions of the problem became obvious. With the Arab oil boycott and the resultant rapid rise in prices for petroleum, it became increasingly clear that energy was a limited resource and the nations of the world must move to conserve it in all its forms, and in particular the fossil fuels such as coal, oil, and natural gas. The energy crisis helped to make the interdependence of nations more obvious, and the world was thrust into an international recession, partially due to the increased cost of energy. The industrialized nations of the world are seeking to become energy self-sufficient and have funded research in nuclear fusion, solar, and hydroelectric energy, and other forms which cannot be cut off by an oil cartel or in times of war. With the rapid increase in the cost of energy, the poor nations suffered the most, with inflation rates of upwards of 30 to 50 percent.

quality of life

A problem related to the world population growth and energy shortages is the worsening quality of life for much of humanity. This can be measured by the polluted air and water, lack of adequate health care, unemployment and underemployment, lack of protein, and malnutrition and starvation. It has become increasingly obvious that these problems do not stop at national boundaries, but are world-wide in scope. Air pollution is carried across continents and over the oceans.

A nuclear holocaust would spread radioactive death throughout most of the northern hemisphere and possibly cover the whole earth. It has slowly been dawning upon the people and power structures of the rich nations that their excessive consumption of the world's resources means less available for the poor, and the continued despoliation of the environment. Quality of life is also affected by wars, crimes in the streets, bombings, hijackings, assassinations, dishonesty in the highest levels of government, and numerous other events that indicate that much of the glue holding together the societies of the world appears to be disintegrating.

maldistribution of wealth

Per capita income figures give some indication as to the gross inequities which exist in the last quarter of the twentieth century. The United States and some of the newly rich oil nations lead the world with per capita incomes of $4,000 or more. They are followed by other European countries, Australia, Japan, and the Soviet Union with $1,000 to $3,000 per person, with the nations of what has been called the Third World having per capita incomes of $100 to $1,000 per year. There now has been added another group called the Fourth World countries, who have been described by at least one international statesman as economic basket cases, due to the extreme nature of their poverty, with per capita incomes of under $100 per year. It has been estimated by some economists that upwards of half the world's population fall into the last category. Within individual countries, too, there are gross inequalities and inequities. Many nations with per capita incomes of $2,000 to $4,000 a year have within them large numbers of people living at near starvation levels. Traditional economic viewpoints suggested that with the development of a nation's total economy, the poor would be brought up with the rest of the population to a decent standard of living. There seems to be considerable evidence, however, in recent years, that both the gap between nations and the gap between rich and poor individuals are growing, so that in the 1970s much of the world found itself in worse condition than thirty years previously.

war and violence

Other major areas of concern are international war and internal violence. Partly because of overpopulation government after government has resorted to military power, police-state tactics and the destruction of civil liberties in order to control their own populations. This has led to rapid increases in the expenditures for military hardware and in the levels of violence, both internal and external throughout much of the world. In spite of the nonproliferation treaty, numerous nations have joined the nuclear club, with the resultant threat not only to their enemies, but ultimately to the whole world.

The United States has been unable to bring about an age of peace in the world, and as the number of new nation states grows each year, calls for world federalism are increasingly resisted. During the 150-year period from 1816 to 1957 there were a total of ninety-three wars, fifty of them between countries, and war was in progress during 126 of the 150 years. Twenty-nine million battle deaths were recorded or reported during the same period. The United States in 1970 was spending an estimated $72 billion on its military budget, the Soviet Union $40 billion, with France, Britain, and West Germany each spending more than $5 billion.

In the same year the United States had over 7500 warheads deliverable by missiles, the Soviet Union, some 5600. In the nuclear arsenals of the United States, the U.S.S.R., Great Britain, France, and China there were over 50,000 megatons of explosive force or the equivalent of fifteen tons of TNT for each man, woman, and child in the world. With a disastrous history of peace and with such incredible levels of violence now available to mankind, war and the threat of war must be a major concern of every nation and of every educational system.

Figure 13-1   People the World Over Seek Education

EDUCATION: PROBLEMS AND SOLUTIONS

The educational systems of the world are generally looked upon as one of the major solutions to the problems of overpopulation, consumptive values, economic problems, and war. However, education also can be part of the problem. Through a study of education in four Third World nations, education as both "problem" and "solution" will be analyzed.
tion" will be analyzed.

The American model of compulsory schooling has been or is being adopted by most nations. At one time, Great Britain, France, and other Western European countries served as the models for the educational systems of the Third World, and the elite of Africa, Asia, and Latin America were trained at Oxford and the Sorbonne. Since World War II, however, the United States has become a model. It is a tragedy that a model with so many flaws and in such a wealthy nation is being adopted by others who cannot even afford to provide decent housing, food, clothing, and health care for their people.

There are more illiterates in the world today than at any point in the history of mankind. According to the *Population Bulletin*, the world's illiterate population rose from 700 to 782 million adults between 1950 and 1970. In spite of a drop in the percentage of the world's illiterates during the same period from 44 percent to 34 percent, the nations of the Third World, were, with few exceptions, unable to keep up with their population growth.[1] Famine stalks hundreds of millions of people in the developing nations. The poor are getting poorer, as evidenced by the August, 1976, economic predictions from the World Bank, which indicate that the poorest nations, those with average incomes of under $200 per person, will grow at an annual rate of less than 1 percent for the rest of the twentieth century. That the educational systems of the world are also in crisis is attested to by educational conservatives and liberals alike. Philip Coombs, director of UNESCO's Educational Planning Agency, entitled his 1968 book *The World Education Crisis*,[2] and things have not improved much, if at all, since that time. The model of schooling found in the United States, Western Europe, and the Soviet Union is involved in the process of keeping people illiterate, poor, hungry, and ignorant. What evidence bears out such an outrageous statement? Let us share the example of two countries which have followed the United States, Western European or Soviet models of schooling, and two which have rejected them. References will also be made to programs and experiments in other Third World countries in an attempt to indicate possible connections between formal, Western-style schooling and the problems of illiteracy and poverty.

Nicaragua

One country which has followed the United States model of education is the Central American country of Nicaragua. Although it can hardly be called prototypical of all developing nations, it does contain within its social, political, economic, and educational systems similarities to much of the rest of the Third World. There are a variety of reasons why Nicaragua has chosen to follow the U.S. model of education.

American involvement in the country goes back to the Clayton-Bulwer Treaty of 1850, which gave Cornelius Vanderbilt, the American financier, the opportunity which he had been looking for to construct an interoceanic canal across the country. Although the canal was never built, many hundreds of "forty-niners" heading for California, were transported by Vanderbilt's steamship company across the country of Nicaragua and up the west coast to California. In 1855, an American soldier of fortune, William Walker, had himself elected president of the country, but two years

---

[1]*Population Bulletin*, as quoted in *Africa Now* (January-February, 1976), p. 10.
[2]Philip H. Coombs, *The World Educational Crisis: A Systems Analysis* (New York: Oxford University Press, 1968).

later, the combined forces of Central America, supported by Great Britain and by Vanderbilt, brought Walker's short reign to an end. The next major American involvement was in 1912, when U.S. Marines were called in to "protect foreign lives and property" during a rebellion by the opposition party. The Marines remained in Nicaragua from 1912 until 1925 and returned again from 1927 to 1933, during which time they were involved in guerrilla warfare against Augusto Sandino, a man who has since become a symbol of revolution throughout Latin America. In 1933, Sandino was killed by members of the Nicaraguan National Guard led by General Anastasio Somoza, the commander of the Guard and Minister of War, who was elected president of the country in 1936, with U.S. support. Although others have been elected to the presidency since that time, the Somoza family has remained in power behind the scenes for forty years. The current President is the son of General Anastasio Somoza.[3] In addition to the historic U.S. involvement in the country, there have been large American investments, many Nicaraguan industries and agribusiness firms having either American partners or American control.

Like many Third World nations, Nicaragua has been plagued with natural disasters, the most recent and famous being the December 23, 1972, earthquake which destroyed the capital city, Managua. There have also been volcanic eruptions, hurricanes, droughts, and other natural disasters, during which time the United States has been active in relief efforts. These have been welcomed and desperately needed by the Nicaraguans, but have been one more penetration by the United States into the country.

With a high percentage of its foreign trade being conducted with the United States, large numbers of American television programs being shown on its nationalized system, American movies dominating its theaters, American corporations controlling many of its businesses, and large numbers of Peace Corps volunteers and missionaries working among its people, the Americanization of Nicaragua can only be described as extensive. All of these are evidence of the reasons why Nicaragua has adopted an American model of schooling for its society. With tens of millions of dollars in U.S.-backed loans to help rebuild their earthquake-shattered schools and industries, it is unlikely that there will be any shift in this direction during the coming years.

The constitution of Nicaragua, like the constitutions of most Third World nations, contains legislation very similar to that found in the United States and Western Europe. Some of the articles are as follows: Public Education is a State duty; primary education is obligatory and both primary and secondary education shall be free; the National University will have autonomous status; academic freedom is guaranteed; teaching is nonpoliti-

---

[3]Johnson Research Associates, *Area Handbook for Nicaragua* (Washington, D.C.: U.S. Government Printing Office), pp. 42–49.

cal.[4] In its stated *goals and objectives*, the Nicaraguan educational system also reflects the influence of the United States and other societies. Some of its goals for education are as follows: strengthening national unity; cultivating the capacity to understand and appreciate spiritual values; forming a democratic conscience; teaching the rational distribution of time between work, rest, and recreation; and facilitating the acquisition of basic knowledge and cultivating a scientific attitude to banish superstition, prejudice and fanaticism.[5]

In and of themselves, the laws governing the Nicaraguan system and the goals for education are hard to fault. It is only when one looks at the realities of the society that the laws and goals can be brought into question. To have as a law that primary education is obligatory is all well and good; however, in 1974 only 54 out of every 1,000 students who entered rural primary schools in 1969 were graduating from sixth grade. In the urban areas it was considerably better, where 440 of every 1000 entrants were completing primary school.[6] Many students, however, never enter the formal educational system at all, so that the numbers actually receiving an education up to the sixth grade are considerably less than the 39 percent average given in 1974.[7] Free education is also desirable for a society; however, in a country where 50 percent of the families have incomes of between $100 and $300 annually,[8] any costs, such as school fees, books, or uniforms, almost automatically eliminate the poor from attending. The autonomous status of the national university and the guarantee of academic freedom are to be found in most constitutions in the Third World. When faced with a lack of jobs and meaningful work following graduation and the injustices which they see all around them, students at both the secondary and university levels in Nicaragua, and throughout most of the Third World, tend to be the centers of dissent and opposition to the government. As a result the national universities are often threatened with cuts in their governmental subsidies and the actual amount of academic freedom is suspect.

Goals of national unity and understanding and appreciating spiritual values are important. To speak, however, of forming a democratic conscience in Third World nations controlled by elite groups is to raise a sense of disbelief in the young people of such societies. To talk of a rational distribution of time between work, rest, and recreation in poor countries where a majority of the people are unemployed or underemployed is mak-

---

[4]Nicaraguan Constitution, as quoted in Ministry of Education, *National Plan for Educational Development: 1974—1980* (Managua: Ministry of Education, 1973), p. 28.
[5]Ibid., p. 29.
[6]Academy for Educational Development, *Nicaraguan Education Sector Assessment* (Managua and Washington, D.C., 1975), p. 113.
[7]Ibid., p. 111.
[8]Ibid., p. 26.

ing a mockery of an educational goal. This is not to deny the importance of having ideals or goals; but the society must have within it some semblance of actively seeking to achieve those ideals, or they can only lead to a great deal of disillusionment.

In addition to the dissonance between the society and its educational laws and goals, a major educational problem facing a country such as Nicaragua can be seen through its literacy rates. Although a comparative analysis of census data from 1950 to 1971 indicates a progressive decrease in illiteracy from 63 percent of the population ten years of age and over in 1950 to 42 percent in 1971, in terms of absolute numbers of illiterates, the figures show an increase from 369,000 in 1950 to 511,000 in 1970, and a projected 630,000 by 1980. Thus, even with a rapid expansion of the schools within the society, the number of adult illiterates will continue to grow.[9] This is true not only of Nicaragua but of most of the nations of the Third World. It is not for lack of effort that the formal schools have failed to solve the problem of illiteracy. Primary enrollments in Nicaragua rose dramatically in the 1960s, 144,000 to 283,000, while in secondary education the numbers increased from 26,000 to 51,000, and in higher education in the five years from 1965 to 1970, from 3,300 to over 9,000.[10] Even with this massive increase in formal schooling, there will continue to be a growing number of illiterates in the Nicaraguan society.

Following the earthquake of 1972, some of the first buildings rebuilt were the public schools. This was partially due to the Nicaraguan government's adoption of the Western value of formal education, but also due to the pressures of CARE, World Bank, USAID, and other international organizations, which loaned and gave millions of dollars to replace the thousands of classrooms destroyed in that disaster. Little if any thought was given to whether the schools should be rebuilt first, or if money could not perhaps be better spent in nonformal methods of education or on other sectors of the economy.

The aid given to Nicaragua for its schools is no exception to the policies governing U.S. aid to the rest of the world. One criteria is that, wherever possible, funds will be spent in the United States in the form of purchases of goods or services given by American citizens. American firms provide the printing machines to print textbooks. American firms contract to build schools, often using American-made materials. U.S. advisors are hired to consult on all aspects of the system, and Peace Corps volunteers are provided to develop programs for which there are no trained personnel in the country. In this manner, the Nicaraguan educational system and those of many Third World countries, look suspiciously like those found throughout the United States.

[9]Ibid., p. 137.
[10]Agency for International Development, *Nicaragua: Statistics of The Educational Sector* (Washington, D.C.: USAID, 1975), p. 3.

In the mid 1960s, a team of educators was brought together to produce textbooks for all of Central America, financed through grants from the U.S. government. Although the textbooks are generally of quite high quality, it is obvious that if they are funded by the U.S., they will tend to represent, to some extent, American perspectives of reality. American foundation funds have gone into the development of testing techniques and standardized examinations, through a program being developed in Guatemala. Nicaraguan educators, along with those from other Central American countries, are now developing tests based on the College Entrance Board Examinations and using American testing techniques.

In the late 1960s, an American team of educators went to Colombia in South America to develop a series of comprehensive secondary schools for that nation. American administrators helped to design the school, develop the curricula, train the teachers and produce an institution very similar to the suburban U.S. high school, In 1973, a Colombian UNESCO advisor began work with the Nicaraguans on instituting and building a comprehensive secondary school. Thus, by way of Colombia, another American invention, the comprehensive secondary school, is coming to a Central American country. In the United States, the comprehensive secondary school was seen as a mechanism for providing a variety of educational experiences under one roof while at the same time breaking down class barriers and the stigma attached to vocational programs. To a certain extent this has been accomplished, although numerous research studies have pointed out the tracking that still occurs in most of these institutions, with low prestige in the vocational track. Because they need a large student population and because of the industrial-vocational bias in their technical curriculum, these schools have almost always been located in urban areas. Nicaragua is no exception and the plans are to build a comprehensive secondary school in Managua. This school, along with the placement of almost all other secondary schools in urban centers, has become a cause, if only a minor one, for an increased urbanization within the country. As E. F. Schumacher pointed out, "Technology cannot eradicate the three-fold disease of mass migration into the cities, followed by mass unemployment, and finally the threat or actuality of mass hunger. Because in the end, food is produced not on the balconies in the cities, but in the vast rural areas."[11]

The schools of Nicaragua have attracted young people from the rural areas, where they are needed in the farming communities and into the large cities where they become part of the large unemployed or underemployed population. A basic question can be raised, however, as to what aspects of a traditional society, one in which farming, rural life and smallness are valued, are communicated when students are brought into a large, urban, comprehensive secondary school with an industrial-technical bias.

[11]E. F. Schumacher, "Intermediate Technology," *The Center Magazine* (January–February, 1975).

In addition to the urbanization problem raised by the comprehensive secondary school, a further urban bias is found in enrollment statistics. At the primary school level, although the 1971 census indicated that 53 percent of the population still lived outside of the cities, only 40 percent of the primary school enrollment came from those rural areas.[12] Almost all secondary schools are located in urban centers, thus forcing a student from a rural home to go to a city in order to receive further schooling. Although the Nicaraguan government has recently given rural development as its number-one priority, it remains to be seen how successful new programs will be in upgrading the rural standard of living.

All too often in the Third World, aid is funneled into bureaucracies located in the capital city, and as has happened in the poverty programs of the United States, the people benefiting most have been the educated, urbanized, middle classes. One of the mechanisms traditionally used to reach the rural poor has been agricultural education. This is true also of Nicaragua, where what are known as Escuelas Granjas are located in the countryside. In 1974, while giving a speech in Nicaragua on the importance of agricultural education, one of the authors was interrupted by a young man who stood up and told him in no uncertain terms that agricultural education in the absence of meaningful land reform was a waste of time, money, and energy. Some land reform has taken place, but few Third World countries ruled by an elite landholding class are willing to move rapidly in this area. Vocational and agricultural education are all too often a mechanism for maintaining the status quo and improving the lot of the rich, while doing very little for the poor.

Ivan Illich[13] and other authors have pointed out that the schools of the world tend to exacerbate the problems of social class and status, and perpetuate elites rather than break down barriers. Evidence of this can be found in Nicaragua, and also throughout most of the developing world. At the primary level, one finds most social classes represented. By the time one reaches *ciclo básico*, the equivalent of junior high school, and certainly by the time the student comes to the end of senior high or university, the poor, be they urban or rural, are seldom to be found in the schools. Nicaragua is no exception to this pattern in which the schools tend to perpetuate the wealthy of the society. This is not to say that some students do not make it up through the system on their own merit, but for the most part, the elites of the world use the mechanism of a supposed meritocracy to perpetuate themselves in their positions of economic, political, and social power.

In a 1968 study in Thailand, one of the authors attempted to analyze the social class makeup of the Thai universities. While 80 to 90 percent of the people live and work in rural farming communities, less than 8 percent of the university population was made up of this particular class. University

---

[12]*1971 Nicaraguan Census*, as quoted in Academy for Educational Development, *Nicaraguan Education Sector Assessment*, p. 3.
[13]Ivan Illich, *Deschooling Society* (New York: Harper & Row, Publishers, 1971).

students came from business, government, and military families.[14] In Nicaragua the wealthy send their children to the private parochial schools and to the private university, while the middle class tends to send its children up through the public system to the national university. Most of the rural poor are gone from the system by second or third grade, and the poor in the towns and cities drop out by the end of the primary grades.

Nicaragua serves as an interesting example in the area of teacher training. An American model was adopted in the early 1950s, when advisors went to Nicaragua to structure the secondary level normal schools. Along with the Americanization of the teacher training which occurred at that time, there has been the inexorable process of upgrading the amount of education the teachers have needed. At one time a secondary school degree was sufficient. Today, the pressures are building for them to have two or four years of college or a *licenciatura*, which is similar to a U.S. master's degree. As teacher-educators, we would be hard put to deny the value of education in upgrading teachers. One must ask, however, where scarce resources should be used. Is it really necessary for all teachers to have a master's, four years of college, or even a secondary normal school degree, or could the money perhaps not be better spent on in-service training to upgrade the quality of instruction, with more emphasis put on literacy and basic adult education programs?

Another evidence of the effort to emulate the American school system can be found in the pressures to expand the number of secondary school years from five to six. This would, of course, put a tremendous strain on an already overburdened economy. In addition, there are pressures to have guidance counselors in all schools and to begin a program of preschool education. The overwhelming problems of health, poverty, and malnutrition facing Nicaragua and other Third World countries make the adoption of an expensive educational system, based on a United States, Russian, French, British, or other developed-nation model, difficult to justify.

Nicaragua is representative of much of the Third World in the large numbers of students and members of the middle and upper classes who go to the United States to study or live. The exact number of Nicaraguans residing in the United States is difficult to estimate. From the size of the Nicaraguan *barrios* in San Francisco, New Orleans and Los Angeles, however, it is known to be many thousands. As with many countries of the Third World, when students have received their training in Western Europe or the United States, they often remain in the developed countries even though their skills are desperately needed back home.

From the standpoint of teaching methodology, the Nicaraguan educational system has also adopted a traditional style. This methodology can be described as a model in which students compete against each other for scarce places both within the educational system and the society. An au-

---

[14]Richard J. Kraft, *Student Background and University Admission* (Bangkok and East Lansing, Michigan: National Education Council and Michigan State University, 1968), p. 20.

thoritarian relationship predominates in the schools between principals and teachers, and between teachers and students, as opposed to a more democratic model, and the schools are seen as a mechanism for the creation of a labor force attuned to the needs of the factories of the society. Traditional lecture-recitation-memorization techniques predominate in the schools, which in their organization also tend to reflect the hierarchical nature of the society.

In many respects the Nicaraguan educational system is a mirror image of thousands of U.S. school districts. The question has yet to be seriously faced as to whether such a system makes much sense in a predominantly poor, rural nation, with massive problems of illiteracy, poverty, disease, and malnutrition.

Ivory Coast

On the African continent is another nation which has adopted a Western educational system. In this case, the Ivory Coast, owing to its colonial history, has opted for a French model. It is one of the "richest" nations of black Africa, with a per capita income of slightly more than $380. As with most developing nations, however, the per capita figure is highly misleading in that the wealth is concentrated in Abidjan, among the wealthy Ivory Coast citizens and the large numbers of French advisors, who live and work in the capital. The 80 percent of the people who live in the rural areas have incomes far below the $380 figure. In addition, there is high, urban unemployment due to people moving from the rural areas and also from immigration from neighboring countries.

For a nation which is comparatively wealthy in African terms, the literacy rate is a low 20 percent even though the government is spending almost one-third of its revenues on the formal educational system. It is not from lack of funding that the Ivory Coast government has been unable to deal with the problems of illiteracy and the shift from rural to urban areas. It has adopted a position of gradualism in its approach to educational reform. This means that the curriculum is still basically French, 30 percent of the students receiving baccalaureate are expatriates, and the educational system is still largely in the hands of French citizens. Ninety-five percent of the nation's industrial capacity is still in French hands.[15]

One experiment which the Ivory Coast government is attempting is the "radical transformation" of the country's primary schools by the use of instructional television. The Ivory Coast was faced, as are many African nations, with large numbers of languages, in this case up to sixty different tribal languages, and thus educational television was instituted in an attempt to teach a national language. The country has rapidly expanded its

[15] Peter Muncie, *Torches in the Night* (Washington, D.C.: World Bank), pp. 39–43.

educational television system with the goal of reaching 720,000 students in 16,500 classes by 1980. The problems with the educational television system, however, are numerous. In the neighboring country of Niger, the plans for educational television failed to materialize, after it became obvious that a rapid expansion of the primary schools would lead to space problems at the secondary school level. In the initial years of using educational television, the Ivory Coast has experienced many difficulties; first of all is the impact of educational television on the desire of primary school graduates to leave the rural areas and move to the large city. Seventy-five percent of all classrooms experienced television breakdowns, and at any one time, up to 8 percent of the TVs were not functioning. The costs to the government were considerable, with many millions of dollars spent on the initial acquisition of equipment and a continuing expenditure of millions of dollars to maintain it. In addition, the social class bias found through the use of instructional television was not dealt with. Middle-and upper class Ivory Coast and French citizens continued to send their children to the elite schools, where they would receive instruction from well-qualified teachers in small classes, while it was the poor who were to be educated through television.

This is not to say that all aspects of educational television in the Ivory Coast have been a failure. It has stimulated curricular and teaching methodological reforms, and through its use large numbers of children who were unable to go to school are now receiving some kind of education. The concepts of education and modernization given by television in the Ivory Coast, however, are basically French in milieu and culture. Thus, children are being prepared to reject their own society and adopt foreign ways. Observers of Ivory Coast educational television have remarked that the system is preparing better-educated taxi drivers, manual laborers, and discontented farmers.[16]

educational technology

Educational technology has never been the success story that its backers at IBM, General Electric, Sony and a host of other manufacturing firms in this country, Japan, and Europe have hoped that it would be. Pressures have been applied to take this educational salvation to many other countries of the world. Mexico, El Salvador, Turkey, Thailand, and India are just a few of the other countries currently making attempts at providing education of one sort or another through educational television or radio. If one is to believe researchers, the success of these technological systems has been dramatic with great cost savings to the countries involved.

Carnoy and Levin in their article, "Evaluation of Educational

[16] Ibid., pp. 47–57.

Media: Some Issues," in *Instructional Science*, October, 1975, suggest however, that much of the research on the success of educational television may not be as accurate as the researchers indicate. They quote James Q. Wilson, who set forth two laws which he believes apply to all cases of social science evaulation of public policy:[17]

> *First Law*: All policy interventions in social problems produce the intended effect—*if* the research is carried out by those implementing the policy or their friends.

> *Second Law:* No policy intervention in social problems produces the intended effect—*if* the research is carried out by independent third parties, especially those skeptical of the policy.

Carnoy and Levin admit to being critics and cynical or skeptical of the effects of educational technology in the developing world. Their first objection is that the cost of instructional technologies is almost always understated, in that most studies do not include all aspects of the projects such as technical assistance, the inputs of existing government agencies and other institutions, and the use of existing buildings and other resources. Perhaps more importantly, however, they question the standards by which effectiveness of educational television is measured, suggesting that in most cases the researchers use an extremely narrow measurement standard to assess educational outcomes. Although cognitive outcomes may be quite high, the authors point to other research that indicates that noncognitive factors, such as socialization, appear to be far more important than the cognitive ones. They go on to point out that the use of educational technology tends to force curricula and teaching into a straightjacket.[18]

A further problem, seldom faced by the developing nations, is that with the use of educational technology, there will be a large increase in the numbers of students graduating at the various levels in the educational system. Evidence from Mexico, El Salvador, Samoa, the Ivory Coast, and Korea indicates that technological innovations tend to increase the number of years of schooling in the potential urban labor force, but that vast numbers of these graduates become unemployed and thus put downward pressure on the wages of both skilled and semiskilled labor. Another criticism is the effect that the use of educational technology has on the exposure of children and young people to a diversity of experiences and institutions, and perhaps most importantly the possibilities of misuse of educational mass media by the authoritarian regimes, which currently control much of the world's population.[19]

---

[17]J. Q. Wilson, "On Pettigrew and Armor: and Afterword," *The Public Interest*, pp. 30, 132–34, as quoted by Martin Carnoy and Henry M. Levin in "Evaluation of Educational Media: Some Issues," *Instructional Science*, 4, no. 3–4, p. 387.
[18]Carnoy and Levin, "Evaluation of Education Media," p. 388–90.
[19]Ibid., p. 404.

With little evidence of success in the United States or other developed societies, one would be hard put to predict any great success in the Third World through the use of educational television, and one can only conclude that the basic motivation for its use is the pressure from large multinational corporations and their governments on Third World countries, including pressures on the bilateral and multilateral aid agencies which provide the funding with which these products can be bought.

In a nation such as the Ivory Coast, so thoroughly controlled by an external power, it is understandable why the educational system reflects French culture and technological desires. However, with a large majority of its people illiterate and living outside the money economy, the formal educational system and recent educational television can only be viewed as destructive of a sense of national pride, as perpetuators of social inequality, and as purveyors of Western values and culture.

Cuba

A nation which followed the American–Western model of schooling for some sixty years and later rejected it to develop its own is Cuba. If anything, Cuba has been more deeply involved with the United States than Nicaragua. Much of this involvement has to do with its proximity, only ninety miles off our coast. Its domination of the entrances to the Gulf of Mexico and the principal routes to the Panama Canal have made it of great importance to the United States.

Throughout the nineteenth century, Cuba and the Caribbean were seen as an American sphere of influence. In fact, in 1864, the Polk administration made an informal offer to buy Cuba from Spain. The Treaty of Paris, signed on December 10, 1898, provided that the "civil rights and political status of the island should be determined by the Congress of the United States." It was at this point that the client status of the island to the United States became obvious. The *Platt Amendment*, in 1900, required Cuba to sell or lease lands to the United States for naval stations, limited Cuba's treaty-making power and its capacity to contract debts, and gave the United States the right to intervene and to preserve independence and maintain law and order. These U.S. rights were written into the new Cuban Constitution and on May 20, 1902, Cuba was formally independent.[20] With the Platt Amendment, Theodore Roosevelt wanted to teach the Cuban population to "behave decently." He felt that the best way to help was to Americanize them in education, law, and government.[21] For the next thirty years the Platt Amendment dominated Cuban-American relations and was resented by the Cubans as an extreme example of American paternalism.

[20]John Plant, ed., *Cuba and the United States: Long-Range Perspectives* (Washington, D.C.: The Brookings Institution, 1967), pp. 12–13.
[21]Ibid., p. 13.

In May, 1934, a new treaty replaced the permanent treaty, and the Platt Amendment was dropped, except for a provision regarding Guantanamo Naval Base. It was at this time that Fulgencio Batista was installed as provisional president and maintained his rule off and on for the next twenty-four years.[22]

During the two periods of direct U.S. intervention from 1898 to 1902, and from 1906 to 1909, the American-style, Cuban education system was founded. The new school law, based on that of Ohio, created local school boards, called for compulsory school attendance, and set up teacher-training schools, textbooks, and curricula based on an Ohio model. Some have suggested that in addition to organizational and structural kinds of changes, American middle-class values were also embedded deeply within the Cuban educational system.[23]

During the Batista regime in Cuba, American investment increased dramatically. Although there was a decrease in the percentage of American ownership within the country, the U.S. total investment rose from $624 million in 1950 to $955 million in 1959. It is also true that the Cuban ownership also was centered in the hands of an elite and of a middle class, while the vast majority of peasants did not receive the benefits from most of the American investment.[24] By 1959 Cuba had the highest per capita income of any country in Latin America, was an unhealthy imbalance in the spread of the wealth, and intense poverty, unemployment, and other problems still existed.

This American dominance of the culture and the society, along with a twenty-year decline in the amount of education and other benefits for the common man, were some of the causes which led to the Fidel Castro revolution in 1958–59. That revolution wrought significant educational changes. Not all aspects of the Cuban revolution have been admirable, but in education, much of what has occurred can be highly instructive for Third World nations faced with similar problems.

In revolutionary Cuba, education is a major part of the societal attempt to change the country. The revolution had, and still has, four basic goals, (1) to expand and utilize fully the society's productive capacities; (2) to eliminate economic, political, and cultural dependence on the United States; (3) to replace the rigid class structure of capitalist Cuba with a classless and egalitarian society, to eliminate sexism and racism, and to end the urban bias in the economy, culture, and politics; and (4) to transform work into challenging and creative activity for the new socialist man.[25] In addi-

[22] Ibid., pp. 22–24.
[23] Roland G. Paulston, "Education," in *Revolutionary Change in Cuba*, ed. Carmelo Mesa-Lago (Pittsburgh: University of Pittsburgh Press, 1971), pp. 377–78.
[24] Plant, *Cuba and the United States*, p. 29.
[25] Samuel Bowles, "Cuban Education and The Revolutionary Ideology," *Harvard Educational Review*, 41, no. 4 (November, 1971), p. 474.

tion to these four overall goals of the society, three objectives were stated for the school system: (1) stagnation in education was to be replaced by rapid growth in enrollments, (2) national scientific and cultural dependency was to be eliminated by the expansion of high-level educational, technical, and research facilities, (3) the class structure of Cuban education was to be destroyed and education was to be made available to all, and (4) the social relations of Cuban education were to be transformed to develop a new socialist man.[26]

Cuba, prior to the revolution of 1958–59, had a literacy similar to Nicaragua's. Although between 1899 and 1953 the percentage of illiterates dropped from 43.8 percent to 23.6 percent, in absolute numbers the number of illiterates had grown from 690,000 to an estimate of over one million.[27] In 1961, when the Castro regime attempted to register all illiterates in preparation for a massive literacy campaign, over 900,000 were registered. In the one year of the campaign, over 700,000 illiterates were taught to read and the illiteracy rate was brought down to 3.9 percent.[28] This campaign has been seen as one of the most successful of its type in educational history, and yet as one looks around the rest of Latin America and the Third World, one sees very few similar attempts at trying to wipe out illiteracy. Most nations are attempting to deal with the problem in the traditional manner of public schooling.

Such attempts appear to be doomed to failure. The will of the elites, who have seen the successful Cuban example yet refuse to restructure their educational plans to wipe out illiteracy must be questioned.
out illiteracy.

In addition to the problem of the growing number of illiterates prior to the revolution, the Cuban educational system was going through extreme stagnation from 1938 through 1958, a period in which the number of primary-school-age children never attending school rose from 20 percent to close to 35 percent.[29] In comparison, from 1959 to 1969 the total primary school enrollment more than doubled from 717,000 to over 1,560,000.[30] Perhaps more important than the overall statistics on enrollment have been attempts to balance urban and rural areas in literacy and primary education. This is partially reflected in the dramatic expansion during the ten-year period in adult enrollment, which went from 27,000 in 1958–59 to 425,000 in 1967–68.[31] The educational system of Cuba appears to have been successful in dealing with problems of illiteracy and basic skills

[26] Ibid., pp. 481–82.
[27] Nelson P. Valdes, "The Radical Transformation of Cuban Education," in *Cuba in Revolution*, eds. Rolando E. Bonachea and Nelson P. Valdes (Garden City, N.Y.: Anchor Books, 1972), p. 423.
[28] Ibid., p. 428.
[29] Bowles, "Cuban Education," p. 480.
[30] Ibid., p. 484.
[31] Valdes, "The Radical Transformation," p.430.

for young people and adults, something which cannot be said for most of the Third World, following the traditional American or European patterns of schooling.

Secondary school enrollment also rose dramatically after the revolution, from 63,000 in 1958–59 to 177,000 in 1967–68.[32] Similar figures can be found in technical and higher education. Perhaps more dramatic than the statistics of number of students in higher education since the revolution is the breakdown by departments in which the students study. Before the revolution, 32 percent of the students were in the humanities; following the revolution that number dropped to only 5.8 percent. Agriculture rose from 4.3 percent to 11.9 percent and the sciences rose from 7.9 percent to 11.3. Technological fields grew from 10.3 to 28.4, and medicine went from 22 percent to 24.8 percent.[33] A change of emphasis following the revolution led to education being seen as a service to the people and not just to satisfy the individual needs and interests of the students involved.

Other evidences of the attempt to provide a more egalitarian educational system can be found in the number of state scholarships, which rose from 15,000 in 1958 to 277,999 in 1970.[34] Education is a big business in Cuba. The state education budget rose from 77 million pesos in 1958 to 280 million by 1969. In addition, one-fifth of Cuba's total productive capacity was devoted to schooling in 1968–69, a figure unsurpassed among the major countries of the world. Education rivaled sugar as Cuba's largest productive sector.[35] Cuba has shown that large expenditures on education, when tied to productive activity and when part of an egalitarian ethic, need not lead to increased poverty and ignorance. Whereas most nations have seen their schoolroom class sizes rise from twenty to thirty to fifty, sixty or even higher, the Cuban revolution has seen its class size drop at the primary school level from 41.3 in 1958–59 to 29.8 in 1968–69. There have been some increases at other levels, but once again, the Cuban government has attempted to provide good quality at the lowest grades.[36]

In most nations the elite and the newly educated middle class want nothing to do with manual labor. The Cuban revolution has attempted to dignify it. This has been done through a variety of mechanisms, one of which is the *escuela al campo*, or literally "the school goes to the country." In this program students spend summers in the countryside, and during the cane-cutting season, entire schools are moved into the fields. "Interest circles" are found in all schools and are centered around productive kinds of activity, in which the students learn practical things to be used in farming or in other ventures. Through these programs, government propaganda,

[32] Ibid., p. 434.
[33] Ibid., p. 437.
[34] Ibid., p. 440.
[35] Ibid., p. 439.
[36] Bowles, "Cuban Education," p. 487.

and the involvement of Premier Castro in the manual occupations, labor has been dignified within the country to an extent found in few other Third World nations. Attempts have been made to tie schooling to factories and farms of the country rather than replicate these activities in technical or agricultural schools, as has been the tradition in most other nations.[37]

Another way in which the Cuban revolution has attempted to deal with education has been to encourage students to study in groups, rather than compete with each other. Teachers are charged with becoming more democratic in their outlook rather than authoritarian, and the system is being changed to provide a more egalitarian milieu in which racial, social, and sexual barriers are broken down. In an attempt to change the elite nature of higher education, a process known as the universalization of the university has taken place. In this program, students are to be integrated into the productive activities of the country and are asked to carry out projects in which they put their theories into practice. The Castro regime hopes that in this manner a new elite will not develop, as it has in the Soviet Union, Eastern Europe, and some of the other communist-socialist countries.[38]

Universities or higher education, however, are considered necessary in order to break away from the dependence upon what was previously American control and what currently is seen as Soviet control of much of the society. Today, one can find Cubans themselves in almost all positions of power and control, something not to be found before the revolution. With the abolition of private schools following the revolution, the elite had no place to send their children. Of course, a very high percentage of the elite left the country and emigrated to the United States and to other parts of Latin America. In one sense, this made the task easier to change the society, and yet also very difficult, for Castro was left without a trained cadre to run the country.

All of this is not to say that the Cuban educational revolution has been a dramatic success in all areas. The problems of elitism can still be found, and there is some question as to the quality of the teachers, following the rapid expansion which occurred after the revolution. There is also a lack of materials, furniture, and equipment in many of the schools, and even though the vast majority of young people are currently receiving a primary education, secondary schools and universities still take only a small percentage of their age groups. Whether Cuba will be able to emphasize primary schooling and basic education and still produce the high level of technical, scientific, and administrative skills needed is still a question to be answered. There is little arguing, however, with the success of the Cuban educational model in dealing with the massive problems of adult illiteracy

[37] Ibid., pp. 488–89.
[38] Ibid., pp. 489–90.

and primary education within the broader context of a society dedicated to wiping out poverty, disease, and malnutrition.

Tanzania

An African nation which has rejected much of Western-style schooling, in a British model, is Tanzania. For the first six years following its independence in 1961, the country continued in a basic British pattern of education and society. Unlike the Ivory Coast, Tanzania is one of the poorest nations in Africa. It is over 90 percent rural, with large numbers of people not even entering the money economy. It is a nation of about 11.9 million people, and has a harsh environment, used primarily for unintensive types of agriculture. About two-thirds of the nation is infested with the tsetse fly, which severely limits its agricultural potential. The nation is 99 percent African, with small numbers of Arabs, Asians, and Europeans making up the rest of the population. It has about 120 tribes, the largest having less than 10 percent of the total population. Approximately half the people have traditional religious belief systems, one-quarter are Moslem, and another quarter are Christian. The language of Swahili has been the "lingua franca" of the people, although the schools at a higher levels are conducted in English.[39]

Like the Ivory Coast and Nicaragua, Tanzania has a tremendous problem with a literate population of only 10 to 15 percent in Swahili and less than 1 percent in English. The problems of school attendance are also great, with fewer than 50 percent of the appropriate age groups to be found in elementary school, only 3 percent at the secondary level, and a small fraction to be found in higher education.[40]

In 1967, President Nyerere, one of the most important intellectuals and leaders of the Third World, made what has come to be called the Arusha Declaration.[41] In that declaration, a strong ideological base was set down for the development of Tanzania, and the nation's only political party, TANU, laid down the direction in which Tanzania was to move over the coming years. The TANU creed states that all human beings are equal and that every individual has the right to dignity, respect, freedom of expression, movement, religious belief, and association. Every citizen has the right to participate in the government at all levels, and the right to receive a just return for his labor. The natural resources of the country belong to all of its citizens. The state must have effective control over the principal

---

[39]Lewis S. Kurtz, *An African Education: The Social Revolution in Tanzania* (Brooklyn: Pageat Poseidon Ltd., 1972), pp. 12–15.

[40]Muncie, *Torches in the Night*, p. 14.

[41]Julius K. Nyerere, "The Arusha Declaration," *Freedom and Socialism* (Dar es Salaam–London: Oxford University Press, 1968), pp. 231–50.

means of production, in addition to the right to intervene in the economy to prevent exploitation of individuals or groups and to prevent the accumulation of wealth to an extent inconsistent with the existence of a classless society.[42] The subtitles of the "Arusha Declaration" were "Socialism and Self-Reliance," and those words summarize where the country of Tanzania has attempted to move since 1967. This is obviously a very different direction than that followed currently throughout most of the Third World.

In 1966, President Nyerere could point to increases in the total numbers of students receiving an education: in first grade, from 121,000 to 154,000 between 1961 and 1966, a 27 percent increase; in the last year of secondary school, from 176 to 761, a 332 percent increase.[43] The number of students receiving no education at all or not being enrolled at any particular level, however, was staggering, and thus it became obvious to the president and to the other Tanzanian leaders that the formal educational system could not meet the society's needs. In addition, President Nyerere stated there were four major problems with the system that needed to be changed. First, it was elitist in orientation and benefited mainly the few who were able to climb up through it. Second, the system alienated the people from the countryside and from the society, turning them into "Europeans." Third, the system was geared towards a perspective that education was acquired from books and that formal education was a criterion for goodness and success. Lastly, the formal educational system was not contributing to the economic output of the society, but was basically a consumption item.[44] These statements, if given by somebody of less stature than the president, would no doubt have led to a revolt on the part of the people. However, Nyerere being the father of his country and having great prestige with most of his people, was able to make such a harsh analysis.

In a 1967 speech entitled "Education for Self-Reliance" Nyerere set forth the basic principles which were to be followed in the Tanzanian society for the years to come. Whereas the education inherited from the British was geared to preparing an intellectual elite, the formal and nonformal educational system under the new plans were to become part of a socialist state. Whereas the colonial educational system had tended to emphasize modern, Western values, the new educational system was to emphasize "Ujamaa," the Swahili word for familyhood. Nyerere expanded this word to include all the tenets of an egalitarian socialism. The exploitation and control of one man by another and the accumulation of wealth were antisocial acts, while traditional forms of landholding were to be abolished, and familyhood, group, or societal control of the land was to become one of the bases for the new society. The people of Tanzania were to be educated to

[42]Kurtz, *An African Education*, pp. 88–89.
[43]Ibid., p. 136.
[44]Muncie, *Torches in the Night*, p. 14.

extend the concept of family beyond tribe, community, or nation, and to look at all men as their brothers.[45] This was a very big order for any educational system, particularly one which reaches such a small percentage of its people, and to say it has been a dramatic success would be an overstatement. However, the reforms were put in practice between 1967 and 1977, and some interesting, even exciting things occurred in Tanzania.

The people have been moved into Ujamaa villages through persuasion, not force, for Nyerere adopted a gradualist approach and not a dramatic, violent revolution. The work of creating the new cooperative society is done by the villagers themselves and is not forced on them. This has been done through a decentralization of the Tanzanian government, so that there are eighteen nearly autonomous regions, which are further decentralized all the way down to the village level. In this way, every Tanzanian citizen participates in the decisions affecting his or her own life. "Self-help, self-reliance and cooperation" is the creed adopted throughout the whole society and in the educational system.[46] In contrast to the Nicaraguan and Ivory Coast examples, the emphasis of the Tanzanian society and educational system had not been on its capital city or upon industry, but upon the rural areas where most of the people live and work in agriculture.

Educational reform, as outlined in "Education for Self-Reliance" has come through three major areas: (1) curricular reform, (2) the reorganization of the schools, and (3) an increase in the age of those entering primary schools.[47] Recognizing that the vast majority of young people would be unable to attend or graduate from primary school, the president declared that primary schools must prepare students for life and not just the academics. In an astute recognition, however, that a child of ten, eleven, or twelve, on graduating from primary school, is not capable intellectually, physically or economically, of being an independent productive citizen, Nyerere declared that young people would enter school at a later age. Thus upon completion of their primary education, they would be both old enough and well trained enough to become productive citizens within the society.

A great deal of emphasis has been put on eliminating illiteracy. A successful regional program has been under experimentation for eight years in the Lake Region, and the literacy rate has risen from 14 percent to 67 percent, with over 300,000 people attending over 10,000 classes. Taking seriously the ideals of radical theorist Paolo Friere, the literacy training deals with specific kinds of problems faced by the people. Thus the books talk about how to use pesticides and fertilizers, how not to be cheated by middlemen, and how to develop a cooperative. The materials used are per-

---

[45]Julius K. Nyerere, "Education for Self-Reliance," *Freedom and Socialism* (Dar es Salaam–London: Oxford University Press, 1968), pp. 267–90.
[46]Muncie, *Torches in the Night*, p. 29.
[47]Ibid., p. 15.

ceived by the rural poor as having direct relevance to their lives. Many hundreds of thousands of adults are learning to read and write in Swahili. All primary school teachers and civil servants must conduct classes, as literacy is seen as a major tool for economic betterment of the rural poor.[48]

In order to break down the elitism so rampant in the educational systems of the Third World, each school is attempting to become self-reliant. Teacher-training schools have their own farms and workshops to raise the funds needed for their institution. Agricultural students at the University of Dar es Salaam no longer become pencil-pushing bureaucrats, but also clean out barns and milk cows. In an attempt to deal with the problems of people moving to the cities and of the rural population being ignored, Rural Training Centers have been created in at least half of Tanzania's districts. Health education, family planning, and agricultural training are all aspects of what occurs in these centers. Village leaders are trained and taught how to plan and conduct meetings, keep books, and form cooperatives. Ministry of Agriculture Training Institutes are also located throughout the country. In these, young people who have graduated from primary school are trained to work in the rural areas, with an emphasis on crops, animal husbandry, irrigation, and land use. They must spend at least two years living in a thatch or mud hut in one of the Ujamaa villages and help the rural poor improve their lives.[49]

"Learning through living" has become the ideal for education throughout Tanzania. Teachers in special teacher-training institutes no longer study a British curriculum, for the curriculum has been Africanized, with African history and culture replacing British history and culture. Examinations designed by and for Tanzanians are used in deciding who continues for more education. In spite of its goals and obvious efforts towards a just society, Tanzania still has tremendous problems. Illiteracy, famine, malnutrition, and lack of work are faced by many of its people. There is great hope and enthusiasm, however, as the country has recognized that a model based upon that of Great Britain, France, the Soviet Union or the United States does not meet the needs of its 90 percent rural poor, and that only a dramatic restructuring, as has been attempted since 1967, will begin to solve the problems of its society.

a critique of world education

With world population doubling in thirty-six years, solutions must soon be found to the related problems of illiteracy, poverty, malnutrition, and starvation. The particular educational model that the powerful nations of the world encourage or permit to exist has life-and-death implications for hundreds of millions of the world's poor.

[48] Ibid., pp. 33–36.
[49] Ibid., pp. 15–29.

Figure 13-2   Can Formal Education Solve the Problems of the Third World?

With a gross national product of a trillion dollars, the United States can, possibly, afford expenditures on education in excess of $100 billion annually. With the possible exception of the newly rich oil nations, the Third World countries must carefully shepherd their scarce resources, spending them only on education that benefits all members of their society and not just the elite. In the export of its curricula, teaching materials, technology, textbooks, structure and organization, idealized educational objectives, and other things being directly copied by other nations, the United States must be careful that it doesn't become an indirect party in keeping the poor of this world illiterate and starving. To speak of spending 5 or 10 percent of the gross national product in a trillion dollar economy, or of 15 to 20 percent of a national budget that runs into the hundreds of billions of dollars, is very different from speaking of spending 20 to 50 percent of the national budget for education when only a few million dollars are available for all sectors of a society. Each dollar spent on an educational system that tends to perpetuate elites takes food from starving children. Every dollar spent on massive comprehensive secondary schools and university education prevents other children and adults from being educated at the most basic literacy or primary school levels. Every dollar spent in education is one less dollar that can be spent on economic improvements to provide jobs for the unemployed graduates coming out of primary and secondary schools or universities. In the absence of an egalitarian ideology, education tends to secure the positions and power of the elites, and wastes scarce resources desperately needed in health and agriculture.

That the poor nations of the world cannot afford Western-style schooling should now be obvious to all. Why such schooling is being adopted world-wide may not be quite so obvious. Following earthquakes or other natural disasters, which seem to regularly strike the poor nations of the world, the schools are some of the first structures to be rebuilt with international aid. All too often the motives of powerful nations are not strictly humanitarian. The school is a major socializing agent in all countries of the world, and it has been suggested by some social scientists that it serves an even greater role in the Third World than it does among the developed nations. The socialization which takes place in the schools leads towards a greater acceptance of urbanization, mechanization, a Western-style attitude toward work and achievement. Numerous studies have been made with grants from the various American foundations and funds from USAID to discover the reasons why the Third World nations refuse to or seem incapable of adopting Western attitudes toward work, industry, capital savings, and other aspects of our culture. The schools, with their emphasis upon achievement, future-orientation, and industrial-type work training, are a major socializing influence toward Western style of life. The question is seldom raised as to whether other, more traditional value systems might have some qualities worth maintaining and that the adoption of a Western set of values may not be the best thing for the whole world.

It appears to have been accepted on face value that there are vast benefits to be derived by the Third World in interaction with the developed nations of the West or the Communist-bloc nations. Few have asked what are the costs of that economic or educational interaction. One cost has been the massive brain drain to the United States and Europe. Large numbers of individuals are trained to very high levels within their own country or in the United States, and find themselves caught between the traditional values of their families and homeland and those given to them by Western-style schooling. Confronted with the opportunity to make a better living in the United States or Europe, many jump at the chance.

Not all of the Third World peoples live in abject poverty, despair and disease, nor do all people suffer from a great deprivation of culture or opportunity. Many have enough to eat and live a satisfying existence; yet the mass media and the Western-style educational systems create a sense of deprivation, a desire for an ever greater standard of living, and a dissatisfaction with traditional values and culture. Few nations have been able to resist the cultural, economic, and educational penetration by the United States, Western Europe and the Soviet Union.[50] Few countries have either the leadership or the motivation to take an independent road, but it is pre-

[50] K. J. Holsti, "Underdevelopment and the 'Gap' Theory of International Conflict," *The American Political Science Review*, 69, no. 3, pp. 827–29.

cisely this type of independence that much of the Third World possibly needs. It is probably too late for those countries which are rich in mineral resources to prevent constant contact with the developed world. However, those nations with few natural resources and little wealth, those that have recently been called the Fourth World, might find it to their benefit to follow the lead of Tanzania and attempt a policy of noncooperation and nonpenetration with and by the developed nations.

Before concluding that such direction is absurd, we should look at "developed" societies with their rising crime rates, mental illness, child brutality, pollution, waste, depletion of natural resources and a host of other problems pointed out by numerous commentators, and ask: Is this the type of society towards which the poor of the world ought to strive? The current model of interaction and involvement by the rich nations with the poor, whether in political, military, economic, or educational terms, has almost always led to the rich getting richer and the increasing poverty of the poor. It is perhaps not too far-fetched, then, to suggest that Western-style economics, politics, values, and education should be rejected by Third and Fourth World nations.

The American, British, French, and Soviet educational systems and their copies in the poor nations of the world are based on a hierarchical, factory, product-oriented, and quality-controlled model of education. Whether such a model has worked for a modernized, technological society will not be debated here. That it has not worked and is not working in the traditional agricultural nations is all too evident. Carnoy suggests that "knowledge itself is colonized."[51] Although we and the Europeans no longer have colonies of our own, there are power elites in most nations who are more than willing to adopt an educational system which continues to perpetuate inequality and protect their positions. The schools become one of the major socializing agents in the shift from a traditional rural, agricultural existence to an urban, factory-oriented one, and these modern institutions are all too often controlled by multinational corporations. Is it any wonder that we support school systems throughout the world which promote domestic tranquility, profits, and a continued flow of the raw materials and manufactured goods to the United States, Europe, and the Soviet Union and the development of a society of consumers along Western lines?

Knowledge has become curricularized and the school is the only means by which the oppressed of this world are permitted to obtain the sacraments necessary for their own salvation. The poor are given an unequal chance in this colonized, curricularized lottery, which at best will only enslave them in an urban factory setting, little better and possibly worse than

[51] Martin Carnoy, *Education as Cultural Imperialism* (New York: David McKay Company, Inc., 1974), p. 3.

their traditional feudal farms. The poverty-stricken of the world seldom rebel, for they suffer from what Friere calls the "culture of silence" and a "pedagogy of oppression."[52] Individuals attempting to break the power of the controlled school systems and institute a pedagogy of liberation find themselves exiled or imprisoned by the power elites of their countries. Nations attempting to break away from the domination of their economies or educational systems by world powers soon find themselves blacklisted and open game for covert and overt pressures. The oppressive aspects of modern schooling have become too clear to many people throughout the world, and unless the United States and other powerful nations become cognizant of the role they play in educational colonialism, we shall become increasingly isolated and lose what international moral integrity we might still have.

THE INTERDEPENDENCE OF MANKIND

The problems listed earlier of population, energy, pollution, war and quality of life indicate the increasing interrelatedness of all nations. Marshall McLuhan heralded the new age in the title of his book *War and Peace in the Global Village*. No longer is mankind separated in time or in space, but we now live in the world of "all at onceness," in which we are not just observers of other men's tragedies and wars but participants. The same theme was struck by Kenneth Boulding who said that mankind no longer lives on an "illimitable plane," where there was always somewhere to go over the horizon and neither man's ignorance nor his armies could be considered a fatal flaw. Instead, we now find ourselves on a crowded and precarious spaceship which is being destroyed through lack of an appropriate organization, ethic, and conduct.[53] It is imperative that mankind recognize the nature of the global village and spaceship earth and the demands that such a changing concept puts on societies in general, and the schools in particular.

At one time it was possible for humanity to exist in small, separate, isolated cultures or nations. Such a possibility has been wiped out with the development of modern methods of warfare, our interdependence for raw materials and manufactured goods, and new forms of transportation and instantaneous communication.

Barbara Ward in her book *Spaceship Earth* summarizes the point:

[52]Paulo Friere, *Pedagogy of the Oppressed* (New York: The Seabury Press, 1970).
[53]Kenneth Boulding, "Education for the Spaceship Earth," *Social Education* (November, 1968), as quoted in David C. King, *International Education for Spaceship Earth*, Foreign Policy Association, 1971, pp. 135-37.

Most of the energies of our society tend towards unity. . . . We have become neighbors in terms of inescapable proximity and instant communication. We are neighbors in economic interest and technological direction. We are neighbors in the risk of total destruction.[54]

Traditionally the schools have emphasized the nation-state and the geographical differences between nations. Within the United States we have placed the emphasis upon the melting pot, and it is only recently that our society has moved towards cultural pluralism and an acceptance of diversity on a worldwide scale. Humanity must come to value differences in religion, race, language, culture, economic system, forms of government, and in that acceptance reach an understanding that will lead to a world of peace, freedom, and justice. In that process the role of the schools assumes great importance.

CASE STUDY: Education in the Third World

Place yourself in the position of the Minister of Education in a Third World nation. It is your duty to appear before the Cabinet and make a case for the educational system. In preparing your speech, you realize that you must deal with the following questions: What percentage of students will be enrolled in the formal educational system at the primary, secondary, and higher education levels? What type of informal educational programs do you propose for those who cannot obtain formal schooling and for the vast numbers of adult illiterates in the country? What mechanisms do you propose to prevent the continuation of the urban migration and make life in the rural villages better for the people? What type of education should be offered at each level in the formal schools? How much education do your teachers need and what should they be paid? Considering that the cost of living in the capital city is similar to that in the United States and Western Europe, you must somehow build schools, pay teachers, and pay for all the other parts of the educational system. What mechanisms do you propose to the Cabinet to save money and yet educate your people fairly and well?

THOUGHT QUESTIONS

1. Many poor nations see American and other international pressure on the part of the rich nations for birth control as a form of imperialism. Population control follows economic and social justice, it does not precede it, according to this view. If this position is right, and there appears to be some evidence to back it up, what can be done to prevent mass starvation from

---

[54]Barbara Ward, *Spaceship Earth* (New York: Columbia University Press, 1966), p. 14.

overpopulation in the years while the poor nations are "catching up" economically?

2. What are ways in which birth-control information can and should be advanced within the schools and the rest of the society?

3. Should people have the right to breed without limit, or should national and/or international controls be instituted?

4. The Green Revolution, which only a few years ago was seen as the solution to humanity's problems of feeding itself, has sputtered to a halt as a result of values differences, lack of capital, poor water control, inadequate land reform, and inequitable farm wages. What role can the educational systems of the world play in these areas, so that the promise of "miracle grains" can be at least partially realized?

5. With the United States consuming many times its "share" of the world's energy and resources, what can the schools contribute to resolving questions of consumption and environmental pollution? What societal, economic, and political changes might be necessary in the future to deal with problems of overconsumption?

6. In what ways have the schools been part of the "military-industrial" complex? Can education for peace ever really succeed, given the history of man's violence towards other individuals and nations? What practical steps do you see which can be taken?

7. With the vast amounts of wealth in the world, and the unequal distribution among rich and poor individuals and nations, what can be done to bring about a greater balance? What values support the superiority of the rich over the poor? Can and should the schools attempt to change those values?

8. Many questions of environmental concern also have tremendous economic implications. From your own experience, describe a case involving some problem of environmental concern which affected the lives, jobs, and economic security of a sizable group of people .How was the issue resolved? How might it have better been resolved?

9. Rank-order the "values" which you consider to be the controlling ones in your life. Do any of yours conflict with others? Do they conflict with any in the society at large? In what ways do we as individuals regulate our conflicts? In what ways can and should societies regulate their conflicts?

10. In what sense can it be stated that the schools in the Third World perpetuate elites, promote the status quo, and socialize their citizens into a Westernized value system?

PRACTICAL ACTIVITIES

1. Talk with Peace Corp recruiters when they visit your campus, or inquire at the National Action/Peace Corps office concerning a teaching position in another country.

2. Compare the U.S. system of education with that found in one of the other "developed" nations of the world. What percentage of young people attend high school and college in each society? What are some of the similarities and differences in curriculum and organization? Which system is more egalitarian or elitist?

3. Study the curriculum of a local school district for evidence of "internationalization." Look at course titles, units, short courses, textbooks, and the training which teachers have had. Look for evidence of ethnocentrism or a Western bias in the curriculum. In particular, deal with the war/peace emphases in textbooks, teaching materials, and other aspects of the curriculum.

4. Design an educational system for a developing nation which takes into consideration the following realities: a high adult illiteracy rate; extreme poverty; a dictatorial government of the right; other budget priorities besides education; a poorly educated teaching staff; a dependence upon agriculture in the nation's economy; a lack of other communication facilities, i.e., roads, radio, and television.

5. From your observations of the community in which you live, your own background, an analysis of the media (radio, TV, advertising, newspapers, and magazines), and any other relevant materials, what appear to be the dominant values of American society? and are these compatible with the ecological dilemmas and possible catastrophes facing modern man?

BIBLIOGRAPHY

international education

BECKER, JAMES B., AND HOWARD D. MEHLINGER, eds., *International Dimensions in the Social Studies*. Washington, D.C.: National Council for the Social Studies, 1968.

BEREDAY, GEORGE Z. F., AND JOSEPH LAUWERYS, eds., *Education and International Life*. New York: Harcourt, Brace & World, 1964.

EVERETT, SAMUEL, AND C. O. ARNDT, *Teaching World Affairs in American Schools*. New York: Harper & Row Publishers, 1956.

SHANE, HAROLD G., ed., *The United States and International Education*. Chicago: University of Chicago Press, 1969.

TAYLOR, HAROLD, *World as Teacher*. New York: Doubleday & Co., Inc., 1969.

WILCOCK, J. B., ed., "Preparing Teachers for Education for International Understanding." New York: UNESCO Publications, 1964.

comparative education

CARNOY, MARTIN, *Education as Cultural Imperialism*. New York: David McKay Company, Inc., 1974.

COOMBS, PHILIP H., *The World Educational Crisis: A Systems Analysis*. New York: Oxford University Press, 1968.
FRIERE, PAULO, *Pedagogy of the Oppressed*. New York: The Seabury Press, 1970.
ILLICH, IVAN, *Deschooling Society*. New York: Harper & Row Publishers, 1971.

14

FUTURES
SOCIETAL AND EDUCATIONAL

Society will be transformed from the "primary" or agricultural level to the "secondary" or industrial level to the "tertiary" level—that of a "learning society."[1]

As a species, humankind is unique in several respects, one of which is the ability to transport itself mentally from present to past to future. To understand fully oneself and one's world, requires that perspectives from the past and future both converge on the present. Conjectures of the future are partly factual and partly imaginative, a combination of extrapolation and intuition.

Education also is influenced by concepts of time—as in the use of instructional and learning objectives, the administrative emphasis on planning and policy studies, the tradition of relying on "olders" to be the teachers of "youngers," and the custom of grouping students by age for instruction. Most of all, education is cumulative and antientropic; it is cumulative both in the residue retained by the individual and in the collective value to society of diversely educated individuals; it is antientropic in that the knowledge created in the process is an energy source (actual and metaphorical) equal to if not greater than the energy expended to create it.

Knowledge seekers are time travelers, in the sense that learning is a

---

[1] M. S. Iyengar, "Can We Transform Into a Post-Industrial Society?", in Alvin Toffler, ed., *The Futurists* (New York: Random House, Inc., 1972), pp. 190–191.

process, a "continuous reconstruction of experience," to use John Dewey's phrase. Learning is an integration of past experience with one's present condition, together with the potential for future applications. For the teachers of children and adolescents, the future is the broad realm in which their clients will spend 80 or 90 percent of their lives. The students of the young teacher in the late 1970s will probably experience more than half of the twenty-first century.

The twenty-first century will require a crucial attitude for the survivors aboard Earth: to view the human condition from a global perspective. More and more, one's immediate, local needs and concerns are inextricably entwined with those of other human beings in many other places on the planet. The energy crisis can be viewed as a practice round for other immanent cases of global confrontation, all signaling the advent of the era of global interdependence.

A FRAMEWORK OF THE FUTURE

If we wish to enter the twenty-first century in advance of its arrival, we not only need to acquire a global orientation, but we need a framework and

Figure 14-1   Spaceship Earth: What Is Its Future?

384 ALTERNATIVE, GLOBAL, AND FUTURE PERSPECTIVES

some tools for probing the future. Further, since our special interest is the future of education, and since education is but one societal institution, we need to look to both national and global futures for clues about education's future. Finally, because biological and technological inventions and discoveries tend to affect all social institutions, we need to see what effects and applications these have in education.

As a framework for approaching the future, we use as a model a three-sided pyramid or tetrahedron (Figure 14-2). The base of the pyramid represents the infrastructure of the future—current and emerging values and attitudes that form the consciousness base for the present and the future. The visible side on the left represents current and emerging state of knowledge, including technology. The visible side on the right represents current and projected problems, crises, and those fears which tend to incapacitate or immobilize. Then there is the invisible side of the pyramid, hidden by the exigencies of the present and the placid appeal of a once-secure past. This unseen side is the future, partly known and determined by emergent aspects of the base and two visible sides, and partly at the mercy of our intuition and caprice, but still amenable to human intervention, to plans, and to self-fulfilling and self-defeating prophecies.

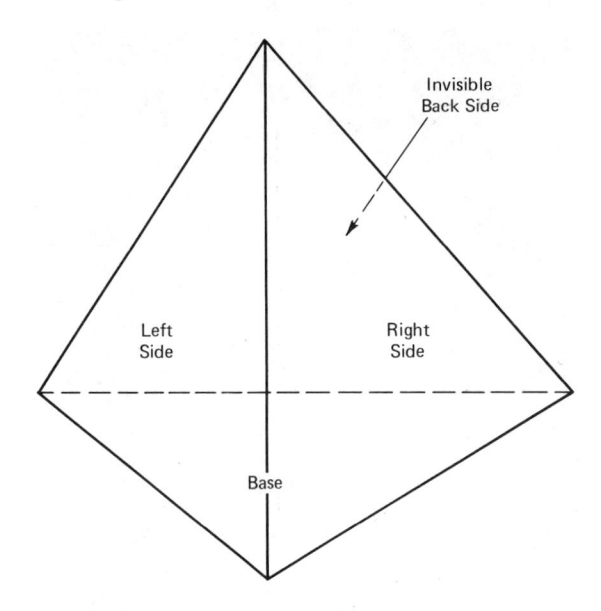

Figure 14-2 A Framework of the Future

Base = Current and Emerging Ideologies, Values and Attitudes
Left Side = Current and Emerging Knowledge, Technology
Right Side = Current and Emerging Problems, Crises and Fears
Back Side = The Future: "Known" and Unknown

CURRENT AND EMERGING VALUES

A society is constructed on a base of shared common values and an ideological view of human nature and human society. All societies possess a values/ideology infrastructure, which is in a state of relative stability and flux. By this is meant that a society's values/ideology base is constantly evolving, the pace varying from nearly stable to revolutionary change. When the pace is rapid, one observes (1) a set of dominant values on which the present society is based, and (2) a different set of emergent values, among which are those values upon which the future society will be built. Thus, in the United States today, there are present a set of traditional, dominant values *and* a set of emergent, future values. Of course, any society of the future—national or global in nature—will reflect a synthesis of *both* traditional and emergent values, and not a total substitution of emergent values for traditional ones. Even cataclysmic social upheavals, such as those which occurred in Russia (1917) and China (1949), do not eliminate completely the values that prevailed prior to the revolutions. The general principle is that since values are broad cultural-meaning patterns, they are relatively stable. Even at the threshold of the 1980s, in the United States and in Western nations in general, even in the midst of rapid technological change and knowledge growth, the values/ideology base of a culture, a society, a nation remains relatively stable.

"The unity of a culture consists in the fact that all valuations are mutually shared in some degree."[2] In the United States today, in the face of new, emerging values, and despite the rhetoric of "cultural pluralism," a cement of shared values binds individuals and groups to the commonwealth, to the national society.

In his classic study, *An American Dilemma*, Gunnar Myrdal called this body of mutually shared values an "American Creed."[3] What this creed is comprised of, however, is difficult to determine. Myrdal only alludes to the tenets of the "creed," without ever attempting a formal analysis. For him, the "creed" embodies a group of ideals: "the essential dignity of the individual human being, . . . the fundamental equality of all men, . . . certain inalienable rights to freedom, justice, and a fair opportunity"; a concept of democracy elucidated in the Declaration of Independence, the Preamble of the Constitution, the Constitution, and the Bill of Rights; Woodrow Wilson's fourteen points and Franklin Roosevelt's four freedoms; "a humanistic liberalism developing out of the epoch of Enlightenment"; the perfectibility of man, reliance on the will of the majority, the use of several processes by which the consent of the governed is obtained. All of these rested

---

[2]Gunnar Myrdal, *An American Dilemma* (New York: Harper and Brothers, 1944), p. xlviii.
[3]Ibid., p. lxvi.

upon the foundations of rationality, science as method, and democracy—the American trinity. Myrdal asserted that "the main norms of the American Creed as usually pronounced are centered in the belief in equality and in the rights to liberty."[4]

American society derived the "creed," in Myrdal's judgment, from at least three sources: (1) the eighteenth-century philosphy of the Enlightenment, (2) the Judeo-Christian tradition and moral code, and (3) the principles embedded in English law. The Enlightenment provided the concepts of perfectibility, rationality, science as method, and democratic nationalism. From the Judeo-Christian tradition, especially from European Protestantism, came the ideas of individualism, bourgeois capitalism, and freedom or free will. Finally, English law yielded political democracy, the "principles of justice, equity, and equality before the law," and the "concept of a government 'of laws and not of men.'"[5]

We have generated our own list of traditional value orientations which seem to us to undergird American society:

1. Values of the Puritan/Protestant Ethic
   a. self-denial and endurance of distress
   b. deferred gratification
   c. sex taboos or sexual constraints
   d. thrift
   e. striving to achieve/hard work yields success
   f. punctuality
   g. self-control
   h. "survival of the fittest" (the elect of God)
   i. volunteerism and charity
2. Values of Capitalism
   a. unlimited demands (wants) with limited supply leads to scarcity
   b. competitiveness
   c. profit motive
   d. contrived demand or "invention is the mother of necessity"
   e. social class distinctions based primarily on wealth
   f. materialism, acquisitiveness, and conspicuous consumption
   g. meritocratic hiring and promotion
   h. desire for upward socio-economic mobility and fear of downward mobility
   i. protection of private property ownership rights
3. Values of Democracy
   a. enhancement of human dignity
   b. rational consent of the governed
   c. majority rule
   d. constitutional guarantees of individual and minority rights and of "due process"
   e. freedom or liberty or independence
   f. equality and equity
   g. conjoint living

[4]Ibid., pp. 4–8.
[5]Ibid., pp. 8–12.

4. Values of American Nationalism
   a. patriotic loyalty
   b. parochialism and exlusionary attitudes
   c. territoriality and desire for hegemony
   d. preference for monolingualism (English)
   e. friendship, paternalism, arrogance, or animosity toward other nations.
5. Values of Western Philosophy
   a. rationalism
   b. empiricism
   c. scientism
   d. dualistic analysis
   e. humanism
   f. reductionism and quantification

Since the 1960s, many observers of American society have noticed value shifts occurring among adolescents and young adults. Such shifts may presage a new, emerging value base for the total society. One could view these challenges and alternatives to traditional values as the first, tentative, experimental manifestations of an emergent ethic. This gradual movement from traditional to emergent values seems to have the following general directional flows:

From	*To*
self-denial, endurance of distress, and deferred gratification	pursuit of immediate pleasures or hedonism
sexual taboos and constraints	sexual permissiveness and openness
self-control; striving to achieve, or hard work yields success	self-actualization and self-expressiveness; acceptance and expression of feelings; self-realization
"survival of the fittest"	"survival of the wisest"; the individual's survival is entwined with species, global survival
progress equated with growth; promotion of increased consumption and number of consumers	limits to growth; search for ecological balances; stress on qualitative, rather than quantitative aspects of progress
competitiveness; a win-lose, either-or attitude	cooperation; conflict resolution and reduction; win-win attitude
materialism, acquisitiveness, and conspicuous consumption	focus on essentials; greater desire for quality and durability of goods
social class distinctions based primarily on wealth	greater concern for equality and equity; class distinctions based on multiple criteria (de-emphasis on accumulated wealth) which will tend to blur class lines
preoccupation with private property ownership rights	increasing pressures to insure basic human rights—nationally and globally; greater concern for "the commons" which are shared collectively (e.g., water, parks, air, neighborhoods)

From	To
government by isolated elected officials in state and national capitals	government by association, involvement, and participation of the entire citizenry; increased interest-groups pressures
nationalism; exclusive national sovereignties as loci of loyalties; independence of nation-states	world order models; transnational economic groupings as bases for regional political groupings (e.g., European Common Market); regional and world federalisms; interdependence of nations
freedom or liberty or independence; individualism	mutuality of concern; cooperative processes; greater attention to interpersonal relations and quality of conjoint living
rationalism, empiricism, scientism, dualistic analysis, reductionism, and quantification	renewed reliance on faith and feeling; practice of meditative modes; global humanism; blending of Taoist and Buddhist world views with those of Judeo-Christian tradition; abandoning the search for value-free knowledge; greater trust in all human ways of knowing

Pointing to three obsolescent premises upon which the industrial-state era is based (as contrasted with pre- and postindustrial eras), O. W. Markley suggests that the coming postindustrial society era will require a new "image of mankind." The outworn premises are (1) "that human progress is synonymous with economic growth and increasing consumption," (2) "that mankind is separate from nature, and that it is the human destiny to conquer nature," and (3) "that economic efficiency and scientific reductionism are the most trustworthy approaches to fulfillment of the goals of humanity."[6]

For Markley, "an adequate image of mankind for the postindustrial future" would possess six conditions:

> 1) an *ecological ethic*, emphasizing the total community of life-in-nature and the oneness of the human race, 2) a *self-realization ethic* . . ., 3) be *multi-leveled, multi-faceted*, and *integrative*, suiting various culture and personality types, 4) [provide for the] *balancing and coordination of satisfactions* along many dimensions rather than . . . along one narrowly defined dimension such as the economic, 5) convey a *holistic* sense of perspective . . . , [and] 6) be *experimental, open-minded*, and *evolutionary*.[7]

Lester Brown believes that "the sixties witnessed a quickening of the social conscience of people" over such issues as war (particularly Vietnam),

[6]O. W. Markley, *Changing Images of Man* (Melno Park, Calif.: Stanford Research Institute, Center for the Study of Social Policy, Policy Research Report #4, May, 1974), pp. vii–viii.
[7]Ibid., p. ix.

racism, sexism, overpopulation, poverty, and hunger—issues calling for empathy and political action. This social concern led to the formation of new values, especially among the young of all nations, and as a result "a new ethic may be emerging."[8]

For Brown, this "new ethic encompasses a new naturalism [emphasizing] harmony with nature. . . ," a recognition of "the finiteness of our biosphere . . . , a new childbearing ethic" in response to threats to our "very life-support systems . . ., [and] one designed to eventually stabilize population . . ., a much greater emphasis on distribution and sharing" of the world's material wealth and technology, the attitude that "I am my brother's keeper" in order "to eliminate territorial discrimination" as well as "religious, racial, and sexual discriminations . . ., [a broadening of] the social scope of decision making . . . [by being] much more cooperative, acting in terms consistent with the collective welfare . . .," and the expansion of loyalties "to include all mankind."[9]

Dorothy Skeel's study "How Do Children Rank Their Values?" revealed that "sixth grade children in varying geographic areas and subcultural groups across the United States do not have difficulty in deciding what values are most important to them. Nor do they show any apparent misunderstanding in the meanings of those values." The composite rankings for all subjects in the study appear in Table 14-1. "Terminal" values and "instrumental" values were defined in this study as: *terminal—* "preferred end states of existence that people strive for"; *instrumental—* "preferred modes of behavior."[10]

What was also significant in the Skeel study "is the low correlation between what teachers value and what children in all geographic areas and subcultural groups value. Is this low correlation a result of the age difference, the fact that the adults have thought through their values or had them challenged, or are values changing?"[11]

CURRENT AND EMERGING KNOWLEDGE

For over two million years our human ancestors have been learning, and, more significantly, accumulating knowledge for the use of each successive generation. Moreover, *Homo sapiens* has employed an ever-widening range of ways of knowing, of methods of creating relatively reliable knowledge. In our search for knowledge, we stand on the shoulders of those who

[8]Lester R. Brown, "Issues of Human Welfare," in Robert Bundy, ed., *Images of the Future* (Buffalo, N.Y.: Prometheus Books, 1976), p. 91.
[9]Ibid., pp. 91–94.
[10]Dorothy J. Skeel, "How Do Children Rank Their Values?" *Bulletin of the School of Education at Indiana University*, 52, no. 1 (January, 1976), pp. 55–72.
[11]Ibid., p. 61.

Table 14-1 Rankings of Terminal and Instrumental Values for All Children's Groups[11] (N=312)

Rank	Terminal Values	Rank	Instrumental Values
8	a comfortable life (a prosperous life)	8	ambitious (hard working, aspiring)
6	an exciting life (a stimulating, active life)	14	broadminded (open minded)
16	a sense of accomplishment (lasting contribution)	15	capable (competent, effective)
1	a world of peace (free of war and conflict)	5	cheerful (light-hearted, joyful)
7	a world of beauty (beauty of nature and the arts)	3	clean (neat, tidy)
11	equality (brotherhood, equal opportunity for all)	11	courageous (standing up for your beliefs)
2	family security (taking care of loved ones)	7	forgiving (willing to pardon others)
3	freedom (independence, free choice)	4	helpful (working for the welfare of others)
5	happiness (contentedness)	1	honest (sincere, truthful)
17	inner harmony (freedom from inner conflict)	17	imaginative (daring)
12	mature love (sexual and spiritual intimacy)	13	independent (self-reliant, self-sufficient)
15	national security (protection from attack)	16	intellectual (intelligent, reflective)
9	pleasure (an enjoyable, leisurely life)	18	logical (consistent, rational)
10	salvation (saved, eternal life)	2	loving (affectionate, tender)
13	self-respect (self-esteem)	12	obedient (dutiful, respectful)
18	social recognition (respect, admiration)	6	polite (courteous, well-mannered)
4	true friendship (close companionship)	10	responsible (dependable, reliable)
14	wisdom (a mature understanding of life)	0	self-controlled (restrained, self-disciplined)

Dorothy J. Skeel, "How Do Children Rank Their Values?" *Bulletin of the School of Education at Indiana University*, 52, no. 1 (January, 1976), pp. 59–63.

have preceded us. And this will also be true for those who succeed us.

This is not to say that all paradigms and models of knowledge and all ways of knowing are already known. Knowledge growth occurs *both* by evolutionary development and by revolutionary "leaps," "shifts," discoveries, or inventions.

What we as a species know at any point in time cannot be known or comprehended by any one human being or computer. Our collective knowledge is stored in a variety of respositories: books and other visual media, libraries, cultural technologies (e.g., a factory or a corporation), specialists in academic disciplines (e.g., physicists or linguists), and an individual's genes, mind, unconscious, and feelings. Our contributions to and uses of species knowledge must always be specific, partial, and selective, even though we may seek more simplified, generalized, and comprehensive understanding. Furthermore, each human society in each of its historical areas "chooses" a focus for its efforts in producing and using knowledge. It selects certain arenas for investigation and prefers certain modes of inquiry, procedures, techniques, or methodologies. This selectivity derives primarily from the economic, political, and other needs of a society in a particular stage of development. Thus, in a preindustrial society such as ancient Egypt, the primary arenas for the creation of new knowledge were in agriculture, religion, religion-related architecture, and military science, and the chief creators of knowledge were the clergy and the governmental aristocracy. Or, in the case of a Western industrial society such as the United States in the nineteenth century, the knowledge created from both basic and applied research was mainly in fields related to industrialization and corporate capitalism, such as physics, chemistry, metallurgy, mechanical engineering, medical science and technology, and especially that peculiarly American province of physical/mechanical inventions by tinkerer-inventors.

In general, we can conclude that knowledge is appropriate and sufficient to a particular time and place, to the survival of a people; and yet its nature is to continually be incomplete, to always challenge human beings to extend its alterable frontiers, to steer its growth and flow in those directions most useful to a society's images of the future.

In industrialized, technologized societies like the United States, the premises underlying the creation of knowledge are probably either almost obsolete or inappropriate for postindustrial societies. Drawing on the work of James Conant, Markley lists these "outdated" axioms:

> Reason is the supreme tool of man.
> Knowledge, acquired through the use of reason, will free mankind from ignorance and will lead to a better future.
> The universe is inherently orderly and physical.
> This order can be discovered by science and objectively expressed.
> Only science deals in empirically verifiable truth.
> Observation and experimentation are the only valid means of discovering scientific truth, which is always independent of the observer.[12]

In the 1960s and 1970s, one or more of these premises has been called into question by several philosophers and social scientists. Herbert Marcuse insisted that sole reliance on the rational-scientific mode led to "one-dimensional" beings, while Theodore Roszak described the "wasteland" created by dependence on scientific and technological world views, and applauded the movement toward a counter-culture which could lead to a new, balanced, holistic conceptions of knowing and knowledge.[13,14,15]

---

[12]Markley, *Changing Images*, pp. 82–83.
[13]Herbert Marcuse, *One-Dimensional Man* (Boston, Mass.: Beacon Press, 1964).
[14]Theodore Roszak, *Where the Wasteland Ends* (Garden City, N.Y.: Doubleday & Company, Inc., 1972).
[15]Theodore Roszak, *The Making of a Counter Culture* (Garden City, N.Y.: Doubleday & Company, Inc., 1969).

Questions have been raised about the claims to knowledge of such "mystical" methods and conceptualizations as meditation, Gestalt psychologies, extrasensory perception, Zen and Yoga techniques, intuition, and feelings-as-truth. Criticisms abound on the proliferation of specialized disciplines, the creation of discipline-specific technical terms, and the reductionist tendency to fragment wholes by analysis. Also, "recent developments on numerous fronts [have challenged] the idea that the objective world explored by the various scientific probes is essentially separate from and independent of the subjective experience of the investigator."[16]

Factors affecting knowing and the known in the future will probably include (1) the creation of new knowledge based on current assumptions and paradigms, (2) the emergence of new paradigms and models which incorporate subjective experience, values, and other elusive dimensions, (3) the development of new procedures for "discovering" knowledge, among which are policy research and forecasting skills, and (4) new technological inventions, some mere amplifications of present systems, and probably a few startlingly new ones.

the frontiers of knowledge

When physicists learned during the first two decades of the twentieth century that light took the forms of particle and wave, they then knew that paradox and uncertainty had reemerged as ingredients of their science. In a sense, electrons were found to be both there and not there, to be both trace and geometric pattern. The universe began to become more mind than material, more idea than matter, more dynamic than static, until

> now we know that we are part of an immense galaxy [the Milky Way] of about 100,000 million stars, arranged in a disc-shaped spiral 100,000 light years in diameter, about three-fifths of the way out from the center of the disc, and moving further out at a mere 35 kilometers per second, [toward] the "edge" of the universe . . . now billions of light years away and full of strange wonders: quasars, pulsars, and black holes; and even stranger, though logical, postulates of antimatter, time flowing backwards, negative mass, and particles travelling faster than the speed of light. . . . Modern physics and cosmology have placed the human in a universe inestimably more rich and extraordinary than the mechanical vision ever prepared him for . . . ; the cosmic man of modern physics bears strong resemblance to the image of man-in-universe of Eastern philosophies.[17]

In the biological sciences, the more promising search has to do with population, ecosystems, cellular, molecular and atomic levels of analysis, developmental-evolutionary factors and patterns, and extraterrestrial organisms. Or consider the implications of cryogenics (ultra low temperature

[16]Markley, *Changing Images*, p. 92.
[17]Ibid., pp. 93–96.

effects), of recombining the structures of DNA molecules to modify the nature of existing organisms or species or to create new organisms, and of cloning or the capacity to replicate organisms.

Then there is brain research. In regard to the effects of biochemical substances on the mind, Kenneth Clark suggests:

> We might be on the threshold of that type of scientific, biochemical intervention which could stabilize and make dominant the moral and ethical propensities of man and subordinate, if not eliminate, his negative and primitive tendencies.[18]

Also in this category is split-brain research, which focuses on the differing functions of the left and right hemispheres of the brain. Tentative conclusions point to the left side of the brain as being "analytic and reductionist," while the right side is "more holistic and integrative."[19]

Another area of increased scientific interest is "in the ways altered states of awareness can affect perception, thinking, feelings, and behavior."[20] This research probes consciousness "indirectly" through the use of such indicators as hypnosis, biofeedback training, dreams and dreaming, meditation or relaxation training, psychedelic drugs, and subliminal stimulation.[21]

new paradigms or models of knowledge

Willis Harman forecasts that by 1994 we will have a new knowledge model or pattern.

> The new knowledge paradigm will be hospitable to some sort of systematization of subjective experience, the domain which has heretofore largely been left to non-science—the humanities and religion. Science will include the study of those experiences from which we derive our basic value commitments.... Thus the paradigm will allow a much more unified view of human experiences now categorized under such diverse headings as "creativity," "intuition," "mysticism," "psychic phenomena," "religious experience."—The new paradigm will also permit a more unified view of the processes of personal change and development which take place within the contexts of psychotherapy, education, "growth centers," religion, and crisis confrontation.[22]

Difficult as it is for students and scholars to accept, it seems an inescapable conclusion that the current modes of organizing knowledge by

---

[18]Ibid., p. 106.
[19]Ibid., p. 107.
[20]Ibid., p. 111.
[21]Ibid., pp. 111–121.
[22]Willis W. Harman, "The Coming Transformation in Our View of Knowledge," *The Futurist*, 8, no. 3 (June, 1974), pp. 126–28.

separate, specialized academic disciplines will not be appropriate for the future. If the construct "quality of life" is the focus for investigation, it is clear that no single academic specialty is sufficient to comprehend and inquire into such an all-encompassing concept. What is called for is a multi- or interdisciplinary approach, or the creation of one or more new, comprehensive, integrating fields of study.

Only dim clues exist to point our way toward holistic approaches. Some potentially rewarding directions are general systems theory and the principles of cybernetics; general semantics and the search for a metalanguage; zetetics or the study of the ways human beings create knowledge, their modes of inquiry; the advancement of policy studies and research, or the process of individual, group, and mass problem-solving and decision-making; the relationships among high-level concepts such as growth, number, time, form, space, entropy, love, beauty, and goodness; and the study of "limiting" principles such as uncertainty, coincidence, paradox, and unpredictability (or synergy).[23]

the frontiers of technology

The technological base of a culture comprises the tools and techniques used to carry out the functions of the culture's social institutions. As was mentioned in Chapter 5, these social institutions are the family, the educational system, the economy, the political system, the health and welfare system, and the religious or moral system. By defining a culture's technology as a collection of tools and techniques, we emphasize that technology embodies both physical, material objects (a set of tools), *and* processes, procedures, and organizational structures (a set of techniques). Such a definition suggests that an automobile, a factory, and a corporation are all technological inventions, as are solid state circuitry, Congress, voting and elections, jet airplanes and space satellites, computers and computer programs, schools, school district bureaucracies, and school curricula. Technology includes "hardware" and "software," that is, machines and processes, e.g., a teaching machine and the substantive lessons programmed into it.

That the existing state of technological development in industrialized nations causes ambivalence among both leaders and citizens is an indication that technological advance is a mixed blessing. We enjoy the convenience provided by cars and jet planes, but not the pollution and energy drain associated with their use. We admire the precision and efficiency of automated tasks, but not the resultant worker alienation, job insecurity, and increased unemployment. We applaud the discovery of miracle drugs and the procedures and inventions that make organ transplants possible, but then shrink from the concomitant problems of an aging population. We are com-

---

[23]John D. Haas, "For Lack of a Loom: Problems in Integrating Knowledge," *School Science and Mathematics*, 75, no. 1 (January, 1975), pp. 4–14.

ing to suspect that further technological development may threaten our quality of life, may cancel many of our material and physical comforts, and may even jeopardize our individual and collective mental health.

Often our naive faith in the gadget, the machine leads us to expect miraculous discoveries and inventions to appear in timely fashion and save us from the brink of disaster. Or conversely, we may become so jaded with the trends in technology that our cynicism blinds us to possible shifts toward a more benign and humane technology. Neither of these outlooks is particularly helpful for coping with either the development or control of technology, now or in the future. Perhaps a more useful attitude toward future technological developments should combine hope and cautiousness, with a questioning hesitation that asks, What will the discovery or invention mean for a definition of being human, what impact will it have on global interdependence and quality of life, what will it mean for human relations at all levels from the interpersonal to the intersocietal, and what will it mean for the long-term survival of the species?

By the twenty-first century, we can expect a new, vast array of technological products and processes. Some will be expected and some unexpected; some will be hardware and some software; and, most significantly, some will have limited, inconsequential effects on human conditions of living, but some will have profound implications for the quality of life on earth. Following are *some* of the technologies that today's forecasters envision:[24]

1. There will be improvements in the type and use of contraceptives for fertility control. Oral and male contraceptives will be perfected. National and international fertility control programs will be implemented.

2. Continuing progress in medical science (e.g., prosthetic devices, surgical procedures, vaccines), will allow U.S. citizens to expect an average 100-year life span. Improvements in cryogenics could make possible longer, interrupted life spans.

3. Pharmacology will develop a number of nonnarcotic and nonaddictive personality modification and control drugs. Also, there will be drugs to enhance intelligence and learning.

4. Weapons research will grow apace with the more benign technologies, producing *both* lethal and incapacitating biochemical weapons. (A weapon on the drawing board even in the late 1970s is the neutron bomb, which kills human beings but doesn't destroy buildings.)

5. New generations of computers and new computer applications will be developed, including home computer terminals and new versions of computer-assisted instruction.

6. Artificial forms of life will be created as outcomes of research on self-replicating molecules, recombinant DNA, and procedures for cloning.

7. Genetic control products and procedures will be developed that will eliminate

---

[24]This far from comprehensive list is adapted from and expanded on Olaf Helmer, "Simulating the Values of the Future," in Kurt Baier and Nicholas Rescher, eds., *Values and the Future* (New York: The Free Press), pp. 202–204, and Herman Kahn and Anthony J. Wiener, "The Next Thirty-Three Years: A Framework for Speculation," in Daniel Bell and others, *Toward the Year 2000: Work in Progress* (Boston, Mass.: American Academy of Arts and Sciences, 1967), pp. 705–732.

many hereditary defects and allow for "choices" by prospective parents of a range of hereditary human characteristics for their planned offspring. Also, ova/sperm banks will be established.

8. Household robots will be created, first to do just a few simple tasks, and then many complex chores.

9. Space exploration of our galaxy and solar system will continue, with a manned landing on Mars and a space colony established equidistant from Earth and its moon to collect solar energy and transmit it to Earth.

10. There will be improvements in and increased use of nuclear energy—both fission and fusion reactors. Other energy sources will be investigated for availability and economic feasibility: sources such as geothermal and solar energy, wind, and evaporation.

CURRENT AND EMERGING PROBLEMS, CRISES, AND FEARS

The second visible side of the "framework of the future" pyramid comprises the problems, crises, and fears now being faced by humankind; and also the barely visible emergent issues which will likely impinge on us in the near future. Both current and emerging social problems grow out of the imbalances and excesses of the industrial era in human socio-politico-economic development, and also out of the dislocations and uncertainties of the transition to a postindustrial society.

At present, the most industrially and technologically developed (some would say "overdeveloped") nations, the United States, Soviet Union, Japan, and almost all nations of Western Europe, are in various stages of transition from an *industrial* to a *postindustrial* society. These nations have already evolved through their preindustrial eras and nearly through their industrial eras, and have begun to encounter the problems of advanced industrialization and the first symptoms of postindustrial development. Basically, a preindustrial society is one that relies on agriculture and manual labor for its survival; an industrial society combines manufacturing with farming, but both rely heavily on technology and industrial organization and process; and a postindustrial society is one where farming and manufacturing are largely technologically automated, and where human occupations have changed from goods-producing types to service-providing and knowledge-producing types.

In essence, the transition from industrial to postindustrial society is a change from maximizing growth and quantitative factors to optimizing growth (which may mean stability or even some decreases) and emphasizing qualitative factors. Industrial nations have become expert at "doing," which has led to excesses. The new society will require expertise in "undoing" and in "doing well."[25]

[25]Bertrand de Jouvenel, "On Attending to the Future," in William R. Ewald, Jr., ed., *Environment and Change* (Bloomington, Ind.: Indiana University Press, 1968), p. 24.

In this period of transition for Western nations, the developing or less developed nations will be affected mainly by the problems of attempting to accelerate industrialization (with limited capital and resources, and often in the face of overpopulation) and by the effects on their population of comparisons between the quality of life in their nations and that in the most developed nations. Such comparisons, of course, may yield envy and demands for redistribution of wealth and resources, but also they may lead to the wisdom to avoid many of the problems of the more "advanced" societies. Few nations, however, will avoid the traumas of transition which in the late twentieth century plague those nations moving toward a postindustrial era.

In addition to the overall movement of developing nations toward industrial development and of developed nations toward postindustrial society, a number of other conditions contribute to late twentieth-century crises, problems, and fears. Worldwide urbanization brings overcrowding, unemployment, and disillusionment. The modern nation-state, in order to deal with intranational and international interdependence, complexity, and conflict, tends toward the centralization of authority and decision-making, in turn alienating citizens from their government making them feel less and less able to influence public decisions. Social problems become more and more complex, involving dozens and even hundreds of related factors, and calling for considerable expertise to arrive at feasible, desirable solutions. And each problem is never totally solved, but leads to a new problem, setting in motion a problem-solution-new problem sequence that seems to go on forever. These conditions tend almost to overwhelm many citizens and even some leaders, too often stimulating feelings of hopelessness and helplessness.

The increasing pace of change characteristic of this century, especially the rapid accumulation of scientific and technological knowledge, creates the twin plagues of human obsolescense and fear of the future. These diseases are further complicated by the intrinsically dangerous nature of many new technologies: the overkill potential of nuclear weapons, the potential thermal and radiation effects of fission and fusion nuclear reactors, the potentially destructive effects of many biological and chemical products, and the threats to human values of techniques of "mind control," genetic engineering, and imposition of order.[26]

Historical accident, timely inventions, and exploitation of readily available, inexpensive natural resources (including human labor) have enabled some nations to develop economically, technologically, and industrially more than other nations. These uneven growth patterns have also been affected by such factors as how much devastation a nation experienced in war, and how it was hindered or enhanced by its status as a colony

[26] Herman Kahn and Anthony J. Wiener, "Faustian Powers and Human Choices: Some Twenty-First Century Technolgical and Economic Issues," in Ewald, *Environment and Change*, pp. 101–131.

or as an imperial power. Clearly, twentieth-century colonialism and imperialism are more economic than political or military. All these historical and contemporary forces have led to unequal distribution of wealth (both within and among nations); unequal access to education, medical care, natural resources, leisure, and food; and differential distribution of overpopulation (within as well as among nations).[27]

World citizens will undoubtedly continue to face a myriad of sociopolitico-economic problems, virtually all solvable only partially or by spawning new problems. Among problems likely to persist past the end of the twentieth century on a worldwide scale, in the developed or developing nations are

1. starvation, hunger and inadequate nutrition,
2. depletion of natural resources, such as arable land, water, air, and fossil fuels,
3. inequality of material wealth and natural resources within and among nations
4. national, regional and local overpopulation
5. threats of nuclear war, threats of wars of "acquisition" (by the rich nations for natural resources or markets for goods), and wars of "redistribution" (by the poor nations to obtain wealth, natural resources, or food),
6. death due to plagues, other diseases, and inadequate medical care,
7. crime and other violations of property and human rights,
8. shortages of many kinds, including energy, medicines, fertilizers, and an array of "necessary" and "unnecessary" products and services,
9. credibility gaps: between political leaders and scientific experts on the one hand and the citizenry on the other,
10. illiteracy and its opposites—overeducation and overspecialization,
11. an increase in specific psychoses and neuroses, including fear of the future, insecurity, and hopelessness.

There are other problems, however, which differ in kind from those in the above list. These we call "consciousness problems," such as:

1. lack of a comparable substitute vision for waning Western secularism, Judaism, Christianity, Marxism, humanism, and primitivism,
2. racism, sexism, elitism, ethnocentrism, nationalism, chauvinism, and paternalism,
3. lack of global and future orientations or predispositions,
4. overemphasis on competitiveness, unbridled individualism, and hedonistic presentism,
5. lack of replacements for the presently prevailing concepts of "ascending progress," "self-evident superiority," and "unlimited growth,"
6. need to harmonize the dualisms of intellect $v.$ feeling, analysis $v.$ commitment, nature $v.$ nurture, victory/mastery $v.$ harmony/acceptance, values $v.$ science/rationality,
7. lack of epics and myths of universal, global, species-wide appeal,
8. lack of positive images and symbols of collective, communal living,
9. tendency for individuals to immobilize themselves: "I'm unable to cope!"[28]

[27]John D. Haas, "Making It On This Planet," *The Educational Forum*, 41, no. 2 (January, 1977), pp. 189–98.
[28]Many items on this list are derived from essays in Robert Bundy, ed., *Images of the Future* (Buffalo, N.Y.: Prometheus Books, 1976), pp. x, 239.

To return for a moment to the futures pyramid in Figure 14-1, interactions will occur along all its edges. The nature of the future is determined by these interactions: among the values/ideology base, the knowledge/technology plane, and the problems/crises side. As future trends appear in barely visible outlines, these also interact with all the other planes—chiefly by self-fulfilling and self-defeating "pushes."

EDUCATIONAL FUTURES

Thus far, almost no mention has been made of education and schooling in the future. As a social institution, education primarily reflects and conserves the values, norms, and practices of a particular society; only secondarily, and then rarely, does it initiate change and innovation on its own. Thus, educational futures are drawn mainly, and by implication, from societal futures, on all levels from family, through state and nation, to planet. For example, Harry Broudy has suggested that the major future demand *by* U.S. society *on* schooling will be for vocational competence, civic competence, and humanness (i.e., individuality, personhood, and freedom).[29] Dwight Allen concluded that "to get past [rigid prerequisites and lockstep credentialing] . . . , we need to implement nonlinearity, simultaneity, and random access to education . . ., by allowing students to learn what they want, when they want it, . . . to make education self-directed, continuing, and enjoyable."[30]

A growing number of educators have become interested in the study of educational futures, or as it is sometimes referred to, educational policy studies or policies research. Their forecasts vary, both in terms of the educational topics they choose to study and in terms of their actual projections. Among the topics education futurists have selected for study and research are curriculum content (i.e., knowledge, skills, values, and attitudes), materials and methods; school and curriculum organization patterns; preservice and in-service education of teachers; schemes for financing public, private, and parochial schools; teachers' organizations or unions, and salaries and benefits; student demographic characteristics; educational media and technology; politics and control of education; global, international education; functions of nonschool educative agents, such as publishers, commercial television, families, and community agencies; and school buildings and other learning environments.

---

[29]Harry J. Broudy, "Education: 1975–2000," in Theodore W. Hipple, *The Future of Education: 1975–2000* (Pacific Palisades, Calif.: Goodyear Publishing Company, Inc., 1974), pp. 28–35.

[30]Dwight Allen, "What the Future of Education Might Be," in *The Future of Education*, p. 6.

What follows are some of the educational futures envisioned by a sampling of late twentieth-century futurists:

Theodore W. Hipple. This prognosticator sees these changes in schools and schooling in the "distant and not-so-distant future":

> An enlarged and broadened base for financing public education will[31] evolve.
>
> Teachers' salaries will continue to increase, though the percent raises will be barely ahead of inflation.
>
> Alternative schools (both the "fundamental" and the "open" varieties), schools-within-a-school, and schools-without-walls will flourish, especially beyond the elementary school level.
>
> A school will become a community center, as well as a user of community facilities and human resources.
>
> The time students spend in schools and classrooms will be shortened, while student time in out-of-school, community agencies and programs will increase.
>
> Older students will teach younger students, under adult supervision and for pay or for credit as volunteers.
>
> Curricula will incorporate computers and data retrieval systems, and will emphasize such learning "economies" as concept learning and basic communication and problem-solving skills.
>
> Teaching methods will change to accommodate more small-group and independent-study modes.[32]

David J. Irvine. According to this educational futurist, an educational system of the future should be able to:

> deal with large numbers of students,
>
> accommodate to new and different population patterns (e.g., metropolitan government or abolition of state boundaries),
>
> capitalize on the many "non-school educational forces which exist in society (e.g., marketplace, corporations, museums, colleges, libraries, clubs, and commercial television stations),"
>
> accommodate to changes in natural resources available, such as air, water and fuel,
>
> provide learning-to-learn and other survival skills,
>
> allow greater learner autonomy in deciding educational needs and programs,
>
> teach a variety of human relations skills: intrapersonal, interpersonal, and multicultural,
>
> provide means for individuals to determine overriding purposes in their lives, and
>
> move students away from the dichotomy between work and play.[33]

---

[31] Most forecasters, although they realize the future is probable and problematical, use the definite-sounding verb "will" because it reads simply.

[32] Theodore W. Hipple, "Some (Specific and Not-So-Specific) Notions about the (Distant and Not-So-Distant) Future of Education," ibid., pp. 119–135.

[33] David J. Irvine, "Specifications for an Educational System of the Future," in Richard W. Hostrop, ed., *Foundations of Futurology in Education* (Palm Springs, Calif.: ETA Publications, 1973), pp. 75–83.

Wilbur J. Cohen. This dean of the school of education at the University of Michigan and former Secretary of Health, Education, and Welfare suggests that educational futures will occur mainly in "ten areas of change":

> formulas and bases of financing school expenditures,
> emphasis on early childhood education,
> continued desegregation, busing, and concern for quality in urban education,
> expanded collective bargaining,
> substitutions (e.g., equivalency tests and competencies checks) for teacher certification,
> continued innovation and experimentation (e.g., voucher plans and challenges to compulsory attendance laws),
> continued teacher surplus, but with shortages in selected areas (e.g., special education),
> greater parent involvement and student participation in decision-making,
> dissatisfaction with and greater expectation from public education,
> changing community institutions—family, government, and economy.[34]

Harold E. Mitzel. "I predict that the impending instruction revolution will shortly bypass the simple idea of individualizing instruction and move ahead to the more sophisticated notion of providing *adaptive education* for school and college learners. By adaptive education we mean the tailoring of subject matter presentations to fit the special requirements and capabilities of each learner."[35]

Margaret Mead. In her volume *Culture and Commitment* this noted anthropologist claims that people learn from each other in three age-related modes, but that one of these modes has been dominant in most past cultures. The three modes are prefigurative learning—the old learn from the young; cofigurative learning—children, adolescents, and adults learn from their peers; and postfigurative learning, historically the typical mode—the young learn from the old. Mead suggests that today in industrial, technological societies like the United States, postfigurative learning is the norm of formal schooling, but that in other contexts (e.g., the adolescent subculture) cofigurate learning (peer learning) is the rule, and this is a crucial determinant of the phenomenon of the generation gap. In the future, Mead observes, there will be a need for all three modes of learning to occur in a culture.[36]

Taking a broad perspective on education in the future, two general, long-term trends seem to pervade public education in every nation. These are (1) the tendency of systems of schooling to first maximize the number of persons served by the system, and then to maximize the quality of service

---
[34]Wilbur J. Cohen, "Changing Influences in American Education," ibid., pp. 93–108.
[35]Harold E. Mitzel, "The Impending Instruction Revolution," ibid., pp. 235–236.
[36]Margaret Mead, *Culture and Commitment* (New York: Doubleday & Company, Inc., 1970).

to special client groups and to individual clients, and (2) the tendency of curricular and decision-making orientations to shift from local, to national, to worldwide concerns and arenas.

Using the United States as an example, the historical pattern has been for each level of public education—elementary, secondary, and higher—to grow toward serving a maximum number of potential clients or students. This has been a progression "upward," of saturating each level in turn. By 1900, well over 50 percent of the elementary school age population was in elementary school (public, private, or parochial), and about 10 percent of the high school age youth were in secondary schools. By 1970, over 95 percent of the potential elementary school clientele were in school, while over 90 percent of the corresponding youth group were in secondary schools. Today in the United States, the elementary and secondary schools have virtually reached their quantitative limits, except in their adult education programs, where they compete with higher education for new clients.

From at least the 1950s and more so in the 1960s and 1970s, elementary and secondary education focused more and more on qualitative factors. This is especially so for federal legislation and funding during the sixties and seventies. For example, the Elementary and Secondary Education Act of 1965 supplied funds to state and local education agencies to improve the quality of education in several ways: to improve instruction and support services in schools with a high percentage of poverty-level students, to improve the holdings of school libraries, to improve state department of education services to local schools, and to foster exemplary, innovative instructional and curricular practices. Other federal categorical-aid acts (as distinguished from general-aid acts) have provided funds for assisting local school districts with desegregation problems, for bilingual education, and for the education of the handicapped. Undoubtedly the future will see greater support at all levels for special-client groups and for the development of individualized approaches to education.

Two other broad tendencies of educational systems are toward the centralization of authority and power at "higher" levels—from local school districts to state departments of education to federal or national government; and the broadening orientation of curriculum from local to national to global. For example, the U.S. Congress in the late seventies was pressured by many groups, such as private and parochial school educators and big-city superintendents and school boards, to enact legislation to provide general financial aid to all forms of elementary and secondary education in the nation. At the same time, school curricula more and more reflected national concerns (e.g., the push to get back to fundamental skills) and the necessity for global citizenship (which was highlighted by the energy crisis, but which grows out of the recognition of interdependence in multiple worldwide contexts).

CASE STUDY: A Problem in Space Travel

Imagine that you are a first-class passenger on a huge spaceship travelling through space at the speed of 66,000 mph. You discover that the craft's environmental system is faulty. Passengers in some sections are actually dying due to the discharge of poisonous gases into their oxygen supply. Furthermore, you learn that food supplies are rapidly diminishing and that the water supply, previously thought to be more than adequate, is rapidly becoming polluted because of fouling from breakdowns in the craft's waste and propulsion systems.

To complicate matters, in the economy sections, where passengers are crowded together under the most difficult of situations, many are seriously ill. The ship's medical officers are able to help only a fraction of the sick, and medicines are in short supply.

Mutinies have been reported, and although some of the crew and passengers are engaged in serious conflict in one of the compartments, it is hoped that this conflict is being contained successfully. However, there is widespread fear as to what may happen if it cannot be contained or resolved within that compartment.

The spacecraft has been designed with an overall destruct system, the controls of which have been carefully guarded. Unfortunately the number of technologists who have gained access to the destruct system has increased, and all of the crew and passengers have become uneasy at the evidence of instability in some of those gaining this access.

What can or should be done to save the spaceship and its inhabitants?

THOUGHT QUESTIONS

1. For each of the following potential developments, decide if you think it "will occur" or "won't occur" by the year 2020. Also, regardless of whether you think it will or won't occur, decide if you think the development would be "desirable" or "undesirable."

Potential Development	Will Occur	Won't Occur	Desirable	Undesirable
A cure for cancer				
Extensive use of home computers				
Existence of space colonies as satellites of moon and/or earth				
World government or world federation				
A life expectancy in U.S. of over 100 years				
Production of test-tube babies				
Nuclear war				

404 ALTERNATIVE, GLOBAL, AND FUTURE PERSPECTIVES

Potential Development	Will Occur	Won't Occur	Desirable	Undesirable
The three-day work week in United States				
Elimination of use of individually owned and operated automobiles in U.S.				
Almost total reliance on nuclear and solar energy				
Zero population growth in U.S.				
The death of capitalism				
Continued urban growth				
Farming and mining of the seas				
Genetic manipulation and control of DNA (e.g., cloning, elimination of birth defects)				

2. Which one of the following four metaphors[37] comes closest to your conception of the future? If none seems appropriate, create one of your own. Explain!

>   1. The future is a great *roller coaster* on a moonless night. It exists, twisting ahead of us in the dark, although we can only see each part as we come to it. . . .
>
>   2. The future is a *mighty river*. The great force of history flows inexorably along, carrying us with it. Most of our attempts to change its course are mere pebbles thrown into the river: they cause a momentary splash and a few ripples, but they make no difference. The river's course *can* be changed, but only by natural disasters like earthquakes or landslides, or by massive, concerted human efforts on a similar scale. On the other hand, we are free as individuals to adapt to the course of history either well or poorly. . . .
>
>   3. The future is *a great ocean*. There are many possible destinations, and many different paths to each destination. A good navigator takes advantage of the main currents of change, adapts his course to the capricious winds of chance, keeps a sharp lookout posted, and moves carefully in fog or uncharted waters. . . .
>
>   4. The future is entirely random, *a colossal dice game*. Every second, millions of things happen which could have happened another way and produced a different future. . . . Since everything is chance, all we can do is play the game, pray to the gods of fortune, and enjoy what good luck comes our way.

3. Supply evidence to support or refute each of the following hypotheses:

>   The value base of American society has remained rather stable and constant for the past 200 years, and will likely remain so for at least another 200 years.

[37]Draper L. Kauffman, Jr., *Teaching the Future* (Palm Springs, Calif.: ETA Publications, 1976), pp. 64–65.

American values have evolved over hundreds of years, but are today being challenged and will probably change considerably between now and the year 2000.

4. On the blank lines, indicate whether each of the following potential educational developments in the United States will occur "by 1984," "by 1994," "by 2020," "by 2050," or "never."

____ 1. a complete environmental-education curriculum, kindergarten through grade twelve
____ 2. year-round school, broken up by holidays every quarter-year
____ 3. abolition of compulsory attendance laws in most states
____ 4. abolition of public schools
____ 5. emphasis on global/futures education
____ 6. gradual decrease in public school enrollments
____ 7. elimination of the local property-tax base for funding public schools; all funds derive from state and federal governments
____ 8. the option to "test out" of high school in all states
____ 9. few, if any, significant changes in public education
____10. use of computers to replace some teachers for almost half the school day
____11. extensive use of drugs to enhance student learning and to increase studdents' abilities to learn
____12. special schools and programs for the elderly
____13. greater uses of educational TV and computer-assisted instruction in homes
____14. free child-care and prekindergarten education
____15. abolition of teacher tenure

PRACTICAL ACTIVITIES

1. With respect to the following future possibilities, ask a number of children or adolescents in what ways their lives would be affected if each possibility were to occur:

   you could travel to other planets as you now can visit other cities or countries
   you were only allowed to work for pay a maximum of twenty hours per week
   you were required to retire from paid employment at age forty-five
   you were expected to live to age 150
   you could communicate with others by the use of extra-sensory perception (ESP)
   twenty babies the exact genetic duplicate of you were artificially produced
   automobiles were only available for rent or lease
   gasoline for cars was priced at $4.00 per gallon
   your occupation became obsolete every ten to fifteen years

406 ALTERNATIVE, GLOBAL, AND FUTURE PERSPECTIVES

you and your family could only dispose of one small garbage can full of garbage each month

you lived in a city under the ocean

you could only obtain food in capsule form

you were only allowed to raise artificially produced "sons" and "daughters":

Write up a summary of your findings.

2. Build a futures wheel! Using Figure 14-3 as a starting point, complete the first, second, and third rings. In your projections, assume that a suburban school district is losing its student population at the rate of 2 percent per year. In 1976, there were 120,000 students in this district, and by 1979 this number had decreased to 113,000.

3. Write a science fiction short story, drama, or scenario that describes the lives of children and adolescents in their homes and schools in the year 2000.

4. Write a unit or lesson plan on "Alternative Futures" to teach in a class.

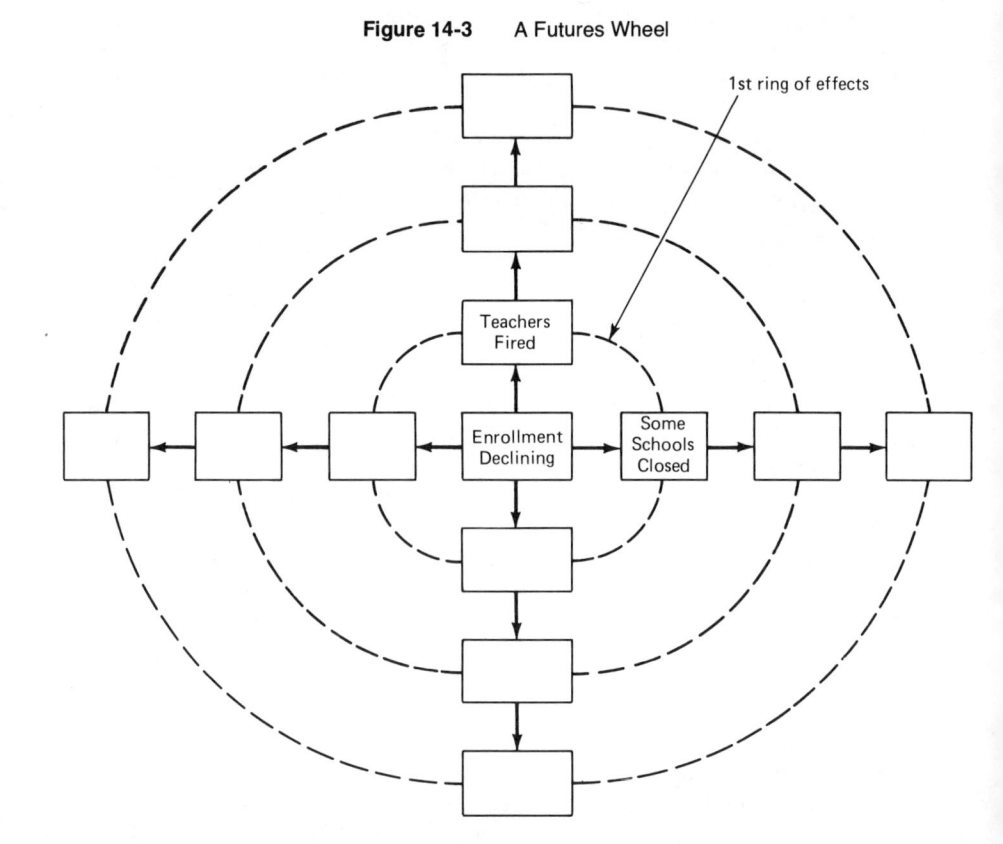

Figure 14-3 A Futures Wheel

5. Become an active member of some organization which you feel is dealing with a crucial issue involved with future world survival (e.g., peace coalitions, Planned Parenthood, ecology groups, energy groups, etc.). Describe the organization, its importance, and your involvement.

BIBLIOGRAPHY

BAIER, KURT, AND NICHOLAS RESCHER, eds. *Values and the Future*. New York: The Free Press, 1969.

BELL, DANIEL, ed., *Toward the Year 2000*. Boston, Mass.: Houghton Mifflin Company, 1968.

BOULDING, KENNETH E., *The Meaning of the Twentieth Century*. New York: Harper & Row, Publishers, 1964.

BUNDY, ROBERT, ed., *Images of the Future*. Buffalo, N.Y.: Prometheus Books, 1976.

CHASE, STUART, *The Most Probable World*. Evanston, Ill.: Harper & Row, Publishers, 1968.

CLARKE, ARTHUR C., *Profiles of the Future*. New York: Harper & Row, Publishers, 1963.

COMMONER, BARRY, *The Closing Circle*. New York: Alfred A. Knopf, Inc., 1971.

DE CHARDIN, TEILHARD, *The Phenomenon of Man*. Evanston, Ill.: Harper & Row, Publishers, 1955.

DE JOUVENEL, BERTRAND, *The Art of Conjecture*. New York: Basic Books, Inc., Publishers, 1967.

DRUCKER, PETER F., *The Age of Discontinuity*. New York: Harper & Row, Publishers, 1969.

EURICH, ALVIN C., *High School 1980*. New York: Pitman Publishing Company, 1970.

EWALD, WILLIAM R., Jr., ed., *Environment and Change*. Bloomington, Ind.: Indiana University Press, 1968,

FULLER, R. BUCKMINSTER, *Operating Manual for Spaceship Earth*. New York: Pocket Books, 1969.

GORDON, THEODORE J., *The Future*. New York: St. Martin's Press, 1965.

HARMAN, WILLIS, *Alternative Futures and Educational Policy*. Menlo Park, Calif.: Stanford Research Institute, 1970.

HEILBRONER, ROBERT, *An Inquiry Into the Human Prospect*. New York: W. W. Norton & Company, Inc., 1974.

HIPPLE, THEODORE W., ed., *The Future of Education: 1975—2000*. Pacific Palisades, Calif.: Goodyear Publishing Company, Inc., 1974.

HOSTROP, RICHARD W., ed., *Foundations of Futurology in Education*. Palm Springs, Calif.: ETC Publications, 1973.

KAHN, HERMAN, AND ANTHONY J. WIENER, *The Year 2000*. New York: The Macmillan Company, 1967.

MARIEN, MICHAEL, AND WARREN L. ZIEGLER, eds, *The Potential of Educational Futures*. Chicago: National Society for the Study of Education, 1972.

MEAD, MARGARET, *Culture and Commitment*. New York: Doubleday & Company, Inc., 1970.

RUBIN, LOUIS, ed, *The Future of Education*. Boston, Mass.: Allyn & Bacon, Inc., 1975.
SHANE, HAROLD G., *The Educational Significance of the Future*. Bloomington, Ind.: Phi Delta Kappa, 1973.
TOFFLER, ALVIN, *Future Shock*. New York: Random House, Inc., 1970.
────── ed., *The Futurists*. New York: Random House, Inc., 1972.
────── ed., *Learning for Tomorrow*. New York: Vintage Books, 1974.

INDEX

Abington v. Schempp (1963), 151, 154
Absenteeism, among women, 223
Absolute relativism, 164–65
Academic freedom, case study of, 316
Academy, 11, 19
  Plato's, 118
Acculturation, 188
Achievement
  definition, 129
  in school context, 130–31
Achievement motivation, 225–26
Achievement tests, comparison of by sex, 227
Administrative personnel, male predominance in, 230, 237
Administrator, high school, qualities necessary for, 237
Adolescence, and junior high schools, 267
Adorno, T.W., 191
Affirmative action programs, 220–21
Affluent Society, The (Galbraith), 88
Aggression, sex differences in, 229, 231
Alienation, and education, 133
Alien Exclusion Act (1924), 184
Alien Land Law (1913), 184
Allen, Dwight, 399
Alternatives, to schooling, 344–45
Alternative school movement, 323–46
  major premises of, 343
  origins of, 326–27
  perspective on, 326–33
  rationale for, 343–44
Alternative schools
  case study on, 346–47
  definitions, 325–26
  emerging new concepts, 333–34
Amalgamation, 188
American Anthropological Association (AAA), 199
American Association of School Administrators, 62
American Dilemma, An (Myrdal), 168, 193, 385
American Education: The Colonial Experience (Cremin), 8
American Federation of Labor (AFL), 91
American Federation of Teachers (AFT), 256, 308–10
American High School Today, The (Conant), 24, 93
American Indian. *See* Native Americans
American Psychological Association (APA), 199
American public education, conflict in, 137–38

Analytic philosophy
  applied to education, 40
  scope of, 39–40
Andelin, Helen B., 214
Apperception, and learning, 7
Aquinas, St. Thomas, 41, 212
Architecture, school, lack of aesthetic quality in, 301
Aristotle, 6, 41, 212
Arusha Declaration, 370, 371
Assimilation, 187–88
Athletics, and sexism, 218–20
Atkinson, John, 225
Atlantic Monthly, The, 200
Attendance, 1924–1974, 247
Attendance, compulsory, 27
  and child labor abuses, 13–14
Authoritarian Personality, The (Adorno), 191
Axiology, 43
  scope of, 39

Barber, Benjamin, 213
Barnard, Henry, 12, 13, 16, 254
Barth, John, 54
Barth, Roland, 330
Beatty, Willard, 332
Behaviorism, 158
Belief system, 170
Belief systems continuum, 171
Bereiter, Carl, 28–34
Berg, Ivan, 101–2
Bestor, Arthur, 324
Bible reading, in public schools, 151, 153
Bill for the More General Diffusion of Knowledge (Jefferson), 11
Bill for Religious Freedom (1786), 150
Biofeedback, 158
Black Americans, discrimination against, 179–81
Black Muslims, 181
Blake, William, 157
Board of Education v. Allen (1968), 152
Boards of Cooperative Educational Services, 139
Boston English Classical High School, 268
Boulding, Kenneth, 100, 112, 156, 160
Brain, and metaphoric mind, 160–61
Brameld, Theodore, 52
British Infant School(s), 262, 328, 337
Bronowski, Jacob, 160
Broudy, Harry, 342, 399

409

Brown, Lester, 388–89
Brown v. Board of Education (1954), 181, 195
Bruner, Jerome, 160, 161, 273, 332
Bureaucracy
  and common schools, 15–17
  incipient, 16
Bureaucratization, effect on schools, 298
Bureau of Indian Affairs (BIA), 186
Bureau of Refugees, and education, 250
Burroughs, William, 54
Busing, effects on achievement levels of minority children, 198
Butts, R. Freeman, 90

Capitalism
  and private production, 88–89
  welfare, 88
Capitalist economic theory, 85–88
Cardinal Principles of Secondary Education, 20
Career education, in secondary schools, 290–91
Carnegie Units, 284, 285
Caroline Pratt's Play School, 328
Carter, James, 12, 13
Carter, Jimmy (President), 309
Carter, Rosalynn, 216
Case study(ies)
  academic freedom, 78–79, 316
  alternative schools, 346
  changing school organization, 269
  compulsory attendance, 32–33
  controversial elementary curriculum, 293
  educational politics, 65–67
  education in the Third World, 378
  equalization of educational opportunity, 113
  the newly integrated school system, 207–8
  problems in space travel, 403
  reporting student achievement, 141
  school holidays, 173
  the sexist curriculum, 238–39
  stone age education, 57–58
Castro, Fidel, 369
Celler, Emanuel, 217
Center for the Study of Public Policy at Harvard University, 336
Centering, definition, 299–300
Certification, of teachers, 255–56
Channing, William Ellery, 13
Character types, 305
Chauvinism, and sports, 218–19
Chavez, Cesar, 183
Citizenship education, 288
Civilian Conservation Corps (CCC), 251
Civil rights, and American Indians, 186
Civil Rights Act
  1875, 180
  1964, 109, 195, 217
Civil Rights Bill (1968), 186
Clark, Kenneth, 393
Clayton-Bulwer Treaty (1850), 355
Cochrane v. State of Louisiana (1930), 152
Cohen, Wilbur J., 401
Coleman, James, 109–10, 195, 196, 282, 292, 335
Coleman Report, 195–98, 204
College education, expansion of, 90
Colonial schools, 274
Commissioner of Education, U.S., 62
Commission on the Relation of School and College of the Progressive Education Association (PEA), 332
Commission on the Reorganization of Secondary Education, 20, 268, 276
Committee of Ten on Secondary Studies, 19
Common schools, 10–12. *See also* Public schools
  and bureaucracy, 15–17
  and Horace Mann, 12–13

Community activity, function of, 126
Compulsory attendance, case study, 32–33
Compulsory schooling, 354
Computer(s), 289
  and curriculum, 273
  in education, 285
Conant, James, 24–25, 159, 160, 324, 391
Conant Report, 93–95
  and secondary education, 93
Congress, U.S., 62
Congress of Industrial Organization (CIO), 91
Constitution, U.S.
  and education, 61, 249–50
  First amendment to, 148–50
  Tenth amendment to, 249
Constitutional authority, and education, 249–50
Coombs, Philip, 355
Cooperative Research Program (1954), 251
Counseling programs, sexism in, 235
Counts, George S., 51, 140, 283
Cremin, Lawrence, 26, 31
Cremin thesis, implications of, 138–39
Crisis in the Classroom (Silberman), 277
Critical analysis, and value dilemma, 169–70
Cuba, education in, 365–70
Cultural pluralism, 188
  in education, 204–5
Curriculum, 272–93
  content of, 272–74
  core, 284
  correlated, 284
  decisions about, 71–72
  elementary school, 278–81
  factors determining, 132
  hidden, 28–29, 128, 277
  junior high school, 281–82
  middle school, 281–82
  reform, 273
  sexism in, 238–39
  societal influences on, 273
  sources of, 273
  student-centered, 274–75
  subject-centered, 274–75
Custodial care, function of, 125

Dare the Schools Build a New Social Order (Counts), 283
Darwin, Charles, 42, 198
Decentralization, and alternative schooling, 334
Decision-making
  economic, 85
  educational, 71–74
Decter, Midge, 214
Democracy and Education (Dewey), 22, 50
Democratic values, and education, 170–73
Dennison, Edward, 99
Dennison, George, 330
Departmentalization, in secondary schools, 283–84
Departmentalized schools, 263
Department of Education Act (1867), 251
Deschooling Society (Illich), 28
Detroit Area Study (1958), 194
Dewey, John, 21–23, 25, 27, 30–32, 41, 42, 46, 47, 50, 136, 165, 168, 275–76, 277, 331, 332, 343
DiCenso v. Robinson (1971), 152
Discipline, colonial, 7–8
Discrimination, 191–92
  Black-American, 179–81
  Oriental-American, 184–85
  reactions to, 192–93
  school, 183
  sexual, 227–29
    in secondary schools, 234–37
    in vocational studies, 234–35

Discrimination, *(cont.)*
    and sexually segregated want-ads, 223
    Spanish-American, 182–83
    and sports, 219
District power equalizing, 111–12
Dobzhansky, Theodosius, 200–201
Dollard, John, 190
Dred Scott decision (1857), 180
Dropouts, 293
DuBois, William Edward B., 180
Due process, 315
Dysgenics, 200–201
Dyson, Freeman, 160

Early childhood education, 260–61
    criticisms, 261
    focus of, 261
Earnings, median, comparison by sex, 221
Earnings, total, comparison by occupation and sex, 222
Economic growth, education's contribution to, 99–100
Economics
    command, 85
    and production imbalance, 88–89
    traditional, 85
Economic system, and American education, 89–96
Education
    American assumption about, 26
    Athenian, 4–5
    colonial, 7–10
    diversity and choice in, 334–43
    and earnings, 96–97, 98
    ecology of, 31–32
    economic effects of, 96–99
    and federal government, 249–53
    function of, 121–22
    history of, 3–35
    incidental, 134–35
    informal, 329–30
    intentional, 134
    manipulative, 29
    mass, functions of, 92–93
    multicultural, 203–4
    multiple domains of, 134–35
    philosophy of, 37–58
        synopsis of, 53
    political issues in, 75–78
    political pressures on, 69
        external, 69
        internal, 70–71
    and politics, 13
    politics of, 61–81
    progressive, 22–24, 27
    and schooling, 68
    and social change, 140–41
    as social institution, 118–19
    sociology of, 117–43
    Spartan, 4
    specialized, 121
    and state governments, 253–56
    struggle for control of, 74–78
    twentieth century, 26–32
    and worker productivity, 102–4
Educational futures, 399–402
Educational opportunity
    case study, 113
    equality of, 104–10
    court cases in, 105
    criteria for, 104
Educational reform, 24
Educational system, 62–63
Educational vouchers
    and alternative schooling, 335–37
    objections to, 335–36

Educational Vouchers Agency (EVA), 335, 336
Education for All Handicapped Children Act (1975), 315
Education Professional Development Act, 252
Education and Jobs: The Great Training Robbery (Berg), 101
Education and the Rise of the Corporate State (Spring), 93
Educative institutions, configuration of, 135–37
Educator, expanded concept of, 135
Edwards, Ninian, 12
Eight-Year Study (1932–40), 332
Eisley, Loren, 160
Elementary education
    changed by expansion of secondary education, 275
    in colonial times, 274
    goals of, 274–81
    objectives of, 274–78
Elementary school(s)
    educational goal, 262
    organization, 262–64
    sexism in, 229–31
    subject areas, 278–81
Elementary and Secondary Education Act of 1965 (ESEA), areas of involvement of, 251–52
Elliot, Charles, 19, 23, 24, 25
Emile (Rousseau), 6
Employment and sexism, 220–24
Energy crisis, 351–52
Engel v. Vitale (1962), 151
English-language arts, in secondary schools, 286–87
Enrollment, 248
    1899–1973, 246
Environment, family, 127
Environment-heredity controversy, 198–201
Epistemology, 39, 43
Equal Employment Opportunities Commission (EEOC), 217
Equal Rights Amendment (ERA), 216
Erhard, Werner, 158
Escuela al campo, 368
Escuelas Granjas, 360
Essentialism, 47–48
    synopsis of, 53
EST (Erhard Seminars Training), 158
Esthetic values, 158
Ethics, definition of, 39
Ethnic differences, median test scores for different groups, 197
Ethnicity, 178–208
    research on, 193–94
Ethnocentrism, 189
Everson v. Board of Education (1974), 152
Evolution, Darwinian, 42
Existentialism, 52–55
Experience and Education (Dewey), 23
Extracurricular programs, in junior high, 282

Family, influence on children, 126–27
Family Educational Rights and Privacy Act (1974), 315–16
Fantini, Mario, 337
Fascinating Womanhood (Andelin), 214
Fear of Success (FOS), 225–27
Featherstone, Joseph, 330
Federal education programs, history of, 250–52
Federal government, and education, 249–53
Federalism, and education, 249–50
Feminine Mystique, The (Friedan), 211
Feminist movement, basic premises of, 213
Feminization, of schools, 231–34
Finances, decisions about, 73–74
Fine arts, in secondary schools, 289–90

412 Index

First amendment
   and education, 149–53
   Establishment Clause of, 150–51, 153
   Free Exercise Clause of, 151, 155
Fischer, Louis, 311
Follow Through, 262
Forbes, Roy H., 228
Ford, Betty, 216
Ford, Gerald, 216
Foreign Language in the Elementary School (FLES), 279
Foreign languages, in secondary schools, 289
Forum, The, 20
Fourth Force, 158
Fraenkel, Jack, 167, 168, 169
Franklin, Benjamin, 11, 268
Free the Children: Radical Reform and the Free School Movement (Graubard), 327
Freedman's Bureau, and education, 250
Freedom
   academic, case study of, 316
   and teaching, 299
Freedom and Beyond (Holt), 27
Freedom of association, 314
Freedom of expression, 311
Freedom of the press, 314
Freedom of religion, 314
Freedom of speech, 313
Free schools, 337
Friedan, Betty, 211
Friedman, Milton, 87, 335
Froebel, Friedrich, 6–7, 260, 330
Fromm, Erich, 305
Funding
   federal, 248
   and government control, 252
   local, 248
   state, 248
Future
   educational, 383–402
   framework of, 383–84
   societal, 383–402

Galbraith, John Kenneth, 84, 156, 160
Gaming techniques, 285
Garvey, Marcus, 181
Gestalt therapy, 158
Ginzberg, Eli, 102
Global survival, 351–78
Goldberg, Stephen, 213, 214, 215
Golden Age (Greek), education in, 118–19
Gonzalez, Rudolfo "Corky," 183
Goodlad, John, 300–301
Goodman, Paul, 27, 30
Grammer, prescriptive *vs.* descriptive, 287
Grammar schools, Jefferson's idea of, 11
Grange, 91
Graubard, Allen, 327
Great Depression, and education, 251
Greece, ancient, education in, 4–6
Greene, Maxine, 54
Greer, Colin, 204
Griffiths, Martha, 217
Guidance programs, 94–95

Harmin, Merrill, 163
Harvard Educational Review, 198
Harvey, O.J., 170
Hawkins, David, 159, 330
Hawley, Gideon, 12, 254
Head Start, 262
Health, in secondary schools, 290
Heideigger, Martin, 54
Heilbroner, Robert, 85, 351
Herbart, Johann Friedrich, 7
Herndon, James, 324

Herrnstein, Richard, 199
High school(s), 267–69
   comprehensive, 20, 25, 284
   early curriculum, 19
   history of, 267–68
   origins of, 18–19
   reshaping, 24–25
Hipple, Theodore, 400
History, in secondary schools, 287–88
Holt, John, 27, 324, 330
Horner, Matina, 225
How Gertrude Teaches Her Children (Pestalozzi), 6
How We Think (Dewey), 22, 332
Human potentials group, 158
Hunt, Maurice, 168

Idealism, 41
   and education, 44
   synopsis of, 43
Illich, Ivan, 28–34, 84, 360
Immigrants, and education, 14–15
Independence
   definition, 129
   in school context, 130–31
Indian Heritage of America, The (Josephy), 185
Indian Reorganization Act (1934), 186
Individualized instruction, 301
   programmed material, 289
Industrialization
   effect on public schools, 13–17
   expansion of, 90–91
Inevitability of Patriarchy, The (Goldberg), 213, 214
Inner-city schools, 293
Inquiry into the Human Prospect, An (Heilbroner), 351
Instrumental values, 148
Integration, in schools, 195–98
International Education Act, 252
IQ
   and heredity, 200–201
   and life success, 199
   and role of school, 201–2
IQ tests
   bias of, 199
   misuse of, 202
Irvine, David J., 400
Isaacs, Susan, 330
Ivory Coast, education system of, 362–63

Jackson, Philip, 302, 343
James, William, 41, 42, 157
Jefferson, Thomas, 11, 25, 150, 155
Jencks, Christopher, 103, 204, 335, 336
Jensen, Arthur, 198–200
Jones, Richard, 159
Josephy, Alvyn M., 185
Journalism, muckraker, and education, 20
Junior high school(s), 264–67
   and adolescence, 267
   curriculum, 281–82
   extracurricular programs, 282
   purposes, 265
   replacement by middle schools, 281

Kallen, Horace, 188
Kearney, Nolan, 276
Kindergarten, growth rate, 260–61
King, Dr. Martin Luther, 181
Kluckhohn, Clyde, 190
Knowledge
   emerging, 389–96
   frontiers of, 392–93
   new models of, 393
Kohl, Herbert, 324, 330
Kohlberg, Lawrence, 165–67

Index 413

Kozol, Jonathan, 324, 327–28
Kuhn, Thomas, 159
Ku Klux Klan, 180, 181

Laboratory School, 21
Labor unions, and public schools, 91
Laissez-faire capitalism, 85
Language arts, in elementary schools, 278–79
Latin grammar school, 11, 268
Law, educational
  Brown v. The Board of Education, 109–10
  colonial, 8–9
  compulsory attendance, 13
  Kalamazoo case, 19
  Serrano v. Priest, 111
Learning objectives, imposed, 132–33
Learning readiness, 275
Learning style, sex differences in, 231
Leiberman, Myron, 297
Lemon v. Kurtzman (1971), 152
Leonard and Gertrude (Pestalozzi), 6
Lewis, Michael, 228
Lewis, Samuel, 12
Life Adjustment Movement, 332
Life-enhancing experience, 343
Life in Classrooms (Jackson), 302
Linguistic analysis, scope of, 40
Linguistics, 278
Local school district. *See* School district, local
Logic, 43
  definition of, 38, 39
Logical positivism, definition of, 39
Loomis, Arthur K., 332

McClelland, David, 225
McCollum v. Board of Education (1948), 151
Madison, James, 10, 149–50
Mailer, Norman, 214, 215
Mainstreaming, 315–16
Making of Economic Society, The (Heilbroner), 85
Man: a Course of Study (MACOS), 279
Mankind, interdependence of, 377–78
Mann, Horace, 12–13, 16, 25, 254
Marcuse, Herbert, 391
Margaret Naumberg's Children's School, 328
Marietta Johnson's Organic School, 328
Marshack, Alexander, 160
Maslow, Abraham, 158, 304
Massachusetts Bay Colony
  education in, 256
  schools in, 9
Maternal deprivation, 224
Mathematics
  in elementary schools, 280
  in secondary schools, 288–89
Mead, Margaret, 401–2
Media, mass, 131
  and education, 24, 287
Melting pot, 187–88
Merleau-Ponty, Maurice, 54
Metaphysics. *See* Ontology
Metcalf, Lawrence, 168
Metro School, 345
Mexican-Americans. *See* Spanish-Americans
Middle school(s), 264–67
  advantages of, 267
  curriculum, 281–82
  purposes, 265–66
  as replacement of junior high school, 281
Mills, Caleb, 12
Mind, metaphoric, 160–62
Minicourses, 285
Minorities, categories of, 188
Minority groups
  in American society, 179
  blacks, 179–81

Minority groups, *(cont.)*
  definition, 179
  native Americans, 185–87
  Oriental-Americans, 184–85
  Spanish-American, 181–84
Mitzel, Harold E., 401
Montessori, Maria, 261, 273, 330
Montessori schools, 201, 333, 337
Moral reasoning, 165–68
  as approaches to values education, 166–67
  levels of, 165
  stages of, 165–66
Moral values, 148
Morgan, Marybell, 214
Morrill Act (1862), 251
Myrdal, Gunnar, 168, 193
Myths, social, 28–29

NAACP. *See* National Association for the Advancement of Colored People
National Assessment of Educational Progress (NAEP), 227, 228
National Assessment Project, 251
National Association for the Advancement of Colored People (NAACP), 180–81
National Association of Manufacturers, 69, 91–93
National Association of School Boards, 62
National Consortium on Options in Public Education, 326
National Council for the Accreditation of Teacher Education (NCATE), 255
National Defense Education Act (NDEA), 251, 279, 280
National Education Association (NEA), 19, 20, 62, 69, 256, 276, 308–10
National Federation of Teachers, 62
National Foundation of the Arts and Humanities, 252
National Institute of Education, 251
National Organization of Women (NOW), 213
National School Lunch Act, 153
National Science Foundation (1950), 251, 279, 287–89
National Youth Administration (NYA), 251
Native Americans, 185–87
Naturalists, 215–16
Nature *versus* nurture, and sex discrimination, 227
Neil, A.S., 327
Neorealism, 42
Neo-Thomism, 42
New England Primer, 7, 9
New Industrial State, The (Galbraith), 156
"New math," 280, 289, 332
New Reformation: Notes of a Neolithic Conservative (Goodman), 30
Niagara Movement, 180
Nicaragua
  American involvement in, 355–56
  education system in, 356–60
  teacher training in, 361
Nongraded schools, 262
Northwest Ordinance (1787), and federal involvement in education, 250
Nuclear family, 214
Nursery schools, sexism in, 229–31
Nyerere, Julius, 37–72

Ocean Hill-Brownsville community, 334
Office of Economic Opportunity (OEO), 336
Office of Education, U.S., 62, 139, 251, 287, 288
Oliver, Donald, 168, 169
Ontology, 43
  definition, 39

Open campus concept, 136
Open-space schools, 337–38
Organization, decisions about, 72–73
Oriental-Americans, 184–85
Ornstein, Robert, 160
Outward Bound, 346
Overlapping continuum model, 337

Paraprofessionals, 264
Parker, Francis W., 20, 332
Parkway Program, 345
Parochial schools, 333
 financial aid to, 152–53
"Peak experiences," 158
Peer groups
 functions of, 128
 influence on children, 127–28
Peirce, Charles S., 41
Perennialism, 48–49
 synopsis of, 53
Pericles, 118
Perls, Fritz, 158
Perrone, Vito, 330
Personal appearance, and student's rights, 315
Personality traits, of model teacher, 305–7
Personnel, decisions about, 73
Pestalozzi, Johann, 6
Philosophy
 analytic, 39
 definition, 38
 of education, 37–58
 methodology of, 38
 personal education, 56–57
 realms of, 38–40
Phonics, 278
Physical education
 basic objectives, 290
 and sex-segregation, 234
Physical facilities, decisions about, 72
Piaget, Jean, 165, 261, 273, 331
Pierce v. Society of the Sisters of the Holy Names of Jesus and Mary, 256
Plato, 5–6, 41, 212
Plato's Academy, 118
Platt Amendment (1900), 365
Plessy v. Ferguson, 180
Plowden Committee, 329
Pluralism
 educational, 31
 institutionalized, 30–32
Polanyi, Michael, 159
Politics (Aristotle), 212
Politics
 definition, 64
 and education, 26
 educational, 62–67
  definition, 64–65
  five battlegrounds in, 74–78
Pragmatism, 42
 and education, 45–46
 synopsis of, 43
Prejudice
 and authoritarianism, 190–91
 and behavior types, 189
 and ethnocentrism, 188–89
 as a learned attitude, 190
 origins of, 189–90
President's Panel on Youth, 292
President's Science Advisory Committee, 292
Process of Education, The (Bruner), 273–74, 332
Profession, definition, 297–98
Professional organizations
 benefits of, 308–9
 local-level, 310
 state-level, 309–10
 for teachers, 307–10

Programmed material, individualized, use of, 289
Progressive education, 51–52, 274
Progressive Education Association, 22–23, 51, 140
Progressive schools, 20–21
Progressivism, 49–51
 synopsis of, 53
Proposals Relating to the Education of Youth in Pennsylvania (Franklin), 11
Psychoanalysis, 158
Psychology
 humanistic, 158
 transpersonal, 158
Psychotherapy, 158
Public Education (Cremin), 31
Public education, in the United States, 245–49
Public options, and alternative schooling, 337
Public schools
 inadequacies of, 16
 origins, 13
 reform, 16–17
Public school systems, progressive, 332
Pygmalion in the Classroom (Rosenthal and Jacobson), 206

Quality of life, 352
Quintilian, Marcus Fabius, 6

Racial isolation, 140
Racism, 140–41, 178–208
 research on, 193–94
 and schools, 195–201
 and teachers, 202
 in textbooks, 202
Raths, Louis, 163
Ravitch, Diane, 31
Realism, 41–42, 43
 and education, 44–45
Reconstructionism, 49, 51–52
 synopsis of, 53
Reimer, Everett, 28–34
Relativity, 42
Religion
 and colonial education, 9–10
 and colonial schools, 149
 "establishment of," 149
Religious experience, 148
Religious groups, minority, 149
Religious holidays, school celebration of, 154–55
Religious schools, 153. *See also* Parochial schools
 use of public funds for, 151–53
Religious values, in American education, 148–55
Republic (Plato), 212
Rice, Joseph, 20
Rickover, Hyman, 324
Riesman, David, 123
Riis, Jacob, 20
Rilke, Rainer Maria, 54
Rodriguez v. San Antonio Independent School District, 203
Rogers, Carl, 158, 304
Rogers, Vincent, 330
Role, social, definition of, 122
Rolf, Ida, 159
Rolfing, 158
Roosevelt, Franklin Delano, 184
Roosevelt, Theodore, 365
Ross v. Eckels, 182
Roszak, Theodore, 157, 391
Rousseau, Jean Jacques, 6, 330
Russell, Bertrand, 42
Russell Sage Foundation, 276
Ryans, David, 302

Sagan, Carl, 160
Salaries, 1929-1975, 247-48
Salk, Jonas, 159, 161
Sarason, Seymour, 303-4
Scapegoating, 190
Scheduling
  flexible, 284
  modular, 284-85
Schimmel, David, 311
School-attendance areas, 259
School In Between. *See* Junior high school; Middle schools
School board, function of, 257-58
School district. *See also* School-attendance areas
  local
    financial considerations, 258
    history of, 256
    organization, 257-58
    powers of, 257
School financing, 104-10
  estimated costs per pupil, 106
  foundation system, 107-8
  local initiative in, 111
  reform of, 111-12
  shared, 107-8
  state obligations toward, 110-13
  through program reduction, 112
School holidays, case study, 173
Schooling
  alternatives to, 344-46
  and annual income, 97
  compared with physical product, 101
  economic benefits of, 110-11
  economics of, 83-113
  and education, 68
  emerging problems, 396-99
  and employment, 101-2
  and lifetime incomes, 98
  politics of, 68-69
Schooling industry, 84
School Is Dead (Reimer), 28
School Organization, 245-69
  levels of, 259-60
School resources, impact of, 109
Schools
  alternative, 325-47
  child-centered, 276
  colonial, 274
  common characteristics, 277
  feminization of, 231-34
  high, 18-19, 24-25, 267-69
  influence on children, 128-31
  junior high, 264-67, 281-82
  Middle, 264-67, 281-82
  Montessori, 301, 333, 337
  open-space, 337-38
  parochial, 152-53, 333
  personnel, 61-62
  progressive, 20-21
  sex-segregated classes in, 232
  social functions of, 120-26
  as socializing agent, 276
School and Society, The (Dewey), 21
Schools of Tomorrow (Dewey), 22
"Schools without walls," 337, 345
Schultz, Theodore, 99
Schurz, Mrs. Carl, 261
Science
  in elementary schools, 280-81
  in secondary schools, 288
Scientific-technological development, 155-57
Scriven, Michael, 168
Secondary education
  goals for, 282-93
  reform of, 291-93
Secondary schools. *See also* High schools

Secondary schools, *(cont.)*
  colonial, 11
  curriculum, 286-91
  growth of, 18
  innovations, 284-85
  sexism in, 234-37
Secularism, religion of, 155
Segregation, 191-92
  according to sex, 232, 234
  age, 292
"Self-actualization" theory, 304
Self-contained classroom, 263
Separation principle, effect on education, 150-53
Seven Cardinal Principles, 269, 276, 282
Sex differences, 227-29
Sexism, 211-40
  and athletics, 218-20
  and employment, 220-24
  in guidance programs, 235
  in higher education, 237-38
  in history books, 236
  history of, 211-12
  and language, 224-25
  and the law, 216-18
  in literature, 235
  in nonformal educational aspects, 231
  in secondary schools, 234-37
Sex-role stereotyping, 219, 228-29, 233-34
Shaver, James, 168, 169
Shockley, William, 199, 200
Silberman, Charles, 26, 134-35, 276-77, 329-30
Silva, José, 158
Silva Mind Control, 158
Simon, Sidney, 163
Sizer, Theodore, 24, 335
Skeel, Dorothy, 389
Skills, basic, 31
Slavery, 179-80
Smith, Adam, 85, 86, 335
Smith-Hughes Act (1917), 251
Smith-Lever Act (1914), 251
Social change, and education, 140-41
Social-class bias, 129
Social classes, 123
Social Darwinism, 198
Social influences, on children and adolescents, 126-31
Social institutions, 118-19
Socialization
  and education, 119-20
  school as institution for, 95-96
Social norms, learned in schools, 129
Social-role selection, function of, 122-25
Social studies
  in elementary schools, 279-80
  in secondary schools, 287-88
Social values, transmission of, 125
Society
  deschooling, 27-30
  nature of, 117-18
  pluralistic, and education, 133
  relationship to education and schools, 118-19
  survival requirements of, 118
Society for the Psychological Study of Social Issues (SPSSI), 199
Socrates, 4-5
Socratic Method, 5
Southeast Alternatives Program, school types in, 338
Southern Christian Leadership Conference, 181
Space travel, problems in, 403
Spanish-Americans, 181-84
  and equal-rights struggle, 183-84
  history of, 181-82
  housing discrimination against, 182

416   Index

Specificity
  definition, 129
  in school context, 130–31
Spencer, Herbert, 198
Spring, Joel, 93, 95
Staffing, differentiated, 263–64, 284
"Stasis Process Continuum," 304
State Boards of Education, responsibilities, 253–54
State governments, and education, 253–56
  expanding role of, 254–56
  organization of, 253–54
States' rights, and education, 252
Status
  American determinants of, 124
  definition, 122
  groupings of, 122–23
Steffens, Lincoln, 20
Stereotyping
  institutionalized, 229–30
  sex-role, 228–29, 230, 233–34
Stoddard, Elwyn, 183
Stone Age education, case study, 57–58
Student Non-Violent Coordinating Committee, 181
Students, legal rights of, 313–16
Success, male vs. female, 232–33
Summerhill schools, 327
Superintendent of schools, responsibilities, 258
Supreme Court, U.S., 62
Survival of the Wisest, The (Salk), 161
Swett, John, 12
System types, and values education, 172–73

Tanzania, education in, 370–73
Teacher(s)
  authority-centered, 305
  certification of, 255–56
  expanded concept of, 135
  goal-centered, 307
  good, 301–4
  guardian-centered, 305
  ideal, qualities characterizing, 301–2
  legal rights of, 311–13
  loyalty oaths for, 312
  making of, 298–300
  model, 304-7
  as person, 312
  professional organizations, 307–13
  self-centered, 306
  skills needed by, 299
  task-centered, 306–7
  tradition-oriented, 306
Teacher behavior clusters, 308
Teacher, personnel, female predominance, 229–30, 232–33, 237
Teaching
  art of, 298
  as a profession, 296–307
Team teaching, 263, 284
Technology
  educational, 363–65
  effect on secondary curriculum, 285
  frontiers of, 394–96
Television, in classroom, 285, 287
Tenure laws, 312–13
Testing, as school function, 94–95
Tests
  achievement, 227
  Stanford-Binet IQ, 94
Textbooks
  public funds for, 152–54
  sex-stereotyping, 230–31
Thailand, education in, 360–61
Thelen, Herbert, 297
Thematic Apperception Test (TAT), 225
Third Force, 158

Third World, 375–76
  education in, 28, 378
Thorndike, Edward L., 275
Training, function of, 92
Transactional analysis, 158
Transcendental Meditation, 158
Transformation of the School, The (Cremin), 21, 26
Transportation, public funds for, 152–54
Treaty of Paris (1898), 365

Unions, for teachers, 307–10
Universalism
  definition, 129
  in school context, 130–31
Universal schooling, 17–20
Urbanization, and education, 92–96

Value(s)
  definition, 147
  democratic, 170–73
  emerging, 385–89
  instrumental, 390
  interpersonal and intrapersonal, 168–69
  terminal, 390
  traditional to emergent, 387–89
  types, 148
Value conflict, 168
Value dilemma, and critical analysis, 169–70
Value education, and social studies, 288
Value orientation in American society, 386–87
Values analysis, 168–70
Values clarification, criticisms of, 164
Values education, 162–70
"Values voting," 163
Valuing, criteria for, 163
Vanderbilt, Cornelius, 355
Verbal abilities, sex differences in, 229
Vilar, Esther, 214
Violence
  and global survival, 353
  in secondary schools, 293
Vocational Educational Act (1963), 251
Vocational education in secondary schools, 290–91
Vocational programs, 95
Voluntarism, paternalistic, 16n
Vonnegut, Kurt Jr., 54

Walberg, Herbert, 110
War, and global survival, 353
Warren, Earl, 184
Washburne, Carleton, 332
Washington, Booker T., 180
Wealth, maldistribution of, 352–53
Wealth of Nations, The (Smith), 85
Weisskopf, Victory, 160
Weisstein, Naomi, 213
Western culture, and religious authority, 148
Where the Wasteland Ends (Roszak), 157
Whitehead, Alfred North, 42
Wiley, Calvin, 12
Wilson, James Q., 364
Wirth, Louis, 188
Wolman v. Walter (1977), 152
Women's liberation movement, 213–16
  critics of, 214
World education, critique of, 373–77
World Education Crisis, The (Coombs), 355

Yale-Fairfield Study of Elementary Teaching, 276
Yoga, 158

Zacharias, Jerome, 324
Zangwill, Israel, 187
Zorach v. Clausen (1952), 151

AuthorHouse™
1663 Liberty Drive
Bloomington, IN 47403
www.authorhouse.com
Phone: 1-800-839-8640

© 2011 by Ted Obomanu. All rights reserved.

No part of this book may be reproduced, stored in a retrieval system, or transmitted by any means without the written permission of the author.

First published by AuthorHouse   10/31/2011

ISBN: 978-1-4670-4106-5 (sc)
ISBN: 978-1-4670-4108-9 (hc)
ISBN: 978-1-4670-4107-2 (ebk)

Library of Congress Control Number: 2011917567

Printed in the United States of America

Illustrations depicted in stock imagery provided by Shutterstock are models, and such images are being used for illustrative purposes only.
Certain stock imagery © Shutterstock.

This book is printed on acid-free paper.

Because of the dynamic nature of the Internet, any web address or link contained in this book may have changed since publication and may no longer be valid. The views expressed in this work are solely those of the author and do not necessarily reflect the views of the publisher, and the publisher hereby disclaims any responsibility for them.

Drive to Passion

Ted Obomanu

authorHOUSE

CONTENTS

INTRODUCTION 1

CHAPTER 1 "Colonel" Harland Sanders:
Greatness After Sixty-Five 7

CHAPTER 2 Winston Churchill:
A Glow-Worm 13

CHAPTER 3 Joseph Kennedy:
Craved Recognition and Privilege 63

CHAPTER 4 Sidney Poitier:
A Slot of My Choosing 126

CHAPTER 5 Abraham Lincoln:
Appetite for Politics 150

CHAPTER 6 Suze Orman:
Like What You Do 170

CHAPTER 7 Barack Obama:
Life Beyond His Father's Dilemma 181

CHAPTER 8 Oprah Winfrey:
Determined To Achieve Fame 242

CHAPTER 9 Realizing Our Powers 259

CHAPTER 10 Success and Greatness 276

Illustration 297

Acknowledgements 299

About Author 300

Notes 301

INTRODUCTION

I began writing this book with the aim of delving into a distinctive subject that would be valuable and enjoyable for readers. I had an idea of approaching personal development from a new angle—something fresh that would give readers a new perspective in this area and a new way of looking at things. An autobiography or a fictional book was out of the question. I had written my first book, an autobiographical fiction, in the early nineties and had lost all two hundred and fifty pages of it on my first laptop. In addition to this predicament, I had begun to harbor the notion that autobiographies were for those with accomplishments of epic proportions or those with things about their lives that would be significant or noteworthy or profound to their readers. So as I wrote and simultaneously prodded my thoughts on how to create a valuable reading experience for my readers, it occurred to me to explore the lives of highly successful individuals. I became convinced that there were manifestations of certain aspects of their lives that could be prototypical or shed some light on a new perspective of significance regarding their approach to success and greatness. As an ardent student of personal development, and having read countless autobiographies and biographies, I decided that an eclectic analysis of these subjects would be a worthwhile undertaking.

Numerous books have been written about success, greatness, and their rewards. However, I felt there was still more that could be learned directly from individuals of great accomplishment by looking at their lives and exploring the intricacies of how they conducted their activities in parity with their needs, ambitions, and principles in order to attain great heights. I also wanted to see if there would be an opportunity to demystify some of the myths about the quest for success.

Some of the popular assertions and advice promulgated by self-improvement gurus, as well as various accomplished individuals, have been around for quite some time. These individuals have contended that the key elements of success and greatness include the following: self-confidence, tenacity, a relentless work ethic, persistence, assertiveness, and risk taking. These are all key ingredients in any plan to make enormous strides in life. Yet, some of us who are tenacious in our endeavors and are hardworking have still not achieved any remarkable level of success; hence, some of these theories are at times still tantamount to myths, or they have left us scratching our heads and wondering what we are missing. So I felt that there is still a lot to learn about success—as there is about most things in life.

* * *

I also approached this book from an introspective point of view, by looking at myself and trying to decipher the lessons I have learned from being an entrepreneur. When I left my sales position in corporate America for entrepreneurial pursuits, I had no doubt that I wanted to take this bold step. The staffing industry was the outcome of the questions I had asked myself. I asked myself if I had the capability of making business-to-business sales calls; I detested selling to individuals, and I did not want to be involved in any endeavor that entailed such sales calls. Next, I asked myself if the initial cash outlay would be minimal because I did not have a lot of cash. I also asked myself if I had any transferrable business skill that I could utilize in this new venture; I had some skills in marketing, sales, and customer service.

Once I embarked on my quest as an entrepreneur, the task was arduous and I had my moments of doubt and episodes when I almost gave up. I underwent an experiential learning process that was different from anything I had learned in corporate America or through the study of other business models in school or from a business plan. I was taken by surprise by my indirect expenses and some uncontrollable variables. However, I stuck to my guns and made it work.

Upon my initial foray into the world of entrepreneurship, I knew little to nothing about the pursuit of a passion, and I had not given much thought to success and its trappings; I just wanted to make headway in business. I knew that I enjoyed the work immensely. I was also absolutely riveted by the new venture, finding ways to outperform my competitors, and offering exceptional customer service to my clients.

Once I had surmounted the initial hurdles, my company's sales increased, along with my desire to become a serial entrepreneur. Within four years, my company's revenue was right at $4.5 million. Following this, I delved into the restaurant and real estate industries.

This abbreviated chronicle of the progression of my primary business is by no means an indication of how quickly a business can ascend into prominence; it is merely a way to show how we can make success out of an activity we enjoy. After all, there have been countless businesses that have achieved unprecedented successes within four to five years with revenues in excess of $100 million.

As I explored the lives of the individuals whom I featured in this book, an interesting phenomenon began to unravel: They were passionate about their undertakings, something I had inadvertently mirrored in my entrepreneurial quests. In addition, I discovered that these individuals possessed a few other qualities that would be endearing to my readers—qualities that could potentially elucidate the true path to success and greatness. The enjoyment of my entrepreneurial endeavors had been evidenced by my success and my excitement about owning a business. However, I failed to recognize all the ramifications of drive and passion in the achievement and sustainability of success. For all intents and purposes, the individuals featured in this book may have been in the same predicament—being driven to do the right things to achieve and sustain the pinnacle of success and greatness without the awareness of all the factors responsible for their success. In addition to discovering the unique qualities of these great individuals, I also discovered another true passion of mine: writing.

The relativity of success and greatness, and the link between personal development, spirituality, and passion also became of interest to me, although they are not the focus of this book. There are societal and individual parameters for defining success and greatness. As we continue in our quest for success and greatness, could they, inexorably, be linked to happiness and spiritual fulfillment? Could there be an intertwining of success, greatness, religion, spiritual fulfillment, and personal development? Better yet, could there be a convergence of all these factors? Through the lives of the successful individuals featured in this book, we can examine what they have done right to see if there are any consistencies we can incorporate into our own lives. As imperfect as these individuals may be or may have been, there are lessons we can learn from their lives.

Accomplishments are deemed important in society—thus, the nations of the world and their people are grouped by their economic power and achievements. We humans are defined by our vocations, incomes, successes, and the strides we make in life, individually and collectively. The world is defined by the successes of its inhabitants. The industrialized nations or the group of twenty (the G-20), developing nations, and emerging markets are all categorized by their gross domestic product (GDP). It is a given that this categorization is ultimately linked to success and advancement in the world—the achievements of the various nations and their citizens. These accomplishments are instrumental in the improvement of the quality of life for mankind and in making a difference in the world.

What is the relationship between passion and the enjoyment of what we do? Could this hold the key to success and greatness? How can we sustain our passion? How does our drive factor into this equation? According to *Forbes*, 87 percent of Americans do not like their jobs. How do we go about identifying an activity that we enjoy? Where would we be as a nation if more people were to take delight in their jobs?

All of the individuals featured in this book achieved great success and fame by U.S. and world standards. What do they all have in common? What can they teach us that we have not been able to learn from success and achievement pundits? Obviously, there are factors to be learned that can enhance the number of highly accomplished individuals in the world; things that can be learned about ways of embarking on the pursuit of our goals in an adept manner that will provide substantial results, which will increase the number of accomplished individuals—impacting the world positively.

What if more people in the world were to become more passionate about their vocations? Would that give rise to the enhancement of the quality of life for all mankind? An increase in the pursuit of our passion will lead to more innovations in the world. More innovations and increased efficiencies in the world will make a difference in the lives of all humans.

Naturally, we all have diverse aptitudes in varied activities, different niches, drives, opportunities, passions, circumstances, interests, and numerous other attributes. The path to greatness and success depends, to a large degree, on how well we are able to develop and harness all of these elements through our thinking, dedication, and the pursuit of our passion to make something of ourselves.

One advantage of studying the lives of luminaries is that certain aspects of their lives are prototypical; these individuals are comparable to pioneers in education, inventors, and discoverers. They have established great models that are discernible and emblematic by virtue of the portrayal of their lives. We can pattern ourselves in our quests after some of these experiential models, for more effective results.

As depicted in the lives of the highly accomplished individuals featured in this book, the acquisition of our drive and subsequent pursuit of our passion will enable us to not only enhance the quality of life for humans, but also to achieve phenomenal success. The individuals featured in this book led interesting and exemplary lives with respect to going from drive to passion and becoming highly accomplished. By examining their lives, we can learn how to acquire our drive and pursue our passion.

*   *   *

Early man had to contend with sticks, stones, earth, water, and other bare necessities of life, but the world has made tremendous strides since then. Looking around today, I marvel at the advancement around me with humility and gratitude. Futurists contend that we as humans are still in the infancy of our development, so one can only imagine what advances will be made in the future. As long as we continue to shed light on the correct ways of going about the quest for success and greatness, many more achievements will be made in the world at breakneck speed. Making strides in life should be a perpetual process that we owe ourselves and our society.

CHAPTER 1
"Colonel" Harland Sanders: Greatness After Sixty-Five

Although it is imperative that we should be mentally and physically capable of embarking on any project, old age has minimal impact on the pursuit of our passion and the achievement of success and greatness. This is evidenced by "Colonel" Harland Sanders and a host of others who found success in their sixties. Sanders, founder of Kentucky Fried Chicken (KFC), did so at the age of sixty-five. If we think we are too old to pursue our passion, we should look around us at all the people who made great accomplishments in their fifties and sixties.

* * *

Harland Sanders was born in 1890, and at the tender age of six, he was burdened with the responsibility of taking care of his younger siblings; his mother had to go to work, so she taught him how to cook a variety of dishes, including fried chicken. She worked in a shirt factory to support the family. Sanders took care of the domestic work, cooking for his siblings and watching them. His father, who had labored in the coal mines of Kentucky, had just died.

The cooking skills that Sanders acquired from his mother would remain with him for the rest of his life and would prompt his foray into the restaurant industry. Although Sanders did not start off working in a restaurant, over the years he modified his fried chicken recipe, and it orchestrated a drive in him to make something of this recipe—which would take him to unprecedented heights.

Sanders held several jobs, including his endeavors as a street car conductor and a railroad fireman. While working with the railroad, Sanders took a correspondence course in law. He eventually became a lawyer and practiced law in Little Rock, Arkansas. He brought his law career to a screeching halt when he got involved in a scuffle with one of his clients in a courtroom.

Later, as Sanders got older, he opened a service station, where he also operated a small eatery for customers. The more he exhibited his great cooking skills, the more his business grew. He eventually expanded into a restaurant next to the service station. His specialty was fried chicken, which included other Southern dishes such as vegetables and biscuits. His restaurant grew into a 142-seat establishment. To sharpen his skills in restaurant management, Sanders took an eight-week course in restaurant management at Cornell University.

For Sanders, the acquisition of knowledge in the area pertaining to his passion was instrumental in propelling him to great heights. Other individuals featured in this book, as depicted in subsequent chapters, mirror Sanders in embarking on avid quests for education in the activities encompassing their passion.

As great as a higher education may be—with respect to enabling us to increase our level of information, polish, flexibility, and learning capacity—the amount of effort that we put into education, preparation, and practice in those activities relating to our passion will contribute immensely toward our success and greatness in our chosen field. This is evidenced not only by the personalities featured in this book, but also by American technology titans such as Bill Gates, Steve Jobs, Michael Dell, and Mark Zuckerberg. All were college dropouts who went on to achieve greatness by founding multibillion-dollar technology companies. These individuals were able to attain great heights through preparation, practice, and education in their chosen activities.

Following his course at Cornell and the growing success of his 142-seat restaurant, Sanders became a burgeoning force in the restaurant industry. His popularity and skill in the industry earned him the honorary title of "Colonel" from the governor of Kentucky, an honor that was bestowed upon him again by the lieutenant governor of the same state. Following this recognition, he began dressing in a white suit with a black string tie and black shoes, carrying a cane, and wearing a white goatee and mustache, portraying the image of a Southern gentleman.

Sanders' budding success came to an abrupt end when the construction of a new highway diverted traffic from his restaurant. As a result of this, his business dwindled and eventually failed. So he retired at the age of sixty-five and proceeded to collect Social Security.

Sanders decided to come out of retirement after collecting his first monthly check of $105. He was sixty-five years old and completely broke. His decision to come out of retirement is commendable. He was deterred neither by age nor by failure. Sixty-five is an age when most people generally throw in the towel and opt for an easier life: lounging, playing golf, or doing something that requires minimal mental or physical exertion. Sanders proved that the paradigm of being undeterred by failure or advanced age is a good one.

Sanders was confident in himself. He had learned valuable lessons from his failure. Still passionate about cooking, he believed that he could be successful at operating another restaurant. Armed with his passion and driven by the need to make something of his fried chicken recipe, Sanders went from place to place trying to sell it, and at the same time he sold chicken cooked with his pressure cooker out of his car. He decided to take full advantage of his fame and cooking skills by convincing some people he knew to invest in his fried chicken recipe. He encountered obstacles; they rejected his idea. His persistent efforts finally paid off when he found a couple who embraced his concept and was willing to invest in it. That was the advent of the famous Kentucky Fried Chicken restaurants, or KFC, as we know it today. From then on, he built and franchised his restaurants.

Sanders often paid surprise visits to his restaurants and scolded employees for not doing things correctly. He was a perfectionist. He was also fastidious about cleanliness and all other aspects of the business. Perhaps in Sanders' time, the chastising of employees was not looked upon with the same amount of disdain as it is today; however, the fact still remains that in any given era, the scolding of one's employees would not have been looked upon in a positive light. Colonel Sanders was definitely not without his faults. But in spite of his weaknesses, he was a tenacious and resilient individual. He was also passionate about his endeavors.

When Sanders sold his stake in his KFC restaurants for $2 million in 1964 to John Y. Brown and his group of investors, little did he know KFC would change ownership a few times and become a behemoth. Twenty years later, in 1984, R.J. Reynolds Industries sold the company to PepsiCo for $840 million. KFC is currently owned by Yum! Brands, Inc, a spinoff from PepsiCo. Yum! Brands operates several franchises including Taco Bell and Pizza Hut. More than two billion dinners of Sanders' fried chicken are now sold annually in over eighty countries. According to Encyclopedia.com's article, "KFC Corporation," as of 2007, KFC made $520.3 million in sales and had 11,000 locations in 80 countries, with 5,300 domestic restaurants. The company's sales peaked at $4.8 billion in 2002. KFC has been plagued by problems pertaining to the unhealthiness of fried foods.

* * *

Although Sanders met with many failures and challenges, he had some remarkable successes in his imperfect yet extraordinary life. He started a few businesses that he eventually closed for one reason or another. Success did not come easily for him, but he was persistent and resilient. Sanders had a difficult time convincing other restaurateurs to stock and cook with his secret recipe. Also, he tried his hand at many careers and professions, including law and sales. He continued and did not give up until he arrived at his real love and passion—cooking fried chicken with his secret recipe. This led to his tremendous achievement: the advent of KFC.

Sometimes, we can easily recognize our passion; at other times, it is not so easy. We all need jobs to make an income, but to make achievements of significance that would mirror Sanders', we should ultimately choose the endeavor we enjoy the most. If that endeavor is not immediately apparent then, similar to Sanders, we should go the trial and error route until we can truly identify what we enjoy doing. People who are close to us can also be instrumental in helping us identify areas that could potentially be our niche. This, invariably, could be where our passion lies. As the Greek philosopher Socrates said when giving a young man advice about passion, the endeavor we want as much as we want the air we breathe is our passion.

Another basic component of success and greatness is the commitment of time, energy, and patience in finding that passion. Since our passion does not always manifest itself readily, time, energy, and patience are vital ingredients for us as we search for our passion. In some cases, for instance, a child may know at age five that she wants to be a neurosurgeon, and she goes on to do just that; this, however, is rare. Identifying our passion is often not that simple. Thomas J. Perkins, a Silicon Valley billionaire and venture capitalist, said in a *60 Minutes* television interview that he tried his hand at ten different ventures and only two of those ventures were successful—the two that elicited his passion.

Some important elements in Sanders' remarkable life were that he was undeterred by age and was driven to go on the quest for his passion. We should be undeterred by age unless we are underage or our vocation involves activities that are too physically demanding for people in our age group. Sanders was driven by some factors: Initially, he grew up in poverty, and he was driven to elevate himself through the pursuit of cooking, with the recipe he had obtained from his mother; later on, he set out to make something of his recipe.

Sanders identified his passion for cooking fried chicken and Southern dishes. How do we recognize our passion when we find it? If we enjoy an activity so much that we are willing to work without immediate financial rewards while in pursuit of that endeavor—this is a good indication that we have found our passion. If we have a niche in that activity, then there is definitely something to build on. If we pursue an endeavor with conviction, it is also a sign that we may have found our passion. In his book *The 21 Indispensable Qualities of a Leader*, John C. Maxwell contended that John Schnatter of Papa John's Pizza lives and breathes pizza. "And he enjoys it so much that he is always in the thick of things." Of course, our passion should be a value-added activity—something that would add value to or enhance people's lives.

How do we acquire passion similar to Sanders'? Can we learn to be passionate and driven? Certainly, we can learn to be passionate and driven. Once we have identified a cogent reason for desiring success, the next step entails identifying a passion that can bring our desire to fruition. Everyone has a niche or a calling, which we need to identify, in order to pursue our passion. Our success depends on ensuring that there is a correlation between our niche and passion. It also depends on fervently pursuing that passion. Of course, some of the key factors that are orchestrated by passion—customized education, preparation, enjoyment of the activity, courage, resilience, tenacity, confidence, and ability to take risks—have to be present to ensure the successful pursuit of our passion.

CHAPTER 2
Winston Churchill: A Glow-Worm

Winston Churchill's childhood was mired by his inconsistent performance in school and a distant relationship with his parents. He came in at the bottom of his class a few times, and at other times, he did well. In general, he struggled with some subjects such as Latin and mathematics, and excelled in history and English literature. Despite Churchill's troubled beginnings, including his less than stellar performance in school, he rose to become one of the world's greatest leaders and an intellectual powerhouse who was driven to write volumes of books and to win the Nobel Prize in Literature—thus making unprecedented accomplishments through the successful pursuit of his passion.

The care of Churchill and his younger brother, Jack, was relegated to a nanny, Mrs. Everest. At that time in Britain, it was not uncommon for people of considerable social status, of the caliber of Churchill's parents, to surround themselves with servants and nannies. Churchill's nanny practically raised him. Most of the time, his parents were too busy with social engagements and travels to really concern themselves with the intricate details of child rearing.

Churchill's impetuous behavior contributed to the distance between him and his mother. According to Martin Gilbert in his biography of Churchill, *Churchill: A Life*, once, upon returning to his Brighton boarding school after a brief holiday with his parents, he wrote back to his mother saying, "You must be happy without me, no screams from Jack or complaints. It must be heaven on earth." Despite the distance between them, Churchill loved his mother dearly.

While in boarding school, young Churchill communicated with his parents through letters. In most of his letters to his parents, he craved their ever-so-elusive attention, especially his father's. When Churchill's father, Lord Randolph, once visited the town of Brighton on official business without stopping to see him, young Churchill was sad after he read about his father's visit in the local newspapers. According to Gilbert, he wrote his father saying, "I cannot think why you did not come to see me while you were in Brighton. I was disappointed but I suppose you were too busy to come." Despite the distance between him and his father, Churchill revered him and decided to follow in his footsteps by going into politics. He followed his father's political career through the newspapers.

As much as Churchill revered his father, he was also cognizant of his mistakes. Lord Randolph was a minister—a cabinet position in the British government. The elder Churchill was terminated from his job as a minister due to problems that ensued from a bad decision he made while in office. Churchill would later forge a closer relationship with his own children than he had with his father because he did not want them to go through the experiences he had as a child.

Upon completion of high school, Churchill, at the persuasion of his father, opted for a military career. Lord Randolph was convinced that his son was academically ill-prepared to attend a university. The Sandhurst Military Academy, which prepared young men for a career in the infantry, was Churchill's last option. He lacked proficiency in mathematics, which was the prerequisite for a career in the Royal Artillery or Royal Engineers. Churchill passed the entrance exam to Sandhurst Military Academy on his third try.

Already, Churchill's early years were riddled with disappointments and failures. He craved the love of his parents, which he did not get. His behavior was deemed wanting by both parents. Although he had a flair for English and history, he was anything but academically gifted; hence, it took him three attempts on the entrance exam to gain admission to Sandhurst. In spite of these failures and disappointments, Churchill would later in life show the mark of a great individual and the resilience it would take to reach great heights.

The discipline at Sandhurst Military Academy was good for Churchill. While there, his father's health, unbeknownst to young Churchill, began to deteriorate. He wrote letters to his father about his progress. Churchill's father often responded with letters decrying his conduct. Churchill did not let his father's denigrating letters foster a sense of inadequacy in him. Rather, as he indicated in his letters to his mother, he resolved to do better and to make something of himself at Sandhurst.

Unaware of his father's malady, syphilis, and his continuing deterioration, both physically and mentally, Churchill continued to write letters to Lord Randolph, assuring him he would do better. The replies from his father, due to his poor health, were sporadic, sometimes confused and incoherent because he was also mentally incapacitated and disoriented. Despite his father's nasty letters, Churchill continued to idolize him. His father died a few months prior to his commission as a second lieutenant.

Churchill was now driven by the memory of his father, and he was prepared to prove that he was not the tepid young man his father had made him out to be. This served as one of Churchill's drives, responsible for impelling him to greatness. Resolving to make something of ourselves in order to prove a point to others, or even to prove them wrong, is pervasive among success-oriented people. This drive stems from the avoidance of negative perceptions that others might have of us; it is characteristic of the drive that spurs passions and eventually propels many individuals to greatness. Churchill was determined to prove to the memory of his father that he could make something of himself. It is crucial that we acquire a strong driving force that will impel our achievements.

Churchill graduated close to the top of his class at Sandhurst Military Academy—twentieth in a class of 130 graduates. He did not receive a four-year college degree upon graduating from Sandhurst because it was not a full-fledged college. It was a military academy that prepared individuals to become officers in the British military after two years of study.

Once Churchill received his commission as a second lieutenant, it immediately became obvious to him that his education in the military was narrow in its scope. He had a thirst for more knowledge; thus he indicated to his mother that his life in the military was not sufficiently intellectually stimulating to him. He further said he had read and practically memorized all of his father's speeches in an effort to improve himself. He was despondent and unfulfilled at that point. He also indicated to his mother that if he knew with certainty he would be stationed in London, he would seek the help of a tutor to help him with the study of economics or modern history.

What Churchill needed was a mentor who would point him in the right direction in his intellectual pursuits. He would become adept in seeking mentors. Churchill would also utilize his mother both as a mentor and a bridge between him and other potential mentors, who would become instrumental in facilitating the accomplishment of his goals.

Churchill sought the advice of Bourke Cockran, a friend and an activist, in trying to determine how he should proceed with his studies. Having noticed his fascination for reading and his quest for knowledge, Cockran encouraged Churchill to study sociology and political economy, contending that he saw in the young officer a curiosity and a zest for life that was unprecedented and could only lead to a promising future in politics.

Thus Churchill, with the help of his new mentor Cockran, was able to set about educating himself in the activities encompassing his passion. Churchill was already driven and motivated to become educated. He had a drive that stemmed from his need to make something of himself and to dispel any notion that anyone, including his mother, may have harbored to the contrary.

Churchill's readings up to that point had been fragmented; however, all of that would change once he embarked on a more organized syllabus, in an effort to become erudite and successful. It was as if he had become a student—he studied with an undying appetite, reading far and wide in the fields of politics, economics, and history. He craved the kind of sophistication and refinement that came with an Oxford or a Cambridge education. Ironically, this type of polish, which Churchill so ardently sought, would elude him for the rest of his life; hence, at the peak of his political career, a critic would characterize him as being uncouth and pompous. This goes to show that as accomplished as we may be in life, some of our aspirations may still remain elusive. Churchill's zest for knowledge in the area of his passion contributed toward the many accomplishments he would make.

At the age of twenty-one, Churchill decided to go to New York and Cuba. It would be his first trip across the Atlantic. While in New York, Churchill observed that there was a marked difference between New York and London. The pomp and pageantry associated with protocol and class that was the order of the day in London was absent in New York. In a letter to his brother, Churchill told him that everything was pragmatic in America—there was even an absence of the wearing of wigs and robes in court.

Following his trip to the U.S., Churchill continued to pursue his aspirations. His drives were discernible, and they fueled his passion. His inclination toward politics would culminate in a passion for it. He enjoyed writing, literature, and history. While in the military, Churchill pursued another passion of his, journalism. He also wrote great speeches. He, in essence, became an eloquent orator. Neither Churchill's inheritance from his father nor his salary from the military was enough to support his lavish lifestyle. He became driven by extravagance and the desire to become wealthy and famous, and these drives would contribute to fueling his passion in writing and journalism.

* * *

Churchill was assigned to India on a military mission. Prior to his departure, he begged his mother to exert her influence on some of the prominent people she knew in government to enable him to experience some combat in the Matabele War in South Africa. He wanted to make his mark on the battlefield in order to be decorated with medals of valor. Churchill was prudent enough to realize that a distinguished career in the military would enhance his political ambitions. He also asked his mother to convince one of the British newspapers to hire him as a war correspondent.

Upon his arrival in India, Churchill found his assignment to be boring. He was surrounded by too many servants and did not have enough to do. He told his mother in a letter that India was pervaded by boring individuals who were snobs. This situation enabled him to occupy himself with his studies of history and literature.

Churchill did not get his wish to be deployed to South Africa; rather, he was deployed to the frontier of Afghanistan and Malakand. There he served a dual function as a soldier and a war correspondent. His mother was able to secure a position for him as a war correspondent with *The Daily Telegraph*, one of the most influential British newspapers at the time. Churchill did well in both roles. He experienced some combat, filed some good stories, and gained acclaim for his writing.

Churchill definitely knew the value of mentorship and how to leverage his mother's and other people's influence to achieve success. Introductions, connections, powerful friends, a name, and good advice well-followed were all basic ingredients for success according to Churchill's letters to his mother. On the other hand, he reasoned that these factors had their limitations, and that people were ultimately judged by the public on their own merits.

Despite Churchill's youth, he was precocious enough to know what he needed to do to make something of himself. He leveraged his mother's influence, and he sought help from his mentors. He became passionate about a few activities: journalism, writing, the military, politics, and public speaking. Churchill enhanced his passions by reading voraciously. Remarkably, he was savvy enough to realize that irrespective of the number of mentors he had and the amount of influence he could leverage through them, he still had to exhibit excellence in his endeavors.

Mentors are usually instrumental in helping with the creation of opportunities for individuals who are driven and in pursuit of their passion. Churchill utilized mentors for this purpose. Most of us have heard stories or know of extremely skilled and passionate individuals in one vocation or another who never got discovered. The main reason for this is that these individuals never sought mentors to facilitate the creation of opportunities—the type that would have brought the right amount of attention to their passion or skill.

Churchill received accolades and financial compensation for his successful newspaper coverage of the Afghan war. Even his mother, Lady Randolph, was proud of him. She indicated to him that his writing was too good for him to remain in the military where his talent as a writer would be underutilized. Churchill made money from his coverage of the war; this helped to renew his confidence in himself. It also enabled him to realize that he could earn an extra income as a writer to augment his earnings from the military. In fact, this realization of his income-earning potential as a writer enabled him to dispel any notion he previously harbored of possibly engaging in litigation with his mother to recover some of his inheritance from her, for fear of her extravagance and the fact that she might marry a man who would stand in the way of his inheritance.

Churchill was eager to go to the war front as a soldier and a correspondent. He was a unique individual in the sense that he actively sought combat in the war, while his fellow officers were content to let the war come to them. In addition to this excitement that stemmed from his youthful exuberance, Churchill was wise enough to realize that a great military career would enhance his political ambitions. He would eventually get his wish. He experienced wars and all of their unpleasantness as a soldier, and he also had the opportunity to cover these wars as a journalist.

* * *

While on leave in England, Churchill tested the waters in politics by delivering his first political speech. He had asked his mother to assemble an audience of about two thousand people for the occasion. Lady Randolph did as she was told, realizing the leadership qualities of her son, who was becoming a young man with great potential and a matching ambition. Churchill's speech was a resounding success. It lasted for about an hour. He reported to his mother and some friends that his audience interrupted him about six times with very loud applauses lasting about ten minutes each time. Also, they yelled out to him, indicating that they wanted more.

Churchill's war experience had elicited the theme for his first book titled *The Story of the Malakand Field Force*, which was published in 1898. His book received acclaim all over Britain. Top politicians and military officers also gave him accolades for the book. No sooner had Churchill published his book than the prime minister, Lord Salisbury, invited him to Number 10 Downing Street, the official residence of the prime minister of Britain, to both compliment and congratulate him on his well-written book. Churchill recounted to family and friends how well he was received by the prime minister.

By the age of twenty-two, Churchill was already a young author, military officer, nascent politician, and war veteran. He had delivered a successful political speech and was on his way to greatness. At an age when most young people are preoccupied with the enrichment of their social lives, exploring and satisfying their sexual tendencies, and discovering the throes and excitement of adulthood without giving much thought to long-range ambitions, Churchill was busy, engrossed in charting the course of success in his life.

Churchill showed unrelenting persistence and willingness to leverage his relationships to achieve his ambitions by asking the prime minister's private secretary and a host of other noteworthy individuals who were his mother's friends and acquaintances to intercede on his behalf by asking the commander-in-chief of the elite British Expeditionary Force in the Sudan to nominate him for an assignment there. However, these recommendations and interventions on Churchill's behalf fell on the deaf ears of the commander-in-chief, who let it be known that there were a host of other qualified officers ahead of him in line for consideration into the force. Most people would have given up at that point, but Churchill pushed ahead in his effort to gain entry into the Expeditionary Force. Through the channels of influence and his relentless efforts, he was able to get the Army's adjutant general at the War Office to intervene on his behalf. Soon after a telegraph was sent to the commander by the adjutant general, Churchill was on his way to Egypt to join the Expeditionary Force. He later confessed to a friend that the only reason he was able to get into the Expeditionary Force so quickly was that two officers had died prior to his arrival, thus creating openings.

Churchill had an almost paradoxical yet pragmatic philosophy about his service in the military and his attraction for combat on the battlefield. In a letter to his mother written on his way down the Nile River, Churchill acknowledged that he was well aware of the imminent dangers in his undertakings; on the other hand, he had an inexplicable attraction for battle and killing the enemy. He was quite ambitious. He wanted to survive the war in order to accomplish his goals in life. Churchill's paradigm about his own fate prompted the following reflections to his mother, according to Gilbert's biography: "I may be killed. I do not think so. But if I am you must avail yourself of the consolations of philosophy and reflect on the utter insignificance of all human beings."

Again, Churchill was able to achieve his objective of being a soldier and a war correspondent for a newspaper, against all odds. However, this time, his commander in the Expeditionary Force was initially opposed to his bid to perform a dual function, but he eventually gave in to his request. Churchill's commander was the same individual who had been opposed to his admission into the Expeditionary Force. The commander had been critical of Churchill for leveraging undue influence to gain admission into the unit. The commander's criticism was centered on the fact that Churchill, whom he perceived to be a precocious and non-career military type, vied for and occupied a position that would have been more fitting for another worthy and well-meaning career soldier, whose career could have been greatly enhanced by a position in the Expeditionary Force.

Although Churchill, in his newspaper reports, was quite critical of the commander for the barbaric acts perpetrated by the British soldiers against the Sudanese, he was at the same time cognizant of his political future. His criticisms in his news filings caused him to make quite a few enemies. As powerful as these criticisms were, they did not derail his career trajectory in politics. Churchill continued to push ahead with all of his aspirations. The Sudanese War was brutal and unforgiving to the Sudanese Army. The British Expeditionary Force emerged victorious. The war gave rise to Churchill's idea for a second book, titled *The River War*. Following the end of the war, Churchill began planning to give more political speeches in anticipation of his return to England. He asked his mother to work on assembling an audience for him again.

* * *

As introspective and philosophical as Churchill seemed to be, he was not religious, as portrayed in Gilbert's biography, in a letter he had written to his mother during the Sudanese War: "But I can assure you I do not flinch—though I do not accept the Christian or any other form of religious belief." He did not entrust his fate in the war to a higher power. Churchill exuded confidence; he believed that he had a mission in life. He reasoned that the dangers of military operations would not terminate his existence, thereby preventing his life from unraveling, as he had envisioned it, into a life of enormous accomplishments in literature and politics. His sense of purpose became a good omen, which served to protect him from danger. Churchill was an existentialist who relied on his resilience, tenacity, and passion to achieve his goal.

In his views on Catholicism and Protestantism, Churchill espoused his preference for Protestantism. He contended that its practices and tenets were less ritualistic than those of Catholicism. He asserted that Protestantism was a bit more logical to him. He was like most other people who are passion-driven and on a quest for excellence: He constantly sought knowledge and questioned the meaning of human existence. Although Churchill preferred Protestantism to Catholicism, he believed in neither of the Christian denominations. Churchill told his cousin that people who believed in religion never experienced any marked level of prosperity because they were too preoccupied with the euphoria of their beliefs and too pacific to engage in the type of internal dialectic and conflict that usually gave rise to prosperity and progress. Rather than concentrating his efforts on religion, Churchill directed his philosophical and empathetic attention to the rights of the poor. He advocated the right of the poor to have the basic necessities of life. Churchill questioned the usefulness of religion when it allowed its followers to wallow in poverty with no gratification for their beliefs.

* * *

"When one door closes, another opens; but we often stare so long and so regretfully upon the closed door that we do not see the one which has opened for us." The first part of this quote by Alexander Graham Bell, the Scottish-born American inventor and educator responsible for the invention of the telephone, depicts Churchill's life thus far. The second part of it has relevance to those of us who continue to look in the wrong places for our passion—areas in which we have no niche. We should focus on our strengths and possibilities, not on our weaknesses, mistakes, and stumbling blocks. Churchill closely patterned his quests after the first part of this quote, in the sense that he was undeterred by the closed doors in his life. He did poorly in mathematics, Latin, and Greek, so he fervently pursued those subjects that encompassed his niche such as history, economics and literature. He could not get into a four-year university, so he chose a non-degreed military academy into which he still had some difficulties securing admission. Churchill did not spend time concerning himself with the fact that he could neither make good grades on certain subjects like Latin nor pass the entrance exam into a university. He circumvented barriers to reach his goals. Churchill ardently focused on his niche, which subsequently led to his quest for his passion in writing and politics.

Churchill's failure to obtain high marks in some of his subjects in school and his inability to gain admission into a four-year university illustrate the notion that there is not a straight path to success. Failure is an integral part of success. Achievement is a factor of succeeding at something more times than we fail or looking for ways to get beyond failures. Churchill utilized failure as a stepping stone to success, and he was confident in himself and his abilities.

Churchill, thus far, had led a multifaceted and dynamic life. His life had also been interesting. His father was a politician during his childhood, but he was not born into wealth. While in the military, he pursued his niche in writing. He went on to develop a passion for politics, journalism, and writing books. He submitted war news reports for newspapers on a part-time basis. He was able to juggle a military career, a career in journalism, writing books, and a foray into politics. He was passionate about all of these activities, which is indicative of the fact that we can be passionate about more than one thing at a time. It also shows that we can achieve excellence in all of our pursuits if we are able to allocate enough time to all of them. However, we must not ignore the inherent danger in trying to do too much at once; it may cause a lack of focus, among other things. Churchill had plenty of energy to sustain all of his adventures in the military and the pursuit of his other passions. He was able to cover the news as a journalist in the same wars in which he fought. Churchill was multidimensional and had varied interests, but he considered politics and leadership to be his ultimate objective. He wrote political speeches and tried them out on his audiences while he was on vacation in England.

In spite of his weaknesses, Churchill continued to make enormous strides in his endeavors. Although he was considered by his parents to be tepid as a child, he was highly opinionated, energetic, and spontaneous as a young adult. He was openly critical of religion, including Christianity, but he minimized any negative backlash from this stance by being an advocate for the poor. Although he harbored some racist views, which was not uncommon in his time, he tried to be fair by criticizing the barbaric acts perpetrated against the conquered, black Sudanese people by some of his fellow British soldiers.

Churchill was courageous and confident, and he believed in his capabilities. He truly subscribed to the notion that practice makes perfect. He was known to practice his speeches for long periods of time prior to delivering them. His commitment to practice, customized education, and preparation led him to visualize himself in his ultimate role as an accomplished politician and a leader. Churchill believed that he possessed unique qualities that made him an extraordinary individual. He was cool under fire on the battlefield, and he was a brave soldier. His coolness, awareness of the dangers of battle, and sense of purpose helped to keep him alive while in combat.

* * *

After the Sudanese War, Churchill returned to his old regiment in India, and shortly thereafter, he decided to leave the Army and return to England. On his way back to England, he stopped in Egypt for some time to work on his book. Churchill was intent on researching the Sudanese War and the path his regiment took down the Nile River. He had already encountered some difficulties with his criticisms of the Army earlier in his newspaper reports; so this time, he sought to curb his biases in his new book. He complained to his mother about how monotonous his endeavors were and how difficult it was, sometimes, to concentrate on his writing—a predicament I am sure most writers encounter.

Churchill's objective was to enter politics upon his return to England. There was an opening in Parliament due to an illness, which brought the total number of open positions in Parliament to two instead of one. He was invited to run for a political office by a friend, who suggested that they represent each of the constituencies with the openings. In preparation for this election, Churchill gave many speeches. In fact, he spoke at eight different venues every day—a heavy campaign schedule. His colleague who had initially invited him to join in the election died suddenly. Churchill decided to continue with the elections, not allowing the death of his friend to become a deterrent. He ran under the platform of establishing a type of program for the elderly that would later serve as a prototype for the United States' Medicare program. He abhorred any type of prohibitive measures of liquor trade and licensing by law, but supported voluntary control by individuals and liquor establishments.

Yet again, Churchill faced a setback, losing the election to Parliament; however, the experience he gained was invaluable. He was neither handsome nor tall, but he made up for these imperfections by being eloquent, affable, and having a good sense of humor. His passion for the English language, literature, and history enabled him to not only compose good speeches, but also to become a great orator. He spoke with an upper-class accent, which gave him more credibility.

Soon after his failed campaign, Churchill headed to South Africa to cover the Anglo-Boer War as a journalist. The *Daily Mail* had initially made him an offer to cover the war as their correspondent. He had two newspapers compete for his services in order to get the best pay. Churchill, in his shrewd way, immediately sent a letter to *The Morning Post* telling them of the offer he had received from the *Daily Mail*. *The Morning Post* offered Churchill the British pound equivalent of approximately $106,000 in 2009 U.S. dollars, topping the *Daily Mail's* offer, to cover the war from coast to coast for four months. Here again, Churchill was staying close to his passion, journalism.

Churchill had the uncanny ability to maneuver the system to his advantage: In addition to being a journalist in the South African war, he also desired to join the military again and serve there as a soldier. He presumed that it would be easier for him to get commissioned in South Africa than it would be to be commissioned in Britain; he knew the adjutant of the British Army in South Africa, which made it easy for him to get commissioned there. Prior to his departure, Churchill made sure all his contacts were adequately arranged: He requested and received a letter of introduction from Joseph Chamberlain, the British colonial secretary, to the British High Commission in South Africa. In his usual manner, he was once again leveraging the influence of his friends and mentors to achieve his goals.

The war in South Africa was between the British and the Dutch settlers who occupied the Boer Republic. It was triggered by an ultimatum issued by the Boers to the British, demanding a withdrawal of all British forces from South Africa. The war ensued as a result of the refusal of the British to comply with the withdrawal ultimatum.

Once Churchill got to Cape Town, the atmosphere in the British colony was quite tense. He caught a train in hopes of traveling to Ladysmith in an attempt to uncover some news events for the newspaper. Apparently, over a thousand British soldiers had already been captured by the Boer forces. Through a combination of maneuvers involving catching the first train and chartering another, Churchill was able to get close to Ladysmith, which was already under siege and surrounded by the Boer troops.

His newspaper reports and findings were informative. The capture of pockets of British forces by the Boer troops was endemic at that point. In light of this fact, Churchill's findings and reports became quite crucial to the British. He was appalled at the sheer number of British forces who were surrendering to the Boers. Churchill, in his opinionated fashion, suggested to the adjutant general of the British forces in South Africa, Sir Evelyn Woods, that the British commanders who were surrendering to the Boers be punished.

Meanwhile, Churchill's book *The River War* had been published back home in Britain, while he was covering the Boer War in South Africa. It received rave reviews, which contributed to his already burgeoning popularity engendered by his newspaper reporting and political aspirations.

From the outskirts of Ladysmith where Churchill had been filing news reports, he decided to travel to Ladysmith in an armored train because other means of transportation were in jeopardy of ambush by the Boer forces. The situation was dangerous. He was in the company of some British soldiers on the train. Once the train stopped, Churchill and a friend decided to go up the hill to get a good view of the surrounding territory in order to assess their options. As they stood at the top of the hill—with shadows of their profile on the ground, caused by a reflection from the sun—a few British soldiers came upon them, thinking they were the enemy. Once they were able to prove to the soldiers that they were also British, the encounter and potential disaster was successfully defused, although their potential captors seemed somewhat disappointed. Churchill immediately took pictures of the soldiers and filed a report of this incident to *The Morning Post*. The men were pleased to have their pictures taken for the London newspaper report.

That evening at dinner with a military officer, Churchill's military instincts were manifested when he voiced his opinion about the officer's proposed retreat, with the soldiers in his command, from the frontlines for fear of an attack by a large contingent of Boer troops. Churchill made a strong case against the withdrawal, with some very valid reasons. He contended that the attack from the Boer troops was not imminent due to his perception of a reluctance on the part of the Boer command to cross the river, which was close by. After dinner, following the departure of the officer, Churchill and his friend observed that the British forces were unloading their truck, which was an indication that the officer had a change of mind about the retreat. Churchill gloated and immediately took credit for the change of mind by the officer.

A captain who was also Churchill's friend received an order to prepare an armored train with 150 men to ride, once again, in the direction of the enemy for a possible attack. When the captain informed Churchill of his orders and invited him to join him, Churchill was initially reluctant, but upon further consideration, he changed his mind and decided to go on the train ride toward enemy territory. It was to be one of the most dangerous assignments he would ever undertake.

The train throttled along for quite some time without incident. Then the captain received information that fifty Boer troops had been spotted. Soon after that, Churchill and the soldiers in the train came under intense attack. The Boer troops had placed a stone on the railroad tracks, causing the derailment of two trucks in front, close to the engine. Soon, the entire train was ambushed by the Boer troops. Churchill immediately put on his soldier's hat, instinctively, and offered his services to the commander, who quickly became aware of Churchill's capabilities as a soldier.

Churchill proceeded to organize some men to help him repair the derailed train tracks; they pushed the derailed coach off the line in order to conjoin the remaining coaches in sequence to the engine. By this time the enemy fire was fierce, with two enemy soldiers dead. Four British soldiers had also been killed and thirty wounded. Churchill and the British soldiers were under heavy fire from a combination of machine guns and heavy artillery. The shots clanged loudly on the engine of the train and the metal frame of the coaches. All efforts to repair the train lines proved futile.

The soldiers and Churchill decided to give the coupling of the engine of the train to the coach one last try. He positioned himself properly, in order to get a good grip, to exert the force needed to try to get the coach and the train's engine to couple, to no avail. The coupling hook had been badly damaged by a shell from the Boer artillery. Churchill threw his revolver and field glasses down in order to help the engineer carry several wounded men into the engine compartment of the train. The engineer had also been wounded. He was hit in the head by a piece of shrapnel. It was mind-boggling to one of the soldiers, who observed him, as this soldier tried to conjecture how Churchill could have escaped injury even though the engine had been struck over fifty times by enemy shells. Churchill would emerge unscathed through it all, even as he helped to load wounded soldiers onto the train.

The soldiers and their officers were completely enthralled and impressed by Churchill's bravery. His coolness under fire was also remarkable. They were so impressed that one officer would later tell a newspaper reporter that Churchill was one of the bravest men he had ever known. Some of these men would later make their admiration for Churchill known to their peers and the British military. As a result, reports of Churchill's heroic efforts became public knowledge.

Once Churchill had finished loading the wounded soldiers onto the train, he advised the engineer to pull the engine out slowly. He rode the train for several yards in order to tend to the wounded soldiers. Once he ascertained that the wounded soldiers and the engineer could ride to safety without him, he calmly stepped out off the train and walked back toward the sight of the ambush and derailment to see if he could be of assistance to the captain.

Churchill observed from a distance a white handkerchief held up high—by the British forces—an indication of surrender by the captain and his forces. He deduced that the captain had no choice because he was cornered and surrounded by the Boer troops. He turned back and walked in the direction of the railroad tracks. He was not quite two hundred yards from his previous vantage point when he observed two men in the distance who seemed to be railroad service attendants. As soon as they saw Churchill, they pointed their guns at him, and Churchill realized who they really were: Boer soldiers. He started back toward the train, running. He spotted a river embankment ahead and dropped into it for cover.

The Boers fired at him as he ran. The bullets came whistling by as he ran in a zigzag manner. He ducked and dropped down for cover on occasion. Churchill maneuvered himself into the bushes and made a mad dash for the river bank, determined to escape. Suddenly, another Boer soldier came out of nowhere, galloping toward him, with his gun in one arm pointed at him. Churchill tried to reach for his side arm. It was not there. He had laid his gun and binoculars on the ground prior to helping with the derailment and the wounded soldiers. The soldier on the horse pointed his weapon at Churchill and was about to fire when Churchill, sensing the dire situation, raised his hands in surrender. He had no choice; he was captured and taken prisoner.

The soldiers who had ridden the train to safety with the wounded spoke highly of Churchill's bravery. Even though he was not officially a soldier, his gallantry in the derailment ordeal made national headlines in the newspapers. Everyone was impressed with him; it was rumored that he would be awarded a medal of valor. Churchill's mother was informed that Churchill had been taken prisoner and that he was unhurt.

Churchill showed the guards his press credentials informing them that he was a journalist. He and the rest of the prisoners were marched toward Pretoria, to a prisoner-of-war camp. He looked longingly at his surroundings as they passed Ladysmith, wishing for his freedom. Later, all the prisoners were carted away by train to Pretoria.

Once Churchill and the other prisoners arrived at the prison camp, he immediately dispatched a letter to the secretary of State for the Boer Republic, explaining that he was a journalist and ought to be released. Unbeknownst to Churchill, he was already an internationally famous figure; the Boer government knew who he was from the news accounts of his bravery and valor during the ambush of the British train. There were newspaper accounts of how he helped with the wounded soldiers and was instrumental in the escape of the train engine, carrying the wounded British soldiers. The Boer general in charge of the forces who took Churchill prisoner informed the secretary of Churchill's activities during the train derailment. He strongly advised the secretary against releasing Churchill.

The Boer captain who led the ambush also gave a full account of Churchill's activities during the battle. He said further that when Churchill was ordered by the soldier on the horse to surrender, he refused and only complied when the soldier pointed his gun at him. Churchill, in the meantime, wrote more letters in an attempt to obtain his release, insisting that he had no part to play in the battle, but to no avail. He also wrote to his mother asking her to help gain his release.

Churchill's time in prison in South Africa was spent reading and writing, and it was also marked by periods of mixed feelings and ambivalence. Although he eagerly anticipated his release, there were moments when he was resigned to his fate in captivity. The prisoners had access to a library, so he took full advantage of it, writing several letters to friends, family, and the Boer government requesting his release.

Amid the uncertainties of the war, Churchill still tried to take matters into his own hands, with regard to his fate and well-being, while in prison. Although he was totally powerless there, he never gave up hope for his release. He took control of his fate, as much as possible, and as was oftentimes typical of him. He wrote several letters requesting his release; he even reminded a guard, who frequently harassed and goaded prisoners, including himself, that the war would one day end and that both sides had an equal chance of emerging victorious. He further suggested to the guard that he was sure that he would not want an example made of him for cruelty to prisoners of war, and the guard backed off. Churchill tried as much as possible to positively influence the outcome of his stay in captivity. He also worked on his third book while there. Meanwhile, news of the success of the Boer forces in battle was pervasive.

Churchill began to plot his escape with the British captain who was ambushed with him and a British sergeant-major who was born in South Africa. He became excited and animated about the prospect of escaping. Churchill's excitement was noticeable by the other prisoners. The trio agreed that on the night of the escape, they would scale the fence behind the outhouse and try to go undetected by the guards.

On the planned day of the escape, Churchill was particularly energized and somewhat agitated. He could neither sleep well the night before nor get himself to relax that afternoon. Unfortunately, on that particular night, things did not go as planned. The guards were there all night and as vigilant as ever.

For the following two nights, the trio did not have the opportunity to escape. Finally, on the third night, they tried again. Churchill climbed over the fence, but the other two were unable to follow suit without detection. All attempts by Churchill to get his accomplices to join him proved futile. He considered it impossible to escape alone—having neither knowledge of the Dutch language nor a compass. He decided that the only way to make it alone would be to hop on a cargo train. He rode the train undetected, concealing himself among the cargo as it headed toward the coast into the British-held territory.

Churchill disembarked from his train ride and walked in the direction of what he perceived to be a railroad station. Luckily, he was dressed in civilian clothes. He passed some civilians on the streets as he walked, but no one appeared to notice him. He whistled and tried to appear as casual as the people he saw on the street. Finally, he spotted the railroad tracks and a railroad station. He walked up to a spot where there was an incline, close to the tracks. His rationale was that the train would be very slow as it approached the incline, thereby making it easy for him to hop on it. He was right. Shortly thereafter, a cargo train carrying bags of coal arrived. He waited and jumped onto another train in between two wagons at the coupling point, as it slowed down on the incline. He hid among the bags of coal and alighted when the train stopped. He spotted what appeared to be a coal mine in the distance.

Meanwhile, news of Churchill's escape had spread through the Republic. A reward was posted for twenty-five pounds, along with his full description and picture, for anyone who could capture him or turn him in, dead or alive. The Boers were intent on capturing Churchill, but his escape instincts were good—he had too much at stake. He was at that point driven by his sense of purpose, which would engender a good omen for his escape.

Once Churchill was out of the train, he spotted a house at the coal mine and ran toward it. In dire need of food and water, he approached the house and knocked on the door, hoping to encounter a friendly face. The door opened, and the face of a man emerged. As the door opened further, the full silhouette of the man appeared; Churchill noticed that he had a revolver pointed at him. Luckily for Churchill, he was British and the manager of the mine. After Churchill identified himself, the manager invited him into his house and gave him some food, an opportunity to take a bath, and a change of clothes. Churchill went back into hiding on the premises of the coal mine until the road was clear enough for him to catch another train.

As soon as the opportunity presented itself, the mine manager and some of his British colleagues escorted Churchill to the train station, sending him off with a revolver for protection. There, Churchill boarded another cargo train, hiding among bales of cotton. The train was heading to the coast of the Indian Ocean through the Portuguese territory of East Africa. At one of the stops, prior to the train's arrival at the Portuguese territory, some Boer Republic agents climbed onto the wagon in which Churchill was hiding and proceeded to search it. They stopped after a short while and left, empty-handed, obviously convinced that their search was pointless. Churchill was fortunate.

Churchill was able to tell by counting the number of stops the train was making that it had entered the Portuguese territory. He was a free man. In celebration, he fired some shots from his revolver, given to him by the mine manager, into the air. Once the train reached Durban, South Africa, there was a large crowd awaiting Churchill's arrival. The news of his impending arrival had spread like wildfire. The crowd cheered as he disembarked from the train. He had become a celebrity.

In addition to re-enlisting, Churchill wrote extensively about his escape and experiences from the war. He also maintained his status as a correspondent and continued to submit news reports about the war to *The Morning Post*. Shortly thereafter, Churchill rejoined the military as a lieutenant. He was eager to return to the war front. He did something brave that not too many people would have done—he returned to the war front through the same

Drive to Passion

route he had traveled previously as a prisoner of war. He remained in South Africa and contributed to the fight against the Dutch.

Churchill's third book, *Savrola*, was published while he was at war and performing his other function as a journalist. His book received rave reviews. This was quite an accomplishment for someone under the age of twenty-six with dual careers. In one of his news submissions to *The Morning Post*, Churchill reported on the liberation of Ladysmith by the British troops. Once the troops reached Ladysmith, he said, the atmosphere became jubilant. Everyone was happy and excited. Soldiers throughout the ranks were excited and animated, shaking hands and hugging each other like long-lost friends. Churchill reported that he shouted for joy and for being alive to witness such a momentous occasion.

Captain Percy Scott, the military commandant of Durban who had the opportunity to meet Churchill, was so impressed with him that he predicted he would one day become the prime minister of Britain. He further stated that he knew of no one more capable and deserving of a position of such high honor and esteem than Churchill.

Similar to Scott's foresight about Churchill, friends, mentors, relatives, managers, and acquaintances may make predictions or observations about our capabilities as we pursue our passion. We should always pay close attention to them; they could be right. There is always a high probability of accuracy in these predictions and assessments, especially if we find consistencies in what we are being told. Even if these observations seem exaggerated, they may still serve as a guiding force to us in our drives and our passion. Others oftentimes see in us what we fail to see in ourselves—things that are not directly apparent to us. Churchill was told a few times that he would make a good prime minister.

As Churchill proceeded with his military and journalistic duties, he demonstrated his perceptiveness and great foresight in his warnings to the British government. He had the uncanny ability to sound an alarm whenever he felt that Britain was on the wrong path. This esoteric, or perhaps arcane, ability would later help him in warning his country against the imminent dangers of World Wars I and II.

Churchill continued to advocate respect and fairness to the enemy in his writings and news reports. He believed in the rebuilding of postwar South Africa. He contended that the purpose of the war was to win peace, not to destroy it. He also warned the British government of the ills of driving the enemy to the brink of guerilla warfare and how that would be disruptive, if not detrimental, to the victory that the British so desperately sought. He received criticism for this opinion from people who believed in revenge.

Churchill demonstrated fearlessness and bravery in battle. He had a close call during a reconnaissance expedition in combat. He and a colleague, while on a scouting mission, happened upon the enemy. When he dismounted his horse to take a closer look at the enemy position, the animal accidentally galloped off without him. The two men suddenly came under fire. They were no match for the Boer forces that were closing in on them. Capture or death seemed imminent, so he took off running. Suddenly, his colleague began to ride toward him. Churchill shouted out to him for help, and the man scooped him up; they rode off to safety.

However, Churchill's colleague manifested his insensitivity when his horse was hit by a bullet. He yelled out that his horse was bleeding, to which Churchill responded that he should be more concerned about their safety than the horse's injury. Bluntly, he told Churchill that he was more concerned about his horse than he was about him. Despite the man's tactlessness, Churchill eventually was able to persuade the British government to award him a medal of valor for saving his life.

Churchill had great qualities. His willingness to persuade the British government to give a commendation to his colleague who had tempered an act of bravery with stupidity demonstrated Churchill's astuteness. He felt that hatred was ineffective, and he abhorred it. He believed in the coexistence of friends and foe and was an advocate for the rights of the enemy in the Anglo-Boer and the Sudanese wars. He was an advocate for the poor. He did not hate his father for being distant from him and always being critical of him as a child. His bravery and tireless energy were remarkable. Without a doubt, Churchill possessed the type of courage that is a basic ingredient for success and greatness. He

Drive to Passion

was a great leader during the most difficult period in his country's history. Courage, among other qualities, propelled Churchill to great heights.

* * *

Johannesburg had almost completely fallen to the British forces by the time Churchill got there, and he made sure he got firsthand information on the situation there for his news reports. Meanwhile, Churchill's fourth book—*London to Ladysmith via Pretoria*, which comprised a collection of the first twenty news reports he had submitted to *The Morning Post*—was published. Wanting to give a full account of the state of affairs in the city to *The Morning Post*, he rode through the city on a bicycle, in disguise, with a Frenchman. There were still Boer forces in Johannesburg when Churchill undertook this risky venture. He was advised by the Frenchman to speak French if they were ever accosted by the Boers. So they rode casually through the city, clad in civilian clothing. The few suspicious stares they received every now and again did not serve as a deterrent. The two men encountered a Boer trooper, who rode up to them on a horse, but just as quickly lost interest in them. Next, they ran into a British soldier with whom they went to the location of the British forces, after convincing the man that it was unsafe for him to continue to the city due to the presence of pockets of Boer troops. Upon their arrival at the British lines, Churchill warned British troops of the presence of a cluster of Boer forces in Johannesburg. The commander who summoned Churchill to a meeting was tickled and impressed by his adventure and his propensity for risk taking.

As soon as the British forces completely secured Johannesburg, Churchill proceeded to Pretoria with them. They entered Pretoria without much resistance. An incident occurred in Pretoria that took Churchill's breath away. Within a few yards of the British soldiers was a very large contingent of Boer forces leaving in a train pulled by double engines. As the train pulled out, both forces, within an arm's length of each other, eyed each other with awe and contempt. Churchill's description of the encounter was vivid. He said that the situation was very tense, and the slightest mistake on either side in firing first would have resulted in a catastrophe for both sides.

Following the nerve-wracking encounter with the Boer troops, Churchill immediately headed to the school compound where the British prisoners of war were held. When he opened the gate and went in, the atmosphere became immediately jubilant. Many of them recognized Churchill. He had once been one of them. He raised his hat in triumph and jubilation as excitement filled the air. They were elated to be liberated.

Churchill wrote to his mother, saying he was planning to return home. He expressed his desire to get involved in politics in England. In his letter, he also indicated his interest in making more money and seeing Pamela upon his arrival. Pamela was a young female friend of Churchill's, with whom he had been in communication for some time.

Unbeknownst to Churchill, he would have a few more close calls with danger, one of which would involve a reconnaissance mission, prior to his final departure from South Africa. Churchill was involved in one of the fiercest battles of his life when he participated in a push to rid Pretoria of all Boer troops. The Boer forces lay in hiding at the crest of the mountain in Pretoria. He joined the British forces assembled to attack these remaining Boer forces. Churchill took it upon himself to climb up to the peak of the mountain on an investigative mission—an attempt on his part to scout out the enemy position. It was nighttime, and he was at the crest, within a stone's throw of the Boer forces. From this vantage point he signaled the attack on the Boers, thus purging them completely and ensuring that they would never re-enter Pretoria. This would be the major turning point in the war. When Churchill narrated this incident, he never took credit for his pivotal role—an example of his modesty.

In another harrowing situation, during Churchill's final departure from South Africa, he took a train packed with British soldiers heading to Cape Town. Suddenly, the train came to a screeching halt. Churchill disembarked in an attempt to investigate the reason for the sudden stop. He then discovered that the train was under attack by a faction of Boer troops. As the only officer there, Churchill immediately took charge and ordered the engineer to prepare to take the train backward to the previous station. While he was on the ground commanding the soldiers, a Boer shell fell next to his foot. Once again, he emerged unscathed. Upon ensuring that all the British soldiers were safely back on board, he ordered the retreat of the train. Churchill came to the realization that his luck was beginning to run out so he left South Africa for good.

* * *

Back home he had more speaking engagements and published more books, bringing the total number of his books to five and making him an accomplished author at the tender age of twenty-five. He earned about ten thousand pounds, the equivalent of almost one million dollars in today's money, from his books. He was becoming quite popular.

As Churchill became adept at public speaking, he had more speaking engagements, which validated his increased skill level. He often practiced in front of friends and in the bathtub, carefully punctuating each line to denote his pauses and rewriting each paragraph until he was satisfied that the finished product was excellent. He delivered his speeches with emotion and enthusiasm, which helped to make him more credible and interesting. Churchill went on a lecture circuit in the United States and Canada, speaking about the war in South Africa. He also spoke to various audiences throughout Britain.

As exemplified by Churchill, preparation, practice, and customized education comprise the key to expertise. No matter how passionate we are about a particular profession, or how high our natural propensity is toward a field of endeavor, we should prepare and continuously strive to improve our skills in that profession in order to gain the degree of expertise necessary for remarkable accomplishments. Improved skills will help our proficiency in that field. While this will yield rewards, our focus for the most part should be on the process, the work, and our passion. When we are passionate about an activity, we invariably derive pleasure from it, and this diminishes the arduousness of the preparation, practice, and education involved in that endeavor.

A critic of Churchill's once used a few strong words and some complimentary language to depict his character. She described him as an obnoxious and narcissistic individual, who was impulsive and had a narrow scope on things. She went on to say that although he lacked formal education and polish, he was charismatic, eloquent, and tenacious, and had a bright future in politics. This critic's review of him was mixed. Churchill was sometimes rude, yet dazzling, with warmth and sincerity. There are few very highly accomplished people today in America who would compare favorably to some of Churchill's paradoxical characteristics.

Churchill had absolute belief in himself and his capabilities, as illustrated in the following remark to a friend, recorded in Gilbert's biography: "We are all worms. But I do believe I am a glow-worm." This remark depicts Churchill's confidence in his capabilities, which invariably contributed to his greatness and tremendous success. From his statement, a deduction can be made that Churchill utilized a combination of visualization and self-actualization to accomplish his goals. He was already convinced that he was a great leader. Hence, some of his behavior and utterances were indicative of this conviction. He believed that nothing could stop him. This is symbolic of the great power we possess as humans. When we truly believe that we can accomplish something, then we inevitably do. Similar to Churchill, when we believe and truly see ourselves reaching our goal and completing the task, it then becomes a reality. This type of belief and confidence in ourselves can be prompted by customized education, practice, and preparation in the activity involved in our passion.

* * *

Churchill became fully engaged in politics, winning a seat in Parliament and becoming one of the two representatives of his constituency in Oldham, England. He became a vocal member of Parliament. He spoke out courageously about military spending, warning Britain about an imminent war in Europe—World War I. On occasion, he criticized his own party members and entertained the idea of breaking away from his party to form a more liberal party. Many people admired him for speaking out with audacity. Churchill's career progressed nicely. He ran for Parliament three times and won. His initial election to Parliament was as a Conservative. After another successful election, he switched to the Liberal Party.

Churchill is credited, through his affiliation with another member of Parliament, with orchestrating a large number of social programs: unemployment insurance, employment exchange to help the unemployed locate work, welfare programs for the poor, and a national pension program, which served as a prototype for the Social Security program in America.

In spite of some of his unorthodox beliefs and shortcomings, Churchill's career proceeded on a trajectory. After his stint in elected office, he secured his first government job as an under-secretary for Colonial Affairs at the Colonial Office. Churchill eventually gained a promotion to the position of Home secretary. Like his colleagues, he believed that through colonization, the British helped the indigenous people of their colonies achieve improved lifestyles and economic stability. He and his colleagues also subscribed to the notion that white people were more intelligent than the colored people whom they colonized. Everyone has shortcomings and may harbor certain unconventional beliefs; however, these aberrations will not serve as a deterrent in our ability to make great achievements and make a difference.

In the midst of his burgeoning political career, Churchill got married at the age of thirty-three. His wife, Clementine Hozier, was ten years younger. She would become his voice of reason, his confidante, and someone who would always tell him the truth, even when everyone else was afraid to do so. She also told him when she thought he was behaving badly.

As Home secretary, Churchill was in charge of the police and prisons. Making many strides in this position, he pushed for prison reforms as well as sentencing reforms. He was a friend to the prisoner, having been a prisoner of war himself during the conflict in South Africa. He pushed for reforms such as reduced sentences for victimless crimes, especially sentences he considered to be too harsh and unsuitable for their crimes. Sentences, he argued, should be commensurate with the crimes committed. He pushed to put a stop to the law that required people who could not pay fines levied on them by the courts to be automatically sent to prison. One of his main objectives was to reduce the prison population.

Churchill also pushed for prisons to be equipped with libraries. His rationale was that people who were incarcerated had the right to develop their minds unless they had committed grievous crimes that would make their education an exercise in futility. He was definitely ahead of his time; his underlying intention of pushing for books for the inmates was to help rehabilitate and transition them into useful citizens of society, especially those who were petty offenders. His contention was that prisoners could be caught in the vicious cycle of crime if no efforts were made to help them become productive and useful citizens again.

Churchill meant well and wanted to modernize the prison laws. However, some of his proposed changes would have been decried today. He proposed that rape should not be considered a heinous crime. As leaders, we may be well-intentioned, but we cannot always be right, and Churchill was no exception. Also, the appropriateness, rightness, or wrongness of any endeavor could be relative and dependent upon the context in which those endeavors are made.

As Home secretary, Churchill had the responsibility of resolving a miners' uprising. He sent in soldiers to quickly quell the disturbance and restore the peace. Many people thought he overreacted, and he resigned due to mounting pressure from this incident. Thus, he experienced the first major failure in his career trajectory.

Churchill's loss of his job would not stop him from reaching the pinnacle of his career in politics. The true measure of success and greatness lies not with the avoidance of failure, but with thriving and succeeding despite our failures. Put another way, success should be measured by the acquisition of a greater burst of success than our aggregate failures.

Although the prime minister decided to give Churchill a second chance by appointing him to the position of first lord of the Admiralty of the Navy, another cabinet-level position, this job was not without incident. He built up the Navy even though initially he was against military spending. Churchill had a sixth sense of an impending war. He was right. Shortly thereafter, World War I ensued. As the war raged, Churchill also lost this position due to another mistake: He suggested that the British government send a reinforcement of its forces through the coast of Turkey to help its allied forces, including the Soviets, attack the Germans from the east. This advice turned out to be disastrous and resulted in the loss of many lives.

The loss of Churchill's job broke his heart—he was depressed for some time, but he eventually took some positive steps toward alleviating his situation. He sought solace and relaxation through painting. Churchill learned how to paint from the experts in this field. Although he initially deemed it an outlet for his frustrations, he continued to improve his painting skills and was able to produce some decent works of art. After a while, he became very restless and decided to re-enlist in the military to fight in the war.

As a veteran of the Boer War, Churchill was quickly accepted as an officer in the army, albeit he continued in his attempts to exonerate himself and indicate his availability for better opportunities in the government. As a result of demonstrating great skills as a soldier, he quickly was promoted to the rank of lieutenant colonel and put in command of a unit. Meanwhile, Churchill and his wife continued to fight fervently to clear his name. In the midst of all this, he was provided another opportunity. When one of his friends became prime minister, Churchill was immediately appointed minister of Munitions. He later was promoted to secretary of State for War and Air, a position he held for some time.

Churchill's resilience after the loss of his job was demonstrative of his resolve to continue in the pursuit of his goals despite his obstacles. There is no straight path to success. The loss of his job is also a great lesson for individuals who have been previously successful, but experienced setbacks. Churchill was unashamed to re-enlist in the military even though he had previously held some cabinet-level positions. His situation, with respect to the loss of his jobs and subsequent recoveries, is emblematic of the fact that there are numerous opportunities to rebound after a setback.

Churchill began to experience some regularity with respect to his career and other aspects of his life, but amid the volatility thus far in his government appointments, he continued to pursue his passion for writing. He was later made secretary of State for Colonies. He led and organized a team to the Middle East to discuss the future of the Arab states. He was also in support of the establishment of a Jewish state by the Jews in Palestine. Churchill never gave up his writing. He wrote his war memoir, which was published in six volumes, and it was considered to be among his best writing.

Following the period of calm, Churchill encountered a chain of unpleasant events: he lost one of his children to an illness; he later lost this job during a general election; and he took ill and was unable to secure another job for a period of time. While he was ill with appendicitis, his wife went around delivering speeches on his behalf, but in spite of this, he failed to secure any new position. This unpleasant chain of events encountered by Churchill was by no means indicative of a curse. He was not besieged by an evil force. It was a random chain of unfortunate events, all occurring around the same time. Any notion that a power stronger than us could hold us back, or afflict us with ill-luck should be dispelled. We are responsible for charting our own trajectory and dealing with the uncontrollable variables in our lives with tenacity, resilience, and a positive outlook. It is also vital that we avoid any temptation to conform to negative self-fulfilling prophecies.

Churchill took his family on a long vacation for some rest, as a means of deflating some of the tension he and his family were experiencing during his period of unemployment. He continued with his writing. He expressed his feelings about his predicament by saying he encountered a problem with his appendix, lost his office, and lost his party, almost in an instant. It is often a good idea to take a break in order to rest. It enables us to clear our heads, revitalize ourselves, and get a better perspective on things. We return from our vacation refreshed and better equipped to solve our problems.

Upon his return from vacation, Churchill encountered another opportunity, which is indicative of the fact that as we pursue our passion and prepare, educate, and position ourselves

Drive to Passion

to reach our goals, opportunities will abound. In a unifying gesture, a Conservative Party leader in office made Churchill the chancellor of the Exchequer. He was in charge of the Finance Ministry. This was not a suitable position for him because he lacked the requisite knowledge in finance. His lack of knowledge in the finance sector was apparent in his decision to return the British currency to the gold standard, causing the value of the British pound to increase, making it harder to sell British goods outside the country. Unemployment and strikes ensued.

It is remarkable that Churchill, in addition to his job as the chancellor of the Exchequer, took on the extra responsibility of publishing *The British Gazette*, the government's newspaper. He was able to do this because of his high energy level and his capacities to multitask and to delegate. Churchill was an individual who was motivated and energized to embark on multiple projects within the same period of time: When he was a soldier in South Africa, he was simultaneously a correspondent for a newspaper. In the midst of all of his responsibilities, Churchill still found time to write his books. He never lacked energy.

Once we initiate an endeavor about which we are passionate, we will be energized and delighted to perform the activity and find ways to accomplish the tasks involved. Churchill utilized the principles of multitasking and delegating to accomplish his enormous tasks. He had a personal secretary who took dictations from him and trusted confidants to whom he delegated responsibilities.

In our quest for success and greatness, we should always be cognizant of the fact that effective multitasking, delegation, and time management are of the essence. There is truly not enough time in the day to get everything done. Time management and multitasking, if done correctly, can enable us to be productive. One of the best ways to multitask is to perform minor tasks such as reading our mail while we are placed on hold on the telephone. However, trying to do too many things at once will reduce our accuracy and efficiency if done incorrectly. We should not text message while driving. An effective way to manage our time is to be organized and to delegate tasks to others. We should delegate, not only to our subordinates, but also to paid professionals and contractors, such as lawyers, accountants, house cleaners, and landscapers. Minor tasks, requiring two minutes or less to accomplish, should be handled immediately. This is an effective approach of accomplishing tasks in a timely manner and efficiently, compared to allowing the minor tasks to accumulate. Quite a few books have been written on how to manage our time and the proper way to multitask. David Allen's *Getting Things Done* is a great book on time management.

Although we have ultimate responsibility for the things we delegate—"The buck stops here," according to Harry S. Truman, the 33rd president of the U.S.—we should delegate to efficient people whom we can also hold accountable. The utilization of a viable system of checks and balances and a great status update process are of the essence, when we delegate tasks. We should bear in mind that while we try to keep mistakes and problems down to a bare minimum, they are sometimes inevitable and should not be a deterrent to delegation.

I was once held accountable, in a peculiar manner, for a task I had delegated. I was in the civil magistrate's court, where I had an eviction case against one of my tenants; the magistrate was appalled by my unawareness of the fact that the deed to the property in question was problematic. My name was not on the deed as the owner of the property; the previous owner's name was still on the deed. When he questioned me about this, I expressed confidence in my closing attorney for this property, and indicated that there was a low probability that the deed was incorrect. I further suggested that if indeed there was a problem, I was sure it could be easily resolved. The magistrate seemed even more perturbed by my self-assurance and said, "Before you go around playing real estate mogul, you need to know how to research the title of your properties and make sure that you actually own them." He behaved as if he was unconvinced that I actually owned the property. Also, it appeared as though my unflinching confidence in myself and my closing attorney for this property bothered him.

After about ten minutes of researching the deed to the property in his computer—and as I mulled over his suggestion that I learn how to research the deed to my properties—the magistrate finally found my name on it, but I was neither jubilant nor thankful because I felt I had delegated the closing of my properties and proper research of my deeds to the right attorney. He immediately behaved as if he had made a record-breaking discovery. I was neither impressed nor had the slightest inclination to learn how to research titles in the computer. "I do not have the time for that," I thought to myself, but did not dare to express my sentiments aloud to the magistrate. "That's what I pay my attorney for, and if indeed my deed had been problematic, I would have had my attorney resolve it." The magistrate's suggestion that I learn how to research the deeds to my properties would have made more sense if I owned one property, but—in addition to my involvement in other business ventures—I owned about $3 million worth of properties, comprising an array of single-family homes. So I was right in my deliberations that, although I was ultimately responsible for all my properties, it was a good business decision to delegate all of my deed issues to my attorney and trust that he would be diligent in the performance of his job.

One more story on delegating. I was once in the process of selling my restaurant to a gentleman whom I took on a tour of the establishment. As we walked around in the kitchen, he tried turning on a particular stove, but was unable to do so; he asked me to turn it on for him. I told him that I was unfamiliar with it; he was dismayed and proceeded to decry my lack of knowledge of the operation of the stove in my restaurant. I thought, "Whatever. Just buy the restaurant." He was oblivious of the fact that I was running the restaurant and my other ventures simultaneously. I did not have the time to learn the intricate details of the operation of the stoves in my restaurant because I had delegated all those functions to my restaurant manager. The deal was concluded, and he bought the restaurant.

* * *

Due to a change in political leadership, Churchill again found himself with neither an appointed government position nor an elected political office, which marked the beginning of his "wilderness years." These years, as described by Gilbert, comprised a period in Churchill's life marked by political turbulence, impasse, and inactivity. He held no political positions during this ten-year period preceding the 1940s. Churchill was disappointed because he had not been chosen to head the Conservative Party.

Although Churchill held no political position during his "wilderness years," he was nonetheless quite vocal; he disagreed openly with the head of his party about the sovereignty of India. Some of his colleagues believed it was time to grant India its independence, but Churchill disagreed with this notion—openly being derisive toward Mahatma Gandhi. Gandhi became an Indian icon because of his doctrine, which entailed utilizing nonviolent demonstrations to achieve independence for his people. Churchill's racist remarks and inflexibility angered his colleagues. This pattern of behavior emblemized his weaknesses, despite his obvious strengths.

Churchill lucratively utilized his "wilderness years" to write and spend time with his family. He entertained, wrote his books, and spent more time with his children. He was determined not to mirror his parents, who did not spend much time with him as a child. He kept a busy schedule, often working late into the night and waking up at eight o'clock in the morning, eating a heavy breakfast in bed, and doing more work in bed before taking a bath.

Churchill seized the opportunity of being politically inactive to go to New York City. He had a fascination with America. He had invested heavily in the American stock market prior to the stock market crash and the ensuing Great Depression. He lost a lot of money and almost went bankrupt. While in New York City, he was hit by a car while crossing the street. Also, during this period, he suffered food poisoning and was ill for some time.

Churchill's problems were exacerbated by his support for King Edward VIII, who abdicated because of his unwillingness to give up his marital pursuit of an American divorcee. He went against the masses and his colleagues on this issue. This support for the king cost Churchill some political dividends; he was ostracized by his colleagues. Once again, Churchill demonstrated guts and courage.

Churchill, at that point, was beginning to worry about the emergence of Germany and Hitler as a threat to the stability of Europe and the world at large. He began to issue warnings and to make his opinions known about Hitler's intention to conquer Europe. Germany, which had been impoverished as a result of World War I, was beginning to build up its military again. Churchill advocated a military buildup for Britain. There were a few problems that prevented this from happening: Churchill's colleagues refused to heed his advice because he was no longer a cabinet member; Britain had spent so much money fighting wars in its colonies that it lacked the funds to build up its military. Churchill even suggested that Britain forge strategic alliances with the United States and the Soviet Union to stop Germany's expansionist efforts. His warnings and suggestions fell on deaf ears.

A series of events marked Churchill's return to the limelight. Britain declared war on Germany after Germany broke an agreement between the two countries by invading Poland. This triggered the official beginning of World War II. The invasion of Britain by the ruthless and indomitable Hitler was imminent. A chain of events occurred soon after this. Churchill was called back to office to assume his former position as the secretary of the Navy. The prime minister lost support in Parliament due to the failed "appeasement" agreement with Germany, and he was forced to resign. Churchill became prime minister. Some of the other events preceding the installation of Churchill as the prime minister were the invasions of France, Luxembourg, Belgium, and Holland by Germany.

Some would argue that Churchill became prime minister of Britain fortuitously, but this is not the case; he had been working hard all his life in preparation for an opportunity of this magnitude. When the previous prime minister resigned, Churchill was not the king's first choice for the job. The king offered the job to the Foreign secretary, the equivalent of the U.S. secretary of State. He turned it down because he lacked the passion for the job. The king then offered the job to Churchill. He was the most logical choice: He had been a brave and experienced soldier, was passionate about the job, and had held cabinet-level positions.

The timing was perfect for Churchill. This situation demonstrates that when we prepare and educate ourselves in the activity encompassing our passion, opportunities will become available to us. We can take advantage of these well-deserved opportunities by leveraging the help of mentors and other well-wishers who have our best interest at heart. Churchill was the most suitable person for the job. Let us consider a hypothetical scenario where the Foreign secretary, who was the king's first choice, had accepted the job of the prime minister. As ill-prepared and indifferent as he was, he would have faltered, which would have in all probability still resulted in an offer of the job to Churchill because he would have still been the most prepared, most suitable, and most logical choice.

Was Churchill lucky to get the job of prime minister, or did he seize an opportunity? Churchill was not lucky to have been chosen by the king for the job. Although luck and opportunity are not the subject of this book, they are nonetheless still worthy of mention. The definition of luck in *Merriam-Webster's Collegiate Dictionary, Tenth Edition* puts it in perspective: "a force that brings good fortune or prosperity." It defines opportunity as "a good chance for advancement or progress." As we work diligently toward our goals and passion, our luck becomes manifested to us in the form of opportunity; several opportunities or chances will be presented to us by our mentors and others. Through persistent efforts and resilience, we can strategically position ourselves to take advantage of the opportunities that are accessible to us. The more we pursue our passion through perpetual and customized education, practice, and preparation in our endeavors, the more opportunities we encounter. Someone is bound to recognize our excellence and present us with an opportunity. Those who run into opportunities without adequate preparation may not be able to take advantage of them, and if they did succeed in taking advantage of them, they may not be able to sustain the conditions created by the opportunities.

Churchill was delighted when he was offered the position of prime minister. He felt as if he had been preparing for this job all his life. He told some close associates that upon being offered the position by the king, he immediately experienced a profound sense

Drive to Passion

of relief. He concluded by adding that he felt as if the trajectory of his career had finally hit its target.

In his new role as prime minister, Churchill met the challenges he encountered with much vigor and enthusiasm. Most of the qualities that had made Churchill difficult and irritating as a minister made him a great prime minister. He was already detail-oriented and energetic, so he proceeded to plunge into his new role with great energy and momentum. His strength and fortitude enabled him to assume two other roles in addition to that of prime minister: first lord of the Treasury and minister of Defense. He was a source of strength, encouragement, and energy to all. It was as if he was already experienced in the job. He reorganized things, dictated memos. He also wrote the great speeches that he delivered. Whenever he came into the House of Commons, there were no great cheers; however, the words he spoke were both memorable and comforting.

All great leaders are great motivators and orators. They are able to motivate their followers by effectively communicating their ideas to them. Churchill and Abraham Lincoln are considered to be among the greatest leaders and orators of all time. Great leaders have charisma and can truly touch people's hearts with spoken words.

* * *

World War II raged, and the battle of France began to wind down in favor of the Germans, which prompted Churchill to make a few attempts to convince President Franklin D. Roosevelt to join the war, to save Britain and all of Europe from the wrath of Hitler. According to Gilbert, Churchill gave a remarkable speech to the House of Commons that may have played a great part in convincing Roosevelt to eventually join the war. Churchill said, "I expect that the battle of Britain is about to begin. . . . The whole fury and might of the enemy must very soon be turned on us. Hitler knows that he will have to break us in this island or lose the war. If we can stand up to him, all Europe may be free . . . but if we fail, then the whole world, including the United States, and all that we have known and cared for, will sink into the abyss of a new dark age."

Churchill was resolute in his desire to lead the British and its allies to victory against Germany and its "Axis" alliance. The Germans made gestures of peace on condition that Britain would surrender, but Britain turned them down. After the fall of France, Churchill was so determined not to allow Germany access to any of the French naval vessels that he ordered their destruction. The destruction of these vessels was carried out despite its collateral damage, which resulted in the killing of over one thousand French sailors on board these vessels. This demonstrated how determined Churchill was to achieve victory. America was impressed and sent destroyers to help.

Despite Roosevelt's resistance to joining the war, Churchill tirelessly pressed his diplomatic efforts with the United States and the Soviet Union. He met with Roosevelt and signed a treaty in which Roosevelt pledged to defend democracy. However, Roosevelt was reluctant to send American soldiers to fight in a foreign war. Churchill then proceeded to orchestrate a meeting between himself, Josef Stalin of the Soviet Union, and Roosevelt to discuss the possibilities of forging an alliance between the three world powers. He needed to forge this relationship with the two superpowers in order to impede and subsequently halt Germany's genocidal, totalitarian, and expansionist efforts.

* * *

Churchill was sometimes rude, abrupt, and abrasive, although he was an effective leader who was compassionate. At one point, he was so petulant and sarcastic with his friends and associates that one of them complained to his wife, prompting her to tell him that he was taking the risk of being loathed by everyone around him as a result of his bad behavior. She also acknowledged that the strain of the war had a direct impact on his rudeness. Churchill was also a true leader in spite of his weaknesses. He delivered many motivational speeches to keep his people's spirits up. He cried on occasion, due to the atrocities of the air raids, during his visits to those sites that had been bombed by the Germans. He was truly touched by the injuries, destruction, and human suffering.

Churchill's courage, tenacity, resilience, perseverance, and unwavering dedication to those things about which he was passionate were apparent all through his life. He had an image of where he wanted to be in life, and he ultimately got there, albeit it occurred in his sixties. He was energetic, diligent, and courageous. Churchill was able to forge a cogent passion for writing, speaking, and politics at the same time. He took up these intellectual pursuits despite his lack of a four-year college education. Churchill reinforced the idea that true accomplishment is prompted by customized education, practice, and preparation in the area of our passion. He had good instincts and insight that enabled him to warn Britain about imminent wars and the West about the possibility of the eradication of its freedom by a brutal dictator.

There are advantages of living in these modern times compared to Churchill's era. More progress has been made now in the areas of personal development, life skills, and the pursuit of our goals than previously. We are poised to greatly benefit from these advancements by virtue of our existence in this modern era. We can take advantage of the wealth of information that exists in all these areas to better prepare us as we undertake accomplishments of epic proportions. In view of all the tools available to us now, in self-improvement, leadership, and other similar areas, we are more capable of making many more strides than our predecessors.

* * *

Britain achieved some victories in North Africa, but as the war raged, Churchill worried that Japan might try to seize some British colonies. Japan was already at war with China, in an effort to gain control of disputed land from China. Japan was truly a burgeoning power in Asia at that time.

The tide of the war began to turn in Churchill's favor. Germany invaded the Soviet Union, and Churchill sent aid to the Soviets. The Soviet government was impressed, and the Soviet Union finally aligned itself with Britain against Germany. The blessing in disguise for Churchill occurred when Japan bombed the U.S. Pacific Fleet at Pearl Harbor. Churchill knew at that point that America, the sleeping giant, had been awakened, and the outcome of this egregious act by Japan would ultimately be beneficial to England. He was right. America then joined the war.

The Second World War did not end easily, even after America joined the fighting on the side of Britain and the Soviet Union. There were certain issues that needed to be resolved: America's war with Japan, in which Britain had promised to help; the manner in which the invasion of France was to be executed by the American, British and Allied forces; and the concern harbored by Britain about the imminent domination by the Soviet Union of Eastern Europe. Churchill hated Communism and was worried that the Soviet Union would take over Greece, Poland, and other parts of Eastern Europe. Little did he know that things would get worse before they got better.

In the midst of the war, Churchill suffered a mild heart attack, but he could not be told so by his doctor for fear that he would not be able to take the recommended time off to rest. He was beginning to age and was visibly stressed. Churchill's wife and daughter worried about him.

Stalin and Churchill did not agree on many things, but they managed to work out their differences to ensure the continuation of the coalition. Stalin was beginning to get impatient with Britain over supply issues. The ships that carried supplies to the Soviet Union had come under heavy attacks by Germany, causing the suspension of these shipments by Britain. The immersion of Britain in the North African conflict was bothersome to Stalin because it contributed to Britain's inability to ensure the shipment of supplies to the Soviet Union. The cumulative effects of these factors created discord between Churchill and Stalin. Churchill met with Stalin and resolved these issues.

There were some major shifts in the war. The Soviets began to gain a few victories over Germany on some battle fronts. The D-Day invasion of Normandy called Operation Overlord was planned. Even though there were initial disagreements on the specifics of it, a consensus was later reached among the Allied leaders, stipulating that the invasion be led by an American general.

Drive to Passion

D-Day was tough, yet momentous. Many American lives were lost, but in the end, the battle of Normandy was won. The invasion of Normandy continued into France, creating a disagreement between Churchill and General Dwight Eisenhower of the U.S., who led the invasion. The general continued his march to the south of France, much to the objection of Churchill. Shortly thereafter, France completely fell into the hands of the Allied forces. Churchill marched on the streets of Paris with French General Charles de Gaulle, drawing criticism from the British people, because the war was still raging on other fronts.

Churchill made strides in his negotiations with the Soviets as victories piled up for the Allies. He was instrumental in the resolution of the issue of the spread of Soviet influence across Europe. Greece was left alone by the Soviets, and Churchill helped to broker peace there. There were signs of victory, and strides were made against Germany and Italy by the Allied forces. The end of the war was in sight. Germany was overrun by the Allied forces. Italy's Mussolini was killed, and Hitler committed suicide. Germany surrendered. The Allied forces dropped atomic bombs on two Japanese cities. Despite these victories and the approaching end of the war, grievous atrocities had already been committed by Hitler against the Jews and others whom he deemed, in his distorted mind, subhuman.

The Second World War finally came to an end. President Roosevelt's death directly preceded the end of the war. In the meantime, Churchill faced increased criticism in Britain. His critics alleged that he had been traveling too frequently and for long periods of time, thus ignoring his duties domestically. In other words, Churchill seemed to be a foreign policy expert who had failed in domestic policy. Also, Churchill was beleaguered by ill health for reasons not unconnected to the stresses and demands of the war.

* * *

As evidenced by Churchill's confidence in his skills and abilities, and his mention of the need for humans to experience some discomfort in order to foster creativity and advancement, he managed his thoughts effectively. His erudition in his endeavors spurred his confidence. Also, Churchill used thought management effectively to propel himself to success and greatness. The purpose of thought management, which could stem from asking ourselves self-directing questions, is to impel us to take the necessary action to accomplish our objective. It is not known exactly that Churchill utilized self-directing questions to manage his thoughts in order to propel himself to great heights; however, it is an effective means of making phenomenal achievements.

Personal development can be utilized in a multifaceted manner. We can use it to pursue wealth, prominence, and our passions, but we cannot ignore the use of these same techniques to manage other aspects of our lives, such as stress reduction and the achievement of happiness. As is often the case in some Eastern cultures, the pursuit of peace of mind, serenity, and happiness is ubiquitous and therefore takes precedence over the pursuit of excellence. Thus it is implied or oftentimes stated directly that the acquisition of tranquility and joy will automatically spur us into action with regard to the pursuit of excellence. This is not necessarily the case since happy people and individuals who are content do not automatically seek excellence.

It is likely that Churchill was a good stress manager, since he lived to be ninety. Leaders and others who are in pursuit of their passion invariably are good stress managers. Proper stress management technique is a necessity for leaders and others who are resilient, tenacious, and courageous. Churchill was a pragmatist who saw life for what it truly was. He philosophized about religion, poverty, progress in the world, and his fate in the wars in which he fought. He once suggested to his mother that in the event of his untimely death in battle, she should utilize the occasion to philosophize about the sheer insignificance of life as an alternative to mourning his death. Similarly, Barack Obama, our current president, manages stress well. We often hear people assert that he does not show anger and emotion as often as he should, which may be a part of his stress management technique. He seems to maintain his composure in the face of uncertainty.

One of Churchill's major strengths was his courage. *Merriam-Webster's Collegiate Dictionary, Tenth Edition*, defines courage as "firmness of mind and will in the face of danger or extreme difficulty." Courage is not the absence of fear. It entails taking positive action in spite of our fear. Highly accomplished individuals take action in spite of their fears. They do not wait for their fears to subside before taking action. In fact, some of the most successful soldiers in battle are those who use fear to their advantage, thus enabling them to avert danger when necessary. Paying attention to our feeling of fear means heeding the warning signals we receive from fear and acting upon them—using them to our advantage without cracking. We often hear actors discuss stage fright, and how they use it to their advantage. Courage is a requisite attribute for making great achievements.

Churchill had an inclination toward risk, which was also one of his strengths. Major achievements are not made by being risk-averse. He sought action on the battlefield while most of his colleagues were satisfied to allow the war to come to them. He did this in spite of its imminent danger. He knew that a distinguished military career would enhance his political career trajectory. There are risks involved in the pursuit of our passion; key among them is the abandonment of a secure lifestyle in pursuit of the uncertainties involved in making significant accomplishments.

Fear, stress, and negative thoughts are natural phenomena we can choose to control. We have the power and ability to manage all of these factors. Fear can be used as a warning signal of impending danger. We can respond accordingly to maintain the desired level of action necessary for our safety or for solving the problem. Stress, however, is triggered by negative thoughts and deserves to be terminated by changing the negative thoughts that produce it. Stress can be injurious to our health. By dealing effectively with the thoughts that produce stress, we can reduce its potentially injurious effects on our health. Negative thoughts and worry go hand in hand. We can always immediately replace negative thoughts or our worries with positive thoughts. We can affirm positive thoughts or use visualization to engender positive thoughts. An effective method of eliminating negative thoughts is by asking ourselves self-directing questions designed to terminate these thoughts or redirect them to more positive aspects. Meditation is also a good tool for thought management.

* * *

By the time World War II ended, Churchill was overconfident and out of touch with reality regarding his political stature. He assumed everyone would go along with his idea of absolute class distinction among the citizens of Britain. Also, he incorrectly thought that whatever views he espoused would be accepted by the people. He reasoned that they owed him a debt of gratitude due to his courageous and successful execution of the war. He was absolutely wrong; he was voted out of office immediately after the war.

Churchill lost his job as prime minister because his thinking was outdated. It was not in line with the postwar period, which was at the time considered to be the modern era. The British people wanted class distinction minimized or completely eliminated in terms of its effects on the people's ability to be progressive and upwardly mobile. They wanted a fair chance to participate in the national prosperity. The British people also wanted their government to be responsible to them by providing them opportunities to improve their lives. They had experienced a feeling of common effort and a certain degree of equality during the war; everyone had to contribute and work together in order to bring the war to a successful end. Most people advocated and sought a continuation of this trend.

Churchill did not react positively to the loss of his job. He was surprised by it, and his wife acknowledged that he was depressed for a while following this loss. Churchill also experienced some financial problems upon relinquishing his job as the prime minister—a hardship that was remedied by publishing and selling more of his books. He also suffered some health problems after losing his job.

The period immediately following the end of the war was marked by a food shortage, which preceded a period of economic boom. There was an over-abundant supply of employment during the economic boom. Everyone who needed a job had one due to the rebuilding efforts. At this point, Britain was one of the wealthiest nations in the world.

Churchill took to painting, writing, and delivering speeches after the loss of his job. He delivered a speech in Fulton, Missouri, in the United States, which turned out to be historic. In this speech, according to Gilbert, he spoke of unity among all nations including those "in front of the iron curtain." He used this famous "iron curtain" phrase, which he had first used when he expressed to President Harry Truman his feelings about the Soviet Union's ominous intentions toward the West. He further predicted, in his usual fashion, that the possibility of war existed between the Soviet Union and the West if both sides did not work collaboratively to prevent it. This speech took everyone by surprise.

Although the Soviets were upset by Churchill's speech, as usual, he would be right about this foresight of an imminent war; luckily, however, he would only be partially right this time. He delivered this speech during the period preceding the Cold War. The Cold War would ensue shortly thereafter and would last for several years. Fortunately for us, and perhaps as a result of Churchill's warnings, it always remained a cold war and not a hot war.

Even though Churchill was older, he was still determined to become prime minister of Britain again. He did not give up hope. In his usual manner, he demonstrated resilience in spite of his advancement in age, willpower in spite of his frailty, and resolve in spite of his physical limitations. He campaigned hard and was elected prime minister for the second time at age seventy-six.

We have much to learn from Churchill regarding his courage, resilience, and how he allowed neither his declining health nor old age to impede his decision to run for office again. Regardless of how old we are, or what our limitations are, we can still pursue our dreams. He demonstrated a perfect example of mind over matter when he ran for prime minister and won despite the obstacles he encountered with his age. Everyone has an incredible gift of having a mind that can actually do much more than he or she can conceive. Once we dream it, prepare our minds similar to Churchill, and take the necessary action, then it will come to pass.

How do we get ourselves to take the action necessary to propel us to greatness? The answer lies with acquiring the drive necessary for action. We can be driven by intrinsic rewards, like the need to be an expert or the best in what we do or the need to make a difference in society. Conversely, we can be driven by extrinsic rewards such as wealth and fame. We can also be driven by other factors such as revenge and the avoidance of the mistakes made by our parents. Once we acquire the drive, we should then identify a passion that will be fueled by our drive. Our passion will, in turn, fuel our accomplishments. In Churchill's case, his passions consisted of writing, politics, and speaking. He was driven by the need to prove to his parents that he was not the tepid boy they believed he was. He was also driven by the need to achieve excellence in his endeavors and the desire to be wealthy and famous. Churchill felt that he was poised to do great things, which was a drive he acquired through self-actualization and visualization. He was convinced that he was a "glow-worm" among regular worms. If we are sufficiently driven, then it invariably propels us into action.

Once we are motivated or driven to do great things, we can then identify our passion. The process of identifying our passion entails asking ourselves questions. What is our niche or calling, or for which activity do we have a high aptitude? What do we take pleasure in doing that will enable us to create value? What are our hobbies? For what activity have we received compliments regarding our proficiency in it? What are our strengths? We cannot be passive while trying to identify our passion. We should simultaneously proceed with the trial-and-error method while trying to identify our greatest pleasures. Sometimes we may have to try several activities before we can identify one for which we have a niche and passion.

Churchill's positive attributes contributed to his excellence: He was always prepared; he educated himself in his areas of interest; he practiced incessantly; he was energetic; he derived pleasure from the performance of those activities about which he was passionate. Churchill was always prepared for his speaking engagements. He practiced his speeches incessantly. In fact, he was known to have practiced a speech prior to delivery over and over—a few hundred times—until he was satisfied. Churchill was a voracious reader. He read widely on such subjects as literature, politics, and history. His preparation could be considered obsessive. His extreme sense of preparedness led to the statement he made when he was initially offered the job of prime minister by the king, in which he remarked to a friend that he felt as if he had been preparing to become the prime minister of Britain all his life. Preparation, practice, and customized education—attributes possessed by Churchill—are key factors in enabling us to achieve expertise in the activities encompassing our passion.

There have been reported cases of professionals whose obsessive practice habits mirrored Churchill's. The Beatles were known to have logged more hours of practice than other bands, enabling them to achieve phenomenal success. Bill Gates and Paul Allen had access to a computer room when the ownership of personal computers was virtually nonexistent. As teenagers, they took advantage of this and worked on computers relentlessly for twenty to thirty hours a week—including weekends, skipping athletics—until they were familiar enough with computers to write programs. Through their efforts in customized education, preparation, and practice, they were able to make immense contributions to the introduction and operation of personal computers, which have greatly enhanced our quality of life and added value to the world, while providing Gates and Allen with unprecedented wealth.

* * *

Churchill settled into his position as the prime minister and reverted to some of his old ways. He gave his old associates key cabinet positions; he spent less time getting acclimated to domestic issues, while spending more time on international matters. Also, at that point, his age became an issue even though he refused to admit it. He was visibly more tired and slower. He visited America a few times for speaking engagements and was committed to fostering a good relationship with the United States, especially because he was born to an American mother. Also, most importantly, his intentions were to stop nuclear proliferation and to make sure that nuclear weapons did not lead to the obliteration of the world. Churchill had been through many wars and knew the devastating effects of war. He also knew that if there were to be another world war or if America and the Soviet Union were to clash militarily, inevitably, nuclear weapons would be used, and more than likely it would result in the annihilation of the world.

In addition to being plagued by declining health, Churchill's latter years in office were marked by noteworthy events. In fact, he almost resigned from office at one point due to his illness. Somehow he found the strength to continue. The king of England died suddenly and his daughter was installed as Queen Elizabeth II. Churchill was honored with the Nobel Prize in Literature. He had become a great writer, in addition to being a great politician and soldier.

Churchill stayed on as prime minister of Britain despite his age and poor health because he was worried about the imminent destruction of the world by nuclear weapons. He reasoned that if he continued in his position as prime minister, he could utilize his influence to orchestrate meetings between the world powers to foster nuclear disarmament. This magnanimous concern for world peace contributed to Churchill's greatness. He postponed his retirement even though his ability to govern was greatly diminished by age. He continued with his speaking engagements and orchestrating meetings with other world leaders. Churchill continued to push his agenda: nuclear disarmament and nonproliferation. There was no call for his resignation because his people felt indebted to him for all he had done for the country. He finally resigned in 1955.

Churchill died in 1965, at the age of ninety, after a distinguished and accomplished life. Although he had many faults, he was still a great man. He was deemed the savior of his country. By the time of his death, he had published fifty books, created five hundred paintings, written over one thousand newspaper and magazine articles, given speeches that filled eight volumes, been prime minister of his country twice, won the Nobel Prize in Literature, and the list goes on. The success and greatness depicted in Churchill's life is a cogent lesson to all.

His courage, energy, drive, and passion were the most outstanding attributes of his life. How could he have had such an inexhaustible supply of energy? Energy is acquired through activity; the more active we are, the more energy we can muster. Conversely, the more inactive we are, the less energetic we become. Drive, energy, passion, and enthusiasm are self-feeding: The more we project these attributes, the more we acquire them. As we take the initiative to take steps in the right direction, the more driven and passionate we become.

Churchill's exemplary life dispels the mythology of natural-born talent. As we can see from his life, his accomplishments were due to his incredible drive and passion for those activities that he enjoyed and for which he had a niche. We as individuals can become great despite our shortcomings, as long as we have the energy, courage, and drive to initiate our pursuits, and as long as we are able to identify an endeavor for which we are passionate. Once our pursuits are underway, we should push forth relentlessly in our efforts to maximize our passion.

With tools and resources on how to reach our goals available more so now than ever before, we should not only experience more advancement and value at a faster rate than those before us, but we should also see more people utilizing these available tools to go from drive to passion, in order to achieve greatness and success.

CHAPTER 3
Joseph Kennedy: Craved Recognition and Privilege

As a six-year-old, sandy-haired, blue-eyed boy with good looks and freckles, Joseph Patrick Kennedy caught the eye of John Fitzgerald, who was visiting the small boy's father at the house in East Boston where he was raised. Little did Fitzgerald know at the time that this handsome little boy would not only become his son-in-law and one of the wealthiest and most famous people in the United States, but he would also become the father of a U.S. president. Fitzgerald had gone to see the six-year-old's father—P.J. Kennedy, a political opponent—to mend fences following an election in which Fitzgerald emerged victorious.

Early narratives indicate that young Kennedy and Rose Fitzgerald, John Fitzgerald's daughter, met during their childhood. The freckle-faced lad was seven years old, while Rose was five at the time of their initial meeting. Their storybook romance would blossom ten years later.

Joe Kennedy and Rose Fitzgerald had much in common. They came from similar backgrounds. Their families were involved in politics. Joe Kennedy's father was one of the ward bosses of East Boston, and Rose Fitzgerald's father was the mayor of Boston. They both shared an enthusiasm for life. Also, they both grew up as the favorite child in their respective families. It was as if a parallel could be drawn between their upbringing and the upbringing of the modern-day Generation Y children, reared by overzealous Little League-coaching dads and soccer moms.

Rose, whose last name would change to Kennedy, would recall in her old age that Old Orchard Beach in Maine was a place of magic, a place where she and Joe first fell in love. This would become her most memorable encounter with anybody of the opposite sex prior to her marriage to Kennedy. Her sweet sixteen summer romantic encounter at Old Orchard Beach would leave an indelible memory in her heart. Despite her travels with her father and family, and a long period of minimal contact with the young Kennedy, as fate would have it, her memories of Old Orchard would remain intact, and he would be the man with whom she would spend the rest of her life.

Rose would also later recount how she and Kennedy, during their romantic interludes, would always talk about their futures and ambitions. It was then that she realized how driven and determined Kennedy was. He was resolute about becoming a financial powerhouse and an eminent force.

Kennedy proceeded to college at Harvard, while Rose went on to attend a convent. It was at Harvard that Kennedy's restlessness and feeling of wanting to belong began to form. Harvard was the college for the wealthy. However, by the time Kennedy got there, it had begun to open its doors to individuals of modest means like him.

The dichotomy between Kennedy and the children of privilege from private high schools was blatantly enshrined in the fabric of Harvard. The children of the upper crust arrived at school with their servants and took up well-furnished suites with steam heat and chandeliers. On the other hand, Kennedy and his colleagues who had attended public schools were relegated to dormitories in the basement without central heating or plumbing systems. It was as if the wealthy had a way of recognizing each other, even if they had not gone to the same private schools. The affluent youngsters recognized each other from their parallel lifestyles. It is a known fact that people of similar backgrounds gravitate toward each other.

The exclusive Gold Coast club at Harvard, where Kennedy was denied membership, is worthy of mention because it helped shape his earlier, uneasy feelings of social inadequacy. These thoughts also helped to spur his drive and passion to succeed. He wanted to eventually elevate himself to those high levels and standards that were out of his reach.

As Kennedy recalled, it was a beautiful fall day at Harvard and three young men who were members of the Gold Coast club walked past him without acknowledging his presence. This exclusive club, like a few others that existed then at Harvard, boasted memberships from the young offspring of the elite upper crust of Boston. These young men from the Gold Coast club dressed alike, in blue jackets and white pants. As they approached him, they looked almost regal, as if they were royalty who happened to be visiting from a much more civilized kingdom. Kennedy observed how handsome their faces were. They had high cheek bones, with smooth and tanned skin that made them appear to have stopped over at an exotic resort—on an exclusive island in the Caribbean reserved for colonial masters and their families—prior to their arrival at Harvard. It became immediately apparent to him that these young men were not the regular students who were streaming into the dining hall for dinner that evening. There was not a shred of evidence that they took any notice of him. They were so engrossed in their conversation that they appeared oblivious of their surroundings. There was no exchange at all between him and them. At that point, Kennedy felt unimportant.

The incident with the three young men who ignored Kennedy served as a turning point in his life. He felt these individuals belonged to a distant world that was out of reach to him, and he wanted to permeate their world of opulence. There was a yearning in his heart for this world. Kennedy felt wistful for not being a member of the upper echelon of society. From this occurrence, his desire to succeed grew. He wanted to make a name for himself, a recognizable name that would allow him access to this world that was elusive to him.

At any early age, Kennedy manifested an unusual thirst for success, an ego, and an incredible drive to experience the lifestyle of the elite. At this stage in the lives of most college students, their lifestyles and preoccupations are usually centered around

Drive to Passion

the blitheness of youth, not an insatiable appetite to belong to the upper echelon of society. Young Kennedy had a longing to belong to the Gold Coast club, so he learned who the Gold Coasters were: Vincent Astor, Jacob Astor IV's son; Kermit Roosevelt, son of Theodore Roosevelt; Edward Atkins, son of Atkins of Westinghouse Electric; and Herman Schwab, Charles Schwab's son.

Despite young Kennedy's yearnings for success, he still led a normal college life. He was surrounded by close friends whom he knew from high school. His life was typical in many ways except for his quest and appetite to belong to the upper crust.

On the other hand, Kennedy's father, known as P.J., was a good man, a perfect gentleman who was perceived as a clean-cut politician. His bushy mustache coupled with his rather excellent fashion ensemble gave him a trustworthy image. In an upcoming election for street commissioner, everyone thought that the winning of the election would be a certainty for P.J. Kennedy. Much to the disappointment of his supporters, he lost to a government employee who was relatively unknown. This loss came as a surprise to all. P.J. in his usual fashion seemed to take the loss fairly well. He was a dignified man who took things in stride. However, Kennedy saw a hurt in his father's eyes, which P.J. tried to conceal with humor. Following the loss of the election, Kennedy also saw in his father a quiet resignation to life. P.J. quickly became deeply engrossed in the affairs of his small business again. Right then, the young Kennedy decided that politics was not his forte. He wanted a more successful and riveting life than his father had, a life that would afford him a taste of affluence.

Kennedy exhibited a common element possessed by great and successful people in wanting a life and a career that would circumvent the drudgery he saw in his father's life. He looked at his father's life critically. P.J. was a local ward boss who ran a small business and was successful in his own right. To him, it was a limiting lifestyle. Kennedy did not want to lead a lifestyle that would mirror his father's in any form. He had the desire for affluence, prominence, and an achievement that would emulate or supersede those of the Brahmins who were at the epicenter of wealth. Kennedy had his eyes set on success and greatness. He wanted power and money. Kennedy's desire and drive had been obvious to him from the start and more so at that point, when the lifestyle of the ever-so-elusive upper class became alluring to him.

Kennedy decided that the world of finance was his best route to the eminence he sought; he decided that it would become his passion. He saw power and money as being synonymous. He wanted both, and it was obvious that he was driven. What better activity in which to establish his passion than business and finance? He was fascinated by both areas.

Passion is a key ingredient in the achievement of excellence, more so than anything else, and is in turn fueled by our drive. Kennedy's drives comprised the avoidance of his father's predicament and the need for opulence. As evidenced by Kennedy, once the drive to succeed, which consists of the motivating force to excel, exists, we must then find a passion that can be fueled by our drive. Passion is successfully established when there is a niche or an aptitude and an affinity or a strong liking for an activity. Kennedy found his passion in business and finance. As is typically the case, Kennedy's passion would in turn fuel his desire to meet his goal of making phenomenal accomplishments.

An intense focus on rewards such as money may derail the realization of our passion. Our passion should be something other than a reward. For instance, we cannot be passionate about wealth, fame, and power, or we may try to obtain these rewards through unscrupulous means. A passion should be value adding and an activity for which we have a niche. If we think about some of the renowned individuals whose passions have touched our lives—Thomas Edison, Martin Luther King Jr., Alexander Graham Bell and Henry Ford—none of them dwelled on the rewards that they would obtain from the pursuit of their passion; otherwise, they would not have made such a huge difference.

Drive is a precursor to passion, and in his book, *Drive*, Daniel H. Pink said that there are two types of motivations: intrinsic and extrinsic. Those who are intrinsically motivated or driven to become successful are usually motivated by the quest for excellence, or the need to be the best at what they do, which Pink calls "mastery." They are also motivated by, among other reasons,

Drive to Passion

the need to make a difference and the need to make strides for altruistic or magnanimous purposes. Conversely, those who are extrinsically motivated or driven to become successful, do so for external rewards. Some common external rewards are wealth and fame. Pink asserted that while extrinsically motivated individuals may have an edge over their intrinsically motivated counterparts in the short run—in the long run, intrinsically motivated individuals have a tendency to experience a greater and more sustainable level of success.

Regardless of what our drive may be, we have to identify an appropriate passion that will be energized by it. All the key components of the quest for our passion should be present: the existence of a niche in the endeavor; enjoyment of the activity involved; continuous education, preparation, and practice in that activity; seeking to be the best or an expert in it; mustering courage, resilience, and confidence, while in pursuit of our venture; and having a tolerance for risk.

* * *

As a child, Kennedy had been involved in selling candies, peanuts, and soap. This may have initiated his attraction to business. It was also a good indication of the existence of a niche in business. Propelled by a conquering will, an attraction for opulence, and the urgency to escape the discomforting identification with his placid father's predicament of dawdling in middle-class existence, young Kennedy became determined to master the world of business.

The idea of starting a tour bus business while at Harvard came naturally to Kennedy and his friend Joe Donovan. This was a stepping stone for him into the world of entrepreneurship. Kennedy and Donovan happened to be taking a tour on a bus one afternoon when they learned the owner intended to sell his company. They made an offer to buy the tour bus service, but it was too low. Much to their surprise, the owner agreed to take their offer as a down payment and finance the balance. As a result of this transaction, a business was born. Prudent entrepreneurial reasoning led them to spruce up the bus by painting it and naming it Mayflower. Kennedy surmised that their revenue would be greatly enhanced by choosing a great location to position the bus—right in front of Boston's South Station.

The next challenge was obtaining a license to operate the tour bus. The licensing board was controlled by Mayor Fitzgerald, whose daughter Rose was romantically involved with Kennedy, much to the disapproval of Fitzgerald. Kennedy courageously and unabashedly approached the mayor for the license. He was confident that he would obtain the permit from the mayor. Kennedy conjectured that the mayor would issue him the license with the intention of causing Kennedy to be obligated to him, so that he could leverage that obligation in the future, in any possible manner. Kennedy was right in his assumptions. He got the license, took it, and never looked back. Also, this did not cause him to have any sense of obligation to the mayor, especially with respect to his advances toward his daughter. He maneuvered the mayor with his shrewdness.

The entrepreneurial venture between Kennedy and Donovan turned out to be lucrative. They made $10,000, a portion of which Kennedy later invested in a real estate deal. As the story goes, this investment in real estate gave him an important insight into business and the world of finance. He was able to see and appreciate the intricacies of business and real estate finance. It was the onset of his lessons in business: credit negotiations, liens, and the different types of loans. He was greatly intrigued by his newfound knowledge in business and finance.

Before Kennedy graduated from Harvard on June 23, 1912, he decided that banking was the aspect of finance he wanted to pursue. Somehow, he presumed that banking was the one area of business that intertwined with all other aspects of business. It served as a bridge through which all business entities remained connected to money—the lifeblood of business. Kennedy's deduction was that banking was the profession that would lead him to prominence and wealth.

Young Kennedy was not the studious type, neither was he at the top of his class at Harvard. In fact, it was reported that he had some problems in an accounting course. Apparently, he was failing this particular course and wound up dropping it. Despite his lack of academic excellence and the challenge he had in accounting, he still chose the world of finance as the arena in which he would display his prowess.

Kennedy, in essence, acquired the drive that propelled him to seek his passion in banking. He longed to achieve expertise or "mastery" in financial services. Kennedy also was driven by the desire to amass the type of wealth that would give him access to the upper class and enable him to circumvent and supersede his father's status as a mediocre local politician and small businessman.

Kennedy had already acquired quite a few of the qualities necessary for success. He took the time to purchase and run a small business. He demonstrated courage and willingness to take risks. He was confident and did not think twice about approaching the mayor, his future father-in-law, for the bus tour license, knowing full well that the mayor did not support his relationship with Rose. Another step Kennedy took toward his future in business was to invest his part of the profits from the bus tour business in real estate. This enabled him to create a return on his investments. The fascination he held for real estate finance was demonstrative of his passion for finance.

Although Kennedy lacked academic proficiency in accounting, he was neither intimidated nor deterred by this fact as he pursued his passion in finance. He did not see his lack of aptitude in accounting as a stumbling block as he later pursued his passion in finance—a related discipline to accounting. He was savvy enough to discern the fact that despite his lack of proficiency in accounting, he could still acquire expertise in finance. He realized that he could learn enough accounting to enable him to achieve "mastery" in his passion. This demonstrates that we can still become experts in our passion in spite of our weaknesses in related subjects.

One key aspect of the pursuit of passion worthy of mention is that ineptitude in life or in college can definitely be overcome as we begin to actually practice, prepare, and educate ourselves in those activities encompassing our niche. In fact, an area of weakness in college can be turned into an area of expertise and passion after college, as long as we ensure that we have an aptitude in that field. We should have the resolve to acquire the necessary skills needed to enable us to become proficient in our passion. The fact that a good number of successful entrepreneurs and Chief Executive Officers (CEOs) were average students in school goes to show that we can achieve excellence in our passion later on in life in spite of our poor performance in school. Nevertheless, I highly recommend higher education. Doing well in school is an enhancement to our pursuits: It gives us discipline, knowledge, and a footing.

Kennedy was undeterred by the fact that the banking industry was controlled by a select few. In that era, names like John Pierpont (J.P.) Morgan, Kidder, Peabody, Lee, and Higginson dominated the banking industry. In Boston, the bankers comprised the Brahmin families for the most part. This circle of bankers was close-knit, but despite this fact, Kennedy was determined to break into this clique. Little did he know that he had embarked on a daunting task. Youthful exuberance and a certain degree of naiveté made him oblivious to the fact that the banking industry was not only going to be a difficult nut to crack, but it was also going to be a world that would remain elusive to him.

As demonstrated by Kennedy's naiveté and lack of trepidation for the daunting task ahead of him, we should not focus on obstacles in our path as we proceed in the pursuit of our passion. Rather, it is crucial that we focus on the desired results and our passion. In the performance of our due diligence, care should be taken not to amplify its effects. This is by no means a minimization of the importance of due diligence. In any undertaking—business or nonbusiness—research and business plans can serve a useful purpose. They can also reveal the challenges and obstacles inherent in the venture. It is then up to us to focus on the possibilities and our passion, rather than the challenges or obstacles. We should utilize our business plan or due diligence as a guide rather than an absolute prediction of the outcome of our venture or a hindrance to it. In fact, it has been said that a certain degree of naiveté, with respect to the knowledge of the obstacles inherent in a business venture, can be beneficial: It forces us to focus on its positive aspects, so that when the challenges do occur we are able to surmount them.

Soon after Kennedy graduated from Harvard, he found a job at a small, local bank in South Boston that was co-owned by his father. His enthusiasm, eagerness to learn, and willingness to take on whatever tasks were assigned to him were impressive to Alfred Wellington, his boss and mentor at the bank.

Kennedy possessed a quality that was seldom found in young people in his time: He considered loyalty to one organization and routine stagnating, and a hindrance to one's progress and upward mobility. Even though he reasoned that loyalty was imperative and a positive attribute, he also knew that banks either failed or got acquired, and that if either of these incidents occurred, he would be faced with a potential career derailment that would be devastating. Kennedy also reasoned that remaining in one organization for too long would stymie the diversification and growth of one's knowledge base—a critical element to one's success—compared to the type of growth and experience a variety of organizations would provide. His sentiment on this issue was so strong that he expressed this notion to a reporter at the tender age of twenty-five, when his colleagues were still oblivious to this type of sophistication in their thinking. His sentiment was depicted by Doris Kearns Goodwin, author of *The Fitzgeralds and the Kennedys*: "[Kennedy] emphasized the vast difference between those who 'made their jobs routine' because they let routine entrap them and those who made 'routine a part of their education for better jobs.'"

Through a combination of instinct and observing his father's shortcomings, Kennedy knew that he wanted to do things differently from him. In spite of the immense respect he had for his father, he saw in him certain qualities that he did not wish to emulate. His father was loyal and dedicated to his constituents, yet he was voted out of office. What a great repayment for his loyalty and dedication to them. Therefore, loyalty to one organization over an extended period of time was out of the question for Kennedy.

Kennedy's quest for his passion would take him to a number of industries such as banking, real estate, movies, liquor, and the financial services, where he would accumulate most of his wealth. This is comparable to Winston Churchill who was a writer, correspondent, soldier, and politician before he became the prime minister of Britain in his sixties. Most often, as we strive to immerse ourselves in our passion in order to become highly accomplished, we may have to embark on the trial-and-error method of problem solving by delving into a few industries prior to identifying our niche and subsequently engaging in our passion. It is also possible to have more than one passion.

It is beneficial to discern our dislikes as we embark on the process of identifying our niche. Doing so enables us to have a basis for comparison. It will also enable us to rule out areas of incompatibility with our goals. Our passion will seldom occur to us through deliberations alone. We should take the necessary steps to identify our niche and passion. Through trial and error and the elimination process, we can identify the activities we truly enjoy. Additionally, friends, well-wishers, bosses, and mentors may be instrumental in helping us to identify our strengths and niches. Kennedy knew he did not want to become a politician and a small businessman like his father. However, he came to the realization that he had an affinity for business and finance.

Similar to Kennedy and Winston Churchill, it is possible to have multiple passions, but it is difficult to single-handedly initiate more than one successful project at the same time. Engaging in two activities concurrently can potentially stymie excellence in both projects and cause ineptitude. Once an existing passion is well underway, it is possible through effective delegation and time management to pursue other passions.

* * *

The turning point in Kennedy's career occurred when his mentor, Wellington, sensing his aptitude for the financial services sector and his eagerness to learn, suggested that he take the state's civil service test to become a bank examiner. Wellington's rationale for this suggestion was that the job of a bank examiner would afford Kennedy the opportunity to acquire a comprehensive knowledge of the banking industry. What better place to experience firsthand the intricacies of the banking industry than on the job as a bank examiner, Wellington reasoned. Wellington helped him study for the test, which Kennedy passed. There were less than a handful of openings for bank examiners in the state of Massachusetts.

Drive to Passion

Competition was stiff for those few openings. Bank examiners were the governor's direct appointees.

Rather than waiting for an appointment from the governor, with the knowledge that the odds were against him, Kennedy took matters into his own hands. He approached Mayor Fitzgerald and asked him to speak to the governor on his behalf. Kennedy gave the mayor a full-fledged presentation with charts and graphs. His presentation demonstrated that there was not a single Irish bank examiner in the state of Massachusetts. His contention to the mayor was that this constituted gross discrimination against Irish Americans. As an Irish American in good standing, Kennedy thought he should unequivocally get the job.

It is interesting and commendable on Kennedy's part to note his willingness to use Fitzgerald as his mentor, even though he knew that he was opposed to his relationship with his daughter. The importance of having mentors and being unafraid and unabashed to leverage their help or influence cannot be overemphasized. Mentors can present us with new opportunities or enable us to take advantage of existing opportunities.

Once again, Kennedy exemplified the traits of an individual willing to circumvent any obstacle in his path to success. Similar to approaching Fitzgerald for a license for his bus tour business, he approached him again for help, with the full understanding that Fitzgerald's opposition to his amorous relationship with his daughter had not changed. However, Kennedy knew that he had a strong and legitimate case, irrespective of Fitzgerald's personal feelings toward him. So he went into Fitzgerald's office, fully prepared—as was typical of him—with charts and graphs and delivered a full-scale presentation that was based solely on merit. His case was so strong that Fitzgerald could not turn him down.

Kennedy's intense preparation for his meeting with Fitzgerald mirrored Churchill's tendency to be well-prepared for his speaking engagements. Kennedy had charts and graphs to prove his point, and he did not take for granted the fact that Fitzgerald had come to his aid previously by issuing him a license to operate his bus tour business. Intense and unremitting practice and preparation is ubiquitous among those who are on the quest for their passion. This trait engenders huge accomplishments.

The mayor agreed to talk to the governor. He was convinced that this was more important than his personal feelings for Kennedy. Fitzgerald saw it as a case of discrimination, so he went to the governor to make a strong case for Kennedy in a very succinct manner. He brought to the governor's attention the fact that there was not a single Irish American bank examiner in the state of Massachusetts. When it appeared as if Fitzgerald's discussion with the governor was not going to yield positive results, he threatened to make this case of discrimination public by going to the press. The governor capitulated, and Kennedy got the job.

Kennedy utilized a winning strategy that worked to convince Fitzgerald to meet with the governor on his behalf. What he used here was a resoundingly persuasive effort that yielded success. In addition to delivering an excellent presentation to Fitzgerald, he provided him with a vital tool that was needed for his discussion with the governor: There was not an Irish American bank examiner in the entire state of Massachusetts, and it was time the governor appointed one; it was overdue.

Kennedy orchestrated an opportunity for himself by approaching Fitzgerald for help, and he took advantage of it once it came to fruition. We all encounter opportunities in varying degrees and in different forms; the more driven and passionate we are, the more capable we are of initiating and taking advantage of them. We have to be able to orchestrate, recognize, and seize opportunities when we encounter them. Additionally, we have to leverage the help of our mentors and others who have our best interest at heart, with respect to the creation and recognition of opportunities. Kennedy had been preparing for a long time to become an awesome force in the world of finance and banking. Kennedy and Churchill, just to mention a few, strategically positioned themselves to take advantage of opportunities. They orchestrated, recognized, and took advantage of those moments. They also leveraged the help of their mentors.

Fitzgerald, who served sporadically as Kennedy's mentor, would attempt to take credit for Kennedy's ascension to prominence. Fitzgerald would insist that Kennedy's exposure to the financial world was a direct result of his meeting with the governor, in which he had insisted that he hire Kennedy as the first Irish bank examiner. On the contrary, Kennedy would contend that his mentor, Wellington, was responsible for his success. Whichever was the case, a path to success had been carved as a result of Kennedy's appointment as a bank examiner. However, fundamentally, the credit for Kennedy's incredible journey to prominence would primarily belong to him.

* * *

Kennedy's days as a bank examiner were marked by excitement, hard work, and his acquisition of a plethora of knowledge about the banking industry. He demonstrated a propensity to amass a lot of information within a short period of time. He had both the affinity and aptitude for banking. He absorbed the intricate details of banking with relative ease. It was noted that what Kennedy learned about banking in a couple of years as a bank examiner would have taken him ten years to learn as a bank employee under normal circumstances. Incidentally, this would not be the last time Kennedy would accelerate his career exponentially, several years ahead of its normal course, by sheer creativity and passion.

Kennedy traveled to different parts of the state to do his job and to truly take an inside look into the world of banking. He found many mistakes and irregularities in the banks, which led him to see the banking world for what it truly was: an environment that was rather ostentatious. Behind the glitz and glamour of tall buildings, shiny floors, and polished desks and chairs were men who—though they were attired in impeccable suits and appeared so very powerful and untouchable—faltered and quivered on their jobs like everyone else.

Most often, Kennedy's gang of examiners took banks by surprise—descending upon them, swarming their offices, and taking possession of their books and cash like a squad from a sheriff's department of old, raiding a gang of criminals. This was the only way to truly see the banks in their element. If the banks had so much as a couple of hours notice or tip prior to the arrival of the examiners, it would have given them more than ample time to stage their operations to look perfect for the examiners. Kennedy performed his job with such discipline and excellence that he began to gain the attention of the executives in the banking industry. By this time he was considered one of the best in his profession. He left a positive and an indelible impression on everyone he met. Kennedy made contacts in the closely knit financial world, giving him the leverage he needed to make strides that he would not have otherwise been able to make. His ascension in the world of business and finance became imminent.

Many things began to surface in Kennedy's mind, including engagement to Rose Fitzgerald and an itch to make a career move, having already decided that being dynamic in his career and learning as much as he could in the process was the best way to get to the top in business. He was seriously considering proposing to Rose. On the other hand, a perfect career opportunity emerged as Kennedy was contemplating his next move. Columbia Trust Company, a bank his father had co-founded and where Kennedy had previously worked, was on the verge of being acquired by another bank, First Ward National Bank in South Boston, in a hostile takeover. First Ward had made a great offer to the stockholders of Columbia Trust, an offer they could not refuse. The challenge, then, became raising enough money to make a counteroffer to the stockholders of Columbia Trust to buy them out and stop the takeover bid by First Ward. This became a perfect opportunity for Kennedy to step in and prove himself.

Kennedy's father and Wellington, Kennedy's mentor, had raised some of the money to buy out the stockholders of Columbia Trust in order to stop the takeover bid by First Ward. There was a $15,000 deficit in the total amount needed for the buyout of Columbia Trust's stockholders, so Kennedy stepped in to help. This was his moment to shine and to demonstrate he was capable of raising the money needed to prevent the takeover.

Kennedy now had the opportunity to leverage the financial resources of one of his contacts—an executive he had met as a bank examiner—Eugene Thayer, president of Merchants National Bank, one of the largest banks in Boston. Thayer was a young man and a Brahmin who was very much impressed with Kennedy. A lot was at stake here. Kennedy needed $15,000 to make up the total amount needed to prevent the buyout from First Ward. The situation was tense for Kennedy; he knew that if he could not

Drive to Passion

secure the loan from Thayer, Columbia Trust would be subject to acquisition by First Ward.

So he headed to Thayer's office to request the loan. Although Kennedy was nervous as he proceeded to Thayer's office, he managed to maintain his composure. As soon as he walked into Thayer's office, the two men greeted each other. Kennedy proceeded to give Thayer a flawless presentation about the need for a loan. At the conclusion of the presentation, Kennedy waited in anticipation of Thayer's decision. His wait was short, but it was nonetheless nerve-wracking, as he knew full well that the fate of the bank rested on his shoulders. Thayer quickly informed Kennedy that the money was his.

The atmosphere at Columbia Trust was jubilant because of Kennedy's success in securing the loan from Thayer. Kennedy, his father, and Wellington now had enough money to ward off a potential takeover bid by First Ward. Kennedy's efforts were lauded by all. Thus Columbia Trust successfully prevented the takeover bid—thanks to Kennedy.

It was now obvious that Kennedy should lead Columbia Trust. The question became how to appease Wellington. Kennedy's father, P.J., decided to step down in order to give Wellington the opportunity to become both the executive vice president and chief financial officer of the bank. Wellington was pleased. Kennedy's ascension to the presidency of the bank was touted by the local newspapers and some national and international newspapers. At the tender age of twenty-six years, he was considered to be the youngest bank president in Massachusetts. There were others who suggested that he was the youngest bank president in the nation or even the world.

Opportunity presented itself to Kennedy as he prepared for a career move from his position as a bank examiner to that of bank president. His new position was not handed to him even though his father was involved in the bank. There was an opportunity to rescue a bank in a takeover bid, and Kennedy rose to the occasion. As a result of his role in the prevention of the takeover, he became the president of the bank. What a huge career move it was for Kennedy. He did a great job in preventing the takeover of the bank without giving much thought to its relative impact on his own fate. Similar to Kennedy, as we pursue our passion, we will encounter opportunities. They will emerge in different forms and in varying degrees. We should position ourselves to recognize these opportunities and take advantage of them.

After his ascension to the presidency of the bank, Kennedy was ready for marriage, and Rose Fitzgerald was definitely the girl for him. Kennedy had achieved considerable success, and he was on a fast track to making huge accomplishments; he was ambitious. He knew that Fitzgerald was not a great fan of his relationship with Rose. Although Kennedy was not very sure of what Fitzgerald's reaction would be if he asked him for his daughter's hand in marriage, he knew that Rose loved him, and he was in love with her. In fact, their love for each other epitomized a storybook romance. Rose definitely knew that if Kennedy asked for her hand in marriage, she would accept. She had relinquished the opportunity to pursue a college education at Wellesley for her parents and was not about to give up the man she loved for her father, no matter how much he objected to the marriage. She and Kennedy had shared their hopes and dreams together at Old Orchard Beach, and she definitely wanted to live that dream.

Fitzgerald was so engrossed in his personal and political problems that he was unwilling to risk the love of his daughter by objecting to her marriage to Kennedy. Kennedy's newly acquired status in the community also helped to sway Fitzgerald's position on the marriage. Kennedy and Rose Fitzgerald were engaged. They got married shortly thereafter and started a family.

Kennedy's three-year tenure as the president of Columbia Trust saw its deposits and loans almost double. He worked hard, putting in ten to twelve hours a day, six days a week. A combination of his affability and open-door policy impressed his existing customers and enabled him to gain new customers.

There is something to be learned from Kennedy's amiability to his customers and its direct relationship to the bank's increase in revenue. We should treat everyone we encounter with the same degree of respect as we would our bosses and clients. Not all battles are worth fighting, nor is retaliation necessary in all cases. Therefore, we should pick our battles and deliberate carefully on

Drive to Passion

when to retaliate. Conforming to these principles enables us to attract more mentors, clients, and opportunities.

* * *

With the advent of World War I came Kennedy's struggles with his opposition to the war. All of his friends were enlisting, including his former Harvard classmates. On more than a few occasions, he engaged his friends in intense debates about the justness of the war. The progression of the war saw Kennedy's position go from adamant opposition to resigned acceptance of it as a necessary evil.

If anything, Kennedy saw the war as an interruption of his ambition—an ambition that had so far been characterized by a major accomplishment such as being on the board of Massachusetts Electric. This board membership was very important to him because it afforded him the opportunity to make important contacts with some of the elite Brahmins of Boston. Prior to being elected to the board, he had been rejected twice by the same board on the basis of his Irish ancestry. The president of Massachusetts Electric would later apologize to him about this act of discrimination.

As the war progressed, Kennedy became increasingly restless about his military draft status. He had a nagging feeling of wanting to be of service to his country in some way, but he did not want to be drafted into the military. He knew that he would eventually be called upon to serve in the military. His foresight in this regard led to his covert aim to circumvent a possible draft into the military. He wrongly assumed that if he were of service to the U.S. government by being employed in a job linked to the military, directly or indirectly, he would not be drafted to face direct combat—a situation that could potentially lead to his death, thereby bringing to an end his life's ambitions and dreams.

There is a dichotomy here between the lives of Kennedy and Churchill. Kennedy sought to avert service in the military, believing that such service could imminently end his life, thereby potentially ending the realization of his dreams and ambitions. Conversely, Churchill utilized his service in the military as a means of leveraging himself to prominence, believing that his ambitions and sense of purpose would keep him alive in the military.

Bethlehem Steel had just acquired a new government contract to build ships for the United Stated Navy. As a result of this new contract, the company expanded its facilities and was in need of a new administrative employee. Kennedy saw an opportunity here and capitalized on it. At the recommendation of an attorney whom Kennedy knew, he had an interview with Joseph Powell, a vice president at Bethlehem Steel, and Samuel Wakeman, the general manager of the new shipbuilding facility. He was one of several candidates being interviewed for the position of assistant general manager of the company's new plant. During this interview with Powell and Wakeman, Kennedy not only exuded vigor and confidence, but he also demonstrated a very sound knowledge of finance, which Powell considered integral to the position of assistant general manager. Recognizing Kennedy's attributes, Powell immediately offered him the job, with a starting salary of $15,000 per year, without bothering to interview the remainder of his candidates.

Kennedy was offered the job even though only a few of the candidates competing for the position had been interviewed. This is a rare occurrence, and a remarkable phenomenon. Very seldom will an interviewer stop his interviews right in the middle before interviewing all the candidates, even if he feels he has found the right candidate. Kennedy impressed Powell tremendously. During the interview, Kennedy was prepared, as usual, and demonstrated an in-depth knowledge of business and finance. Even though he was not at the top of his class at Harvard, once he was out of school, pursuing his passion in finance and business, he achieved a high degree of excellence in these areas through preparation and customized education. Kennedy had a thirst for knowledge that was unprecedented as a bank examiner. The cumulative effect of ardent practice, preparation, and education in the finance sector led to his impressive knowledge and background, which earned him his new position at Bethlehem Steel.

Kennedy exemplified the notion that once we set our eyes on our passion, we should do so without any apprehension about our weaknesses. Total confidence, once we identify our passion,

Drive to Passion

without any trepidation about our capabilities, is what we need to propel us toward phenomenal heights in our passion. Invariably, we will seek and grasp the knowledge required to further enhance our passion to the point of excellence—the point at which we can become an expert in our chosen field.

Kennedy was fascinated by the upbeat tempo at the Bethlehem Steel shipyard once he got there. He plunged into his job with youthful exuberance. He was quoted as saying that he worked harder at the shipyard than he had ever worked.

* * *

The prototypical lives of the individuals featured in this book are of the essence because they epitomize the achievement of success and greatness in spite of life's challenges. Kennedy was not at the top of his class in school, but he had the drive and passion for success. Churchill was not at the top of his class at Sandhurst Military College either. As a matter of fact, Sandhurst, a top-rated military academy, was a last resort for Churchill. Both of these men were great despite their academic challenges and the other obstacles they encountered. The process of making great accomplishments has been exemplified by Churchill, Kennedy, and the rest of the subjects in this book. It is up to us to identify areas of relevance to us and to emulate and mirror these individuals in those areas, as we deem appropriate, for the enhancement of our own lives.

There is a parallel between Kennedy and General Colin Powell, who went on to become a great man even though he graduated from The City College of New York with a C average. When Powell was commissioned as a second lieutenant in the U.S. Army, he immediately had two strikes against him: He was black in a newly integrated military, and he was not a graduate of one of the nation's top military academies. To exacerbate these handicaps, he had not graduated at the top of his class at City College. What Powell had was a niche in the military, prompted by the drive to succeed and rise above the immigrant status and label that characterized his background. Powell studied and prepared as he pursued a military career. He was passionate about the military. He became so articulate that he caught the attention of a commanding general after delivering a flawless presentation. Today, his impeccable resume and accomplishments include chairman of the Joint Chiefs of Staff, national security adviser, and secretary of State.

Along the lines of the implications and results of excellence similar to Kennedy's, The Beatles' Paul McCartney gave his opinion on the essence of making great accomplishments. He was asked interesting questions about his children in a radio interview and he had some fascinating answers. The questions were rather humorous and came from Howard Stern of SiriusXM Satellite Radio. Stern wanted to know what type of inheritance plans McCartney had made for his children, in view of his tremendous financial resources prompted by his accomplishments in music. He said he had made adequate provisions for them, the details of which he did not care to disclose publicly. Another question from Stern was centered on his children's musical abilities. Stern asked McCartney if he thought any of his offspring would become a huge star like he is. To that McCartney replied that his son was actually a very talented musician, and they had previously collaborated in music and were planning to do some more work together in the future. He further stated that, although his son is a very talented musician, he lacked the same type of "hunger" that he and his fellow Beatles had when they were his age. Stern agreed. This "hunger" is synonymous with passion—the same passion that Kennedy and Churchill had, and the same passion that McCartney has for music.

* * *

Although Kennedy was embedded in the rigors of Bethlehem Steel as the war raged, he was still faced with a looming problem—the probability of being drafted into the military. He experienced a heightened sense of alienation from his friends who were serving in the military. Some of his letters to them were unanswered. He felt a terrible sense of loneliness and isolation from them. Later, Kennedy's draft status was elevated to a readiness status despite his initial request to be excluded from military service due to his perception of the essential nature of his job relative to the war effort. His contention was that his contribution to the war effort would be more valuable with his involvement in building ships for the United States Navy, as opposed to being a part of the infantry in battle. The draft board, after conducting a thorough investigation of Kennedy's activities in shipbuilding at Bethlehem Steel, concluded that he lacked technical knowledge—that his involvement in it was indirect and in an administrative capacity; as such, he was eligible to be drafted.

Kennedy's request to be excluded from the draft was denied; however, Joseph Powell was able to save the day. Powell intervened on his behalf by writing a letter to the draft board, first to no avail. Finally, Powell was able to get Kennedy's draft canceled by leveraging his political contacts in Washington, D.C. Kennedy never heard from the draft board again. He experienced a sense of guilt after successfully maneuvering himself out of the draft. Kennedy was unable to get rid of this guilt. A combination of the guilt he felt and the alienation from his friends who were all in the military caused a sense of gloom in him. He buried himself in his job out of guilt. He also did this because of his intense work habit.

The influenza epidemic—one of the worst in recorded history—set in and claimed several thousand lives. Kennedy was visibly stressed. His job, coupled with his efforts in ensuring that the sick at the plant were properly cared for, while maintaining the work flow as much as possible, were the culprits. Charles Schwab, owner of Bethlehem Steel, met and liked Kennedy during one of his visits to the plant and urged him to take a much-needed break to rest and recuperate from his ailments: exhaustion and a stomach ulcer. Schwab was so impressed with the young man that he promised him a position at the corporate headquarters.

No sooner was the end of the war in sight than Kennedy began to develop his usual itch to move on. He cultivated this itch despite Schwab's promise of a position in the corporate office. Bethlehem Steel had served its purpose for Kennedy; the demand for warships built by the company had dwindled, and had almost come to a screeching halt following the end of the war. The plant that once bustled with activity was now almost desolate. Kennedy felt he needed to move on to the next exciting field—his real passion.

Kennedy had decided that his next career move would be the stock market. During the war, he had tried his hand at the stock market and made a healthy profit. Now, he was determined to pursue a career as a broker in a stock brokerage firm, and the company he chose was Hayden, Stone, and Company. He had first met Galen Stone, one of the partners of the firm, when he was on the board of Massachusetts Electric. Kennedy had been impressed with Stone's knowledge and quiet demeanor. He felt that he could learn a lot about the stock market from him.

The years following the end of the war were marked by an economic boom of epic proportions. Kennedy had the foresight to recognize the signs of an imminent economic boom. By choosing to become a stock broker, he was positioning himself to take advantage of it. He believed that the stock market was a direct reflection of the economy.

Meanwhile, Kennedy's resignation from Bethlehem Steel came as a surprise to his mentors there, in view of his bright future in the company. Initially, it appeared to be a seamless resignation that would be accompanied by a severance package. When this severance package was withdrawn unceremoniously, he protested to one of the board members, Eugene Thayer, who was a friend. Thayer was attentive to Kennedy. He took up Kennedy's case with the appropriate executives tactfully. This situation had a happy ending; his severance was reinstated.

Prior to Kennedy's intended undertaking as a stock broker, he had the opportunity to extend a nice gesture to a friend who had done him favors. When Thayer, who had also provided Kennedy with the loan that he had utilized to prevent the takeover of Columbia Trust, lost his job as a bank president, Kennedy immediately offered him as much as $75,000. Although Thayer did not need his money, it was an excellent gesture nonetheless.

The economic boom that Kennedy had predicted began to set in. It was a time of prosperity; there were signs of it all over the country. He was poised to take advantage of it with his foray into the industry.

Kennedy's initial experiences at Haden, Stone, and Company turned out to be enthralling, even though his starting salary was lower than his earnings in the past. No sooner had Kennedy settled into his new job than his postwar life began to unfold. His salary of $10,000 a year was not of concern to him because it was augmented by a commission structure. His new job, its surroundings, and its atmosphere were all exhilarating to him. The company was located in the middle of Boston's financial district, along with other powerful brokerage firms in New England. It was what he had envisioned: The huge board where all the trades were listed was there, along with the staff responsible for making changes to the board based on the changes in the market. Kennedy enjoyed the vigorous work environment of his new employer and wanted to learn as much as he could. The distinction between this job and the other jobs he had held was obvious: This was his passion.

Kennedy executed trades for clients: buying and selling stocks. As he began to purchase stocks, it became clear to him that the most concrete way to ensure success in the stock market was to isolate a few companies that he deemed progressive and viable, study and research these companies thoroughly before executing his trades in the ones he felt had the most potential of yielding the highest returns. He proceeded to do that. In his usually detailed and unrelenting manner, Kennedy researched these companies: their management style and talents, products or services, prospects for longevity, financials, and all available information that was pertinent to the prospective companies. He was frequently seen at his desk with his head buried in volumes of books and periodicals doing his research. He could be likened to a hungry man at this point, with an itch to satisfy his hunger. He was on the right path to becoming a successful stock broker—adept at his craft.

Preparation and studying were not alien to Kennedy. In fact, he had an insatiable appetite for knowledge. As always, high achievers have a common denominator: the quest for knowledge, practice, and preparation in their areas of expertise. Kennedy, Churchill, and others ardently made preparations and engaged in practices in the activities for which they were passionate. Despite Kennedy's charm, good looks, and ability to make high-powered friends easily, he still maintained his voracious appetite for knowledge, preparation, and practice.

It was obvious to Kennedy from the onset that the profession of buying and selling stocks was not an exact science. No matter how much research he conducted or how in-depth his studies were on the prospective companies in which he intended to invest, the investment of securities was always considered to be an art rather than a science. This fact he wholeheartedly embraced.

As Kennedy delved further into the stock market, he uncovered an interesting fact about it. The burgeoning, postwar, unregulated stock market was not free from the canny insider information among investment experts and influential men with whom he closely aligned himself. Some of these men were board members of several companies and company presidents. Through these associations, Kennedy was able to see which way the tide was going and to make appropriate changes to reflect the tidal waves of the stock market. These men exerted enough influence to cause a substantial shift in stock market prices. Kennedy's knowledge of the industry grew to the point of being able to discern the combination of the complex details of his recently acquired knowledge from his new associates and the human, unforeseen element in investment—speculation.

Kennedy also observed his teacher and mentor, Galen Stone, very closely in order to absorb all he could about the stock market. He listened to his conversations and observed his moves for clues on how to accomplish the best deals. Knowing full well that Kennedy watched him very closely, Stone never divulged clues easily; he wanted Kennedy to acquire the erudition to seek and decipher his own information. He also wanted him to be able to make his own decisions and mistakes—and most importantly, to learn from them.

Kennedy had great listening skills. He had listened to his customers and had an open-door policy with them at Columbia Trust Company; hence, he had more than doubled the bank's revenue during his tenure as president. He also listened to and observed his mentor, Stone, and others as he studied the art of investing in the stock market. Listening is a vital skill that we need to develop as we pursue our passion.

One of the twenty-two companies on whose board Stone sat was Eastern Steamship. It was not an unusual practice for major investors of Stone's caliber to sit on the boards of companies whose stocks they sponsored and managed. This practice ensured their protection by these powerful investment brokers. Kennedy picked Eastern as the company in which he would make his first major personal investments. He studied this company in his usual detailed manner and was pleased with what he found. Furthermore, it was a company whose board Stone chaired. Besides, Kennedy liked and used the services of Eastern Steamship.

Kennedy became skilled in the use of lines of credit and bank loans to finance his stock purchases, and he used this capability to purchase a large number of Eastern's shares. He was right in his assessment of Eastern's stock. Over a period of about one year, its shares almost doubled in price. He cashed in, making several thousand dollars, but he still held some of Eastern's stock due to his strong belief in the viability of the company.

No sooner had Kennedy had the time to relish his success than a recession hit the stock market. It had a negative effect on his investments. The much anticipated postwar boom ended in a recession in 1919, a recession that would last two years. The Dow Jones Industrial Average plunged from 119 to 63, and Kennedy experienced his first bad loss. He bought a substantial amount of shares for $160 that plummeted to $80, depleting his cash reserves. For the first time, Kennedy made a bad error in judgment that cost him a substantial loss. He had failed to research the organization in which he had invested, in his usual detailed fashion, and the repercussions were horrendous.

Following Kennedy's mistake, he sought consolation from his mentor, Stone. He told Kennedy that failure was a normal process in business. Stone also told him that anyone who had not failed at least once in business was still green. He in essence implied that failure was not only normal in business, but it afforded everyone the opportunity to learn from her mistakes. He further indicated to Kennedy that as long as he learned from his mistakes, he would likely not repeat them. Some mistakes can be fatal; however, the path to success also entails learning from other people's mistakes. Kennedy vowed to re-ignite and maintain his habit of meticulously researching the companies in which he made his investments and to continue to learn from his mentor.

In keeping with Kennedy's initial prognostication of an economic boom, subsequent to the war, the 1920s became vibrant economically despite the minor impediment caused by the brief recession that had just ended. The 1920s become the "Roaring Twenties"—a period of economic boom and prosperity. Kennedy was right in his foresight; the country and the stock market rebounded from a brief period of recession. The Dow Jones Industrial Average climbed to an unprecedented level of 380. The period of prosperity had emerged. The stocks Kennedy had acquired began to climb again. Kennedy had learned from Stone to buy stocks individually from companies after a thorough due diligence and based on his perception of the companies' capabilities. He held on to those stocks because he knew they would appreciate in the long run.

The 1920s symbolized an important era. To Kennedy, it marked the passing of the baton from Stone to him. His period of wealth accumulation had arrived. He had made the right choices and landed in an industry that afforded him the opportunity to begin to make his mark in the world.

Due to Kennedy's reluctance to discuss business at home, his wife, Rose, was oblivious to his business dealings, which may have contributed to the strain on his marriage. His rationale for refraining from business discussions at home was that he wanted to separate his business life from his home life. This factor, however, alienated his wife. Rose was known to have once commented that her husband switched jobs so frequently that it was difficult to tell what business he was involved in at any given time. Kennedy's business involvements also put him in the company of some beautiful women. He was often out in the company of his single friends. Although Kennedy and his wife had shared so many dreams together, it was reported that at that point her dreams of a perfect marriage began to crumble.

Kennedy's family was growing by leaps and bounds, and the rigors of raising a family had begun to take its toll on the romance in his marriage. He had five children. He and Rose were so engrossed in the day-to-day affairs of running a family that they seldom had time for real romance—the type of romance they used to have at Old Orchard Beach, when their love for

Drive to Passion

each other was passionate and intense. They were youthful and idealistic then. Their future was bright and held a lot of promise. It was as if they were going to conquer the world together. At that stage, their relationship also bore the semblance of the forbidden fruit because of her father's opposition to it. This resistance by her father added to the excitement and intensity of their love affair. However, their marriage was now more like a partnership—a partnership that centered mostly on the children and the running of the household. In spite of the emotional distance in their marriage, Kennedy and his wife still had tremendous respect for each other. He was impressed with her organizational skills in running the household: The house was always impeccable, and the children were well-behaved and neat.

* * *

Kennedy arrived at a crossroads in his employment with Hayden, Stone, and Company. The challenge that lay ahead of Kennedy was that his mentor, Stone, was approaching retirement, and he had begun to ponder the next step in his employment at the company subsequent to Stone's retirement.

One day, during that period, Kennedy emerged unscathed by a bomb explosion that occurred close his job. He was fortunate to be uninjured in the incident triggered by the blast.

At that point in his life, Kennedy had attained considerable success, and had begun to contemplate a golf club membership, which he felt he deserved. He had become an avid golfer and sought a club membership, where he could engage in this recreational activity and mingle with people of like mind. He felt that he had earned his place among the elite of Boston by virtue of his financial status and accomplishments in the stock market. Also, he was, by reason of his marriage to the mayor's daughter, a member of the first family of Boston. The club of choice for Kennedy was the Cohasset Golf Club, which was exclusive and reserved for the upper-crust Protestants of Boston. His emergence in the limelight had momentarily caused a reduction in the level of his awareness of the acute class distinction that existed in Boston. He thought it would not be difficult to gain membership to the club. Kennedy would find out that Boston was still what it had always been: a place highly stratified by class—where the Protestant bluebloods looked down on the Irish Catholics.

Kennedy applied for a club membership in the hope that his friendship with Dudley Dean would be an asset in his quest for the membership. Dean was a noteworthy member of the club who worked in an organization that shared the same office building with Hayden, Stone, and Company. He made his intentions of wanting to join the club known to Dean. Dean agreed to propose his membership to the club officers.

Kennedy's intention had been to join the club before the start of the summer, in order to take advantage of the lush golfing atmosphere of the Cohasset Golf Club, which was located on one of the finest shores Massachusetts had to offer. He wanted to relax on the shore with his family that summer, play golf at the club, and mingle with some of the notables in the community. After all, he had, so far, made financial strides in the stock market and was the mayor's son in-law. He was becoming a known figure in Boston.

Little did Kennedy know that he was in for a rude awakening. At first, days went by with no word from Dean on the status of his membership application. Then, weeks elapsed, and finally Kennedy approached Dean about his membership application, only to be promised by Dean that he would follow up on the matter, though he was unable to guarantee Kennedy a successful outcome. Dean wrote to the treasurer of the club. The treasurer responded by indicating that he had communicated with another club officer and was awaiting an answer. To Kennedy's dismay, the matter dragged on for quite some time. The long span of the application process was disconcerting to Kennedy, to such an extent that it caused him to relive his rejection to the Gold Coast club at Harvard. The hurt that Kennedy suffered from his inability to gain admission into the Gold Coast club had left an indelible scar on him. He wrongly thought that this time, the outcome would be different—he would definitely gain admission into the golf club because he now had a salient image in the community, but he was wrong. Finally, it became obvious to Kennedy that his membership application to the club was going nowhere.

Kennedy could not conjecture what was more disheartening to him, the actual rejection itself or the excuse given for his rejection. The Cohasset Golf Club claimed it was not just a club for golfing, but it was also a meeting place for individuals of like mind and similar family backgrounds; a club for a very cohesive group of people, comparable to a meeting ground for relatives. In essence, they were birds of a feather and Kennedy was of a different flock. Kennedy had been dejected when he was refused membership to the Gold Coast club at Harvard. His despondency at this second rejection was of enormous proportion. This was the last straw for him because soon after this, he would uproot his entire family and move to a different city. It dawned on Kennedy that his financial success was not enough to thwart the cronyism and discrimination that was prevalent in the Boston of the early twentieth century. He detested all clubs and contended that they were a waste of time.

As a result of the rejection he suffered, Kennedy became more determined to move forward with his career, and this served to fuel his drive for more accomplishments. His drive at that point was geared toward the attainment of a higher level of success than the Brahmins who had discriminated against him. He also became resolute about being defined by his own standards. These drives became so strong that they served the purpose of intensely fueling his passion. He transferred his drives into an ardent passion for the stock market. He had something to prove. The more he was snubbed and rebuffed, the more persistent and resilient he became. Kennedy's desire to make a legend of himself was born. His passion for his endeavor grew stronger.

The discriminations and rebuffs that Kennedy encountered may have been a blessing in disguise because they were contributing factors in the spurring of his drive and consequently his passion. Had he been in a less socially stratified environment, his circumstances may have been different. He may have been less driven, and his quest for his passion may have been less zealous, thereby causing his ascension to prominence and power to be reduced or nonexistent.

Kennedy would become a huge success. He would become so well-accomplished that he would contemplate a dynastic setup for his family. When he came to the realization that the presidency of the United States was out of reach for him, he would then envision it for his first son.

* * *

Kennedy had the extrinsic drive to become wealthy and the intrinsic drive to become an expert in the activity encompassing his passion: financial services. Wealth is a good extrinsic drive; however, it is not a passion unless it is associated with a value-creating activity such as investment banking. Kennedy's passion was in financial services. He educated and prepared himself in this field; he was driven by the need to become an expert in it and to become very wealthy in order to outperform those who had rebuffed him. Most experts in the field of personal development contend that for an individual to be defined by money is neither a good sign nor a good path to success and greatness. Money, rather, is a by-product of the pursuit of our passion, and in Kennedy's case, his passion was financial services, rather than money itself. We can acquire wealth when we create value through the pursuit of our passion. Once value is created, the general population will be more than willing to pay for that value. This value could be in the form of great services or products. In Kennedy's case, he created value by executing excellent stock trades for his clients and himself, which resulted in wealth accumulation for him through commissions and his personal return on investment (ROI). Whenever our sole passion is the acquisition of wealth, it may lead to unscrupulous activities because it does not engender the creation of value. It also means that we want wealth at all costs. The desire to be wealthy is a cogent extrinsic drive or motivator that can lead us to seek a passion that will be fueled by this drive. Pink in his book, *Drive*, offers an excellent explanation of motivation and drive.

Whenever individuals or companies lose sight of their passion and only focus on the acquisition of revenue or wealth, it often leads to a decline: closure of business, loss of wealth, or a significant reduction in revenue. We should seek excellence in our craft through the fervent pursuit of our passion, in order to keep the wheels of our achievements in motion. This leads to the creation of value, which in turn leads to prosperity.

* * *

As the roaring 1920s progressed, Kennedy charted his course financially, with the intention of pursuing his passion in the financial services industry more ardently and increasing his financial status. It was time to seek his next great deal. He wanted to increase his level of prominence; he was very ambitious. Kennedy was intent on continuing the quest for his passion with more vigor than ever; he wanted to prove himself as a financial powerhouse to his rivals. Deep down he knew that if he continued to propel himself on the path of success and greatness, it would serve as an equalizer for the acts of discrimination he had encountered. He wanted to become the envy of the snobs. Kennedy's success model, which triggered his continuous quest for great accomplishments, was that the best defense against life's inequities is success and more of it.

Kennedy did not need to search too long for another investment opportunity before he conceived of the idea of investing in the automobile industry. Automobiles had gone from being a luxury item only the wealthy could afford to a necessity for the working class. They had become an affordable means of transportation.

Once Kennedy decided to invest in the automobile industry, he immediately sought to capitalize again on his relationship with Galen Stone, his mentor, who had already given him privileged information about the automobile industry. Stone had informed Kennedy confidentially that Pond Creek Coal, a company whose board he chaired was about to delve into the automobile industry. Pond Creek was a manufacturer of soft coal, which was used for the production of illuminating gas. Stone wanted to be of help to his protégé, so he informed him of his chairmanship of the board of Pond Creek, and then gave him confidential information he believed would be tremendously useful to him. He informed Kennedy that he was engaged in secret discussions with Henry Ford—the famous automobile magnate of the most popular brand of cars in America, Ford automobiles—to integrate the capabilities of Pond Creek with his automobile company. The news of the association of Pond Creek with the automobile industry was expected to have a huge impact on the price of its stock. Kennedy bought several thousand Pond Creek shares at $16 a share by leveraging his lines of credit and all other credit resources at his disposal in anticipation of the stock price going up once the news of the purchase of Pond Creek by Ford was made public.

A few months elapsed, and the negotiations between Ford and Pond Creek dragged on. Kennedy became more nervous because he was aware of the fact that if the negotiations were to encounter a stumbling block, he would be wiped out financially. He was heavily leveraged in this deal. Kennedy's wait was finally over when Ford and Pond Creek reached an agreement on the purchase. Soon after that, *The New York Times* published an article announcing the sale. Pond Creek stock shot up and continued to rise. Once the stock reached $45, Kennedy unloaded his shares for a substantial profit. He almost tripled his profits on his original purchase price of $16 a share. By the time Kennedy paid off all his debt and credit lines, he was sitting on a profit of close to three-quarters of a million dollars, which in today's money would be close to $10 million. Kennedy was definitely on his way to becoming super wealthy.

This kind of insider trading information would be subject to criminal prosecution and jail time in today's world; however, in Kennedy's time, even if it was against the law, it was still the order of the day. He was not alone in this practice. Most of his friends were deemed honest, respectable, and law-abiding citizens, but they routinely provided each other insider trading information. It was considered privileged information, passed around by the wealthy to each other, especially those in the world of finance.

Kennedy, in his usual fashion, masterfully utilized the help of Stone and other mentors in his ascension to wealth and prominence. He also leveraged the assistance of acquaintances as he moved up the ladder on his career path. At the onset of his career in banking, his mentor was Alfred Wellington at Columbia Trust Company. Wellington suggested that Kennedy become a bank examiner in order to learn all there was to learn about the banking industry and to facilitate his career in the industry. Wellington even helped him to study for the examination to become a bank examiner. Kennedy leveraged Mayor Fitzgerald's influence to get the bank examiner's job, despite Fitzgerald's dislike for him. Later, Eugene Thayer, president of Merchants National Bank, loaned Kennedy the $15,000 he needed to avert the takeover of Columbia Trust by First Ward National Bank. Joseph Powell and Samuel Wakeman simultaneously became his mentors at Bethlehem Steel. In fact, Joseph Powell helped Kennedy evade the draft during the First World War by writing a letter to the draft board. After that letter, Kennedy never heard from the draft board again. As a mentor to Kennedy, Galen Stone was one of the important figures in his life. He hired Kennedy in his investment firm, much to the objection of his partner, Hayden, a Brahmin who did not think that an Irishman should be employed in the firm that he co-owned with Stone. Stone was pivotal in Kennedy's life because he helped him to make his initial millions in the stock market.

A mentor is defined by *Merriam-Webster's Collegiate Dictionary* as "a trusted counselor or guide; tutor, coach." In essence, a mentor could be a teacher, and in some cases an adviser. Jack Welch's book—*Winning*, co-authored by his wife, Suzy Welch, former editor of the *Harvard Business Review*—augmented the dictionary's definition of a mentor; he gave an insight into mentoring from his experience as former chairman and CEO of General Electric, a *Fortune* 25 company. He stated that a mentor is someone who can teach us something important. She can be someone younger or older than us. A mentor can even be a subordinate, as long as that subordinate has something to teach us.

Welch and the dictionary show that there is no single individual who fits the typical mold or stereotype of a mentor. Welch said in his book, "Mentors don't always look like mentors." Contrary to popular belief, a mentor is not always the gray-haired fatherly figure, clad in a worn but neatly pressed suit, a nice white shirt, and a bow tie, who seems to have all the answers and helps us in every step of our career path to achieve our ultimate objective. Welch contended that "there is no one right mentor. There are many right mentors." We could have a mentor without realizing it. Acquaintances, friends, colleagues, associates, subordinates, and bosses are all individuals with whom we share a common bond in our bid to actualize our passions, and they could all be mentors to us. As we proceed from drive to passion, people will be an integral part of this progression. We need people to make anything possible.

Although Kennedy had help along the way from certain individuals, he was also snubbed and rebuffed by some others, thus causing him some pain and heartache. It is therefore important to consider that, while some people may be of tremendous help to us, there are others who may have an adverse effect on us. It is extremely helpful to improve our human relations skills as we pursue our goals and our passion in order to attract more people who may have a positive influence or impact on our lives. Kennedy had good human relations skills and empathy for others; a prime example is when he immediately offered his assistance to Eugene Thayer when he was in trouble.

While in pursuit of our passion, we will encounter a good number of people, or we may find ourselves in leadership roles. Our ability to interact with others will be critical to the success of our endeavors. As exemplified by Kennedy, we will need great human relations skills. In the past, many leaders governed or led by intimidation. That is neither feasible nor practical in today's world, especially in the Western world. The quickest and best way to get to the top is through civility. Leading by fear or intimidation is fast becoming outdated. However, civility should be tempered by firmness, strength, and courage. In fact, Welch, in his book, also discussed the balancing act. We should aim to achieve a balance between fraternizing with our subordinates in the bid to be congenial and being too aloof in an effort to garner respect. We should build alliances with our subordinates, without fraternizing. Also, we should garner respect without appearing stern, draconian, or dictatorial. It also helps if we are liked by our subordinates.

People go the extra mile for those with whom they enjoy working. Getting our associates to enjoy working with us is the key to promoting a creative and efficient workplace. Some technology companies, including Google and Facebook, are now in the forefront of promoting an enjoyable workplace;

Drive to Passion

it fosters creativity. In today's world, Churchill and Colonel Sanders would be anomalies with respect to some of their styles of leadership. Our path to greatness becomes smoother if the people with whom we work enjoy working with us. Many other factors could also be linked to the human relations dynamics: fairness, clear communication, building loyalty and consensus, good interactions with others, and motivating others, to mention a few. Welch contended that he made sure that he was fair to his subordinates and treated them with respect.

When Welch was one of the contenders for the position of the CEO of General Electric, his subordinates became his advocates for the position as well as his mentors; they did so by approaching the chairman of the company and making a strong case on his behalf. They informed the chairman that he was fair and great with people. The other two contenders for the position each had strong support from each of the two vice chairmen. Welch, without support from either of the vice chairmen, became the next CEO and chairman of GE. The underdog, in essence, won.

The aim of any driven and goal-oriented individual should be to manage every relationship with the utmost care. In fact, the same amount of effort and care should be put into managing relationships up as is put into managing relationships down, with up being people to whom we report and down being our subordinates. We need people even when we are asleep. Actualizing our passion requires people. Without people, the transitioning of our drive to passion is either imperiled or hampered.

* * *

The other element worthy of mention in Kennedy's life was his willingness to take risks. Even though he was reluctant to risk his life during the war, he was unafraid of taking business risks. There are risks inherent in all business ventures and in the pursuit of our passion. High-risk ventures often yield high returns. If we are risk-averse, then we do not belong in the arena of trying to discover our passion. Somewhere in the process of making a transition from our drive to our passion, we have to take some risks, such as risking a comfortable job for the pursuit of our passion, which does not have a guaranteed outcome. Embarking on the pursuit of our passion always entails some uncertainty. Kennedy took a few major risks in his time. When he bought the share of Eastern Steamship, he was highly leveraged. Had those shares taken a nose dive, he would have been wiped out financially. Would it have been a career stopper? It is often difficult for failure to stop people who are intent on making successes of themselves. The second major investment Kennedy made with Pond Creek Coal was risky as well. He was also highly leveraged in that instance and stood the risk of losing everything had the price of those shares declined.

* * *

Following Stone's retirement in 1923, Kennedy found himself in a position where he was the master of his own fate. He had risen within the organization from a customer man to the head of the stock exchange. Yet he knew that he would never become a partner at Haden, Stone, and Company. Hayden, who was Stone's partner, had initially been opposed to Kennedy's employment at the firm. Kennedy was of course an Irish Catholic, while Hayden was a Protestant with a lineage that dated back to the founding fathers. Hayden would have never conceived of the idea of having someone other than a full-blooded Brahmin like himself as a partner. Kennedy wanted to take his future into his own hands. He did not want a position that would not entail decision-making authority in the company. Thus, he resigned and formed his own organization. He set up his own office—a modestly furnished but nice office. In choosing a name for his business, Kennedy made a conscious decision to add "banker" at the end of it rather than "financial services" or "stock broker." He wanted the name to resonate well with people, depicting class, distinction and his strong banking background. So he chose the name "Joseph P. Kennedy, Banker," for his company. With this new name, he felt confident about the future and ready to take on the financial services industry.

No sooner had Kennedy started his own company than an opportunity came literally knocking on his door. One night, at about midnight, Kennedy was awakened by Walter Howey, a noteworthy editor of a popular newspaper. Howey had invested his life's savings in Yellow Cab Company, owned by John Hertz. He was about to lose all his money due to a sharp decline in the stock price of Yellow Cab, instigated by some unscrupulous private equity investors who were in the process of trying to make a bid for a hostile takeover of the company. He begged Kennedy to go with him to New York that night, via the overnight train, to meet with Hertz, the owner of Yellow Cab. Their final destination was the Waldorf-Astoria Hotel, where they would meet with Hertz to strategize on how to ward off the prospective hostile takeover bid by the stealth equity investors. Kennedy agreed to go, sensing the potential opportunity.

Even though Kennedy was tired upon his arrival in New York City that morning, the hustle and bustle in the lobby of the Waldorf excited him. The attendants and bellmen rushed around in different directions; the people there were in some cases gathered in small clusters, conducting their businesses and carrying on discussions. Kennedy was wide awake, with an adrenaline rush despite his fatigue; it was his type of environment.

Kennedy joined Hertz and his vice president, Charles McCullough, in one of the cafés at the Waldorf, where they had been awaiting his arrival. While the exact identity of the group of individuals engineering the takeover was unknown, it was speculated that a competitor of Yellow Cab's—Checker Cab Company—was behind it. Hertz had been poring over the previous day's stock market figures with a worried look on his face. The meeting quickly commenced after the men exchanged brief greetings, with Hertz immediately explaining the situation to Kennedy. The price of Yellow Cab stock had been plummeting. Kennedy quickly devised a plan to buy and sell Yellow Cab shares at will in a maneuver intended to confuse the hostile takeover artists and stop the stock from its downward spiral. Kennedy further explained that his intentions were to put the individuals who were shorting the stock out of business. Hertz told Kennedy that he had a cash reserve of $5 million that would be made available to him to buy and sell the stock as he deemed fit.

As Kennedy later indicated to Rose over dinner in Rhode Island that weekend, the riveting scenario in the lobby of the hotel that morning when he arrived from Boston elicited in him a sense of renewed ambition. He wanted to possess all of the opportunities that the wealthy had, like the ability to come and go as he pleased and the ability to make important decisions. He craved the recognition and privilege that opulence bestowed on the wealthy.

Kennedy chose a suite at the Waldorf as his office. He went to work there for about four weeks, with his aide and trusted friend, Eddie Moore, assisting him. He dug in at his suite, with Moore helping him in all regards: ordering meals, admitting visitors, and running errands. Kennedy stayed on the phone for hours on end, talking to various brokers and ordering the purchase and sale of huge amounts of Yellow Cab stock in order to manipulate the price of the stock. He did this masterfully and skillfully, covering his tracks to avoid detection. After some time, the effects of his maneuvers began to be felt by his adversaries; they could no longer control the price of the stock. Kennedy was in control of the ball. He had utilized the laws of supply and demand to frustrate the takeover artists.

This was Kennedy's moment to prove to the world of finance that he was an emerging phenomenon in the stock investments industry, worthy of notice. As the price of Yellow Cab stock started to stabilize and rise, Kennedy began to instigate articles in the press that were favorable to the company by means of an effective public relations strategy. Consequently, Kennedy and all the individuals on the side of Yellow Cab began to see some light at the end of the tunnel. Also, Kennedy began to encourage the legitimate investors of Yellow Cab stock to buy and hold its stock. He contended cogently that the company was a sound investment.

Kennedy's brilliant thinking and efforts in averting the takeover bid for Yellow Cab earned him a substantial reward; it also earned him a reputation in the industry as a clever financial expert. He received a sizeable amount of cash and Yellow Cab shares. His earnings from this deal helped to propel him to new heights of wealth and influence on Wall Street. Not only did

Kennedy become very wealthy by thwarting the efforts of the takeover artists, but he also became well-known in the industry and was considered a budding force in financial circles. Hertz was so impressed with Kennedy's skills that he offered him a stake in his newest venture—Hertz Drive-Ur-Self System—which would later become Hertz Rent-A-Car. Hertz also offered Kennedy a stake in another new operation—Omnibus Corporation—which provided inexpensive bus services in New York City.

At the age of thirty-four, Kennedy was not only a millionaire, but he also had made some powerful friends, and he had established himself as a burgeoning mind on Wall Street. What an accomplishment. He continued to befriend some of the most powerful men on Wall Street, exchanging correspondence on stock tips and trades. Kennedy befriended Matthew Brush, the president of American International Corporation, a large investment bank. Brush was also a stock speculator, with a net worth of $15 million. In their correspondence, Brush sought Kennedy's opinion on a particular investment strategy—wanting to know if Kennedy agreed with him in his assertion that the stock of a certain organization was going to double. Kennedy's answer was a resounding yes; his rationale for being so confident in his reply to Brush was that Stone was at the helm of that particular company. Brush had another question on Eastern Steamship, which was also headed by Stone. Eastern was expanding and was about to double in size. Brush wanted to confirm Eastern's expansion with Kennedy prior to purchasing some Eastern shares. Kennedy agreed and, of course, Brush invested heavily and made money.

There was minimal regulation of the stock market in Kennedy's era. He belonged to an exclusive club of men who freely traded information on stocks without any guilt or the notion that they were necessarily breaking the law; it was a common practice. These men were a close-knit group of individuals who belonged to a privileged class, and they epitomized the adage that "the rich get richer." In a capitalist society such as ours in the United States, where a group of individuals were amassing wealth legally, who could blame them for taking advantage of all the loopholes that were available to them? Most people would have done the same thing given similar circumstances. Kennedy and his cohorts were smart enough to know that the market was not going to remain unregulated forever. They knew they were getting away with a lot.

By the mid-twenties, Kennedy had amassed $2 million dollars in wealth, highlighting a sharp dichotomy between him and his father, P.J. Kennedy. Kennedy was now a capitalist to the core who exploited the system for what it had to offer. His father, however, was an honest, forthright individual who would practically give the shirt off his back to his neighbor, even to the disapproval of his wife or the inconvenience of his family. The dichotomy between Kennedy and his father is nothing new among a significant number of driven and passionate individuals. For them, drive is also spurred by a desire to rise above their perception of their parents' weaknesses or the prevailing environment of their childhood.

* * *

Kennedy had been interested in the movie industry for some time—it was nascent, and it provided great entertainment to the masses. He knew that the industry had great potential. It was one of the few forms of escape in an era when the masses comprised immigrants and uneducated workers who subsisted on menial jobs and other forms of dreary employment. These individuals had neither the means nor the sophistication to engage in any marked form of entertainment or amusement, such as vacations and fine dining. So, in Kennedy's thinking, going to the movies was a good way to ease the doldrums of their mundane existence and possibly the only form of entertainment that would ever be accessible to them. Kennedy also realized that the movie industry was in its infancy and could become one of the best forms of entertainment for everyone. The industry was similar to the automobile industry in a few ways: They were both burgeoning industries, targeted toward the masses, and were affordable.

Kennedy began his foray into the movie industry by buying a controlling interest in a small chain of movie theaters in New Hampshire and Maine. He immediately realized that he was in stiff competition with the more established chains such as Loew's

Theater and others. Furthermore, he realized that movie production companies made all the profits while squeezing theaters out of their profits; theaters had low margins. Consequently, he began to set his tentacles on movie production companies.

Film Booking Offices (FBO), a movie production company that made action-packed movies, was in a predicament due to its inability to obtain credit from banks, an endemic problem in the movie industry at the time. FBO was owned by some British investors. In Kennedy's time, movie companies were considered risky investments by traditional lending institutions. Banks considered loans extended to movie companies as high-risk loans because of the high salaries they paid their employees and the large inventories of movies they carried. As a result, movie companies were unable to get loans from banks. They resorted to "loan sharks" who were unethical in their lending practice and charged very exorbitant interest rates on their loans. FBO found itself caught in this cumbersome quagmire. The company was losing money. It paid high interest rates for loans because it was forced to borrow money for its working capital from unscrupulous loan operators.

While at Hayden, Stone, and Company, Kennedy had been assigned the task of finding a buyer for FBO, for a sale price of $1.5 million. He had been promised a substantial commission of $75,000 as the sole broker for this deal, but he was unable to find a buyer for the company. After unsuccessful attempts by Kennedy to unload the company, he was consequently made an advisor to FBO for a fee of $1000 per month. All along, Kennedy had wanted to buy the company but did not have enough money for the purchase.

As Kennedy began to make plans to purchase FBO, he called on his father-in-law, Fitzgerald, to make an investment in the company. Although their relationship had a rocky start, both men had grown to respect each other over the years. Fitzgerald thought Kennedy was a financial genius, and Kennedy admired his father-in-law for his tenacity, youthful vigor, and ability to push forward with alacrity in spite of setbacks. Fitzgerald not only commanded respect in Boston as the consummate Irish politician, but he was also quite influential in other circles. Kennedy called on Fitzgerald to invest in his bid to

Joseph Kennedy: Craved Recognition and Privilege

purchase FBO and to help him assemble a group of investors for the project. Fitzgerald wound up investing $10,000 in the deal.

Kennedy was poised to purchase FBO. He was no longer with Hayden, Stone, and Company, and he had made a couple of million dollars in securities trading. He travelled to London, met with the owners of FBO, and offered them a million dollars for the company. They turned him down. The British investors had already sunk $7 million into the sinking ship in an attempt to revamp it, in the years following Kennedy's departure from Hayden, Stone, and Company. They rejected Kennedy's offer; they felt their company was worth much more because of the substantial investment they had made in trying to restore it. Kennedy returned from London disappointed and dejected.

Soon after Kennedy returned from London, he planned a golf trip to Florida with three of his friends. It was the middle of the winter, and the men had been working hard in their various professions, so the vacation was well-deserved. They all assembled in New York City, at the Harvard Club, the night before their departure. The following day, they were to take a cab to the train station where they would catch the train to their vacation destination. No sooner had their cab been loaded up with their suitcases and golf clubs than one of the porters came rushing toward their vehicle from the hotel, in an attempt to stop them from taking off. The porter approached the vehicle and told Kennedy he was wanted on the phone at the hotel; it was very important.

Kennedy returned to the hotel for a few minutes, came back, and announced to his friends that he had just bought a movie studio and would not be going to Florida with them after all. He was needed in Boston due to the acquisition he had just made and would be departing that night.

After Kennedy consummated the purchase of FBO, the newspapers touted Fitzgerald as the principal in the purchase of the movie studio—thanks to Fitzgerald, who was anything but reticent to the press. Prior to the conclusion of the purchase of FBO, Fitzgerald was vocal to the press; he talked to the newspapers extensively about the deal, to such an extent that they all thought he had actually orchestrated it. Kennedy was upset because the

Drive to Passion

Boston press did not give him the accolades and recognition he deserved for the FBO deal. He felt that no matter how much he achieved, he never got the respect he deserved in Boston.

As a result of his disappointment with the press's bias in the FBO deal, Kennedy continued in his resolve to achieve more success in order to prove himself. We definitely can rectify the injustices we encounter as a result of life's challenges and inequities by deciding to persistently achieve and make more strides in our endeavors. We should always demonstrate our resilience by prevailing over our problems more times than we are beaten by them. This is certainly one way to guarantee ourselves success. Kennedy channeled and refocused his anger in a positive direction.

Kennedy quickly concentrated on running the day-to-day affairs of FBO. He was undoubtedly going to make the studio a success. Once again, the motivation of trying to prove himself to the elite of Boston became a tremendous driving force for Kennedy. He became the president of FBO, with the primary objective of turning the company around. He started by offering preferred FBO stock to raise capital for the company. He then proceeded to set up a bank loan and a line of credit for FBO. Next, he brought in his own team of trusted employees and aides—a group of individuals who had moved with him from place to place.

The marketing strategy of FBO was redefined by Kennedy. He wanted FBO to represent to the movie industry what Ford represented to the automobile industry and Woolworth to the retail industry. In essence, he wanted his target market to be the masses rather than a select few people who were deemed sophisticated and in the upper echelon of society. He aimed to position the company in a manner similar to the positioning of the Ford automobiles, by making FBO's movies affordable to the general population. Also, Kennedy redefined the corporate culture and mission of FBO. The company was no longer going to compete with the large movie companies; rather, it was going to concentrate its efforts on movies with mass appeal that required minimal cash outlay.

Kennedy always controlled his excitement whenever he was involved in a new and lucrative venture; this limited any hindrance in his judgment, thus increasing his capability of making good decisions. He was always able to channel his attention and energy to the appropriate areas of the business at hand in order to be productive. This also minimized any impediments to his shrewdness and creativity. In the first year of Kennedy's presidency at FBO, the company's revenue reached $9 million. His ambition, at that point, was dominated by his passion for the movie industry.

Once Kennedy settled into his new role as the president of FBO, he began to contemplate his next move. In his quest to make a name for himself in Boston, to advance his business, and to further his philanthropic agendas, Kennedy decided to travel back to Harvard. He had been disappointed, rebuffed, and actually rejected a few times, but he was still driven and motivated to make a name for himself. He wanted to circumvent the stereotype of being the Irishman and Catholic whose lot in life was predetermined by circumstances beyond his control. As he entered Dean Wallace Donham's office in the Harvard School of Business, he had already mapped out his strategy. He wanted Harvard to bestow honor and recognition on the movie industry under his auspices. His objective was to enable the movie industry to gain credence at Harvard and the nation at large. In 1926, the movie industry was still in its infancy, but it was beginning to gain a foothold in the American landscape. It was an industry that would benefit further from Kennedy's contributions and propitious endeavors.

As Harvard's de facto advocate in the movie industry, Kennedy's aim was to convince the dean that Harvard needed to set up a curriculum for cinema in order to join the momentum of a burgeoning industry. It was already commanding several million patrons daily, on a national basis, and it was growing by leaps and bounds. The movie business could no longer be ignored, in spite of some of its negative attributes at the time: scandals, drugs, and sexual improprieties.

Were there personal gains for Kennedy in all of this? Whatever successes he could achieve in establishing a cinema curriculum at

Harvard would revert back to him as the one who orchestrated the idea. Kennedy also pledged a donation of $30,000 for a proposed film library—a great act of benevolence. Not only were there historical implications here, but there was an opportunity for him to gain recognition if he could make this significant stride. Recognition of this magnitude would definitely not go unnoticed by the elite of Boston, most of whom he had already surpassed in wealth and fame at that time.

In Kennedy's proposal to Donham, the event that would enable the Harvard students to get acquainted with the movie business would be kicked off with a series of lectures about the emergent industry. His arguments in favor of the event were compelling. Despite strong opposition from some influential members of the Harvard community, the decision makers at Harvard decided to go ahead with the lectures.

Preparations for the lectures about the movie industry at Harvard proceeded in earnest, and all of the Hollywood heavyweights with whom Kennedy had some areas of commonality agreed to participate. In addition to being in the same industry, they all shared a cohesive bond: the quest for personal recognition, as well as the need to legitimize the industry. Another area of commonality among the Hollywood moguls, including Kennedy, was their immigrant lineages and need for acceptance by others. The fact that they had the opportunity to gain recognition by virtue of their involvement with one of the nation's best institutions of higher learning and a monumental national symbol was an honor to them. This endeavor also gave Kennedy the opportunity to get to know some of his colleagues in Hollywood better. The industry was fairly new to him. What better way to get to know the other industry titans and to gain their respect than to orchestrate an event of this magnitude?

We do not make progress in life without aspiring to do so. We sometimes get things we do not actively seek, but they may not last. Even when we play the lottery, we make a conscious effort to play in order to win. The only exception may be in the case of an inheritance. However, a potential beneficiary of an inheritance will often make a conscious effort to conform to whatever stipulations are set by his benefactor to avoid being disinherited. In other words, if we choose to be in a state of inertia, greatness will elude us. Kennedy was actively in pursuit of great accomplishments, which would be augmented by his benevolence at Harvard.

When corporations, individuals, and business people get involved in community or philanthropic activities and take actions geared toward corporate responsibility and good corporate citizenship, are these actions orchestrated by a hidden agenda? Individuals and businesses that are benevolent should benefit from their acts of benevolence, as long as these kind deeds are truly beneficial to their beneficiaries. There is nothing wrong with an unemployed individual volunteering for a Habitat for Humanity project in the hope of meeting a potential employer, as long as he actually works once he gets there. In other words, it should be a "win-win" situation. This assessment is not designed to issue a guideline on the morality of philanthropy; it merely serves as a projection of the "win-win" paradigm between the benefactor and beneficiary of charity. As most self-improvement and religious pundits have contended, when we give, we get it back in other forms. This is a good incentive to give. A certain amount of gratification and recognition accompanies philanthropy.

Did Kennedy initiate his endeavors at Harvard for purely selfish reasons? The morality of his charitable ventures is outside the scope of this book. However, when we measure the benefits to the benefactor compared to the benefits to the beneficiary, the results tell the whole story. In Kennedy's situation, both he and Harvard University benefited from his gestures. He offered students a taste of the inner workings of a burgeoning industry that was still, to a degree, elusive and esoteric—an industry whose image was riddled with fables and innuendos with regard to drugs, sex, money, and other endemic problems. Kennedy benefited from this act of benevolence by gaining recognition from the upper crust of Boston and his peers in the movie industry. This brought him in direct contact with other movie executives. The cumulative effects of these activities would propel Kennedy to great heights in the movie industry.

Kennedy exemplified Malcolm Gladwell's contention in his book, *Outliers*, that attitude is more important in the quest for success than innate ability. Gladwell further stated, "Success is a function of persistence and doggedness and the willingness to work hard for twenty-two minutes to make sense of something that most people would give up on after thirty seconds." The statement came about as Gladwell tried to prove that proficiency is not so much a factor of natural prowess as it is a factor of resilience and the willingness to continue to think through a problem, step by step, relentlessly, and without quitting until a solution is found. In all his undertakings, including the project he orchestrated between the movie industry and Harvard University, Kennedy epitomized resourcefulness, tenacity, and resilience.

Like Kennedy, we should always take our future into our own hands by asserting ourselves and charting our own course in life, while simultaneously embarking on a trajectory for our ambitions. We should not harbor the mentality of being victims of our circumstances. Kennedy's move into the position of a bank examiner gave him, within a short period of time, the prominence in the banking industry that was equivalent to ten years of experience in a bank. Also, his creativity in orchestrating the lectures at Harvard and his other benevolent activities there, in the words of Goodwin, Kennedy's family biographer, "made more of an impact in his standing in the Hollywood community than he could have made with years of hard work." In essence, Kennedy knew how to catapult his career several years ahead of its normal course and to orchestrate a trajectory of the highest velocity and magnitude to springboard himself to tremendous success.

Kennedy gave himself a short period to relish the impacts of his accomplishments at Harvard before he set out to capitalize on them. He began to set his sights on other aspects of the movie industry with the intention of fully capitalizing on both the industry's potential and his own newly acquired prominence. He was well-positioned to take advantage of his popularity among other movie executives. He was also poised to take advantage of the newest innovation in the industry: talking movies. Once Kennedy was rested and had fully enjoyed his achievements and newly acquired fame, he moved on to the next phase. He proceeded to inquire about one movie company after another. He was intent on making acquisitions.

Finally, Kennedy decided to acquire a chain of theaters: the Keith-Albee-Orpheum (KAO) theaters. His bid to acquire KAO,

Joseph Kennedy: Craved Recognition and Privilege

and his subsequent acquisition of it, was not without incident. KAO comprised a chain of three hundred theaters. Keith Albee, a fellow Bostonian, was at the helm of the company. KAO had previously merged with another company—Pathe-De Mille—bringing John Murdoch, who was the president of Pathe, into the equation. Murdoch, recognizing Kennedy's prudence and tenacity, quickly aligned himself with him. He saw Kennedy as an aggressive and shrewd businessman. Albee, the majority stockholder of KAO, was the only stumbling block in Kennedy's way as he sought a controlling interest in the company. Kennedy made Albee an offer to buy two hundred thousand shares of KAO's common stock at $21 a share, for a total of $4.2 million. Albee refused, even though the offer would be of benefit to him; the stock was actually worth only $16 a share. Pressure mounted on Albee to sell. Kennedy and Murdoch, who by this time had formed a powerful alliance, asserted to Albee that Kennedy's experience, energy, and financial backing would be good for the company. Although Albee was initially reluctant to sell, he began to see things their way. However, he did not equate the loss of all these shares with the loss of his controlling interest in the company: Having $4.2 million dollars to himself became his main focus, and it overshadowed his good judgment. The deal was enticing. Albee finally yielded to Kennedy's persuasiveness and decided to sell.

Under the agreement, Albee would still maintain the presidency of KAO, while Kennedy would join forces with him to aggressively grow the company. Once the sale was concluded, Kennedy immediately acquired a controlling interest in KAO and became its chairman. However, Albee still thought he was running the company—apparently misconstruing the dynamic setup of corporate mergers and acquisitions with respect to voting rights and control of the power structure predicated upon a sale. He also underestimated Kennedy's shrewdness. One day, subsequent to the sale, he walked into Kennedy's office to offer his opinion on a matter at hand; Kennedy seized the opportunity to tell him that he was fired, and Albee was forced to resign. Feeling betrayed by Murdoch and Kennedy, he became acrimonious and despondent. He died shortly thereafter.

Drive to Passion

Kennedy, in his usual quest for excellence, took KAO to great heights—increasing its sales and further penetrating the market, thus positioning the company for growth. Soon after Kennedy made these accomplishments, he began looking for other possibilities of growth and expansion. He was a firm believer in the mantra that we cannot hold steady in business; we have to either grow or decline.

With Kennedy's reputation as a tenacious businessman on the rise, he was invited by the declining First National Exhibitors' Circuit, a production company, to take over its production and distribution unit, with an option to purchase twenty-five percent of its stock. Kennedy accepted. Everything was on track for his participation as a stakeholder in the company. This caused an industrywide buzz that created an air of anticipation. Suddenly, everyone was talking about better things to come for First National. Following Kennedy's acceptance as a stakeholder in the company, he began to orchestrate a takeover bid. Kennedy wanted to quickly add First National to his arsenal of companies.

The board of First National, which had anticipated Kennedy's arrival, suddenly began to show ambivalence, and eventually it resisted his ideas and actions. Finally, the board rescinded its offer to him. Kennedy had been planning to merge First National with all of his companies and form a large production company. After much deliberation, the board refused to extend Kennedy's contract, forcing him to resign. This action by the company's board was sudden and took everyone by surprise. The board's dissension resulted from Kennedy's desire to acquire complete power in the company and his inability to show discretion in discussing issues pertaining to First National. Reportedly, Kennedy had dinner one night with a very pretty woman, and in the midst of that dinner, he became braggadocios about his involvement in First National—boasting to the woman that, in a short while, he would be at the helm of one of the nation's largest movie companies. Kennedy also insinuated to this woman that he was smarter than all his colleagues in the industry. Unbeknownst to him, this woman was the mistress of one of the board members of First National. This served to reinforce the board's decision to kick Kennedy out.

Kennedy had derailed a nascent deal, with First National that had great potential, because of his own actions. He once again proved that there is no straight path to success. His failure was partially attributable to his own indiscretion. Not only did Kennedy cross the boundaries of his marriage by having a dinner date with this woman, but he also failed to use good judgment with respect to his dissemination of confidential information. Kennedy also faltered by being overly aggressive: He pushed the board of First National too hard by initiating a takeover bid of the company too quickly. He wanted too many changes too soon. We all have faults, and we are prone to errors in judgment, but we should be resilient in spite of our shortcomings.

In Kennedy's typically progressive style, he was undeterred by this failure and mistake. He considered this a minor setback. No matter how driven and passionate we are, mistakes and failures are unavoidable. Earlier, Kennedy had learned from his mentor that failure was normal as long as one learned from it. Thus, he began plotting his next move; he had his eyes set on other deals. He did not dwell on his mistakes and failures. Before long, it was announced by a newspaper that Kennedy and Joseph Sarnoff of RCA were in merger talks and would be joining forces to form a huge conglomerate, one of the largest in Hollywood, to be called Radio-Keith-Orpheum (RKO).

Soon, the merger became a reality accompanied by accolades and recognition for Kennedy. RKO had combined assets of $80 million. The media went crazy with fanfare. Kennedy had finally arrived. The newspapers heralded him as one of the most prominent movie moguls in Hollywood, and certainly the youngest among them. His youthful exuberance and good looks definitely did not go unnoticed. He finally achieved a combination of both wealth and fame. He gained the recognition and adoration he had so actively sought. Kennedy at that point took over from Fitzgerald as the most popular Irish man in Boston: He was no longer referred to as the son-in-law of Mayor Fitzgerald; rather, Fitzgerald was referred to as the father-in-law of movie mogul Joseph Kennedy.

Kennedy had followed the path that typically would lead anyone to greatness: He was driven and focused on his passion;

Drive to Passion

he was resilient and persistent in his pursuits; he had the courage to set his ambition on a trajectory; he never allowed mistakes or failures to stop that momentum; he was affable and sought mentors; he had an insatiable appetite for knowledge in the activity encompassing his passion; and he prepared and practiced ardently in that area.

Kennedy's ascension to prominence in Hollywood came with his initiation into the amorous and peculiar traditions of the industry. He was introduced to Gloria Swanson, an actress with whom he collaborated on a few movies. He also had an affair with her. He initially served as her financial advisor, and the liaison progressed from there. At the height of Kennedy's professional and intimate relationship with Swanson, they were both married to other people. However, much later in their relationship, Swanson divorced her husband.

Although Kennedy was at the pinnacle of success in Hollywood, a series of events led to his decision to return to Wall Street. His father had passed during this period. He was often away from his family because he was in California, working in the movie industry, and he wanted to be closer to them. Swanson, now a single woman, had begun to put more pressure on Kennedy to spend more time with her, and he was discontented with her increased demands. The cumulative effects of the aforementioned factors, coupled with Kennedy's itch to move on after spending a certain amount of time in one profession, caused him to initiate the liquidation of his assets in Hollywood and return to Wall Street.

By the early part of 1929, Kennedy began to reduce his entire stock portfolio and assets in Hollywood. The stock market was experiencing its highest boom ever. The Dow Jones Industrial Average was at an all-time high of 191. Kennedy knew that the value of the stock market was too high to sustain itself; it was overvalued. There was a consensus among Kennedy and his friends that stock prices had risen to unprecedented levels and the economy would not be able to sustain the inflated prices much longer. Kennedy remembered what Stone, his mentor, had taught him: The price-to-earnings ratio of each individual stock must not be too high and flighty to sustain its earnings and dividends.

In an attempt to get a pulse of the nation's economy, Kennedy decided to talk to one of the heavyweights in the financial industry. He had become a very confident man. He had made national news headlines several times; he was a national figure and a celebrity. Kennedy was also very wealthy; he was worth $4 million. He walked into the office of J.P. Morgan II and announced his presence to the receptionist, expecting to be seen by Morgan. After a brief moment, he was informed by the receptionist that Morgan was too busy to see him. Once again, he was snubbed by a white Anglo-Saxon Protestant.

Kennedy did not dwell on this rebuff by J.P. Morgan; instead, he decided to meet with a friend, Guy Currier, to discuss the economic conditions and to determine his next move. Currier confirmed Kennedy's fears. Both men were right about the impending doom in the U.S. economy. Stock prices were too high and overpriced. The financial system was unable to support that level of activities in the stock market. There was an exaggerated sense of affluence that was unsustainable by the economy. Kennedy initiated the sale of all of his other shares. With the exception of Pathe, Kennedy completely liquidated his holdings in the movie industry. He moved his money to less risky securities such as bonds and treasury bills.

What was Kennedy's drive at this point? He was still driven by the same things that had motivated him all along. He was wealthy, yet he was still rebuffed by the white Anglo-Saxon Protestants. There was definitely a need for him to continue to accumulate wealth in order to prove himself; he still had the drive for expertise, and he was still passionate about the stock market. He resorted to short selling stocks and became incredibly wealthy as a result.

October 24, 1929, marked the arrival of doomsday in the stock market and the American economy ("Black Tuesday"), the day when the Dow Jones dropped by 31 points, or lost 12 percent of its value. Prior to this drop, the Dow had risen to an unprecedented level of 381 points. The Dow would continue its plunge to a low of 41 points by 1932 and would not regain its pre-Depression high until 1954. Following the plunge in the stock market, the Great Depression ensued. The nation was thrown into its worst economic malaise. Nevertheless, Kennedy, who had sold all of his stocks prior to the plunge, was now a very wealthy man.

In fact, Kennedy was one of the wealthiest men in the nation. By 1935, he would amass $180 million in wealth. Kennedy increased his wealth exponentially without regard for the economic climate and out of distaste for the banking elite. A member of this select group of individuals who were influential in the banking industry had rebuffed him. He purchased an estate and was living lavishly though not ostentatiously. He was now operating exclusively in his own self-interest. He was directing his anger for the elite in the banking community into wealth creation. By his continuous success and pursuit of wealth, Kennedy conformed to the mantra that the best defense against the injustices of life is continuous success. The channeling of Kennedy's anger and frustrations into the accumulation of enormous wealth served as a great outlet for him.

Kennedy severed his ties with Pathe, his remaining tie to Hollywood, in the latter part of 1930, causing a ruckus among investors. It was with a sigh of relief that he unloaded the company for $5 million. However, this whole situation was not without incident. Pathe's stocks had plummeted from about $14 a share to slightly over $1 a share. There was substantial public backlash against Kennedy by some of the stockholders following the sale of Pathe. These individuals had lost their life's savings due to the steep decline in the stock market, and they felt that Kennedy was eluding them and the company, especially those who had purchased Pathe's stocks because of their faith and confidence in his competence and abilities. He was at the helm of the company, navigating its course with his erudition, which was the reason for their confidence. There were a few threats on his life as a result of this sale.

Kennedy's enormous wealth enhanced his ability to increase and maintain the size of his family and to become the patriarch of the Kennedy clan. He and his wife already had nine children who were well-behaved, and this was attributable to Rose. She did an excellent job managing their household affairs. Kennedy admired his wife for her skills in this regard. They had mutual respect for each other.

Achieving acceptance by his peers who were of the white Anglo-Saxon Protestant breed became ever so elusive to Kennedy, thereby turning his quest for recognition and acceptance into a perpetual challenge. The primary drive in Kennedy's life at that point became his need to prove himself to the banking community and all of the people who had either discriminated against him or rebuffed him. This factor continued to fuel the quest for his passion in the financial industry. He became so wealthy and powerful that he superseded most of the people who had snubbed him. However, in spite of his tremendous accomplishments, gaining acceptance into some of the groups in which he sought recognition would remain unattainable.

Similar to Kennedy, the quest for our passion is a journey in perpetuity. No matter how wealthy or successful we get, we should constantly challenge ourselves, rekindle our drives, set new goals, and seek new passions. These factors will also enable us to lead more meaningful and interesting lives.

* * *

No sooner had Kennedy begun to savor his burgeoning affluence and to spend some much-needed time with his family than a nagging concern set in. The nation's economy was in such shambles that he was worried that it could decline further and diminish his wealth. In fact, amid the disconcerting economic turmoil, Kennedy was noted as saying that he would be willing to give up half of his wealth if he would be guaranteed the safety and security of the other half. To Kennedy, the answer to this cumbersome national problem would entail his involvement in politics despite his aversion to doing so earlier in life.

Kennedy's emerging intuition to intervene in national politics in order to preserve his wealth immediately led him to align himself with Franklin D. Roosevelt (FDR), who was then governor of New York. Roosevelt was congenial and diplomatic, yet aloof, while Kennedy was extroverted, exuberant, and candid. Despite their differences, the men became instant friends. Roosevelt found the

Drive to Passion

Irishman to be intelligent and high-spirited, while Kennedy felt that Roosevelt was the right candidate to preserve the beleaguered American capitalist system.

Kennedy rallied his wealthy friends around FDR and campaigned for his presidential bid. He made contributions to FDR's campaign and went on a cross-country train ride with him. After FDR won the election, there was a victory celebration in Florida at which Kennedy's in-laws, John and Josie Fitzgerald, were in attendance. According to Goodwin, Josie, his mother-in-law, remarked to her dancing partner, "Isn't it wonderful? My son-in-law Joe Kennedy has made FDR president." Despite its hyperbole, this comment by Kennedy's mother-in-law reflected Kennedy's level of involvement in FDR's campaign.

Similar to Kennedy's situation, unfairness, racism, injustice, and the ills of life exist at every level of society; however, wealth and affluence tend to serve as buffers against certain social ills. For instance, a wealthy and powerful person is able not only to hire the best attorneys to defend her in litigation but also to approach other influential and powerful people in various positions of authority to help rectify whatever inequities she may encounter. However, as epitomized by Kennedy's perpetual challenges, it is a fallacy to harbor the notion that once an individual reaches a certain level of affluence, the challenges and unfairness she may face will be diminished. Although certain challenges are cushioned by wealth and affluence, challenges and unfairness exist in all levels of society.

Despite his affluence, Kennedy faced yet another injustice after the elections, which caused him to lose steam and become tepid. It was a disheartening ordeal for Kennedy to sit waiting day after day, expecting a phone call from FDR for an appointment to a government position that never came. He watched other colleagues, who may not have contributed as much as he did in time and money, receive their phone calls with appointments to top-level political positions. Kennedy was exasperated. He could not imagine what FDR's rationale could be for not appointing him to a political position.

The problem, as Kennedy would later find out, was that there was a debate between FDR and his assistant, Louis Howe, who was vehemently opposed to his appointment to any political position. He argued that Kennedy was too unscrupulous to hold any political position, although he was perhaps more motivated by his jealousy of Kennedy's friendship with FDR. As soon as Kennedy found out about Howe's intervention in his appointment to a political position, he began to work to circumvent Howe's influence on the president. The lesson to be learned here is that Kennedy did not take the situation lying down; he sought to minimize Howe's adverse effect on the president with regard to his appointment to a government position.

In the meantime, Kennedy returned to Wall Street with a vengeance while continuing with his persistence in politics. Once again, he had been rebuffed; yet he remained resilient and optimistic with regard to his bid for a political appointment. Kennedy's return to the world of finance and stock trading was more or less a continuation of his previous efforts in the stock market: short selling. He pursued stock deals with intensity and revenge. Kennedy thought he had been discriminated against by FDR, a man he had helped get elected to the presidency of the United States. He focused his energy on making money again with careless abandon and without remorse over the moral ethics of his stock trading methods. This was his outlet, a way of implementing redress of the inequities he was facing.

Short selling stocks was not necessarily illegal at the time; however, given the economic conditions, the degree to which Kennedy participated in short selling made him morally culpable. He was buying and selling large amounts of stocks—large enough to manipulate the prices of stocks up or down to suit his purposes. Paradoxically, he was contributing to the delinquency of a system he was ostensibly trying to save. Kennedy was smart enough not to use his name in his short-selling deals. Had the press been made aware of his short-selling activities in the stock market, it would have ended his bid for a political appointment.

Kennedy mentored FDR's son, Jimmy Roosevelt, a resilient young man who did not want to live in the shadow of his father. Kennedy helped him grow his insurance business by introducing him to new accounts such as Hayden, Stone, and Company, and First National Bank. The young Roosevelt accompanied

Kennedy on his mission to London to negotiate liquor imports. His influence had a positive effect on Kennedy's business deals. The British had high regard for the young man and treated him like royalty, which in turn enhanced Kennedy's transactions. Although the young Roosevelt was a renegade, FDR did take notice of Kennedy's efforts to mentor his son.

Kennedy was briefly involved in the liquor business during Prohibition. The extent of his involvement in the shady aspects of the business at the time is arguable. Given gangsters' dominance of the industry, Kennedy could not have been that deeply involved in too many shady liquor deals. Nevertheless, he still made some income in the business on the prescription end.

Soon, Kennedy's name surfaced as a possible candidate for the chairmanship of the Securities and Exchange Commission (SEC). He eventually got the position after much ado about his background and possible involvement in unethical Wall Street deals. The position was a good fit for Kennedy. What better person to police Wall Street than an insider who understood the game? It was a smart move on FDR's part.

While in Washington, D.C., Kennedy's friendship with the president continued to flourish. FDR was known to spend quite a few evenings at Kennedy's house in the Washington, D.C. area, dining and relaxing with him and a few friends. The differences in their personalities, which served as a bond that initiated their friendship, continued to hold it. It was this same friendship that prevented FDR from appointing Kennedy to a cabinet-level position. He knew him well: Kennedy was too outspoken and direct to be a member of his cabinet.

Kennedy was engrossed with his new appointment, but it did not stop him from being fully involved with his family. He surrounded and pampered his children with the wealth and privilege that were absent in his own upbringing, without enabling them to lose sight of the need to excel and strive for excellence. His children, having been surrounded by the trappings of wealth and aristocracy all their lives, were not as driven to succeed as their father was. Despite their privileged upbringing, their father encouraged them to succeed. Kennedy's children possessed a certain aristocratic quality and ease of character that were absent in their father, having been surrounded by servants and the trappings of wealth all their lives. They never pushed themselves to either join high-caliber clubs or make friends in the upper echelon of society; those things came to them with ease.

Joe Kennedy Jr., the eldest of Kennedy's children, was said to be as handsome as a movie star. Kennedy and his son Joe had a close relationship. He attended his father's alma mater, Harvard. From the onset, it appeared as if his father had already charted Joe's course; he was being groomed for the presidency of the United States.

Though not as goal-oriented as his elder brother, Jack, the second son, was nonetheless confident and precocious. He did not apply himself as much as his elder brother, but he always felt he was innately smarter than Joe. Jack was saddened by the fact that Joe was his father's favorite and received more attention. As a result, he sought to be his own person and did not follow in the footsteps of his elder brother. Thus, he attended college at Princeton rather than Harvard. This need to prove himself to his father would contribute to Jack's ascension to the presidency of the United States later in life. Jack's life had the interference of frequent bouts with illness. These illnesses caused Jack to depart from Princeton and transfer to Harvard eventually.

Kennedy later resigned from his position as chairman of the SEC. This was followed by a brief stint as a consultant in the movie industry and the world of finance. By this time, Kennedy was one of the revered financial minds in the country. He was also regarded as one of the nation's top business moguls.

Kennedy received an appointment from FDR to another political position. Although he expected a cabinet-level position, FDR, who knew him well, still considered him to be too independently minded to be in his cabinet; thus, FDR offered Kennedy the chairmanship of the Maritime Commission, a position he accepted with reluctance. The period following Kennedy's brief stint as the Maritime Commission chairman was marked by more consulting work. His short-selling days were over. However, he was considered by many to be infallible in business.

FDR subsequently made Kennedy an offer he could not refuse: He was appointed United States ambassador to Britain, a position

Drive to Passion

everyone thought was a perfect fit for him. Once again, Kennedy received the adulation of the press for his new appointment. He was the first Irish American to receive such an appointment. He was heralded by the press throughout the country as someone who epitomized the American success story. Some even went as far as saying that Kennedy was living the American dream.

Kennedy's new position as ambassador of the United States to Great Britain was kicked off in England with pomp and pageantry. He and his family were accorded a warm welcome by the British. There was much ado about him and his large family in the press. The British people were charmed, enthralled, and fascinated by the handsome and vivacious young family.

As soon as the frenzy of the press and the honeymoon died down, the difficulties and challenges that lay ahead for Kennedy began to set in. Hitler, the leader of the Nazi Party, was wielding power in Germany. He had spread his fascism to Austria and was threatening to invade Czechoslovakia and Poland. The British prime minister, Neville Chamberlain, who shared Kennedy's views on the avoidance of war with Hitler at all costs, was involved in "appeasement" efforts with Hitler, in which Chamberlain attempted to make all sorts of concessions to him, short of surrender, all in the name of keeping the peace and avoiding direct conflict between their countries. In the meantime, Hitler was amassing a colossal military strength in Europe.

Kennedy aligned himself with Chamberlain too openly, much to the discomfort of FDR and the State Department. The American government felt it was not the ambassador's prerogative to openly agree or disagree with the domestic policies of its host nation. In essence, Kennedy's career as a diplomat, which started off on the right foot and with much acclaim from the locals, began to veer off course. He shared the views of the isolationists: the avoidance of war at all costs unless America was directly attacked.

Kennedy's appointment as the ambassador of the United States to Great Britain was one of his biggest failures. His efforts as the ambassador and pacifist opinions on the Second World War were focused on his self-serving interests: the protection of his wealth and the well-being of his family. He valued these beliefs above the protection of democracy and the free world from fascist dictators.

Kennedy condoned coexistence with fascism in the interest of half-hearted peace, which he wrongly perceived to be good for mankind. In an effort to calm the waves created by Hitler during the initial stages of his genocide of the Jews, Kennedy proposed a resettlement plan for Jews in Africa or South America, a plan that garnered much attention but was fruitless nonetheless. Kennedy's position somewhat mirrored his self-interest and ambitions, which he had placed above service in the military during World War I.

As Kennedy proceeded in his quest for his passion, he exhibited weaknesses and failures like any other human being; however, he was undeterred by the adverse effects of these shortcomings. His persistence and relentlessness were epitomized by the unyielding efforts he put into his beliefs and passion. He was an individual who seized an opportunity whenever he was presented with one. In fact, as an Irish Catholic, he broke many barriers for his people in his time. Kennedy was tenacious and resilient in spite of his failures.

The irony of Kennedy's distaste for war was manifested by the fact that his three oldest male children, unlike their father, had no reservations about enlisting in the military during World War II. Jack displayed unprecedented gallantry in the U.S. Navy, and Joe, the oldest boy, who was slated for greatness in politics, volunteered for some of the most dangerous missions in the Army Air Corps, in an attempt to not only define himself as his own person, but perhaps to establish a record of valor similar to or better than Jack's. After all, he was the "chosen one," destined for greatness in politics. Joe's tendency to take on the most dangerous assignments would later cost him his life. Bobby, the youngest of the three boys, also enlisted and was eager to go to battle.

In essence, Kennedy's sons, who placed excitement, valor, and service to country ahead of their father's fears, would thwart his unfalteringly parochial endeavors with respect to war. Little did Kennedy know that his sons would not hesitate to join the war effort; in fact, they seemed to have an affinity for acts of bravery and gallantry. Also, Kennedy failed to realize that his wealth and pacific needs would be more secure in a world where democracy prevailed, a world aligned with freedom. Even though his family made the ultimate sacrifice during the war—the loss of a son—Kennedy's other fear did not materialize. His perspective was wrong on the issue of the coexistence of the free world with fascist dictators the likes of Mussolini and Hitler, who would have stopped at nothing until the entire world was under the grip of their distorted ideology.

* * *

Eventually, Kennedy resigned as the ambassador of the United States to Britain. He waited for another political appointment, to no avail. His chances of even being closely aligned with FDR were grim. Kennedy delivered a great campaign speech for FDR during his campaign for a third term. However, he flatly refused to go on another train ride with FDR, like the old days. Obviously, his relationship with FDR had been strained from the cumulative effects of his actions during his tenure as the U.S. ambassador to Britain. His inflexible views of the war did not help things.

FDR's death preceded the end of World War II, and his closeness to Kennedy was never re-established; their friendship remained strained until his death. To a man such as FDR, a close friendship with Kennedy could have been politically motivated in the first place.

Subsequent to the end of the war, the Kennedys finally emerged as the Irish version of the Boston Brahmins. Jack's arrival on the political scene created excitement among the people of Boston; the general population was enthralled by him. His status as a war hero combined with his family ties made him an instant celebrity. The Kennedys gave the Irish hope. The achievements and social status of the Kennedys made it possible for the Irish to believe in the realization of the American dream. As Kennedy advanced in age, most of his dreams began to be realized. He now had a high status in the nation, not just in Boston. He was very wealthy, there was no longer an impending war of any significance or threat to the stability of the world, and his son was running for a political office in the hope of becoming a major political figure one day.

Kennedy's mark of greatness, the end product of his drive to become a force to be recognized, was exemplified in his passionate pep talk to his son, Jack, in which he urged him to run for the presidency of the United States. Jack demurred for the following reasons: He felt that he was too young to be president; he was a Catholic and did not think the country was ready for a Catholic president; and he did not think he could garner enough support from the Democratic Party. According to Goodwin, Kennedy said in rebuttal to his son's objections, "There's a whole new generation out there and it's filled with the sons and daughters of immigrants from all over the world and those people are going to be mighty proud that one of their own is running for president." With this statement, Kennedy became forever remembered as a kingmaker and great motivator.

CHAPTER 4
Sidney Poitier: A Slot of My Choosing

Sidney Poitier, the son of a poor tomato farmer, had two choices: accept his lot in life with quiet resignation like his parents and wallow in poverty, or take charge of his life, define his own circumstances, and rise above the abject poverty in which he found himself. He chose the latter. Poitier set out to carve his path to success and greatness. He was thrown out of a theater when he auditioned unsuccessfully for a part in a play; consequently, he was determined to prove to the man who had thrown him out that he could become a great actor. Neither his very humble beginnings nor the fact that he was functionally illiterate hampered his drives, which would spur his quest for his passion in the movie industry, and would ultimately lead to the honor that would be bestowed upon him as one of the greatest actors of all time.

* * *

Born in the United States while his parents were briefly here, Poitier grew up in the Bahamas, the birthplace of his parents and ancestors, under poverty-stricken circumstances. Poitier's childhood in the islands was mired in the absence of an adequate supply of food and other basic necessities. However, he was neither engrossed in self-pity nor initially conscious of the deprivation in his surroundings. Young Poitier's carefree youthful spirit made his obliviousness to his environment possible. Also, there was the absence of affluence on the island, so he did not have a basis for comparison. There were no modern amenities such as radios, televisions, or other types of outside influences, so he was free of the pressures from the outside. He was from a close-knit family, and as such, there was enough love and warmth within the household to satisfy his emotional needs. As Poitier got older, it would occur to him that his father was one of the poorest people around—a fact he would come to detest. This would also serve to drive him to rise above his impoverished environment.

Poitier grew up in a small house with a thatched roof, surrounded by the barest necessities. As a child growing up, his life was predictable. His parents were tomato farmers and daily worked the land. Rice was the special meal eaten on Sundays. There was no electricity or running water. The temperature was much the same from day to day, and there were no refrigerators. So the delicacy of salted and sun-dried fish that hung in the kitchen was prepared only on special occasions, and it made a "terrific" dish, according to Poitier, in his autobiography, *The Measure of a Man*. Poitier's family routinely spent the evening hours on the porch with his parents utilizing the heavy "smoke from green palm leaves [they were] burning to shoo away the mosquitoes and the sand flies."

Cat Island, Bahamas, a small island of about 138 square miles, is where Poitier grew up. The small roads and paths were unpaved. It was a small, sleepy island, pervaded by trees, sand, insects, and other creatures. It also had the smells and sounds of the ocean, with the accompanying sea breeze and wind. When Poitier was a child, the island was more or less a dichotomy between a hamlet and gorgeous beaches populated by coco plum trees, sea grapes, cassavas, and wild bananas.

The island was Poitier's to explore and roam as a child. He was a typical boy: climbing to retrieve and feast on wild, tasty fruits; sustaining scratches and scrapes; getting stung by wasps; exploring the terrain to satisfy his boyhood curiosity, which was inundated with adventurous escapades; and getting in enough trouble to authenticate his boyish tendencies. In Cat Island, as in most tropical hamlets, whenever it rained, the children stayed in, impatiently waiting for the rain to stop so that they could get back out and play.

* * *

At the age of ten, Poitier's family set sail for Nassau, Bahamas, after bidding farewell to family and friends who came to see them off. For his parents, the tomato farming that was slightly above the subsistence level was no longer lucrative; there had been an embargo in Florida on imported tomatoes from the Bahamas. As a child, Poitier did not have the depth of understanding to comprehend the reasons for his family's departure to Nassau. All he knew was that the city's dazzling fascinations were beckoning, and he as a child was in great anticipation of it all. In all of its promise of things to come, urban life was a shock to young Poitier's system: the city's bright lights, hotels, automobiles, restaurants, movie theaters, bars, and clubs.

It was in Nassau that young Poitier began to get a picture of life as it truly was: racism, friendship, love, crime, wealth, and poverty, just to mention a few. Once, a white boy, who was a few years older than he was and a total stranger, rode his bicycle directly toward him as he walked on foot. As he got close to him, the white boy dealt Poitier a heavy blow to the face and rode off. Poitier gave the boy a good chase on foot, but to no avail. His foot chase was no match for a bicycle. By this time, Poitier had acquired the maturity and the introspection to realize that his family was very poor. He had contrasted his lifestyle with those of others in Nassau, and there was a crystal clear distinction to him between the haves and the have-nots. Young Poitier witnessed his best friend's incarceration for stealing a bicycle—a crime in which Poitier could have easily been involved. Poitier also had a brief encounter with love, involving a girl who was the sister of a friend of his. He had met this boy on the road randomly, and they had formed a bond of friendship. Poitier had a strange sensation all over his body whenever he saw his friend's sister, and he imagined she felt the same way about him. These incidents summed up his initial experiences in Nassau.

Poitier started school at the age of eleven and dropped out shortly thereafter, at age thirteen. It is self-evident that two years of schooling was not much education for him. Young Poitier was functionally illiterate. Little did he know that this level of education would be all the formal education he would ever get. However, his lack of education would contribute toward the discomfort in his life that would stimulate his drive and passion.

One of the luxuries available to Poitier and his family then was the movies. He and his brothers and sisters went to the movies on occasion. Upon their return from the movie theater, they would act out the parts they had seen on the screen. According to Poitier in his autobiography, at the age of twelve, his sister asked him what he wanted to be when he grew up, and he replied, "I would like to go to Hollywood and become a cowboy." He said this without the concept of what Hollywood cowboys did. Poitier's indelible impression of cowboys came from the first cowboy movie that he had seen.

How many childhood premonitions come to fruition? Poitier's imagery of himself as a Hollywood cowboy is ubiquitous among children. All children, including me, had one image or another of something we wanted to be when we grew up and probably forgot about those things as fast as we thought of them.

There was something else that struck a nerve with Poitier: When he discovered his father was one of the poorest people in Nassau, he did not like that, and this would spur the drive in him to undertake the shaping of his destiny. This distaste for poverty was permanent in Poitier's memory and more of a driving force for him than acting out movie parts and hoping to be a cowboy. The avoidance of a negative situation, such as destitution or poverty, caused Poitier to resolve to steer clear of a predicament similar to that of his parents. He detested the fact that his parents were among the poorest people in town. It became obvious to Poitier that he had to do better than his parents. Leading a life of deprivation was unacceptable to him.

Poitier's father made the tough decision to send him away to Florida to live with his brother. Poitier's brother was ten years his senior. He was getting older, and his other elder brother in Nassau had been incarcerated for extortion. The incarceration of Poitier's brother set a negative precedent for him. Had he remained on

Drive to Passion

the island, his father reasoned, he too would have been prone to incarceration at some point.

Once Poitier got to Florida, he instantly disliked what it had to offer. Though the lifestyle was similar to that of the Caribbean, "its culture and mores were of the American South, 1940s Jim Crow style," Poitier said in his autobiography. This was evident in his first job as a delivery boy. On his delivery route one day, he approached the front door of a house where he was to make a delivery, knocked on the door, and an elderly white woman emerged with a look of disgust on her face. He politely indicated that he was there to make a delivery. She immediately told him to take his delivery to the back door, where he belonged. She then proceeded to slam the door in his face. Poitier stood there with mixed feelings of shock, anger, and bewilderment, not quite knowing what to do. He finally decided to ignore the woman's rude order. He dropped the delivery in front of the house, left, and did not think too much of it after that day. A few days later, Poitier returned home one night to find his brother's entire family lying on the floor, huddled together, terrified, and sobbing. The hate and racist group Ku Klux Klan had apparently paid them a visit as a result of Poitier's encounter with the elderly white woman.

Poitier was an assertive and strong-willed young man who knew right from wrong; he knew that he was not going to tolerate hatred and racism from others. He encapsulated this in his autobiography: "I had become conscious of being pigeonholed by others, and I had determined then to always aim myself toward a slot of my choosing."

Great accomplishments often stem from unrest, the dialectic occurrences of ideas, the rejection of the status quo, and the belief that we can change our circumstances by changing ourselves. Harv Eker asserted in his book, *Secrets of the Millionaire Mind*, "The only time you are actually growing is when you are uncomfortable." The progress that mankind has made, in looking around us and looking back to history, has occurred for the most part as a result of dissatisfaction and the urge to solve unique and pervasive problems.

Poitier was not going to accept whatever serendipity was going to assign to him. He was going to take his destiny into his own hands. He was driven: He was dissatisfied with the poverty-stricken environment in which he found himself; he was dissatisfied with the 1940s Jim Crow-style oppression and racism; and he was not going to be defined by his environment or by other people's concept and expectations of him. Poitier was determined not to accept a life of destitution with defeat like his parents.

Armed with the knowledge that racism was less severe in the northern parts of the United Sates, Poitier decided to get as far away from the South as he could. He did not necessarily intend to go to New York City initially, but it sounded good, and it was the farthest away he could get—with his limited bus fare—from the harsh racism of Florida and the southern United States. Poitier's spirit of unrest and intolerance for the status quo propelled him to New York City.

While in New York City, young Poitier endured the brutal elements of life, which led to his brief stint in the U.S. military. He bounced around from place to place in Harlem, taking any low-end job he could find, including dishwashing. He endured a severe winter without adequate clothing, using rooftops as shelters on occasion. Prior to the arrival of the following winter, he opted for the military, thinking that it would give him the security of a regular income. No sooner had he joined the Army than he quickly realized it was not the answer to the harsh realities of life at the bottom. He had three square meals and shelter there, but it was not the answer to his restless quest for a passion that would satisfy his drives.

Poitier, who was only seventeen, quickly devised a scheme to get out of the Army. It was 1944; World War II was still raging, although the end of the war was near. There was a need for an able-bodied young man of his stature in the military; thus, he had some planning to do if he wanted to get out of his obligations with the military. He conceived of a plan that would enable him to be discharged. He decided to throw a chair at a window that would miss an officer's head by a few inches, which it did. The chair crashed through the window adjacent to the officer without hitting him. Poitier got his wish: He was taken into custody by the

Drive to Passion

military police immediately pending a comprehensive psychiatric evaluation and a possible trial, with a sentence of twenty-five years if convicted.

Poitier's objective in throwing the chair was to portray himself as an individual who was mentally incompetent to serve in the military. He was transferred to a hospital for psychiatric evaluation. Poitier contended in his autobiography that his psychiatric evaluation sessions with the young psychiatrist who was in charge of assessing his mental state were arduous for both of them; they "were teachers to each other." He was eventually discharged from the Army. He successfully avoided languishing in jail for concocting a scheme to avoid military service.

Was Poitier unscrupulous for getting out of his military commitment the way he did? He was underage and had lied when he applied in the first place. Throwing a chair at a senior officer was not the best way to terminate his military obligations. Poitier castigated himself for these actions in his autobiography. He alluded to the fact that there were other options he could have pursued to gain a discharge from the military without resorting to the method that almost earned him jail time.

Similar to Poitier, we should aim to embark on the pursuit of our passion once we can identify an activity about which we are passionate. We should also be willing to make the sacrifices necessary to bring our quest to fruition. Service in the Army could have provided Poitier with the security he needed: money, food, and shelter. It could have also provided him with the financial stability he needed to return to his passion at a later date. Joe Kennedy avoided military service during the First World War in order to pursue his passion in financial services. Bill Gates, one of the wealthiest men in the world, left the security of a degree from Harvard University to pursue his passion of building a computer software company. Michael Jordan left college before the attainment of a four-year college degree to pursue his passion of playing basketball at the professional level. Could Gates and Jordan have delayed the pursuit of their passion until a later date, after the completion of their four-year college degrees, and could Poitier and Kennedy have waited to pursue theirs until after completing military service? Timing is everything. If we have a strong drive to pursue our passion, we should do so immediately, as long as our drive is strong enough to sustain our passion and bring our dreams to fruition. We do not know what could happen in the future to change things if we delay the pursuit of our passion. Conversely, we can usually return to the safer path if things do not work out: returning to school or a job.

Poitier had no idea what his passion was in his earlier years, which illustrates that our passion is not always immediately discernible. There are a few ways to identify our passion. Similar to how Poitier would later identify his passion, we can stumble into it. Our passion can be made obvious to us by the observations of friends and mentors. It may stem from something we enjoy, such as a hobby or an activity for which we have a niche, or sometimes we may find our passion through trial and error. However, occasionally a small child may know that he or she wants to become a renowned physician, and that child eventually embarks on this passion and accomplishes it. Even though we may have a strong drive to do something extraordinary in life, we may not initially be clear on how to achieve our objective.

How do we know when we have found our passion? There are several "litmus tests" we can use to identify our passion or an activity for which we could develop a passion. If we have a niche or an aptitude for a particular activity, then we could successfully embark on the pursuit of our passion in it. If we can work on an endeavor for an extended period of time without any financial rewards, then there is the potential of the existence of passion for that activity. Another method of identifying our passion, similar to Socrates' contention, is that our desire for that activity should be comparable to our need for the air we breathe. Also, similar to John Schnatter of Papa John's Pizza, if an activity for which we have a niche consists of our "predominating thought" and we take delight in the performance of that activity, it is a clear indication of the existence of a passion for it.

* * *

After Poitier left the Army, he found himself once again in the streets of Harlem. He was dejected and wanted to return to

Drive to Passion

Nassau. The deterrent in his bid to go back was that he lacked the funds to pay for the trip from New York to the Bahamas. Had Poitier been able to raise enough funds to defray the cost of his trip back to his home, the world would have been denied the pleasure and impact of this great actor's works.

Back in civilian life, Poitier knew that he wanted to do something great with his life, but he could not identify a suitable vocation. He maneuvered himself from one odd job to another. Dishwashing became the easiest job he could get. Poitier worked as a dishwasher at various places. He had no clue about what other vocations he could seek. He could have wallowed in poverty as a permanent member of the underclass because he was practically illiterate and had no concrete plans. However, Poitier was armed with some key attributes that would be vital in his ascension to prominence: He was dissatisfied with the status quo; he had a drive to surpass his parents' condition and to chart his own course.

Poitier would unintentionally stumble into his passion when he responded to an advertisement for a theater audition while he was going through the help wanted section of the newspaper in search of a job. On a whim, he decided to go to the theater audition, with no apparent rationale other than the fact that it was just another job and it sounded better than his previous jobs as a dishwasher. What happened at the theater audition was pivotal in giving Poitier the impetus, courage, and determination to chart the right course for success in his life. His poor reading skills and sing-song Caribbean accent triggered the disapproval of the man in charge of the Negro Theater where he was auditioning. He showed his contempt and disgust for Poitier's poor performance by shoving him out of the theater and telling him to seek a job as a dishwasher. Poitier felt insulted and decided to prove this man wrong. His ego kicked in, and he wondered how this man could have conjectured that dishwashing was the job in which he had been engaged.

Poitier became determined to prove to this man that he was capable of acting. He began to work on improving his reading skills by reading the newspapers. During his break periods on his job as a dishwasher, he would sit in a corner, reading the paper aloud to himself, imitating the sounds he heard on the radio. A waiter who saw him struggling took pity on him and decided to help him. This waiter, a Jewish man, became Poitier's tutor and mentor, helping him during their break periods with his reading and pronunciation. Most often, they would sit together in a corner of the restaurant working on Poitier's reading and speaking skills. In his autobiography, Poitier said of his desire to conquer his illiteracy and prove that he was capable of auditioning for a play, "There's something inside me—pride, ego, sense of self—that hates to fail at anything. I could never accept such a verdict of failure." In essence, his ego and pride served the purpose of driving him to take a leap at that point, and, of course, he backed it up with an intense passion for acting.

Poitier would give an interview in 1964 to the British Broadcasting Corporation in which he stated that he went back to the Negro Theater a few times to audition but was thrown out each time. Not only did Poitier's reading skills improve each time he went back to audition, but he also discovered that he actually enjoyed auditioning and trying to become an actor. He then realized he had found his passion. He had an aptitude for acting.

Once Poitier acquired the passion for acting, he followed it up with ardent practice and customized education, and he was riveted by it. Similar to Winston Churchill, he practiced in perpetuity to improve his knowledge, performance, and level of expertise. With the help of his mentor, Poitier utilized whatever written material he could find to prepare and work toward improving his English and acting skills.

* * *

I used to think that business was my only passion until recently. During one of my introspective sessions, I started reflecting back to my childhood and my college days to see if I had other activities about which I am passionate. It occurred to me that in college, in the house I shared with my college roommate, I once had my essay for an English class lying around on the kitchen table, and a friend who was an upperclassman picked it up and read it without my knowledge. As he was finishing it, I realized he had been reading it. He put the essay back on the table, smiled, and complimented me on my writing skills; this experience preceded the reading of my essays in class on a few occasions by my English instructors.

The other incident that made evident the existence of my niche in writing occurred in an evening class that I took while I was a graduate student working on a master of business administration (MBA) degree. It was an accounting class, and most of my colleagues were plant managers, scientists, and other high-caliber professionals, some of whom already held doctorate degrees and master's degrees in other disciplines. They had returned to school to get an MBA in order to move up the corporate ladder. The high-caliber student population was a bit intimidating, and it exacerbated my introversion and reticence. The fact that I was one of the youngest the individuals in the class did not help matters. Also, accounting was alien to me at that point. My reserved demeanor probably portrayed me wrongly to the professor.

We had an assignment from this professor to write a three-page essay on selected topics. My selection was ROI. I turned in my essay and forgot to put my name on it. The following week in class, the professor, upon returning everyone's paper, said that although my paper had no name on it, it was the best paper in the class. When he disclosed the topic of my paper, I raised my hand, informing him that it was mine—to which he replied, "No, it's not." Embarrassment is an understated description of my feelings at that point. It was something much worse than that; humiliation, perhaps. He had assessed my capabilities incorrectly, due to my reticence in class.

To resolve the matter, I picked up the handwritten draft of my essay from my typist, took it to the professor's office the following day and slammed it on his desk. The professor, sensing my anger, said with his hands raised in a flight mode, "Take it easy, take it easy." I retrieved my essay from him, dropped his class, and moved on.

One positive aspect of my introspection about the incident with my accounting professor in college was that it enabled me to realize, as humiliating as that incident had been, I was proud that he thought my essay was the best in the class. I knew if I worked on improving my writing skills, I could become an excellent writer.

Sidney Poitier: A Slot of My Choosing

* * *

After much persistence in auditioning for plays and hard work in trying to improve his reading skills, Poitier eventually secured a small part in a play at the Negro Theater, which lasted a short while. He had built up the confidence, through practice and education, to go back there a few more times to audition. He improved with each audition. He showed tenacity and resilience by convincing the theater administrators to hire him as a janitor. This was a pragmatic approach that helped him tremendously. His intention was to be close enough to the casting director and other decision makers to convince them to cast him in future plays.

Due to "my lack of education and experience, after a couple of months I was flunking out," Poitier said, with regard to his pursuit of self-education and his efforts to secure more parts in plays at the theater. He experienced an interlude of failure, which did not serve as a deterrent. He realized that in order to succeed, he would have to be resilient. If the path to success was plotted on a graph, it would have peaks and valleys as it edged up, rather than a straight-line trajectory. Failure serves as a teacher. Poitier was smart enough to realize all of these factors at such a young age.

There are different schools of thought on failure. One of the most remarkable lines of reasoning on failure is that there can be no success without failure. If we do not experience at least a certain degree of failure, we will not know what corrections to make in our endeavors to steer our efforts in the right direction; an engineer or an inventor who is working on a new contraption will have to fail and make adjustments many times before coming up with the right prototype. This phenomenon could also be deemed trial and error, with error equating to failure.

Poitier continued to work fervently on his acting skills, diction, and reading while working as a janitor, and his efforts began yielding some success. He encountered an opportunity when he learned of an upcoming large theater production in which he thought he would have a significant role. He met with disappointment when another budding actor, also from the Caribbean, who had a combination of good looks and talent in both acting and singing, was cast for that role in his place. For some reason, this budding actor—Harry Belafonte—could not keep his appointment on the opening night, which was an especially important night due to the potential presence of an influential casting director. Poitier got the opportunity he so ardently sought. He was cast in Belafonte's place. The visiting casting director liked his performance.

As a result of Poitier's outstanding performance in the play, the casting director invited him to participate in another play, *Lysistrata*, on Broadway. He was excited and accepted immediately. On the opening night of the play, Poitier suddenly found himself on stage on Broadway and "staring into a sea of white faces," according to him. He was nervous and had an acute case of stage fright. He fumbled his lines and delivered what he thought was an abhorrent performance. He was dejected and described his performance in his book by saying he felt that his "career was over before it had begun." As a result of what he deemed a terrible performance, he did not attend the cast party afterward.

Yet an interesting thing happened. The critics who reviewed the play in the press totally disliked it, just as Poitier had thought; however, they liked his performance. Despite the accolades he received from the press, he was still hard on himself. In fact, he began to harbor self-doubts. He almost lost confidence in himself, which would have inevitably led him to rethink his acting career. Following the end of *Lysistrata*, Poitier secured another acting job on a road show, *Anna Lucasta*. After this stint in theater, he experienced a long dry spell, without much work as an actor.

Poitier's break in the movie industry came with the casting of the Twentieth-Century Fox movie, *No Way Out*, for which he auditioned and secured a part. He had found out about the movie by chance. The accolades he had received in his performances in plays worked in his favor. This movie with Fox would become the first movie his parents would see. Poitier made a remarkable achievement. He had gone from his days of talking about wanting to become a movie cowboy to actually starring in a movie. Good things began to happen to him in his acting career.

As Poitier was finishing the Fox movie in California, the director gave him a referral to a movie producer in New York. Once Poitier arrived back in New York City, he went to see the producer, who invited him to London. Before he knew it, he was on his way to London, flying first class. He had come a long way, so soon, from his days as an impoverished dishwasher to an actor who was now flying first class to London. Following his meeting in London with the producer, he was asked to play a part in the movie, *Cry the Beloved Country*. Poitier was cast as a young priest, and he flew to South Africa to shoot the movie. His circumstances suddenly became propitious.

Following his role in *Cry the Beloved Country*, Poitier went home to the Bahamas to visit his parents and to make amends for his long absence. He had been gone for eight years. In that time, he had experienced remarkable success: He had been in a number of movies and a few plays. Poitier had made his parents very proud. We can only imagine the type of a hero's welcome he received from family members and other citizens upon his arrival in the Bahamas.

In spite of his initial successes, Poitier was unable to maintain the momentum of continuous achievement. Before he knew it, he was back in his previous profession as a dishwasher. He began to experience a dry spell. There were no acting jobs for him. Some people would have given up at that point, but Poitier pushed ahead and even got married. In his book, Poitier said of this particular time in his life, "Perhaps I had a gift from Cat Island buried within me, because despite the setback, I still had faith in myself and in the future." Poitier's resilience, drive, and passion kept him going. He and a friend later opened a rib shack.

Poitier, similar to other great individuals of tremendous accomplishments, was not lacking in resilience and confidence. He had enough faith in himself to push ahead despite the obstacles. Winston Churchill never doubted that he would one day become a top political figure in Britain. He kept up his relentless preparations and education. Churchill was confident in his abilities. Poitier believed that he would one day achieve the pinnacle of success in the acting profession, so he continued to be persistent and confident in his ability despite his setback.

Poitier was still working at the rib shack when he received a call from an agent who had secured an acting job for him. By this

Drive to Passion

time, Poitier and his wife were already parents of one child, and they were expecting a second; he still had no gainful employment in his chosen field of acting. Unbeknownst to Poitier, this arrangement entailed an appointment with a movie producer and director who, following their meeting, offered him the part of a janitor in a movie. This was an inconsequential part, depicting a passive and spineless janitor. Despite being destitute, Poitier turned down the offer, which was supposed to pay $750 a week, a considerable sum at the time and over $5,500 in today's dollars.

Poitier turned down this offer of a role as a janitor in a movie, much to the dismay of the agent who had obtained the offer. The agent could not understand why he would turn down this part in spite of his critical financial position. According to Poitier, his rationale for turning down the movie role was, "The character simply didn't measure up. He didn't fight for what mattered to him most. He didn't behave with dignity." For someone who was practically destitute, this was a determined position to take. Poitier was simply not passionate about the role; he could not see himself in it and was too proud to be typecast in this role. Poitier depicted his courage and tenacity in this instance—a vital ingredient in the pursuit of our passion.

In spite of his very limited educational background, Poitier had an in-depth understanding of the movie industry. He did not want to be typecast in certain nominal roles that would cause him to be forever branded exclusively in those roles. Poitier was a man of conviction, high self-esteem, and dignity who believed in being in control of his destiny. He knew exactly what he wanted. The summation of Poitier's mind-set at the time is illustrated in this statement from his autobiography: "I do what I do for me and for my wife and children, of course. And I do it out of a certain professional ego drive and ambition like anyone else. But everything I do, I also do for Reggie and Evelyn." These were his parents.

We are who we want to be. The thug who wants to acquire an intimidating demeanor and portray himself as a tough and heartless individual will always find a way to portray that image and become that person. By the same token, an individual, who wants to portray an image of being a high-caliber professional, who is erudite, or who aspires to be learned, will find a way to get there and be that person. In Poitier's case, he had chosen to portray himself as an intelligent black man. Although Poitier had minimal formal education, he had native intelligence and he was well-read. He portrayed his intelligence by turning down the demeaning role about which he was not passionate. He waited until he was able to find one that suited his purpose and passion. This is emblematic of the courage and tenacity of individuals who are on the path to greatness.

Poitier received a call from Marty Baum one day while he was engaged in what had become his daily routine of toiling away for a meager income. He was pleasantly surprised to hear from Baum, who was a noteworthy agent. Baum informed Poitier that he heard about him turning down a substantial role as a janitor and wanted to know why. Poitier explained to him that it was a demeaning role. Baum still could not understand why Poitier had opted for a life of destitution in place of an income of $750 a week. He thought that Poitier's decision was stupid and incomprehensible. According to Poitier, Baum concluded the meeting by saying, "Well I'll tell you what. I don't know what's going on with you, but anybody as crazy as you, I want to handle him." Poitier consented to Baum becoming his agent, and at that point a turnaround ensued in his acting career.

Although it took courage and tenacity for Poitier to turn down the offer for the role of a janitor, it also enabled him to distinguish himself as a high achiever. He was driven and was bent on expressing his drive through what had by that time become his passion: a passion for acting in dignified movie roles. Poitier's niche or aptitude for acting was probably no greater than the next actor's. However, what he demonstrated was that he was more driven and passionate than the next person, and he backed up his passion with fervent practice, customized education, and preparation. He had come this far, so he wanted a role that would stimulate his intellect. Had he settled for the role of a janitor just because he needed the money, he would have wound up like many other actors of his time who, although they were good actors, never stood out in the crowd.

Drive to Passion

Although he was already an actor with considerable experience, he was passionate enough to engage in continuous education and preparation in his chosen profession. Poitier wanted to become an expert and one of the best in his profession. Similar to Churchill, Poitier believed in continuous education and practice; thus, he took acting lessons, and it was during this period that he met Louise, a classmate who contributed immensely to his education.

Poitier's brief encounter in his acting classes with Louise—a young lady who turned out to be a friend, teacher, and mentor—left an indelible impression on him. His description of her was very vivid: "saintly, volatile, edgy, raucous . . . introspective, sensuous, a talented and daring taker of risks. . . . In acting classes she was a riveting, hypnotic presence." Louise awakened in Poitier a love and passion for the English language. She caused him to realize how important and enriching it was to have a great command of the language. She often used some electrifying words, expressions, and phrases: "Bourgeoisie Negroes; this hypocrisy democracy; disingenuous; rhetorical." Poitier was enthralled by Louise's knowledge. For a man with very minimal formal education, she rekindled in him a quest for knowledge; it was an awakening of sorts for him. Education for him consisted of whatever he could learn from anybody who had some knowledge to impart to him. He also learned from the streets and from whatever reading material he could find that was of substance and interest to him. Following his encounter with Louise, Poitier's quest for knowledge became heightened.

Although Poitier's career turned around for the better after his meeting with Baum, it did not happen immediately. He and his young family continued to be in a dire financial situation. During this period, Poitier tried his hand at a few jobs without much success. He sought jobs in a few vocations and was engaged in different businesses, all to no avail; he was a restaurateur, bricklayer, and carpenter. As a matter of fact, Poitier demonstrated his lack of aptitude for bricklaying during this dry spell in acting. He asked his father-in-law, a master bricklayer, to teach him the trade. His father-in-law assigned Poitier's brother-in-law the arduous task of acclimating him to bricklaying. Poitier gave an account of that experience in the following words: "I tried and tried, but I

Sidney Poitier: A Slot of My Choosing

evidently didn't have the knack." This shows that there are certain vocations or activities that cannot be deemed our niche no matter how hard we try to get acclimated to them. Michael Jordan found out the hard way that he had no niche in baseball when he tried to play on a professional level in 1994.

No sooner had Poitier begun to secure a few movie roles than he encountered blatant racism. He was asked to sign loyalty oaths, renouncing his friendship with Paul Robeson and others. During the preliminary stages of the movie *Blackboard Jungle*, he was preparing for a read-through when he received a call from someone in the studio office inviting him to the office. No sooner had Poitier stepped into the office than a man, possibly a lawyer, confronted him with accusations of being associated with other black individuals—Paul Robeson and Canada Lee—who were considered dubious characters. This lawyer then asked Poitier to sign "a loyalty oath," which entailed swearing to disassociate himself from these individuals whom he respected. He considered the proposition to be an insult and refused to sign the document. Poitier thought his refusal to sign the loyalty oath would cost him the part in the movie. After much ado, he was asked to continue with the movie. Prior to the shooting of another movie, *A Man Is Ten Feet Tall*, Poitier was again summoned to the office by the attorney for NBC and asked to sign another "loyalty oath" regarding his friendship with Paul Robeson. Similarly, he was being asked to distance himself from Robeson. Once again, he refused to sign the document. This time, Poitier was on the verge of losing his part in the movie, but the producer, who was on his side, prevented that from happening. Consequently, they were able to complete the shooting of the movie without interruption.

The NBC studio was flooded with phone calls from angry viewers who had watched *A Man Is Ten Feet Tall*, in which Poitier's character's wife was played by a light-skinned black woman whom they perceived to be white. In 1955, America was not ready for interracial marriages anywhere, including the movies. Even though the viewers' perception was wrong, it still caused an uproar.

While Poitier was in Atlanta promoting the movie *Blackboard Jungle*, he experienced a racial incident that was pervasive in the South during that time. He had gone to a restaurant to eat, and unbeknownst to him, blacks were not served in white-owned restaurants. If they were going to be served at all, then they were made to sit in a secluded section of the restaurant, away from the view of the white patrons. Even though the restaurant had a few black employees, comprising a black maitre d' and black waitresses, Poitier was still refused admission into the main area of the restaurant. He was told that he could only be admitted into the restaurant if he would consent to being seated in a corner, screened off and secluded from the main restaurant. Poitier turned this offer down and refused to eat in the restaurant.

Poitier's uniqueness lies in the fact that despite his handicaps—a lack of education, being black in an all-white industry, initially lacking fluency in the English language—he still made remarkable strides. He was undaunted and undeterred by racism and the rest of the stumbling blocks in his way. Most importantly, he did not settle for just any job or movie part that came his way; he set out in pursuit of his passion, which consisted exclusively of movie roles that were dignified and worthwhile.

Poitier's career did not improve significantly until he played the leading role in the movie *Something of Value*. It was unheard of for a black person to play the leading role in a movie in the 1950s. This actually marked the major turning point in Poitier's career. With his earnings from *Something of Value*, Poitier purchased a small two-story house in a black middle-class neighborhood located in a suburb of New York City. He and his family lived on the ground floor, while he rented the top floor to generate extra income. Poitier had a commendable business savvy, as evidenced by his previous ownership of the rib restaurant.

Poitier intrinsically expected to do well; he was confident in his passion and truly believed he would do well. His mindset was based on the premise that his performance should always be of the highest caliber and that he should play dignified roles that would portray him and the black race in a positive light. He did not want to dwell on the fact that his objectives and aspirations could be deemed unusual and far-fetched for a black person in that period. In fact, his goals were lofty and required an extraordinary achievement on his part. Poitier was employing powerful mind exercises: visualization and self-actualization. He already saw himself in these powerful movie roles in his mind's eye. He had already claimed these roles and achievements without dwelling on how difficult they were to attain or what type of historical implications they were going to have. He was just focused on the work without allowing its potential rewards to become a distraction. When we are passionate about an activity, it entails continuous preparation, practice, and education, which in turn enable us to attain the kind of expertise and excellence that will engender unwavering self-confidence and belief in ourselves.

After the movie *Something of Value*, Poitier was asked to do another movie, *The Defiant Ones*. This particular movie stirred up the critics, especially the black ones who said, "We aren't ready for oneness." This was triggered by a scene in the movie where Poitier opted to extend a hand to Tony Curtis and pull him onto a freight train rather than leaving him behind. In his attempt to pull Curtis on to the train, Poitier fell off. The train had been their only hope of escape.

In 1964, following the movie *Lilies of the Field*, Poitier was awarded an Oscar. He made history by being the first black in a leading role to receive an Oscar. The first black ever to receive an Oscar had been Hattie McDaniel in 1939, for a supporting role in *Gone with the Wind*. Poitier's Oscar was a major accomplishment of historical proportions. He had come a long way since his days as an uneducated dishwasher who could barely read or write. He was at that point an articulate actor who had propelled himself to greatness through sheer resilience and the persistent pursuit of his passion for acting. He was deemed an intelligent actor by members of the media. Following the Oscar award and the movie *Lilies of the Field*, Poitier and his family moved to a huge estate in Pleasantville, New York. It was an expensive neighborhood, and he and his family were well received by their neighbors.

"I'm not always satisfied with my work in every scene in every picture," Poitier said. This profound statement by Poitier was interesting because he was not one to sit back and continually relish his successes. Consider all the accomplished individuals in the world; if they became complacent, they would atrophy and cease to strive for more achievements, even if they had all the money they would ever need. The belief that we can either move forward or go backward, and we are never at a standstill, holds true. This rationale by Poitier of never being satisfied with his work was one of his intrinsic drives that kept him passionate about acting. It was an intrinsic drive that could be summed up as the perpetual quest for expertise. Poitier's philosophy of never being satisfied with his work made it possible for him to continuously challenge himself and to set new goals for himself. We can choose to constantly seek new and better ways of doing things or desire expertise in perpetuity in order to keep us driven. In the final analysis, our drives will serve the purpose of fueling our passion.

The persistent quest for improvement, excellence, and "mastery" caused Poitier to seek new and better ways of performing his acting roles. This need for unending improvement, in essence, is a drive that is motivated by an intangible desire or an intrinsic attribute. It spurs the quest for our passion, gives us great confidence, and prompts a high level of sustainable accomplishments in us. This may explain why Poitier believed in his capabilities as an actor to such an extent that he refused to settle for the role of a janitor, even though he desperately needed the job. It is invigorating to think that there are always better ways of doing things. Thus, the constant quest for improvement also fosters the "aha moment," which stems from the sudden emergence of a new idea. This may engender the saying that we wish we knew yesterday what we know today. Intelligence is not invariable; it can be enhanced. The world is dynamic. There will always be better ways of doing most things. We will continue to have room for improvement. The incessant need for improvement has always been one of Poitier's strongest drives.

Poitier considerably influenced the outcome of some of his latter-day movies. In the movie *In the Heat of the Night*, for instance, the original scene called for one of the characters, the white businessman who lived in a mansion up the hill, to give Detective Tibbs, played by Poitier, a slap on the face when Tibbs would ask for his alibi on the night of the murder. However, Poitier insisted on having the scene changed, enabling him to retaliate with a backhand slap. His contention was that the retaliation would give the movie a more interesting and exciting twist. The director agreed to the change in the scene, and it worked out just as Poitier had envisioned.

In the midst of Poitier's successes and accolades, he became estranged from his family: He fell in love with another woman and divorced his wife; his young children paid a heavy price emotionally as result of the divorce. Through it all, his friend and mentor, Harry Belafonte, stood steadfastly behind him, giving him advice regarding his relationship with his children, which helped him tremendously. He learned from Belafonte how to be there for his children, even when they were tepid with him, or when they had strained and infrequent communication with him. Poitier was prone to mistakes in his family life just like anyone else. We hear of divorces among the rich and famous, and turmoil in their families, especially in Hollywood. However, somehow we hold highly accomplished people to different standards than ourselves, but they experience trials and tribulations in the same manner as the general population.

* * *

The following is a summation of Poitier's introspective analysis of his belief system, with respect to his spirituality: "I simply believe that there's a very organic, immeasurable consciousness of which we're a part. I believe that this consciousness is a force so powerful that I'm incapable of comprehending its power through the puny instrument of my human mind." This is not necessarily the perspective of someone involved in organized religion. Poitier conforms to the belief pattern of most of the individuals featured in this book: the absence of a consistent involvement in organized religion. Poitier also evaluated Christianity and his traditional island culture: "I'm enriched by the language and imagery of both traditional Christianity and old island culture." He concludes by referencing his reverence for a culmination of the range of his perceptions in a universal power: "I just give it respect, and I think of it as living in me as well as everywhere else."

Poitier's autobiography depicts his eruditeness and self-education in many areas, including philosophy. He delves into his findings and perceptions with a certain rhetorical colloquialism that is suggestive of someone who had invested a substantial amount of time exploring these subjects on a non-scholarly basis. In his book, Poitier also portrayed his interpretation of his world, his perception of the reasons for his success, and his discernment of the forces that guide the earth—both visible and invisible.

Poitier explained how success can be achieved in his autobiography: "Before you can achieve a better life, you've got to be able to spell out what a better life means. What it means for you." We get what we desire; it may not come in the exact specifications that we want, or it might not come as easily as we hoped, but it does come nonetheless. We have to define what we want, which is tantamount to identifying our drive; we have to ascertain whether it is intangible and intrinsic, such as the acquisition of expertise and freedom, or whether it is tangible and extrinsically motivated, such as wealth and fame. The next step is to establish our niche and how to pursue our passion in that niche.

As I alluded to earlier, there is never a straight path to success. Everyone experiences failure. Our resilience enables us to push ahead. Poitier was no exception to this predicament. In his autobiography, he states his feelings about the outcome of his collaborative effort with a friend: "Our first effort at a one-man show met with failure, and oh, how I hate to fail." Of course, failure also serves the useful purpose of enabling us to learn from our mistakes and to fine-tune our efforts.

* * *

How can we determine the prolificacy of a venture or ascertain that an endeavor is going to lead to fruition? It is always obvious to us whether an endeavor is proceeding according to plan or not. Time and progress are good indicators of our success, or the lack thereof, in a venture. If we make quantifiable progress in a reasonable amount of time, it is indicative of the fact that we are in the right field. According to Malcolm Gladwell's book, *Outliers*, it takes ten thousand hours of intense preparation, or at least three hours a day, seven days a week of intense preparation for ten years, to achieve expertise in our chosen field. However, the determination of whether our venture will lead to fruition depends on whether we are in pursuit of an endeavor that comprises our niche. It also depends on how strong our passion is and whether we are able to create value with our quest. Confidence and belief in our capabilities, which are qualities possessed by Poitier, are important attributes, essential to ensuring success in our venture.

Intense preparation could be relative, but it involves grueling and repetitive practice. For maximum results and efficacy, our mode of practice may need to be varied. It is not uncommon to find ourselves reaching a plateau during prolonged and ardent practice of the activity encompassing our niche and passion. At that point, we should vary and tweak our methods of practice to continue on an upward trail of improvement. We should practice under pressure to maximize our performance and ensure the sustainability of our endeavor. In *Drive*, Daniel H. Pink discussed practice: It should be deliberate and consistent; it demands focus and concentration; and we should be mentally prepared for it. Other aspects of preparation include research, analysis, human relations, and networking.

Education is crucial in our quest for excellence and success. While practice entails repetition, education consists of seeking more knowledge and better ways of executing the activity encompassing our passion. Knowledge is infinite, and the more knowledge we acquire in our field of endeavor, the better our chances of achieving excellence in it. Education is complementary to practice and preparation and augments our quest for expertise in our field of endeavor.

The word failure has a negative connotation; however, it is not negative if we consider the fact that it enables us to identify the correct path to our goal. Failure is what happens before we succeed. In solving a problem, failure teaches us how to arrive at the solution; it enables us to learn and to grow, as long as it is not fatal. We should also learn from other people's failures and mistakes. Failure is negative only when we fail to learn from it. No one is immune to it; not even Sidney Poitier.

CHAPTER 5
Abraham Lincoln: Appetite for Politics

Abraham Lincoln was the greatest U.S. president of the nineteenth century and one of the greatest American presidents of all time. He was the sixteenth president of the United States and was instrumental in the prevention of the secessionist efforts of the Southern states. He was born in 1809. The slavery issue was contentious in Lincoln's time. There was also a strong abolitionist movement in that era. Lincoln was responsible for signing into law the Emancipation Proclamation, which was a key step in ending slavery. He was an eloquent speaker who used uncomplicated speeches to articulate his impressive thought process. He knew the value of words and used them well. His remarkable life exemplified the American dream as well as greatness and success.

Lincoln's father moved the family a few times in search of a good deal on land for farming and finally settled in Indiana. He also chose Indiana as a final place to settle because of his opposition to slavery, which stemmed from his religious beliefs. He wanted to settle in a state where slavery was outlawed.

The early years of Lincoln's life were marked by poverty. Although his father was a farmer who owned his land, the farming of this land was solely his responsibility, without much outside help. Young Lincoln served as his father's helper. The farming that he and his father did was done mostly by their physical labor, which defined Lincoln's hardship-ridden lifestyle as well as his father's.

Young Lincoln worked hard on the farm with his father, but he never liked farm work. It is often easier for us to find out what we do not like than it is to find our passion. In young Lincoln's time, it was uncommon for people to openly make known their distaste for manual labor, so Lincoln worked hard for his father without complaining. As a matter of fact, his dislike for manual labor caused him to later remark that although his father had instilled a strong work ethic in him, the inculcation of this work ethic in him did not include a fondness for manual labor. This notion led to speculations that he was lazy. Quite to the contrary, he was actually hardworking.

Dissatisfaction with the status quo during childhood seems to be a common denominator in the lives of great people and a driving force behind their quest for other more fulfilling endeavors. Lincoln definitely did not want to follow in his father's footsteps of being a farmer. His dislike for manual labor farming—a line of work with a meager income—served as one of the drives that propelled him to seek his passion. He once built a small rowboat with which he transported two men to their steamer, which was anchored up the river. Upon arriving at their boat, each of them tossed him half a silver dollar, giving Lincoln a glimpse of how lucrative life beyond the grueling and practically unrewarding labor of the farm could be. The idea of making a half dollar in a day, much less in a couple of hours, was inconceivable to him. This experience helped to open his eyes to the world beyond the confines of his hamlet.

Although young Lincoln did not know initially that he wanted to be the president of the United States, what he did know was that he liked to debate and read. His favorite books were biographies and history. Lincoln was known to have walked for miles to borrow a book. Oftentimes, he read his books without much light. Once, after the lantern that he used to read burned out, he proceeded to use the ray of light emanating through a crack from the fireplace to continue his reading.

When Lincoln left home, he found it both adventurous and financially rewarding to navigate a rowboat up and down

Drive to Passion

the Mississippi River from New Orleans to Illinois, where he impressed both his colleagues and employer with his skill and common sense. He finally settled in New Salem, Illinois, where he went to work for a store owner. While in New Salem, Lincoln practiced his oratory skills by engaging in public debates about politics and current affairs. He was also a good storyteller. He engaged his customers at the store in public policy discussions.

Once, Lincoln agreed to engage the town's wrestling champion, who was a bully, in a wrestling match to establish his presence and gain recognition there. The champion, Jack Armstrong, though considerably shorter than Lincoln, was much more muscular and was five years older. The day of the match elicited much excitement and frenzied anticipation among the town's people because the match was orchestrated by a newcomer who had enough nerve to go against the town's bully. The mantle of leadership in the town was at stake here. Even though Armstrong was strong and more muscular, Lincoln was nonetheless a viable challenger who was taller, with longer, far-reaching and strong arms. As the fight progressed, the two wrestlers locked arms for some time with no one at an advantage. After a while, Armstrong became frustrated and lost his grip. Technically, Lincoln had emerged victorious, but he agreed to call it a draw, and both men shook hands. Even though Lincoln was the de facto champion, by agreeing to call it a draw, he gained something more important than winning a wrestling match. He demonstrated his strength and audacity and scored diplomatic dividends with the people in his new environment. Lincoln also mitigated the importance of the town's gang and the bully at its helm—while securing acceptance from the males in the locale—and, importantly, he portrayed himself as a viable candidate for leadership of the group.

A combination of his public speaking efforts, superior performance during the wrestling match, and his maturity enhanced Lincoln's popularity, which engendered his notion of a possible bid for a political office. Lincoln's wisdom and astuteness were commendable. His willingness to forgo the title of a champion in order to garner support and turn potential foes into friends, allies, and supporters was a good move that made common sense and made him suitable for a political office. He demonstrated an ability to muster support. He portrayed himself as an individual with leadership potential and the capacity to build a coalition of different factions. Lincoln also through his actions demonstrated and affirmed the existence of the "win-win" paradigm.

Lincoln was driven by the need to gain acceptance and public support. In his biography, *A. Lincoln,* Ronald White, Jr. quoted Lincoln as saying, during his candidacy for the state legislature of Illinois, "Whether it be true or not, I can say for one that I have no other so great as that of being truly esteemed of my fellow men, by rendering myself worthy of their esteem. How far I shall succeed in gratifying this ambition is yet to be developed." This statement by Lincoln showed his drive to become a politician of the highest caliber. He also wanted to be respected, liked, and held in high esteem. These factors encompassed his drive.

Lincoln was driven by multiple factors, including the need to avoid manual labor and the need to pursue his niche in public speaking. He had a healthy dose of ego as well: He wanted to stand out in the crowd; he wanted to be liked and respected by his peers; and he wanted a life for himself that would transcend mediocrity. He was both intrinsically and extrinsically driven. Lincoln was driven by his need to avoid the type of poverty that he had experienced in his childhood. This was an extrinsic drive. At the same time, he was driven to explore his passion for debating, public speaking, and politics.

Although Lincoln lost his race for the Illinois state legislature, he volunteered in the local militia, campaigned for the position of captain, and won. He was tall and strong, and his physical features worked in his favor. His bravery, courage, and strong sense of right and wrong contributed to his selection as captain. As captain, he once stopped his men from murdering an Indian whom they accused of being a spy. He re-enlisted twice in the militia.

Lincoln used the proceeds of his service in the militia to open up a general store, which turned out to be an unsuccessful venture. He soon discovered he was not a businessman. His partner consumed most of the liquor that was for sale to customers. The business failed, and he accrued some debt as a result. Business was not the only venture that did not work out for him; his initial foray into politics proved unsuccessful as well.

Lincoln increased his credibility in the community by the way he handled his debt after his business failure. He earned a reputation for being honest, which in turn earned him the nickname "Honest Abe" because he made contact with all his creditors, promising to repay all of his debt, and he did. This was unusual in his time. It was not uncommon for debtors to skip town. His reputation as an honest and steadfast member of the community was later helpful in his political career.

We cannot be deterred by our failures. In fact, they always have lessons to teach us. Lincoln learned that business was not his niche, but he enjoyed politics. Although his first attempt at running for a political office was unsuccessful, in the words of Ronald White, Jr., "He had discovered his appetite for politics," and it was riveting to him. Politics and campaigning excited him. We all have our passion, and it is up to us to identify it. The process of uncovering our passion can sometimes be arduous. It should be initiated by ensuring the existence of a niche. Like Lincoln, we may have to try our hands at various things before we can accurately pinpoint our passion.

Once Lincoln identified his passion, similar to Winston Churchill, he began to work ardently toward improving his skills in all aspects of his passion. He became involved in a local debating society. This was an organization where men congregated to debate the issues of the day such as education for women, slavery, and the use of public money to build roads and canals. Lincoln also imitated the oration of preachers and used his boyhood friends as his audience as he practiced and sought to improve his speaking skills. He was passionate about speaking because he knew it intertwined with politics.

Lincoln's qualities of success were evident. He was a trusted leader who had a great sense of fairness. He enjoyed debating and telling jokes. He also enjoyed telling stories. He was courageous. Although Lincoln's level of formal education was low, and he could not afford the pursuit of higher education, he enjoyed reading and believed in education. He had tried his hands in business and politics but discovered that he preferred politics to business. Lincoln was passionate about politics and public speaking.

Lincoln decided to run again for the state legislature of Illinois, as a member of the Whig Party. At this point he was beginning to earn a reputation as a good speaker. His speeches were usually short and humorous. In one of his campaign speeches, Lincoln said, "My politics are short and sweet, like the old woman's dance. I am in favor of a national bank. I am in favor of a high protection tariff. These are my sentiments and political principles. If elected, I shall be thankful; if not, it will all be the same." He won the seat by a landslide. Lincoln was considered to be a great consensus builder. Even though he ran for this election under the Whig Party, he received a surprising amount of support from the Democratic Party.

Lincoln's involvement in politics could be considered a turning point in his life; he had found his true passion and was bent on developing his skills further. He was urged by a friend, John Todd Stuart, to become a lawyer because most successful politicians were lawyers. Lincoln never knew he could become a lawyer without attending college. He later found out that there were quite a few lawyers in the state legislature who had not attended college. They had studied law in an attorney's office. Thus, he borrowed law books from Stuart and proceeded to study law.

Stuart and Lincoln, who had been colleagues in the Black Hawk War, developed a mentor-protégé relationship. Stuart, already a successful attorney, became Lincoln's mentor and ushered an opportunity into Lincoln's life by serving as the attorney under whom Lincoln studied for his law degree. The use of mentors who serve the purpose of orchestrating opportunities for their protégés is a common denominator among individuals who are in pursuit of their passion and who go on to achieve success and greatness. Similar to Lincoln, Sidney Poitier and Winston Churchill utilized the help of mentors, at one point or another, while pursuing their passion.

Here, we see some of the same qualities in Lincoln that are typical of other highly accomplished people: He was a hard worker; he did not settle for a profession for which he had no passion; and he tried his hands at several things until he identified his fascination for politics and speaking—two activities that were absolutely riveting to him. Lincoln fervently practiced and prepared himself to become an effective public speaker. Then he took the necessary step to become a successful politician: He became a lawyer by educating himself.

Lincoln told a young man, a protégé who sought his advice on how to become a lawyer, to muster the resolve and tenacity to proceed toward his goal of becoming an attorney. He further told this young man that if he could muster the doggedness to embark on this undertaking, he should consider most of the job done. Lincoln explained to him that the willpower to succeed was always the key determinant of success. This is a clear indication of Lincoln's belief in personal development. Lincoln's belief is also in parity with thought management; if we can manage our thoughts to the point of focusing intensely on our drive and passion, then most of the job is done. The remaining fraction of our efforts in fostering the accomplishment of our goal consists of taking the necessary action to get the wheels in motion. In Lincoln's time, information on the power of the human mind was nowhere near as ubiquitous as it is today. However, through reading books such as George Washington's biography and the Bible, Lincoln was able to conjecture that in the human mind lies great power and potential.

When we compare Lincoln's time to the modern era, when all sorts of studies have been conducted and assertions made on the potential of the human mind, it would behoove us to think that we are at a great advantage compared to Lincoln in his day. There are more biographies, autobiographies, and an abundant supply of other pertinent books and information on personal development, motivation, and success available now.

* * *

Lincoln received his license to practice law in the state of Illinois and joined Stuart in his law practice as a junior partner. As a lawyer, he once again had a reputation for being honest. He analyzed his cases objectively without regard to his fees or the appeasement of his clients. In his usual manner, he listened to his clients carefully, interrupting occasionally with questions. Once, after listening to a client, he spent some time away from the client to deliberate on the case. Upon rejoining the client, Lincoln flatly told him he was wrong. In another situation, he advocated a concession on the part of his client. Most lawyers would have been reluctant to be brutally honest with clients for fear of the resultant loss of business and revenue.

Although Lincoln was already considered a good speaker and a relatively successful lawyer, he had an insatiable appetite for self-improvement. He was always seeking to improve his oratory skills. He believed so much in the power of speech that he once commented that spoken words rewarded those who bothered to master them.

Following the establishment of his career as a lawyer, Lincoln became a husband and a devoted family man who deeply loved his wife, Mary, despite her tempestuousness. Once, his wife asked him to take care of the fire and he forgot. She asked him again. It skipped his mind a second time. When she came around the third time, the fire had burned out. She got angry and hit him on the nose with a stick. As a result of her frequent outbursts and quarrelsome nature, history has not been kind to her with regard to her mental state. However, despite her bad temper, she supported her husband throughout his political career. She was protective of him and defended him vehemently whenever his political opponents made malicious comments about him or misrepresented his character. Lincoln took her outbursts in stride. In fact, he rationalized her episodes by referring to them as a passing storm.

Lincoln approached most things—including his wife's tempestuousness and petulance—rationally. He was able to put his wife's erratic behavior in perspective. While most men would have fought back, injured, or abandoned their wives due to this type of behavior, he stuck it out with her and dwelled on the positive. He was a patient man who approached things reasonably and sensibly. He was always in control of his emotions. He was not idealistic about marriage. When we pick our battles and meet our challenges with a degree of calmness, we are able to better assess the people with whom we interact.

Lincoln, meanwhile, continued his tenure in the Illinois state legislature for four terms, after which he successfully ran

Drive to Passion

for the United States House of Representatives. His term in the House was marked by his strong opposition to the United States' war with Mexico. He was convinced that the circumstances surrounding the war were shrouded in deceit, orchestrated by James Polk, who was the president at the time. This is comparable to the sentiment shared by many regarding the conditions that prompted the Iraq war. Lincoln's criticism of Polk was that he had lied to the American people about the cause of the war. Polk and his administration claimed Mexico had started the war. Lincoln and some of the president's other sharp critics contended that the only reason the United States went to war with Mexico was to seize more land from them. At the end of the war, Mexico signed a peace treaty with the United States. Under this peace agreement, the United States gained several territories, including California, New Mexico, and Arizona.

While in the House of Representatives, Lincoln was involved in another hot debate. This debate was centered on the issue of whether slavery should be allowed in the new territories gained from Mexico. It was no secret that Lincoln was opposed to slavery. This was to be the platform on which he would later run for the presidency of the United States.

After a brief stint in Congress, Lincoln returned full time to his law practice in Illinois. He liked the practice of law and often appeared in court while his law partner was engaged in the research aspect of the practice. Lincoln's momentary loss of interest in Congress may have been attributable to the fact that he had served his purpose there. He was ready to move on to more elaborate challenges.

It is not uncommon for success-oriented individuals to have a momentary loss of drive while in the pursuit of their passion, and to come back to it later, or to refocus their quests on a new passion. Similar to Lincoln's loss of interest in Congress, Winston Churchill's "wilderness years" symbolized a period when his political activities came to a screeching halt. Churchill refocused his attention on other activities such as painting, writing and speaking. Similarly, Lincoln refocused his energy on his law practice at the end of his term in Congress. Whenever we lose steam in our existing passion, we should not despair as long as we continue to be driven. We can always rekindle our existing passion or refocus our energy on another passion. We should revisit our drives, passion, and activities for which we may have a niche.

Lincoln focused his energy on his law practice. He was a good lawyer who used a combination of eloquence and good humor to win cases. When Lincoln once represented a farmer who had been swindled during a horse trade, the defendant's lawyer rambled on for two hours about horses without realizing that he had worn his shirt inside-out. When it was Lincoln's turn to plead his case on behalf of his client, he proceeded to tell the jury that his colleague on the opposing side had spent two hours talking about horses with a seemingly demonstrable knowledge of the subject. Lincoln went on to say that his colleague, with all his knowledge about horses, had however talked the entire time with his shirt worn inside-out. Lincoln was ostensibly the only one who had noticed it before then. He further contended to the court that, in spite of his colleague's elaborate speech about horses, his knowledge of horses could not be validated if he did not have the good sense to wear his shirt correctly. The entire court roared with laughter, and Lincoln and his client won the case.

Lincoln, in a number of cases, encouraged his clients to settle. His rationale for encouraging settlement was that the plaintiffs and the defendants were frequently from the same town; usually, after the case, they faced the prospect of returning to the same community to live together. Lincoln's thought process was sophisticated for an era when people sometimes settled their differences by shooting things out. His exceptional reasoning ability was one of his key leadership qualities.

Some time elapsed before Lincoln decided to re-enter politics, and when he did, he ran unsuccessfully for the United States Senate. He ran in opposition to slavery while his opponent's platform was that Congress had no right to either force slavery or remove it from a given territory. They held several debates, which were centered on this critical topic. Lincoln was the subject of cynical comments from his opponent during these debates. In one incident, Lincoln's opponent sarcastically referred to the Negro as Lincoln's relative. He further asserted that unlike Lincoln, he believed Negroes belonged to an inferior race, and they were definitely no kin to him. This drew laughter from the crowd.

Lincoln did not take his loss well. He felt badly about it and hoped that he could run against his opponent again at the expiration of his opponent's term in office; however, there was something else in store for him. Although Lincoln's sight was set on the Senate, he had gained tremendous popularity due to his eloquence in debates during his campaign. As a result, there was a movement by the Republicans to draft him for a presidential bid. Initially, the movement to draft Lincoln to run for the presidency of the United States started with local newspapers in small towns. His reaction initially portrayed him as lacking confidence because of his frequent self-deprecating comments. Although Lincoln later began to acquiesce to his supporters about the prospect of becoming president, he did not think he had the luck or the people's goodwill for the job.

The turning of the tide for Lincoln came with his sudden realization of his popularity as a candidate for the presidency. According to White, Lincoln consented to the notion of his presidential bid by saying, "The taste is in my mouth, a little." His acceptance of an invitation to speak in Brooklyn, New York, was another indication of his newfound confidence in his viability as a candidate for the presidency.

The effort, thought, and preparation Lincoln put into the campaign speech he delivered in New York were unprecedented. He went to New York in the hope of impressing everyone, and he accomplished that. Lincoln impressed the nation with his eloquence, power of persuasion, likeability, and fairness. He also traveled to New England to campaign and to see his son, who was in college there.

Following Lincoln's campaign speeches in New York and New England, he became certain of his prospect for the presidency; his confidence level increased. He also became convinced of the enormous support he wielded in the nation. After a tedious campaign, Lincoln emerged victorious as the presidential nominee at the Republican convention.

Lincoln's unique ability to build a coalition of diverse advisers consisting of individuals who were often intelligent, opinionated,

Abraham Lincoln: Appetite for Politics

and pigheaded was very visible during his campaign and after he won the Republican nomination. These individuals were difficult to assemble in one room due to the differences in their opinions. He had the great ability to listen and harness the confluence of their various prodigious ideas, deciphering and utilizing certain aspects of this immense resource to the extent that they complemented his weaknesses and improved his capabilities.

Lincoln was elected the sixteenth president of the United States on November 6, 1860, by a landslide, but along with this cheerful occasion came a predicament. Shortly after his election to office, Lincoln became aware of the fact that the Southern states were in the process of trying to secede from the Union. He had underestimated the Southern states. Lincoln had conjectured that the Southerners were too intelligent and patriotic to attempt to disrupt the Union.

Lincoln made a miscalculation when he thought that the South was too savvy to secede, but he quickly corrected his assertions and adjusted to the simmering discontent among the Southern states. A trait of highly successful individuals is their ability to quickly learn from their mistakes and get beyond them. Lincoln quickly came to grips with the extent of the dissatisfaction among the Southerners; thus, he became intent on focusing his efforts in the right direction, which comprised a proper assessment of the situation and a determination of an appropriate line of action. Similarly, when Joseph Kennedy's contract with First National Exhibitors' Circuit was terminated by the board due to his mistake, he did not allow this to become a hindrance. He quickly refocused his efforts on other deals.

As time elapsed, Lincoln became cognizant of a looming civil unrest between the North and the South. According to White, Lincoln's premonition of the seriousness of what lay ahead of him led him to make the following statement in his address to the crowd that gathered in Springfield, Illinois, to bid him farewell prior to his departure to Washington D.C.: "I now leave, not knowing when, or whether ever, I may return, with a task before me greater than that which rested upon Washington."

Similar to his diverse group of advisers, Lincoln made sure his cabinet included political opponents whose views were different from his. He sought the most intelligent people for his cabinet rather than yes men. Also, he wanted at least one Southerner in his cabinet to show the Southerners that his administration would be inclusive. He attempted to make the contentious issue of slavery a subject that would be on the forefront of his agenda, and he made this known to the Southerners to avoid potential problems from lack of communication. The South wanted the extension of slavery and contended that it was justified. Conversely, the North thought slavery was unjustified and should be restricted.

Lincoln's astuteness, sense of logic, and diplomacy were unprecedented in his time. Seeking highly intelligent people in his cabinet, irrespective of their party affiliation or political ideology, was a rarity among presidents in his era. Lincoln's perceptiveness and intuition were refreshing and worthy of commendation. He behaved as if he was a leader who had been chosen by a higher power. In actuality, these are qualities inherent in all of us who are of sound mind, if we would summon them or invoke our rational sense.

No sooner had Lincoln begun to settle into his role as president than an incident occurred in Fort Sumter, South Carolina, that could be said to be the straw that broke the camel's back with regard to the tension between the North and the South. The issue of sending supplies to the stranded troops on the island of Sumter, after the secession of South Carolina, would become pivotal in the initiation of the Civil War between the northern Union and the southern Confederates.

The high degree of deliberation and diplomacy utilized by Lincoln prior to the commencement of the war is noteworthy. The commander of the United States' forces in Sumter sent word to Lincoln indicating that his supplies were low and that the Confederate forces were threatening to invade the fort. Lincoln had a tough problem to solve. He deliberated on this dilemma for a few weeks: Should he allow the Confederate forces to capture Sumter, or should he send his forces to liberate the island? He reasoned that if he allowed the capture of Sumter, it would send a signal of weakness to the Confederates. On the other hand, if Sumter was rescued, the rescue mission would be perceived as an act of aggression. Finally, he decided to simply send supplies to the United States' troops in Sumter, despite the counsel he had received to the contrary. His rationale was that sending supplies to Sumter would not constitute an act of aggression on the part of the federal government.

The Confederate forces reacted exactly as Lincoln had predicted: They fired at the supply vessel. The firing at the supply vessel by the Confederate forces served as a turning point in the history of the United States; it symbolized the beginning of the Civil War because it was an act of aggression perpetrated by the South against the northern Union. Lincoln had met and passed some of the tests of a successful leader: problem solving, courage, resilience, and patience. These are also some of the characteristics of greatness.

As the war raged, Lincoln indeed confirmed the notion that patience is a virtue and a quality he was glad he possessed. He utilized the metaphor of the ripening process of a pear to stress the importance of patience in the war. Lincoln contended that the ripening process of a pear must not be forced without running the risk of destroying the tree and the fruit. If the process were allowed to take its natural course, then the fruit would drop on its own, thereby becoming easily accessible. Therefore, similar to the ripened fruit, patience to Lincoln was a requisite virtue in the successful execution of the war.

Lincoln's opposition to slavery sometimes was a lonely endeavor, but he continued to push ahead in spite of his lack of popular support. He was a fair man and fought hard for what he believed in. This fight would lead to the Emancipation Proclamation, which he believed would placate the border states and prevent them from joining the Confederate states. Lincoln would also continue his fight against slavery until a few years later when the Thirteenth Amendment, which outlawed slavery in the entire country, would be approved and ratified, albeit shortly after his death.

The Civil War triggered several challenges for Lincoln. One of the challenges was the replacement of many of his generals, who did not live up to his expectations with regard to their execution of the war. Also, Lincoln was running out of soldiers. This led to the enlistment of African-Americans in the military.

Drive to Passion

The majority of the African-American soldiers who fought in the Civil War against the Confederates were men who had fled the South. The fact that the Confederates were afraid to recruit African-Americans to fight on their side, for fear that they would defect or turn against them, worked in Lincoln's favor.

As Lincoln continued to replace his generals and to indentify and appoint those whom he deemed capable of successfully executing the war, his efforts began to pay dividends. The Confederate troops took a beating from the Union forces; they suffered a crushing defeat by the Union soldiers in the battle of Gettysburg—thanks to General George Meade, who led his troops to victory there. This important victory marked the turning point of the Civil War.

Following this important battle, Lincoln was invited to participate in a somber celebration, in Gettysburg, to mark the victory. He was actually one of the last speakers invited to speak at the event. His invitation appeared to be an afterthought. Other more rhetorical speakers—who would speak for great lengths of time at this event and were considered to be better orators than Lincoln—received their invitations before Lincoln. Upon his arrival, he proceeded to settle into the Wills residence, which was the most magnificent home there. On the appointed day, November 19, 1863, he showed up at the square promptly at 10:00 A.M.

President Lincoln and other prominent individuals proceeded to address the public at the Gettysburg event. The dignitaries there included governors and other politicians. Close to fifteen thousand people were present. Lincoln's speech was preceded by Edward Everett's oration, which lasted slightly over two hours. Everett, a New England politician, was considered a great orator. Lincoln had a tough act to follow. In White's biography, he noted that Lincoln started his address by utilizing a Biblical inference in his reference to the founding fathers of the United States, the date of the creation of the nation, and the reason for the founding of the nation: "Four score and seven years ago our fathers brought forth, on this continent, a new nation, conceived in Liberty, and dedicated to the proposition that all men are created equal." Lincoln skillfully tied liberty and equality for all to the successful outcome of the war. He then dedicated the land and the occasion to the fallen soldiers who had given their lives to the cause and the living soldiers who had made immense contributions as well: "But, in a larger sense, we can not dedicate—we can not consecrate—we can not hallow—this ground. The brave men, living and dead, who struggled here, have consecrated it far above our poor power to add or detract." Once again, Lincoln invoked the Bible to give credence to his speech by using the word consecrate and by referencing a higher power.

Lincoln capped off his address with his famous aphorism and another reference to God: "That this nation, under God, shall have a new birth of freedom—and that government of the people, by the people, for the people, shall not perish from the earth." In essence, Lincoln had succeeded in tying the freedom of the United States to the successful ending of the Civil War, thereby formulating his legendary adage.

Initially, newspapers and critics decried the speech. It was considered to be too short, especially since it was preceded by Everett's long oration. His address was also considered by his critics to be flat and simple. Lincoln himself harbored doubts about his eloquence during the address; thus, he remarked to a friend that he thought his speech was flat and had descended on his listeners like a "wet blanket." Although Lincoln's Gettysburg Address was unusually short, over time it became known as one of the most eloquent political addresses ever given in the United States.

The success of this speech came as a surprise to Lincoln. It is not uncommon among great achievers in a given situation to consider themselves to have rendered a sub-standard performance, due to their high expectations of themselves, when in fact they delivered an outstanding performance. Sidney Poitier thought his first major performance on stage was a total failure, but the audience and critics thought differently. Lincoln's days of trying to improve his speaking ability by joining the debating society and practicing his speeches in front of his friends had paid off. He had become a member of a revered group of eloquent speakers. Lincoln was considered to be a great orator by many.

Drive to Passion

Although the popular adage "practice makes perfect" holds true, practice also enhances our confidence and passion. All of the men and women of passion in this book enhanced their skills and consequently their passions through rigorous practice. This mode of perpetual practice led these individuals to become experts in those activities encompassing their passion. It also led them to develop unrelenting and unshakable confidence in their abilities.

* * *

Persistence paid off for Lincoln. He was dogged in his efforts to find generals who could successfully execute the war. He did not give up hope of finding the right generals for the job. Persistence leads to opportunity and the accomplishment of our goals. The more persistent we are, the more strides we can make in our endeavors. If we are convinced of the potential of our endeavors, we must continue to strive to achieve the type of success that will match our aspirations.

The Union forces began to experience more victories as the war progressed. Lincoln finally had brought generals on board who were winning battles; however, these victories came with a heavy loss of lives on the Union side. Some southern states including Virginia, Tennessee and North Carolina began to be liberated by the Union forces.

Lincoln's second term in office was marked by a turnaround in the war in favor of the Union forces. His swearing-in ceremony was not accompanied by pomp and pageantry; rather, it was solemn and was celebrated by a short speech, similar to his Gettysburg Address. He economized his words, as usual; they were powerful words, centered on the end of the war and reconciliation.

Lincoln visited Virginia at the invitation of one of his generals. Many people gathered around him to welcome him. The African-American slaves who had just been freed recognized him and seemed particularly excited; they cheered for him.

The cheering by the African-American ex-slaves was symbolic of Lincoln's charisma and popularity among the general population. He was empathetic toward others, and this heightened the admiration of many. Even though members of his staff set a schedule for him to receive visitors, he seldom adhered to it. He received guests and saw people with varied problems and concerns past his scheduled time for doing so, which was remarkable considering how busy he was. He was drawn to people and actually enjoyed helping others. This is an attribute of great leaders. Most often, nothing can be achieved alone. We always need other people's involvement in our endeavors. Lincoln helped people and, in turn, received help and advice from them. We may not always be charismatic, but we can always learn to like people—learn to respect and cherish our differences with others, and learn to treat everyone fairly. It is of utmost importance that we develop and maximize our listening skills in our bid to be congenial as we work with others, even when their ideas may seem outrageous or inconsequential. There is always something we can learn from our interactions with others.

Another quality possessed by most highly accomplished individuals is the ability and willingness to take on responsibilities. This is evident in Lincoln's case. He had many responsibilities, but he never shied away from them. Looking at challenges and tasks in their totality can be quite daunting. However, if we compartmentalize our tasks or problems, we can gain clarity and increase our efficiency and effectiveness. Doing so also enables us to minimize our stress levels by reducing the overwhelming effects of our tasks. Lincoln compartmentalized his tasks and problems; thus, he was able to execute the war and attend to other pressing domestic issues simultaneously.

Leadership and greatness are not for those who lack courage, resilience, and the ability to take risks. We should have tolerance for risks while in pursuit of our passion. We often take a leap of faith or relinquish the security of a job in order to make remarkable strides. While in pursuit of excellence, it is paramount that we muster the courage to push forward and summon the resilience to bounce back from a failure or mistake. The progression to leadership positions and greatness is neither consistent nor clearly defined. Winston Churchill experienced a failure, which preceded his appointment to a cabinet-level position and subsequent appointment to the position of prime minister of Britain. Lincoln would make the ultimate sacrifice with his life in his second term in office, which stemmed from the risk involved in the presidency in his time, and it was a tragedy of epic proportions.

In addition to his capacity to handle huge responsibilities, Lincoln was effective as a leader and president. He had great listening skills. Lincoln was able to assemble highly opinionated advisers; he listened to and discerned their various opinions and ideas, utilizing those that were relevant, while discarding the irrelevant ones. In some cases, his calm demeanor and great listening skills were mistaken for reticence and naiveté and deemed an opportunity to be irreverent toward him. However, in his unshakable resolve, Lincoln dispensed appropriate discipline to those who misconstrued his superb qualities for weakness. His ability to delegate tasks to the right people fostered his effectiveness. He delegated tasks to his generals, cabinet, and governors, just to mention a few. He also motivated and inspired those he led. The cumulative effects of these qualities made Lincoln a great leader and president.

Lincoln enjoyed politics and giving great speeches, but he certainly did not enjoy the war and the ensuing loss of lives. Certain aspects of our passion may not be as enjoyable as others; nevertheless, we still need to perform those tasks we deem mundane or the ones we dislike, in order to bring our quests to fruition. Delegating the mundane tasks without compromising their excellence could alleviate this predicament.

Although there are individuals who may inherently have charisma and the ability to lead, competence in leadership similar to Lincoln's can be learned. There are many great books on this subject, including biographies and autobiographies of great leaders. Lincoln was a fair, honest, and charismatic leader. Importantly, he had great listening skills and was willing to be connected to people with opposing views, from whose pertinent insights and opinions he learned. He won people over because of his fairness and sincerity. Our leadership skills can be enhanced by being empathetic toward others and by having the ability to motivate our subordinates. Lincoln's style of leadership is one that we can emulate. As we pursue our passion, we will also increase our chances of being in leadership positions.

* * *

After a few years of the brutal Civil War and the deaths of over six hundred thousand soldiers, peace was within reach. The end of the war was marked by the capitulation of the leading Confederate general to the top Union general. Lincoln was elated about the end of the conflict and the prospect of peace. There were celebrations all over Washington, D.C., and the rest of the country.

Although Lincoln demonstrated his outstanding leadership skills and greatness by delving immediately into the resolution of the main issues of the day such as rebuilding the South and the fate of the freed slaves, he and his presidency were doomed. Lincoln's line of reasoning was sophisticated and ahead of its time because he deliberated on all the intricate details that were of relevance in bringing the war to a successful end. Some of the key political figures in the Union wanted the South punished, but Lincoln's approach was more conciliatory and reasonable. He advocated reconciliation between the North and South. He also talked about voting rights for African-Americans in some of his public speeches. Lincoln's presidency ended tragically—an ending so unjust and paradoxical for such a great man. He was assassinated in a theater as he watched a play. The difference Lincoln made will forever keep him and his legacy at the forefront of history.

CHAPTER 6
Suze Orman: Like What You Do

Born on the South Side of Chicago, Suze Orman grew up in the 1950s and 1960s. She had a speech impairment as a child and was less than confident in the academic arena. She felt inadequate in her reading class. Her reading score was far below the reading scores of her three best friends. Despite these setbacks, Orman developed into the great television personality and financial expert we know today.

In Orman's book, *Suze's Story*, she said of herself, "I knew I would never amount to anything, so why even bother to try?" Her Scholastic Aptitude Test score was low; nevertheless, she still gained admission into the University of Illinois at Urbana-Champaign, much to her surprise.

In her meeting with her guidance counselor upon her arrival at the University of Illinois, Orman ironically told him that she wanted to be a brain surgeon, in spite of her low grades. It was incongruous and humorous to her counselor that a student with low grades would want to be a brain surgeon. However, Orman became more realistic and later settled for social work—a major less academically challenging than brain surgery.

Judging from Orman's early academic performance and her impression of herself, one would be inclined to believe she would not amount to anything, or at best she would achieve a life of mediocrity. Her self-esteem was low, and she was ashamed of her performance relative to the performance of her peers. All of these factors pointed in the direction of an individual who should have resorted to low-level employment.

Orman stopped short of graduating from college with a degree in social work in 1973, due to her inability to fulfill the course requirement in languages. Her lack of confidence in her ability reared its head again. Orman described it in the following words in her book: "Once again, it was the shame of my grade-school years holding me back. If I had trouble with English, what made me think I could learn a foreign language?" Orman would later earn her degree in social work in 1976 from the University of Illinois after meeting the degree requirement through the completion of a Spanish class at Hayward State University.

Similar to Orman, there are a substantial number of accomplished individuals who either showed mediocre academic aptitude in school or did not finish college. Sidney Poitier had minimal formal education, yet he turned out to be one of the best and most articulate actors of his generation. Winston Churchill passed the entrance exam into a non-degreed, two-year military academy—where he received his postsecondary school education—after more than one try. General Colin Powell, who graduated with a C average from City College, New York, would become one of the best career military officers and one of the most erudite individuals to serve the U.S. government. Of course, there are a few titans in the high-technology industry without college degrees, as well.

The importance of a college education cannot be overemphasized; however, one's level of higher education has minimal direct impact on one's level of achievement later in life. Rather, rigorous and perpetual practice and education in the activity encompassing our passion are necessary to become accomplished and an expert in that endeavor. I highly recommend higher education as a solid foundation and a framework from which to begin our pursuit for our passion. Driven and passionate people such as Sidney Poitier and Suze Orman usually acquire the necessary education and make the preparations needed along the way to enhance their passion. Success and greatness are orchestrated and heavily influenced by one's drive and passion primarily. If we do not have a passion that

Drive to Passion

we enjoy and for which we have a niche, we may never attain the degree of accomplishment that we desire.

Higher education is not the only measure of our astuteness or eruditeness; making value-added strides in society is also a way to measure it. This is not a minimization of the importance of higher education. It serves the useful purpose of broadening our perspective and making us trainable. Education also serves to potentially spur an appetite for more knowledge in the minds of those who seek it.

Intelligence is linked to our ability to think or our ability to acquire information through education. It could also be relative. There are "those who subscribe to an 'incremental theory' [of intelligence]"—believing that, while humans may have intelligence in varying degrees, it can be increased, according to Pink, in his book, *Drive*. Conversely, there are others—"entity theorists"—who believe that intelligence is fixed. In some circles, a person with high verbal skills may be deemed intelligent, while in others, an expansive memory or excellent quantitative skills may be a measure of intelligence. Pink cited an experiment in which students who believed that intelligence can be enhanced performed better than those who believed that it is fixed. The former group of students tended to be more dogged in their approach to the performance of their task, while the latter group gave up more readily, with the assertion that their capabilities were fixed and could not be further enhanced. Emotional intelligence is an aspect of intelligence that also contributes significantly to performance because it fosters our human relations skills. Orman, who initially deemed herself unintelligent, would go on to become an expert in her field. Obviously, the quest for learning in the activity pertaining to our passion enhances our attainment of expertise and intelligence in it.

* * *

After Orman left college in 1973 without graduating, she drove to Berkeley, California, with a couple of her friends. No sooner had they arrived in Berkeley than Orman found a job with a tree-clearing company. As a matter of fact, she secured this job just as she was driving into the city and was in a traffic holdup that was triggered by the clearing of trees. On a whim, Orman asked the man in charge of the clearing if there were job openings, and sure enough, she was offered a job with the tree-clearing company.

Orman's next job was as a waitress at a coffee and pastry shop, Buttercup Bakery. She stayed at this coffee shop for six years, earning $400 a week. While at this coffee shop, she conceived of the idea of opening up her own restaurant. Orman was great at customer service. She won her customers over with her affability and smile. She may have had a passion for the restaurant industry at the time, or maybe it was simply a passion for customer service. Orman's first step toward the pursuit of her dream of opening up a restaurant was to attempt to borrow $20,000 from her parents. They did not have the money.

Luckily for Orman, she discussed her aspirations with one of her habitual customers at the restaurant, Fred Hasbrook, who not only gave her a check for $2,000 but also approached other regular customers on Orman's behalf. Before long, the restaurant's customers had contributed $50,000 toward her restaurant venture. She had ample time to repay the loan: ten years. Orman was elated; these customers had enough confidence in her to risk their money in support of her dream. They were angel investors, investing in Orman to make her dream come true. They could also be deemed her mentors. They gave her the opportunity of a lifetime.

Through Hasbrook's advice, Orman decided to invest all of the money she received from her customers at Merrill Lynch. She neither had a clue of who Merrill was nor what a money market account was prior to her introduction to the company. She just had enough faith in Hasbrook to follow his advice and recommendation. Unbeknownst to Orman, her Merrill representative was not forthright. Following their initial meeting, the Merrill representative cajoled her into signing a virtually blank contract, which he later filled out, placing her funds in a high-risk security known as buying options. Due to her investment, Orman began to follow the markets closely by reading financial circulations such as *The Wall Street Journal* and *Barron's* and by watching an investment program on Public Broadcasting Service

Drive to Passion

(PBS) television every Friday night. Although Orman's portfolio initially made money, soon the losses started, and she eventually lost everything. Her dream of becoming a restaurateur vanished with the loss of her funds.

There was a positive aspect to Orman's loss of her investment. In tracking her investment, she had learned about the markets, and she decided to become a financial advisor. She thought she could do better than the disingenuous Merrill representative who had lost all her money. At that point, Orman had no clue what her passion would be. All she knew was that she could do well enough in this profession to outperform this dishonest representative. Financial services would become her passion due to her enthusiasm for investment, her perpetual practice and education to achieve expertise in it, her niche for it, and her affinity for excellent customer service.

It could be said that Orman stumbled across financial services, in a similar manner to Sidney Poitier, who prior to inadvertently coming across the advertisement in the newspaper for actors, had no idea that he wanted to become an actor. Orman dressed up and went to a job interview with Merrill, the same company that had lost all her money.

Orman demonstrated resilience, courage, and tenacity as she proceeded to make headway at Merrill subsequent to the loss of her funds there. Every organization has at least one unscrupulous individual similar to the representative responsible for Orman's predicament. She had the tenacity to delve into unfamiliar terrain and the courage and resilience to move forward despite her losses and her lack of aptitude in math. Orman's fortitude mirrors Joseph Kennedy's pursuit of his passion in business and finance despite his weakness in an accounting course in college. Highly accomplished individuals never throw up their hands and give up in despair in the wake of failure or adversity; they continuously demonstrate tenacity, courage, and resilience.

To exacerbate Orman's disconcerting situation with regard to the loss of her money, her experience at the job interview with Merrill was less than inviting. According to *Success* magazine, she was told by the branch manager during the interview that "women belonged barefoot and pregnant." Despite this comment from the manager, she was hired at a salary of $1,500 a month.

She believed that the only reason she was offered the job was that the manager had a female quota to meet. Orman, who initially thought her calling in life was to own a restaurant, was now in a different industry, primarily out of necessity. All of her seed money was gone; she had no choice but to move forward. She now owed a huge sum of money—$50,000—to a few people. The prospect, especially to a young person in her twenties, of owing such an amount in the 1970s would have been unnerving to most people, considering it is worth over $180,000 in 2011.

Orman had a new job. She updated her wardrobe, which was less than adequate. Her initial experience on the job was unsettling. She was intimidated by the other representatives, who were relatively well-to-do and very knowledgeable. Her car was a clunker, compared to her colleagues' European luxury cars. Orman had no prior business experience. She was told by the manager that she would not last longer than six months in the organization, so she had something to prove.

Orman was faced with the challenge of studying for the Series 7 Exam, a standardized test required to qualify for her new position. While studying for the exam, Orman came across a stipulation in the code of conduct that required brokers to acclimatize their clients with the securities in which they were investing prior to making any investment. They had to find out if their clients were risk-averse or predisposed to high-risk investments in their investment objectives; in other words, it was stated in her reading, "Know your customer." The Merrill representative who had lost her money did not adhere to these principles; he had lost all of her borrowed capital in a high-risk security without her knowledge.

Orman confronted the branch manager with her findings. The manager responded by holding her accountable for signing a document without reading it, and he asserted that the unscrupulous representative was a top producer in his team. According to Orman, he also reminded her that he had told her she "wouldn't last six months." At that point she had three months to go before the exam—so she decided to concentrate on her exam rather than delving further into the issue of her lost investment. She passed the exam and became a broker.

*   *   *

Pacific Gas and Electric had utilized the services of the brokers at Merrill for the purpose of educating their potential retirees and employees about the intricacies of retirement planning. However, none of Pacific's employees was retiring, so the venture was an exercise in futility. As a result, many Merrill brokers began to shy away from the job of giving seminars to the employees of Pacific.

Once Orman became aware of the requests by Pacific for a financial advisor, she volunteered for the job of teaching its employees about retirement planning without giving it much thought. She was enthusiastic at the prospect of conducting these seminars. Orman designed her brochures and other presentation materials and truly enjoyed giving the seminars. According to *Success* magazine, Orman said of the seminars, "Before you knew it, it took four full weeks to give all the seminars, and nobody was retiring." Thus, Pacific repeatedly asked Orman back to give the seminars.

In the interim, Orman said she had specialized in an investment vehicle called "single premium whole life." She loved this form of investment and described it "as a legal tax loophole." One day, as she was driving and happened to be listening to a San Francisco radio station, a financial advisor was discussing single premium whole life. This individual's explanation of the investment strategy was incorrect, so Orman called the radio station's program director and told him so.

Following Orman's complaint to the program director, she was invited to the radio station to host a show on single premium whole life. At that point, her media career was born. She was so impressive as a radio financial counselor that several invitations were extended to her to be a guest host of financial advice programs at various radio stations. Orman enjoyed her job as a financial advisor, and she also loved being on the radio. Not surprisingly, she became proficient at hosting financial advice programs on radio. Orman, in essence, developed a passion for both aspects of her career: hosting radio shows and dealing directly with clients.

Suze Orman: Like What You Do

On the other hand, after a few years of conducting frequent seminars without any financial rewards to Orman, Pacific Gas and Electric suddenly laid off ten thousand employees. All of this business from the company was up for grabs. The other brokers, who had been reluctant to give free seminars initially, suddenly became interested in becoming financial advisors to the employees who were either forced to retire or laid off. Her colleagues were told, "No thanks. Suze's our girl." She was well rewarded financially because of her efforts and persistence. The Pacific employees she counseled also did well. Orman became one of the most successful brokers at Merrill.

Orman then sued Merrill to recover her investment that had been illegally lost by the company's unscrupulous broker. As the case proceeded, Orman found that Merrill could not fire her while the case was in progress. Merrill decided to settle out of court. The company paid her back all the money she had lost, with interest. She in turn repaid all the money she owed to all of those who had loaned her the money for her restaurant project.

The business from Pacific culminated in a successful career for Orman, which encompassed the establishment of her own company, writing books, and a foray into television as a guest and host of programs. Orman is a best-selling author of financial advice books. She has written eight books, six of which have been on *The New York Times* bestseller list. She is a nationally acclaimed TV personality. Orman has been a guest on CNN's *Anderson Cooper 360*, NBC's *Today*, and other programs. She now has her own TV show on CNBC, *The Suze Orman Show*. It is certain that she will be making many more strides in the future.

* * *

In reviewing Orman's activities, she was driven to make phenomenal achievements, and she initially harbored aspirations of owning a restaurant; however, she stumbled upon her real passion for the financial services industry. She had been a waitress for over six years—so she was conversant with the restaurant industry. She thought she was passionate about the prospect of owning and running a restaurant. Orman, perhaps, was passionate about customer service at that point, making her failure to enter the restaurant industry a blessing in disguise. Due to her proficiency in customer service, her customers had rallied around her in support of her aspirations. They had supported her with their investment of $50,000. Although Orman was driven to success, she came upon her niche and subsequently her passion for financial services unexpectedly. This exemplifies a manifestation of a niche and passion.

The exploration of Orman's drive to become successful uncovers her resilience in pursuing a job interview that was deemed out of her league following the loss of her seed money for her restaurant venture. Her incredible drive led her to interview for a job in a predominantly male environment that required a high aptitude in math, finance, and a proficiency in academics—areas in which she was deficient. Orman was challenged and therefore driven by two factors: Her manager, a male chauvinist, told her that women did not belong in the financial services industry; he also told her that she would not survive in the industry beyond six months. In essence, Orman's ego kicked in to augment her drive in her bid to overcome this stereotype and prove her manager wrong. This became a powerful driving force that would propel her to enormous heights. So, she set out to prove that not only was she going to gain admission into the financial services profession, but she was also going to excel in it.

Orman had discovered a new passion; she conducted seminars without pay and enjoyed it tremendously, which was not typical. Most people will experience a loss of interest in a job if there is an absence of immediate financial compensation in it. Hence, most jobs have a reward system based on regular paychecks combined with incentive plans. Those jobs whose rewards are based solely on incentives or commissions are fewer than jobs with regular rewards and are often taken by those who are willing to work in an environment where their rewards are based solely on merit. Working in this environment could in most instances be symbolic of the existence of a niche and passion.

Passionate individuals are easy to identify. Those potential retirees who had been to Orman's seminars could tell that not only did she enjoy giving the seminars, but she also had an aptitude for it. She cared about them. She was passionate about her job, and she was proficient in it. The decision to turn over all of the business from the laid-off employees at Pacific to Orman was an easy one. Orman met all the criteria of being passionate about her profession: She enjoyed her work; she educated herself in it; she was always prepared for the seminars at the gas company in spite of the absence of foreseeable financial reward; and she had become an expert in her profession.

Success magazine reported Orman as saying that there are three principles that comprise the key to her success: "Find your niche and become an expert; do the work; like who you are and what you do." There is a complimentary relationship between niche and passion. In striving to become an expert in our niche, it is essential that we acquire the passion for that niche, and in doing so, we will become the best or one of the best in that activity. Niche is defined by *Merriam-Webster's Collegiate Dictionary, Tenth Edition* as "an activity for which a person is best fitted." If we are best fitted for an activity, but we lack the passion to become an expert in that activity, then we will never maximize our potential in it. Liking what we do is a basic component of passion, and liking ourselves is a factor of our self-esteem and spirituality. The choice is ours to utilize the best methods of enhancing our spirituality and self-esteem to engender the best results for us.

A niche or an aptitude for an activity without passion, which entails practice, preparation, and education, can render us dormant in it; hence, Thomas A. Edison said, "Genius is one percent inspiration and ninety-nine percent perspiration." I once heard a Grammy Award-winning star say in a television interview that on one of his recent visits to his old neighborhood, he encountered an individual whom he considered to possess a superior talent in music to his during their early years. He further stated that this individual did not make accomplishments in music despite his talent. The artist then attributed his accomplishments in music and good fortune to divine powers. Be that as it may, anyone who knows this musician will find that he exudes a tremendous drive, passion, tenacity, resilience, and confidence. These attributes were primarily responsible for his success in music. According to *Merriam-Webster's Collegiate Dictionary, Tenth Edition*, passion is

Drive to Passion

defined as "a strong liking to some activity." Choosing an activity for which we are best suited is as important as having "a strong liking" for it.

CHAPTER 7
Barack Obama: Life Beyond His Father's Dilemma

Barack Obama was raised by a single parent and his maternal grandparents, and through sheer drive and passion, he rose from relative obscurity to become a U.S. senator and the first African-American president of the United States. He is a resilient and deliberate president, who is also an intellectual. Some in the media have portrayed him as being overly measured at times because of his contemplative demeanor. He was able to refurbish some of America's foreign image and relationships and to stop the ominous downward spiral of the U.S. economy prompted by the collapse of the housing market and the ensuing financial crisis. It remains to be seen if he can pull the economy up to the status of prosperity.

Who were the major influences in Obama's life? He was raised by his grandparents and to some degree by his mother, who was single for most of his childhood. She had two brief, failed marriages. He was influenced by the limited contact he had with his father as well as his images of him. Obama was also influenced by his contact with his stepfather when he lived in Indonesia. There was no sign earlier in Obama's childhood that he was going to make history by becoming the first black president of the United States. His drives stem from the cumulative effects of his upbringing and his experiences with his mother, grandparents, father, stepfather, and mentors. Obama experienced a transformation as he transitioned from Occidental College to Columbia University. This change he owed to the principles and ideas instilled in him by his mother. It was during this time that he became more pensive and studious. The culmination of his new environment and his various drives orchestrated his initial quest for his passion. He would relocate from New York to Chicago in his bid to further the pursuit of his objective.

Obama was driven by the need to avoid the mistakes made by his father. In his autobiography, *Dreams from My Father*, he referred to his father as an alcoholic, a womanizer, "an abusive husband," and a "defeated lonely bureaucrat," who was penalized by his superiors for being outspoken. He set out to learn from his father's predicament and to pattern himself into a person of his own choosing—an individual of drive and passion who would make a difference.

Obama was also driven by the need to avoid the mundane existence of his grandfather. In his autobiography, he said his grandfather was "always searching for that new start, always running away from the familiar." In other words, he never established himself in a profession he liked. "The awkward mix of sophistication and provincialism, the rawness of emotion that could make him at once tactless and easily bruised [were among his characteristics]," Obama further said. His grandfather and his peers were "men who embraced the notion of freedom and individualism and the open road without always knowing its price, and whose enthusiasms could as easily lead to the cowardice of McCarthyism." Obama's intellectual pursuits and the molding of his character could be said to also stem from wanting to be a man who was more certain than his grandfather of what he wanted out of life.

Obama is one of the most intellectual presidents of the United States. The driving force behind his great intellect is evident. His grandfather lacked both intellectualism and accomplishment, so he chose to acquire both of these attributes. His father, though an intellectual, was unable to realize his full potential. Obama emulated his father's intellect while decrying and rejecting his shortcomings, choosing to succeed in politics and government—areas where his father had failed. He also chose to pursue other positive traits that were lacking in his father. He is not a womanizer; he is affable and liked by those around him.

Some of the individuals featured in this book emulated their fathers' characteristics to a certain extent, and at the same time, similar to Obama, they sought to avoid some of their fathers' shortcomings. Winston Churchill loved and admired his father in spite of his weaknesses. Although he aspired to follow in his father's footsteps in politics and intellectual prowess, he was still cognizant of his father's mistakes and wanted to prove that he could accomplish more than his father intellectually and otherwise. Sidney Poitier was cognizant of his father's limitations and mistakes. His father, though an honest and forthright man, was stuck in abject poverty, so Poitier resolved to be assertive, resilient, and a master of his own fate. Abraham Lincoln wanted more for himself than being a poor farmer like his father. Although he learned his work ethic from him while doing manual labor on the farm, he detested the fate to which his father was relegated, so he sought to become an intellectual and a politician. Kennedy sought opulence and recognition, which was in sharp contrast to his father's middle-class existence. All of these individuals, including Obama, derived some of their drives from the most influential people in their lives. As a result of their different drives, they went on to identify their passion successfully.

The drive to make something of ourselves can stem from several avenues, which include: wanting to emulate our parents, seeking to avoid the mistakes of a parent, desiring to prove something to ourselves or a group of people, needing to make a difference in the world, wanting to be the best at what we do, and seeking to be wealthy and famous.

* * *

Obama, the offspring of an interracial marriage between a Kenyan foreign student and a Caucasian woman from Kansas, spent his childhood in Djakarta, Indonesia, his stepfather's country of birth. Similar to his father, his stepfather, Lolo had also been a foreign student at the University of Hawaii in Honolulu. Obama and his mother moved back to Indonesia with Lolo when he had to return home abruptly. His stepfather and his mother had married after her divorce from his father, who had won a scholarship to Harvard University to work on his graduate degree in economics. Obama's father had then gone off to Harvard, leaving him and his mother in Hawaii.

In Indonesia, the standard of living for Obama, his mother, and his stepfather was close to that of the indigenous Indonesians. It was definitely not at the level of the well-positioned, white expatriate officials at the American embassy where his mother worked, teaching English to Indonesian businessmen. Although his mother worked at the embassy, she was neither entitled to the luxurious fringe benefits the embassy officials enjoyed nor the affluence experienced by the foreign oil company employees and other similar employees of entities where there was a high concentration of white expatriates.

As a child, Obama did not have a yearning for the higher standard of living experienced by other American children; he was immersed in his childish quests, the Indonesian culture, and the day-to-day activities of his new environment, similar to a typical Indonesian child. Obama encapsulates this in his autobiography with the following statement: "With Lolo, I learned how to eat small green chili peppers raw with dinner (plenty of rice), and, away from the dinner table, I was introduced to dog meat (tough), snake meat (tougher), and roasted grasshopper (crunchy)."

Obama was enrolled in a regular school in Djakarta. His mother and his stepfather did not have the means to send him to the International School, where the sons and daughters of diplomats and other foreign noteworthy individuals were educated. The quality of education Obama was getting, especially in the English language, became a subject of great concern to his mother—so much so that she supplemented his education with a correspondence course in English from the United States.

A popular story often told by Obama, even before he became president, was that while in Djakarta, every weekday his mother would come into his room at 4:00 A.M., feed him breakfast, and proceed to go over his English lessons with him for at least three hours before he went to school. Whenever he would complain of being tired and make excuses for not wanting to go through with his work, or when he would claim to be too sleepy to stay up for the lessons, she would say to him, "This is no picnic for me either, buster."

Once, Obama's mother was frightened by his disappearance and subsequent re-emergence after a few hours. Upon his arrival, he discovered that she was already organizing a search party for him. She was both furious and relieved to see him. He had been out with a friend hiking at their family farm. Shortly thereafter, a heavy rainfall had ensued, creating what he referred to in his autobiography as a "terrific place to mudslide," which caused him to sustain an ugly cut from the barbed wire that was nearby. The cut ran from his wrist to his elbow and was wrapped with a muddy sock. His mother took him to the hospital, where it was stitched.

Obama's mother inculcated in him her midwestern American virtues: a sense of right and wrong. She did the best she could as a white mother trying to instill in her black child confidence, pride in his race, and basic American principles of freedom. She pointed out to him, on more than one occasion, that she thought Harry Belafonte was the best-looking man on the planet. She also talked about how his father, as a foreign student, did not cut corners; he worked diligently, to the point of excellence.

The reasons Obama's mother decided to send him back to the United States to live with his grandparents were varied. She wanted the best education for him, and she could not afford it in Indonesia. There was a volatility and lack of temperance in the Indonesian environment that fostered her uneasiness because it threatened Obama's safety in a way that could have been obvious only to a maternal instinct. The incident that had led her to initiate a search party for him was no exception to this precariousness that she feared. The culmination of these factors prompted her decision to send him back to America.

Prior to his departure, Obama's mother sat down with him and outlined her reasons for sending him back to the United States to live with his grandparents. She had exhausted all of the lessons in the English correspondence course she had acquired and wanted him in an American school, which she could not afford in Djakarta. She underscored other incentives Obama would have for going back to America: He could have as much ice cream as he wanted, and he would not have to wake up at 4:00 A.M. anymore. Obama's mother also told him that she and his younger maternal half-sister would be joining him for the holidays that Christmas.

When Obama arrived at the airport in the United States, his white maternal grandparents were there to pick him up. His grandfather had left the furniture sales industry and switched careers to the life insurance sales profession. Obama's vivid recollections of his grandfather's career as an insurance salesman helped shape his perceptions of a job without passion. He observed him undergo a certain level of apprehension as Sunday evening approached. His grandfather would usually get him and his grandmother to leave the living room, and then he would reluctantly pick up the phone and try to set up sales appointments for the following day. Obama observed his grandfather go through what seemed like an endless torture stemming from one rejection after another as he tried to set up his sales appointments. He summed up his grandfather's predicament in the following words: "He was unable to convince himself that people needed what he was selling." This was indicative of his lack of passion for his job. Not surprisingly, he did not do very well as a life insurance salesman. Obama's grandmother worked at a bank in a mid-level management position and was the breadwinner of the family.

According to Obama, his grandfather harbored dreams of writing poetry and painting. He had "the book of poems he had started to write, the sketch that would soon bloom into a painting." Those were activities about which he was passionate, which turned into unrealized dreams that would go to his grave with him. Could Obama's grandfather have pursued his passion in the fields of poetry and painting even though he lacked the necessary skills and formal education in those fields? If they comprised his niche and passion (with the appropriate drive), he could have sought the education, practice, and preparation necessary to achieve proficiency and expertise in them in a manner similar to Sidney Poitier, who had no formal education but put in the requisite effort to attain his goals. This is an example of how passion, education, and practice have an intertwining relationship. In essence, people who are ardently in pursuit of their passion seek the necessary skills and education to bring their passion to fruition. The more we are convinced of our passion, and the more we are willing to engage in education and practice to attain the level of proficiency needed to be an expert in our field, the less likely we are to fail or be outdone by competition.

The situation regarding Obama's grandfather exemplifies a scenario endemic in most jobs. If we do not like and believe in what we are doing, there is a good chance we will function on a level of mediocrity in it. If, on the other hand, we enjoy and believe in what we are doing, we have a good chance of becoming passionate about it.

Obama's grandmother—who initially took a position as a secretary at a local bank, primarily, in Obama's words, "to help defray the cost of my unexpected birth"—also harbored some dreams. She would eventually rise to the position of vice president at the bank, the prospect of which, at that period in history, would neither sit well with his grandfather nor make for total harmony between them, given that she became the breadwinner of the family. Toot, as Obama knew her, divulged to him her own dreams. She had always dreamed of owning a home "with a white picket fence." Similar to his grandfather, whom he called Gramps, Toot's dreams never materialized—neither did she indicate to him any passion that could have been fueled by this drive to own a house "with a white picket fence." Toot neither worked in a liberal era with regard to the height of the glass ceiling for women nor possessed a college degree. She was caught in a dichotomy between the pride and enthusiasm she had for her job and her awareness of her limitations at the bank. Also, Toot was caught in the same dreams in which a majority of people are caught: dreams of the trappings of success, without a clue about the exact passion that would spur the success. In the case of Gramps, it was his dreams of his passion for poetry and painting without the drive to fuel it.

In contrast to the unrealized dreams of Obama's grandparents, the best dreams that will inevitably guarantee success are the dreams that are accompanied by specific passions that can be fueled by those dreams. Unlike his grandparents, Obama would choose to muster the courage and drive to pursue his passion in

Drive to Passion

public service to the underserved, in making a difference in the lives of others, and in seeking power. He armed himself with a great education before seeking a career in politics. Obama's rationale and aspirations consisted of being the best grassroots organizer there was, getting the best education possible, becoming one of the best politicians, and acquiring the power that comes with politics.

Similar to Obama, General Colin Powell sought his passion in his career because he knew all about passion. He made history more than once: He was the first black secretary of State, the first black chairman of the Joint Chiefs of Staff, and the first black national security adviser. He was passionate about military service and public service; hence, he had such an outstanding career in both arenas. Powell, however, once disclosed to Larry King on CNN that he had been misconstrued by the media all along with regard to the prospect of his presidential bid. It had been rumored that he had dismissed the idea of running for the presidency of the United States because his wife, fearing for his safety, had been opposed to the idea. Powell disclosed to King that the real reason he never ran for president was that he truly had no passion for politics. In examining Powell's attributes, we can conclude that his recognition of the fact that he had neither the drive nor the passion to become a politician put him in a class by himself, in terms of his greatness. It is not too often that people recognize ahead of time that they have no passion for one of the highest positions in the world. We have seen some terrible past presidents who absolutely had no drive or passion for the job other than a desire for the trappings of the office. To this day, quite a few people, including journalists and politicians, still contend that Powell would have made a great president.

* * *

Following Obama's arrival at his grandparents' home from Indonesia, he enrolled in school. Punahou Academy, an elite prep school in Honolulu, was the school of choice for his grandparents. It was the school to which Obama had gained admission upon his return, and his first day in school was fast approaching. This made

Gramps and Toot proud. They both had reached a stage in their lives when most people embark upon a quiet resignation to their lot in life, resorting to living vicariously through their offspring. Gramps was so proud of Obama's admission into Punahou that he told all his friends about it, having been instrumental in his grandson's admission into the school by approaching his boss, who used his influence as an alumnus of the school to secure the admission.

Obama met his first day of school with the same sense of trepidation pervasive among most children transferring from out of town to a new school. Gramps walked him to school. They met someone while waiting for classes to begin—a boy named Frederick to whom Gramps introduced Obama as Barry. Upon Gramps' departure, both boys headed to class.

Once they were seated in class, the teacher, Miss Hefty, introduced herself and then proceeded to take attendance. Once she got to Obama, she called out his full name, Barack Obama, which immediately elicited giggles from the other children in class. According to Obama, Frederick immediately said to him, "I thought your name was Barry." Miss Hefty overheard that, and asked Obama if he preferred to be called Barry. She proceeded to tell the class that Barack was a beautiful name. She further explained that she had learned from Obama's grandfather that his father was from Kenya. Miss Hefty told the class that she had lived and taught school in Kenya.

Miss Hefty's explanations and attempts to silence the boys and girls in the class with her adulations for Obama and Kenya had the opposite effect, which heightened Obama's nervousness about his first day of school. Following her explanations, she asked him what tribe his father was from. By this time, the class was really worked up; more giggles ensued, which turned into laughter and chaos. Obama reluctantly answered, "Luo," in a subdued tone after the teacher managed to control the class. To make matters worse, one of the boys echoed the tribal name "in a loud hoot, like the sound of a monkey," Obama said. Due to the children's inability to contain themselves, Miss Hefty admonished their rude behavior. Embarrassment would be an understatement in attempting to describe Obama's feelings at that point; he was dismayed. As if Obama had not had enough humiliation for one day, one of the girls in class asked him if she could touch his hair and was seemingly upset when he turned down her request. Another kid in class, a boy, wanted to know if his father was a cannibal. Obama's initial sense of trepidation and reservation about his first day of school turned out to be justified.

Life at school for Obama gradually began to take a fairly normal course except for some minor incidents. His friendship with the other African-American in his class—a dark-skinned and plump black girl, whose camaraderie his classmates misconstrued as a very close friendship—resulted in a teasing episode by the entire class, who referred to them as boyfriend and girlfriend. He wound up hurting her feelings through his vehement assertions that they were not an item. The second situation was normal for a ten-year-old boy who was seeking acceptance and perhaps an elevation in status in his peer group. He lied to his classmates by telling them that his father was a prince.

Not long after his return from Indonesia, Obama received word from his grandmother that his father was coming from Kenya to visit. He would arrive two weeks after his mother's arrival from Indonesia for the Christmas holidays. He had been in a car accident and was coming to the United States as part of his convalescence from the accident. This was a major event in Obama's life; he would finally get the opportunity to meet the father he had never known. His reaction to the news of his father's impending visit was not one of exhilaration; instead, he embraced the news with a sense of apprehension.

Obama did not know how to prepare for his father's arrival. His mother, whose arrival from Indonesia for the Christmas holidays preceded his father's arrival, spent time with him, imparting whatever knowledge she had about Kenya and the Luo tribe. She attempted to paint an image to him that was rich in history by linking the origins of the Luo people to ancient Egypt. Obama even went to the library in a futile attempt to research the Luo tribe and its connection with ancient Egypt. The more he read, the more difficult it was to ascertain a connection, and he left the library disappointed by his inability to establish a direct link between the Luo and ancient Egypt.

The period directly preceding and following the senior Obama's visit was marked by the rattling of the mundane structure Obama had grown accustomed to in living with his grandparents. His father's arrival meant that he would have to adjust to the prolonged presence of another adult whom he did not really know. The fact that his father would have a separate apartment did not lessen his anxiety. Obama's father had an intellectual power, and its effect was keenly felt by the entire family—a power that stopped short of intimidation. Following his arrival, Obama said, "Gramps became more vigorous and thoughtful, my mother more bashful; even Toot, smoked out of the foxhole in her bedroom, would start sparring with him about politics or finance."

Obama's father even attempted to discipline Obama on occasion. This Obama met with quiet resistance. When his father abruptly cut short his television time, referring to television as a machine that was an impediment to his schoolwork, Obama's mother came to his defense, citing the Christmas holiday season as a reason for him to catch up on a Christmas show. According to Obama, his father retorted by saying to his mother, "Anna, this is nonsense. If the boy has done his work for tomorrow, he can begin on his next day's assignments. Or the assignments he will have when he returns from the holidays." Then, turning to Obama, he admonished him: "I tell you, Barry, you do not work as hard as you should. Go now, before I get angry at you."

Shortly after his father's arrival, Obama received the nerve-shattering news that his father had been invited by Miss Hefty, his teacher, to speak to his class. According to Obama, with a heightened sense of trepidation, he spent part of his days and nights imagining the faces of his "classmates when they heard about mud huts" he thought his father would be discussing in his speech. He also had another worry: His "lies [would be] exposed, the painful jokes afterward."

The day of the senior Obama's speech to his son's class finally arrived. The teacher introduced him to the class, with a mention that he was on a visit to the United States from Kenya. Much to Obama's surprise, the boys and girls in the class appeared attentive and eager to hear what his father had to say.

Drive to Passion

The senior Obama gave an outstanding speech to the boys and girls in his son's class—a speech that would set a precedent for Obama's future oratory skills. In that short class period, he covered Kenya's struggle for independence, which he skillfully compared to the American fight for independence. He drew an analogy between slavery in Kenya and slavery here in the United States. He talked about the wild animals that wandered through their natural habitat in Kenya and talked about his tribe, the Luo—its hierarchy of leadership, respect for elders, rites of passage for young men, and how people there were just as hardworking as people here in America. At the end of the speech, the senior Obama received a resounding applause from the entire class. Obama was told by his teacher that his father was "impressive." According to Obama, the boy who had previously asked if his father was a cannibal said to him after the speech, "Your dad is pretty cool."

Toward the end of his visit, Obama and his father had a better understanding of each other. It was as if they had come to terms with their roles in each other's life. His father understood that he had been an absentee father who had suddenly re-emerged. He was trying hard to garner respect from his son and be the father of an American child who needed discipline, a father figure, and to know from whence he came. Obama, at that point, reached the understanding that he was his father's child, although he had been raised almost single-handedly by an American mother. There was an unspoken, though clear, understanding between father and son. His father recognized that his son would not be relegated to the background and that he needed reassurance, attention, and love from him. Obama had a better appreciation for his father; he momentarily came to terms with his father's absence and realized that he was trying to play his role as a father with him in his own way. Obama encapsulated their times together in his autobiography: "For brief spells in the day I will lie beside him, the two of us alone in the apartment sublet from a retired old woman . . . and I read my book while he reads his."

Just before the end of his visit, Obama's father presented his son with a forty-five record consisting of songs from his homeland. He engaged him and the entire family in a dancing session, with the songs from the record oozing out of Gramps and Toot's stereo. He recalled his father's slender frame moving to the pulsating beat of the song emanating from the stereo as he let out a high-pitched shriek of enjoyment. Obama tried to move to the beat of the music like his father, but to no avail. Those were his last memories of his father. Soon after that, his father would be forever gone, never to be seen by him again.

* * *

Five years had elapsed since his father's visit, and Obama was now in high school, had a best friend, Ray, and had moved in with his mother. She was separated from her husband and was back from Indonesia, pursing a master's degree in anthropology at the local university. She was a single woman raising two children on higher education grants, and without a doubt, on a very tight budget. Life was stressful for her and her children.

Obama's high school years consisted of his emergence as a skilled basketball player and his friendships with his best friend, Ray, and some of the other black teenagers who were beginning to move into the area. Obama described his emergence in the world of basketball in the following words: "And I could play basketball, with a consuming passion that would always exceed my limited talent." Apparently, his niche in basketball was not strong enough to sustain his passion.

Obama, as a teenager in a unique situation, observed and coveted the popularity of the young black men who had been recruited to play basketball for the University of Hawaii. He observed how they were cheered on the court by many and how they winked at the girls on the sidelines. At that point, he and his friends were laden with adolescent maladies that would exacerbate his own confused feelings about some of life's challenges. Obama had the enormous responsibility of trying to single-handedly raise himself as a black man in a world where his immediate family comprised Caucasians; this was a daunting task.

Racism, his biracial heritage, and other adolescent issues were beginning to surface in Obama's mind; he sought answers to these tangled feelings from books. He was trying to handle

Drive to Passion

his identity as a young black adult in a white environment. He immersed himself in books he felt would shed light on some of his unanswered questions and, at the same time, give him a better perspective on his dialectic feelings, spurred by race and adolescent hormonal changes. He read books from the likes of James Baldwin, W.E.B. DuBois, Ralph Ellison, and Langston Hughes, but he failed to achieve the solace he sought in these books. He saw in these writers, similar to himself, a degree of fallibility and the inability to relieve the pain thrust upon them by society. They all exhibited the presence of their anguish in different ways: one went on a self-imposed exile to Europe; another retired to Africa; yet another immersed himself in the depths of the enclaves of Harlem. If Obama expected a direct answer to the questions stemming from his peculiar situation as a biracial adolescent being raised by a white single mother and white grandparents, he certainly did not get it from his readings. The authors who had written the books he read did not have any direct answers for him. Like all humans, they had their own demons to fight. However, what Obama did gain from his readings was the unending desire for knowledge and an incessant stream of questions to which he sought answers. He would continue on his quest for answers from mentors, friends, and more books.

The elusiveness of the answers that Obama sought was exacerbated by an argument one morning between his grandmother and grandfather. Gramps was reluctant to drive Toot to work. She had been catching the bus to work. The sudden adjustment of having to drive Toot to work every morning was a bit difficult for Gramps to swallow. Obama intervened and tried to end the commotion by volunteering to drive his grandmother to work. He thought that his gesture would bring a resolution to the problem. Little did he know that the problem was a bit more complex than that.

The circumstance leading to the argument was manifested in stages. Gramps told Obama that Toot had been accosted at the bus stop, while waiting for the bus the previous day, by a man who had asked her for a dollar. He experienced momentary relief when he thought he had heard the entire story. Toot then interjected by saying the man who had asked her for money was aggressive. She told Obama she felt threatened by his aggressiveness and said she was certain he would have attacked her had the bus not arrived right in the midst of this incident. The panhandler had been rather insistent in his demands for more money after she had given him a dollar, Toot added.

It was not the end of the episode, for no sooner had Toot finished with her side of the story than Gramps further disclosed to Obama that Toot, who had been approached by panhandlers previously, was so agitated this time because the man who had approached her at the bus stop was black. Obama vividly captured his reaction to this information in his book: "The words were like a fist in my stomach, and I wobbled to regain my composure." The incident between Obama's grandfather and grandmother further complicated his situation and feelings toward them. His grandmother—whom he loved and who was helping to raise him—harbored racial biases. This was hard for him to accept.

Obama sought solace in a mentor's wisdom—a friend of his grandfather's, who was black, and a poet by vocation. Frank was a knowledgeable, older black man who had become good friends with Gramps over the years. Frank symbolized to him an individual capable of the type of empathy that his grandfather lacked by virtue of his race as a white man. Obama went to Frank that day seeking solace, empathy, and advice from someone capable of helping his young mind decipher some of life's dichotomies and paradoxes. Frank helped Obama make sense of the situation between his grandmother and the black panhandler. He shared his wisdom with him. He told him that although Gramps was doing his best to be a good man and a good grandfather to him, he would never understand what it truly felt like to be black because he had never been black—something all whites, no matter how hard they tried to empathize, will always lack. By the same token, Frank told Obama, his grandmother had the right to be scared of the black panhandler because she knew that blacks were downtrodden and as such had a basis for hatred against whites. Frank presented more than one side of the situation to Obama. He instilled in him empathy and the ability to see things from different perspectives.

Obama's mother was instrumental in the molding of his character at the initial stages of his life and in his adolescent years when all of his turmoil with his identity as a biracial child were setting in. His tumultuous adolescent period coincided with his mother's return from the completion of her fieldwork for her graduate degree. Upon her return, she observed a certain degree of shiftlessness in his behavior. It was at this time that he began to have a brush with what he referred to in his book as "getting high." Obama was in his senior year in high school, a time when teenagers exhibit their independence and other characteristics associated with adolescence. He was also at the stage when young people generally decide on a college to attend, a time when they hopefully go off to an institution of higher learning to arm themselves with the tools necessary to make a successful transition into adulthood. Obama's mother continued to instill in him a sense of direction. Had she relented, Obama may not have had the drive and passion to become the first black president of the United States.

Obama was accepted into several good colleges, but he chose Occidental College in Los Angeles for the following reason, according to him: "mainly because I'd met a girl from Brentwood while she was vacationing in Hawaii with her family." Obama hoped that he would establish a relationship with her upon his arrival there. For a young person in the initial stages of teenage independence, this reason for choosing a college was not out of place.

Prior to his departure to Occidental College, Obama paid Frank a visit again to seek counsel. According to Obama, Frank advised him in the following words: "They'll train you to want what you don't need." He further admonished Obama not to leave his people behind or get too caught up in the trappings of success to the extent of forgetting to think for himself. Obama said in his book that Frank capped off his advice to him by saying, "Keep your eyes open. Stay awake." At that time, the full impact of Frank's words may not have resonated with Obama; but as time went by, some of those words of wisdom began to reverberate with him. These words helped to shape how he would pattern his life from the time he graduated from college in New York, to when he would embark on his objective of becoming a grassroots organizer in Chicago, fighting for the rights of the poor.

Upon Obama's arrival at Occidental, he demonstrated the rambunctiousness of a typical teenager who was gaining independence from his parents for the first time; however, he also cultivated some good qualities there. His level of intellectual awareness increased. He became actively engaged in the quest for intellectually stimulating discussions, so much so that, according to him, he often "discussed neocolonialism, Franz Fanon, Eurocentrism, and patriarchy" with his friends. By the same token, he and his friends wore leather jackets, smoked cigarettes, and put out their cigarette butts on the carpet in the dormitory. In essence, Obama and his friends exhibited traits that comprised a dichotomy between a spirit of rebelliousness and a growing sense of intellectual prowess—qualities that are ubiquitous among youth.

Life at Occidental would be different from life at Columbia University in New York, where Obama would later transfer after a few years at Occidental. His decision to transfer to Columbia would have a major impact on the strides he would make later on in life, not only because it was a better school, but because it was for him an environment that fostered solace and the opportunity for much deliberation about his future. Conversely, life at Occidental for Obama engendered a set of experiences that he would have been unable to acquire at Columbia. At Occidental, Obama was active in campus life. He had a great degree of camaraderie with the other black students. On the other hand, he was also eclectic in his choice of friends, a quality he would take to the Illinois Senate and the U.S. Senate.

Similar to other offspring of interracial unions, especially those of white and black parents, Obama continued to undergo an internal dialectic with regard to his identity and race. He later emerged from it seeking to be strongly identified with the black students at Occidental. He did not want to be considered a "sellout." Frank's advice, in which he stressed to Obama the importance of not forgetting his people, resonated with him. A black person can be considered a "sellout" if he embraces the white culture with such alacrity that he forgets his culture and begins isolating and ostracizing himself from the black community—not wanting to reach back and help lift other blacks. Obama did not

Drive to Passion

want to be seen in this light—not after his conversation with his mentor, Frank.

Occidental could be said to be instrumental in the molding of Obama's passion for politics. He began taking a more active role in politics, while simultaneously experiencing an awareness of his excitement for the subject. Obama also made a significant discovery: People were interested in what he had to say. At Occidental, he got involved in "drafting letters to the faculty, printing up flyers, arguing strategy," Obama said, and inviting outside speakers like "the representatives of the African National Congress to speak on campus."

The rally organized by the students on campus during the trustees' meeting, in an attempt to dramatize the situation in South Africa, epitomized Obama's oratory skill. He was to give a speech to depict the plight of the activists in South Africa. During the speech, he was to be pulled away from the stage by other students after a few minutes, in an attempt to portray an activist being hauled off by the police. His speech, which was also supposed to be a simple opening remark, wound up being the highlight of the occasion. Obama mounted the stage, stepped up to the microphone like an athlete in the zone and proceeded to speak, remembering, fleetingly, his father's excellent speech to his class in Hawaii. It was as if, at that moment, he was separated from his voice; he heard his voice ring out to the audience. Suddenly the noisy audience was at a standstill; there was absolute silence. "There's a struggle going on," he heard himself say. "It's happening an ocean away. But it's a struggle that touches each and every one of us. Whether we know it or not. . . . A struggle that demands we choose sides. Not between black and white . . . a choice between right and wrong." Obama had much to say, to such an extent that when the two students who were supposed to haul him off the stage after a few minutes approached the stage, he was not ready to be removed. So, the act of Obama being removed from the stage became an actual event rather than an act. In the midst of this activity came a boisterous applause from the audience, and accolades later followed from his colleagues and friends for his great speech.

Unbeknown to Obama, a passion was born after he delivered his speech, but similar to Sidney Poitier, who wrongly assumed his first major theatrical performance was an absolute disaster, Obama thought he had not done that well with his speech. When Obama's fellow students gave him compliments on his speech, which they thought had come from his heart, he brushed them aside with self-deprecating comments about it, implying that it had all been an act on his part. Obama finally came to terms with the fact that he had delivered a great speech when he was made aware of it by one of his colleagues and fellow students, Regina.

Regina could have possibly served as the catalyst that spurred an introspection in Obama, enabling him to look at all aspects of his life. She told him that she was disappointed by his selfishness in attempting to repudiate his great oratory skills. She implored him to come to terms with it, and to look at his skills from a realistic perspective. Regina also lashed out at Obama regarding his rather childish and rebellious ways: He and his friends were boisterous at odd hours of the night and littered the halls, leaving the garbage for someone else to clean. She invariably led him to a more serious realization of what college truly entailed.

Occidental had initiated a transfer program with Columbia University in New York, and Obama astutely took advantage of it. He based this decision on the premise that he needed to be in an environment with more black people, where he could make a difference in some way; he needed to make a clean break and subsequently a transition from his rather immature and self-indulgent lifestyle at Occidental to a more responsible one at Columbia. He had been struggling with his own identity and was finally beginning to see himself in a more positive light following the lecture he had received from Regina. Obama was never in doubt of his racial identity; rather, his struggles stemmed from the absence of a black male father figure in his life.

Prior to his departure to Columbia, Obama embarked on a journey to Pakistan because he had a propensity for travel. He did so with his Pakistani friend at Occidental. He visited the rural villages in Pakistan, and it enabled him to come face to face with the class distinction between the peasants of Pakistan and their masters—a phenomenon that is absent in America.

He experienced the type of abject poverty he had encountered at an early age in Indonesia. This trip was good for him because it enabled him to formulate part of his drive: helping the poor.

Obama's awareness of his passions came relatively early in his life. This awareness served as a turning point for him. His decision to transfer to Columbia University and the pursuit of his passion came simultaneously. He knew he had an aptitude for delivering convincing speeches. He also knew he had a niche in politics and the ability to reach out to people with his assertions and opinions. It was then that he seriously began to harbor the notion of becoming involved in politics or public service in some capacity.

Our passion may stem from activities for which we have received compliments or activities for which we have an aptitude. The compliments given to Obama for delivering a great speech at Occidental are an example of getting accolades for an activity about which we are passionate. Also, similar to Obama's mention of his affinity for politics and his discernment of the fact that people were always interested in listening to his ideas, we can recognize our capabilities in activities for which we may have a niche. Even if others disagree with our judgment of our own capabilities and strengths in those activities, as long as we have the conviction of our niche and passion in them, we should not allow ourselves to be deterred by the adverse opinions of others with regard to the pursuit of our passion.

Obama was not only influenced by his father's great speech in his school as a boy, but he was also driven by his perception of his father's status in public service in Kenya. He had an admiration for his father's intellect; he conjured up images of his father in his high government role in Kenya, talking to other government officials and important people, handling vital business, negotiating import deals, and giving orders to his subordinates. He wanted to be successful, just like his father. The speech given by his father played a role in the success of his first major speech at Occidental. His father's voice echoed in him briefly, in a flashback of his excellent speech in Hawaii to his class. This enabled Obama to drive his point across to the audience during the delivery of his speech at Occidental.

* * *

Obama's transition from Occidental to Columbia was not easy, given the differences between the impersonal atmosphere at Columbia and the small college environment at Occidental; however, it was positive. At Columbia, he experienced a certain degree of solitude, though not completely by design, which enabled him to apply himself to his studies. New York had its usually uninviting atmosphere. No matter how intensely Obama explored the communities in Harlem and Brooklyn to see if he could somehow fit in, he continued to harbor the feeling of looking in from the outside. Obama said of his changed demeanor and increased studiousness: "I ran three miles a day and fasted on Sundays. . . . I applied myself to my studies." His roommate even told him that he was becoming boring when he began opting out of going to bars with him.

Obama's mother and half-sister, Maya, paid him a visit in New York City, and while there, they found a changed young man. He had assumed a more serious disposition and had become diligent in his schoolwork. He had actually become a bookworm. He bought his sister novels to read and got angry with her for watching television instead of reading the novels. He was so well-read that he lectured his mother on the ills of neocolonialism: the ever-increasing dependency by the Third-World countries on the economic powers of the West.

During this visit from Obama's mother and Maya, Obama had the opportunity to receive a family history lesson from his mother, mainly about his father, their marriage, and his maternal and paternal grandparents. He learned that his mother had been accepted into the University of Chicago, but Gramps did not approve of her choice to go there. According to Obama's mother, she was the one who had divorced his father. The marriage had met some obstacles, including the disapproval of Obama's maternal and paternal grandparents. Obama, in his book, reported his mother as saying that his paternal grandfather had written Gramps a stern letter of disapproval of their marriage, saying, "He didn't want the Obama blood sullied by a white woman." Gramps had been enraged by this letter. Obama's father had responded by saying that he would go ahead with the marriage and would be returning to Kenya upon the completion of his studies with his wife and son. She added that Obama's grandfather had responded by "threatening to have his student visa revoked." To exacerbate the situation, Toot had been reading about the Mau-Mau rebellion, which had been spawned by the struggle for Kenya's independence from the British. She had been greatly perturbed by the ensuing violence and was concerned that her daughter's head would be cut off upon her arrival in Kenya and that Obama would be permanently taken away from them. There was also the issue of the legality of his father's first marriage. He had married his first wife in Kenya under the native law and custom without legal documents.

Obama's mother also gave Obama some insight into her romance with his father. Obama described her as saying that on one of their earlier dates, she was fully dressed and awaiting his arrival; as was typical of him, he was running late, and she had fallen asleep only to be awakened one hour later by three men staring down at her, including his father who said to them, "You see, gentlemen. I told you that she was a fine girl and that she would wait for me." At that moment, his mother's vulnerabilities, fears, and disappointments became apparent to Obama. It was as if she was a young, impulsive girl again who was pursuing love for the first time without the faintest idea of its full ramifications and demands.

Obama's mother gave Obama further insight into his father's actions. Shortly after his birth, his father had won two scholarships for his graduate studies, one from Harvard, which paid only his tuition, and the other from The New School in New York City, which was a full scholarship with tuition and board. He had stubbornly opted for Harvard even though it was a partial scholarship, saying he could not refuse an education from the best university in the world. Had Obama's father opted for The New School, with his full scholarship there, he could have afforded to take her and Obama with him, she asserted. On the other hand, Harvard's partial scholarship did not give him that option. So, they stayed behind while he went on to Harvard.

* * *

The period preceding Obama's graduation from Columbia was marked by his father's death. One of his aunts called from Kenya to inform him that his father had died in a car accident. His mother had loved his father without a doubt. Obama said that this was discernable by "her cry over the distance" on the telephone, when he called to inform her of his father's death. He mourned his father's death and saw him in his dreams. He encapsulated his mourning period and what the father he did not quite know meant to him in his book: "And I realized, perhaps for the first time, how even in his absence his strong image had given me some bulwark on which to grow up, an image to live up to, or disappoint."

It was also during the period prior to his graduation that Obama decided to pursue a career in community organizing, a career whose full functions he did not completely fathom and could not articulate to his fellow students and colleagues. They applauded him for his initiative in wanting to embark on such an altruistic and magnanimous endeavor; nevertheless, his classmates continued unflinchingly to mail out their graduate school applications.

Similar to Obama, whenever we formulate our goals and objectives, they should be based on our passion, whether or not they seem abstract, unattainable, or illogical. Most major accomplishments and discoveries initially sounded far-fetched, outlandish, and, perhaps, illogical to others, including, in some cases, friends and relatives of the individuals who made these achievements. Had these individuals conceded to the scoffers, naysayers, or skeptics, they would not have accomplished their dreams. Our dreams may parallel Obama's in that they may be abstract; nonetheless, we should continue on our quest for our passion, as long as we are convinced of it.

When Obama had engaged Frank, his mentor and adviser, in a conversation about his future, he had also counseled him about "the real price of admission" to a college. Frank had alluded to the fact that some of the burgeoning young black people of that era were selfish and oblivious to the history of how they had earned

Drive to Passion

the right to attend college. Frank had concluded by saying that this behavior by progressive young black people was tantamount to "leaving your race at the door; leaving your people behind." Obama heeded this advice, and resolved to touch the lives of the less fortunate through his grassroots and community organizing efforts.

Obama's passion was prompted by the culmination of several factors: advice from his mentor, Frank; his niche in politics and organizing political gatherings; defending the rights of the poor and oppressed; and acquisition of power through politics, perhaps, with the aim of using it to continue his advocacy for the poor. In charting his progress, the development of his passion for politics would become obvious.

In the months prior to his graduation, Obama said he wrote to civil rights groups, "to any black elected official in the country with a progressive agenda, to neighborhood councils and tenants rights groups" for a job, to no avail. He decided to accept a job in the interim with a consulting firm.

Obama had a lucrative job in this consulting firm, where he was the only black person in a professional capacity in the entire company. As a matter of fact, he had a promising career there. The black secretaries in the firm became surrogate mothers to him—taking a liking to him and an interest in his well-being. In essence, they were proud to have him in their midst—a twenty-two-year-old with a bright future and, perhaps, with the prospect of becoming an executive in the company one day.

When Obama made it known to some of the blacks in the consulting firm that his goal was to become a community organizer, they were not thrilled with his ambition. Although they did not necessarily express to him their disapproval of his intentions, he knew that his close-knit group of surrogate mothers and admirers did not approve of his plans. According to Obama, the only individual who summoned enough courage to advise him against his career move was the black security guard in the lobby, who said to him, "Forget about this organizing business and do something that's gonna make you some money. . . . I can see potential in you. Young man like you, got a nice voice—hell, you could be one a them announcers on TV."

Over an extended period of time, Obama began to allow the notion of becoming a community organizer to progressively slip away from him. He was becoming complacent. He had just been promoted to a new position with the consulting firm, and he now had a secretary. He was also beginning to enjoy the financial security that came with the job and some of its other entitlements. One day, Obama caught a glimpse of his reflection on the elevator wall leading to the office; with briefcase in hand and attired in suit and tie, he liked what he saw. He imagined himself "as a captain of industry, barking out orders" and closing important deals. This closely paralleled his image of his father earlier, in his government position in Kenya. At that point, he felt a twinge of guilt for deviating from his goal.

A few occurrences preceded Obama's resignation from his job. These incidents directly or indirectly influenced his resignation. He felt that he was losing sight of his passion, due to his emerging complacency. Obama's paternal half-sister put off her intended visit to the United States, due to a fatal motorcycle accident in Kenya that claimed the life of their brother. Following these incidents, he resigned from his job and became unemployed.

Obama's resignation from one job without another one at hand is a typical example of what most parents might deem an irrational decision on the part of their offspring. It takes tremendous tenacity to quit a job without securing another one. Had Obama not plunged full force into the quest for his passion, he may never have been able to bring it to fruition. The pursuit of our passion necessitates plunging in, in full force, at some point, based on our level of confidence, which was what Obama did when he quit his job and embarked on the quest for his passion on a full-time basis. One way to look at this is that, if we fail, we can always resort to seeking employment. A friend once advised me to go with my gut feeling, when I was trying to decide between pursuing a business venture and getting a job. She further stated that jobs are always available; the opportunity to start a business is much rarer than the opportunity to secure a new job. As indicated in other instances in this book, the pursuit of a passion is always going to be accompanied by an element of risk and uncertainty.

As if quitting his job was not enough risk, Obama turned down a job offer he deemed an imperfect fit. It was an offer from a top civil rights organization of great reputation. Similar to Sidney Poitier who turned down a $750 per week acting job because it was not the right fit despite being almost destitute, Obama was without an income when he declined this job offer. To the bystander, it would have seemed preposterous for Obama to turn down the job offer. The job was, after all, close to the ideal career he was seeking. It was a job that his potential employer said entailed forging "links between business, government, and the inner city." It seemed natural that he would have accepted the offer in hopes that it would be fulfilling to him; if nothing else, he could have accepted the offer until he found the exact job he desired. Also, the job offer was a munificent one. He had no income, so why not accept the offer? Obama's rationale for declining the offer, in his own words, was that he "needed a job closer to the streets."

Sometimes our passion may sound highly speculative or absurd; it is up to us to bring it to fruition. Creativity, intelligence, and innovation are oftentimes too abstract and unrealistic for the average person to comprehend; hence, some pioneers and inventors were mocked and dismissed derisively by others when they openly professed their ideas. Nevertheless, when their dreams became a reality, they made sense to the masses. If a concept is not immediately comprehensible to the masses, this should not deter the pursuit of the idea.

Obama and Poitier both proved that, while in pursuit of our passion, we should not settle for less. There is a clear distinction between the pursuit of a passion and seeking employment. When we are in search of employment, we tend to accept any job offer that comes close to what we desire. When we are in pursuit of our passion, it would behoove us not to settle for less. If we settle for anything less than our real passion, then that activity may never fit the boundaries of our passion, and we may never truly be passionate about it. We may not have a niche in the endeavor, and we may never be able to bring ourselves to take delight in it or attain excellence in it.

As evidenced by Obama's decision to leave his job and switch careers, money should never be at the forefront of our choice to pursue a passion. In other words, it would be to our disadvantage to abandon a passion because there is not an abundant supply of financial rewards in it. If we decide to embark on an activity based on its income or revenue potential, we may never deliver peak performance or reach our full potential in it, because passion elicits peak performance. This is by no means an espousal of the idea that we should not be involved in the creation of value through our passion. Once we begin to create value, invariably, people will be willing to pay for it, subsequently generating income for us.

Our reward is guaranteed when we create value in society because value engenders demand from those who seek the value we create, which in turn gives rise to a business transaction involving supply and demand. Rather than focusing on the rewards of a given passion, we should focus on ensuring that it is truly our niche; we should make sure we enjoy the activities involved in it; we should be in a perpetual state of education, preparation, and practice in it; we should ardently work toward the achievement of "mastery" in it; we should make sure that our passion is geared toward adding value in society.

* * *

Obama had a brief stint with one of Ralph Nader's causes relating to recycling, followed by a call from a community organizer. While he was employed by Ralph Nader, he was assigned to City College of New York, where he said he had the responsibility of "trying to convince minority students . . . about the importance of recycling." Shortly thereafter, Obama said, he received a phone call from a Jewish man, Marty Kaufman, who had started a grassroots community organizing project in Chicago "to pull urban blacks and suburban whites together" to save endangered manufacturing jobs. Kaufman was looking for someone to spearhead the project. He proposed a job interview with Obama in New York City. Following the interview, Obama was offered the job of an organizer in Chicago, which was exactly what he wanted. The job had a starting salary of $10,000 a year and a $2,000 car allowance. He accepted the offer.

Drive to Passion

Obama packed up and drove to Chicago. Upon his arrival, he began to get acclimated to his new environment. He visited the neighborhood barbershop, where he had the opportunity to pick up the latest gossip in the neighborhood and the latest tidbit about the politics of the city. In local gossip, Obama learned that a man had found his wife in bed with another man. On the political front, Obama heard that Harold Washington, the mayor of Chicago and an African-American, was much revered by the city's black people. The barber summed up what Mayor Washington meant to the blacks in Chicago: "Before Harold, seemed like we'd always be second-class citizens."

Within a day of his arrival in Chicago, Obama was off to his first rally, which was being organized by Kaufman and some of the other activists in the community. The purpose of the rally was to celebrate $500,000 in funding from the state of Illinois to an organization headed by Kaufman for the purpose of embarking on a computerized program that would provide job placements for members of the community. It was a much-needed program in view of the rapid loss of manufacturing jobs in Chicago. Upon his arrival at the venue for the rally with Kaufman, Obama had the opportunity to meet some of the other members of the organization: Wilbur, co-president of the organization, Angela, Shirley, and Mona.

Obama found out that Will, as Wilbur was known, was a Vietnam veteran who had worked for a bank. Upon his return from Vietnam, he had secured a job in the management trainee program of one of the burgeoning local banks in Chicago, and soon after his completion of the program, he had become a manager at the bank. He had quickly risen through the ranks to an executive-level position, where he had enjoyed the trappings of success, including nice cars and a big house. As a result of attrition and reorganization at the bank, he was laid off. Subsequently, Will ran into some financial problems, renewed his faith in the Lord and drew closer to God—taking a job as the janitor of a church.

The organization, to which Will and the rest of the group belonged, included steel workers, who had been laid off from their jobs, and other blue-collar workers. These were individuals with minimal disposable income who ate out sparingly, shopped mostly at mass merchandizing outlets for most of their nonfood items, and drove American-made automobiles. Most of them were overweight and smoked too much for their own good. As depicted by Abraham Maslow's philosophy on the hierarchy of needs, they neither had the means nor the time to take good care of themselves because they were too preoccupied with the acquisition of the most basic needs of life: food and shelter.

Obama received his first real assignment from Marty the day after the rally. Marty gave him a list of individuals to interview saying, "Find out their self-interests. That's why people become involved in organizing—because they think they'll get something out of it." As Obama began setting his appointments and subsequently going to his interviews, he concluded with a hint of nostalgia that it reminded him of Gramps setting his "insurance sales" appointments on Sunday nights. The difference here was that unlike his grandfather, he did not demur in the performance of his job. He enjoyed his task. Initially, setting the appointments and conducting the interviews were challenging, but after he learned how to overcome objections, the travails of the job began to diminish.

The potential for danger and disappointments were inherent in Obama's new assignment of conducting interviews. There was the danger of walking up to people's houses without knowing what to expect. He neither knew the caliber of individuals with whom he would be interacting nor the type of reception he would get. On occasion, by the time Obama got to his appointments, the people with whom he was supposed to meet had either forgotten about the appointment or had purposely avoided him. Generally, however, Obama found that the people he interviewed were genuinely interested in organizing and bringing about changes in the community: alleviating some of the endemic problems such as crime and unemployment.

Soon after his arrival, Obama dug into the history of the neighborhood. Its predicament was pervasive in many cities throughout the United States: As blacks moved in, whites moved out in great numbers. The neighborhoods that were once perceived as nice and safe suddenly became crime-ridden. The reason for the decline of the neighborhood in which Obama

Drive to Passion

conducted his interviews was not because it had become heavily populated by black people—although those who had moved into the neighborhood had lower incomes compared to those who had moved out—it was that the new transplants in the neighborhood could not afford the mortgages. Their properties had begun to be foreclosed on, and some of the houses in the neighborhood were already boarded up.

Obama's initial interview report, which he submitted to Kaufman, did not receive a good review from him. According to Obama, Kaufman critiqued his report as soon he turned it in. He needed to make it more in-depth, less academic, and less "peripheral and abstract," Kaufman said. Obama found this critique to be irritating, even though he knew Kaufman was right.

In addition to his interviews, Obama had been meeting with some community groups in an attempt to push his agendas. The black church ministers with whom Obama had previously met were still unsympathetic to his attempts to use them to reach out to their congregations, to address pressing issues in the neighborhood. He scheduled a meeting in which he gave a great presentation to the ministers and sought their help in disseminating information to their congregations for a meeting he intended to hold to address the recent issue of gang violence. One minister, Reverend Smalls, who arrived at the meeting late, was indifferent to Obama's wishes. After Smalls had been updated on what he had missed and was introduced to Obama, he took some time to think before he quipped and called him "Obamba" and did not apologize for mispronouncing his name. Reverend Smalls said, "Listen, Obamba, you may mean well. I'm sure you do. . . . White folks come in here thinking they know what's best for us, hiring a buncha high-talking college-educated brothers like yourself who don't know no better and all they want to do is take over." He further made it clear to Obama that he and his colleagues were against Jewish and Catholic organizations coming into the neighborhood to dictate how they should run their lives and conduct their affairs. The deliberate mispronunciation of Obama's name was not a good sign. It depicted Small's arrogance, wit, and contempt.

Obama had his hurdles earlier in Chicago. He had lost his bid to have the preachers of the churches in Chicago's Southside assist him in promoting his neighborhood meetings. He was also unable to garner support for his programs. Obama had intended to address a recent gang shooting in the neighborhood at the meeting. A failed meeting with the police district commander, who sent a lower-ranking officer in his place, exacerbated Obama's plight. Only thirteen people in the entire neighborhood showed up for the meeting.

On the other hand, Obama scored his first victory. He prevented the mass resignation of some of the volunteer organizers who were about to quit due to their frustrations, stemming from their perceived inertia of the organization—Developing Communities Project (DCP)—which was Obama's employer as well as theirs. The $500,000 award from the state for the computerized job placement program had been a flop. The project had been relegated by the state to a local college with the necessary computer access to administer the program. For months no placements were made. This contributed to the DCP members' frustrations. Fortuitously for Obama, from outside the venue for his meeting with the disgruntled DCP members, there came the sound of shattering glass: Some kids were breaking the windows of a dilapidated house nearby. He capitalized on the vandalism by asking the prospective quitters what the fate of those children would be if they all were to quit: "Who's going to make sure they get a fair shot? The alderman? The social workers? The gangs?" With these successive questions, Obama dramatized his point and drove it home; it worked. By a combination of a persuasive argument and pep talk, he was able to prevent the mass resignation of his employees.

Obama's next achievement was prompted by a discovery he made while at the Mayor's Office of Employment and Training (MET). He and some of the other organizers had driven forty-five minutes to the MET office, and soon after their arrival there, Obama's inquisitive mind went to work. He surreptitiously poked around until he discovered a brochure that listed the locations of the MET offices across the city; none of those locations was on the Southside. Obama alerted the other organizers to this situation. He and his colleagues unanimously decided to push for a location of MET on the Southside. Soon after they got back from their

Drive to Passion

visit, they drafted a letter to the director of the MET program on this issue.

Obama and the other members of DCP were paid a visit by the director of the MET program, Cynthia Alvarez. Even though the meeting did not produce a direct answer from her, Obama had initiated a project that would ultimately yield good results. The meeting ended with Alvarez promising to initiate a proposal for the establishment of the MET on the Southside, but without a definite commitment on when it would happen.

* * *

Obama's paternal half-sister, Auma, decided to visit him from Germany, where she had been attending college on a scholarship. As soon as Obama picked his sister up from the airport, they began to form a strong sibling bond, even though they were meeting each other for the first time. The instant bond Obama formed with his sister gave him the opportunity to learn much more about his father and to make his own assessments about him. He learned from Auma that his father had married another white American woman upon returning to Kenya, and that he had other biracial siblings. He also learned from her that his father had been a womanizer; he had maintained close contact with his African wife, who was Auma's mother, and had been seeing her on occasion even though he was married to another woman.

His sister recounted their father's life history with regard to his career: entanglements with his colleagues, the government, and the eventual the loss of his job. According to her, after his return from the United States, everything seemed to go smoothly for him: He had a great a job with an oil company; he later switched jobs and secured a top government position with, perhaps, some political ambitions; he established friendships with top government officials, including ministers, who would all, from time to time, come to his house to drink with him. At that point, he was married to his other white American wife, and they had children. According to Obama's sister, the turning point in their father's life came when he began to criticize the government for its corrupt practices: The tide took a turn for the worse for him; he became instantly blacklisted by the president for speaking out so boldly against the government. Consequently, he lost his government job, his house, and his American wife; he lost everything. Their father, in effect, became destitute. He later managed to secure a low-level job, which he eventually lost as well. He took to drinking, and as a result, he was in a bad car accident. His recovery period from this accident lasted about a year. Upon the death of the president of Kenya, Obama's sister recounted, things significantly turned around for their father. He secured another lucrative job with the government prior to his death.

Auma's revelations contributed significantly to Obama's resolve to do better and conduct his life more propitiously. The story he heard from her shed significant light on who his father really had been. Obama saw weaknesses in his father that he did not want to emulate, especially in those areas where he had failed; at the same time, his father and other role models in his life had made a positive impact on him in some ways. Subsequent to this disconcerting information he had gained about his father, Obama said about him in his book, "I now felt as if I had to make up for all his mistakes." Conversely, there were some positive aspects of his father that he wanted to emulate. His father had instilled in him a solid work ethic when he visited him and his family in Hawaii; he had said to him, "Barry, you do not work hard enough." He had an ardent work ethic, which Obama copied. This would propel him to great heights academically. On the other hand, he saw his father for who he really had been: "a defeated lonely bureaucrat" and a "womanizer."

Obama was now at a crossroads in his life; his passion and how he would conduct his life came to a confluence. What would prevent his life from taking an insidious turn, similar to his father's? He would have to take control of his fate and chart a course for his life that would be positive and a total deviation from his father's.

Upon his sister's departure, Obama resumed his work in earnest, and in that process he met Rafiq a-Shabaaz—a businessman and a long-winded, rhetorical, inner-city, self-styled member of the intelligentsia—with whom he forged an alliance, much to the displeasure of his colleagues. Rafiq wanted Obama to have the mayor's office locate its MET program in a building close to his office. Obama was open to Rafiq's proposal. His alliance with Rafiq did not garner enthusiasm and support from the other DCP members because they did not see any potential benefit to the organization from this alliance.

The disagreements that Obama had with Rafiq were directly related to Rafiq's ineptitude rather than his views on nationalism, in which he blamed all the ills of the black community on circumstances triggered by the white race. Obama said he requested a collaboration with Rafiq's supporters in the event that "a public showdown with the city became necessary," thinking that a solid alliance had been forged between the two of them. Rafiq refused his request, citing rhetorical excuses relating to the fact that Obama should concretize his agreements with the city to prevent them from reneging. Rafiq also alluded to the fact that the people in the neighborhood did not care enough to participate in such an undertaking.

The city delivered on its promise to locate an MET center in Roseland, in Chicago's Southside, and the mayor was invited to the center's ribbon-cutting ceremony. Rafiq, pleased with the outcome, helped with the decorations and final touch-ups at the new center. Prior to the mayor's arrival for the opening ceremony, Obama instructed Angela, a DCP employee, who was to receive the mayor upon his arrival, to make sure that she got his commitment to attend the fall rally.

The excitement engendered by the mayor's arrival was similar to that of a high-caliber celebrity. As his motorcade approached, it set off a boisterous atmosphere around the center. When the mayor alighted from his vehicle, the crowd that gathered to welcome him chanted his first name, Harold. He quickly walked toward the building with his security detail. At that point the DCP women became animated. Cameras were flashing left and right. Angela was star-struck and busy trying to ensure that one of her colleagues would be able to take a good picture of her and the mayor. The mayor's official appointment at the ribbon-cutting ceremony happened quickly. It was over in ten minutes, and he was off to his next engagement. As the mayor walked off, Obama yelled out to Angela, inquiring about the mayor's commitment to the fall rally. Angela and the other women were busy talking and laughing. Everyone was still animated from the mayor's visit. Angela hardly even remembered what Obama had told her. She and her colleagues continued to talk to each other about how enchanted they were with the mayor's visit.

Obama lost his temper and walked away. When Will saw him walking away in exasperation, he followed him. Will caught up with him and asked why he was so agitated. Obama retorted: "We're trifling." He explained to Will that he was angry because Angela had forgotten to get the mayor's commitment to the fall rally. It was Will's turn to give Obama a pep talk. "You want everything to happen fast," he said. "Like you got something to prove out here.... You don't have to prove nothing to us, Barack. We love you, man. Jesus loves you."

Will was able to pinpoint Obama's ambition, his drive, his ego, and his commitment to excellence. He was right; Obama wanted to maintain his momentum with regard to his accomplishments. Obama was similar to others in this book who were in pursuit of their passion: A healthy dose of ego combined with courage and drive enabled them to become resolute about realizing their dreams rather than settling for mediocrity. In fact, settling for a substitute for our passion may mean that we will not enjoy that substitute for which we are settling. If we do not enjoy the activity in which we are engaged, we will not pursue it with zest and alacrity; as such, we may never become an expert in it. If all of these factors are not present in our pursuit, we may never create any significant value that will engender the law of supply and demand in the general population, thus creating substantial rewards for us, or we may never gain any significant acclaim. Ego, courage, and drive contribute immensely to the pursuit of a passion.

Obama, Winston Churchill, and Sidney Poitier are similar with respect to their tendencies to never be satisfied with the strides they made. Obama wanted a future meeting with the mayor; he was displeased and frustrated with Angela for not getting the mayor to commit to it; he was not satisfied with the accomplishments he had already made. Churchill was never satisfied with his success as a writer, a speaker, and a soldier; hence, he continued to strive for more accomplishments. He rehearsed his speeches for hours on end prior to his speaking engagements because he was never satisfied. He continued to strive to give great speeches that some deem among the best of all time. Poitier continuously strived to be better in acting, and as such, he indicated that he was never satisfied with his work: "I'm not always satisfied with my work in every scene in every picture." Therefore, never being satisfied is a key component of our drive. Satisfaction breeds contentment and lack of drive. Proficiency, excellence, and expertise in our craft should always be viewed as work in progress, and so should our passion.

* * *

Obama's success in securing the MET program gained him accolades and popularity. He began to receive invitations to participate in various grassroots events. Even the alderman of the ward in which he was located now knew who he was. The preachers who had rebuffed him began to try to collaborate with him and to make announcements in their churches about his events. As a result of Obama's success with the MET program, Kaufman attempted to recruit him for another project in Indiana. Kaufman appeared to have lost his momentum for the Chicago project and was shoring up for new challenges in Indiana. He had already decided he would hire someone to replace Obama. His argument in trying to convince Obama to go to Indiana with him was that Chicago was too large for him to make any significant difference; he needed a smaller territory where the impact of his accomplishments would be better felt. According to Obama, Kaufman also used career advancement and what he termed "development" as a tool to attempt to lure him to Indiana. Kaufman was wrong in his assessments; hence, Obama turned out to be who he is.

Obama rejected Kaufman's offer, sensing a philosophical difference between them. Kaufman neither had outside loyalties other than to his family nor attachment to the individuals with whom he collaborated in his organizing efforts. Rather, his ambitions and efforts were driven by the actual projects and the accomplishment of the tasks at hand. Conversely, Obama's passion was driven by the relationships he forged and by making a difference in the lives of the people with whom he interacted.

Next, Obama focused his attention on Altgeld, one of the public housing complexes under the umbrella of the Chicago Housing Authority (CHA). The plight of the teenage mothers there was disconcerting, poignant, and often a case of children raising children, with no end in sight to the vicious cycle. They were teenage mothers raised by teenage mothers themselves, oftentimes with more than one child to rear—usually on welfare, with little or no education, and no knowledge of what proper nutrition and childcare entailed. The conditions at Altgeld were deplorable. The buildings were poorly maintained, resulting in several problems, including leaky pipes, clogged toilets, faulty heaters, and broken windows.

When Sadie, a resident of Altgeld, approached Obama with an advertisement she had seen in a small publication, it triggered his concern and heightened his curiosity. They were about to uncover a major problem. The advertisement, which was run by CHA, requested that contractors submit bids for asbestos extraction from the Altgeld office. Sadie was concerned about the possibility of the existence of asbestos in the apartments at Altgeld as well. As a result of her concern, Obama suggested she set an appointment with Altgeld's project manager.

The project manager was a man nearing retirement, and he was taken aback by Obama's presence at the meeting, which was supposed to be between him and Sadie. He immediately tried to dispel Sadie's concern about the potential existence of asbestos in the units by explaining that, during renovations, one of the pipes in the office had been found by the maintenance crew to have asbestos insulation, which was the reason for the advertisement that Sadie had seen. He further contended that the dwelling units had been tested and found to be free of asbestos insulation. Obama felt empathy for him, the type of empathy that one might feel for a father figure who was about to make a grave mistake due to a degree of ineptitude or laziness over a matter that could be easily solved by telling the simple truth. As they were about to leave, Sadie asked to see the documents authenticating that tests had been conducted in the dwelling units to show the absence of asbestos. She contended that it was for the benefit of the other residents who were concerned parents and who did not want their children's health compromised by asbestos. The project manager said that the documents were at the CHA headquarters in downtown Chicago, and he promised to make a copy available to Sadie.

After a few weeks of silence from the project manager and some of the higher ups whom Obama and Sadie had initially approached, including the executive director, they decided to take a bus downtown to the CHA headquarters. In a move to depict solidarity among the residents, Obama and Sadie requested the participation of the other residents in the bus ride. They also sent a press release announcing their impending visit to the downtown office of the CHA. This sparked the interest of the local TV station, which sent a camera crew and a reporter to cover the story.

Although Obama and Sadie were unable to meet with the director, their mere presence, along with the TV coverage, enabled them to get some answers from the assistant to the director who had previously been unsympathetic to their demands. Now the assistant went out of her way to be nice to them. They discovered the truth. No tests had been conducted to substantiate the absence of asbestos in the dwelling units at Altgeld.

The trip to the downtown office of CHA made a positive impact on Obama's career in organizing. It enabled him to gain exposure in the community, while providing him with a sense of accomplishment. He began to see the possibilities of making strides in organizing. He saw how things could turn around for the better within a short period of time by pursuing the right objectives with dedication and passion. Some of the individuals who had previously rebuffed Obama began to give credence to him and his work. Obama and the women at Altgeld got the meeting they sought with the director. He agreed to a meeting with the residents of the housing complex.

On the day of the meeting between the CHA director and residents of Altgeld, once again the TV news crew was present; local politicians were also present to try to capitalize on the situation for their own political gain. The church preachers who had previously declined Obama's requests for a working relationship were all present. They suddenly were treating him with respect and offering to help him in any way they could. The politicians' and preachers' affability toward Obama was underscored by their quid pro quo intentions. They wanted visibility and whatever their affiliation with Obama and his causes could add to their individual agendas. Kaufman, who had offered Obama another position in Indiana and had told him that Chicago would cause his professional stagnation, was also present. He was very animated about Obama's accomplishments.

While awaiting the director's arrival, Kaufman tried to lead the residents who packed the development's gymnasium in a chant. When Obama asked him what he was doing, he explained that the crowd was beginning to thin down due to the long wait for the director's arrival. Obama admonished Kaufman on the awkwardness of the situation he was creating by saying, "Please sit down, will you please."

Obama told the individual who would be handling the microphone to hold it up for the director, and not to allow him to handle it himself. In so doing, they had hoped to prevent the director from rambling and talking for too long. No sooner had the director arrived and gone to the front to speak than a struggle ensued for control of the microphone. The director, who wanted to handle the microphone himself, engaged in a tug of war with the woman holding the microphone. Neither of them was willing to give up the microphone. As each of them pulled it, a ruckus developed among the crowd. The director finally gave up the microphone and headed toward the door in a mad dash. He made his way through the crowd, got in his car, and was gone. The woman involved in the tussle with the director sobbed. Obama tried to console her.

The unsuccessful attempt by Obama to host a meeting, in which the executive director of CHA would have had the opportunity to address the asbestos debacle, resulted in a major mistake. Unbeknown to Obama, not allowing the CHA director to have control of the microphone triggered a blunder. He and his team had anticipated neither the microphone tug of war nor the director's precipitous exit. They were surprised by the uproar that ensued.

Some days later, a few men in work gear showed up at the housing complex and began removing asbestos from the pipes. Although the microphone incident at the meeting had been a mistake, ultimately, some progress emerged from it, and it served as a learning experience for Obama. The Department of Housing and Urban Development, which is responsible for appropriations to individual housing authorities in the cities and towns across the United States, became involved in the matter. A representative was sent to Altgeld to meet with the residents and discuss the issues; promises were made to resolve the asbestos issue in the entire complex within the budgetary constraints of the federal government.

Obama learned that there is not a straight path to success. There are always mistakes and problems that require resolution, and there are pockets of failure in any endeavor. The microphone blunder resulted in the failure of that one meeting; nevertheless, the problem of asbestos in the units received attention, and consequently, the project was not a total failure. Failures serve the purpose of making us more aware of problem areas. They also teach us how to seek solutions to problems. Mistakes can enhance our knowledge, if we learn from them. Obama gained experience from that incident, emerging as a smarter, wiser, and more mature individual. He also learned that no endeavor is immune to failures and mistakes. Most importantly, he learned that our quest for our passion and excellence must continue in earnest, despite our mistakes.

As we pursue our passion, we can minimize the effects and incidents of failures and mistakes by being cognizant of their possibilities, taking the needed precautions to avoid them, and staying persistent to ensure our continued quest for excellence. We should make sure that adequate due diligence is conducted prior to embarking on a project. As the project is initiated, we should ascertain its sustainability and use best practices to maintain its momentum, keeping in mind that the process may entail learning from other people's mistakes as well as our own.

* * *

Obama proceeded to hire an assistant and to focus on other projects including the public schools and black churches, but there were some inherent risks and an endemic crime problem in the midst of his activities. Johnnie was his new assistant with whom he instantly established a good rapport. Obama hoped to acclimatize his assistant to the functions of the organization including his foray into the public schools. On their way back from dinner one night in Hyde Park, they suddenly heard two popping sounds as they approached Johnnie's car. In the distance and coming around the corner, not too far from them, was a teenager, not more than fifteen years old, running for his dear life with the determination of an Olympic athlete gunning for the finish line. Right behind him were two other teenagers chasing him, one with a pistol in his hand. Johnnie and Obama immediately dropped to the ground simultaneously. When the two young men realized they were not going to catch up with the teenager in flight, the one with the gun fired three more shots and then stopped, cursed, and laughed insidiously. Also, there was the ever-present sound of police and ambulance sirens, which, more often than not, terminated at the crime scenes. The shooting scenes were always similar: victim on the ground, with fresh blood beside him or her.

After he hired Johnnie, Obama shifted his focus to the public schools in the community. His objective was to tackle some of the problems in these schools through his organizing efforts. There were several endemic problems that required attention: They had a 50 percent graduation rate; there was an acute shortage of textbooks and other supplies; and the buildings were in disrepair. Obama chose one of the schools on the Southside that characterized all of the problems. He and Johnnie paid a visit to Dr. Lonnie King, the principal of the school of their choice, to discuss the problems. Dr. King was receptive; he immediately referred them to a male counselor of the school, who was starting a mentorship program for the young male students.

The counselor, Asante Moran, whose first name symbolized a tribe in Africa, was an Afrocentric man whose office had the type of African décor emblematic of someone in touch with his

Drive to Passion

roots. Obama learned that Moran had visited Kenya, and it had been a riveting experience for him; he was warmly received by the Kenyans he met there. Moran was glad when he found out that Obama's father was from Kenya. He, however, was disappointed to learn that Obama had never been there.

Upon learning that the discussions with Moran had gone well and that considerable progress had been made by Obama and Johnnie with regard to the mentoring program, Dr. King proceeded to exhibit a peculiar behavior. He submitted his wife's resume, with the suggestion that she would fit in as the director of the program. As if that were not enough, he also submitted his daughter's resume with the suggestion that she would make a good counselor for the mentoring program. This incident was absurd to Obama and Johnnie. They had a good laugh about Dr. King's nepotistic tendencies.

Obama, in his organizing efforts, turned his attention to the black churches, where he met an influential and intellectual minister, with whom he had a lengthy discussion about the black church. According to Obama, Reverend Philips, a scholarly black minister, educated him on the intricacies of the establishment of the "black church as an institution, the black church as an idea." The minister recounted to him the origins of the black church. It started during the days of the black slaves who, upon their arrival to the shores of a distant land—the United States—resorted to blending their original traditions with some of their newly found beliefs, in an effort to find solace in the harsh and unwelcoming expanse of their new environment. Reverend Philips continued in his enumeration of the history of the black church up to the era of Dr. Martin Luther King Jr. He then delved into his own church and some of the challenges he faced with his current congregation. These problems consisted of the church's suburbanite members who, even though they still drove into the city to attend church, were now advocating better security on the grounds of the church and a fence around the church compound to safeguard their vehicles from the deteriorating conditions of the inner city and the ensuing high crime rate. Reverend Philips worried that, upon his departure, the congregation would disband, forming new churches that would more closely mirror their burgeoning middle-class status. Obama interjected by saying, "If we could bring just fifty churches together, we might be able to reverse some of the trends you've been talking about."

Reverend Philips suggested that Obama meet with Reverend Jeremiah Wright, pastor of Trinity United Church of Christ, a key player and a budding force in the community of black churches. His church was widely attended by the up-and-coming black professionals of Chicago: lawyers, doctors, corporate executives, engineers, entrepreneurs, and other types of professionals.

Obama met with Reverend Wright to further discuss his efforts to organize the black churches. He had a productive discussion with him. Following their conversation, he suggested that Obama meet with other members of his congregation, and he did. In the process of meeting with the church members, they suggested that he join their church. Their rationale was that anyone soliciting help from churches in some manner should, at least, be a member of one of the churches. So, early one Sunday morning, Obama attended Trinity. The sermon delivered by Reverend Wright was "The Audacity of Hope," which would become the title of Obama's second book.

Neither Obama's mother nor his grandparents were ardent churchgoers. His stepfather, his father, and their families were Muslims. His mother was not deeply religious; rather, she had instilled in him Western ethics and morals, and the spirit of decency. Her orientation had been built on a foundation of Western ideals, spirituality, and distrust for religion.

Obama's religious beliefs had not been deeply entrenched in any particular religion prior to his arrival in Chicago. His spirit of decency, instilled in him by his mother, would become one of the strongest guiding forces in his life. He would exemplify it by his desire to negotiate rather than cause discord and his desire to seek a common ground among the individuals with whom he interacted. Obama later decided to not only become a member of Trinity but to become baptized there. This decision, he would later admit, was not based on a religious epiphany, but was a calculated choice predicated on his need for community affiliation and his desire to identify with the African-American experience.

There are similarities between Obama, Oprah Winfrey, Abraham Lincoln, Winston Churchill, and Sidney Poitier with regard to their religion and beliefs. In reviewing their backgrounds, none of them maintained strong affiliations with religious organizations or institutions. The general pattern of belief depicted in their lives is that, although God is responsible for all humans, to a great extent, we humans have a significant part to play in the outcome of our lives. Oprah advocates personal development and the power of intention; Lincoln advocated self-actualization, visualization, and other self-enhancement techniques he had picked up from the Bible and autobiographies of highly accomplished individuals such as George Washington. Among all of these individuals, Churchill was the only one who openly decried religion as being either irrelevant to the progress of mankind or actually responsible for human suffering and confusion. He warded off criticisms for this stance by being an advocate for the poor. Abraham Lincoln read the Bible for inspiration and quoted from it in his speeches. The general notion portrayed by these individuals is that personal development is an effective method of achieving our objectives rather than waiting for manna from heaven.

* * *

Obama began to contemplate a Harvard law school education. He had a discussion with Reverend Wright, in which he told him of his plans to pursue a law degree at Harvard University. He indicated to Wright that he thought a law degree would be a necessary augmentation to his credentials in his efforts to pursue a career in politics. Here, Obama mirrored Abraham Lincoln, who also realized that a law degree would enhance his political aspirations. However, unlike Lincoln who studied at home because it was possible to do so at the time and because he lacked the financial resources to pursue a law education in a formal setting, Obama took advantage of student loans to enable him to further his education at one of the best institutions of higher learning in the world.

During the application process to Harvard, Obama effectively leveraged his mentors' help with obtaining letters of recommendation from influential individuals. An influential New York attorney, Percy Sutton, agreed to give Obama a letter of recommendation, at the urging of one of his mentors. Obama also obtained a letter of recommendation from John McKnight, a professor at Northwestern University in Chicago, who would serve as his mentor and with whom he had an interesting discussion about his aspirations. McKnight wanted to know how Obama would use his Harvard law degree. Obama said he was contemplating the practice of civil rights law and an eventual bid for political office. He urged Obama to make sure politics and law would be satisfying to him, because both professions required compromise. Obama in turn responded by saying that he did not mind compromise.

After his acceptance into Harvard Law School, Obama announced to everyone who was closely associated with him his intentions of going to Harvard to study law. He received mixed responses from the different individuals in his community circle: Some were not surprised because they knew he was destined for greatness; others congratulated him and wished him luck; some of the female DCP members were upset that he was leaving; Will predicted that he would be back upon graduating from Harvard; and Johnnie, his assistant, said that he knew right from the onset that Obama was not going to remain at DCP for long. Obama made sure the organization had adequate funds to cover that season. He also had discussions with Johnnie to ensure that he would take over for him as the lead organizer.

After two and a half years with DCP, Obama left to pursue his dream and passion. What was his passion at that point? It is fair to say Obama's passion was at its nascent stage. He enjoyed organizing people for a common cause; he believed that there was strength in numbers. Similar to Abraham Lincoln, Obama realized the potential of politics as a means of effecting positive change in society. Consequently, it became obvious to him that he would need to utilize his zest for organizing in the political sector. Also, similar to Lincoln, Obama realized that law and politics have a symbiotic relationship.

Obama contended that his decision to go to law school was spurred by his need to expand his knowledge in a way that would aid

Drive to Passion

his efforts to effect cogent changes in the community. Obama, in his autobiography, outlined his reason for going to law school: "I would learn about interest rates, corporate mergers, the legislative process; about the way businesses and banks were put together; how real estate ventures succeeded or failed." All of these components comprised the much-needed knowledge he would bring back to the impoverished communities for whom he intended to be an advocate.

* * *

Obama's initial meeting with Asante Moran, though short, nevertheless made a lasting impression on him, awakening his curiosity about his roots. The tinge of disappointment in Moran, when he realized that Obama had never been to Kenya, helped to elicit in him a need to seek out his origins. Right after that meeting, he had flown to Washington, D.C., to meet and bond with his half-brother, Roy, for the first time. This interest in his roots led to Obama's decision to go to Kenya. The timing was right. He now was on his way to Harvard, and he was, in the meantime, done with DCP. His half-sister who was previously in Germany had returned home to Kenya and was now teaching at a university. What better time would there be to visit Kenya and experience things for himself than that particular period? Obama took advantage of the time in between the end of his service at DCP and the commencement of his studies at Harvard to not only visit Africa, but also to spend a few weeks touring some countries in Europe on his way to Africa.

In addition to meeting his relatives in Africa, Obama had the opportunity to learn about and experience life in Kenya. He also became acclimatized to its corruption, tribalism, and nepotism. He discovered that post-colonial Kenya still suffered from neocolonialism. Another cultural experience for Obama consisted of learning how family traditions and interdependence among family members were interwoven in the fabric of Kenyan society.

Following Obama's arrival in Kenya, he and his half-sister Auma went out to an upscale restaurant, where they were ignored by the waitresses and waiters. They were considered to be indigenous Kenyans and deemed less affluent than foreign, white customers who spent lavishly on food and tips in restaurants. It was a surreal experience. After he and Auma seated themselves, they tried to catch the eye of one of the waiters for service, but to no avail. They were ignored by the entire wait staff. One of the waiters, an older man, reluctantly brought menus to them, which he dropped off with disdain and disappeared. The white family who came in after them was waited on promptly and enthusiastically. They had their food and were eating while Obama and his sister were still without service. Auma was fuming by this time and demanded to speak to the manager. The waiter at whom the brunt of her anger was initially directed simply responded by saying that he had mouths to feed, which meant that he was inclined to prioritize by servicing those whom he perceived to have money ahead of others. Obama and his sister stormed out of the restaurant.

When Obama first arrived at the airport in Kenya, his luggage did not arrive with him due to a mistake by the airlines, and the circumstance surrounding the retrieval of his luggage was absurd. He had been promised by an airline employee that the problem would be resolved and that he would receive his luggage in a day. After a few days elapsed and he still had not heard from the airline, he and his sister decided to go to the airport, where they made a futile attempt to retrieve his luggage. They were rudely referred to the downtown office by a small group of airline employees whose behavior suggested that Obama's inquiry was an intrusion into their conversation.

Luckily for Obama, upon their arrival to the downtown office of the airline, they ran into a distant relative whom his sister knew and who happened to know the airport manager. This relative interceded by alerting the manager of the problem. The manager, in turn, immediately resolved the problem by having Obama's luggage delivered to that office later that afternoon.

When Obama and one of his aunts visited another aunt who was estranged from the rest of the family, he had the opportunity to experience firsthand the degree to which poverty and family interdependence were ubiquitous in Kenya and ingrained in the culture. Auma refused to go on this visit due to previous squabbles with the aunt who would be hosting the visit. Upon their arrival there, the estranged aunt proceeded to explain that

Drive to Passion

her mother was Obama's blood grandmother, and that the other grandmother, whom everyone called Granny, was actually his step-grandmother. The situation there became awkward when an argument ensued between both aunts. Obama's estranged aunt unabashedly asked him for financial assistance. He was boxed into a corner and proceeded to give her a thirty-dollar equivalent of Kenyan shillings from his wallet.

Obama had the opportunity to meet his father's other white wife—his half-brother Mark, who was her son—and her entire family. She had extended a dinner invitation to Obama and Auma. This invitation provided Obama an opportunity to meet Mark for the first time. Although dinner was somewhat awkward, Obama gained an insight into how his father was viewed by one of the women he had married. His father's former wife had very little regard for the late Obama; she incessantly barraged them with his flaws. She seemed to have invited them over to make a comparison between Obama and Mark, who was in school at Stanford University in the United States, and to complain about his late father's shortcomings. Obama's conclusion, when he and Auma left, was that their father's previous wife still had a lot of unresolved issues with their father. She was a chronically wounded animal who would forever bear the burden of her wound.

Obama invited Mark out to lunch, and in the process, he found out that he had consciously disconnected himself from everything relating to their father, including the country of Kenya. In fact, he drew an analogy between his brother's efforts in detaching himself from Kenya and a rock climber who was always careful not to lose his footing, inferring that both of them went to great lengths to maintain the status quo.

Obama was surprised by the degree to which tribalism and stereotyping was pervasive in Kenya, even among his own relatives. This must have dashed all his previous hopes of Pan-Africanism. Obama said he heard from his relatives such stereotypical comments as, "The Luo are intelligent but lazy . . . those West Africans are all crazy anyway. You know they used to be cannibals."

Obama brought up the subject of going on a safari. Auma initially objected on the grounds that it was for white tourists.

However, due to his insistence, she gave in, and shortly thereafter, they left for the safari. On their way to the safari, the driver of their transport vehicle, who was also a coffee grower, criticized the government's corrupt practices. He talked about how the government practically confiscated coffee from the coffee farmers. This act of coercion by the government was the antithesis of the government subsidies, which were prevalent among other governments. According to the driver, the Kenyan government set the coffee prices at a reduced and subsistence rate, which made it difficult for the farmers to survive, much less make profits. The government in turn sold the coffee in foreign markets at several thousand percent profit. The driver also talked about how the roads on which they traveled showed unusually early signs of wear and poor construction due to unscrupulous government officials who believed in building poor roads with much less money than was allotted for the roads and using the remaining cash to build mansions for themselves, thus profiteering from their corrupt practices. The safari experience, though a bit dangerous, was well worth it for Obama. He was able to see the wild animals and the much talked about Masai tribesmen, who were great warriors.

Next, Obama, Auma, and Roy, his brother who lived in America, packed up and headed to the hamlet where his father was born to visit his step-grandmother, Granny, and his father's grave. It was there that Obama got a good dose of the family history from Granny. She talked elaborately about his father, his grandfather, and great-grandfather. She even delved into his roots several generations back.

Obama's pilgrimage to Kenya to discover his father's family was worth it because of its significance in his own self-discovery. In his autobiography, Obama discussed the questions he had asked his half-brother Mark, who acknowledged a perpetual feeling of numbness due to their father's absence and ensuing ineptitude with his family life: "Don't you ever feel like you might be losing something? And that doesn't bother you? Being numb, I mean?" Unlike Mark, who suppressed his feelings about his family background and their father's shortcomings, Obama went all the way to their father's village, in order to come to terms with his own identity and his father's memory. In that bid, he tried

Drive to Passion

to discover the circumstances surrounding his father's childhood. He also searched for evidence of the conditions that could have contributed to the molding of his father's character. This discovery helped shape Obama's character and make him who he is. It also helped allay any fears that he may have harbored about being struck with a curse or the same ill fortune that had befallen his father. He was able to reaffirm to himself that his future was in his own hands. Obama became more convinced that he needed to avoid those things that had contributed to his father's demise.

Upon Obama's return from Kenya, he proceeded to tackle the next significant challenge that lay ahead of him: law school at Harvard. As the summer approached during his first year at Harvard, he thought about seeking employment in Chicago for the summer. He needed a job, especially one that would be lucrative enough to not only sustain him while in Chicago, but to also enable him to accumulate enough funds to defray some of his expenses at Harvard.

At this juncture, Obama leveraged the help of a mentor to enable him to secure a job at a prestigious law firm, Sidley and Austin, in Chicago. He used the help of one of his law professors at Harvard, Martha Minow, who thought he was absolutely brilliant. Minow's father, Newton Minow, was one of the senior partners at Sidley. Obama came highly recommended to Sidley, and he also came with great credentials. He wrote an excellent letter of introduction of himself, which the senior partner brandished around the office, with praises of how poetic some of his phrases were.

Following Obama's arrival at Sidley and Austin his internship began in earnest. This was also a homecoming to Chicago for him. It was there that he met Michelle Robinson, who would become his wife and the first lady of the United States. She was assigned to mentor him, and show him the ropes at the law firm. Although she was younger than Obama, she had already graduated from law school at Harvard University and was working permanently at Sidley. Initially, she was reluctant to go out with him because she did not want to infringe on her professional capacity as his mentor. However, due to Obama's unrelenting insistence, she gave in—they had their first date, and the rest is history. Thus, the law firm turned out to serve a dual function for Obama: It fulfilled his summer employment need and turned out to be where he met his future wife.

Similar to Winston Churchill, Oprah Winfrey, and Joseph Kennedy, Obama utilized mentors to enhance the progression of the pursuit of his goals. The importance of utilizing mentors to help us along the way as we chart our course in life cannot be over-emphasized. Mentors can be younger or older than us; they can be our subordinates or our superiors, as long as there is something we can learn from them. Mentorship can also be symbiotic: A mentor can become a protégé and vice versa. While in search of a mentor, we should always be prepared to serve as a mentor as well. Mentors are instrumental in helping to educate us and create opportunities for us.

* * *

While at Harvard, Obama was elected the first black president of the *Harvard Law Review*. He received several accolades for this, including the prospect of writing a book. Obama summed up his law education in the following words: "I went to Harvard Law School, spending most of three years in poorly lit libraries, poring through cases and statutes. The study of law can be disappointing at times, a matter of applying narrow rules and arcane procedure to an uncooperative reality."

Four years after law school, Obama—now a married man—ran for an open seat in the Illinois state legislature and won. His experience as an organizer and a civil rights attorney made him a good candidate for the position. Obama made the decision to run for the Illinois Senate while he was teaching law at the University of Chicago and was also involved in a law practice at a small civil rights law firm. He based his decision to run for office on two main factors: the need to initiate his political career from a vantage point that would afford him the opportunity to prove himself; and some of his friends, who saw his passion for politics and public service, had encouraged him to run.

Although Obama and his wife had huge debts accrued from college loans taken out to defray the cost of their education at

Drive to Passion

Harvard law, he did not practice law at a large law firm with a hefty income or seek a high-profile and high-paying job to enable him pay off their college loans. He did not go in these directions for the same reason that he had initially quit his job at the consulting firm where he had worked upon graduating from Columbia; Obama had also turned down a high-paying civil rights job in place of a job as a community organizer, on an initial salary of $10,000 a year. He was in pursuit of his passion in politics and public service, without regard for the relatively low financial rewards involved in the activities encompassing his passion. He also was unperturbed about his financial liabilities because he was focused on the achievement of his passion. Deep down, Obama knew that the successful attainment of his passion and the ensuing value he would create would yield substantial financial rewards and enable him to meet his financial obligations.

Whether we are extrinsically driven, intrinsically driven, or both in the pursuit of our passion, one fact remains constant: We need financial resources to survive. However, regardless of our drive and motivation, we cannot focus on rewards. Our focus should always be directed toward our passion. Our drive fuels our passion and enables us to stay focused. A deviation from an intense focus on our passion could potentially derail our success. Once we create value with our passion, it will invariably be financially rewarding to us because the laws of economics will apply: supply and demand—people paying us in exchange for the value we create.

Did Obama know how far he would go in politics? He wanted to go as far as he could, while allowing his extrinsic drive—his quest for power—to fuel his passion for politics and public service. Christopher Andersen, in his biography of Obama, titled *Barack and Michelle*, mentioned comments made by Obama and his family about his drive and aspirations. Before his return to Harvard from Chicago, Obama said to Michelle, "When I go back to Harvard, I think I'm going to run for president of the *Law Review*." Andersen also noted that Obama harbored an interest in becoming the mayor of Chicago. When Michelle met his grandmother, Toot, she said about her grandson, "He is a dreamer." Andersen also said that Obama's mother "told her son to aim for the White House." Later, Obama told Michelle, "I think maybe I'll run for the Senate, then president—why not?" He also told Michelle's brother, Craig Robinson, about his senatorial and presidential aspirations. He was driven to acquire some of the highest political positions of the land. Obama successfully used this drive to fuel his other passion: advocacy for the needy and underserved.

Obama's burgeoning passion for politics, which was nascent in his earlier days, would also be fueled by his intrinsic drives, as he depicted in his second book, *The Audacity of Hope*: "I know that my satisfaction is not to be found in the glare of television cameras. . . . Instead, it seems to come more often now from knowing that in some demonstrable way I've been able to help people live their lives with some measure of dignity." Obama concluded by noting a similarity between his goal and Benjamin Franklin's goal. He quoted Franklin as saying, "I would rather have it said, 'He lived usefully', than, 'He died rich.'" Obama's sincere desire to bring about prolific changes that would enhance the conditions of the disadvantaged individuals whom he was accustomed to helping is another example of his intrinsic drive.

Cindy Moelis, one of Obama's friends, observed that he was solemn and pensive because he was so smart, and she teased him once by saying, "Come on, let's talk about the last movie you saw," which was her attempt to engage him in more light-hearted discussions. Apparently, at that time, a few of his friends found him to be boring; he was serious and often engaged in political discussions. Obama talked about his political aspirations so much that some of his friends nicknamed him "governor"—others even suggested that he run for president. Moelis was mistaken in her assessment of Obama. Rather than being boring, he was intently focused on politics because it was his passion. Obama's serious demeanor and his frequent mention of his political ambition also stemmed from his passion for politics. He had an enthusiasm for politics and a desire to take his passion to great heights. Obama lived and breathed politics, which was why he appeared so intense to his friends. It was not so easy for him to socialize with those who were not, in John Maxwell's words, "people of passion." This is why Maxwell espoused the paradigm that people who are in the quest

Drive to Passion

for their passion should "associate with people of passion [because] passion is contagious."

* * *

Obama's tenure in the Illinois Senate was not without sacrifice on his part and his wife's. In fact, Michelle was not too thrilled with his decision to become a state legislator. Obama, in his second book, said about this period in their marriage, "Michelle put up no pretense of being happy with the decision. . . . Leaning down to kiss Michelle good-bye in the morning, all I would get was a peck on the cheek." In essence, Obama's foray into politics at the state level had the potential of derailing his marriage.

Obama's indifference to the hundreds of thousands of dollars he and his wife owed in college debt is typical of passionate individuals who are usually more concerned about the pursuit of their passion than any sense of trepidation they or the people around them may harbor about their undertakings or other circumstances surrounding them. Obama attempted to assuage his wife's concerns over their mounting college debt and other monetary worries by saying, "There will be plenty of time to make money—lots of it. Right now is the time to make a difference."

Following the prototype of Obama's approach to focusing on his passion rather than distractions, when there is an opportunity to explore our passion, we should always take advantage of it, without apprehensions. The opportunity to pursue our passion occurs less frequently than the opportunity to seek gainful employment, so we should seize the moment to explore our passion. If we are unsuccessful with the pursuit of our passion, we can always seek other more traditional means of supporting ourselves.

Obama set out to utilize his extrinsic and intrinsic drives to fuel his passion for politics. Although he was not driven by money, he was however extrinsically driven by power and the need to hold a high office. This was evidenced by the statements he made to Michelle and his brother-in-law about his desire to run for the U.S. Senate and possibly the presidency. At the same time, Obama was intrinsically driven by the need "to make a difference." This was also demonstrated by his statement to Michelle in this regard. Obama made his social conscience known to his friends at different times. One of his goals was to help the poor. Perhaps his extrinsic drive was prompted by his intrinsic drive: the need to become powerful in order to muster enough influence to effect real changes in the lives of the poor and the disadvantaged. Nevertheless, Obama immersed himself in his passion for politics, similar to any other individual on the quest for his passion. Regardless of what our drive or motivation may be, the key to achieving our goals is to totally immerse ourselves in our passion by transferring the focus from our drive to our passion and allowing our drive to fuel our passion.

The difficulties Obama encountered earlier as a young newlywed may be similar to the challenges we will encounter when we set out in pursuit of our passion. He had been a state senator for three years, had an eighteen-month-old child, and he and his wife were in debt; the family was just doing okay on both of their salaries. His wife was quite displeased with his political aspirations; she detested the fact that politics was taking him away from her and his child-rearing responsibilities. Obama was under tremendous pressure from his family as a result of his decision to delve into politics—the type of pressure that could potentially lead to the dissolution of a marriage—but he neither buckled nor quivered under pressure.

The pursuit of our passion is not for risk-averse or fearful individuals. Assertiveness, courage, and resilience are among the requisite attributes for the quest for our dreams. All of the individuals in this book were courageous and took considerable risks in the pursuit of their passion. Sidney Poitier took a few risks. He not only had the courage to move to New York City, despite all the uncertainties that lay ahead, but he turned down a job that he deemed unsuitable, even though he was near destitution. "I don't get as tensed or stressed," Obama said, in reference to his family's financial situation and his wife's discomfort about it. "I'm more comfortable with uncertainty and risk." Abraham Lincoln and Winston Churchill were both heads of state during difficult wars. They both pushed ahead with unflinching courage despite these uncertainties. Suze Orman lost a huge amount of borrowed seed money in the mid-1970s when she was only in her 20s. Yet, she pushed ahead with confidence until she recovered all the lost funds. All these individuals displayed tremendous courage in the face of risks, which is what we should do once we decide to pursue our passion.

Amid his wife's dissatisfaction with his political aspirations—the lack of abundant income in the family and some potential risks inherent in the quest for a political office, such as the loss of personal funds—Obama decided to run for U.S. Congress, representing Illinois. Although he knew that it would be difficult to unseat the incumbent congressman, Bobby Rush, Obama was undaunted. He took on the enormous challenge of running against a popular incumbent. His advisers, including his wife, pointed out that the task he was about to undertake was practically insurmountable. Obama still followed his passion and proceeded with his bid for congressional office. He lost.

Like Abraham Lincoln, who lost his senatorial bid but was not impeded by it, Obama could not be hindered by his failed congressional bid. Naturally, he felt saddened by the loss and even sulked about it. But he quickly got over his defeat and frustrations and moved on. Again, like Lincoln, Obama would continue in his quest for his passion with zest and alacrity. Setbacks will always occur in all pursuits and endeavors that lead to success and greatness, but we cannot allow ourselves to be deterred by them. The best approach for us is to learn from our disappointments and remain tenacious and resilient. Success and greatness will abound through our persistent quest for our passion.

Obama almost caved in to pressure and the need to make more money to meet his family's mounting financial obligations when he interviewed for a $300,000 a year job. However, he was unsuccessful at securing this position either by design or as a result of a lack of desire for it, which may have been inadvertently manifested by him during the interview. His aspirations were more important to him than earning this sum of money over the short term. However, in the long run, he knew that, through the successful quest of his passion, he would be able to make more than enough money to meet his financial obligations.

Despite the post-September 11 association of Obama's name with the name Osama, his wife's apprehensions toward his political aspirations and its imminent threat to his marriage, and his bleak financial situation, Obama was courageous enough to run again for political office. He consulted with his powerful friends and advisers and geared up to run for the U.S. Senate. Some of his confidants met his enthusiasm with skepticism; nonetheless, others were excited about the prospect of Obama becoming a senator.

Obama had one more thing to do prior to running for office: He had to persuade his wife, who was less than enthused about his continuous bid for political positions, to be amenable to his intention of running for the Senate. His selling point was that, if he failed in his bid for the Senate, he would completely give up any further attempts to run for a political office and concentrate on acquiring a job that would enable him to generate the type of income they needed to meet their financial obligations.

Obama decided to attend the annual Conference of the Congressional Black Caucus in Washington, D.C., in an attempt to garner support for his Senate bid. What he discovered was both disheartening and distasteful. According to Christopher Andersen's biography, *Barack and Michelle*, rather than getting the support and validation he so ardently sought, Obama discovered, much to his dismay, that he was being propositioned by some of the women at the event. "I don't care if you're married," Obama was told. "I am not asking you to leave your wife—just come on." He, of course, did not yield to the advances made by the women at the Congressional Black Caucus. Obama's experience is a reminder that we should be cognizant of temptations and distractions and their potential to derail our quest for our passion.

Once Obama began to test the waters—to determine his viability as a political speaker, by addressing various gatherings—his delivery and method of response to questions came under scrutiny by his wife. She told him that his delivery at these gatherings was suggestive of someone who was talking down to his audience, which comprised blue-collar people. She also told him that he hesitated too long when responding to questions. Michelle recommended that Obama speak the language of his audience; she said that this would be the best way to communicate with his potential constituents. She suggested that he emulate great

Drive to Passion

orators such as Reverend Martin Luther King Jr. and other eloquent ministers.

Obama took Michelle's suggestion and began to emulate the oratory skills, in certain cases, of great black speakers. He demonstrated that in our bid to attain excellence in those activities relating to our passion, people whom we admire for their attainment of excellence and expertise in our field of endeavor, or in a related field, can serve as teachers in our education and practice sessions, as we pursue our passion.

Amid the rigors and excitement of Obama's Senate campaign, his wife remained steadfast in her support for him, and it was evident that he valued her advice and opinions. She made a 180-degree turnaround from her initial reservations about his Senate bid by ardently supporting him. Already his confidante, she became his adviser, critic, cheerleader, and the force that would keep him grounded. According to Andersen, Michelle would give Obama crucial advice such as, "Stick to your guns," in an effort to encourage him to disallow the editing of his speech at the Democratic National Convention (DNC). She was also instrumental in convincing him to adopt the "Yes We Can" slogan for his presidential campaign and further underscoring its potential effectiveness. Obama's wife would be actively involved in orchestrating the dismissal of a campaign staffer who was allegedly not only flirting with Obama, but was also developing a closeness with him that made her uncomfortable.

All hands were on deck and efforts underway in Obama's bid for the Senate. In conjunction with his mentor at the Illinois State Senate, Obama engineered the passage of a few bills, thus establishing a track record of accomplishments. He positioned himself to raise funds. His opponent for the U.S. Senate seat was found to have a blemish in his background; this served to minimize competition for Obama. This mirrored the situation that he had encountered during his bid for the Illinois State Senate.

In an effort to bolster his campaign, Obama and his staff, after much effort, secured a spot for him to deliver the keynote address at the DNC, where Senator John Kerry was nominated for president. This was a milestone, compared to the prior DNC for Al Gore's presidential nomination, when Obama was refused admission into the convention. He had flown over 1,700 miles, from Chicago to Los Angeles, for Gore's nomination, and, prior to his drive to the convention venue, had experienced and overcome a setback in renting a car at the L.A. airport because his credit card was declined. He had to return to Chicago to explain to his wife that he was refused entry into the DNC.

Obama wrote and delivered an excellent speech at the DNC. He revised his speech several times and practiced it to perfection in a manner similar to Winston Churchill. Obama followed in the footsteps of other great orators such as Abraham Lincoln and Martin Luther King Jr. Passion in place, speech in hand and, according to Andersen, a word of advice from his wife saying, "Just don't screw it up, Buddy," Obama proceeded to the podium to deliver his speech. His wife's word of advice was designed to be humorous and relaxing, yet candid. He started his speech by talking about his father's humble beginnings as a goat herder and then a Kenyan foreign student in Hawaii, who subsequently married a girl (his mother) from Kansas. Obama then delved into the highlight of his address, in which he made his game-changing remark: "There's not a black America and white America and Latino America and Asian America; there's the United States of America!"

Andersen further said, with Michelle "struggling to maintain her composure," and the crowd electrified, the keynote address turned out to be eloquent and the catalyst that would propel Obama and his family from relative obscurity to fame overnight. Things were never the same for Obama and his family. They were now public figures. Of course, with popularity came certain problems that accompany such recognition: Political groupies showed up frequently to the places he went; women groped him from time to time, sometimes slipping their phone numbers into his pocket. He became an instant celebrity and an overnight sensation of rock star status.

Obama went on to receive a sweeping victory to the U.S. Senate and joined the exclusive group of the few blacks who have made it to the U.S. Senate. No sooner had Obama been elected to the Senate than he began to face some of the realities of being a U.S. senator: the heavy work load; maintaining two households, one in

Drive to Passion

Washington, D.C., and the other in Chicago; being away from his family; and relearning how to live by himself.

Before long, there was buzz about Obama running for president, followed by a fortuitous sequence of events. He and his wife were guests on *The Oprah Winfrey Show*, when Oprah suggested that he consider running for president. He refused to promise anything or to comment on the suggestion. One of Obama's former colleagues at the Illinois Senate and a friend also suggested that he run for president. Obama's response was that he did he not think his wife would go along with it. He had to make sure she would be on board with him, should he decide to engage in such an arduous undertaking. *Time* magazine featured Obama on the cover with the headline, "Why Barack Obama Could Be the Next President."

Obama got to the point where he felt prepared to run for the presidency: He was passionate about politics; he had a knack for politics that he recognized earlier in his days at Occidental College; and he had the drive to seek high political positions and to make a difference. His success was based on his niche in his endeavors and his ability to transfer his drive of wanting to seek the presidency or another high office to his intense passion for politics and public service. Many of us are driven intrinsically or extrinsically at certain points in our lives, but we fail to find the appropriate niche and passion to actualize our drive; hence, many of our dreams go unrealized. The techniques in this book will enable us to identify our passion and niche. Once we identify them, it will behoove us to ensure that we focus on our niche so intently and with all amount of passion that it becomes our dominant thought. When we cease to be preoccupied with the potential rewards for our endeavors, and we become so entrenched with our passion that we live and breathe it, then we will be invariably involved in the creation of value, and subsequently, financial rewards and accolades will abound. At that point, our rewards could become so copious that they may seem to the layman like we are endowed with an overabundance of natural abilities and good fortune. Similar to Obama, we should identify a niche and muster our passion for it to actualize our drive.

Once Obama made sure his wife was on board with his passion to become president, he proceeded to initiate all the preparations to run for the office. With Obama's mentors, friends, and family on board, his campaign proceeded in full force. He assembled an eclectic and diverse group of supporters to help with his campaign. All the detractors, problems, and difficulties typical of political campaigns were present. The challenges of the campaign were even more pronounced than usual because it was a unique campaign with the potential of leading to a history-making event: An African-American who had a good chance of winning the United States presidential election was in the race.

Four years after emerging in national politics and at the age of forty-seven, President Obama became not only one of the youngest individuals to be elected president of the United States of America, but the first African-American to hold the position. He is a black man who was elected president in one of the toughest economic periods in the history of the United States, which many have styled "the Great Recession." With at least one challenging war raging and the economic conditions still below par, it remains to be seen what his legacy will be. Regardless of his legacy or whether he is a one-term or a two-term president, one fact will remain true: Obama accomplished a colossal feat that is unprecedented by becoming the first African-American president of the United States of America.

CHAPTER 8
Oprah Winfrey: Determined To Achieve Fame

Oprah Winfrey is a billionaire, a business mogul, a philanthropist, and a celebrity from humble beginnings, whose appeal spans the globe. Born to an unwed mother in rural Mississippi and partially raised by her grandmother, Oprah's upbringing was marked by abject poverty at her grandmother's house. They used an outhouse, boiled their clothes in a pot, fetched water from a well, and fed chickens and pigs. She and her grandmother slept in the same bed. Despite these lowly circumstances, she has risen to become who she is today. As a popular and wealthy former television talk show host and owner of her own television network, Oprah is a recognizable figure all over the world. She joined the ranks of one-name celebrities such as Prince and Madonna several years ago, when she came to be known simply as "Oprah." Her media empire is an awesome force. Oprah's net worth was recently estimated at $2.7 billion.

The circumstances surrounding Oprah's conception and birth were deeply rooted in promiscuity, poverty, and youthful abandon. Her mother, Vernita Lee, was a teenager; her father, Vernon Winfrey, was a twenty-year-old soldier who was on leave in Mississippi when she was conceived. Oprah's grandmother, Hattie Mae Lee, was entrusted with her care until she was six, when Vernita, who lived in Milwaukee, was able to send for her.

There, the vicious cycle of poverty would continue for Oprah, at least for a while.

Oprah's grandmother read the Bible in her spare time, and she taught Oprah how to read the holy book as a toddler. Oprah began memorizing and reciting passages from the Bible in church at a very early age. She was deemed precocious by her grandmother and her friends. They greatly admired her smartness, although they also considered her to be chatty.

Oprah's mother sent for her, and as soon as she arrived in Milwaukee to live with Vernita, she discovered that her mother was more destitute than her grandmother. Also, Oprah found out that she had two other siblings who were of a lighter complexion than she was. Her siblings were more favored by her mother and her landlady due to their lighter skin tone. Oprah's mother was young, single, uneducated, and the mother of three, trying to raise her young children without much income. Oprah encountered deplorable conditions; however, she continued to make strides in school.

Three years later, at the age of nine, Oprah's mother decided to send her to Nashville to live with her father, Vernon Winfrey, and his wife, Zelma. Vernon and Zelma did not have any children of their own; she took Oprah in and tried to raise her as her own daughter. The standard of living at her father's house was much better than what she encountered at her mother's house. Vernon was a hardworking man who owned a barbershop and a grocery store. Oprah worked at the grocery store but hated the job. She blossomed in her academic work. Zelma put her to task with regard to her intellectual development. She assigned young Oprah a certain number of books to read every week. Zelma was a disciplinarian who believed in education.

The dislike Oprah harbored for her job at her father's grocery store mirrors Abraham Lincoln's hatred for the manual labor on his father's farm. Our discontent can serve as a driving force, enabling us to seek our passion. If we are content and complacent, we can become less driven to pursue our passion. The dislike that both of these individuals felt for the work they performed in their fathers' occupations led them to conclude that they did not wish to make careers out of those occupations. Lincoln and Oprah, among their many drives, were driven to seek their own passion due to their dislike for their fathers' occupations.

One year later, Oprah was uprooted again and sent back to Milwaukee at Vernita's request. She barely had time to settle into the structure that her father and stepmother were trying to establish for her. Oprah's father was unhappy about the prospect of having to part with his daughter, but he had no choice. Vernita wanted her daughter back because she hoped to get married and create a good home for her. This did not happen.

Oprah's return to Milwaukee was marked by the same turbulence and hardships that existed in her mother's house prior to her departure to Nashville, and their effect on her was devastating. Oprah found herself in a much worse situation than ever. She became a subject of frequent sexual abuse and molestation by some of her mother's male visitors and male relatives. All the structural and disciplinary strides she had previously made at her father's house gave way to waywardness. Once again, Vernon was asked to take her back. Unbeknown to Vernon and her mother, Oprah was pregnant at the age of fourteen. The child was born prematurely and died shortly after birth.

Soon after Oprah moved back to Nashville to live with her father, her life became structured again. Vernon demanded excellence from her at school. By this time, Oprah was a teenager. She was not immune to the traits that are endemic among young adults in her age group, such as obstinacy, mood swings, restlessness, and other peculiarities, brought on by adolescent hormonal changes. Oprah was difficult, but she was not out of the realm of her father's control and discipline, which proved to be instrumental in shaping her character.

Oprah began to carve out her path to success as early as her adolescent years. She knew she wanted to be famous, and she communicated this to her father. She also made no secret of the fact that she wanted to be in broadcast journalism. She astounded judges during her participation in contests and pageants, most of which she won, with her eloquence and poise. She was Miss Black Nashville, Miss Black Tennessee, and the first black Miss Fire Prevention. She also participated in the Miss Black America contest.

Oprah's father demanded excellence from her in all aspects of her education, and she exhibited it by receiving several accolades at East High School in Nashville. She excelled in academics. She became active in the school's extracurricular activities, attaining the positions of president of the Student Council, vice president of her class, and president of the Drama Club. Among her many accomplishments, Oprah was chosen as the most popular girl in school, and she became a member of the Honor Society. An important achievement for Oprah consisted of representing the entire state of Tennessee at a White House conference during President Nixon's administration.

Oprah's drive to become famous, which spurred her passion for broadcast journalism, would contribute immensely to her remarkable accomplishments. She identified an extrinsic drive of wanting to be famous, which she vocalized to her father. She also identified her niche and passion for journalism, which would be stimulated by her drive. This is a typical model for success: having drives that we can use to fuel a passion for our niche.

Oprah abhorred her mother's precarious situation and the poverty-stricken environment in which she found herself prior to living with her father; this detestation also served as a driving force for her. There is a parallel here between Oprah's poor environment in her childhood and Sidney Poitier's poverty-stricken upbringing. Unlike Poitier, Oprah was in school, getting an education despite her challenges. Oprah was driven to become successful to avoid the destitution that she initially experienced in her childhood. Poitier was also driven by the avoidance of poverty. We are driven by many factors, and without these various drives it would be impossible to make remarkable achievements. We should endeavor to identify occurrences in our lives or aspects of our lives that we can use as drives, such as the need to elude certain hardships, or the need to prove something to ourselves or others. We can utilize many drives to prompt our accomplishments.

By indicating to her father that she would be famous, Oprah was both affirming and visualizing her future into existence. Affirmation involves a declaration of what we believe to be factual. As long as our affirmation is realistic and we truly believe it, we can use it to actualize our dream. Visualization entails creating an accurate projected mental picture or image of ourselves in our

Drive to Passion

new role. Here again, as long as our visual image of ourselves is realistic and we truly believe the projection of ourselves, we can bring our dream to fruition.

* * *

Upon graduating from high school in 1971, Oprah enrolled in Tennessee State University on a scholarship from the Elks Lodge, and she also began to make some strides in the journalism profession. When a job opportunity became available to Oprah at a radio station where she had previously been interviewed as a pageant winner during her senior year in high school, she was encouraged by her father to take the job. However, she was ambivalent about accepting the job because she thought it would interfere with her school work. Oprah eventually decided to accept the job. She read the news at the radio station and made quite an impression on her audience. She later took another job at a larger radio station, which led to an opportunity to move to a job in television news.

As is often the case with individuals who are in the quest for their passion, the path to Oprah's passion for communications and broadcast journalism was neither clearly defined nor obvious to her initially. She was ambivalent about her decision to accept a job offer at a radio station due to her concern about the interference the job would cause with her school work. Oprah's father intuitively convinced her to accept the job, which initiated a trajectory in her career in broadcasting. When Oprah first mentioned to her father that she would one day become famous, she had a different career path in mind. She thought she would become a famous movie star. Similarly, Sidney Poitier's passion was not clearly defined initially; in fact, he essentially stumbled into his job as an actor. As a dishwasher, he wanted to try something different. With nothing to lose, he auditioned for a part in a play, knowing full well that he could neither read nor write. Although he was thrown out of the theater, he discovered that he liked acting. Once we have identified our niche, we should then proceed with the pursuit of our passion in that area. We cannot linger until we are guaranteed success or until we are sure of the outcome. We may have to make slight or even major changes along the way, based on how much pleasure we take in the performance of our niche activity—but it will be for the better. The important lesson here is that as changes and adjustments occur for us along the way, while in pursuit of our passion, it would be an error in judgment to reject these changes because of the deviation they may cause from our original intention or because our intention is perhaps much more pleasing to others than our new path. Just think of what would have happened had Oprah given up her career in media in pursuit of an acting job, which was her initial attraction. It is therefore difficult to ascertain the degree to which we will enjoy a niche activity until we actually become involved in it.

Like any other young adult, Oprah was eager to assert her independence by taking a risk and pursuing her passion. The structured lifestyle and discipline established by her father, who was an ex-military man, was a bit much for her. Oprah took a leap of faith similar to other individuals of passion like Steve Jobs, Michael Dell, and Bill Gates, who never finished school. She packed up, quit school, and headed to Baltimore. Taking a leap of faith involves risk, but highly driven individuals who follow their passion are also risk takers.

Oprah accepted a job on television as the co-anchor of an evening news program in Baltimore. She was in her early twenties. Moving from the small southern city of Nashville to a large market like Baltimore—a city with a northern atmosphere—was not an easy transition for Oprah. Her adjustment to the six o'clock evening news anchor spot was a difficult one. For instance, she occasionally got so emotionally involved with the news stories that it interfered with her objectivity in delivering the news. Also, Oprah's employers had a problem with her looks—they felt that she did not portray the right image for the anchor position. They also thought she was unsophisticated. She was sent to New York City for a "makeover" to make her more alluring to her viewing audience, according to Oprah's biographer, Helen Garson. While she was getting the makeover, the permanent hair relaxer that was used to straighten her hair caused it to fall out. This debacle took its toll on Oprah: She felt inadequate for the position. As a result, she was relieved of her duties. So, according to Garson, "She lost her job as well as her hair."

Oprah's demotion was the first major failure in her professional career. Failure, in one form or another, could be considered inevitable in everyone's career path. When we are in pursuit of our passion, we should expect challenges and pockets of failure along the way. What was the delineation of Oprah's failure? Was her passion not in straight news reporting? When we are on the quest for our passion, it may take a failure to point us in the right direction. It is sometimes easier to find out what we do not like, or what we are incapable of, than it is to find our true niche and passion. Oprah enjoyed taking sides or voicing her opinion in a news context. That was her niche. She was also passionate about this aspect of the news. Oprah would later confess that the human relations aspect of the news, and the subsequent emotional connection that she made with people was as "natural as breathing [air]." She enjoyed the bond she forged with the individuals on her show.

The following statements—similar to Oprah's phrase "natural as breathing"—depict the existence of passion in an activity encompassing our niche: We live, sleep and breathe the activity; we cannot wait to wake up in the morning to get involved in it; when we are involved in this activity, we become oblivious to the passage of time; and we take so much pleasure in our involvement in the activity that we are absolutely riveted by it. These statements are relevant to our involvement in a particular activity over an extended period of time. We should exercise caution in choosing activities about which we may be passionate; a heightened sense of excitement for an activity, which quickly fades away, is not an indication of the existence of passion. As long as we are resolute in our decision to identify our passion, we should be able to do so with persistence, resilience, and patience.

Oprah was pointed in the direction of her actual niche and passion by her station manager and mentor, Richard Sher, who liked her and recognized her flair for forming an emotional bond with the people she interviewed. He established a slot for her as a co-host in the morning talk show *People Are Talking*, which reignited her career. As we proceed to identify our niche and pursue our passion, we will come across opportunities. They will be made available to us by our mentors and through other avenues; the more we strive and acquire mentors, the more we are exposed to opportunities. Opportunities come in different forms. There are some intricacies involved in encountering and taking advantage of opportunities: We are better positioned to take advantage of opportunities if we are on the quest for our passion when we encounter such opportunities; we are also better positioned to take advantage of them if we actually have a niche or calling in the activities involved; and opportunities may not always be accessible to us in plain and simple terms—they may sometimes be available to us in the semblance of an obstacle. Therefore, we should have the capability of recognizing and discerning opportunities when we encounter them.

Mentors perform a variety of functions in helping to bring the pursuit of our passion to fruition. Nevertheless, most of the effort and hard work needed to keep the wheels of our passion in motion are still our responsibility, including the job of identifying an appropriate mentor. Mentors could be individuals who provide us with breakthrough ideas or some advice on how to channel our passion to the right avenues to enable us to make great achievements. Mentors could also be individuals who identify our passions, niches, strengths, and capabilities that have gone unnoticed and unused by us. In Oprah's case, Sher not only provided her with the opportunity to maximize her passion, but he also made her aware of her strengths. Our mentors could be our friends, relatives, subordinates, superiors, neighbors, or offspring. Anyone who has our best interest at heart—who genuinely wants to help us and has skills or knowledge to impart to us—could be our mentor. The best way to embrace a mentor is to keep an open mind and have the capability of recognizing her when we come across her.

Oprah's mentor was right: Connecting with people was truly her passion. The ratings of the show *People Are Talking* became larger in the Baltimore area than *The Phil Donahue Show*, which was the number one syndicated show in the nation. Oprah enjoyed making her opinions known and bonding with her audience. She held this job for almost six years, after which she began seeking

Drive to Passion

another position. It became obvious to her that she needed to reach a wider audience.

One of the essential factors that foster the quest for our passion is having the ability and insight to maneuver ourselves from one setting to another to buoy the achievement of our goals. Oprah recognized that her career had stagnated after being in the Baltimore market with the same show for six years. Thus, she began to look around for a larger market to bolster her passion and her profession. Similarly, Joseph Kennedy utilized this method of mobility in his vocation to enhance his quest for his passion. He leveraged his position as a bank examiner to rapidly increase his knowledge in the banking industry. He maneuvered himself from place to place to avoid stagnation and to boost his career and his quest for his passion.

At age thirty, Oprah secured a new job in Chicago hosting *AM Chicago*—a show that would spur the trajectory of her career. She had finally arrived at a setting where she could maximize her passion. One dislike she harbored for her previous position was that she had a co-host. She wanted her own show, which was what she got in Chicago. Her new mentors here comprised Debra DiMaio and Dennis Swanson. DiMaio, who was Oprah's acquaintance and co-worker in Baltimore at the television station, had moved to Chicago before Oprah. She had introduced Oprah to Swanson, the station manager in Chicago and her new boss. After Oprah was hired, Swanson encouraged her to be herself. Initially, Oprah was slightly intimidated by Phil Donahue, whose show was the number one talk show in the nation. She took Swanson's advice and connected with people emotionally rather than trying to compete directly with Phil Donahue. Two years later, at age thirty-two, Oprah's show became a nationally syndicated talk show. Subsequently, it became the number one talk show in America.

Rather than being in direct competition with Phil Donahue, Oprah was advised to concentrate on her niche and conduct her show uniquely. Oprah's niche and passion consisted of empathizing with her audience. According to *Success* magazine, an aspect of Suze Orman's success principles is "find your niche and become an expert" in it. Oprah had great mentors who pointed her in the right direction, which invariably enabled her to zero in on her niche of connecting with people. She cried with her audience when she needed to and rejoiced with them when the occasion warranted. She connected with her audience emotionally, and her show achieved unprecedented success.

We all have a niche, a passion, or an activity that we enjoy. A common misunderstanding is that a passion can only be a hobby or a recreational activity. I once read a magazine article about a high-powered female attorney, a senior vice president in a *Fortune* 500 company, who said that she normally got together with friends in the evenings and on weekends to play music, and that it was her true passion because she enjoyed it so much. My impression from this article was that she may not have been passionate about her career, since music was her true passion. This may conform to the old paradigm that a job is an arduous affair that is not designed to be enjoyed. Today, there are many activities that can create marketable value and be fun at the same time. Jobs should not be deemed activities from which we cannot derive pleasure, or they should not be considered to be activities for which we cannot be passionate. In fact, the more delight we take in our jobs, or the more passionate we are about them, the higher the level of our performance, as long as we have a niche in the activities involved.

Many governments around the world are loosening their tight control on their economies and allowing free market forces to cause propitious conditions for their citizens, who are involved in the creation of marketable value through the pursuit of their passion and niche. This dynamic enables people in these societies to enjoy the fruits of their labor without interference. Here in the U.S., we should be perpetually appreciative of the freedom we have to pursue our passion, which is a key ingredient in "Yankee ingenuity." To attain expertise in our pursuit, we should identify a niche upon which our passion should be predicated. As we begin to create marketable value through the pursuit of this passion, the laws of economics (supply and demand) will ensue, enabling us to benefit financially from it.

While in the quest for our passion, we should remember that we cannot simply sit around deliberating on our passion and waiting

Drive to Passion

for a clear revelation of it. We should, in essence, try our hands at as many endeavors as are necessary, possibly on a part-time basis, to uncover our niche and passion. Once we identify our niche, we cannot maintain a lukewarm attitude toward it; we should "live and breathe" it; this translates into passion. Conversely, the pursuit of our passion may not be for everyone. It takes courage and risk tolerance to pursue our passion. It could still be fulfilling to obtain an education and a job, possibly one that we like, and make our contributions to society in doing so.

* * *

Following her successful foray into the talk show industry, Oprah took advantage of her relationship with her mentors to forge sound collaborative ventures and to propel herself to great heights. Debra DiMaio, who had previously mentored Oprah, now became her key employee, ally, and protégé. Her business associations with the King Brothers and Jeff Jacobs, an entertainment attorney, were instrumental in her monumental ascension in television broadcasting and business. Roger and Michael King, brothers who together inherited a marginally successful syndication distribution company, King World Productions, from their father, used their business acumen to turn it into a successful company. They were responsible for the distribution of Oprah's show to television stations across the nation. Jacobs, who was Oprah's friend as well as a partner, collaborated with her and later owned 10 percent of her company. He eventually became the de facto president of Oprah's company.

AM Chicago was renamed *The Oprah Winfrey Show*. In 1987, she was awarded an Emmy. Over the years, King World maintained sole distributorship of *The Oprah Winfrey Show*; even after the sale of the company to CBS, it retained exclusive rights to distribute the show. Earnings from *The Oprah Winfrey Show* consisted of 40 percent of the total revenue of King World. Oprah, in her sound business judgment, became a major stockholder in King World.

Similar to other cases involving the fervent quest for education and practice by individuals in pursuit of their passion, Oprah learned to perfect her skills by watching tapes of Phil Donahue and Barbara Walters. The people we admire, who are experts in the industry in which we aspire to be an expert, are the ideal people from whom we can learn, as we proceed to educate ourselves in the vocation of our passion. We can also emulate them as we practice, keeping in mind that it is crucial that we maintain our individuality and uniqueness. Oprah was engaged in a rigorous learning and preparation process by striving to learn from some of the best in the industry as she and her show came of age, and I am sure that she is continuously learning and practicing as she persists in her search for excellence and the pursuit of her passion. Sidney Poitier, Winston Churchill, Joe Kennedy, and Abraham Lincoln perpetually educated and rigorously prepared themselves while in pursuit of their passion, throughout their careers. Irrespective of the degree of our drive or passion in our profession, we should strive for expertise in perpetuity. Certain National Basketball Association (NBA) superstars have been known to distinguish themselves from their colleagues by taking several hundred free throws daily, on their own time, as a means of perfecting their skills. Unrelenting practice, preparation and education are imperative as we pursue our passion.

* * *

By 1993, at the age of thirty-nine, Oprah was worth $93 million, and ten years later she would become a billionaire. In the process of her ascension to prominence, Oprah continued to display tremendous business savvy: She acquired a controlling interest in *The Oprah Winfrey Show*; she formed the Harpo Entertainment Group; she bought 8 percent of Oxygen Media, a cable channel devoted to women's issues; in 2000, she partnered with the Hearst Publishing Company to form *O* magazine; and in 2011, she formed the Oprah Winfrey Network (OWN), a television network. Oprah has an aggregate net worth of $2.7 billion with all the trappings of wealth, including a private jet and mansions.

Oprah's philosophy is that of personal responsibility and self-help. We humans could not have advanced this far without being self-reliant and believing in our God-given strengths and capabilities. Oprah's mantras are: "Excellence is the best barrier

Drive to Passion

to both sexism and racism," and "The path to freedom is through education." She is not involved in organized religion, although she attends church on occasion. Oprah believes that God is the guiding force, church exists in all of us, and if we are able to find a "connection to a higher power, anything is attainable." The Biblical tenet that God created humans in his own image and gave us dominion over the earth is relevant here. In essence, God exists in all of us, and we are in control of our own destiny.

Oprah's great qualities consist of her kindness, generosity, and philanthropic drive. She has been known to give her employees and family members expensive gifts. Oprah continues to give even when some of her family members, especially those who have a sense of entitlement, have accused her of not doing enough for them. She was generous toward her half-sisters, who were more favored than she was as children. Patricia Lloyd, one of her sisters, accused her of not doing enough for her and disclosed some of Oprah's secrets to the press to make a few bucks. Oprah forgave her and still continued to give her money. Oprah's philanthropic efforts span the globe. She recently built a school for girls in South Africa at an estimated cost of $40 million. She is known to have donated all of her salary, totaling $500,000, to a scholarship fund, which was matched by ABC television network, her employer. Oprah has given generously to black colleges. She was instrumental in the creation of the Angel Network, an organization that encourages those who are fortunate to give back to the less fortunate.

When we go from drive to passion, we create value through the subsequent realization of our goals. The benefits the world derives from us are associated with the value we create. This could also elicit our acts of benevolence. Therefore, the rewards to society from the realization of our passion are tremendous: We make a difference and foster progress, thus making life more enjoyable.

Oprah, in addition to her philanthropic efforts, has served as a mentor to some and created auspicious conditions for others. Her association with Phillip McGraw—a psychologist who would be known as Dr. Phil—would propel him from relative obscurity in Texas to the national limelight. She would first meet him during her mad cow disease trial in Texas. Dr. Phil, who would be introduced to Oprah as the psychologist who would serve as her adviser on the case, became instrumental in winning the case. They would become friends in the process. At Oprah's invitation, Dr. Phil would become a regular on her show and later branch out into his own show. Creating opportunities for others and mentoring have become two of her trademarks. In addition to Dr. Phil, she has mentored Rachael Ray, Suze Orman, Dr. Oz, and others. She has also created opportunities for several writers by featuring them on her show and book club. She has given full scholarships to youths to go to school. Oprah, whose mentors played a pivotal role in enabling her career to come to fruition, became a mentor herself, helping others realize their dreams. Her experience shows how the mentor-protégé relationship can be symbiotic and how a previous protégé can in turn become a mentor to others.

Books played a great role in Oprah's upbringing, and her affinity for books has remained with her. This love of books is one of Oprah's pivotal reasons for forming a book club in 1996. The book club comprised individuals who shared her interest in books. They got on the air once a month to discuss books Oprah and members of the club had read and liked. Authors were individually invited to answer questions and to participate in discussions. Her book club provided many writers with much-needed exposure and credence. New, relatively unknown writers were able to instantly sell a million or more copies of their books after being featured on Oprah's book club. Oprah officially ended the book club in the summer of 2002. The task of screening one book per month had become arduous for Oprah and her staff. She reinstated her book club in 2003 with a slightly different twist: She focused more on classics. Oprah continues to invite authors to her show, despite the debacle of an author who embellished events in his memoir and lied about his previous substance abuse problem.

Oprah has had the opportunity to explore her other passion: acting. As previously mentioned, she initially thought acting would become her claim to fame. Oprah's foray into the movie industry as an actress consisted of playing roles in a few movies: *The Color Purple*, *The Women of Brewster Place*, and *Beloved*. She still contends that acting is her first love. Oprah has also been the producer of a few movies including *Precious* and *The Women of Brewster Place*.

Some of Oprah's close friends have served as her confidants and mentors, and have supported her whenever she needed it. Quincy Jones, one of Oprah's friends, met her by chance. He was in Chicago for a Michael Jackson trial, and happened to catch Oprah's *AM Chicago* show on television in his hotel room. Jones, who was the co-producer of the movie *The Color Purple*, was absolutely riveted by Oprah and her show. She made such a big impression on him that he decided he had found the right person to play the role of Sofia in the movie. Their relationship blossomed from there. Gayle King, Oprah's best friend, was a production assistant at the same television station in Baltimore where Oprah was an anchorperson. King had admired Oprah from a distance. However, their friendship did not start until King, who had a long commute, was snowed in at work one winter day and Oprah, who lived close by, invited King to stay at her house. Their friendship developed from there. Since then, they have given each other tremendous emotional support. The poet Maya Angelou forged a relationship with Oprah that was instrumental in her life: She served as both a role model and a friend. Although Angelou is more than twenty-six years Oprah's senior, their lives mirror each other in some respects, perhaps explaining their closeness. They had each lived with their grandmothers at an early age, were sexually abused while young, and were both teenage mothers.

Although Oprah is currently unmarried, she does have a companion, Stedman Graham, with whom she has spent the past two decades. Their relationship could be described as sound and unshakable. Even though Oprah and Graham have been together this long, marriage is still out of the question for them. The novelty and sensation-seeking press and tabloids have published several swirling romance stories about them. The fact still remains that they are together and very supportive of each other. Without any children thus far, Oprah continues to maintain that children are out of the question for her. Prior to Graham, Oprah, like most people, went through a few relationships, some pleasant and some not so pleasant, but the cumulative effects of these failed relationships have been instrumental in helping to give her a great perspective on romantic relationships.

Oprah's magazine, *O*, has done very well, despite the high failure rate for magazines. Although the magazine's topics are eclectic, it has middle-class females as its target market. The topics *O* magazine regularly covers include books, cosmetics, dating, and weight. The publication of *O* is jointly handled by Harpo Entertainment and the Hearst Corporation. Its circulation is in excess of two and a half million readers, with annual revenue of over $140 million. The success of *O* magazine could be attributed to its partnership with a reputable publisher and Oprah's quest for excellence—a quest for excellence manifested by the detailed style with which she manages all aspects of the magazine, from such minuscule details as punctuation in its text to its format. *O* currently outperforms older, more seasoned magazines such as *Vogue*. According to Garson, "Every issue of the magazine has a different subject." This is different from the setup of other similar magazines.

Oprah has had numerous challenges, like everyone else. One of the most significant challenges she faced was the mad cow debacle. For Oprah, the ensuing trial from this predicament was rather cumbersome and disconcerting. This fiasco developed when Howard Lyman appeared on Oprah's show to discuss the mad cow disease. This disease stemmed from contaminated cattle feed, which was made partially from cattle infected with the mad cow disease. All of the cattle that ate this feed contracted mad cow disease. This was around 1996, when the disease was prevalent in Britain. The people who had eaten beef contaminated with mad cow disease were also showing symptoms of the disease. When Lyman made this known on Oprah's show, she responded by saying that she was not going to touch another burger. Due to Oprah's immense popularity, the futures market responded with a sharp decline, which set off a chain reaction in the beef industry; beef prices took a nose dive. As a result of this upheaval, Oprah and Lyman were sued by Texas cattlemen.

During the trial, Oprah moved her show to Amarillo, Texas, and her attitude toward this challenge is noteworthy. Much to the dismay of her opponents, her presence in Amarillo caused a media frenzy. Despite objections from Oprah's adversaries about disruptions by star-struck locals and the undue influence her celebrity status might have on the case, people still lined up and waited to catch a glimpse of her. They also wanted to get into the courthouse to witness the trial. These objections fell on deaf ears. Oprah was not sure she was going to prevail, but she demonstrated persistence and never complained. All of her friends rallied around to support her. Gayle remarked during the trial that "Oprah is no whiner and dislikes those who are." Oprah's lawyers brilliantly defended her, and she emerged victorious.

Oprah, who is now middle-aged, is vibrant and has her whole life ahead of her. It will be interesting to see what strides she will make in the future and what more we can learn from her exemplary life. The year 2011 marked the end of *The Oprah Winfrey Show* as we know it, and subsequently, she is devoting her entire efforts to the operation of her network, OWN. I am sure she will remain persistent on her quest for her passion. The prolificacy of Oprah's career will not lie in an impassive bid on her part to increase her net worth beyond $2.7 billion; rather, it will lie in the pursuit of her passion and creation of value. Invariably, this paradigm results in the creation of marketable value and the subsequent increase in such extrinsic rewards as income, revenue, and net worth.

CHAPTER 9
Realizing Our Powers

As we proceed with our mission of finding solutions to the sometimes esoteric challenge of empowering ourselves to become driven to pursue our passion, we should keep in mind that, although philosophy, spirituality, personal development, and other dogmas do not present easy solutions, they contribute tremendously toward spurring our drive and passion. We should utilize whichever aspect of these techniques and in any eclectic mix we deem suitable to accomplish our objectives. It is important to note that, as much as we need to be in the right frame of mind to pursue our passion, the pursuit of our passion helps to make our lives more purposeful and thus healthier—especially as we approach old age. Rather than seeking happiness and peace of mind directly, we can indirectly achieve these attributes by making our lives more purposeful and meaningful through the pursuit of our passion.

There are various views in the world on how to increase our focus and improve our minds and our thoughts in our bid to attain self-actualization, morality, balance, and peace of mind. They entail incorporating personal development, spirituality, philosophy, religion, meditation, and other beliefs that we may have into our lives. Exploring all these views is not the purpose of this book; however, in addition to seeking the best techniques for enhancing our efforts to be driven to attain our passion, we need to make sense of everything in our world in order to increase our comfort level and reduce uncertainties. The absence of any sustainable thought management process in us or a belief system or any notion that there is a collective purpose much greater than our individual goals could mean the difference between a high accomplishment or the lack thereof, as we go from drive to passion.

It is pragmatic to seek to improve ourselves in perpetuity. Life was not designed to be uncomplicated or to make our quest for knowledge, answers, and personal development easy or conclusive; therefore, it is advantageous for us to continuously seek answers to our questions. The idea of maximizing our full potential or embarking on self-actualization through the pursuit of our passion is not born of left-or right-wing idealism, rather, it is born of rational thinking and the need for advancement. The world is dynamic; change is one of the few constants. We humans have so far tremendously influenced the way the world has turned out. We should continue to meet our challenges in order to foster development and make a difference.

We have come a long way from the days of carts and horses to the modern era of iPads and supersonic jets, and we should continue to exert great influence over our future by empowering ourselves to do so through the enhancement of our thoughts and the subsequent pursuit of our passion. It will behoove us to unremittingly direct our thought processes toward solving problems of epic proportions such as eradicating our energy dependence on fossil fuels, preventing earthquakes, and stopping global warming. Two hundred years ago, humans had no idea of how the world would turn out in two hundred years. Why should we not steer our world toward some of the major accomplishments that we expect in the next two hundred years? We all have different niches or callings, and the pursuit of our goals in the areas encompassing our niche—by means of a combination of our drive and passion—will enable us to keep the dynamism of the world in motion for the better.

How can we utilize personal development to become driven and passionate about those activities for which we have a niche in order to make all the accomplishments that we desire? How should we design or pattern our lifestyle to achieve what we want in life? It is useful to constantly be on the quest for answers. Personal development buoys our drive and our quest for our passion; it enhances our resilience, courage, and our ability to tackle our challenges and failures. Visualization, affirmation, positive thinking, meditation, self-actualization, and asking ourselves self-directing questions all fall under the category of personal development. If embarked upon correctly, they will enable us to reach our goals. Personal development is vital in going from drive to passion. Our quest for self-improvement is good for us to the extent that it fosters passion and positive attributes in us. When we fail or make mistakes, we adjust, learn from the situation, and remain resilient through the use of personal development.

Visualization is an important component of personal development and our quest for our passion. While it is imperative that we dream big and visualize ourselves in accomplished positions, we also have to visualize the process of reaching our goals, and see ourselves in our mind's eye going through the process successfully. It is therefore crucial that we make all of our visualizations believable to us. If they are not believable, our objectives may not be attainable. Our drive and passion can be enhanced by our visualizations. As we become more specific about what we visualize, we improve our chances of attaining our goals.

Affirmation and positive thinking are closely linked, and they can enable us to reach our goals. When we affirm, we should ensure that our affirmations are believable to us—otherwise, they may be in vain. For instance, if we repeat to ourselves, "I am one of the best musicians in the world," it may never come to fruition because we may never truly believe it. On the other hand, if we say to ourselves, "I am on my way to becoming one of the best musicians in the world," and we practice fervently with delight, then our chances of accomplishing this dream will become greater because we are more likely to believe this affirmation. Of course, affirmations should be done in current, progressive, and positive terms; they should also be made with emotion and enthusiasm. The latter affirmation is both positive and progressive. An affirmation like, "I will not accept second best," is not positive because it lacks an affirmative plan that we can believe. Positive thinking intertwines with our confidence, which stems from believing in ourselves and our capabilities. We can bolster our confidence through effective action: engaging in customized education, becoming engrossed in ardent practice, and preparing ourselves. Our drives and passion narrow our positive thoughts and affirmations to those specific goals that we want to achieve, thus making them more believable to us and subsequently more attainable.

Meditation enables us to manage our thought process by mustering the discipline to focus on a serene setting or on our inner self, while controlling our breathing and being still for a length of time of our choosing until we are able to achieve serenity, which will in turn enable us to later focus on our goals. Consequently, we can either continue to relax or redirect our thoughts to our drive and the pursuit of our passion.

Asking ourselves the right questions to propel us to great heights is one of the most viable ways of enabling our drive and passion to come to fruition. It is also one of the most effective and pragmatic avenues of personal development. However, similar to affirmations, our questions should be appropriate and capable of stimulating the right action. A good question, assuming we have a niche in music, would be, "How can I become one of the best musicians in the world?" This question should enable us to point our thoughts and actions in the right direction.

* * *

The pursuit of our passion will give rise to more human advancement and discoveries, which will continue to serve the purpose of uncovering some of the enigmas of life including our beliefs, thus making it possible to maximize our full potential. There was a time when certain inexplicable illnesses were attributed to anger of the gods until modern medicine unraveled the actual causes and cures of these diseases. Knowledge will continue to elucidate the mysteries of the world and dispel myths. The maximization of our full potential through the pursuit of our passion also enables us to realize our powers.

Our integrity and the credibility of our beliefs will be greatly enhanced if we lead an exemplary lifestyle, despite our fallibilities. This will help to portray us and our beliefs in a positive light. What good would it do us and society to assert that we are religious or spiritual, if we are in fact malevolent and diabolical, and we commit atrocious acts in the name of religion or for any reason whatsoever?

An illustration of the religious aspects of our beliefs and its relativity to our quest for our passion was manifested in a sermon delivered by an intelligent minister whom I admire, in a Sunday service at his church. He used a story from the Bible in the Book of Acts to demonstrate the fact that we may not always reach the exact goal to which we aspire, but we may, however, reach a similar goal that is more appropriate for us. In this story, a man whose limbs were impaired to the point of losing the function of his legs was positioned daily at the gate of the Temple by his friends and relatives to beg for gold and silver. As Peter and John approached the Temple, he proceeded to beg for gold and silver, and Peter said, "Silver or gold I do not have, but what I have I give you. In the name of Jesus of Nazareth, walk." Peter took him by the hand and pulled him up. He got up, stood on his feet, and walked. This relates to the Chinese proverb, "Give a man a fish and he will eat for a day. Teach him how to fish and he will eat for a lifetime." The lame man's ability to regain the use of his limbs, as he begged for gold and silver, gave him the capability of being self-reliant, while at the same time affording him more propitious circumstances of amassing his own wealth. Oprah aspired to be a journalist and thought she had a passion for straight news reporting, but unbeknown to her, her real passion was in talk show hosting. As we embark on the quest for our passion, we should maintain some flexibility to enable us to adjust our pursuits to suit our exact niche.

Comparable to the need for us to have the ability to recognize our exact passion based on our niche, we should have the capability to discern an opportunity when we encounter it, as illustrated in the following fable. During the massive flood caused by Hurricane Katrina in New Orleans, a woman who was by herself in her house while the flood was raging prayed to God to rescue her. She stood at her doorstep and watched the water rise almost to the base of her door. As she looked out into the distance, she saw a boat approaching her house to rescue her. She waved the rescuers off, telling them that God was going to rescue her. As the rain continued, she climbed onto her rooftop as the water rose. Shortly thereafter, a helicopter approached her house, hovering overhead, ready to rescue her. She waved it off, telling the rescuers that she was waiting for God to rescue her. She drowned and went to heaven where she saw Saint Peter. She complained to him that her prayers had gone unanswered during the flood. Saint Peter expressed surprise to see her there and told her that a boat and a helicopter had been sent to rescue her. This indicates that opportunities are presented to us in various forms. Abraham Lincoln unsuccessfully ran for the United States Senate. He was undeterred by his inability to capture the Senate seat. When the opportunity arose, just two years later, to run for the presidency—although he was initially doubtful of his chances of winning—he recognized the propitious circumstance and took advantage of it, rather than waiting for additional signs.

The espousal of self-help and the work ethic in the Bible depicts an aspect of the pursuit of gainful employment, which encompasses the quest for our passion from a religious perspective. Paul, who was a missionary, a great philosopher, and an apostle, discussed the work ethic in II Thessalonians in the Bible: "If anyone will not work, neither shall he eat." It portrays the decisiveness and finality of the consequence of the choice not to work. This quote from Paul espouses self-reliance as a means of enabling us to obtain the basic needs of life. The quest for our passion goes beyond obtaining employment at the subsistence level. It entails engaging in an endeavor that has the potential of producing employment for others, creating value, producing wealth, and enhancing the quality of life for everyone.

The story in Matthew in the Bible about a businessman who delegated to each of his employees tasks according to their abilities is an example of management, success, wealth, class distinction, niche, and passion. It also illustrates the rewards for our passion and efforts. This businessman gave his employees different amounts of money to invest. To one he gave five talents; to another he gave two talents; to a third, he gave only one talent. The employee who was given five talents doubled the amount he was given, demonstrating his commitment to the business, his passion, and his knack for it. The second employee who was entrusted with two talents also doubled the amount he was given, by investing wisely and showing astuteness and commitment. However, the third individual, to whom only one talent was given, conformed to the assessment of his boss—he was the least dedicated to the business. He did not invest the money given to him; instead, he dug a hole and buried it. Obviously, the money did not yield any return.

Upon the boss's return, all three employees turned in their funds. The first employee delivered his ten talents to his boss and informed him of his success. His boss commended him for attaining a 100 percent ROI and invited him to celebrate the occasion with him, with promises of a great future in the organization. The second individual, who had a total of four talents, also delivered his funds to his boss. He was equally commended and was invited to celebrate with them. He was also promised a good future in the organization. The third employee, who buried his one talent in the ground, turned it in, rudely accusing his boss of being an unscrupulous businessman. His boss had a few harsh words for him as well.

This story ends with a few morals and a hint that the rich will get richer, while the poor get poorer. The businessman decided to turn all the responsibilities and money over to the employee with the ten talents and suggested that those employees without passion and initiative should not expect to do well. The story illustrates the fact that those who continue to strive persistently for their passion will be rewarded with leadership opportunities and wealth—a sharp contrast to the life of destitution to which those who do not strive will be relegated.

We are fortunate to have great books that serve as teaching guides on religion, spirituality, and philosophy that contribute toward enabling us to buttress the development of our drive and, subsequently, the pursuit of our passion. As we continue on our quest for truth and more knowledge based on the dynamics of the world, newer teachings will emerge that will either refute or augment existing teachings. The following are some examples of the repudiation of previous dogmas: The Bible calls for slaves to obey their masters, and slavery is now against the law; the Bible calls for children to obey their parents, but this should not be applicable to cases of child molestation or abuse. The overlapping of the Ten Commandments in the Bible with some of the laws in the United States and other countries serves to delineate the combination of new tenets with the old. The acquisition of more knowledge in religion, spirituality, and philosophy will continue to demystify some of the puzzles that we are confronted with, and it will help us to understand our world better, make it more predictable, and increase our level of comfort. All of this knowledge, if utilized individually in a beneficial manner, will continue to enhance our drive and the quest for our passion.

* * *

Lincoln's position on religion was obvious when he ran for the United States Congress against a Methodist minister who accused him of being against Christianity. According to Ronald White in *A. Lincoln*, to clear the air, Lincoln made his position on religion known: "That I am not a member of any Christian Church, is true; but . . . I have never spoken with intentional disrespect of religion in general, or of any denomination of Christians in particular." Admitting that he was not a member of organized religion was a bold divulgence for a politician in Lincoln's time, or in any era. Most politicians in America probably would not openly declare their lack of involvement in organized Christian religion, for fear of political retribution by voters, especially conservative voters. Lincoln, however, was unafraid to make his position known. Although Lincoln was not a member of organized religion, he believed in God and read the Bible, from which he quoted passages on occasion during his speeches. He also used the Bible as a source of inspiration and an avenue for summoning his powers of self-actualization. In defense of himself against the accusation from his nemesis, Lincoln said he did not see himself supporting anyone running for a political position, who was an "open enemy of, and scoffer at, religion."

Winston Churchill decried religion and did not make any major shift in his position all through his life. He criticized religion for falling short of coming to the aid of the poor and for its contribution to some diabolical situations in the world. He contended that religion failed to serve as a driving force in people's lives. Churchill asserted that religion contributed to heinous situations, such as wars and civil strife in different parts of the world. He also criticized religious organizations for not coming to the aid of the poor and downtrodden with more vigor and frequency. Churchill maintained that those who worried about religion did not do well in life: They spent too much time agonizing over the afterlife that it hampered their progress in this life. He compared religion to a narcotic, which pacified people too much, thus decreasing the type of internal dialectic and discomfort that often led to innovation and progress.

Oprah is not involved in organized religion, but in addition to being spiritual, she has strong moral convictions. She believes that church should exist in each of us. Oprah also believes in God and makes references to God. She maintains that she is not affiliated with any particular church. Her idea of religion is one in which she ascribes to personal responsibility in her relationship with God; hence, she deems membership to a particular Christian religion restrictive. She also espouses self-help, self-actualization, and the power of intention.

Although Barack Obama's father and stepfather were Muslims, he grew up in a Christian household that did not have a strong allegiance to the church, and so he was not initially active in the Christian faith. His mother, who was not officially an agnostic, had a distrust of Christians. The rearing of Obama by his mother was rooted in American ideals and ethics. He was not particularly religious prior to his attempt to organize the black churches in the Southside of Chicago. He joined Trinity United Church of Christ at the urging of church members there, who saw it fit for him to become a church member to augment his bid to organize and energize the black church ministers. Obama also indicated that his decision to join Trinity was not based on a sudden religious consciousness, rather it stemmed from his need to share in the

African-American experience of which religion is an integral part.

One of America's founding fathers, Benjamin Franklin, was instrumental in popularizing the mantra that "God helps those who help themselves," which is the position that most people who are believers in self-actualization take. It is a pragmatic approach that also promotes the popular belief that manna does not fall from the sky. Like Franklin, the successful people featured in this book are proponents of self-help.

When we look around us at all the marvels of nature and human empowerment and progress, it would behoove us to conclude that there is a source responsible for the orchestration of the world as we know it, including the fundamental origins of humans and other living creatures. Our scientific theories are cogent with regard to gene mutations and the evolution of living organisms, but when we consider amazing phenomena such as the perfect food chain among creatures on land and sea and the precision of the intricate bodily functions, the manifestation of extraterrestrial or celestial involvement in our existence on earth becomes palpable. While it is outside the realm of this book to delve into this issue, it is, however, befitting to touch on the marvels of nature and human strides. The Bible, in Genesis, alluded to the creation of humans in the image of God and the empowerment of humans to have dominion over the earth. Although we humans virtually control the plants, animals, and the expanse of the earth, the manipulation and full knowledge of many things still elude us. Humans are among the weakest organisms physically, in contrast to many other forms of life. Many other species are capable of doing devastating bodily harm to humans. Despite our physical weakness, we are able to exert enormous control in the world through our intelligence. In three to four hundred years, human strides will still be considered limited, albeit many more exceptional advancements will have been made by then.

The phenomenal capabilities that humans possess lead to the belief that we have been empowered in ways that are beyond our comprehension; it is, therefore, necessary for us to maintain the realization of our powers in perpetuity. Regardless of our various religious beliefs, there are tremendous powers residing in the entire human race. This idea reinforces the tenet that God created humans in his own image. It also suggests that the Creator or a part of her resides in humans, a notion that is relative to Oprah's contention that the church resides in us. The degree to which we can summon our powers, to a large extent, will determine how we turn out individually and what type of progress we make collectively in our society.

In view of our untold capabilities and powers, the size of our drive and ambitions should be measured not by what we can pragmatically accomplish, but by the passion we are capable of conceptualizing and pursuing. For instance, the idea of humans flying around in airplanes sounded far-fetched at the time of its conception, and the proponents of this idea were thought to be rather eccentric. With this in mind, we should feel empowered to make many more colossal accomplishments. It would not be beyond our scope to think in terms of having the capability of influencing and perhaps stopping such natural disasters as earthquakes and volcanic eruptions. Additionally, there are still infinite strides to be made in many fields including medicine, sciences, technology, and the arts. The world is wide open for the pursuit of our passion—opportunities abound, and human advancement is still considered to be in its infancy. We have countless opportunities to create marketable value while embarking on the pursuit of our passion.

Religion suffers many criticisms when diabolical occurrences are attributed to it. However, in the words of Alexander Pope, the eighteenth-century English poet, "To err is human." There are imperfections in all human endeavors. Therefore, religion should not be looked upon from the point of view of its imperfections. Rather, it should be looked at as an institution that enables us to find meaning and make sense of our environment.

Suze Orman's mantra, "Like who you are," is appropriate in the context of religion, spirituality, and self-help. It stems from our outlook on life and ourselves, and could be orchestrated by our convictions and our belief system. If we like who we are, we are more capable of forging positive relationships, which invariably enhances our quest for our passion. Do all highly accomplished individuals like who they are? What are some of the things people need to do to like who they are? Once again, the answers may lie within the realms of our beliefs including spirituality, religion, and self-improvement. Once we embark on the pursuit of our passion, we should also undertake a quest for spiritual enhancement or personal development. Doing so will help to ensure the success of our pursuits and enable us to cushion the effects of mistakes, challenges, and failures.

Similar to religion, philosophy fosters our thinking capacity, which in turn enables us to muster the power and resolve to spur our drive and passion. The subsequent quotations outline some of the important considerations we face in our thinking process. "How like philosophers! Preening themselves for teaching black-and-white thinkers to see shades of gray and forgetting all about the reds and greens and blues and yellows," wrote Susan Sparks. Sparks, a humorous theologian and attorney, asserted that thinking should involve consideration of all conceivable variables. Similarly, Ludwig Wittgenstein, the Austrian philosopher maintained that, "A thought which is not independent is a thought only half understood," reinforcing the need for completeness in our thought process.

Basic rational thinking is vital and beneficial. It is centered on fundamentals: Most of our worries will never come to fruition; be fair and equitable in our dealings with others because we never know when we will need impartial treatment and who may be in a position to render such assistance to us. If we are in business, for instance, we are better able to direct our business along the right path, ultimately leading to growth and success, when we think straight and clearly. These qualities also enable us to understand and assess people better. Another key benefit of clear and straight thinking is that we are able to lead a worry-free life in doing so. Although most of our worries never materialize, we should concentrate our efforts on the resolution of our problems rather than on worrying. In the bid to think straight and clearly, we should strive to counter our negative thoughts with mature thinking and positive thoughts. Infusing positive thoughts in ourselves should be done in perpetuity. Considering all possible ramifications in our thinking process helps us in numerous ways, including enabling us to pick our battles, recognize our mistakes, and realize our limitations. Rational and cogent thinking aids us in minimizing obstacles as we pursue our passion.

Success in our personal relationships or the lack of it, as we seek our passion, will depend on our thinking and our convictions. The successful pursuit of our passion does not equate to success in our relationships. Sometimes we are so engrossed in the pursuit of our passion that we fail in our relationships with friends, relatives, and business associates. Successful relationships can be relative. Whereas one individual might enjoy the company of others on a regular basis, somebody else might find solace in being reclusive; whereas one individual might find success in relationships by being candid and aggressive, somebody else might find success with others by being diplomatic and subtle. Nevertheless, it is vital to be successful in our dealings with others in order to forge good relationships. We need good relationships to bring the quest for our passion to fruition. Success in our relationships may enhance our happiness. Through our thinking, we are able to discern various relationships, read the people with whom we interact, and decide on the best method of managing each relationship.

Interpersonal communication skills are crucial in our bid to enhance our relationship with others. We need people in various facets of our endeavors, including employees, partners, contractors, mentors, and bankers, to ensure the success of the projects in which we are involved. Our ability to communicate clearly and succinctly is critical to the success of our endeavors. Regardless of whether we are in sales or information technology, human interaction is unavoidable. It is therefore crucial that we communicate with clarity and brevity, whenever we are in a communication context, to foster good relationships.

In our association with others, the old mantra, "Treat others as we would like to be treated," is a great starting point, but it is not applicable in all situations. Our treatment of others should also be unique and relative. We cannot treat two employees with different drives, niches, and interests alike. One employee might be diligent, thorough, and dependable, but may require care and patience while being taught a new concept. This employee's work may not need to be monitored closely for accuracy. Another employee may be quick and an intellectual, yet not quite as dependable and thorough as the previous employee. This employee may not require much time while being taught a new concept, but may need to be checked for accuracy often. Each of these employees will require a different treatment. The businessman in Matthew delegated responsibilities to his three employees based on his perception of their strengths. He gave five talents, the highest number of talents, to the most effective employee, and to the least effective employee he gave one talent. His treatment of his employees in this case was based on his perception of their competences. Our treatment of others should be unique to each individual, equitable, and better than we expect to be treated. This paradigm will elicit improvements in human conditions as it ricochets around.

Fair and equitable treatment of others is vital in our relationships and the pursuit of our passion. Let us consider a hypothetical situation where two employees, Roger and Margie, are hired at the same time to perform similar tasks. After a few months, it is clearly established that Margie's performance is superior to Roger's—with the understanding that there is an insignificant variance in all other aspects of their involvement in the organization, including their conduct. The dilemma here is that Margie is carrying an unfair share of the workload, due to her superior performance—and the owner of the business is trying to decide how to maintain fairness to both employees while continuing to treat them uniquely based on this disparity and their differences. The quickest and easiest way to maintain equity and satisfaction among both employees is to establish a quantifiable depiction of Margie's superior performance, and to ensure, through effective communication, that both employees clearly understand the situation. Next, Margie can either be promoted to a higher position or given a salary increase commensurate with her superior performance.

Another common denominator in our relationships is respect. We should treat everyone we encounter with respect, as if she were a $40 million client, without compromising our assertiveness. One good reason to treat everyone with respect is that we never know when we will encounter our mentor or someone who could be of tremendous assistance to us. This may be a selfish reason; however, we all have a great dependence on others, and, as such, it is imperative that we are respectful of others at all times. Of course, respect is reciprocal; we should respect others, while maintaining our self-confidence.

When dealing with interpersonal relationships, it is essential to keep a few simple rules in mind. Sometimes it is good to walk away from a fight or resort to diplomacy; in other words, we should choose our battles because doing so may help keep us focused on the big picture. Equivalent retaliation should be used with caution because it may not always be the best solution in a conflict or dispute. However, constructive encounters are necessary, as long as we do not deviate from the parameters of the encounter. It is imperative that we become acclimated with proper techniques for conflict resolution. There are several good books on this subject. No one has all the answers, and all humans are imperfect. The acquisition of good interpersonal skills is necessary for our success, and it entails a delicate balance.

Achieving balance between our work and personal relationships is an important factor that contributes to our happiness. Living, breathing, and taking delight in our passion are demanding. Our endeavors may not feel arduous to us if we enjoy them. The pursuit of our passion may take its toll on our family and those closest to us if they do not share our passion. It is then necessary to educate them on our passion and get them to share our dreams.

Mustering the drive to seek our passion, in addition to providing us with other benefits, has the potential of fostering our happiness and longevity. The quest for our passion gives our lives more meaning and purpose, which is an indirect way of enhancing our happiness and consequently our longevity. According to *The Wall Street Journal*, John Kay, in his book *Obliquity*, asserts that people are happy when they "have their minds fixed on some object other than their own happiness." In the same manner that we may indirectly gain fame and wealth by focusing on our passion, we may also indirectly gain happiness, and consequently longevity, by focusing on our passion.

* * *

As we seek to reach our goals—utilizing self-enhancement techniques orchestrated by our spirituality or any other methods that may buoy our drive and passion—it is vital to realize that it is not always possible for everyone to take care of himself or aspire to make these strides, for reasons ranging from physical impairment to mental incapacitation; thus, it is the responsibility of those who are able to make achievements to come to the aid of those who cannot. "Am I my brother's keeper?" is an excerpt from Genesis in the Bible. Clearly, the answer to this question is yes. This adage was also used and popularized by President John F. Kennedy and his siblings in their philanthropic and humanitarian efforts.

A society or an environment where there is a huge disparity between the wealthy and the poor, with no apparent program aimed at alleviating the problems of the needy, is clearly a breeding ground for social upheaval. This disparity could pose a threat to the wealthy and their ability to preserve their wealth. Crime and dissent of epic proportions and gross disenchantment of the poor majority could ensue. This should be enough motivation for us to be our brothers' keepers. We engage in acts of charity for different reasons, but whatever our reasons may be, the pursuit of our passion could, among other reasons, enable us to make a difference and make a positive impact in the lives of those who are in need. Whether we are extrinsically or intrinsically driven to pursue our passion, we would be creating value and perhaps providing jobs or engaging in acts of benevolence on a large scale.

* * *

When we harbor positive thoughts and behave positively, we engender positive outcomes; when we harbor negative thoughts and behave negatively, we attract negative occurrences. Our actions and thoughts have causative effects on us. We are what we think about and what we aspire to be. This notion was espoused by Rhonda Byrne in her book, *The Secret*. An aspect of the Buddhist dogma is predicated on Karma, which is also a tenet of cause and effect. We usually bring our predominant thoughts or actions to fruition, whether they are positive or negative. This is a clear depiction of the powers that we possess. Our thought process and our actions are integral parts of the equation as we pursue our passion. For instance, if we want to be mentored, we should mentor others; if we want to be helped, we should help others; if we want to be respected, we should respect others. The law of reciprocity, in effect, is also an example of how we get back what we give.

CHAPTER 10
Success and Greatness

Success and greatness, initiated by our drive and fueled by our passion, can be relative, and a societal standard measures and rewards these attributes; however, they should be mostly depicted by the difference we can make in society or the lives we can touch. The societal definition of success and greatness is emblematic of the commendations and rewards utilized to recognize significant accomplishments. Periodic or yearly accolades are bestowed upon individuals and entities to symbolize enormous achievements: the *Fortune* 500 list of companies; *Forbes* magazine's list of the world's richest people; Oscar awards for actors and actresses; Nobel Prizes for excellence in various fields; and the list goes on. A single welfare mother who rises above poverty and successfully raises her children—who become educated, with lucrative employment—could be considered by her offspring to be the most successful individual they know. This situation would denote the relativity of her achievements. On the other hand, success and greatness can be epitomized by the creation of value: adding value to the lives of others with our products, services, and endeavors; creating jobs; and engaging in philanthropy.

Making a difference is symbolic of the pursuit of our passion, and the example below is indicative of that. A hypothetical model of greatness would consist of an individual who, in the pursuit of her passion, invents a product that necessitates the employment of several people in her factory, perhaps thousands. Her invention creates tremendous value in society: It is a contraption that enables automobiles manufacturers to make vehicles that are completely independent of crude oil. In addition to providing employment for many people, she embarks on acts of benevolence—donating large sums of money to aid the children of the needy in their education. Ultimately, this individual touches several lives as an employer, a philanthropist, and the orchestrator of a product that partially eliminates American dependence on fossils fuels, enabling people to save money. Although this constitutes a substantial loss to the fossil fuels industry, the aggregate gain to the general population is enormous. She will be considered a great woman. Using a real example—Abraham Lincoln was considered a great man because he touched the lives of hundreds of thousands of African-Americans by orchestrating the end of slavery.

Our passion enables us to tailor our drives, which are usually broad, to something more specific on which we can intensely focus irrespective of the prize, accolade or reward for the achievement. Passion will cause us to tailor an aspiration or drive, such as wanting to become an actor, into something more specific, like playing dramatic roles in movies, based on our niche, without considering the wealth or fame associated with the endeavor. Although Sidney Poitier's dream was to become an actor, he was particularly passionate about dignified roles that would portray him and other African-Americans in a positive light. Our dreams and drives should enable us to identify the direction of our passion and to fuel it.

According to Sharon Good of Good Life Coaching, when an athlete is "running a race . . . he is mentally and physically 'in the zone,' totally focused. . . . If his mind turns to rewards—glory, praise, money or fame—the intense focus is broken." Individuals such as Henry Ford and Thomas Edison were so engrossed in their passion that they had no time to conjecture their rewards or think that they would one day be deemed great men in the history books. Whether we are driven intrinsically or extrinsically, we should direct our focus to our passion. Once we are engaged in our niche activity, it is crucial that we switch our focus from our anticipated rewards to that passion, to ensure peak performance.

In our bid to make great accomplishments, it is imperative that we ensure that our engagement in this process is for the right reasons, to facilitate our success. It is important that we ascertain the existence of true passion for our undertaking. We should make sure that we are not merely engaged in our endeavor for the rewards. Are we truly passionate about our endeavor? Do we really have a niche in this activity? My wife's friend once indicated that her husband was aspiring to mirror my entrepreneurial pursuits. My wife was flattered and wanted to learn more about why this lady's husband was seeking to start a business. She explained that her husband was eager to become an entrepreneur so that he could spend more time with her and their children. She further contended that as a midlevel manager of a retail outlet, her husband worked too hard and put in long hours, without much time for the family. This rationale or drive for wanting to start a business may be misguided. We cannot be driven to pursue our passion by the need to work fewer hours. The pursuit of our passion entails ardent practice, education, and preparation in addition to the performance of the actual task, which will more often than not necessitate long hours. Once we identify our passion, we often enjoy the activity associated with it and are prepared to put in the required time to achieve our objective. It is true that self-employment entails more flexibility, but this should not be confused with working fewer hours. Imagine Thomas Edison worrying about working fewer hours! The pursuit of our passion may actually necessitate more hours than the average job. It may, nonetheless, not feel as arduous as a job because we truly enjoy our work.

If we fail to transition from drive to passion, and instead become utterly focused on our drive, we may never make any remarkable achievement or we may encounter problems. If we are extrinsically driven to accrue wealth, which is a cogent drive, but we fail to identify a specific passion that will lead us to the accumulation of wealth, we may aspire to become wealthy at all costs or we may develop a passion for money. Both of these situations could lead to unscrupulous activities. The need to be independent, which is an intrinsic drive, without an identifiable passion that will lead to independence could also be problematic for us. It may lead to the attainment of independence through shiftlessness or other negative means. The question in this case would be: From what are we seeking independence? Are we uncooperative with authority, or are we shying away from responsibility? We should develop a passion that will lead to wealth creation or independence.

Money managers and stockbrokers who produce high ROI for their clients or themselves are passionate about the creation of value, rather than money. They create value through the delivery of high ROI to their clients. Whenever their focus shifts from the creation of value to activities centered around their extrinsic drives or rewards—such as the accumulation of wealth at all costs, as in the case of Bernie Madoff's Ponzi scheme—then this misplaced passion could lead to criminal activity.

The financial throes that led to the Wall Street meltdown of 2008 and the crisis that occurred in the auto industry in the United States during that period were attributable to misplaced passion or greed. Wall Street and real estate investors shifted their focus from ardently creating value for their clients and themselves to the myopic goals of fattening their pockets. Their passion shifted to their drive and rewards, which was tantamount to wealth creation at all costs. The American auto industry suffered a similar predicament. The industry's emphasis shifted from the high-performance and durable automobiles they previously manufactured, which created value for consumers, to low-quality, poorly designed, and fuel-guzzling automobiles infused with planned obsolescence in order to increase short-term profits and returns for shareholders and executives. In both Wall Street and the auto industry, the focus changed from creating value for their clients to catering to their pockets.

The focus on drive rather than passion and misplaced passion are contributing factors to bribery and corruption around the world. In these instances, the creation of value through the pursuit of passion is replaced by a focus on drives such as wealth, fame, and other rewards. These trappings of success become the passion for the people concerned, rather than value-adding endeavors. Ineptitude sets in because there is the absence of a quest for excellence. Individuals in these instances are more interested in the acquisition of wealth, fame, and other similar incentives, but they do not have any specific passion for the creation of sustainable value that would uplift society and reward them at the same time. They, in essence, resort to bribery, corruption, criminal activity, and other shady deals to reach their goals, while leaving their environments in a state of degradation and disrepair.

Sometimes, our passion may not entail the creation of marketable value such as a nonprofit endeavor; it would, nonetheless, still initiate the addition of value to society, equating to a major accomplishment. Nonprofit organizations enable us to make a tremendous difference in society—bringing value to the lives of others. In such instances, we solicit funds for our nonprofit activity—an integral part of this endeavor. On the other hand, we could embark on a socially conscious project that is for-profit but uses part of its revenue for nonprofit activity. Nonprofit and for-profit hybrids are nascent—a combination of for-profit and nonprofit activities, relying simultaneously on revenue from its for-profit activity and the solicitation of funds. Whether we empower ourselves to make achievements through the nonprofit or for-profit sector, as long as our endeavor is truly our calling and passion, it can be positively impactful in society and rewarding to us, as we accomplish our goals.

* * *

Drive propels us into action, or it enables us to have strong momentum for the purpose of accomplishing great goals and becoming successful. There are several forms of extrinsic and intrinsic drives. Examples of extrinsic drives include the need to be wealthy, the need to be famous, and the need for power. Some examples of intrinsic drives are the need to make a difference, the need to become an expert in our undertaking, and the need for independence. Can we be both extrinsically and intrinsically driven? An individual can start out being driven by wealth, but once she identifies her passion, she may discover that she enjoys it so much that she has an interminable drive to be the best at that activity. In this case, she is extrinsically and intrinsically driven. People who are extrinsically driven and those who are intrinsically driven make great accomplishments once they identify their niche and proceed with the pursuit of their passion. Those who are extrinsically driven may accomplish more over the short run, but they may lose steam once they accomplish their objective. In the long run, however, those who are intrinsically driven tend to accomplish more with a high degree of sustainability. Their drive is intangible and is not materialistically inclined.

Drive precedes passion because it is the force that causes us to explore our passion. As much as we may be driven to make accomplishments, if we are unable to identify a passion that can be fueled by our drive, we may never be able to make any accomplishment of significance. Drive could be prompted by negative and positive factors. Some examples of positive drives are the need to be famous and the need to challenge ourselves to make more accomplishments. Conversely, negative drives could stem from the need to be powerful in order to seek revenge and wanting to excel for narcissistic reasons.

Drive and passion spur attributes such as courage, resilience, and persistence, which are essential components in the accomplishment of our goals. They are the forces that intertwine with our drive and passion. Courage allows us to muster the resolve to take action and maintain our focus despite our fears. Resilience enables us to recapture our drive and passion after setbacks. When we have fortitude and determination, we are able to remain relentless while on the quest for our objectives.

"Colonel" Harland Sanders was driven by several factors. Initially, he was driven by the need to be independent and the need to be in business for himself. He had the challenge of marketing his fried chicken recipe and fostering the sustainability of his restaurant. Sanders went into retirement for a brief period and re-emerged at the age of sixty-five, broke and destitute, to rekindle the pursuit of his passion. He was at that point driven by the avoidance of poverty. Sanders was also driven by the need to become successful at marketing his fried chicken recipe. These drives contributed to the successful pursuit of his passion.

Winston Churchill was driven in many ways, which led to his incredible life. He was a brave and courageous soldier, a literary genius, and a great politician who possessed tremendous drives. One of his key drives stemmed from his desire to make a name for himself to prove his parents wrong. They had the impression that he was petulant and tepid as a child. Churchill's drive to become an eloquent speaker stemmed from his admiration of his father, whose entire political speeches he memorized. He also was driven by the need to top his father's success in politics. When Churchill was appointed prime minister of Britain by the king of England, he asserted to some friends that he felt as if he had been preparing for that day all his life. He was endowed with inexhaustible energy. Despite his lack of a four-year university education, he possessed a tremendous drive for excellence in writing and politics. Churchill was also driven by fame and the desire to amass significant wealth through his writing. He was a true symbol of success and greatness, and one of the world's greatest leaders of all time.

Joe Kennedy was driven to pursue his passion in business by a number of factors, some of which were recurrent in different forms all through his life. He was snubbed a few times—so he longed to outshine and outperform all of those who had rebuffed him. Kennedy also sought to avoid his father's reserved and modest lifestyle. He was driven by wealth, fame, and the quest for expertise in financial services.

Sidney Poitier refused to accept his lot in life. His father, a poor tomato farmer who later peddled cigars in Nassau, was resigned to his fate and accepted it with quiet grace. Poitier was driven to control the outcome of his life. He was tossed out of a theater because of his inability to read his script, but he kept going back, and each time he got better. This spurred his courage, which enabled him to take risks and push the limits and boundaries of his destiny in order to pursue his passion. He maintained the outlook that certain things were beneath him, and he carried himself with dignity and grace, which indicated that he deserved much more out of life than he was entitled to by virtue of his race, lack of education, and humble beginnings. Poitier was never satisfied with his work; thus, he was driven by the perpetual need to master his craft. His quest for excellence led him to positively influence a number of the directors with whom he worked in a manner that added more value to his movies.

Abraham Lincoln was a courageous man who was driven to accomplish great things in politics. He was intent on avoiding his father's fate, which was that of a poor farmer who subsisted on manual labor. Lincoln performed manual labor on his father's farm and disliked it; this served as one of the driving forces that propelled him to seek his passion. He was driven to choose a profession he liked. Lincoln once remarked to some friends that his father taught him how to work hard on the farm doing manual labor, but he did not teach him to like it. He aspired to become an expert in public speaking. He was driven to seek respect from his peers, and he was also driven to the service of others. Lincoln was one of the most courageous presidents that the United States ever had and one of the greatest presidents of all time.

Suze Orman was driven to pursue her passion by many factors, including the need to be successful and the need to prove that, despite her lack of academic prowess, she could become successful. Her drive to become successful led her to borrow $50,000 from her customers, which she slated for the potential opening of her own restaurant. She demonstrated courage and resilience despite the loss of all her borrowed funds in a bad investment deal. Following this loss, she secured a job in the financial services industry, where she sought her passion. Orman was confident she could do the job; she had acquired some knowledge in the money markets due to her interest in monitoring her own investments. After she joined Merrill Lynch, she became driven by the need to prove to her boss—a male chauvinist—that she could, at the very least, be as proficient as her male counterparts. Later on, Orman became driven by the need to be an expert and the best in her field.

Barack Obama was intrinsically and extrinsically driven. He was adhering to his intrinsic drive when he said to his wife, "There will be plenty of time to make money—lots of it. Right now is the time to make a difference." He said this in an effort to allay her concern about their gloomy financial situation. Obama was extrinsically driven by power when he informed his friends of his aspirations to be the president of the United States. Obama had other drives that contributed to his quest for his passion. He was driven by the avoidance of his father's mistakes and his grandfather's predicament.

Drive to Passion

Oprah knew she was going to make something of herself. She felt that she would become famous in the foreseeable future. She told her father so; thus she was driven by the pursuit of fame. Oprah wanted to prove that she could get beyond the predicament that befell her while she was at her mother's house. She was driven by the need to overcome the abject poverty that surrounded her earlier in her life. Of course, Oprah became driven intrinsically with the passage of time; hence, she was propelled by the desire to engage in huge philanthropic efforts and to make a difference.

* * *

In his book *Outliers*, Malcolm Gladwell stressed the importance of intense practice and hard work as a means of achieving success. He further discussed the importance of combining talent with ten thousand hours or ten years of practice, several hours a day, in our area of interest to achieve the desired result. Passion—which encompasses practice, preparation, customized education, and the performance of our niche activity with delight—is the single most compelling factor responsible for success and greatness.

What is the relationship between talent, niche, and passion? *Merriam-Webster's Collegiate Dictionary, Tenth Edition* defines talent as "a special often creative or artistic aptitude." It defines niche as "an activity for which a person is best fitted" and passion as "a strong liking or desire for, or devotion to some activity, object, or concept." There is a parallel between niche and talent: If an individual is best fitted for an activity, then she will invariably exhibit a high aptitude for it. The existence of passion entails a compelling force, capable of spurring accomplishments of epic proportions. Passion necessitates a desire for an activity, which equates to devotion. Pleasure, practice, preparation, and customized education all intertwine in fostering our devotion to an endeavor. However, if we are not best suited for an activity, or if we do not have a high aptitude for it, our passion for it may never lead to an achievement of great significance. Conversely, we may be best suited for an activity or have a niche in it, but if we do not enjoy the activity and prepare, practice, and educate ourselves in it, we may never excel in it; thus niche or talent without passion is tantamount to stagnation. Talent is overrated. We all may know of cases where an individual was well suited for an activity or had a high aptitude for it, but lacked the desire to explore it further.

How do we acquire a niche in an activity or talent for it? Chances are that if a child is reared in a house where all her relatives are musically inclined, she will become musically inclined. The same circumstances may apply to children reared in an environment where all of their relatives are intellectuals. If those same children are placed in an environment that lacks these prolific attributes, their chances of being talented or gifted in these areas will be greatly diminished. On the other hand, a child may have a calling or a high aptitude for an activity innately. Environmental factors do play a role in a child's prodigious aptitude or niche, but this does not detract from the fact that innate abilities also play a role in the manifestation of this phenomenon. We all have a niche or calling. As Sharon Good stated, "Everyone is a genius and an artist [in something]." We should identify that activity that comprises our niche, calling, talent, or genius and devote the requisite drive and passion to it to take it to unprecedented levels. However, regardless of how well endowed we are with niche or talent, as Thomas Edison asserted, it is only one percent of the equation. Ninety-nine percent of the equation is dependent on our perspiration, which reverts to our drive and passion.

The pursuit of our passion requires the ability to harness all of our resources, including human capital, to bring our quest to fruition. It is crucial that if we have employees, we make our work environment pleasant. Not everyone has the opportunity to embark on the pursuit of her passion; therefore, we should keep in mind that those individuals we employ need the best work environment to buoy their motivation and job satisfaction. It is imperative that we understand that, although it is impossible to keep others as driven and impassioned as we are, we should nonetheless strive to keep them motivated.

* * *

"Yankee ingenuity," which corresponds to success and greatness, is driven by a marriage of hard work, passion, and freedom of expression. The United States has excelled in such areas as high technology, higher education, and medicine. While the U.S. lags behind some of its Western and G-20 counterparts in elementary and secondary education (K through 12), according to *U.S. News & World Report*, close to 22 percent or 87 of the world's top 400 universities are located in the United Sates. The United Kingdom ranks a second, with 12 percent of the world's top universities; Germany, Australia, Japan, Canada, and France all have single-digit percentages. What can we learn from all this? This is the typical "Yankee ingenuity" at work—born from passion, hard work, and freedom of expression. I am sure that our number one ranking in the world in higher education is not a direct result of our unprecedented expertise in our methods of imparting knowledge to our young people! American college professors in some of our best universities are unparalleled primarily in the number of their new discoveries, high-caliber postulations, commitment to excellence, and passion. The favorable environment in which they work—an environment that fosters creativity, delight in their work, and freedom of expression—cannot be overlooked.

The key to success, as elusive as it may be, is intertwined with "Yankee ingenuity." We on occasion hear questions posed to business magnates, stars, and individuals of extraordinary accomplishments: "How did you do it? What is the key to success?" Their responses are often not comprehensive enough to enable the masses, who desire success, to readily duplicate their level of success. These answers usually range from, "I did it through persistence and hard work" to "I believed in myself and never took no for answer." The general population treats these answers with a degree of skepticism and reservation because they have tried all of these things without much success. Analogous to "Yankee ingenuity," without drive and passion for our niche activity, and the freedom to seek that passion, there can be no accomplishment of great significance.

In choosing a venture, profession, or an activity for which we are passionate, we should ensure that it will enable us to create value in society. Should we decide to pursue an activity about which we are passionate—such as bird-watching, which may not be value creating—and expect to make a career out of it, then we should ensure that we have a huge inheritance or we should expect to create value with it in some way such as writing, publishing, and pursuing this activity in an academic setting. Conversely, we should not base our passion on the popularity of the profession or its level of income; rather, it should be based on our niche. The decision on what we are passionate about will ultimately rest with us; it should be centered not on the limits of our capabilities, but on our imagination and conceptualization. Whether the activity encompassing our passion is popular or not, we can always make a difference with it and make a name for ourselves at the same time.

A word of caution is necessary on the use of passion to denote our enthusiasm for a recreational activity or a hobby; it is of utmost importance to distinguish between that type of passion in which we have no niche and the type that enables us to undertake the pursuit of excellence in a niche, for the purpose of the creation of value. This type of pursuit of distinction takes daily commitment in customized education, practice, and preparation in the area of our niche and passion. If we enjoy a particular spectator sport, and we participate in that sport occasionally for enjoyment, we will not have met the criteria for the type of passion that enables us to become an expert in that activity. On the other hand, passion for activities encompassing our lifetime goals does not detract from the fact that we can still be passionate about extracurricular activities such as spectator sports or hobbies.

How do we go about the pursuit of our passion? Most experts agree that passion is the most important component in achieving success and greatness. The pursuit of our passion entails the identification of our niche, and subsequently, practicing, preparing, and educating ourselves in that activity. If we have truly identified our niche and passion, then, in all likelihood, we will enjoy the activity that encompasses that passion. As we continue to educate and prepare ourselves in our field of endeavor, we will elevate our level of competence to the point of gaining expertise in it. The quest for our passion also involves courage, tenacity, resilience, a tolerance for risk, and belief or confidence in our skills and abilities. All of these attributes are spurred by our drive and passion.

Drive to Passion

"Colonel" Harland Sanders demonstrated courage and a tolerance for risk when he emerged from retirement at the age of sixty-five to reinitiate the quest for his passion. After the failure of his restaurant and his subsequent retirement, he exhibited resilience and courage in his passion by coming out of retirement to bring the pursuit of his passion to fruition. The Colonel was unafraid to fail again, and he minimized the risk involved in his quest through the fervent pursuit of his passion. He used his persuasive selling skills to sell his fried chicken recipe to a couple, enabling him to set the growth of his franchise in motion. Sanders took courses at Cornell University to enhance his restaurant management skills. He was deemed a perfectionist because of his quest for excellence and expertise in his passion. Sanders engendered the creation of phenomenal value with his fried chicken recipe through the pursuit of his passion.

Winston Churchill had many passions: writing, speaking, politics, and military service. He became one of the world's most acclaimed writers despite his lack of a four-year university education. Churchill was awarded the Nobel Prize in Literature in 1953. He was one of the best British prime ministers and one of the world's greatest leaders of all time. Churchill was known to be an ardent preparer of his speeches—usually spending hours on end in preparation and practice. He demonstrated eloquence in his speeches, putting him in a class with the world's greatest orators. His passion was emblemized by his incessant practice, unremitting education, and unyielding delight in his endeavors. His excellence and passion led him to deem himself a "glow-worm." He was also courageous, as demonstrated by his leadership of his country in the time of war and his bravery while in the military. Churchill was, without a doubt, resilient. Not only did he take his "wilderness years in stride," but he bounced back from them to become prime minister at the age of sixty-five.

Joe Kennedy's passion spanned a few professions: movie production, financial services, and business. Although Kennedy diversified into other industries, he eventually returned to his true passion: the financial services industry. As a young man in the industry, he was often seen at work with his head buried in books and charts, researching the companies in which he executed his stock trades. At the initial stages of his career as a bank examiner, Kennedy embarked on the task of mastering the financial services industry with unprecedented vigor and a thirst for knowledge in the industry that sustained his passion all through his business career. He was a courageous capitalist who took substantial business risks to enhance the pursuit of his passion.

Sidney Poitier was intent on playing movie roles that were commensurate with his passion, dignity, and eruditeness. By an act of courage, he turned down a movie role as a janitor, even though he was near destitution. He did so because it was a stereotypical role for black people, and he wanted more dignified and professional roles that would portray him in a positive light. Poitier demonstrated the components of the pursuit of his passion by being an astute student of his craft and taking delight in it. The pursuit of our passion amplifies our excellence due to our constant quest for knowledge and increased skill level in our endeavor. To successfully pursue our passion, we should firmly believe that intelligence, knowledge, and proficiency are not constant and that we can elevate these components through continuous preparation, practice, and customized education. Poitier had absolute confidence in his capabilities. He was confident that he would be able to find suitable movie roles, and he did. Poitier's confidence and passion led to staggering accomplishments in his career.

Abraham Lincoln was passionate about debating, communication, and politics. He knew with certainty that he detested farm labor, and unlike his father, he was going to steer clear of farming. He pursued the activities he really liked and for which he had received compliments and accolades: speaking and politics. As soon as he learned he could obtain a law degree without actually going to college and that the degree would enhance his political career, he decided to become a lawyer. No sooner had he earned his law degree and commenced his law practice, than he discovered he enjoyed the practice of law. Lincoln ran for political office and eventually became president. While he was president, he demonstrated his passion for public service by maintaining an open-door policy to the public, usually allowing visitors from the general population to exceed their allotted visitation time. As president, he also demonstrated his passion for speaking by giving some of the most memorable speeches in the history of the United States. He demonstrated his courage by his successful conclusion of the Civil War. He was one of the greatest U.S. presidents and world leaders of all time.

Suze Orman failed in her attempt to open up her own restaurant due to the loss of her borrowed funds; however, she was resilient and courageous enough to start a new career in the financial services industry and to attain expertise in it. Orman demonstrated tremendous passion and a niche for financial services by her enthusiasm and enjoyment of the seminars she conducted for the potential retirees at Pacific Gas and Electric, despite a lack of immediate financial rewards for her efforts. Her passion for the seminars paid off when she was awarded the contract of handling the potential retirees' retirement plans following their retirement. When asked about the key to success, Orman stated that finding our niche, being an expert in it, and liking ourselves comprised the key to success. Her passion for financial services has led her to become a huge success in this industry. She has also become successful in the broadcast media industry by demonstrating her expertise as a personal finance adviser.

Barack Obama, through sheer courage and without much money in his bank account, resigned from a lucrative job as a consultant in a "consulting house" and turned down another beneficial position in the nonprofit sector to pursue his passion in community organizing and public service. He was tenacious and courageous. Obama also exhibited the type of resilience involved in the pursuit of our passion. He was not only courageous enough to take the bold steps of quitting one job for which he lacked passion and turning down another unsuitable job offer, but he was persistent enough to continue his job search until he found an appropriate position. He showed his resilience when he bounced back into his new position with vigor after a period of unemployment. Obama's quest for his passion would ultimately lead him to the historical presidency of the United States: the first black person to attain this position.

Oprah is passionate about acting and broadcast journalism, specifically, talk show hosting. She acted in a few movie productions. Similar to Lincoln's hatred for his father's occupation of farming, Oprah made no secret of the fact that she detested her job in her father's small grocery store. She was absolutely riveted by broadcast journalism. It was not until she lost her news anchor position that her true passion for hosting a talk show emerged. She demonstrated courage and resilience when she seized the opportunity of her job loss to make the leap to her true passion. Oprah demonstrated courage and tenacity when she left school prior to graduating to pursue her passion. She prepared for excellence in her passion by reading voraciously and studying the tapes of her idols, comprising Barbara Walters, Phil Donahue, and others.

* * *

What is the relationship between excellence in school and high achievement later on in life? John C. Maxwell, in his book *The 21 Indispensable Qualities of a Leader*, analyzed the school grades of leaders such as CEOs to prove that passion, rather than their brilliance and grades in school, was responsible for their success later in life. While mediocrity in education or the lack of a higher education is not necessarily ubiquitous among successful and great people, we do find that many were not necessarily academically prodigious in school. At the time of Maxwell's survey, more than 50 percent of all CEOs of *Fortune* 500 companies had C or C— averages in college; close to 75 percent of all previous American presidents were at the "bottom half" of their classes; 50 percent of all entrepreneurs who were millionaires never earned a four-year college degree. The people in all of the above categories attained these great heights through their passion for their individual professions. Passion could also be defined as the love of our work and an unyielding quest for expertise in it.

Choosing to be involved in a vocation about which we are passionate greatly diminishes our chances of failure and insulates us from obliteration by competition. Niche and passion give us the confidence to win. The more passionate we are, the more we prepare, practice, and educate ourselves in our passion; thus we buffer ourselves from defeat or failure. We frequently hear of successful individuals who were involved in several failed

Drive to Passion

ventures prior to settling on one that became successful or settling on their passion. The process of identifying a vocation about which we are passionate can be arduous; it could also entail trial and error, but it gives us the opportunity to make phenomenal achievements, thereby protecting us from failure and from the claws of competition.

Passion is the single most important factor responsible for success and greatness. John Schnatter, founder of Papa John's Pizza, was quoted by Maxwell as saying, when asked about the key to success, "Concentrate on what you do well and do it better than anybody else." Passion is responsible for Schnatter's success with Papa John's Pizza. Maxwell said, "Schnatter not only eats Papa John's pizza; he breathes, sleeps and lives it. It is always his predominating thought." Maxwell went on to quote another business titan, David Sarnoff of RCA, as saying, "Nobody can be successful unless he loves his work."

Maxwell told a story in his book about Socrates giving some advice to a young man—his protégé—who had approached him for guidance on how to become successful. Socrates' response to the young man's request was a pragmatic one. He took him to a pool of water and submerged his head in it for a few seconds. Upon bringing his head back up, he asked him to repeat his request. The young man did as he was told, again requesting from Socrates advice on how to be successful. Socrates then repeated the process a few more times, each time submerging his head for a longer time. Finally, after submerging the young man's head for a fairly long time, he asked him again to repeat his request. This time, the young man could barely talk—he was gasping for air. Finally, he managed to blurt out that he needed air to breathe. Socrates then told him that his question had been answered. He further explained to the young man that his passion in life, which would ultimately lead him to success, would consist of any vocation that he would want as much as he wanted air.

We could always run some "litmus tests" to determine if an activity qualifies as a passion. Our passion should add value to society by enhancing the quality of life for others, unless, of course, it is for recreational purposes. It should be an activity that we enjoy. If we could see ourselves improving our skills in perpetuity in this profession to the point of expertise, then it may qualify as a passion. Once we add value to the lives of others, our passion will be income producing, unless we do not wish to make it so. It should be an activity that we could be involved in without immediate expectations of rewards or income. We also should care more about our passion than its potential reward. Our passion should be an activity for which we have a niche or a high aptitude. If we are given compliments on our performance in this activity or for our aptitude for it, then it may qualify as a passion. This endeavor should feel as natural as the air we breathe. If the performance of this activity engenders in us an eagerness to wake up in the morning to get involved in it, then we could be passionate about it. When we are involved in this activity, if we are oblivious to the passage of time, then it could qualify as a passion. The existence of some or all of the above-mentioned phenomena is indicative of our passion for an activity.

The school of thought that the world's advancement is still in its infancy leads to the notion that opportunities abound in the world. Maxwell said, "Human beings are so made that whenever anything fires the soul, impossibilities vanish." If more people would muster the key elements in this book to pursue their passion, the world would benefit tremendously; the number of highly accomplished people in the world would increase, prompting more innovations, more jobs and more wealth; the world would take a leap forward with respect to advancement and the alleviation of human suffering; the world would become a better place.

The notion that there are a select few people in the world who are destined for success and greatness is a myth. It is also a myth that those who are at the pinnacle of success are there because they are lucky or possess an exclusive and special talent from God that they use effortlessly. Top athletes, top actresses, top entrepreneurs, top CEOs, top musicians, and top leaders of nations, just to mention a few, are people who have chosen their niche or calling and have become passionate about it. They possess a driving force that fuels their passion and are able to identify mentors who enable the pursuit of their goals to come to fruition. Regardless of the assertions made by some of these individuals about such factors as hard work, courage, tenacity, and resilience being the key to their success, if we do not identify our niche or calling and become passionate about it, the prospect of reaching the same level of accomplishment as these high achievers will be bleak. Although hard work, tenacity, and other factors are all inclusive components of the achievement of success, the key elements frequently missing from the equation are drive and passion.

Many people in the general population who work very hard and conform to other elements comprising the key to success never make substantial strides in life. The ratio of those who actually achieve success and greatness to those who conform to the so-called key to success, such as hard work, is quite low; thus, only a small fraction of our population is considered to be highly accomplished.

Only a small percentage of the individuals of phenomenal achievement have, thus far, taken the time to critically examine all the reasons for their great accomplishments. This is likely true because they are too busy to analyze the bases of their success. In fact, the great comedian Bill Cosby once admitted that he did not know the key to success. We often find the responses to the key to success to be varied. The key to success simply lies in being driven to identify our niche and becoming passionate about it.

Although we may sometimes be deemed too exuberant when we are passionate about an activity, we should not apologize for our passion or be ashamed of it. If we are excited about an activity, we may exhibit this characteristic by being energetic and vivacious, which may incorrectly portray us in a negative light. According to Maxwell, "[We should] associate with people of passion. Passion is contagious." The adage, "Birds of a feather flock together," also illustrates why we should seek out and associate with people of like minds as we pursue our passion. The quest for our passion requires dedication and commitment; we are able to get support and encouragement from people of similar interests.

Aspirations such as running a business, inventing a new product, writing great literature, or being the president of a country will entail challenges and responsibilities. Not everyone wants the level of accountability or pressure that comes with great achievements. The challenges and responsibilities inherent in being highly accomplished were echoed by Shakespeare and the Bible. In echoing these challenges, Shakespeare wrote in *Henry the Fourth*, "Uneasy lies the head that wears a crown." The Bible underscored the responsibilities involved in remarkable accomplishments in Luke: "To whom much is given, much is expected." We should always be cognizant of the significance of our achievements and behave accordingly—keeping in mind that many people may depend on us for such things as their livelihood and security.

Those of us who are on the quest for our passion should keep in mind that not all aspects of it will be enjoyable; certain aspects of it may be mundane, but we can delegate the monotonous or boring aspects of our passion when feasible. If we decide to handle them ourselves, we should do so with excellence and enthusiasm, keeping in mind that the mundane aspects of our passion may be as vital to our pursuit as the enjoyable aspects.

Whether we initiate our drive and subsequently engage in the pursuit of our passion or not, we should consider the fact that everyone experiences the rigors of life, and we will all need courage, tenacity, resilience, a certain amount of drive and passion in something, and some risk-taking ability, on a daily basis, to survive. It is, however, more riveting and auspicious to be driven to, say, become famous. Once we get in that mode, we can then identify a niche in a discipline like economics, and set out in pursuit of a career in equity management, with the aim of becoming passionate and an expert in it through customized education, practice, and preparation, which will ultimately lead to our goal or reward of becoming famous. Alternatively, the decision to seek employment should also be made with the aim of doing so in an area of our niche and passion to ensure a propitious career path.

I cannot help but constantly marvel at how far the world has come with all the amazing feats of human ingenuity and advancement. The more we study the lives of successful and great individuals in a prototypical manner, and engage in the initiation of our drive and the subsequent pursuit of our passion, the more feasible and attainable greatness and success will be, and the more we will be

Drive to Passion

spurred to embark on remarkable innovations. The world is still in its infancy with regard to human development and advancement. As we continue to make strides individually, the world will undergo more progress and the answers to our questions will continue to unravel.

Illustration

Formula for Success and Greatness

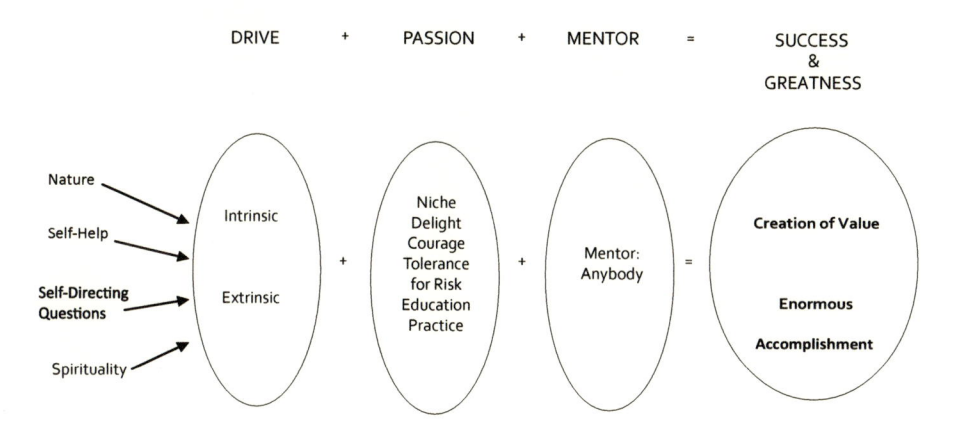

DRIVE + PASSION + MENTOR = SUCCESS & GREATNESS

- Nature → Intrinsic
- Self-Help →
- Self-Directing Questions → Extrinsic
- Spirituality →

+ Niche, Delight, Courage, Tolerance for Risk, Education, Practice + Mentor: Anybody = Creation of Value, Enormous Accomplishment

Drive fuels passion, which leads to great accomplishments. We are fundamentally prompted to be driven by natural means or a number of other factors including spirituality, self-help, and asking ourselves self-directing questions. Our drive can then be expressed intrinsically or extrinsically. The attributes of intrinsic drive include the need to make a difference. An example of extrinsic drive is the need to accumulate wealth. Once we are driven, we can subsequently identify a passion that can be fueled by our drive. This can be done by first ensuring that we have a niche or calling in a particular activity. Everyone has a niche or calling in something. Our passion will then encompass the delight we take in the performance of the activity, courage, the tolerance for risk, customized education in that endeavor, practice, preparation, resilience, and confidence in our ability. Next, we

Drive to Passion

should seek mentors to enable our quests to come to fruition. This will culminate in success and greatness. The end product of the pursuit of our passion consists of the creation of value and the rewards of our efforts.

Acknowledgements

It is time to give credit where credit is due—one of my favorite aspects of this endeavor. My sincere gratitude first goes to my lovely wife—Deborah, with whom I discussed and tested the bulk of my rationale for *Drive to Passion*—for serving as my sounding board and voice of reason. Thanks to my friends who read this book initially and made some good suggestions. Many thanks to the editors and proofreaders who made valuable contributions; I owe all of you a debt of gratitude. Special thanks to Jeff Gilman whose eye for detail and passion for editing and proofreading were invaluable to the outcome of my work.

About Author

Ted Obomanu received an MBA from Marshall University, where he was recognized with the Distinguished Graduate Student Alumnus Award in 2004. He went from a stint in corporate America to a life of entrepreneurship in Durham, North Carolina. In 2001, his company was ranked as number thirty on the list of the fifty fastest growing companies in the Raleigh-Durham area of North Carolina, USA.

Notes

Introduction

Reeves, Scott. December 01, 2005. "Loving the Job You Hate." Forbes.com. *Forbes* magazine, New York, NY.

Chapter 1. "Colonel" Harland Sanders: Greatness After Sixty Five

Rosenschein, Bob. 2005. "Biography: Colonel Sanders." Answers.com Online Dictionary, Encyclopedia & Much More, New York, NY.

Maxwell, John C. 1999. *The 21 Indispensable Qualities of a Leader*. Thomas Nelson Inc., Nashville, TN.

Norton, Frances E. 2008. "KFC Corporation." Encyclopedia.com, Cengage Learning Stamford, CT.

The Associated Press. July 22, 2005. "'Secret' recipe to KFC's success is locked away." *USA Today*, McLean, VA.

Hostetler, John with Hostetler, Dan. 2007-2010. *$ DollarTimes*. H Brothers, Inc, Seattle, WA.

Chapter 2. Winston Churchill: A Glow-Worm

Binns, Tristan Boyer. 2004. *Winston Churchill: Soldier and Politician*. Scholastic Inc., New York, NY.

Macdonald, Fiona. 2003. *Winston Churchill*. World Almanac Library, Milwaukee, WI.

Gilbert, Martin. 1991. *Churchill: A Life*. Owl Books Henry Holt and Company, New York, NY.

Allen, David. 2003. *Getting Things Done*. Penguin Books, New York, NY.

Byrne, Rhonda. 2006. *The Secret*. Atria Books, New York, NY.

Robbins, Anthony. 1991. *Awake the Giant Within*. Free Press, New York, NY.

Gladwell, Malcolm. 2008. *Outliers*. Hachette Book Group, New York, NY.

Pink, Daniel H. 2009. *Drive*. Riverhead Books, New York, NY.

Merriam-Webster. 1994. *Merriam-Webster's Collegiate Dictionary, Tenth Edition*. Merriam-Webster Inc., Springfield MA.

Hostetler, John with Hostetler, Dan. 2007-2010. *$ DollarTimes*. H Brothers, Inc, Seattle, WA.

Chapter 3. Joseph Kennedy: Craved Recognition and Privilege

Goodwin, Doris Kearns. 1987. *The Fitzgeralds and the Kennedys*. Simon & Schuster, New York, NY.

Pink, Daniel H. 2009. *Drive*. Riverhead Books, New York, NY.

Merriam-Webster. 1994. *Merriam-Webster's Collegiate Dictionary, Tenth Edition*. Merriam-Webster Inc., Springfield, MA.

Welch, Jack with Welch, Suzy. 2005. *Winning*. HarperCollins Publishers, New York, NY.

Gladwell, Malcolm. 2008. *Outliers*. Hachette Book Group, New York, NY.

Hostetler, John with Hostetler, Dan. 2007-2010. *$ DollarTimes*. H Brothers, Inc, Seattle, WA.

Powell, Colin, with Joseph E. Persico. 1995. *My American Journey*. Random House. New York, NY.

Chapter 4. Sidney Poitier: A Slot of My Choosing

Poitier, Sidney. 2000. *The Measure of a Man.* HarperCollins Publishers, New York, NY.

Eker, T. Harv. 2005. *Secrets of the Millionaire Mind.* HarperCollins Publishers, Inc., New York, NY.

Maxwell, John C. 1999. *The 21 Indispensable Qualities of a Leader.* Thomas Nelson Inc., Nashville, TN.

Hardy, Darren. May 2009. *Success.* Success Media, Lake Dallas, TX.

Byrne, Rhonda. 2006. *The Secret.* Atria Books, New York, NY.

Robbins, Anthony. 1991. *Awake the Giant Within.* Free Press, New York, NY.

Gladwell, Malcolm. 2008. *Outliers.* Hachette Book Group, New York, NY.

Pink, Daniel H. 2009. *Drive.* Riverhead Books, New York, NY.

Hostetler, John with Hostetler, Dan. 2007-2010. *$ DollarTimes.* H Brothers, Inc, Seattle, WA.

Jordan, Michael. 1998. *For The Love of the Game—My Story,* Crown Publishers, Inc., New York, NY.

Chapter 5. Abraham Lincoln: Appetite for Politics

Roberts, Jeremy. 2004. *Abraham Lincoln.* Lerner Publications Company, Minneapolis, MN.

Sullivan, George. 2000. *Abraham Lincoln.* Scholastic Inc., New York, NY.

White, Ronald C., Jr. 2009. *A. Lincoln.* Random House. New York, NY.

Keyes, Kenneth S., Jr. 1950. *How to Develop Your Thinking Ability.* McGraw-Hill Book Company, New York, NY.

Maxwell, John C. 1999. *The 21 Indispensable Qualities of a Leader.* Thomas Nelson Inc., Nashville, TN.

Chapter 6. Suze Orman: Like What You Do

Orman, Suze. 2006. *Suze's Story*. Suze Orman Media, Beverly Hills, CA.
Pink, Daniel H. 2009. *Drive*. Riverhead Books, New York, NY.
Hardy, Darren. May 2009. *Success*. Success Media, Lake Dallas, TX.
Maxwell, John C. 1999. *The 21 Indispensable Qualities of a Leader*. Thomas Nelson Inc., Nashville, TN.
Merriam-Webster. 1994. *Merriam-Webster's Collegiate Dictionary, Tenth Edition*. Merriam-Webster Inc., Springfield, MA.
Hostetler, John with Hostetler, Dan. 2007-2010. *$ DollarTimes*. H Brothers, Inc, Seattle, WA.
Powell, Colin, with Joseph E. Persico. 1995. *My American Journey*. Random House. New York, NY.

Chapter 7. Barack Obama: Life Beyond His Father's Dilemma

Obama, Barack. 2006. *The Audacity of Hope*. Crown Publishers, New York, NY.
Obama, Barack. 2004. *Dreams from My Father*. Three Rivers Press, New York, NY.
Andersen, Christopher. 2009. *Barack and Michelle*. HarperCollins Publishers, New York, NY.
Pink, Daniel H. 2009. *Drive*. Riverhead Books, New York, NY.
Wales, Jimmy. June 21, 2010. "Maslow's Hierarchy of Need." Wikipedia, The Free Encyclopedia, Wikimedia Foundation, San Francisco, CA.
Poitier, Sidney. 2000. *The Measure of a Man*. HarperCollins Publishers, New York, NY.
Welch, Jack, with Suzy Welch. 2005. *Winning*. HarperCollins Publishers, New York, NY.
Powell, Colin, with Joseph E. Persico. 1995. *My American Journey*. Random House. New York, NY.

Chapter 8. Oprah Winfrey: Determined To Achieve Fame

Garson, Helen. 2004. *Oprah Winfrey: A Biography*. Greenwood Press, Westport, CT.

Welch, Jack with Welch, Suzy. 2005. *Winning*. HarperCollins Publishers, New York, NY.

Pink, Daniel H. 2009. *Drive*. Riverhead Books, New York, NY.

Edgecliffe-Johnson, Andrew. December 10, 2010. "Oprah Winfrey: out on her own." *FT* magazine, Financial Times, London, UK.

Amazon.com. 2010. *Holiday Movie Guide: Oprah Winfrey*. IMDb.com, Inc., Seattle, WA.

Chapter 9. Realizing Our Powers

Byrne, Rhonda. 2006. *The Secret*. Atria Books, New York, NY.

Robbins, Anthony. 1991. *Awake the Giant Within*. Free Press, New York, NY.

Scofield, Cyrus. 1984. *The New Scofield Study Bible*. Oxford University Press, New York, NY.

Covey, Stephen R. 1989. *The 7 Habits of Highly Effective People*. Simon & Schuster, New York, NY.

Gilbert, Martin. 1991. *Churchill: A Life*. Owl Books, Henry Holt and Company, New York, NY.

Cassano James. 2010. "The Electric Ben Franklin." Independence Hall Association, Philadelphia, PA.

Human World Records. 2010. *Famous Quotes*. Answers Corporation, New York, NY.

Stark, Andrew. April 12, 2011. "The Long Way Around." *The Wall Street Journal*, New York, NY.

Sayadaw, Mahasi. 1996-2011. "The Theory of Karma." Buddha Dharma Education Association, Tullera, Australia.

Chapter 10. Success and Greatness

Keyes, Kenneth S., Jr. 1950. *How to Develop Your Thinking Ability.* McGraw-Hill Book Company, New York, NY.

Gladwell, Malcolm. 2008. *Outliers.* Hachette Book Group, New York, NY.

Good, Sharon. 2004. "Accessing Genius." Good Life Coaching, New York, NY.

Pink, Daniel H. 2009. *Drive.* Riverhead Books, New York, NY.

Merriam-Webster. 1994. *Merriam-Webster's Collegiate Dictionary, Tenth Edition.* Merriam-Webster Inc., Springfield, MA.

Morse, Robert. February 25, 2010. "About the World's Best University Rankings." *US News & World Report,* New York, NY.

Garson, Helen. 2004. *Oprah Winfrey: A Biography.* Greenwood Press, Westport, CT.

Obama, Barack. 2004. *Dreams from My Father.* Three River Press, New York, NY.

Andersen, Christopher. 2009. *Barack and Michelle.* HarperCollins Publishers, New York, NY.

Orman, Suze. 2006. *Suze's Story.* Suze Orman Media, Beverly Hills, CA.

Hardy, Darren. May 2009. "Success from the Ground Up." *Success* magazine, Lake Dallas, TX.

Roberts, Jeremy. 2004. *Abraham Lincoln.* Lerner Publications Company, Minneapolis, MN.

Poitier, Sidney. 2000. *The Measure of a Man.* HarperCollins Publishers Inc., New York, NY.

Goodwin, Doris Kearns. 1987. *The Fitzgeralds and the Kennedys.* Simon & Schuster, New York, NY.

Rosenschein, Bob. 2005. "Biography: Colonel Sanders." Answers.com Online Dictionary, Encyclopedia & Much More, New York, NY.

Gilbert, Martin. 1991. *Churchill: A Life.* Owl Books, Henry Holt and Company, New York, NY.

Moncur, Michael. 1994-2010. "Quotation #603—Bill Cosby." Quotation Page.com, Salt Lake City, UT.

Forbes, Steve. December 12, 2008. "$50 Billion Ponzi Scheme." Forbes.com., *Forbes* magazine, New York, NY.
Wales, Jimmy. June 22, 2010. "Financial Crisis 2007-2010." Wikipedia, The Free Encyclopedia, Wikimedia Foundation, San Francisco, CA.
Wales Jimmy. September 24, 2010. "Automotive Industry Crisis 2008-2010." Wikipedia, The Free Encyclopedia, Wikimedia Foundation, San Francisco, CA.
Maxwell, John C. 1999. *The 21 Indispensable Qualities of a Leader*. Thomas Nelson Inc., Nashville, TN.